OXFORD HANDBOOK OF

# Occupational Health

## Published and forthcoming Oxford Handbooks

Oxford Handbook for the Foundation Programme 5e
Oxford Handbook of Acute Medicine 4e
Oxford Handbook of Anaesthesia 5e
Oxford Handbook of Cardiology 2e
Oxford Handbook of Clinical and Healthcare Research
Oxford Handbook of Clinical and Laboratory Investigation 4e
Oxford Handbook of Clinical Dentistry 7e
Oxford Handbook of Clinical Diagnosis 3e
Oxford Handbook of Clinical Examination and Practical Skills 2e
Oxford Handbook of Clinical Haematology 4e
Oxford Handbook of Clinical Immunology and Allergy 4e
Oxford Handbook of Clinical Medicine – Mini Edition 10e
Oxford Handbook of Clinical Medicine 10e
Oxford Handbook of Clinical Pathology 2e
Oxford Handbook of Clinical Pharmacy 3e
Oxford Handbook of Clinical Specialties 11e
Oxford Handbook of Clinical Surgery 4e
Oxford Handbook of Complementary Medicine
Oxford Handbook of Critical Care 3e
Oxford Handbook of Dental Patient Care
Oxford Handbook of Dialysis 4e
Oxford Handbook of Emergency Medicine 5e
Oxford Handbook of Endocrinology and Diabetes 4e
Oxford Handbook of ENT and Head and Neck Surgery 3e
Oxford Handbook of Epidemiology for Clinicians
Oxford Handbook of Expedition and Wilderness Medicine 2e
Oxford Handbook of Forensic Medicine
Oxford Handbook of Gastroenterology & Hepatology 3e
Oxford Handbook of General Practice 5e
Oxford Handbook of Genetics
Oxford Handbook of Genitourinary Medicine, HIV, and Sexual Health 3e
Oxford Handbook of Geriatric Medicine 3e
Oxford Handbook of Infectious Diseases and Microbiology 2e
Oxford Handbook of Integrated Dental Biosciences 2e
Oxford Handbook of Humanitarian Medicine
Oxford Handbook of Key Clinical Evidence 2e
Oxford Handbook of Medical Dermatology 2e
Oxford Handbook of Medical Imaging
Oxford Handbook of Medical Sciences 3e
Oxford Handbook for Medical School
Oxford Handbook of Medical Statistics 2e
Oxford Handbook of Neonatology 2e
Oxford Handbook of Nephrology and Hypertension 2e
Oxford Handbook of Neurology 2e
Oxford Handbook of Nutrition and Dietetics 3e
Oxford Handbook of Obstetrics and Gynaecology 3e
Oxford Handbook of Occupational Health 2e
Oxford Handbook of Oncology 4e
Oxford Handbook of Operative Surgery 3e
Oxford Handbook of Ophthalmology 4e
Oxford Handbook of Oral and Maxillofacial Surgery 2e
Oxford Handbook of Orthopaedics and Trauma
Oxford Handbook of Paediatrics 3e
Oxford Handbook of Pain Management
Oxford Handbook of Palliative Care 3e
Oxford Handbook of Practical Drug Therapy 2e
Oxford Handbook of Pre-Hospital Care 2e
Oxford Handbook of Psychiatry 4e
Oxford Handbook of Public Health Practice 4e
Oxford Handbook of Rehabilitation Medicine 3e
Oxford Handbook of Respiratory Medicine 4e
Oxford Handbook of Rheumatology 4e
Oxford Handbook of Sport and Exercise Medicine 2e
Oxford Handbook of Tropical Medicine 5e
Oxford Handbook of Urology 4e

OXFORD HANDBOOK OF

# Occupational Health

THIRD EDITION

EDITED BY

**Steven S Sadhra, Alan J Bray, and Steve Boorman**

OXFORD
UNIVERSITY PRESS

OXFORD
UNIVERSITY PRESS

Great Clarendon Street, Oxford, OX2 6DP,
United Kingdom

Oxford University Press is a department of the University of Oxford.
It furthers the University's objective of excellence in research, scholarship, and education by publishing worldwide. Oxford is a registered trade mark of Oxford University Press in the UK and in certain other countries



First Edition published in 2007
Second Edition published in 2013
Third Edition published in 2022



Published in the United States of America by Oxford University Press
198 Madison Avenue, New York, NY 10016, United States of America

British Library Cataloguing in Publication Data

Data available

Library of Congress Control Number: 2021943567

ISBN 978–0–19–884980–3

DOI: 10.1093/med/9780198849803.001.0001

Printed in Italy by
L.E.G.O. S.p.A.

# Foreword

This small book is up-to-date and based soundly on evidence and good practice. It provides a compact but remarkably comprehensive guide for all those engaged in Occupational Health, including trainees. Many experienced authors have contributed to this comprehensive text, which has been edited by Steven S Sadhra, Alan Bray and Steve Boorman, with much teaching experience.

Those practicing in Occupational Health have responsibility to respond effectively to unforeseen threats to both individual and population health arising in the context of working life. The recent pandemic has more than confirmed this, with all Occupational Health practitioners in great demand and the importance of the specialty enhanced.

At a time when serious inequalities in health and life chances are on the rise, and after a decade of austerity, we are increasingly aware of the burden, cost, and social consequences of impaired health among people of working age. This book, although written for specialists in Occupational Health, has much useful to say to other health professionals and engaged employers. This is largely because it is now accepted that good work is good for health and that worklessness is harmful to health, and also because not being wholly fit or having disabilities are often compatible with the right kind of work.

This is a book that I would have been very glad to have beside me, had I chosen a career in Occupational Health, and I commend it to all trainees and practitioners in the specialty.

Professor Dame Carol Black DBE FRCP FMedSci

Professor Dame Carol Black (the first National Director of Health and Work) has authored three independent reviews for the UK Government: of the health of the working-age population; of sickness absence in Britain; and of employment outcomes of addiction to drugs or alcohol, or obesity.

# Preface

The *Oxford Handbook of Occupational Health* is intended to be a concise practice-based guide primarily for occupational health (OH) practitioners including general practitioners (GPs) who practice OH on a sessional basis. The book will also be useful to therapists who work with and support OH services, e.g. physiotherapists, rehabilitation, and behavioural therapists, and those preparing for professional examinations in Occupational Medicine.

Although the Handbook is primarily for those practicing in Occupational Health, it meets important and growing needs of much wider readership, particularly those who have responsibility for the following: assessing managing work-related health conditions, managing absence and return to work, development of health, and well-being programmes at work and evaluation of work-based interventions for improving health outcomes. The need for practical expertise in these areas is driven by increasing evidence that good work is good for health. Furthermore, health care professionals now recognize that work should be regarded as a clinical outcome.

Changes in legislation and evidence-based practice also reinforce the importance of making suitable workplace adjustments to support individuals as part of their recovery and rehabilitation at work. The new approaches to the management of work-related health issue advocate a more integrated approach with involvement of employers, employees, OH services, and the National Health Service (NHS). Such collaborations particularly in the development and implementation of health and well-being strategies require good understanding of OH concepts and principles as well as evidence-based practices which are central to the OH handbook and will further broaden its readership.

The third edition has been subject to a major rewrite by Professor Steven Sadhra, who was a joint editor for the two previous editions and also has benefited hugely from the expert knowledge and vast experience of the two new editors, Dr Steven Boorman and Dr Alan Bray. This is evident from the revisions to various sections in particular chapters on OH practice, delivery of OH services, fitness for work policies, and procedures. A number of new chapter writers have helped to broaden the coverage of topics and provided different perspectives based on their experience from working in different occupational settings.

The intention of the Oxford Handbook is not to provide an exhaustive detailed reference to occupational and environmental medicine, as many pre-existing texts already offer this. The third edition maintains the overall approach and the general structure of previous editions but updates the material to reflect important new changes to practice, disease recognition, OH service delivery, guidelines as well as changes to legislation and ethical principles.

Since the publication of the second edition, there has been a major focus on health and well-being in the workplace at national level in the UK. Several development and important guidelines have impacted (and will impact in future) significantly on the practice of OH and its delivery.

The third edition retains the same successful sectional divisions and the primary structure of existing pages within each main section. The new material for the third edition reflects developments in the field of OH and the enhanced attention on health and work (improving employment and work capability, reduced sickness absence, increased productivity) in the political, employment, and the academic research arenas. The principal changes are:

- Updates on section on ethics, work health and disability, infection control, respiratory disorders, and fitness for work
- Guidelines on OH practice and the provision of OH services reflecting current service delivery methods and approaches
- Updated evidence-based guidance published by national and international organizations, including: National Institute for Clinical Excellence (NICE), the Health and Safety Executive (HSE), the British Medical Association (BMA) Occupational Health Committee, the Centre for Work and Health, World Health Organization (WHO), International Commission on Occupational Health (ICOH), and Council for Work and Health (CWH)
- Revision to health and safety legislation, data protection requirement, and HSE guidance documents. Examples include:
  - Reporting of Injuries, Diseases, and Dangerous Occurrences Regulations (RIDDOR) 2013
  - Working with Ionizing Radiation Regulations 2017
  - General Data Protection Regulation 2018
- Updates on health and safety statistics for different occupational diseases throughout the handbook. Examples of information sources include Health and Safety Labour Force Survey, RIDDOR, and voluntary reporting of occupational diseases by specialists and GPs
- Updated diagrams and figures and the inclusion of chemical structures of different substances for the section chemical hazards

We hope the third edition will be as successful as the first two editions, and we look forward to your feedback via the Oxford University Press website: http://www.oup.com/uk/medicine/handbooks. We are particularly interested to hear about the level of detail and topics which may have omitted.

# Acknowledgements

The book editors would like to thank all who contributed to the writing of the chapters in this third edition of the *Oxford Handbook of Occupational Health*. We thank them for their time, dedication, and expertise.

We thank all those who contributed to the first two editions of the book. Special thanks to Julia Smedley and Finlay Dick who coedited the first two editions with Steven Sadhra. Our job in writing this third edition was made easier by all your hard work.

We would like to thank all staff at Oxford University Press for their support in putting together this book. In particular, we wish to thank Elizabeth Reeve, Michael Hawkes, and Jade Dixon.

Steven Sadhra would like to dedicate this book to his father Tarsem Singh (late), a proud man who worked tirelessly (farmer in India and then in metal foundries in the UK) from a young age to support his family. Alan Bray would like to thank his wife Chris and family for their unstinting support as well as thank his students for their encouragement and quest for learning. Steve Boorman would like to thank students for the pleasure of teaching them and his very patient wife, Sharon.

We would like to say a huge 'thank you' to colleagues who kindly gave up their time to update chapters or write drafts for new topics or chapters: Dr Rajaa Ahmed, Dr Kevin Bailey, Dr Jed Boardman, Dr Sally Bell, Dr Richard Caddis, Professor John Cherrie, Dr Epha Croft, Dr Hilary Cross, Dr Roger Cooke, Dr Momeda Deen, Mr Russell Fife, Professor David Fishwick, Dr David Flower, Dr Prosenjit Giri, Dr Cornelius J Grobler, Professor Craig Jackson, Dr Áine Jones, Professor Diana Kloss, Professor Hubert Lam, Dr Ian Mollan, Dr Lanre Ogunyemi, Dr Shriti Pattani, Dr Dipti Patel, Dr Chris Schenk, Dr Alan Smith, Dr Jon Spiro, Dr Gareth Walters, Elizabeth A. Wood, Ruth Wilkinson, Dr Justin Varney, and Dr Philip Wynn.

# Contents

# Contributors

**Rajaa Ahmed**
Consultant Occupational Health Physician
International
London, UK

**Sally Bell**
Chief Medical Advisor
Maritime and Coastguard Agency
Southampton, UK

**Jed Boardman**
Senior Lecturer in Social Psychiatry
Institute of Psychiatry, Psychology, and Neuroscience
King's College London
London, UK

**Steven Boorman**
Consultant Adviser Employee Health, Empactis
Chair Council for Work and Health
London, UK

**Alan J Bray**
Academic Registrar (Director of Examinations) of IRISH Faculty of Occupational Medicine of Royal College of Physicians
Medical Director and Consultant Occupational Physician, South West Independent Medical Services Ltd, West Midlands, UK

**Richard Caddis**
Chief Medical Officer and Director of Health, Safety and Wellbeing
BT Group
London, UK

**John W Cherrie**
Institute of Biological Chemistry, Biophysics and Bioengineering
Heriot Watt University and Institute of Occupational Medicine
Edinburgh, UK

**Roger Cooke**
Consultant in Occupational Medicine
Honorary Senior Lecturer
Institute of Occupational and Environmental Medicine
College of Medical and Dental Sciences
University of Birmingham
Birmingham, UK

**Epha Croft**
Consultant Occupational Physician
Occupational Health Service
Department of Health, Isle of Man
Douglas, Isle of Man

**Hilary Cross**
Honorary Senior Lecturer in Occupational Toxicology
Institute of Occupational and Environmental Medicine
College of Medical and Dental Sciences
University of Birmingham
Birmingham, UK

**Beverley Davies**
Health and Safety Advisor
University of Birmingham
Birmingham, UK

**Momeda Dean**
Independent Consultant Occupational Physician
Modify Medical Services Ltd
Swindon, Wiltshire

**Russell Fife**
Chartered Ergonomist and Human Factors Specialist
Attwood Leighs
Bury St Edmonds, UK

**David Fishwick**
Consultant Respiratory Physician and Hon
Professor of Occupational and Environmental Respiratory Disease, STH NHS
Foundation Trust and the University of Sheffield
Sheffield, Yorkshire

**David Flower**
Senior Health Director
BP International
London, UK

**Kevin GH Bailey**
Kevin GH Bailey Director of Occupational Health at Health Management Gloucestershire, UK

**Prosenjit Giri**
Consultant Occupational Physician
Sheffield Teaching Hospitals and Senior Lecturer Sheffield University
Sheffield, Yorkshire

**Cornelius J Grobler**
Consultant Occupational Physician, Senior Medical Advisor
Jaguar Land Rover
Solihull, West Midlands

**Louise G Holden**
Occupational Medicine and Defence Consultant Advisor in Occupational Medicine
Senior Health Advisor (Army)
London, UK

**Craig Jackson**
Professor of Occupational Health Psychology
Birmingham City University
Birmingham, UK

**Áine Jones**
Consultant in Occupational Medicine
Galway, Ireland

**Diana Kloss**
Barrister
St John's Buildings Barristers' Chambers
Manchester, UK

**Hubert Lam**
Associate Professor
Nuffield Department of Population Health
University of Oxford
Oxford, Oxfordshire

**Ian Mollan**
Consultant Occupational Medical Consultant and Aeromedical Examiner
Royal Air Force and Independent Consultancy
Oxford, Oxfordshire

**Lanre Ogunyemi**
Consultant in Occupational Medicine and Medical Director
Trinity Occupational and Public Health Solutions Ltd
Nottingham, Notts

**Dipti Patel**
Chief Medical Office
Foreign, Commonwealth and Development Office
London, UK

**Shriti Pattani**
Clinical Director and Consultant in Occupational Medicine
London North West University Healthcare NHS Trust
London, UK

**Steven S Sadhra**
College of Medical and Dental Sciences
University of Birmingham, UK

**Chris Schenk**
Specialist Occupational Physician
Guildford, UK

**Alan Smith**
Lighting Consultant, Honorary Research Fellow
Institute of occupational and Environmental Medicine
College of Medical and Dental Sciences
University of Birmingham
Birmingham, UK

**Jon Spiro**
Independent Specialist in Occupational Medicine
Oxford, Oxfordshire

**Justin Varney**
Director of Public Health
Birmingham City Council
Birmingham, UK

**Gareth Walters**
Consultant in Occupational Respiratory Medicine
Regional NHS Occupational Lung Disease Service, Birmingham Chest Clinic
Birmingham, West Midlands

**Ruth Wilkinson**
Head of Health and Safety
Institution of Occupational Safety and Health (IOSH)
Leicester, UK

**Elizabeth A Wood**
Specialist Community Public Health Nurse
Specialist Practitioner Occupational Health
York, UK

**Philip Wynn**
Senior Occupational Health Physician
Durham County Council
Durham County, Durham

# Symbols and abbreviations

| | |
|---|---|
| ↑ | Increased |
| ↓ | Decreased |
| ► | Important |
| ⚠ | Warning |
| 💣 | Controversial |
| ➲ | Book reference |
| 🖱 | Web reference |
| ♀ | Female |
| ♂ | Male |
| AAS | atomic absorption spectroscopy |
| ABS | acrylonitrile-butadiene-styrene |
| AC | air conduction |
| ACAS | Advisory, Conciliation and Arbitration Service |
| ACD | allergic contact dermatitis |
| ACDP | Advisory Committee on Dangerous Pathogens |
| ACGIH | American Conference of Governmental Industrial Hygienists |
| AChE | acetylcholinesterase |
| ACOPs | Approved Codes of Practice |
| Acute tox. | Acute toxicity (Category 1, 2, 3, or 4) |
| AD | Alzheimer's disease |
| ADs | Adjustment disorders |
| ADS | approved dosimetry service |
| $a_{hw}$ | frequency-weighted measurements |
| AIHA | American Industrial Hygiene Society |
| AIOH | Australian Institute of Occupational Hygienists |
| AKI | acute kidney injury |
| ALAMA | Association of Local Authority Medical Advisers |
| ALL | acute lymphoblastic leukaemia |
| ALT | alanine aminotransferase |
| AMED | approved medical examiner of divers |
| AMI | acute myocardial infarction |
| AML | acute myeloid leukaemia |
| AMRA | Access to Medical Reports Act 1988 |
| ANHOPS | Association of NHS Occupational Physicians |
| ARDS | acute respiratory distress syndrome |
| ART | Assessment of Repetitive Tasks |
| ARVs | antiretroviral drugs |
| ASHRAE | American Society of Heating, Refrigerating and Air-conditioning Engineers Scale |
| ATMs | automated teller machine |
| $B_{12}$ | vitamin $B_{12}$ |
| BA | breathing apparatus |
| BAT | biological tolerance values |
| Batneec | best available techniques not entailing excessive cost |
| BBV | blood-borne viruses |
| BC | bone conduction |
| BCG | bacillus Calmette–Guérin |
| BCNU | bischlorethylnitrosourea |
| BEIs | Biological Exposure Indices |
| BeLPT | beryllium lymphocyte proliferation |
| BEM | biological effect monitoring |
| BM | biological monitoring |
| BMGV | Biological Monitoring Guidance Value |
| BMI | body mass index |
| BOHRF | British Occupational Health Research Foundation |
| BOHS | British Occupational Hygiene Society |
| Bot | botanical |
| BP | blood pressure |
| Bq | becquerel |
| BSE | bovine spongiform encephalopathy |
| Byp | bypiridylium |
| CAA | Civil Aviation Authority |
| CAR | Control of Asbestos Regulations 2012 |
| Carc. | carcinogenicity (category 1A, 1B, or 2) |
| CBD | chronic beryllium disease |
| CBI | Confederation of British Industry |

| | |
|---|---|
| CBRN | chemical, biological, radiological, or nuclear |
| CBT | cognitive behavioural therapy |
| CCOHS | The Canadian Centre for Occupational Health and Safety |
| Cd | candela |
| CE | clinical engineering |
| CFS | chronic fatigue syndrome |
| $CH_3Br$ | methyl bromide |
| CHD | coronary heart disease |
| CHIP Regulations | Chemical Hazard Information and Packaging for Supply Regulations 2009 |
| CIBSE | The Chartered Institution of Building Service Engineers |
| CIE | Commission Internationale de l´Eclairage |
| CJD | Creutzfelt–Jakob disease |
| CLAW | Control of Lead at Work |
| CLL | chronic lymphoid leukaemia |
| CLP Regulation | Classification, Labelling and Packaging Regulation |
| CML | chronic myeloid |
| CNAWRs | Control of Noise at Work Regulations |
| CNTs | carbon nanotubes |
| CNS | central nervous system |
| CO | carbon monoxide |
| COHPA | Commercial Occupational Health Providers Association |
| COMAH | Control of Major Accident Hazards Regulations 1999 |
| COPD | chronic obstructive pulmonary disease |
| Corr. | Skin corrosion (category 1A, 1B, 1C) |
| COSHH | Control of Substances Hazardous to Health |
| CRS | chronic rhinosinusitis |
| CSA | chemical safety assessment |
| CSF | cerebrospinal fluid |
| CSM | Committee on Safety of Medicines |
| CSR | chemical safety report |
| CT | computerized tomography |
| CTS | carpal tunnel syndrome |
| CVD | cardiovascular disease |
| CWP | coal worker's pneumoconiosis |
| CXR | chest radiography/chest X-ray |
| DAA | direct-acting antivirals |
| DCLG | Department for Communities and Local Government |
| DEEE | diesel engine exhaust emissions |
| DEFRA | Department for Environment, Food, and Rural Affairs |
| DFG | The Deutsche Forschungsgemeinschaft |
| DH | Department of Health |
| DNA | deoxyribonucleic acid |
| DNEL | derived no-effect level |
| DOB | date of birth |
| DPT | diphtheria, polio, tetanus |
| DSE | display screen equipment |
| DSM III | Diagnostic and Statistical Manual of Mental Disorders |
| DTS | Davidson Trauma Scale |
| DU | downstream users |
| DVLA | Driver and Vehicle Licensing Agency |
| DWP | Department for Work and Pensions |
| EA | Environment Agency |
| EAA | extrinsic allergic alveolitis |
| EAGA | Expert Advisory Group on AIDS |
| EAP | employee assistance programme |
| EASA | European Union Aviation Safety Agency |
| EAVs | (daily) exposure action values |
| EC | elemental carbon |
| ECG | electrocardiogram |
| ECHA | European Chemicals Agency |
| EDE-Q | eating disorder examination questionnaire |
| EDTA | ethylenediamine tetra-acetic acid |
| EEF | UK manufacturers' organization |
| EEG | electroencephalogram |
| EHOs | environmental health officers |
| EIA | Environmental Impact Assessment |
| ELF EMF | exposed to extremely low frequency electromagnetic fields |
| ELF | extremely low frequency |
| ELVs | (daily) exposure limit values |
| EMA | employment medical adviser |

| | |
|---|---|
| EMDR | eye movement desensitization and reprocessing |
| EMF | electromagnetic fields |
| EmT | employment tribunal |
| ENT | ear, nose, and throat |
| EPPs | exposure prone procedures |
| ESA | Employment and Support Allowance |
| ETS | environmental tobacco smoke |
| Eye dam. | Serious eye damage (category 1) |
| Eye irrit. | Serious eye irritation (category 2) |
| F/V | flow volume |
| FCA | flux cored arc |
| $FEV_1$ | forced expiratory volume in 1 s/lung function tests |
| FFP | ferrous foundry particulate |
| FHP | farmer's hypersensitivity pneumonitis |
| FOD | Field Operations Directorate |
| FOM | Faculty of Occupational Medicine |
| FVC | forced vital capacity |
| G6PD | glucose-6-phosphate dehydrogenase |
| GC | gas chromatography |
| GDG | guideline development groups |
| GDPR | General Data Protection Regulation |
| GET | graded exercise therapy |
| GF | glass fibre |
| GHS | Globally Harmonized System |
| GI | gastrointestinal |
| GM | genetic modification |
| GMC | General Medical Council |
| GMOs | genetically modified organisms |
| GP | general practitioner |
| GRADE | Grading of Recommendations Assessment, Development and Evaluation |
| GWBQ | General Wellbeing Questionnaire |
| GWI | Gulf War illness/syndrome |
| HACCP | Hazard Analysis and Critical Control Points |
| HARNs | high aspect ratio nanomaterials |
| HAS | primary hepatic angiosarcoma |
| HAVS | hand–arm vibration syndrome |
| HBIG | Hepatitis B specific immunoglobulin |
| HBV | hepatitis B virus |
| HCN | hydrogen cyanide |
| HCV | hepatitis C virus |
| HCWs | health care workers |
| HDI | hexamethylene diisocyanate |
| HDV | hepatitis D virus |
| HELA | Health and Safety Executive/ Local Authorities Enforcement Liaison Committee |
| HEW | Health, Environment, and Work |
| HIDL | high-intensity discharge lamps |
| HIV | human immunodeficiency virus |
| HPA | The Health Protection Agency |
| HPLC | high-pressure liquid chromatography |
| HR | human resources |
| HSC | Health and Safety Commission |
| HSE | Health and Safety Executive |
| HSL | Health and Safety Laboratory |
| HSW | The Health and Safety at Work, etc., Act of 1974 |
| HTV | hand-transmitted vibration |
| HUS | haemolytic uraemic syndrome |
| HWDU | Health and Work Development Unit |
| IARC | International Agency for Research on Cancer |
| ICAO | International Civil Aviation Organization |
| ICNIRP | International Commission on Non-ionizing Radiation Protection |
| ICO | Information Commissioner's Office |
| ICP-AES | induced coupled plasma-atomic emission spectrometry |
| ICRP | International Commission on Radiation Protection |
| ICOH | International Commission on Occupational Health |
| IES–R | Impact of Event Scale–Revised |
| IgE | immunoglobulin E |
| IHR | ill-health retirement |
| IIDB | Industrial Injuries Disablement Benefit |
| ILO | International Labour Organization |
| ILS | immediate life support |
| IOSH | Institution of Occupational Safety and Health |
| IrCD | irritant contact dermatitis |

| | |
|---|---|
| IREQ | required clothing insulation |
| IRR | Ionizing Radiation Regulations |
| Irrit. | Skin irritation (category 2) |
| IRS | infrared spectrometry |
| ISO | International Standard Organization |
| IV | intravenous |
| IVP | intravenous pyelogram |
| KCN | potassium cyanide |
| KRE | kidnap, ransom, and extortion |
| LBP | lower back pain |
| $L_{Cpeak}$ | peak sound pressure level |
| $L_{EP,d}$ | daily personal exposure level |
| $L_{EP,w}$ | personal weekly exposure |
| LEV | local exhaust ventilation |
| LFT | liver function tests |
| LGV | large goods vehicle |
| LOAEL | lowest observed adverse effect level |
| LOD | limit of detection |
| LOLER | lifting operations and lifting equipment regulations |
| MAC | Manual handling assessment chart |
| MbOCA | 4,4′-methylene bis-2-chloroaniline |
| MCA | Maritime and Coastguard Agency |
| MDHS | Methods for the Determination of Hazardous Substances |
| MDI | methylene bisphenyl isocyanate |
| MDR | multidrug-resistant |
| ME | myalgic encephalomyelitis |
| MEK | methyl ethyl ketone |
| MESs | Medical Employability Standards |
| MHLW | [Japan's] Ministry of Health, Labour and Welfare |
| MHSWR | Management of Health and Safety at Work Regulations |
| MIG | metal inert gas |
| MMA | manual metal arc |
| MMMF | machine-made mineral fibre |
| MMR | mumps, measles, rubella |
| MMSE | Mini-Mental State Examination |
| MOD | Ministry of Defense |
| MOSS | Musculoskeletal Occupational Surveillance Scheme |
| MRI | magnetic resonance imaging |
| MRSA | methicillin-resistant *Staphylococcus aureus* |
| MSDs | musculoskeletal disorders |
| MSLA | minimum school leaving age |
| Muta | germ cell mutagenicity (category 1A, 1B, or 2) |
| MWFs | metal working fluids |
| NaCN | sodium cyanide |
| NCGC | National Clinical Guideline Centre |
| NHS | National Health Service |
| NI | National Insurance |
| NICE | National Institute for Health and Care Excellence |
| NIHL | noise-induced hearing loss |
| NIOSH | US National Institute for Occupational Safety and Health |
| NMC | Nursing and Midwifery Council |
| NNLW | notifiable non-licensed work |
| NOAEL | no observed adverse effect level |
| NPIC | National Poisons Information Centre |
| NRL | natural rubber latex |
| NRPB | National Radiological Protection Board |
| NSI | needlestick injury |
| OA | osteoarthritis |
| OASYS | Obstacle Avoidance System |
| OC | organochlorine |
| OD | occupational dermatitis |
| ODTS | organic dust toxic syndrome |
| OEL | occupational exposure limits |
| OH | occupational health |
| OHNs | occupational health nurses |
| OHP | occupational physician |
| OHS | occupational health service |
| ONS | Office for National Statistics |
| OP | organophosphate |
| OPIDN | OP-induced delayed neuropathy |
| OPRA | Osseointegrated Prostheses for the Rehabilitation of Amputees |
| OSHCR | Occupational Safety and Health Consultants Register |
| OSSA | Occupational Surveillance Scheme for Audiological Physicians |
| P | pyrethrin |

| | |
|---|---|
| Pa | pascals |
| PAHs | polycyclic aromatic hydrocarbons |
| PBT | persistent bioaccumulative and toxic |
| PCB | polychlorinated biphenyl |
| PCR | polymerase chain reaction |
| PCV | passenger-carrying vehicle |
| PD | Parkinson's disease |
| PEF | peak expiratory flow |
| PEFR | peak expiratory flow rate |
| PEP | post-exposure prophylaxis |
| PGD | patient group direction |
| PHE | Public Health England |
| PMF | progressive massive fibrosis |
| PMV | predicted mean vote |
| POPs | persistent organic pollutants |
| PPD | predicted percentage dissatisfied |
| PPE | personal protective equipment |
| PTSD | post-traumatic stress disorder |
| PUWER | Provision and Use of Work Equipment Regulations |
| PVC | polyvinyl chloride |
| QEC | quick exposure check |
| QLFT | qualitative fit testing |
| QNFT | quantitative fit testing |
| RA | risk assessment/rheumatoid arthritis |
| RAPP | risk assessment of pushing and pulling |
| R–CN | nitriles |
| RCS | respirable crystalline silica |
| RCTs | randomized controlled trials |
| REACH | Registration, Evaluation, Authorization and Restriction of Chemicals |
| REBA | postural hazards in repetitive whole-body handling tasks |
| Repr. | reproductive toxicity (category 1A, 1B, or 2) |
| Resp. Sens. | Respiratory Sensitization (category 1) |
| RF | radiofrequency fields |
| RIDDOR | Reporting of Injuries, Diseases, and Dangerous Occurrences Regulations |
| RIPL | Rare and Imported Pathogens Laboratory |
| RMM | risk management measures |
| rms | root–mean square |
| RNA | ribonucleic acid |
| RPA | radiation protection adviser |
| RPE | respiratory protective equipment |
| RR | relative risk |
| RTW | return to work |
| RULA | rapid upper limb assessment |
| SALI | sporadic and low intensity |
| SAR | subject access requests |
| SARS | severe acute respiratory syndrome |
| SBS | sick building syndrome |
| SCL | skin contamination layer |
| SDS | Safety Data Sheets |
| SEA | Strategic Environmental Assessment |
| SEPA | Scottish Environmental Protection Agency |
| SIDAW | Surveillance of Infectious Diseases at Work |
| SIGN | Scottish Intercollegiate Guidelines Network (for Scotland) |
| Skin Sens. | Skin Sensitization (category 1) |
| SLL | Society of Light & Lighting |
| SLM | sound level meter |
| SME | small and medium size enterprises |
| SMR | standardized mortality ratio |
| SNC | sinonasal cancer |
| SOM | Society of Occupational Medicine |
| SOP | standard operating procedure |
| SOSMI | Surveillance of Occupational Stress and Mental Illness |
| SPL | sound pressure level |
| SSP | Statutory Sick Pay |
| STEC | Shiga toxin-producing *Escherichia coli* |
| STEL | short-term exposure limit |
| STOT/RE | Specific target organ toxicity—repeated exposure (category 1, 2, or 3) |
| Sv | sievert |
| SVHC | substance of very high concern |
| SWORD | Surveillance of Work-related and Occupational Respiratory Disease |
| TB | tuberculosis |
| TDI | toluene-2,4-diisocyanate |

| | |
|---|---|
| THOR | The Health and Occupation Reporting Network |
| THOR-ENT | Occupational Surveillance of Otorhinolaryngological Disease |
| TI | total inhalable |
| TIG | tetanus immune globulin |
| TIG | tungsten inert gas |
| TLD | thermoluminescent dosemeter |
| TLV | threshold limit value |
| TOCP | tri-orthocresyl phosphate |
| Travax | travel health information website—run by Health Protection |
| TSEs | transmissible spongiform encephalopathies |
| TST | tuberculin skin test |
| TTP | thrombotic thrombocytopenic purpura |
| TTS | temporary threshold shift |
| TWA | time-weighted average concentration |
| Twc | The Wind Chill Index |
| UKAP | UK Advisory Panel for health care workers infected with blood-borne viruses |
| UKAPOHR | UK Advisory Panel for Occupational Health Registration |
| ULD | upper limb disorders |
| UV-B | ultraviolet radiation B |
| V/T | volume time |
| VA | visual acuity |
| VCM | vinyl chloride monomer |
| VDUs | visual display units |
| VHF | viral haemorrhagic fever |
| VOCs | volatile organic compounds |
| vPvB | very persistent and very bioaccumulative |
| VRMHP | Veterans and Reserves Mental Health Programme |
| VTE | venous thromboembolism |
| VWF | vascular component |
| WB | wet bulb temperature |
| WBV | whole-body vibration |
| WCA | Work Capability Assessment |
| WELs | workplace exposure limit(s) |
| WHASS | Workplace Health and Safety Survey |
| WHO | World Health Organization |
| XRD | X-ray diffraction |
| XRF | X-ray fluorescence spectroscopy |
| XRFS | X-ray fluorescence spectrophotometry |

## Section 1

# Occupational hazards

Chapter 1

# Physical hazards

# Noise 1: Legal requirements and risk assessment

## Definitions

- *Peak sound pressure level ($L_{Cpeak}$)*: maximum value of the C-weighting sound pressure in pascals (Pa) to which a person is exposed during the working day
- *Daily personal exposure level ($L_{EP,d}$)*: daily equivalent A-weighted sound level, expressed in dB (A) or personal weekly exposure ($L_{EP,w}$)
- $L_{Aeq}$: continuous equivalent A-weighted sound pressure level
- *dB(A) and dB(C) weighting*: the human ear is more sensitive to certain frequencies than to others. Allowance for this can be made in the electronic circuitry of the sound meter. Certain frequencies can be suppressed, and others boosted. This technique is called weighting. The most commonly used weighting is the A weighting because it mimics the response of the human ear. The C weighting should be applied when measuring the peak sound pressure level
- *Sound Pressure Level (SPL)* is measured in dB and define as

$$SPL = 20 \times \text{Log } 10 \left(P_a / P_r\right)$$

- $P_a$ is the sound pressure of noise being measured
- $P_r$ is reference sound pressure (threshold of hearing = 0.00002 Pa)

Given the logarithm formula, doubling or halving of measured pressure (or intensity) will result in increase or decrease of 3 dB

## Control of noise at work regulations and exposure limits

The legal requirements are covered in the Control of Noise at Work Regulations 2005 (CNAWRs; see Box 1.1). The exposure action values (EAVs) are the noise exposure levels at which certain actions are required. These actions relate to need for risk assessment, controlling exposure, health surveillance, and the provision of information and training. The exposure limit values (ELVs) are the levels of noise above which employees may not be exposed. The EAVs and ELVs are listed in Table 1.1.

**Box 1.1 The general duties under CNAWRs**

- A formal risk assessment (RA) at or above the lower EAV
- If exposure cannot be reduced by other means, and is likely to be above the upper EAV, then ear protection must be provided by the employer and used by employees
- Health surveillance is required if the RA indicates that there is a risk to health from noise (those regularly exposed above the upper EAV) without taking account of noise reduction from use of hearing protectors
- Information, instruction, and training must be provided for those exposed at or above the lower EAV

**Table 1.1** Noise exposure limits and action values

| | Lower EAV | Upper EAV |
|---|---|---|
| Daily or weekly personal noise exposure ($L_{EP,d}$ or $L_{EP,w}$) | 80 dB (A) | 85 dB (A) |
| Peak sound pressure ($L_{Cpeak}$) | 135 dB (C) | 137 dB (C) |

## Risk assessment and management

### Risk assessment steps

- Systematically identify all noise sources
- Identify individuals exposed to noise
- For those exposed to noise determine daily exposure pattern and exposure duration
- Identify measure used to reduce exposure and their effectiveness (including protection afforded by ear defenders)
- Estimate likely exposure (daily and peak) to noise and compare with exposure limit and action values

*Risk management*

- Where practical eliminate/reduce noise exposure
- Select low-noise tools and equipment
- Modify existing equipment to reduce exposure, e.g. fitting silencers
- Use shields/sound barriers or sound absorbing materials
- Limit noise exposure using noise exclusion zones
- Provide health surveillance (audiometry) for those at risk
- Give employees information and training on safe work practices and hearing protection
- Maintain noise control equipment and hearing protection
- Develop and record action plan to minimize risk
- Review the following: actual work practices, health surveillance data, and new technologies for reducing noise exposure
- Provide hearing protection if noise level exceeds upper EAV or if employees ask for hearing protectors and noise is between lower and upper EAV

# Noise 2: Instrumentation and determination of $L_{EP,d}$

## Instrument types

*Sound level meter*

- Handheld portable instruments with data integrating (averaging) facility (Fig. 1.1a). To take measurements, the sound level meter (SLM) is held at arm's length at the ear height for those exposed to the noise
- Quality (instrument class) is governed by European Standards. Class 1 and 2 are used for noise surveys. Use windshield to protect microphone against air movement and dirt
- Indicates the following: $L_{eq}$ over the measurement period, $L_{Cpeak}$, and the frequency content of noise (octave band analysis)

*Dosimeter (personal SLM)*

- Easily carried around by operator (Fig. 1.1b). Should be placed at least 15 cm from the head (avoid reflected sound) and on the side of head where noise levels are higher
- In addition to data from SLM, dosimeters can indicate $L_{EP,d}$ or noise dose expressed as a percentage, e.g. 200% dose
- May have data logging facility, enabling the visualization, storage, and retrieval of record showing change in sound level with time (work tasks) and data storage

*Calibrators*

- Must provide tight fit around microphone
- Use to check the SLM and dosimeter before and after making measurements
- SLM, dosimeter, and the calibrator should be checked by manufacturer at least annually

## Methods for determining $L_{EP,d}$

*Personal dosimeter*

- Use when the person is highly mobile (e.g. maintenance workers) or where exposure fluctuates greatly
- Place microphone on operator's shoulder and on the side of the head where the noise levels are higher and monitor for the duration of shift

*Using handheld SLM*

- Break the working day into a number of discrete tasks/jobs and measure representative noise level for each task ($L_{Aeq}$) by placing the SLM close to employee's head
- Record time spent by each employee on different tasks over a working day
- The $L_{Aeq}$ for each task is combined with exposure duration to determine $L_{EP,d}$ using either the ready reckoner or the electronic spreadsheet: both are available on the Health and Safety Executive (HSE) website (http://www.hse.gov.uk/noise)

(a)

(b)

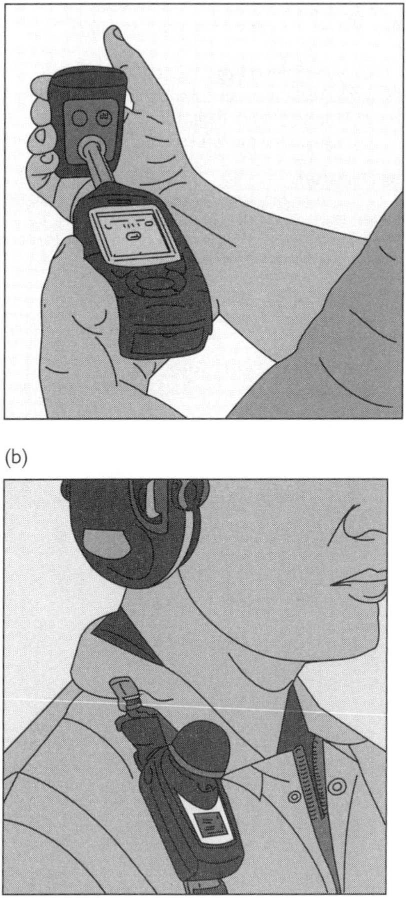

**Fig. 1.1** Sound level meters (SLM) (a) A hand held SLM being calibrated. (b) Personal noise dosimeter worn on shoulder.

## Relevant legislation


- HSE. *Provision and Use of Work Equipment Regulations 1998*. HSE Books, Sudbury. Available at: https://www.hse.gov.uk/pubns/priced/puwer.pdf
- Supply of Machinery (Safety) Regulations 2008. London. Available at: http://www.legislation.gov.uk/uksi/2008/1597/contents/made
- The Control of Noise at Work Regulations 2005. London. Available at: http://www.legislation.gov.uk/uksi/2005/1643/contents/made


## Further information


HSE (2012). *Noise at Work: A Brief Guide to Controlling the Risks (2012)*. INDG362. HSE Books, Sudbury. Available at: https://www.hse.gov.uk/pubns/indg362.pdf

HSE (2019). *Sound Solutions Case Studies*. HSE Books, Sudbury. Available at: https://www.hse.gov.uk/noise/casestudies/soundsolutions/index.htm

# Vibration 1: Whole-body vibration

## Common sources

Whole-body vibration (WBV) refers to vibration transmitted to the worker through the seat or the floor, and therefore may affect those who drive vehicles such as tractors, fork lift trucks or heavy plant, and machinery. However, any vehicle has potential to produce such vibration, especially when driven over uneven terrain. Standing on a vibrating platform may also produce such exposure. Other activities such as driving fast boats, riding helicopters or kite surfing have also been reported as having potential for such exposure.

WBV frequencies of between 0.7 and 100 Hz have been reported as being associated with adverse health outcomes. However, there is a lack of definitive evidence regarding the health effects of WBV. WBV treatment is now targeted at individuals with a range of conditions including disorders of gait, osteoporosis, and low back pain (LBP).

The commonest occupations with exposure are:

- Farm and forestry workers
- Lift truck drivers
- Drivers of heavy plant such as bulldozers, dumper trucks

The commonest industries are:

- Agriculture and forestry
- Construction, mining, and quarrying

## Main factors affecting exposure

- Intrinsic vibration of the vehicle, including design of controls which may affect posture
- Seating and vehicle suspension
- Road surface
- Road speed

## Potential health effects

The primary risk is of LBP, which may be non-specific or resulting from lumbar disc degeneration. A systematic review by US National Institute for Occupational Safety and Health (1997)[1] described evidence on the association with LBP as 'strong' (15 of 19 studies positive), but there is less certainty about the dose–response relationship.

Other suggested effects including hypertension, neck pain and cervical disc degeneration, autonomic disturbance, and digestive and reproductive effects are less well evidenced. Motion sickness and *mal de debarquement* syndrome are well recognized.

## Exposure limits

Two exposure limits are specified in UK and European legislation:

- *An EAV A(8) of 0.5 m/s2*: While there is an overriding duty to reduce exposure to as low a level as reasonably practicable, the EAV is the daily amount above which employers must act to control exposure, and provide appropriate information, instruction, and training to employees

1 NIOSH (1997). Musculoskeletal disorders and workplace factors. A critical review of epidemiologic evidence for work-related musculoskeletal disorders of the neck, upper–extremity and low back, Publication no. 97–141. NIOSH, Cincinnati.

- *ELV A(8) of 1.15 m/s2*: this is the maximum amount an employee may be exposed to on any given day (ELV should not be considered a target; rather, the aim should be to reduce exposure as low as reasonably possible)

## Risk assessment and monitoring

In the UK, the Health and Safety Executive (HSE) has issued guidance about WBV (see following section) and provides an exposure calculator to facilitate the summation of partial doses from several vehicles (http://www.hse.gov.uk/vibration/wbv/wbv.xls)

## Prevention and control

HSE advises that drivers should:

- Adjust their seating
- Avoid rough, poor, or uneven surfaces
- Adjust the vehicle speed to suit road conditions

It also advises on several other measures, including:

- Maintenance of vehicle suspension
- Maintenance of site roadways
- Better choice of seating
- Rest breaks
- Safer systems of work
- Routine health surveillance is unlikely to be helpful in identifying the effects of WBV, although monitoring of back pain among exposed employees may identify individuals with relevant symptoms

## Relevant legislation

Control of Vibration at Work Regulations 2005 Available at: https://www.legislation.gov.uk/uksi/2005/1093/contents/made. UK statutory instrument 2005.

## Further information and guidance

HSE (2005). *Whole Body Vibration Guidance to the Control of Vibration at Work Regulations 2005*, L141. ISBN 978 0 7176 6126 8 publ. HSE Books, Sudbury.

HSE. *Control Back-Pain Risks from Whole-Body Vibration*. INDG 242 06/05. Leaflet published in 2005. HSE Books, Sudbury. Available at: https://www.hse.gov.uk/pubns/indg242.pdf

HSE. *Whole body vibration calculator*. HSE Books, Sudbury. Available at: http://www.hse.gov.uk/vibration/wbv/calculator.htm

HSE. *Whole Body vibration at work*. web links. HSE Books, Sudbury. Available at: http://www.hse.gov.uk/vibration/wbv/index.htm

# Vibration 2: Hand-transmitted vibration

## Common sources

Exposure to hand-transmitted vibration (HTV) arises from many sources, including concrete breakers, chainsaws, handheld grinders, metal polishers, power hammers and chisels, needle scalers, scabblers, powered sanders, hammer drills, and even powered lawnmowers, and motorcycle handlebars. The common factor is extrinsic vibrational energy being transmitted to the hands.

## Occupations and industries

Occupations where exposure is common include:
- Construction workers, ground workers, and road workers
- Metal-working, welders, and maintenance fitters
- Shipbuilders
- Foundry workers
- Forestry and grounds/garden maintenance workers

The main industries are construction and heavy engineering. An estimated 1.2 million individuals in Britain have weekly exposures that may justify health surveillance.

## Main factors affecting exposure

- *Tools*: intrinsic properties of the tool (e.g. size, weight, frequency characteristics, balance between reciprocating forces), age of tools, and their maintenance
- *Material* being worked
- *Type of work* (e.g. cutting, drilling, grinding)
- *Transmission of vibration* to the operator technique (type and force of grip, orientation of the hand-arm)

## Potential health effects

- Hand–arm vibration syndrome, which includes a secondary form of Raynaud's phenomenon (vibration-induced white finger), sensorineural impairment in the digits, and other musculoskeletal effects including possible weakness of grip
- Carpal tunnel syndrome in which vibration may be a contributory factor as well as other factors, such as ergonomics, other underlying disease, wrist structure
- Other effects to the hand and arm are described (see ➲ p. 330, hand-arm vibration syndrome)
- Workers who use vibratory tools have increased risk of high-frequency hearing loss as well as local hand–arm symptoms

## Risk assessment and monitoring

Vibration magnitude is measured in terms of acceleration, averaged by the root–mean square (rms) method. Frequency-weighted measurements ($a_{hw}$) are made in three axes relative to the tool handle, using mounted accelerometers, and values (in m/s$^2$ rms) are determined for each axis and summated.

It is generally accepted that injury relates to the total lifetime exposure, which will reflect years of exposure as well as the average daily exposure.

The daily exposure to vibration (A(8)) of a person is obtained using the formula and expressed as $m/s^2$,

$$A(8) = a_{hv} \sqrt{}(T/T_0) m/s^2,$$

where $a_{hv}$ is the weighted rms vibration magnitude ($m/s^2$); T is the duration of exposure to the vibration magnitude $a_{hv}$; $T_0$ is the reference duration of 8 hours (expressed in same unit as T).

Partial doses from more than one tool can be summed to an equivalent daily dose. HSE provides an exposure ready-reckoner,[1] to estimate A(8) from exposure time and vibration magnitude,[2] and an exposure calculator to facilitate the summation of doses from several tools. In practice, this requires an inventory of tools, data on vibration magnitude, either from equipment handbooks or suppliers' information sheets or measured directly, and an estimate of 'trigger time'—being the time that the tool is held while vibrating.[3]

## Vibration measurement

- Vibration metres should meet the specification for the measurement of HTV in BS EN ISO 8041 and BS EN ISO 5349-2
- Personal vibration magnitudes vary due to several factors, e.g. posture, techniques, changes in force; therefore need to take several measurements for a range of common machine/tool operating conditions
- Measure the vibration for each of the makes and models of machine types in use
- The mean plus one standard deviation of the range of vibration measurements is usually sufficient when operators work on a wide range of machines/tasks
- Examples of vibration magnitude of common machines are included in Table 6 of the HSE L140.[4] Vibration data is also available through technical and scientific publications and from online databases

## Exposure limits

Employers have an overriding duty to reduce exposure to HTV as low as reasonably practicable. Two exposure limits are specified in UK and European legislation:

- *EAV A(8) of 2.5 m/s²*: the daily amount above which employers must undertake specific actions, including health surveillance for workers who are regularly exposed above the EAV, and the provision of information, instruction, and training
- *ELV A(8) of 5 m/s²*: the maximum amount an employee may be exposed to on any given day

1 Hand-arm vibration at work- a brief guide. Published 2012. Issued by the Health and Safety Executive (HSE). http://www.hse.gov.uk/pubns/indg175.pdf

2 Exposure points system and ready-reckoner. Available on the HSE website no date, accessed 22Nov 2021. http://www.hse.gov.uk/vibration/hav/readyreckoner.htm

3 Hand-arm vibration exposure calculator. Available on the HSE website, no date, accessed 22Nov 2021. https://www.hse.gov.uk/vibration/hav/vibrationcalc.htm

4 Hand-arm vibration. The Control of Vibration at Work Regulations 2005. Guide on Regulations L140 (second edition). 2019. Published by TSO (The Stationery Office).

## Prevention and control

A number of steps can mitigate the risk in exposed populations. These may be broadly summarized as:

- Avoidance (e.g. doing the job another way)
- Substitution (of tool or material worked)
- Interruption of the pathway (by isolation or vibration-damping, although 'anti-vibration gloves' are not likely to be helpful in most situations)
- Appropriate selection of tools for the task, and good tool maintenance
- Rest breaks and job rotation to limit individual exposure times

Another common approach involves screening for early health effects and limiting further exposure in those with diagnosed hand–arm vibration syndrome.

## Relevant legislation

Control of Vibration at Work Regulations 2005

## Further information and guidance

BS EN ISO 5349-2. *Mechanical Vibration. Measurement and Assessment of Human Exposure to Hand-Transmitted Vibration. Practical Guidance for Measurement at the Workplace*: British Standards Institution. BS EN ISO 8041. Published in 2017. London.

BS EN ISO 8041. *Human Response to Vibration. Measuring Instrumentation*. British Standards Institution.

HSE web links. HSE, *Hand-arm vibration at work*. Sudbury. Available at: http://www.hse.gov.uk/vibration/hav/index.htm

# Light and lighting 1: Effects and illuminance levels

## Terms, definitions, and units

- *Luminous intensity* is the term applied to the luminous flux emitted per solid angle and is measured in candela (Cd). The candela is one of the seven basic SI units
- *Illuminance* is the amount of light falling on a surface divided by the area over which it is falling and is measured in lux (derivation = lumens.$m^{-2}$)
- *Luminance* is the amount of light emitted by a source in a given direction, measured in Cd.$m^{-2}$

## Lighting and health

In striving for optimum lighting conditions, it is essential to consider the intensity and colour spectrum of the light sources used. Incorrect selection may lead to adverse health and/or psychological effects. The selection of the appropriate illuminance for given visual tasks is vitally important.

- Too much illuminance can lead to the onset of glare
- Too little illuminance can put a strain on the eyes. In some cases, the latter causes the individual to adopt uncomfortable working postures which may lead to musculoskeletal problems

Poor lighting increases risk of fatigue and accidents, reduces productivity, and increases workers dissatisfaction, which may contribute to worker absenteeism.

*Specific health risks*

These include, but are not limited to:

- *Infrared and ultraviolet (UV) radiation*: tungsten halogen (desk top lamps) and other high-powered lamps, e.g. those used in broadcasting studios may emit high levels of UV radiation and cause harm to skin and eyes. These lamps should be fitted with a safety shield or UV filter. For lasers, see ➲ p. 32, Non-ionizing radiation 3: Lasers.
- *Blue light hazard*: in accordance with the 'Position Statement' released by CIE (Commission Internationale de l´Eclairage) in April 2019, the term 'blue light hazard' should only be limited to consideration of the photochemical risk to the retinal tissues of the eye which is technically referred to as 'photomaculopathy'. It is usually associated with staring into bright sources, such as the sun or welding arcs. Reference to 'Blue' in the description is included as the risk of photochemical injury is wavelength-dependent, peaking in the blue part of the optical radiation spectrum around 435 nm to 440 nm. Blue light hazard is particularly important when considering aphakic individuals
- *Photokeratitis*: a tender eye condition typically following exposure of insufficiently protected eyes to the UV rays emitted by either natural or artificial sources, e.g. welder's arc or some artificial light sources

## Unwanted effects created by lamps and lighting

- *Glare* occurs when one part of the visual field is much brighter than others. There are two major types of glare:
  - *disability glare* where the individual is disabled from carrying out a given visual task

- *discomfort glare* where the individual is not disabled from carrying out a given visual task, but where they will experience discomfort, which may be delayed in manifestation
- *Veiling reflections* is the term applied to the scenario where typically out of focus reflections of light sources are viewed on specular surfaces (typically display screen equipment). This throws a veil of light over the screen making reading of text either difficult or impossible. Veiling reflections is a form of disability glare
- *Flicker* is effectively light modulations at frequencies detectable by the human visual system. This can lead to both discomfort and fatigue and may provoke seizures in photosensitive individuals if the flicker frequency lies typically between 5 Hz and 30 Hz
- *Stroboscopic effects on rotating machines*: this is the scenario where rotating elements of machinery appear to be stationary or moving in a different manner (possibly in the reverse direction). It is caused by a combination of the rate of oscillations in light output illuminating the rotating element and the rate at which the human visual system can detect movement

## Recommended illuminance values

- The illuminance requirements of a task depend on performance factors such as level of detail, speed, and accuracy. The Chartered Institute of Building Service Engineers (CIBSE) via the Society of Light & Lighting (SLL) provides a comprehensive schedule of recommended illuminance values for different workplaces.[1] The lighting levels depend on the visual requirements for different tasks (level of detail) in different work environments (Table 1.2)
- Guidance on minimum acceptable levels of lighting is given in the HSE publication *Lighting at work*[2]

**Table 1.2** Typical lighting levels for work environments with different visual requirements

| | Illuminance (lx) | Location/activity |
|---|---|---|
| Increasing visual requirements for tasks (↑) | 1500 | Fine work and precision assembly |
| | 1000 | General inspection, electronic assembly, paintwork |
| | 750 | Drawing rooms, meat inspection |
| | 500 | General offices, laboratories |
| | 300 | Libraries, lecture theatres |
| | 150 | Loading bays, plants room |
| | 100 | Corridors, stores |

1 CIBSE (2009). *SLL Lighting Handbook*. Available at: https://www.cibse.org/knowledge/knowledge-items/detail?id=a0q0O00000F4MeJQAV

2 HSE (2002). *Lighting at Work*. HSE, Sudbury. Available at: http://www.hse.gov.uk/pubns/books/hsg38.htm

# Light and lighting 2: Assessment and surveys

## Assessing lighting in the workplace

Workplace lighting should meet the following criteria:

- Provides suitable and sufficient illuminance on the work piece
- Provides suitable and sufficient discrimination on the surface colours of objects in the working area
- Prevents the onset of glare
- Avoids flicker and/or stroboscopic effects
- Avoids the effects of veiling reflections
- Provides sufficient contrast between work piece and background
- Prevents excessive variation in illuminance and luminance within the vicinity of the working areas. Optimally, the ratio of luminance values (task: near surround: far surround) should be 10:3:1
- Takes into account the requirements of workers with disabilities
- Be located so that access to luminaires (formerly light fittings) and other lighting equipment does not pose a risk of danger to maintenance personnel
- Incorporates appropriate emergency lighting
- Evaluates the risks and in so doing decides if improvement measures are required to protect the employees

## Lighting surveys

- It is desirable to have scale drawings of the interior to be surveyed. Alternatively, draw a sketch plan of room showing position of work surfaces, windows, and luminaires
- *Record*:
  - visual tasks carried out
  - state of cleanliness of the luminaires
  - any luminaires which are damaged or missing
  - any luminaires or windows that cause discomfort or disability glare
  - any flicker from lamps
- Photographs showing areas of particular contention can be extremely useful
- The principal measurements of interest when undertaking a lighting survey are illuminance and luminance
- Illuminance reading should be taken and recorded at all stations and on every work surface
- During measurements, normal workplace lighting should be switched on and natural lighting should be excluded, where possible
- Illuminance measurements are normally taken at the height of the work plane. In situations where there is no specified plane for the visual task, the measurement should be taken at a horizontal plane at typically 0.8 m above the floor
- The minimum number of measurements can be derived by calculating the room index k, where $k = \{(L \times W) \div [Hm\ (L + W)]\}$, L is the room length, W is the room width, Hm is the height of lamps above working surface. For values of $k < 1$, 1–2, 2–3, and $> 3$, the minimum number of measurements are 9, 16, 25, and 36, respectively

- Average illuminance values are calculated by adding all measurements and dividing by the number of measurements and compared with the CIBSE (SLL) guidance values
- Lamps must be in operation for sufficient time to allow light output to stabilize (typically 20 minutes)
- Comprehensive details of required illuminance values in typical workplace locations are provided by CIBSE (SLL)

## Further information

BS 5266–1 (2016). *Code of Practice for the Emergency Lighting of Premises*. British Standards Institution. London, UK.

BS EN 12464–1 (2011). *Light and Lighting—Lighting of Workplaces Indoor Workplaces*. British Standards Institution. London, UK.

BS EN 12464–2 (2007). *Light and Lighting—Lighting of Workplaces Outdoor Workplaces*. British Standards Institution. London, UK.

CIE (2019). The position statement on blue light hazards was published by the Commission Internationale de l'Eclairage (CIE)International Commission on illumination in 2019 (Austria).

HSE) (1992). *Health and Safety (Display Screen Equipment) Regulations (1992)*. HSE Books, Sudbury. Available at: https://www.hse.gov.uk/pubns/priced/l26.pdf

HSE (1997). *Lighting at Work*, HSG38. HSE Books, Sudbury. Available at: https://www.hse.gov.uk/pubns/priced/hsg38.pdf

SLL *Code for Lighting* (2012). Published by Chartered Institute of Building Services Engineering (CIBSE) available at https://www.cibse.org/knowledge/knowledge-items/detail?id=a0q20000008I6xiAAC

Smith NA (2000). *Lighting for Health and Safety*. Butterworth-Heinemann, Oxford.

# Ionizing radiation 1: Types, units, and effects

## Routes and sources of exposure

- The hazard from ionizing radiation can arise from:
  - the uniform external irradiation of the whole body or part of the body
  - internal irradiation due to inhaled or absorbed radioactive material, which may concentrate in organs and tissues
- Natural (background) radiation arises from several sources, including radiation from materials in the Earth's crust (e.g. radon in granite strata), cosmic radiation, food, radioactive aerosols, and gases in the atmosphere. The largest dose of radiation, approximately 84% of the total, received by a person living in the UK is due to natural background radiation. Typically, this can amount to 2.3 millisieverts (mSv) per year

*Sources of ionizing radiation*

- *Sealed*:
  - contained or shielded
  - presenting only an external radiation hazard
- *Unsealed*: can be released into the atmosphere because they:
  - are powders, liquids, or gases
  - can contaminate surfaces and be taken into the body by ingestion, inhalation, or via the skin particularly from a wound, thereby giving rise to an internal radiation hazard, which can be present for variable periods of time

## Types of ionizing radiation

Ionizing radiation is emitted by unstable isotopes of various chemical elements which have an imbalance of mass or energy compared to stable isotopes. The common, medically important, forms of the resulting radioactivity are:

- *Alpha particles*: these are positively charged particles consisting of two protons and two neutrons (the same as a helium atom nucleus) with relatively little energy (they cannot pass through a sheet of paper or intact skin and have a very limited range in air), but capable of causing significant damage to tissue over a short range
- *Beta particles*: these are electrons and are also charged (negatively). They are much lighter than alpha particles and can pass through paper and skin, although they can be stopped by materials such as glass or thin layers of metal
- *Neutrons*: these are uncharged particles with intermediate mass and variable energy, but with a range similar to gamma and X-rays
- *Gamma and X-rays*: these are uncharged and without mass. They therefore cause less damage to tissue, but can pass through many materials, although are attenuated by thick layers of lead or concrete

## Units of ionizing radiation

*Activity*

This indicates the rate of transformations in radioactive material. The unit is the becquerel (Bq).

1Bq= 1 transformation/s.

(In practice, the Becquerel is a very small unit and thus radioactivity is often quoted in terms of kilo-, mega-, and giga-becquerels. It is also usual to indicate radioactivity per unit of mass, i.e. Bq/kg.)

*Absorbed dose*

This is the measure of energy deposition in any irradiated material by all types of ionizing radiation and is expressed as the energy absorbed per unit mass of material. The unit of absorbed dose is gray (Gy):

$$1\text{Gy} = 1\text{J/kg of energy deposition.}$$

*Dose equivalent*

In biological systems, the same absorbed dose of different types of radiation produces different degrees of biological damage. To take account of this, the absorbed dose of each type of radiation is multiplied by a Q (or weighting) factor, which reflects the relative ability of the particular type of radiation to cause damage. The unit of dose equivalent is the sievert (Sv), which is related to the gray as follows:

$$\text{dose equivalent } (\text{Sv}) = \text{absorbed dose}(\text{Gy}) \times \text{Q}.$$

(Occupational doses of radiation are quoted in mSv in view of the levels of radiation received.)

For beta particles, gamma and X-rays, Q = 1. For $\alpha$ particles, Q = 20. For neutrons, on average, Q = 10.

*Effective dose*

Similarly, the risk to various tissues varies from one tissue to another; it is not the same for any given equivalent dose. There is thus a weighting factor for each tissue; when multiplied by the equivalent dose, the sum of all such calculations for the various tissues is referred to as the effective dose and is a single measure of the risk of detriment to health. This includes the so-called committed dose which arises from internal irradiation.

## Health effects

These arise from direct damage to cell DNA or indirect damage due to radiation-induced free radical formation. Cancer, cataract formation, and cardiovascular disease are all associated with ionizing radiation exposure.

- Damage to tissue sustained by an irradiated individual is termed '*somatic*' *effects*. These can be acute or delayed. That passed on to descendants is the hereditary effect
- *Stochastic effects* are those for which *risk* (the probability of the effect) increases progressively with dose received, but there is no detectable threshold, e.g. induction of carcinogenesis and inheritable genetic defects. The risk of developing cancer for radiation workers is calculated as 4% per Sv
- *Deterministic/tissue effects* are those for which the *severity* of the effect increases progressively with dose and will not occur until a certain threshold of dose has been received, e.g. acute radiation syndrome, radiation burn, cataract

# Ionizing radiation 2: Principles of radiation protection

## Justification

The use of sources of ionizing radiation or radioactive materials must be justified in terms of risk and benefit.

## Optimization

Work with sources of ionizing radiation must be such as to reduce risks to levels that are as low as reasonably achievable (in practice, 'achievable' becomes 'practicable').

## Dose limits

- Dose limits are recommended by the International Commission on Radiation Protection, with the aim of preventing non-stochastic (deterministic) effects and limiting stochastic effects
- Current dose limits for UK workers and the public are published in the Ionizing Radiations Regulations 2017 and are shown in Table 1.3

**Table 1.3** UK annual dose limits (mSv)

| | Annual dose limits | | |
|---|---|---|---|
| | Whole body | Skin | Lens of the eye |
| Radiation workers (classified) | 20 | 500 | 20 |
| Trainee (under 18) | 6 | 150 | 15 |
| Radiation workers (non-classified) | 6 | 50 | 15 |
| Others, including members of the public | 1 | 50 | 15 |

The dose limit to the foetus once pregnancy has been declared is 1 mSv during the period of the pregnancy. From TSO (2018). *Ionizing Radiations Regulations*. TSO, London. Available at: http://www.books.hse.gov.uk

# Ionizing radiation 3: Instrumentation and measurement

## Environmental radiation detectors

A wide range of instruments are available. Instruments are based on several types of detectors (gas ionization, solid state detectors, change in chemical systems, and neutron activation) and are used to quantify incident radiation as a count or dose rate. Such detectors include:

- *Installed (fixed) monitors*: used to monitor personal contamination, general radiation, and air contamination level in the working environment
- *Portable (battery operated) monitors*: used to measure levels during specific operations and for contamination surveys

## Devices for personal monitoring

*Film badges*

- The film is developed and analysed for external radiation dose, which is in proportion to darkening of the film
- Various filters inside the badge differentiate types of radiation and energies
- Developed film can be stored to provide a permanent record, which can be read again at a later date
- They are no longer widely used as they are less practical and more expensive than thermoluminescent dosemeters (TLDs)

*Thermoluminescent dosemeters*

- Can measure over a wide range for both whole body and extremity (finger) monitoring
- Popular dosemeter for personal monitoring, as they are small, and analysis can be performed quickly and automatically
- Not as sensitive to the effects of heat and humidity as film badges
- They are more sensitive at low doses than film badges
- Dose information is destroyed at readout, unlike film badges

*Direct reading instruments*

- Use for direct measurement of X-rays or gamma rays
- Self-indicating dosemeters, such as the electronic personal dosemeter, are useful for measuring doses in situations where the dose rate is high, allowing a continuous watch to be kept on the rate of accumulation of dose. They may be fitted with alarms
- Must be calibrated with known dose levels
- May be used alongside other dosimeters, such as TLDs

## Monitoring unsealed radiation sources

- *Surface contamination*: monitoring in the work area and on the worker's skin, and clothing is carried out using portable and fixed monitors, including before workers leave a controlled area
- *Airborne sampling*: as with dusts, certain types of radioactive material can be sampled on filter paper using a high-volume sampler. Particulate or gaseous activity is then measured by scanning the filter for radioactivity using a counter. Radioactive gases can also be collected using a sampling bag or chamber. Employees in areas where there is a risk of internal contamination from radioactive materials wear personal air samplers which utilize these principles
- *Whole-body monitoring*: external radiation detectors in special centres measure gamma or X radiation emitted by radioactive material absorbed by the body
- *Biological monitoring*: total internal dose is determined in special cases by measuring radioactivity in urine or stool samples
- Biological effect monitoring can be done by examining lymphocyte chromosome abnormalities in a blood sample. The dicentric abnormality is characteristic of ionizing radiation exposure. The minimum dose detectable is in the region of 100 mGy

# Ionizing radiation 4: Exposure control

## General requirements

- Demarcating specific areas and classification of personnel based on their radiation exposure. For those workers designated 'classified', personal dosimetry and health surveillance are required under the Ionizing Radiations Regulations 2017. Such workers are classified on the basis of a requirement to work in areas where they may receive at least 30% of the legal, or a lower locally imposed, maximum total body dose, or doses to the eye lens, skin, or extremities above a specified limit
- Appointing a radiation protection adviser (RPA) and radiation protection supervisors
- Arrangement for waste disposal, monitoring exposure, and training on safe work practices and precautions

## Control of external exposure

Exposure to external ionizing radiation can be reduced by time, distance, and shielding.

- *Time*: reduce exposure time to a minimum
- *Distance*: arrange work so that the distance from source to worker is as great as possible. The intensity of point source radiation decreases with increasing distance, obeying the inverse square law
- *Shielding of the worker from radiation*: advice can be obtained from manufacturers or the RPA on the type and thickness of shielding necessary. This is particularly indicated for penetrating radiation, such as gamma and X-rays

## Control of internal exposure

This can be reduced by:

- Containing the source, e.g. in a glove box
- Good housekeeping and personal hygiene
- Use, careful storage, and maintenance of personal and respiratory protective equipment, e.g. gloves, full face respirator, air hood, or pressurized suit

## Classification of work areas

Work areas are classified according to the potential level of exposure:

- *Supervised area*: dose rate is likely to be less than 7.5 μSv/h, but workers in that area may receive an effective dose of greater than 1 mSv per year
- *Controlled area*: dose rate can exceed 7.5 μSv/h and workers in that area may receive an effective dose of at least 6 mSv per year. Access to such areas is strictly controlled

## Relevant legislation

- Ionizing Radiations Regulations (2017)
- Ionizing Radiation (Medical Exposure) Regulations (2017)
- Radiation (Emergency Preparedness and Public Information) Regulations (2001)

## Further information

Cherrie J, Semple S Coggins M, (2021). *Monitoring for Health Hazards at Work*, 5th Edition. Wiley Blackwell.

HSE (2015). *Working Safely with Ionising Radiation Guidelines for Expectant or Breastfeeding Mothers.* HSE Books, Sudbury. Available at: http://www.hse.gov.uk/radiation/ionising/index.htm

HSE (2018). *Work with Ionizing Radiation. The Ionizing Radiations Regulations (2017), Approved Code of Practice and Guidance L121.* HSE Books, Sudbury.

Public Health England (PHE) website. *Radiation: risks from low levels of ionising radiation.* Published by Public Health England (PHE), UK. Available at: www.gov.uk/government/collections/radiation-risks-from-low-levels-of-ionising-radiation

# Non-ionizing radiation 1: Electromagnetic fields

Electromagnetic fields (EMF) radiation (frequencies up to 300 GHz) does not have sufficient energy to break the bonds that hold molecules in cells together, and so it does not produce ionization of matter. Effects on the body depend on the frequency and magnitude of EMF. Static electric fields build up charge on the surface of the body. Magnetic fields can induce flows of electric current in the body. Radiofrequency radiation is partially absorbed, penetrating a short distance into tissues, and can give rise to localized heating. EMFs are present in almost all workplaces, being produced when an electric or electronic item of equipment is used.

## Sources of exposure (occupational and environmental)

*Static and extremely low-frequency fields (ELF)*

- Electrical power lines
- Household electrical appliances
- Electrical transport
- Welding
- MRI scanners

*High-frequency or radiofrequency fields*

- Radiofrequency fields (RF): radar
- Radio and television broadcast facilities
- Mobile telephones and their base stations
- Induction heaters
- Anti-theft devices

## Health effects of EMF

- Various sensory abnormalities, such as vertigo, and local heating effects are described
- Employees with implanted or body-worn medical devices are at increased risk
- ELF have been classified by the International Agency for Research on Cancer (IARC)[1] as a possible carcinogen (2B) for childhood leukaemia in humans but have not been given a carcinogen notation for any other cancer. The evidence for childhood leukaemia is inconclusive and there could be other explanations for the association with ELF
- While until recently the balance of evidence has suggested that there are no important health effects from RF, IARC has also classified this type of EMF as a possible human carcinogen (2B) for glioma

There is currently a high level of public interest and debate regarding exposure to RF (in particular, mobile telephones and masts) focusing on the health effects of long-term low-level exposure. The Interphone study, coordinated by IARC, has yet to show any definite evidence of public health risk. 5G communications, while utilizing higher frequencies than previously, are not expected to be associated with significant health effects, as a result of updated International Commission on Non-ionizing Radiation Protection (ICNIRP) guidelines.

1 World Health Organization International Agency for Research on Cancer. WHO, Geneva. Available at: http://www.iarc.fr/

## Exposure guidelines

Countries set their own exposure standards for EMF, the majority of which are based on ICNIRP guidelines.[2] These follow the precautionary principle in setting separate limits for occupational and public exposure. They cover frequencies in the range 0–300 GHz and are based on short-term acute exposure.

In the UK, the National Radiological Protection Board (NRPB) (now part of Public Health England (PHE)) has defined exposure limits.

The Control of Electromagnetic Fields at Work Regulations (2016) require employers to assess the risks to employees and eliminate or minimize the risks.

## Exposure control

Elimination is not usually possible. Control measures include:

- Careful selection of equipment or working methods
- Effective enclosure, interlocks, and reflective screens
- Control by distance from source
- Personal protective equipment (PPE)
- Medical pre-selection and exclusion of employees with susceptible implantable or body-worn medical devices when risk reduction not possible

## Relevant legislation

Control of Electromagnetic Fields at Work Regulations (2016)
http://www.hse.gov.uk/pubns/hsg281

## Further reading and guidance

International Commission on Non-ionizing Radiation Protection (ICNIRP). Available at: http://www.icnirp.org/

The IARC Report to the Union for International Cancer Control (UICC) on the Interphone Study 2011. Available at https://interphone.iarc.fr/uicc-report-final-03102011.pdf

PHE (2013). *Electric and Magnetic Fields*. Sudbury. Published by Public Health England in 2019, UK. Available at: http://www.gov.uk/government/collections/electromagnetic-fields

The International EMF Project has established a worldwide database of standards.

The International EMF Project has established a worldwide database of standards. Available at: http://www.who.int/peh-emf/standards/en/

World Health Organization (2002). *Establishing a Dialogue on Risks from Electromagnetic Fields*. WHO, Geneva. Available at: http://www.who.int/peh-emf/publications/risk_hand/en/index.html

World Health Organization International Agency for Research on Cancer. WHO, Geneva. Available at: http://www.iarc.fr/

2 International Commission on Non-ionizing Radiation Protection. Available at: http://www.icnirp.de/what.htm

# Non-ionizing radiation 2: Optical radiation

## Relevant legislation

The Control of Artificial Optical Radiation at Work Regulations (2010) aim to protect workers from risks from various sources, such as UV light (excluding sunlight) and lasers. The regulations distinguish between 'safe sources', such as most forms of visible light, and 'hazardous sources', such as high intensity UV and laser sources. There are requirements to consider alternative sources, undertake training, use control measures and, if necessary, carry out a detailed risk assessment. Some workers may be at increased risk due to light-aggravated medical conditions

## Hazardous light sources

Hazardous sources of light that present a risk of harming the eyes and skin of worker where control measures are needed include:

- *Metal working*: welding and plasma cutting
- *Hot processes*: furnaces, hot metal glass
- *Motor vehicle repairs*: UV curing of paints and welding
- *Pharmaceutical and research*: UV sterilization and induced fluorescence
- *Printing*: UV curing of inks and paints
- *Medical and cosmetic treatment*: UV and blue light therapies, laser surgery (Class 3B and 4 lasers), intense pulsed light
- *Industry and research*: use of Class 3B and Class 4 lasers as defined in BS EN 60825–1 (2014). British Standards Institution
- Any risk group 3 lamp or lamp systems as defined in BSEN 62471 (2008), e.g. professional projections systems

## Control measures

- Use alternative safer light sources
- *Engineering measures*: automation, controlled areas, remote control, screening, interlocks
- Use filters, remote viewing, and time delays
- Protect others using screens/curtains/restricted access to hazardous areas
- Provide PPE, e.g. coveralls, goggles, face-shields, gloves
- Provide information and training on safe use and best practice
- Display safety and warning signs
- Monitor use of control measures

► If any workers are overexposed, e.g. damage to skin and eyes, provide medical examination and follow-up health surveillance.

## Ultraviolet

*Subtypes*

UV light is divided into three types, according to wavelength. (Only UVA and UVB from the sun affect humans as UVC is absorbed by the earth's atmosphere).

- *UVA*: 315–400 nm
- *UVB*: 280–315 nm
- *UVC*: 100–280 nm

*Sources of exposure (occupational and environmental)*

- Welding
- Printing
- Germicidal and mercury lamps
- Spectroscopy
- External work (sunlight—not covered by the specific legislation)

*Health effects*

- Skin erythema/burn
- Premature skin ageing
- Cataract
- Photokeratitis
- Photosensitive and phototoxic reactions (associated with external or internal exposure to chemical agents, or skin or systemic diseases)
- Skin cancer (basal and squamous cell types are associated with prolonged sun exposure, while melanoma may be more associated with short, intense exposures)
- Benefits from Vitamin D production, and improvement in some conditions, such as psoriasis

*Control measures*

- Limit exposure time to sunlight, especially in the middle of the day
- Have shaded areas available for breaks
- Use suitable clothing and hats to protect the skin
- Use sun protection creams
- Provide training to workers including the above as well as on maintenance of hydration and observation of the skin for suspicious lesions

## Laser

See ➲ p. 32, Non-ionizing radiation 3: Laser.

## Further information

HSE (2010). *Control of Artificial Optical Radiation at Work Regulations*. HSE, Sudbury.

HSE (2010). *Guidance for Employers on the Control of Artificial Optical Radiation at Work Regulations*. HSE, Sudbury.

HSE, Sudbury. Guidance for Employers on the Control of Artificial Optical Radiation at Work Regulations (AOR) 2010. Published by HSE Books. Available at: http://www.hse.gov.uk/radiation/nonionising/employers-aor.pdf PHE (2017). *Laser Radiation: Safety Advice*. PHE, London. Available at: www.gov.uk/government/publications/laser-radiation-safety-advice

# Non-ionizing radiation 3: Laser

## Characteristics

- *Laser radiation has unique properties*: monochromatic, coherent, bright, high irradiance, and focused to deposit intense energy on small surfaces
- *Lasers are of four types*: solid state, dye (liquid), gas, and semi-conductor
- *Lasers can be operated in two major modes*: pulsed and continuous wave
- *Lasers are grouped into eight classes*: the higher the class, the greater the potential for harm

## Health effects

- Visible and IR-A (short-wave infrared) laser beams can be focused to create very high intensity exposures on the retina
- The effects depend on a number of factors including the wavelength, power, pulse duration, and beam geometry
- Laser beams produce biological damage by thermal burns and photochemical injuries. Visible and IR-A lasers produce retinal damage
- The retina is most at risk; thermal and photochemical damage may also occur
  - inadvertent reflections must be avoided so that beams are not redirected into safe zones
  - a classification system for lasers has been developed to ensure safe use (summary shown in Box 1.2)
  - training programmes are required for users of class 3 and 4 lasers. Medical surveillance is not required by legislation, although has been recommended with the use of class 3B and 4 lasers
  - the American Conference of Industrial Hygienists (ACGIH) publishes threshold limit values standards for lasers emissions (ocular and skin exposures) for IR, UV, and light exposure arising from viewing a laser beam

## Controls

Controls applied to different laser devices are shown in Box 1.2.

### *Engineering*

The main engineering control is enclosure, often in the form of interlocked rooms. Remote interlocks can make up safety chains covering a large area.

### *Administrative*

Administrative controls are used during set up and maintenance. These include designated zones, authorization, and warning signs.

### *Personal protective equipment*

Laser protective goggles must be selected to ensure that they are of appropriate optical density for the type (wavelength) of radiation encountered and its power. Lenses are glass or plastic. Glass lenses are heavier but offer more resistance to direct strikes and let through more light. Glass is often used when average laser power exceeds 100 mW.

**Box 1.2 Laser safety classification and required controls**

*Class 1*

- Safe under reasonably foreseeable conditions of operation
- Protection measures not necessary, PPE not required

*Class 1C*

- Contained in products used on the skin, e.g. for hair removal
- The hazard to the eye is controlled by engineering features

*Class 1M*

- Safe for naked eye, may be hazardous if the user employs optics
- Prevent use of magnifying, focusing, or collimating optics
- PPE not required

*Class 2*

- Safe for short exposures, eye protection afforded by aversion response
- Follow manufactures' instructions for safe use
- Do not stare in to beam
- PPE not required

*Class 2M*

- Safe for naked eye for short exposures, may be hazardous if the user employs optics
- Do not stare in to beam, prevent use of magnifying, focusing, or collimating optics
- Training recommended; PPE not required

*Class 3R*

- Risk of injury is relatively low, but may be dangerous for improper use by untrained person
- Enclosed
- Prevent direct eye exposure
- Training required
- PPE may be required subject to findings of risk assessment

*Class 3B*

- Direct viewing is hazardous and minor skin injuries may occur
- Enclosed and interlock protected
- Prevent eye and skin exposure to the direct or reflected beam
- Training and PPE required

*Class 4*

- Hazardous for eye and skin; fire hazard
- Enclosed and interlock protected
- Prevent eye and skin exposure from direct and diffuse reflection of the beam
- Training and PPE required

# Thermal environment 1: Thermal balance and instrumentation

## Heat stress

Heat stress occurs when the body's means of controlling internal temperature starts to fail. Operations involving high air temperatures, radiant heat sources, high humidity, or strenuous physical activities have a high potential for inducing heat stress.

## Heat balance

- The body core temperature must be regulated to remain typically at 37 ± 0.5°C. Below 31°C leads to loss of consciousness and death. Above 43°C leads to failure of the thermoregulation mechanism
- Heat balance between the human body and its surroundings can be expressed as the equation

$$M = \pm K \pm C \pm R - E,$$

where M is the rate of metabolic heat production (see Table 1.4); K, C, and R are gain or loss of heat by conduction, convection, and radiation, respectively; and E is the evaporative heat loss from skin and respiratory tract

- The heat balance is affected by work performed and the rate of change in the store of heat in the body

## Health effects

- *Exposure to high temperature*: heat stroke, heat syncope, heat exhaustion, heat fatigue, and prickly heat, cataract, susceptibility to other disease (e.g. cardiovascular)
- *Exposure to low temperature*: hypothermia is a condition of low core temperature, and is clinically defined as a deep body temperature below 35°C

## Occupations at risk

Work activities that may lead to heat stress include handling molten metal, metal refining, glass-making, boiler and furnace maintenance, mining and tunnelling, firefighting, and outdoor work in hot climates.

## Parameters and instruments for heat stress

The following four environmental parameters must be assessed:

- air temperature
- air velocity
- radiant temperature
- relative humidity (RH)

Instruments for measuring individual environmental parameters include:

- *Dry bulb thermometers or electric thermometers*: measure air temperature
- *Wet bulb thermometer*: dry bulb covered in a clean cotton wick wetted with distilled water. Used to measure RH. At 100% RH, the wet and dry bulb temperatures are equal
- *Psychrometers*: consist of wet and dry bulb thermometer mounted in a frame. There are two types—the sling and the aspirated. Used to determine the RH

- *Globe thermometer (mercury-in-glass thermometer with its bulb in the centre of a matt black sphere or globe)*: used to measure radiant temperature
- *Kata thermometer*: used for measuring air velocities <0.5 m/s

*Integrating electronic heat stress monitors*

- *Static instruments*: provide a single value for wet bulb globe temperatures (WBGT) and air velocities (Fig. 1.2)
- *Personal heat stress monitors* (Fig. 1.3): signals from various sensors including heart rate and temperature fed into a data logger, which calculates a strain index. The monitor can be set for different age ranges and clothing. An audible alarm, indicating if preset warning and action levels are exceeded, is usually fitted

**Table 1.4** Metabolic rates for activities

| Class | Mean metabolic rate ($Wm^{-2}$) | Example |
|---|---|---|
| Resting | 65 | Resting |
| Low | 100 | Standing |
| Moderate | 165 | Sustained hand/arm work |
| High | 230 | Intense work |
| Very high | 290 | Very intense to maximum activity |

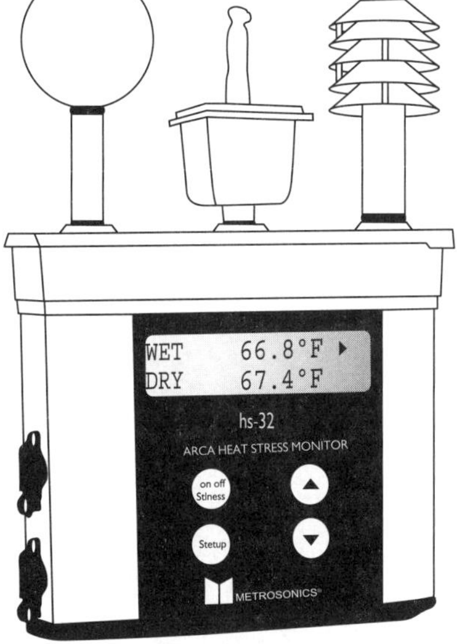


**Fig. 1.2** Electronic integrating heat stress monitor

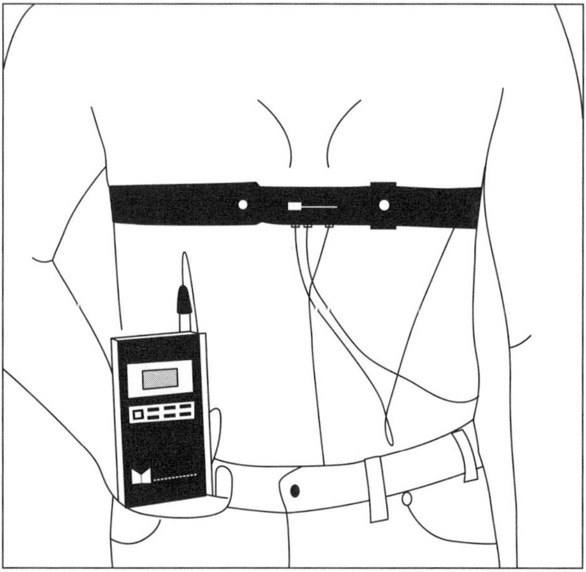

**Fig. 1.3** Personal heat stress monitor

# Thermal environment 2: Assessment of the thermal environment

A number of heat stress indices have been developed for different industries. These form part of a risk assessment with the aim of preventing the deep body temperature from exceeding 38°C.

## Classification of heat stress indices

*Empirical and direct indices*

Wet bulb temperature (WB), effective temperature, corrected effective temperature, WBGT.

*Analytical indices*

Required sweat rate, heat stress index, predicted 4-hour sweat rate.

## Wet bulb globe temperature

WBGT is the most widely accepted index for assessment of heat stress in industry and published as British Standard BS EN 27243 and also in the ACGIH threshold limits values.

WBGT (expressed in temperature units) is calculated as follows:

$$\text{For indoor use, WBGT} = 0.7\ \text{WB} + 0.3\ \text{GT},$$

$$\text{For outdoor use, WBGT} = 0.7\ \text{WB} + 0.2\ \text{GT} + 0.1\ \text{DB},$$

where WB is natural wet bulb temperature; GT is the globe thermometer temperature (°C), and DB is the dry bulb temperature (°C).

Table 1.5 shows reference values of WBGT related to a maximum rectal temperature of 38°C for different metabolic rates and state of acclimatization. The reference values assume the individual is fit, normally clothed, with adequate water and salt intake.

**Example**

In a foundry with still air, a worker is acclimatized and estimated to be working at a metabolic rate of 180 $Wm^{-2}$. Air temperature = 25°C, globe temperature = 27°C, natural wet bulb = 18°C

$$\text{WBGT} = 0.7(18) + 0.3(25) = 20.1.$$

The reference WBGT value of 28°C for this scenario is not exceeded, i.e. heat stress is not a risk in this environment.

## Acclimatization

Acclimatization is a set of physiological adaptations. Full heat acclimatization requires up to 3 weeks of physical activity under the heat stress conditions expected in the work environment. During acclimatization, the ability of the body to sweat is increased and amount of sweat produced is also increased. Salt content of sweat declines avoiding sodium deficiency.

**Table 1.5** Recommended WBGT reference values for acclimatized and unacclimatized people (modified from ISO7243)

| Metabolic rate | | WBGT reference limit | |
|---|---|---|---|
| Metabolic rate (Class) | Metabolic rate ($Wm^{-2}$) | Person acclimatized to heat (°C) | Person unacclimatized to heat (°C) |
| Class 0 (Resting) | $M < 65$ | 33 | 32 |
| Class 1 (Low metabolic rate) | $65 < M < 130$ | 30 | 29 |
| Class 2 (Moderate metabolic rate) | $130 < M < 200$ | 28 | 29 |
| Class 3 (High metabolic rate) | $200 < M < 260$ | 26 | 23 |
| Class 4 (Very high metabolic rate) | $M > 260$ | 25 | 20 |

Modifed from ISO7243. HSE Books under Open Government Licence 3.0

## Risk control: Reducing heat strain

- *Planning of work*: e.g. maintenance work
- *Modifying the environment*: reduce process heat, improve ventilation, evaporative cooling, shield radiant heat sources
- *Worker*: medical pre-selection, acclimatization, report symptoms
- *Managerial*: monitor heat stress conditions, develop work–rest regimes, training and supervision, selection of appropriate controls
- *Protective clothing*: ice-cooled jackets, air-cooled suits

## Relevant legislation

- Workplace (Health, Safety and Welfare) Regulations (1992)
- Management of Health and Safety at Work Regulations (1999)

## Further information

American Conference of Industrial Hygienists (ACGIH) (2022). *Threshold Limit Values for Chemical Substances and Physical Agents and Biological Exposure Indices*. ACGIH, Cincinnati, USA.

British Occupational Hygiene Society (BOHS) (1996). *The Thermal Environment, BOHS Technical Guide No.12*, 2nd edn. BOHS, Derby.

Parsons KC (2014). *Human Thermal Environment*, 3rd edn. Taylor & Francis, London.

Youle A (2005). The thermal environment. In: Harrington JM, Gardener K (eds.), *Occupational Hygiene*, 3rd edn. Blackwell Science, Oxford. Available at: http://www.hse.gov.uk/temperature/index.htm indices

# Thermal environment 3: Assessment of cold workplaces

## Health effects and occupations

- The 1° physiological responses to cold exposure are peripheral vasoconstriction and increase in metabolic heat production by shivering
- Effects of cold include hypothermia (below 35°C), localized tissue damage, and adverse effects on performance at work. Outdoor (construction, telecommunications, maintenance of electrical power lines, agricultural and forestry, fishing industry), indoor (cold stores, meat processing), also inland and offshore work

## Risk assessment

- ISO 1574 (2008) provides methodology and practical tool for assessing and managing cold risk in the workplace. It includes checklists and questionnaires to identify individuals at risk
- The main climate factors for cold stress are air temperature and air speed. As the difference between skin and ambient temperature increases and/or the air speed increases, the rate of heat loss from exposed skin increases
- A wind chill index (equivalent chill temperature) can be calculated for different combinations of air temperature and speed (see ➲ p. 41, Calculating the Wind Chill Index and interpretation of values)
- The equivalent chill temperature is used when estimating the combined cooling effect of wind and low air temperature on exposed skin or when determining clothing insulation requirements to maintain core temperature above 36°C. The model is based on exposed flesh but is a useful first approximation of cold stress

## Risk control

- For exposed skin, continuous exposure should not be permitted when the equivalent chill temperature is −32°C
- If air temperature falls below 16°C for sedentary, 4°C for light, or −7°C for moderate work, gloves should be used by workers
- If fine work is performed with bare hands for more than 20 minutes in an environment below 16°C, provision should be made to keep hands warm
- Total body protection is required if work is performed in an environment at or below 4°C
- The ACGIH recommends that protective measures should be introduced when air temperature is less than 5°C. The equation shown here can be used to estimate the amount of clothing insulation (1 clo) required for a specific task in a given air temperature (*T* in °C) and metabolic rate (*M* in W):

$$\text{clo} = 11.5(33\text{-}T)/M$$

- When cold surfaces below −7°C are within reach, a warning should be given to prevent inadvertent contact with bare hands

## Calculating the Wind Chill Index and interpretation of values

- The Wind Chill Index (Twc) can be calculated using the equation:

$$Twc = 13.12 + 0.6215.Ta - 11.37.v^{0.16} + 0.3965.Ta.v^{0.16},$$

where $T_a$ is the air temperature (°C) and $V$ air speed (km/h)

**Example**

- If the dry temperature is −22°C at 16 km/h then the wind chill factor = −32°C

- Twc values (°C): −10 to −24 (uncomfortably cold), −25 to −34 (very cold, risk of skin freezing), −35 to −59 (exposed skin may freeze within 10 minutes), below −60 (exposed skin may freeze in 2 minutes)

## Relevant legislation

- Workplace (Health, Safety and Welfare) Regulations (1992)
- Management of Health and Safety at Work Regulations (1999)

## Further information

BS EN 511 (2006). *Protective Gloves Against Cold*. British Standards Institution. Published the British Standards Institution (BSI), London, UK

BS EN ISO 7243 (2017). *Ergonomics of the Thermal Environment. Assessment of Heat Stress Using the WBGT (Wet Bulb Globe Temperature) Index*. British Standards Institution.

ISO 11079 (2007). *Evaluation of the Thermal Environment-Determination of Required Clothing Insulation (IREQ)*. The International Organization for Standardization (ISO). Geneva, Switzerland.

ISO 15743 (2008). *Ergonomics of the Thermal Environment—Cold Workplaces—Risk Assessment and Management*. The International Organization for Standardization (ISO). Geneva, Switzerland.

ISO 9886 (2004). *Ergonomics Evaluation of Thermal Strain by Physiological Measurements*. The International Organization for Standardization (ISO). Geneva, Switzerland.

ISO 9920 (2007). *Ergonomics of the Thermal Environment-Estimation of Thermal Insulation and Water Vapour Resistance of a Clothing Ensemble*. The International Organization for Standardization (ISO). Geneva, Switzerland.

# Thermal environment 4: Thermal comfort

## Definition

- Thermal comfort describes the person's psychological state of mind and is defined as 'that condition of mind which expresses satisfaction with the surrounding thermal environment' (BS EN ISO 7730)
- Thermal comfort depends on a range of environmental (air temperature, humidity, air movement, and radiant heat) and personal factors (clothing insulation and metabolic heat). In workplaces, thermal discomfort may only occur when heating ventilation and air conditioning systems either break down or do not work as intended
- Thermal comfort can affect overall morale. Complaints may increase and productivity may fall. Most problems arise when individuals are not able to adapt to their work environment. Localized discomfort can also occur, e.g. due to vertical temperature gradients

## Assessment of thermal comfort

- International Standards (BS EN ISO 7730 and BS EN ISO 10551) provide methods for predicting the general thermal sensation and degree of discomfort (thermal dissatisfaction) in indoor environments. The methods for the objective assessment of the thermal environment included in these standards are based on those proposed by Fanger (1970)
- Thermal comfort is determined using calculations of predicted mean vote (PMV) and predicted percentage dissatisfied (PPD)
- The PMV is an index that predicts the mean value of the votes of a large group of persons on the seven-point thermal sensation scale (Table 1.6) and can be calculated for different metabolic rates, air temperature, air velocity, clothing insulation, and air humidity. Combinations of these parameters, which on average will provide a thermally neutral sensation, can be determined
- The PPD establishes a quantitative prediction of the percentage of thermally dissatisfied people, i.e. those who will vote hot, warm, cool, or cold on the seven-point thermal sensation scale
- The seven-point thermal sensation scale can also be used to assess and compare the actual and desired thermal sensations

## Controlling the thermal environment

A combination of engineering and administrative are required:

- *Work planning*: location of work station and scheduling of work and breaks
- *Assess the type of heating system*: hot air based, combined heat and ventilation, under floor heating, overhead heating
- *Air movement*: consider the type and location of fan(s), reduce draft discomfort by directing ventilation or air movement
- *Air conditioning*: determine whether the unit controls air movement and humidity as well as lowering air temperature. Air distribution from units should be uniform throughout the workplace
- *Assess the need for thermal insulation*: insulation type present and its effectiveness
- Use mechanical aids for physically demanding jobs
- *Allow workers to make adaptation*: clothing, temperature, etc.
- Monitor the environment thermal conditions and staff who have special requirements, e.g. pregnancy

**Table 1.6** Seven-point thermal sensation scale—American Society of Heating, Refrigerating and Air-conditioning Engineers Scale (ASHRAE) scale

| | |
|---|---|
| −3 | Cold |
| −2 | Cool |
| −1 | Slightly cool |
| 0 | Neutral |
| +1 | Slightly warm |
| +2 | Warm |
| +3 | Hot |

## Relevant legislation

- Workplace (Health, Safety and Welfare) Regulations (1992)
- Management of Health and Safety at Work Regulations (1999)

## Further information

ASHRAE (2017). *Standard 55—Thermal Environmental Conditions for Human Occupancy*. ASHRAE Inc., Atlanta.

BS EN ISO 10551 (2019). *Ergonomics of the Physical Environment. Subjective Judgement Scales for Assessing Physical Environments*. British Standards Institution.

BS EN ISO 7730 (2005). *Ergonomic of the Thermal Environment—Analytical Determination and Interpretation of Thermal Comfort Using Calculation of the PMV and PPD Indices and Local Thermal Comfort Criteria*. British Standards Institution.

Fanger PO (1970). *Thermal Comfort*. Danish Technical Press, Copenhagen.

# Chapter 2

# Chemical hazards

# Chemical hazards: Classification and labelling

This chapter provides information on specific hazardous substances encountered in the workplace.

## Relevant legislation

- The Classification, Labelling and Packaging Regulation (CLP Regulation) came into force in all EU member states, including the UK, on 20 January 2010
- The CLP Regulation replaces the Chemical Hazard Information and Packaging for Supply) Regulations 2009 (known as CHIP) in the UK
- The aim of the CLP Regulation is to ensure that users of a substance receive information on its hazards and advice on how to protect themselves, others, and the environment, and that the substance is packaged appropriately
- Under the CLP regulation, information on hazards of a substance is communicated to users by means of signal words, pictograms, and hazard statements (see ➔ Appendix 1)
- The CLP Regulation adopts the Globally Harmonized System for classification and labelling
- A European law on chemicals, Registration, Evaluation, Authorization and Restriction of Chemicals (REACH), came into force on 1 June 2007 (see ➔ p. 588). Under REACH, manufacturers or importers of substances are required to register substances with the European Chemicals Agency (ECHA). REACH places responsibility on industry to manage the risks from chemicals and to provide safety information on substances

## Classification and labelling of specific substances

- The Classification and Labelling (C & L) Inventory is a database containing classification and labelling information on *notified* substances; these are submitted by manufacturers, importers, and downstream users
- The C & L Inventory also contains *harmonized* classifications for those substances with hazards of highest concern (carcinogens, mutagens, reproductive toxins, or respiratory sensitizers) which are approved by the EU following a consultation process
- The C & L Inventory is maintained by ECHA
- In the UK, substances hazardous to health are defined under the Control of Substances Hazardous to Health (COSHH) Regulations 2002. Substances hazardous to health need not be a single substance, but may also include mixtures, microorganisms, or allergens

For each substance reported in the following pages of this chapter:

- Classification and labelling according to the CLP regulations is reported, comprising hazard class and category (e.g. carc 1B; see Table 2.1) and hazard statement (e.g. H350; see ➔ Appendix 1)
- Classification and labelling entries are for 'health effects' only. Those relating to 'physicochemical properties' and 'environmental effects' are not reported here, nor are precautionary statements

## Further information

All MDHS sampling and analysis methods are available are:*Methods for the Determination of Hazardous Substances (MDHS) guidance*. Published by the Health and Safety Executive (HSE). ☞ http://www.hse.gov.uk/pubns/mdhs/index.htm

European Chemical Agency (ECHA), Helsinki. ☞ http://echa.europa.eu/clp_En.asp ☞ http://echa.europa.eu/reach_En.asp

The GB CLP Regulation. HSE website. ☞ http://www.hse.gov.uk/chemical-classification/legal/clp-regulation.htm

UK Registration, Evaluation, Authorisation & restriction of Chemicals (REACH). ☞ http://www.hse.gov.uk/reach/index.htm

☞ https://www.echa.europa.eu/web/guest/regulations/clp/cl-inventory

## Classification glossary

**Table 2.1** CLP regulation—classification categories

| | |
|---|---|
| Acute tox | Acute toxicity (category 1, 2, 3, or 4) |
| Corr | Skin corrosion (category 1A, 1B, or 1C) |
| Irrit. | Skin irritation (category 2) |
| Eye dam | Serious eye damage (category 1) |
| Eye irrit | Serious eye irritation (category 2) |
| Resp sens | Respiratory sensitization (category 1) |
| Skin sens | Skin sensitization (category 1) |
| Muta | Germ cell mutagenicity (category 1A, 1B, or 2) |
| Carc | Carcinogenicity (category 1A, 1B, or 2) |
| Repr | Reproductive toxicity (category 1A, 1B, or 2) |
| STOT/SE | Specific target organ toxicity—single exposure (category 1, 2, or 3) |
| STOT/RE | Specific target organ toxicity—repeated exposure (category 1, 2, or 3) |

# Airborne chemical hazards: Types, sampling, and analytical methods

## Pollutant types

Airborne chemical pollutants can be categorized according to their physical forms. Table 2.2 shows definitions of chemical types (physical form) together with examples of processes that generate them.

Table 2.3 provides a summary of methods for sampling and analysing common chemical airborne pollutants. These sampling methods are based on the Methods for the Determination of Hazardous Substances (MDHS) published by the Health and Safety Executive (HSE).

Examples of sampling devices are shown in Fig. 2.1.

**Table 2.2** Aerosol types

| Type (size range) | Description | Examples: Processes/ substances |
|---|---|---|
| Gases | Formless fluids that expand to occupy the space or enclosure in which they are confined, i.e. a gas at room temperature | Gases arising from electrical arc welding, accidental chemical mixing of chemicals, combustion processes, biodegradation, e.g. carbon monoxide, hydrogen sulphide, and methane |
| Vapours | Volatile form of substance which are normally solid or at room temperature and pressure | Solvents used in degreasing, cleaning, paints, vanishes, plastics and rubber manufacture, e.g. toluene, xylene, acetone, n-hexane |
| Dusts (1.0 to >100.0 µm) | Solid particles | Generated by cutting, handling, grinding, crushing, abrasion, and transportation |
| Inhalable dust (0.05–200.0 µm) | Fraction of total airborne particles that are inhaled through the nose and/or mouth | Wood dust, cement dust, and flour dust |
| Respirable dust (0.05–10.0 µm) | Fraction of airborne particles that penetrate to the lower gas-exchange region of the lung (alveolar region). Respirable particles have a median aerodynamic diameter of 4 µm with a cut-off of 10 µm | Silica, coal dust, pulverized fuel ash, and ferrous foundry particles |
| Fumes (0.01–1.0 µm) | Formed when material from a volatilized solid condenses in cool air. In most cases the hot vapour reacts with air to form oxides | Lead oxide, iron oxide, welding, soldering, diesel, and rubber fume |
| Fibres | Respirable fibre is defined as a fibre >5 µm in length, with a length to width ratio of at least 3:1 and a diameter <3 µm | Asbestos or machine-made sources including glass wool, rock wool, and ceramic fibre |
| Smoke (0.01–1.0 µm) | Aerosol of solid or liquid particles | Generated by incomplete combustion of carbonaceous material, e.g. carbon or soot particles |
| Mists (0.01–20 µm) | Suspended liquid droplets | Generated by splashing, dispersing of liquids, e.g. acid and alkali mists, metal working fluids, and paint spraying mist |

**Table 2.3** Sampling and analytical methods for airborne pollutants

| | Substance | Substrate | Sampling device | Analysis | Comments |
|---|---|---|---|---|---|
| Mists | Chromic acid mist (electroplating) | GF Filter treated with sodium hydroxide | TI sampler, e.g. IOM sampler (Fig. 2.1a) | Spectrophotometry | |
| | Mineral oil mist from metal working fluids (MWF) | GF filter | TI sampler | Gravimetric (weigh filter before and after oil extraction with cyclohexane) | Water mix MWFs are analysed by measuring a suitable marker (sodium, potassium, or boron) |
| Fibres | Asbestos, fibres | Membrane filter | Open face cowl sampling head | Fibre counting by phase contrast light microscopy | For counting, a fibre is defined as >5 μm in length, <3 μm in width, and with an aspect ratio >3:1 |
| Particulates | Dusts, e.g. wood, cement | GF filter | TI sampler | Gravimetric analysis | Balance must be capable of weighing ±0.01 mg |
| | Silica | Membrane filter | Cyclone (respirable dust sampler) (Fig. 2.1b) | IRS or XRD | |
| | Metals, e.g. chromium, nickel, zinc, lead, cadmium, iron, copper | Mixed cellulose ester membrane filter | TI or respirable sampler | Filter dissolved in acids analysis by AAS or ICP-AES or XRFS | |
| | Welding fume | Mixed cellulose ester membrane filter | Open face sampler | Gravimetric followed by AAS or ICP for metals | |

| | Substance | Substrate | Sampling device | Analysis | Comments |
|---|---|---|---|---|---|
| Fumes | Rubber fume | GF filter | TI sampler | Gravimetric analysis (cyclohexane extractable fraction of filter) | |
| | Solder fume (resin acids) | Mixed cellulose ester membrane filter | Solder fume sampler | GC analysis of resin acids (derivatized) extracted from filter | Fix sampler close to head (Fig. 2.1c) |
| Organic compounds | Volatile organic compounds, e.g. solvents used in paints and glues | Solid sorbent tubes | Glass tube containing a solid sorbent, e.g. charcoal | Desorption of solvents followed by GC analysis | The choice of sorbent depends on solvent type to be sampled<br>Sampling for VOCs may also be conducted using diffuse samplers |
| | Aldehydes, e.g. formaldehyde | Chemical coated filter | | HPLC analysis of filter extracted in acetonitrile | Formaldehyde can also be sampled using a diffusion badge |
| | Isocyanates | Chemical coated GF filter | TI sampler | HPLC with UV and electrochemical detection | For vapours use an impinger. For a mixture of airborne particles and vapours use impinger and the impregnated filter in series |
| | Pesticides | GF filter with sorbent tube to collect the more volatile pesticides | TI sampler with sorbent tube | Filter and sorbent tube desorbed in a solvent. Analysis by GC with mass spectrometry | Dermal exposure samples collected using cotton gauge swabs (set at different positions on workers' outer clothing) can also be analysed by this method |

AAS: atomic absorption spectroscopy; GC: gas chromatography; GF: glass fibre; HPLC: high-pressure liquid chromatography; IOM: Institute of Occupational Medicine; ICP: induced coupled plasma; ICP-AES: induced coupled plasma-atomic emission spectrometry; IRS: infrared spectrometry; TI: total inhalable; VOCs: volatile organic compounds; XRD: X-ray diffraction; XRFS: X-ray fluorescence spectroscopy

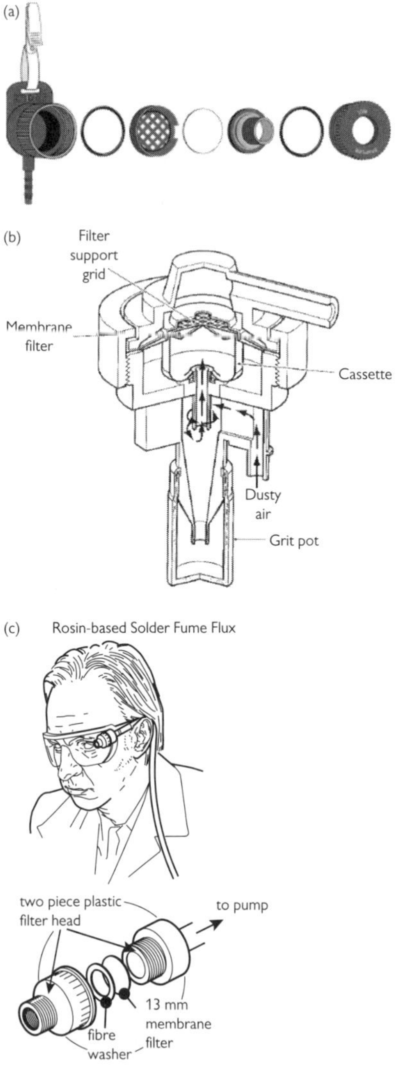


**Fig. 2.1** Sampling devices for collecting airborne chemical pollutants (from MDHS14/4 and MDHS 83/2, HSE Books). Material reproduced with permission from the controller of HMSO

(a) Institute of Occupational Medicine (IOM) inhalable sampler. (b) Cyclone respirable sampler. (c) Sampler for solder fume (resin acids).

# Coal dust

## General substance information

- The Mines Regulations 2014 require that exposure to inhalable dust is prevented or, where that is not reasonably practicable, reduced to as low a level as is reasonably practicable
- Exposure to respirable dust and respirable crystalline silica (RCS) in coal mines should be reduced to below 3 mg/m$^3$ and 0.3 mg/m$^3$, respectively, averaged over a 40-hour working weeks
- *Physical properties*: carbonaceous mineral dust with other minerals, notably crystalline silica (quartz). Quartz may comprise ≥10% of the respirable mass. Composition and physical properties (e.g. hardness) are highly variable

## CLP classification and labelling

Currently no classification.

## Uses/occurrence

Exposure occurs during mining and processing of coal.

## Key health effects

- *Pneumoconiosis*: the quartz content of freshly generated particles accelerates progression of the disease (see ➲ p. 59, Crystalline silica (quartz); ➲ p. 248, Silicosis)
- Emphysema and chronic bronchitis (see ➲ p. 238, Chronic obstructive pulmonary disease)
- Health surveillance is required under The Mines Regulations 2014 for 'significantly exposed' workers who regularly work below ground at mines. and should include respiratory symptom questionnaires (including smoking history), spirometry, and chest X-rays. Health records should be kept in a suitable form for 40 years.

## Measurement

- *MDHS 14/4* Pumped dust sample (total inhalable or respirable sampling head) on to filter followed by gravimetric analysis
- *Miners may also be exposed to RCS* (see ➲ p. 248) *and radiation* (see ➲ p. 20)

Note: high air velocities in mines, e.g. when diluting diesel fumes, may distort sampling for particles. In such cases isokinetic sampling (matching sampler inlet velocity with free stream air velocity) is recommended

## HSE publications

HSE (2015). *The Mines Regulations Guide on Regulations*. Published by Health and Safety Executive (HSE). Available at: https://www.hse.gov.uk/pUbns/priced/l149.pdf

# Cotton dust

## General substance information

- Cotton dust is defined by the HSE as 'the cellulose fibre that grows inside the seed pods (or bulbs) of the cotton plant'. For purposes of exposure monitoring, HSE defines cotton dust as 'the handling of raw and waste cotton including blends containing raw or waste cotton'
- The following are excluded:
  - dust from weaving, knitting, braiding, and subsequent processes
  - dust from bleached or dyed cotton
  - dust from finished articles, e.g. garments
- *Occupational exposure limit (as inhalable dust)*: workplace exposure limit (WEL), 8 hours time-weighted average concentration (TWA) of 2.5 $mg/m^3$
- *Physical properties*: organic fibrous matter

## Classification and labelling

Currently no classification.

## Uses/occurrence

Manufacture of cotton and cotton-based products.

## Key health effects

Byssinosis ('cotton worker's lung'), an asthma-like condition thought to be immunological in origin, although the causal agent is unknown (see ➔ p. 230, Byssinosis).

## Measurement

*MDHS 14/4* Pumped inhalable dust sample on to filter followed by gravimetric analysis. Available at: https://www.hse.gov.uk/pubns/mdhs/pdfs/mdhs14-4.pdf

# Flour dust

## General substance information

- Defined by HSE as 'finely ground particles of cereals or pulses (including contaminants) that result from any grinding process and from any subsequent handling and use of that 'flour'
- Flour dust may contain a number of additives, e.g. enzymes ($\alpha$-amylase, cellulase, hemicellulase, malt enzymes, xylanase, protease, lipase), additives (yeasts, egg powder, milk powder, sugar), flavourings, spices, and chemical ingredients (preservatives, antioxidants, bleaching agents)
- *Occupational exposure limit (as inhalable dust)*: WEL, 8 hours TWA of 10 $mg/m^3$; short-term exposure limit (STEL) of 30 $mg/m^3$; 'Sen' notation
- *Physical properties*: organic dust may be contaminated with bacterial debris

## Classification and labelling

Currently no classification.

## Uses/occurrence

Exposure occurs widely across the food industry in bakeries and prepared foods. Key tasks include handling raw material (bagging, weighing, sieving, etc.), product mixing, production, and cleaning and maintenance.

## Key health effects

- *Acute effects*: eye irritation, irritation of mucous membranes
- *Asthma*: flour and grain dust currently account for 8% of the incidence of occupational asthma. Although not clearly understood, high short-term exposures are thought to be of significance (see ➔ p. 224)

## Measurement

*MDHS 14/4* Pumped inhalable dust sample on to filter followed by gravimetric analysis. Available at: https://www.hse.gov.uk/pubns/mdhs/pdfs/mdhs14-4.pdf

# Grain dust

## General substance information

- Defined by HSE as 'dust arising from the harvesting, drying, handling, storage, or processing of barley, wheat, oats, maize, or rye, including contaminants'
- Grain dust may contain non-grain plant matter such as fungi, bacteria (including endotoxins), and excretions (proteolytic enzymes); mites; rodent excrements; and pesticide residues
- *Occupational exposure limit (as inhalable dust)*: WEL, 8 hours TWA of 10 mg/m$^3$
- *Physical properties*: grain dust may be contaminated with fungi, bacteria (including endotoxins), and excretions (proteolytic enzymes); mites; rodent excrements; pesticide and fertilizer residues; and pollen

## Classification and labelling

Currently no classification.

## Uses/occurrence

Exposure occurs in flour mills, animal feed manufacture/handling, and the transport of bulk grain. Tasks which generate grain dust include harvesting and transferring grain, drying grain, sweeping edges of grain piles, tipping operations (grain elevators), loading open topped lorries, grinding grain, manually bagging operation, and blowing out settled dust from plant/equipment.

## Key health effects

- *Acute effects*: eye irritation, irritation of mucous membranes
- *Asthma*: flour and grain dust currently account for 8% of the incidence of occupational asthma (see ➲ p. 224, Occupational asthma and rhinitis)
- Extrinsic allergic alveolitis (farmer's lung) may occur where fungal spores are present (see ➲ p. 232, Hypersensitivity pneumonitis)

## Measurement

*MDHS 14/4* Pumped inhalable dust sample on to filter followed by gravimetric analysis. Available at: https://www.hse.gov.uk/pubns/mdhs/pdfs/mdhs14-4.pdf

## Further information

HSE (2010). *Current Control Standards for Tasks with High Exposure to Grain Dust.* Research Report RR829. HSE Books, Sudbury. Available at: https://www.hse.gov.uk/pubns/indg140.pdfHSE (2013). *Control of Exposure to Grain Dust—An Employee's Guide.*

HSE Books, Sudbury. Available at: https://www.hse.gov.uk/research/rrpdf/rr829.pdf

HSE (2013). *EH66 Grain Dust*, 3rd edn. HSE Books, Sudbury. Available at: https://www.hse.gov.uk/pubns/eh66.pdf

# Wood dust

## General substance information

- Wood dust is designated as hardwood (from deciduous trees, e.g. beech, ash, oak, mahogany, and teak) or softwood (from coniferous trees, e.g. Scots pine, and cedar)
- Wood workers may also be exposed to organic solvent from adhesives, paints, and stains
- *Occupational exposure limit (inhalable dust)*:
  - hardwood: WEL, 8 hours TWA of 3 $mg/m^3$
  - softwood dust: WEL, 8 hours TWA of 5 $mg/m^3$
  - for mixtures of hardwood and softwood dusts: WEL, 8 hours TWA of 3 $mg/m^3$
- *Physical properties*: organic dust may contain other matter present in wood products, e.g. binders, coatings

## Classification and labelling

Currently no classification.

## Uses/occurrence

Exposure may occur in any process involving the working of wood, chipboard, and fibreboard, including forestry, sawmilling, joinery, construction, and furniture making.

The type of activity determines the nature and level of exposure. For instance sanding produces fine dust, sawing, and routing produces coarse dust.

Cleaning machine, equipment, and work areas often gives rise to high levels of wood dust exposure.

## Key health effects

- *Dermatitis*: may cause contact or allergic dermatitis
- *Asthma*: many reports of asthmatic and other respiratory symptoms
- *Other respiratory effects from chronic exposure*:
  - alteration in nasal mucosa
  - reduced mucociliary clearance (furniture industry)
  - anosmia
- *Cancer*: carcinogenic risk appears to be confined to workers in the furniture industry with heavy use of hardwoods
  - excess adenocarcinoma of nose and sinus cavity
  - some evidence of excess lung cancer but confounding effects of (a) exposure to other occupational agents and cigarette smoke and (b) high historical exposures

## Measurement

*MDHS 14/4* Pumped inhalable dust sample on to filter followed by gravimetric analysis. Available at: https://www.hse.gov.uk/pubns/mdhs/pdfs/mdhs14-4.pdf

## Further information

Free information sheets including HSE (2022). *Wood Dust Controlling the Risks*. HSE Books, Sudbury. Available at: https://www.hse.gov.uk/pubns/wis23.htm

# Crystalline silica (quartz)

## General substance information

- *Occupational exposure limit:*
  - Silica crystalline (respirable): WEL, 8 hours TWA of 0.1 mg/m$^3$
  - Silica, amorphous (inhalable): WEL, 8 hours TWA of 6.0 mg/m$^3$
  - Silica, amorphous (respirable): WEL, 8 hours TWA of 2.4 mg/m$^3$
  - Silica, fused (respirable): WEL, 8 hours TWA of 0.08 mg/m$^3$

## Classification and labelling

Currently no classification.

## Uses/occurrence

Most important sources of exposure are quarries, mines, ferrous foundries, construction, stone masonry, and the ceramics, heavy clay, and brick-making industries. Construction workers may be exposed to silica when cutting or breaking stone/concrete and during abrasive blasting and tunnelling operations. Crystalline silica content of materials varies widely, e.g. sandstone 70–90%, slate 20–40%, and marble 2%. Fine silica dust is referred to RCS.

## Key health effects

- *Silicosis*: usually slow onset over many years or 'acute silicosis' following high levels of exposure over 1–2 years
- *Lung cancer*: IARC Group 1, carcinogenic to humans; possible synergistic effect with smoking
- *Chronic obstructive pulmonary disease (COPD)*: associated with RCS
- *Other respiratory effects*: some evidence that exposed workers may have an excess of tuberculosis, bronchitis, and emphysema. The role of smoking and the causal mechanisms are unclear
- *Other effects*: an excess of autoimmune, immunological, and renal disease has been reported

## Measurement

*MDHS 101/2* Pumped respirable dust sample on to filter. The filter is analysed by infrared spectroscopy (IRS) or X-ray diffraction (XRD). Available at: https://www.hse.gov.uk/pubns/mdhs/pdfs/mdhs101.pdf

## Further information

HSE (2016). *Health Surveillance for those Exposed to Respirable Crystalline Silica (RCS)*. Supplementary guidance for occupational health professionals (amended January 2016) HSE. Available at: https://www.hse.gov.uk/pubns/priced/healthsurveillance.pdf

HSE (2013). *Control of Exposure to Silica Dust -A guide for employees*. HSE Books, Sudbury. Available at: https://www.hse.gov.uk/pubns/indg463.pdf

# Nanoparticles

## General substance information

- Nanomaterials are defined by the EU 'as a natural, incidental or manufactured material containing particles, in an unbound state or as an aggregate or as an agglomerate and where, for 50% or more of the particles in the number size distribution, one or more external dimensions is in the size range 1 nm–100 nm' (nanoscale). One nanometre is $10^{-9}$ m or one millionth of a millimetre
- Currently no UK WELs for nanoparticles

## Classification and labelling

*Uses/occurrence*

- Nanomaterials may be deliberately engineered with certain desired properties (e.g. carbon nanotubes (CNTs), titanium dioxide nanoparticles) or may occur as by-products of industrial or mechanical processes (e.g. vehicle engine exhaust, welding fume). Nanomaterials may also occur naturally in biological systems
- High energy processes may also generate nanoparticles, e.g. welding and grinding. Nanoparticles can be used in the manufacture of scratchproof eyeglasses, crack resistant paints, stain repellent fabrics, self-cleaning windows, and coatings for solar cells

## Key health effects

- Health effects may be influenced by physical properties, such as size, aggregation, surface area, shape, crystalline structure, surface charge and surface chemistry, and their chemical composition
- Nanotechnology is an emerging field and, currently, the risks posed by nanomaterials to human health are not fully understood. In addition, there are uncertainties about the applicability of test methods currently used to assess the harmful properties of nanomaterials
- Available evidence indicates that inhalation of some types of CNTs and other bio-persistent high aspect ratio nanomaterials (HARNs) can cause inflammation and fibrosis in the lungs which may be irreversible. However, there are insufficient data concerning the effects of long-term repeated exposure. Some types of CNTs and HARNs may cause an inflammatory reaction in the skin

## Measurement

Currently there is no HSE method recommended to measure airborne nanomaterials in the workplace.

## Further information

*Nanoparticles*. European Chemical Agency (ECHA) website, Helsinki. https://echa.europa.eu/regulations/nanomaterials

HSE (2013). *Using Nanomaterials at Work*. HSE Books, Sudbury. Available at: https://www.hse.gov.uk/nanotechnology/what.htm#what

# Asbestos

## General substance information

- Asbestos is a group of 'naturally occurring silicate minerals' comprising crocidolite, amosite, chrysotile, fibrous actinolite, fibrous anthophyllite, and fibrous tremolite, or mixtures containing these
- Exposure is regulated by the Control of Asbestos Regulations (CAR) 2012 (see ➲ p. 574), and the associated ACoPs. L143, and L127. CAR prohibits the importation, supply, and use of all form of asbestos
- *Control limit*:
  - 0.1 f/cm$^3$ (equivalent to 0.1 f/ml; all asbestos types) averaged over a continuous period of 4 hours

Note: employers must ensure that no employee is exposed to asbestos above the control limits and exposure should be reduced to the lowest level reasonably practicable.

- in CAR 2012, any exposure to asbestos which exceed the STEL of 0.6 f/ml over 10 minutes is deemed to not be sporadic and of low density
- clearance sampling inside the enclosure is required after asbestos removal (level should <0.01 f/cm$^3$)

## Classification and labelling

Carc (1A), STOT/RE (1); H350, 372.

## Uses/occurrence

- Formerly lagging for pipes and boilers; cement pipes, sheets, and ceiling tiles. Insulation and fireproofing materials, vehicle brakes, cement and floorboard materials, textiles (fire blankets), and outdoor uses such as asbestos roofs, gutters, down pipes, asbestos cement flues
- Now mainly encountered in demolition and renovation operations

## Key health effects (see ➲ p. 240)

Asbestosis, mesothelioma, lung cancer, and cancer of the larynx, pharynx, ovary, and stomach.

## Measurement

Surveys should be carried out following the HSE guidelines:

- *HSG 264*: covers survey planning, sampling, and assessment of asbestos-containing materials, quality assurance, and survey reports. Available at: https://www.hse.gov.uk/pubns/priced/hsg264.pdf
- *HSG 248*: provides information on air and bulk asbestos sampling

Measured volume of air drawn through a membrane filter in a cowl sampler. Fibres on filter visualized and counted using phase contrast optical microscopy counting fibres of length >5 μm, width <3 μm, and a length/width ratio of at least 3:1. Available at: https://www.hse.gov.uk/pubns/priced/hsg248.pdf

CAR 2012 require that air testing for asbestos meets the criteria set out in ISO 17025.

## Further information


HSE (2012). *Managing Asbestos in Buildings—A Brief Guide*. HSE Books, Sudbury. Available at: https://www.hse.gov.uk/pubns/indg223.pdf

HSE (2013). *Managing and Working with Asbestos. Control of Asbestos Regulations 2012. Approved Code of Practice and Guidance*. HSE Books, Sudbury. Available at: https://www.hse.gov.uk/pubns/priced/l143.pdf

HSE (2018). *Asbes tos Essentials. A Task Manual for Building, Maintenance and Allied Trades of Non-Licensed Asbestos Work*, HSG210, 4th edn. HSE Books, Sudbury.

IARC Monographs on the Evaluation of Carcinogenic Risks to Humans. *Arsenic, Metals, Fibres and Dusts Volume 100C. A Review of Human Carcinogens*. International Agency for Research on Cancer 2012. Available at: https://publications.iarc.fr/120

# Machine-made mineral fibre

## General substance information

- *Machine-made mineral fibre (MMMF)*: machine-made vitreous (silicate) fibres, e.g. mineral wools (rock and glass wool) with alkaline oxide and alkali earth oxide content greater than 18% by weight. Refractory ceramic fibres and special purpose fibres have a separate WEL and classification
- *Occupational exposure limit*: WEL, 8 hours TWA of 5 mg/m$^3$ and 2 fibres/ml except refractory ceramic fibres and special purpose fibres; WEL, 8 hours TWA of 5 mg/m$^3$ (total inhalable dust) and 0.3 fibres/ml (respirable fraction)
- *Physical properties*: individual fibres have a diameter of ≤10 μm, with median diameter of ~3–4 μm. Majority of airborne MMMF clouds have a median diameter of <1 μm

## CLP classification and labelling

- *MMMF*: carc (2), skin irrit (2); H351, 315
- *Refractory ceramic fibres*: carc (1B); H350i

## Uses/occurrence

- MMMF materials have excellent thermal and acoustic insulation as well as fireproofing properties, and are widely used in commercial and residential property and in industry
- Mineral wools (glass wool, rock wool) are used in thermal and acoustic insulation of buildings and for fire protection. Ceramic fibres are used mainly in insulation boards and blankets (heat resistance). Continuous glass filament fibres are used to reinforce cement and plastic products. MMMF materials are highly workable, and exposure may occur during fitting or removal. Depending on the application, and whether materials are bonded or unbonded, preformed or applied in situ, exposure may be predominantly in the form of relatively coarse-matted fragments or as respirable fibres; hence the dual WEL

## Key health effects

- *Irritant*: highly irritant to the eyes and skin
- *Cancer*: evidence for excess lung cancer is equivocal; may be partly dependent on particle size distribution

## Measurement

*Gravimetric*

- *MDHS 14/4* Pumped inhalable or respirable dust sample on to filter followed by gravimetric analysis
- Airborne fibre concentration
- *MDHS 59/2* Pumped non-size-selective dust sample on to filter, filter visualization, fibre counting by phase-contrast light microscopy. Fibre defined as particles of length >5 μm, width <3 μm, aspect ratio >3:1

# Diesel engine exhaust emissions

## General substance information

- Diesel engine exhaust emissions (DEEE) are a complex mixture of gases (oxides of carbon, nitrogen, and sulphur), vapours (aldehydes), and submicron particulate matter (soot) emitted from diesel engines
- *UK occupational exposure limit*: none
- The German Maximum Workplace Concentration (MAK) value of 100 µg/m$^3$ for elemental carbon (EC) and 30 ppm for carbon monoxide (work-shift time averages) may be useful as a guidance value
- *Physical properties*: gases include a wide range of compounds, including acrolein, formaldehyde, oxides of nitrogen, and sulphur dioxide (the latter much reduced by use of low-sulphur fuel). Particulate matter is comprised of a carbonaceous core (EC) with adsorbed semi-volatile organics, including polycyclic aromatic hydrocarbons (PAHs) and hydrocarbon species (organic carbon)

## Classification and labelling

*Diesel fuel (liquid)*: Carc (2), Asp tox (1), Sk irrit (2), Acute tox (4). STOT RE (2); H351, 304, 325, 332, 373.

Currently there is no classification of DEEE under the CLP Regulation. IARC classify diesel engine exhaust as a Group 1 carcinogen based on sufficient evidence that exposure is associated with an increased risk of lung cancer.

## Uses/occurrence

Exposure arises from work with road vehicles (garages, test centres, bridge, or motorway toll booths) and off-road vehicles (mines, manufacturing and distribution industry, and construction). The level of diesel fume and its composition depend on workload of engine, the state (tuning) and maintenance of the engine, engine temperature, and quality of the diesel fuel.

## Key health effects

- *Lung cancer*: plausible mechanistic basis for diesel fumes as a carcinogen, but epidemiological evidence is weak, confounded by poor exposure assessment, and co-exposure to cigarette smoke and asbestos
- *Other respiratory effects*: some evidence of a cross-shift decrement in lung function
- Irritation of mucous membranes, particularly the throat
- *Bladder cancer*: some evidence of increased risk of this cancer

## Measurement

- Collect airborne diesel soot using a respirable cyclone sampler on to a quartz filter. The filter is then analysed for EC, which is a surrogate measure for DEEE, e.g. *NIOSH 5040* pumped submicron sample on to filter in single-stage impactor, EC analysis
- Levels of carbon dioxide above 1,000 ppm 8-hour TWA in the workplace may indicate poorly maintained or faulty control systems
- Respirable dust levels can be measured to assess the particulate exposure. However, the levels measured will include particulates from all sources and not just the DEEEs

## Further information

HSE (2012). *Diesel Engine Exhaust Emissions*. HSE Books, Sudbury. Available at: https://www.hse.gov.uk/pubns/indg286.pdf

# Rubber process dust/fume

## General substance information

- HSE have assigned functional definitions to rubber dust and fumes:
  - rubber dust is defined as 'dust arising in the stages of rubber manufacture where ingredients are handled, weighed, added to or mixed with uncured material or synthetic elastomers'
  - rubber fume is 'fume evolved in the mixing, milling and blending of natural rubber and rubber or synthetic elastomers, or of natural rubber and synthetic polymers combined with chemicals, and in the processes which convert the resultant blends into finished products or parts thereof, and including any inspection procedures where fume continues to be evolved'
- *Occupational exposure limit*:
  - rubber process dust: WEL, 8 hours TWA of 6 mg/m$^3$
  - rubber fume: WEL, 8 hours TWA of 0.6 mg/m$^3$; this limit relates to the cyclohexane soluble material
- Where other substances are present in the dust/fume, any WELs for such substances also applies

## Classification and labelling

Currently no classification for rubber fume.

## Uses/occurrence

Exposure may occur in the production of vehicle tyres, components in the automotive industry, and a range of other industries, footwear, and domestic appliances.

## Key health effects

- *Cancer*: workers in rubber industry have a risk of excess cancers at a number of sites, e.g. bladder, lung, stomach, colon, prostate, liver, and oesophagus. There is a lack of epidemiological evidence to support a causal link at all sites. In particular, complex exposures occurring in the industry (solvents, plasticizers, accelerators, etc., in addition to polymers) are poorly characterized. Currently, IARC have concluded that 'sufficient' evidence exists only for leukaemia and bladder cancer
- *Respiratory effects*: emphysema, reduction in lung function, dyspnoea, and chest tightness have all been reported. Cases of respiratory sensitization are attributed to co-exposure to isocyanates
- *Dermatitis*: there are several reports of contact dermatitis among rubber workers. Eczema and vitiligo have also been reported
- *Reproductive effects*: studies of pregnancy outcome are inconclusive and are further limited by lack of exposure data

## Measurement

- *Rubber dust*: *MDHS 14/4* Pumped inhalable dust sample on to filter followed by gravimetric analysis
- *Rubber fume*: *MDHS 47/3* Pumped inhalable dust sample on to filter, cyclohexane extraction, gravimetric analysis Available at: https://www.hse.gov.uk/pubns/mdhs/pdfs/mdhs47-3.pdf

# Rosin-based solder flux fume

## General substance information

- CAS No. 8050–09–7
- *Occupational exposure limit*. Rosin-based solder flux fume:
  - WEL, 8 hours TWA of 0.05 mg/m$^3$
  - STEL of 0.15 mg/m$^3$
  - 'Sen' notation

► Note: compliance with WELs for other components of the fume is required as appropriate (e.g. cadmium in silver soldering).

## Classification and labelling

Currently no classification.

## Uses/occurrence

Rosin (colophony) is widely used in solder fluxes in the electronics and other industries (also in paper products, adhesives, paints, varnishes, printing inks, plasticizers, cosmetics, and medical devices). Alternatives to rosin-based fluxes exist, and where these are used, the WEL is not applicable.

## Key health effects

- *Asthma*: rosin-based solder flux fume is the third most common cause of occupational asthma in the UK (see ➲ p. 224, Occupational asthma and rhinitis)
- *Other respiratory effects*: evidence for reduction in respiratory function is equivocal
- *Dermatitis* (see ➲ p. 268, dermatitis 1)

## Measurement

*MDHS 83/3* Measured volume of air drawn through a membrane filter in a sampling head (non-size selective). The filter is desorbed, the resin acids derivatized and then analysed by gas chromatography (GC) with Flame Ionisation Detection (FID). Available at: https://www.hse.gov.uk/pubns/mdhs/pdfs/mdhs83-3.pdf

## Further information

HSE (2011). WL17. *Soldering: Hand-held with Lead-Based, Rosin-Cored Solders*. HSE Books, Sudbury. Available at: http://www.hse.gov.uk/pubns/guidance/wl17.pdf

HSE (2015). *Exposure to Cadmium in Silver Soldering or Brazing EIS31* (Rev1). HSE Books, Sudbury. Available At: https://www.hse.gov.uk/pubns/eis31.pdf

HSE (2015). INDG248 (rev2). *Solder Fume and You*. HSE Books, Sudbury. Available at: http://www.hse.gov.uk/pubns/indg248.pdf

HSE (2015). INDG249 (rev1). *Controlling Health Risks from Rosin (Colophony) Based Solder Fluxes*. HSE Books, Sudbury. Available at: http://www.hse.gov.uk/pubns/indg249.pdf

# Welding fume

## General substance information

- CAS No. 8050–09–7
- *Occupational exposure limit*: none for total welding fume

► Compliance with WELs for components of the fume (metals and inorganic gases) is required as appropriate (e.g. $Cr_{VI}$, Ni, Mn, $O_3$).

- Check WELs for fume components

## Classification and labelling

Currently no classification.

## Uses/occurrence

- The most important substrates are mild and stainless steel, and their alloys, and aluminium and its alloys. The main types of welding are:
  - manual metal arc (MMA)
  - flux cored arc (FCA)
  - metal inert gas (MIG)
  - tungsten inert gas (TIG)

The composition of fume is influenced by many process factors including material to be welded, composition of the consumable electrode/flux, and the welding technique. In general, MMA and FCA are more likely to produce high levels of fume than MIG or TIG welding. The most important applications are in engineering (e.g. boiler, tank, and vessel assembly), shipbuilding, and construction.

## Key health effects

- *Lung cancer*: IARC concluded that all welding fume can cause lung cancer and may cause kidney cancer, classifying all welding fume as Group 1 carcinogenic substances.
- *Asthma*: mainly due to welding stainless steel (exposure to CrVI)
- COPD
- *Acute effects*: irritation of eyes and throat, tightness in the chest at higher exposures, metal fume fever, acute pneumonia.
- *Asphyxia*: asphyxiant properties of inert shield gases (argon) in confined spaces should also be considered in MIG and TIG welding

## Measurement

- *BS EN ISO 10882: 2011* Sampling of air borne particles (part1) and gases (part2) in the operator's breathing zone (welding fume) Available at: https://www.iso.org/obp/ui/#iso:std:iso:10882:-1:ed-2:v1:en https://www.iso.org/obp/ui/#iso:std:iso:10882:-2:ed-1:v1:en
- Methods and guidance for biological monitoring of metals are available from Health and Safety Laboratory (HSL). Available at: https://www.hsl.gov.uk/online-ordering/analytical-services-and-assays/biological-monitoring/metals--inorganics

## Further information

HSE (2012). INDG297. *Safety in Gas Welding, Cutting and Similar Processes*. HSE Books, Sudbury. ISBN 9780717624737. Available at: http://www.hse.gov.uk/pubns/indg297.pdf

IARC Monograph 118 (2018). *Welding, Molybdenum Trioxide, and Indium Tin Oxide*. Available at: International Agency for Research on cancer (IARC). Lyon, France. Published in 2018. http://publications.iarc.fr/569

# Aluminium

## General substance information

- CAS No. 7429–90–5
- *Occupational exposure limit*:
  - aluminium metal and oxides in inhalable dust: WEL, 8 hours TWA of 10 mg/m$^3$
  - aluminium metal and oxides in respirable dust: WEL, 8 hours TWA of 4 mg/m$^3$
  - aluminium alkyl compounds and soluble aluminium salts: WEL, 8 hours TWA of 2 mg/m$^3$
- *Physical properties*: silver malleable metal, mp = 661°C, bp = 2,467°C
- Aluminium powder is white/grey in colour. Finely divided dust is easily ignited and may cause explosions
- *Exposure route*: inhalation

## Classification and labelling

- *Aluminium alkyl compounds*: skin corr (1B); $H_314$
- *Aluminium powder (stabilized)*: no classification for health effects

## Uses/occurrence

- Occurs mainly as alumina or bauxite ($Al_2O_3$)
- Workers exposed during extraction and refining of ores and during electrolytic reduction of alumina
- Aluminium powder is produced by atomization in air/inert gas
- Used in manufacture of alloys, engine and aircraft components, window frames, roofs, food containers, and electrical wires and cables
- Also used as a powder in protective paints and coating. Aluminium can be electrically coated and dyed by anodic coating
- Welding of aluminium and aluminium alloys produces metal fumes and ozone

## Key health effects

Aluminium metal interstitial fibrosis of lungs associated with repeated exposure.

## Measurement

- *MDHS 14/4* General inhalable and respirable dust followed by gravimetric analysis, then atomic absorption spectroscopy (AAS) for specific metals
- *Alternative method*: *NIOSH 7300* Pumped inhalable dust sample on to filter, acid digestion, analysis by AAS

# Arsenic

## General substance information

- CAS No. Arsenic metal 7440–38–2
- *Occupational exposure limit*: arsenic and its inorganic compounds, except arsine (as As)—WEL, 8 hours TWA of 0.1 mg/m$^3$
- No Biological Monitoring Guidance Value (BMGV)
- *Physical properties*:
  - occurs mostly in compounds of trivalent (e.g. $As_2O_3$) or pentavalent ($As_2O_5$) form
  - arsenic compounds occur in a range of physical forms (crystalline, powder, etc.)
  - pure arsenic sublimes at 613°C

## Classification and labelling

- *Arsenic oxides*: carc (1A), acute tox (2), skin corr (1B); H350, 300, 314
- *Arsenic and some other compounds*: acute tox (3); H331, 301

## Uses/occurrence

- Impurity in ores of other metals such as lead, zinc, and copper
- Major use is as a wood preservative (e.g. chromated copper arsenate)
- Manufacture of pesticides but now declined
- Used in lead (and some other) alloys for hardening
- Manufacture of semiconductors
- Contaminant in drinking water in many countries
- By-product in smelting of copper ores

## Key health effects

- Cancer of respiratory tract
- Cancer of skin and liver
- Irritant and allergic dermatitis
- Irritation of eyes and upper respiratory tract
- Perforation of nasal septum
- Severe haemorrhagic gastritis associated with ingestion of soluble arsenic compounds; may result in death

## Measurement

- *MDHS 91/2* Pumped inhalable dust sample on to filter, analysis by X-ray fluorescence spectroscopy (XRFS) (. Available at: https://www.hse.gov.uk/pubns/mdhs/pdfs/mdhs91-2.pdf
- *Biological monitoring*: arsenic in urine (sample at the end of work week)

## Further information

HSE (2013). *Arsenic and You*. HSE Books, Sudbury. Available at: https://www.hse.gov.uk/pubns/indg441.pdf

MDHS 91/2. Metals and metalloids in air by X-ray fluorescence spectrometry. Health and Safety Laboratory. Available at: https://www.hse.gov.uk/pubns/mdhs/pdfs/mdhs91-2.pdf

# Beryllium

## General substance information

- CAS No. 7440–41–7
- *Occupational exposure limit*: beryllium and beryllium compounds (as Be)—WEL, 8 hours TWA of 0.002 mg/m$^3$
- *Physical properties*: hard white metal; its utility arises from the combination of lightness and rigidity; mp = 1,287°C, bp = 2,475°C

## Classification and labelling

Carc (1B), acute tox (2), eye/skin irrit (2), skin sens (1), STOT RE (1); H350i, 330, 301, 372, 319, 335, 315, 317, 372.

## Uses/occurrence

- Used in alloys with copper or nickel to make springs, electrical contacts, spot welding electrodes
- Beryllium alloys used in specialist structural and component applications in the aerospace (space craft) and nuclear industries
- Hardening agent in alloys (copper, nickel)
- Electronics and computer industries

## Key health effects

- Pulmonary clearance of inhaled beryllium is slow (months to years for sparingly soluble compounds)
- Acute beryllium disease affecting lungs (pneumonitis, alveolitis, dyspnoea, fever), sometimes resulting in chronic fibrosis
- Chronic beryllium disease (CBD), a granulomatous disorder affecting lungs and skin, caused by cell-mediated sensitization to beryllium
- CBD symptoms include wheezing, dry cough, dyspnoea, fatigue, and weight loss
- Sub-clinical CBD can occur, with microscopic granulomas occurring in the lungs
- May cause cancer by inhalation

## Measurement

- MDHS 14/4 General inhalable and respirable dust followed by gravimetric analysis, then atomic absorption spectroscopy (AAS) for specific metals. NIOSH 7102, OSHA 125G
- *Beryllium biomarker*: blood beryllium lymphocyte proliferation (BeLPT)

## Further information

HSE (2011). *Beryllium. A Review of the Health Effects and Evidence for Screening or Surveillance in Workers Exposed to Beryllium*. Research Report 873. HSE, Sudbury. Available at: https://www.hse.gov.uk/research/rrpdf/rr873.pdf

HSE (2013). INDG311. *Beryllium and You*. HSE Books, Sudbury. Available from at: https://www.hse.gov.uk/pubns/indg311.pdf

# Cadmium

## General substance information

- CAS No. Cadmium metal 7440–43–9
- *Occupational exposure limit*:
  - cadmium and cadmium compounds (as Cd): WEL, 8 hours TWA of 0.025 mg/m$^3$
  - cadmium oxide fume (as Cd): WEL, 8 hours TWA of 0.025 mg/m$^3$; STEL of 0.05 mg/m$^3$
  - cadmium sulphide and cadmium sulphide pigments (as Cd): WEL, 8 hours TWA of 0.03 mg/m$^3$
- *Physical properties*: malleable and ductile soft white metal, mp = 321°C, bp = 776°C

## Classification and labelling

*Cadmium and cadmium oxide*: carc (1B), muta (2), repr (2), STOT RE (1), acute tox (2); H350, 341, 361, 372, 330.

## Uses/occurrence

- Manufacture of rechargeable nickel cadmium batteries alloyed with other metals for use in electrical cables, silver solders
- Electroplating
- Metal coating, pigments, and stabilizers
- During heating and welding of metals containing cadmium

## Key health effects

- Cadmium is excreted very slowly, accumulating in liver and kidneys
- Inhalation exposure causes metal fume fever and pulmonary oedema
- Kidney damage may be caused by repeated inhalation of all forms of cadmium (mainly tubular dysfunction, characterized by proteinuria; glomerular damage; glycosuria; aminoaciduria; and renal stones)
- Repeated exposure to cadmium may cause severe lung damage (emphysema, loss of lung function, and radiographic abnormalities)
- Possibility of cancer, based on animal evidence (for cadmium oxide, chloride, and sulphate)
- Impaired fertility and effects on foetus (for cadmium chloride)

## Measurement

- MDHS 91/2 A measured volume of air is drawn through a filter mounted in a inhalable or respirable dust sampler. The filter then analysed by X-ray fluorescence spectrometry.
- *Biological monitoring*: cadmium in blood (ethylenediamine tetra-acetic acid) or urine (sampling time not critical)

## Further information

HSE (2010). INDG391(REV1). *Cadmium and You*. HSE Books, Sudbury. Available at: https://www.hse.gov.uk/pubns/indg391.pdf

HSE (2015). EIS31. *Cadmium in Silver Soldering and Brazing*. HSE Books, Sudbury. Available at: https://www.hse.gov.uk/pubns/indg391.pdf

# Chromium

## General substance information

- CAS No. Chromium metal 7440–47–3
- *Occupational exposure limit*:
  - chromium (VI) and compounds (as Cr): WEL, 8 hours TWA of 0.01 mg/m$^3$; '*carc*', '*sen*'
  - process-generated Cr (VI) compounds: WEL, 8 hours TWA of 0.025 mg/mg$^3$
  - chromium metal and chromium (II) and (III) compounds (as Cr): WEL, 8 hours TWA of 0.5 mg/m$^3$
- *BMGV*: chromium (VI) (as Cr)—10 μmol chromium/mol creatinine in urine (post-shift)
- *Physical properties:* hard brittle silver metal, extremely resistant to corrosion, mp = 1,907°C, bp = 2,671°C

## Classification and labelling

- *Chromium (VI) trioxide*: carc (1A), muta (1B), repr (2), acute tox (2), skin corr (1A), resp/skin sens (1); H350, 340, 361f, 330, 311, 301, 372, 314, 334, 317
- *Potassium dichromate*: carc (1B), muta (1B), repr (1B), acute tox (2), STOT/RE (1), skin corr (1B), resp/skin sen (1); H350, 340, 360FD, 330, 301, 372, 312, 314, 334, 317

## Uses/occurrence

- Chromium is used to manufacture stainless steel (hardening steel)
- Used in chrome electroplating generated during welding of steel
- Used in leather tanning
- Cement use and cement manufacturing
- Production of paint, pigments, corrosion inhibitors, and wood preservatives

## Key health effects

Adverse health effects are mainly from chromium (VI) compounds:

- *Acute*: irritation of upper respiratory tract, skin, eyes
- *Chronic*: lung cancer, skin and respiratory sensitization, nasal corrosion (septum perforation), kidney and lung damage, ↓ fertility, foetal toxicity

## Measurement

- MDHS 91/2 A measured volume of air is drawn through a filter mounted in a inhalable or respirable dust sampler. The filter then analysed by X-ray fluorescence spectrometry
- MDHS 52/4 A measured volume of air is drawn through a membrane filter mounted in an inhalable sampler. The filter is then desorbed with dilute sulphuric acid. Quantification using a spectrophotometer. Available at: https://www.hse.gov.uk/pubns/mdhs/pdfs/mdhs52-4.pdf
- *Biological monitoring*: total chromium in urine (end of shift at end of work week) for soluble chromium compounds

## Further information

HSE (2013). INDG346. *Chromium and You*. HSE Books, Sudbury. Available at: http://www.hse.gov.uk/pubns/indg346.pdf

HSE and SEA (2018). Hexavalent chromium in electroplating: Prevention and Control of Chromic Acid Mist. Available at https://www.sea.org.uk/wp-content/uploads/2018/12/chromic_acid_mist_18169.pdf

# Cobalt

## General substance information

- CAS No. Cobalt metal 7440–48–4
- *Occupational exposure limit*: cobalt and cobalt compounds (as Co)—WEL, 8 hours TWA of 0.1 mg/m$^3$
- *Physical properties*: silver-white metal, mp = 1,495°C, bp = 2,870°C

## Classification and labelling

- *Cobalt*: resp/skin sens (1); H334, 317
- *Cobalt dichloride and sulphate*: carc (1B), acute tox (4), resp/skin sens (1); H350i, 302, 334, 317

## Uses/occurrence

- Manufacture of hard alloys (super alloys) for heavy engineering and aerospace applications
- Pigments in coloured glass, paints, and ceramics
- Production and use hard metal cutting and grinding tools

## Key health effects

- *Skin sensitization*: humans with nickel sensitivity are predisposed to cobalt sensitivity
- *Respiratory sensitization*: leading to asthmatic response at very low exposure levels
- *Diffuse interstitial pulmonary fibrosis*: also associated with repeated exposure
- Short-term gastrointestinal (GI) effects following ingestion

## Measurement

- MDHS 91/2 A measured volume of air is drawn through a filter mounted in a inhalable or respirable dust sampler. The filter then analysed by X-ray fluorescence spectrometry
- Cobalt in urine or blood (end of shift at end of work week)

## Further information

EH68. *Cobalt. Health and Safety Precautions*. ISBN 0717608239. Published by Health and Safety Executive (HSE) 2013.

HSE (2013). *Cobalt and You*. HSE Books, Sudbury. Available at: https://www.hse.gov.uk/pubns/indg442.pdf

# Copper

## General substance information

- CAS No. 7440–50–8
- *Occupational exposure limit*:
  - in dust and mists (as Cu): WEL, 8 hours TWA of 1 mg/m$^3$; STEL of 2 mg/m$^3$
  - copper fume: WEL, 8 hours TWA of 0.2 mg/m$^3$
- *Physical properties*: reddish-brown, malleable, and ductile metal, mp = 1,083°C, bp = 2,595°C

## Classification and labelling

- *Copper sulphate*: acute tox (4), eye/skin irrit (2); H302, 319, 315
- *Copper (I) chloride, oxide*: acute tox (4); H302

## Uses/occurrence

- *Major uses*:
  - smelting and refining of copper
  - production of electrical cables
  - materials for the construction and water distribution industries
- *Other uses*:
  - production of copper chemicals and powders
  - piping and plumbing
  - electroplating
  - coinage
  - antifouling agent on boat hulls
  - pigment in paints and glass

## Key health effects

- Copper is an essential element and effects may arise as a result of deficiency
- Acute oral toxicity characterized by GI symptoms, with nausea being the earliest symptom
- Eye irritation (copper (I) oxide and copper sulphate)
- Hepatotoxicity associated with long-term oral intake; also, effects on kidney and GI tract
- Exposure to freshly formed copper oxide fume has been linked to the occurrence of flu-like symptoms (metal fume fever)

## Measurement

MDHS 91/2 A measured volume of air is drawn through a filter mounted in a inhalable or respirable dust sampler. The filter then analysed by X-ray fluorescence spectrometry

# Iron

## General substance information

- CAS No. Iron metal 7439–89–6
- *Occupational exposure limit*:
  - iron oxide ($Fe_2O_3$) fume (as Fe): WEL, 8 hours TWA of 5 mg/m$^3$; STEL of 10 mg/m$^3$
  - iron salts (as Fe): WEL, 8 hours TWA of 1 mg/m$^3$; STEL of 2 mg/m$^3$
  - ferrous foundry particulate (FFP): WEL, 8 hours TWA of 10 mg/m$^3$ (total inhalable dust) and 4 mg/m$^3$ (respirable dust). (Note: FFP is a surrogate for exposure in ferrous foundries, but components of FFP also have individual WELs)

Note: the airborne pollutants in ferrous (iron and steel) foundries are a mixture of dust, fume, gases, and vapours. The particulate fraction of the pollutants is referred to as FFP. According to the HSE, the airborne concentration of FFP (total inhalable and respirable) is a suitable surrogate for overall exposure assessment in ferrous foundries. However, need to also comply with the components of the airborne contamination with WELs

- *Physical properties*: silver-white metal, mp = 1,535°C, bp = 2,750°C

## Classification and labelling

None.

## Uses/occurrence

- Exposure may occur in smelting/refining of iron and production of steel and other alloys
- Exposure to iron oxide fume may arise during flame cutting of iron or its alloys
- Iron oxide is widely used as a pigment in paint, stains, plastics, construction materials, and ceramics
- In coarse form (rouge) it is used as a polishing material in the jewellery trade
- Iron salts are used as a flocculant in waste-water treatment, the dyeing of textiles, and the production of fertilizer and feed additives

## Key health effects

- Iron is an essential element and effects may arise as a result of deficiency
- Acute iron poisoning associated with accidental ingestion (vomiting, metabolic acidosis, liver and kidney damage); mainly in children
- Chronic iron toxicity associated with hereditary malabsorption condition (haemochromatosis) or excessive dietary intake (haemosiderosis in liver, spleen, heart, and endocrine organs)
- Effects on lungs (fibrosis) caused by long-term inhalation of iron oxide fumes or dust

## Measurement

- MDHS 91/2 A measured volume of air is drawn through a filter mounted in a inhalable or respirable dust sampler. The filter then analysed by X-ray fluorescence spectrometry

## Further information

HSE (2017). RR1115. *Exposure to Substances Hazardous to Health in Foundries*. HSE Books, Sudbury. Available at: https://www.hse.gov.uk/research/rrpdf/rr1115.pdf

# Lead

## General substance information

- Exposure to lead is regulated under the Control of Lead at Work Regulations 2002 (CLAW). Statutory airborne exposure and biological monitoring values apply
- CAS No. 7439–92–1
- *Occupational exposure limit*: WEL, 8 hours TWA all lead (except lead alkyls), 0.15 mg/m$^3$; lead alkyls, 0.10 mg/m$^3$
- *Biological monitoring*: three threshold levels are indicated in the CLAW Regulations (see ➲ p. 572, Control of Lead at Work Regulations 2002):
  - a level at which health surveillance is required
  - 'action level': exposure should be reduced
  - 'suspension level': individual must be removed from exposure
- *Physical properties*: soft, malleable silver-grey metal, mp = 327°C, bp = 1,740°C

## Classification and labelling

- Lead alkyls: repr (1A), acute tox (1), STOT/RE (2); H360, 330, 310, 300, 373
- Other lead compounds (excluding azide, acetate, and chromate): repr (1A), acute tox (4), STOT/RE (2); H360, 332, 302, 373

## Uses/occurrence

- Extraction of lead from its ore (lead sulphide) and melting of scrap lead (2° smelting)
- Manufacture of lead acid batteries, lead compounds, and paints
- Production of solder, ceramics, glass, pigments, and ammunition
- Organic lead (alkyls) added to petrol as an anti-knocking agent
- Exposure during blast removal, stripping and burning of lead paint; hot cutting in demolition work; breaking and recycling lead batteries

## Key health effects

- Organic forms of lead can be absorbed through skin
- *Haematological*: anaemia, reticulocytosis, basophilic stippled red cells
- Encephalopathy, peripheral neuropathy
- Renal toxicity (tubular damage and interstitial fibrosis)
- Effects on GI tract (colic)
- Reduced fecundity in males, impaired foetal neurological development

## Measurement

- MDHS 91/2 A measured volume of air is drawn through a filter mounted in a inhalable or respirable dust sampler. The filter then analysed by X-ray fluorescence spectrometry
- *Biological monitoring*:
  - lead (inorganic): blood, zinc protoporphyrin, ALA
  - lead (organic): urine (end of shift, end of working week)

## Further information

HSE (2002). L132. *Control of Lead at Work. Control of Lead at Work Regulations 2002*. ACoP and guidance, 3rd edn. HSE Books, Sudbury. ISBN 9780717625659. Available at: https://www.hse.gov.uk/pubns/priced/l132.pdf

HSE (2012). INDG305REV2. *Lead and You* (Free). HSE Books, Sudbury. ISBN 9780717663873. Available at: http://www.hse.gov.uk/pubns/indg305.pdf

# Manganese

## General substance information

- CAS No. Manganese metal 7439–96–5
- *Occupational exposure limit*: manganese and its inorganic compounds (as Mn)—WEL, 8 hours TWA of 0.2 mg/m$^3$ (inhalable fraction), 0.05 mg/m$^3$ (respirable faction)
- *Physical properties*: hard brittle grey-white metal found mainly in crystalline form, mp = 1,244°C, bp = 1,962°C

## Classification and labelling

- *Manganese dioxide*: acute tox (4); H332, 302
- *Manganese sulphate*: STOT/RE (2); H373

## Uses/occurrence

- *Major use*: production of stainless and carbon steel
- Used in the production of batteries, fertilizers, ceramics, and glass
- Exposure occurs during refining of ore, smelting, and fabrication operations
- Used in the manufacture of dry cell batteries, pigments, and dyes
- Majority of alloys of aluminium and magnesium contain manganese to improve corrosion resistance
- Welding (steel) in construction and mining manufacturing. Exposure varies widely depending on manganese in the metal welded, welding wires/rods, and flux

## Key health effects

- Central nervous system (CNS) effects associated with repeated exposure by inhalation; early signs include sleepiness, weakness in legs, stiffness, and trembling
- Historically, effects on lungs (pneumonitis) were associated with chronic exposure, although recent studies provide no evidence of this

## Measurement

- MDHS 91/2 A measured volume of air is drawn through a filter mounted in a inhalable or respirable dust sampler. The filter then analysed by X-ray fluorescence spectrometry. ISO 10882-1:2011. Manganese in welding fume.

## Further information

HSE (2017). RR1115. *Exposure to Substances Hazardous to Health in Foundries*. HSE Books, Sudbury. Available at: https://www.hse.gov.uk/research/rrpdf/rr1115.pdf

# Mercury

## General substance information

- CAS No. 7439–97–6
- *Occupational exposure limit*: mercury and divalent inorganic mercury compounds (as Hg)—WEL, 8 hours TWA of 0.02 mg/m$^3$
- *BMGV*: 20 µmol mercury/mol creatinine in urine (random sampling)
- *Physical properties*: silver coloured, mobile liquid metal, mp = −39°C, bp = 357°C. Mercury vapourizes easily and its vapour can condense and accumulate on cold surface, e.g. on stainless steel

## Classification and labelling

- *Mercury (elemental)*: acute tox (3), STOT/RE (2); H331, 373
- *Some organic and inorganic mercury compounds*: acute tox (1), STOT/RE (2); H330, 310, 300, 373

## Uses/occurrence

- Used as an electrode in the electrolytic production of chlorine from sodium hydroxide (chloro-alkali process)
- Widely used in thermometers, barometers, and batteries
- Use in dental amalgam is in decline
- Production of fungicides, biocides, and antifouling paints

## Key health effects

- *Acute inhalation exposure*: respiratory irritation (cough, chest tightness, shortness of breath, decreased lung function)
- *Effects on CNS (psychomotor effects)*: tremor, irritability, nervousness, and hallucinations
- Renal toxicity (tubular damage)

Note: Elemental mercury may readily cross the blood–brain barrier. Mercury accumulates in the kidneys and is eliminated mainly through urine and faeces.

## Treatment

See ➲ p. 842, Mercury poisoning, for management of acute poisoning.

## Measurement

- NIOSH 6009 Mercury & compounds (except alkyl compounds)
- MDHS 16/2 diffusive badges or pumped sorbent tubes, acid dissolution and analysis by cold vapour atomic absorption spectrometry
- *Biological monitoring*:
  - usually based on measuring total inorganic mercury in urine (cumulative exposure—recent weeks/months, elimination half-life of 40–60 days), analysis by induced coupled plasma-mass spectrometry (ICP-MS), or by cold vapour AAS
  - total inorganic mercury blood levels (acute exposure)

# Nickel

## General substance information

- CAS No. Nickel metal 7440–48–4
- *Occupational exposure limit*: nickel and its inorganic compounds:
  - water-soluble compounds (as Ni): WEL, 8 hours TWA of 0.1 mg/m$^3$
  - metal and insoluble compounds (as Ni): WEL, 8 hours TWA of 0.5 mg/m$^3$
- *Physical properties*: hard ductile silvery metal, resistant to corrosion, mp = 1,453°C, bp = 2,752°C
- Nickel tetracarbonyl is a gaseous metal compound

## Classification and labelling

- *Nickel*: skin sens (1), carc (2), STOT/RE (1); H351, 317, 372
- *Nickel oxides*: STOT/RE (1), skin sens (1); H350, 317
- *Nickel sulphide*: skin sens (1), muta (2), STOT/RE (1); H317, 341, 372
- *Nickel sulphate*: resp/skin sens (1), STOT/RE (1), skin irrit (2), muta (2); H317, 334, 372, 315, 341
- *Nickel tetracarbonyl*: carc (2), repr (1B), acute tox (3); H351, 360, 330

## Uses/occurrence

- Used mainly in stainless steel alloys. Alloys with other metals include copper, aluminium, and silver
- Also used in electroplating, as a catalyst and in the production of nickel compounds, rechargeable batteries (nickel-cadmium), and coins
- Exposure occurs when welding and grinding nickel-containing metal alloys
- Workers come into contact with nickel-containing/coated tools

## Key health effects

- Nickel metal and insoluble salts are retained in the lung
- Soluble nickel salts may also be absorbed through the skin
- Skin and respiratory sensitization
- Cancer of the lungs and nasal sinuses
- Fibrosis of lungs, with loss of pulmonary function

## Measurement

- MDHS 91/2 A measured volume of air is drawn through a filter mounted in a inhalable or respirable dust sampler. The filter then analysed by X-ray fluorescence spectrometry

## Further information

HSE (2013). INDG351. *Nickel and You*. HSE Books, Sudbury. Available at: http://www.hse.gov.uk/pubns/indg351.pdf

HSE (2016). *Nickel and Its Inorganic Compounds. Health Hazards and Precautionary Methods*. HSE Books, Sudbury. Available at: https://www.hsl.gov.uk/media/1235788/eh60%20ni%20health%20haz%20&%20prec%20measures%20current%20guidance.pdf

HSE and SEA (2018). *Nickel and Nickel Alloy Plating Operations: Controlling the Inhalation Risk*. Available at: https://www.sea.org.uk/wp-content/uploads/2018/12/sea_-_hse_controling_risk_of_inhilation.pdf

HSE and SEA (2018). Nickel and Nickel Alloy Plating Operations: Controlling the Risk of Skin Exposure. Available at: https://www.sea.org.uk/wp-content/uploads/2018/12/controling_risk_of_skin_exposure.pdf

# Vanadium

- Vanadium is an essential element
- Inhalation is the main route of entry
- Vanadium compounds are poorly absorbed through the GI system and rapidly excreted in the urine

## General substance information

- CAS No. Vanadium pentoxide 1314–62–1
- *Occupational exposure limit*: Vanadium pentoxide—WEL, 8 hours TWA of 0.05 mg/m$^3$
- *Physical properties*: soft ductile grey-white metal; good resistance to corrosion by acids and alkalis

## Classification and labelling

*Vanadium pentoxide*: muta (2), repr (2), STOT/RE (1), acute tox (4), STOT/SE (3); H341, 361, 372, 332, 302, 335.

## Uses/occurrence

- Vanadium occurs in different minerals such as patronite ($VS_4$)
- Also present in carbon-containing deposits such as crude oil and oil shale. The ash from oils may be rich in vanadium and is a hazard for industrial furnace and boiler cleaners
- Approximately 80% of vanadium produced is used as ferrovanadium in the production of steel alloys
- Vanadium salts are used as catalysts in the manufacture of glass, dyes, inks, and pesticides
- Exposure also occurs during refining and manufacture of steel alloys

## Key health effects

- Effects include irritation of the eyes, skin, and respiratory tract, and GI disturbances
- Workers may complain of metallic taste and there may be a greenish discoloration of tongue (indication of exposure rather than toxicity)
- The key health effects of concern for vanadium pentoxide are mutagenicity and respiratory tract toxicity

## Measurement

- MDHS 91/2 A measured volume of air is drawn through a filter mounted in a inhalable or respirable dust sampler. The filter then analysed by X-ray fluorescence spectrometry
- NIOSH 7504. Oxides of vanadium analysed by XRD after collection (total inhalable fraction) on a polyvinyl chloride (PVC) membrane filter

# Zinc

## General substance information

- CAS No. Zinc metal 7440–66–6
- *Occupational exposure limit*:
  - zinc chloride fume: WEL, 8 hours TWA of 1 $mg/m^3$; STEL of 2 $mg/m^3$
  - zinc distearate inhalable dust: WEL, 8 hours TWA of 10 $mg/m^3$; STEL of 20 $mg/m^3$
  - respirable dust: WEL 8 hours TWA of 4 $mg/m^3$
- *Physical properties*: hard, brittle, and lustrous bluish-white metal, mp = 420°C, bp = 907°C

## Classification and labelling

- *Zinc powder (stabilized)*: no classification for health effects
- *Zinc chloride fume*: acute tox (4), skin corr (1B); H302, 314
- *Zinc sulphate*: acute tox (4), eye damage (1); H302, 318

## Uses/occurrence

- Major uses of zinc metal are in galvanizing and the production of batteries, die castings, and construction materials
- Many zinc alloys are of industrial importance, principally those with copper (brass), tin, lead, and aluminium
- Zinc chloride is used in soldering flux, as a battery electrolyte, and in textiles, wood preservatives, and medical products
- Uses of zinc distearate include the manufacture of plastics and pharmaceuticals

## Key health effects

- Zinc is an essential trace element and effects may arise as a result of deficiency
- Metal-fume fever, a transient acute condition associated with exposure to freshly formed fumes of zinc oxide (and some other metals); characterized by fever, chills, dyspnoea, nausea, and fatigue, which occur several hours after exposure

## Measurement

- MDHS 91/2 A measured volume of air is drawn through a filter mounted in a inhalable or respirable dust sampler. The filter then analysed by X-ray fluorescence spectrometry.
- MDHS 14/4 for Zinc oxide

# Acetone

## General substance information

- CAS No. 67–64–1. Formula $CH_3COCH_3$, also known as propan-2-one

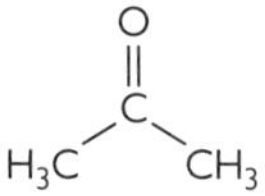

- *Occupational exposure limit*: WEL, 8 hours TWA of 1,210 mg/m$^3$ (500 ppm); STEL of 3,620 mg/m$^3$ (1,500 ppm)
- *Physical properties*: colourless liquid, fruity odour, water-soluble liquid, mp = −94°C, bp = 56°C

## Classification and labelling

Eye irrit (2), STOT/SE (2); H319, 336.

## Uses/occurrence

- Used in polymer synthesis in the plastics, textile, and pharmaceutical industries
- Used as a solvent in manufacturing; in paint, inks, varnishes; and other coatings; and in cleaning materials
- Manufacture other chemicals, artificial leather, and rubber products
- Degreasing agent (removing oils and greases) in the metal industry
- Some use in consumer products, e.g. nail varnish remover

## Key health effects

- Irritation of eyes and respiratory tract
- CNS effects

## Measurement

- *MDHS 96* Pumped solid sorbent tubes, solvent desorption, analysis by GC
- MDHS 104 Laboratory method using sorbent tubes, solvent desorption or thermal desorption and GC. Available at: https://www.hse.gov.uk/pubns/mdhs/pdfs/mdhs104.pdf
- *MDHS 88* Diffusive sorbent samplers, solvent desorption, GC. Available at: https://www.hse.gov.uk/pubns/mdhs/pdfs/mdhs88.pdf
- *Biological monitoring*: Breath sampling (sampling time end of shift). HSE recommend that if breath acetone levels exceed 1,000 nmol/l, then analysis of a post-shift urine sample for acetone

## HSE publications

HSE. 2014. INDG273(rev1). *Working with Solvents—A Guide to Safe Working Practices*. HSE Books, Sudbury. Available at: https://www.hse.gov.uk/pubns/indg273.pdf

# Acid anhydrides (cyclic anhydrides)

## General substance information

- *Phthalic anhydride*:
  - CAS No. 85–44–9. Formula $C_8H_4O_3$

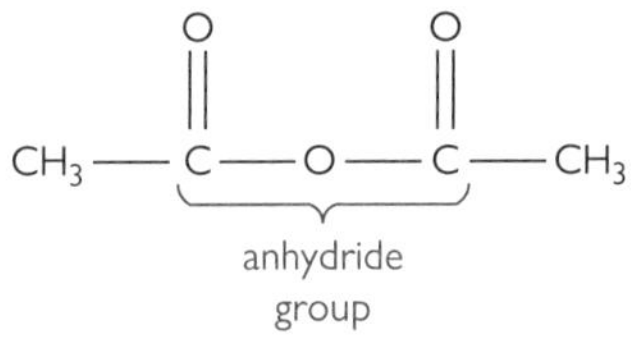


  - occupational exposure limit: WEL, 8 hours TWA of 4 mg/m$^3$; STEL of 12 mg/m$^3$
  - physical properties: white crystalline solid, mp = 131°C, bp = 295°C
- *Trimellitic anhydride*:
  - CAS No. 552–30–7. Formula $C_9H_4O_5$
  - occupational exposure limit: WEL, 8 hours TWA of 0.04 mg/m$^3$; STEL of 0.12 mg/m$^3$
  - physical properties: white crystalline solid, mp = 165–169°C
- *Acetic anhydride*:
  - CAS No. 108–24–7. Formula $(CH_3CO)_2O$
  - occupational exposure limit: WEL, 8 hours TWA of 2.5 mg/m$^3$; STEL of 10 mg/m$^3$
  - physical properties: colourless liquid with a pungent odour, mp = −73°C, bp = 138–140°C

## Classification and labelling

- *Phthalic anhydride*: acute tox (4), STOT/SE (3), skin irrit (2), eye dam (1), resp/skin sens (1); H302, 335, 315, 318, 334, 317
- *Trimellitic anhydride*: STOT/SE (3), eye dam (1), resp/skin sens (1); H335, 318, 334, 317
- *Acetic anhydride*: acute tox (4), skin corr (1B); H332, 302, 314

## Uses/occurrence

- Cyclic acid anhydrides are a group of reactive chemicals that are used as curing agents and plasticizers in the production of epoxy resins, a range of polymers, chemicals, dyes, and pesticides
- At room temperature, cyclic anhydrides are powders
- The most abundant chemicals are listed here

## Key health effects

- Irritation of eyes and respiratory tract
- Occupational asthma and rhinitis
- Sensitization of the skin

## Measurement

*MDHS 62/2* Carboxylic acid anhydrides in dust and fume measured by pumped sampling on to a glass fibre filter with a sorbent (tenax) back-up tube. During desorption, acid anhydrides are converted to the corresponding acids, analysis by high-performance liquid chromatography (HPLC). Available at: https://www.hse.gov.uk/pubns/mdhs/pdfs/mdhs62-2.pdf

# Acrylamide

## General substance information

- CAS No. 79–06–1. Formula $H_2C{=}CHCON{=}H_2$

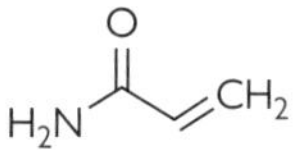

- *Occupational exposure limit*: WEL, 8 hours TWA of 0.1 $mg/m^3$
- *Physical properties*: white crystalline solid, soluble, mp = 84–85°C, bp = 125°C

## Classification and labelling

Carc (1B), Muta (1B), Repr (2), acute tox (3), STOT/RE (1), eye/skin irrit (2), skin sens (1); H350, 340, 361f, 301, 372, 332, 312, 319, 315, 317.

## Uses/occurrence

- Used in the synthesis of polyacrylamides which are used in the treatment of drinking water and waste water, paper industry, metal ore processing, dye, adhesive and textile manufacturing, as an oil recovery agent in the oil industry, and in construction
- Other examples of workers exposed to acrylamide include manufacture of toiletries, construction workers involved in constructing sewers and tunnels

## Health effects

- Can be absorbed through skin
- Irritation of the skin
- Neurotoxicity; symptoms include fatigue, muscle weakness, numbness of extremities, and other sensory effects
- Possibility of cancer (based on animal studies)
- May cause adverse effects in offspring

## Measurement

*MDHS 57/2* Acrylamide in air—collection of pumped samples into a midget impinger (containing water), analysis by HPLC Available at: https://www.hse.gov.uk/pubns/mdhs/pdfs/mdhs57-2.pdf

# Acrylonitrile

## General substance information

- CAS No. 107–13–01. Formula $H_2C{=}CHCN$

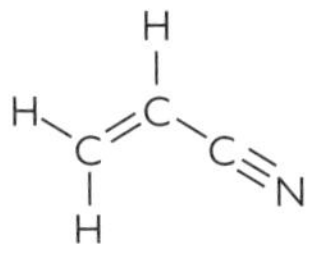

- *Occupational exposure limit*: WEL, 8 hours TWA of 4.4 mg/m$^3$ (2 ppm). Limit values are currently under review by HSE
- *Physical properties*: colourless, soluble liquid, mp = −83°C, bp = 77°C

## Classification and labelling

Carc (1B), acute tox (3), STOT/SE (3), skin irrit (2), eye dam (1), skin sens (1); H350, 331, 311, 301, 335, 315, 318, 317.

## Uses/occurrence

- Major use as a monomer in the production of synthetic fibres, elastomers, and plastics
- Polyacrylonitrile fibres are used in the manufacture of tennis rackets, fishing poles. Acrylic fibres are similar to wool, hence used in clothing, carpets, and upholstery
- Used in the manufacture of acrylonitrile-butadiene-styrene (ABS) rubber, plastics, and in the production of acrylamide and other chemical intermediates

## Key health effects

- Can be absorbed through skin
- Acrylonitrile is a suspected carcinogen (based on animal studies)
- Dermatitis may result from prolonged or repeated skin contact
- CNS effects (headache, nausea, fatigue)
- Diarrhoea and jaundice
- Respiratory tract irritation
- Simultaneous exposure to some other organic solvents may enhance acrylonitrile toxicity

## Measurement

- Pumped sorbent tubes, followed by either thermal or solvent desorption, analysis by GC (MDHS 96 MDHS 104)
- Diffusive sorbent samplers, followed by solvent or thermal desorption, analysis by GC (MDHS 88)

# Benzene

## General substance information

- CAS No. 71–43–2. Formula $C_6H_6$

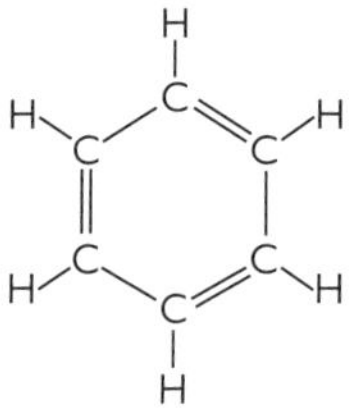


- *Occupational exposure limit*: WEL, 8 hours TWA of 1 ppm
- *Physical properties*: colourless liquid, slightly soluble in water, mp = −6°C, bp = 80°C. The main natural source of benzene is crude oil

## Classification and labelling

Carc (1A); Muta (1B), STOT/RE (1), Asp tox (1), eye/skin irrit (2); H350, 340, 372, 304, 319, 315.

## Uses/occurrence

- Used in the synthesis of other organic compounds (e.g. styrene, phenol, aniline) and the synthesis of polymers used in the manufacture of plastics, resins, and textiles (synthetic fibres)
- Also used in tyre and shoe manufacturing
- Exposure occurs in oil refineries, petrochemical plants, and in areas where benzene or petrol is stored/distributed
- Benzene also found in cigarette smoke
- Benzene is no longer used as a general solvent because of its high toxicity

## Key health effects

- Can be absorbed through skin
- Effects on blood and blood-forming tissues (anaemia, leukaemia, and other blood disorders) (see ➔ p. 364, Haematological malignancies)

## Measurement

- *Air monitoring*:
  - Pumped sorbent tubes followed by either thermal or solvent desorption, analysis by GC (MDHS104)
  - Diffusive sorbent samplers followed by solvent or thermal desorption, analysis by GC (MDHS 88 )
  - Real-time portable monitors
- *Biological monitoring*: S-phenylmercapturic acid (benzene metabolite) in urine (sample end of week)

## HSE publications

HSE. 2013. INDG329. *Benzene and You*. HSE Books, Sudbury. Available at: http://www.hse.gov.uk/pubns/indg329.pdf

# Carbon disulphide

## General substance information

- CAS No. 75–15–0. Formula $CS_2$
- *Occupational exposure limit*: WEL, 8 hours of TWA of 15 $mg/m^3$ (5 ppm)
- *Physical properties*: colourless liquid, mp = −112°C, bp = 47°C (highly flammable)

## Classification and labelling

Repr (2), STOT/RE (1), eye/skin irrit (2); H361fd, 372, 319, 315.

## Uses/occurrence

- Most important use is the production of viscose rayon and cellophane
- Also used in the production of carbon tetrachloride and as a pesticide and fungicide
- Solvent for oils, resins, and phosphorous

## Key health effects

- Can be absorbed through skin
- Irritation of skin, eyes, and respiratory tract
- Repeated or prolonged skin contact may cause dermatitis (see ➔ p. 242, dermatitis 1)
- Effects on nervous system (acute and chronic encephalopathy, peripheral and cranial polyneuropathy, central and peripheral nervous system dysfunction)
- Effects on cardiovascular system (coronary heart disease)
- Possible effects on reproduction (based on animal data)

## Measurement

- *Environmental monitoring*:
  - *MDHS 96* Pumped sorbent tubes, solvent desorption, analysis by GC
  - *MDHS 88* Diffusive sorbent samplers, solvent or thermal desorption, analysis by GC (MDHS 80 and 88)
- *Biological monitoring*: 2-thioxothia zolidine-4-carboxylic acid (end of shift)

## Further information

Public Health England (2017). Carbon disulphide. Available at: https://assets.publishing.service.gov.uk/government/uploads/system/uploads/attachment_data/file/839737/Carbon_disulphide_general_information.pdf

# 2,2′-Dichloro-4,4-methylene dianiline (MbOCA)

## General substance information

- CAS No. 101–14–4. Formula $C_{(13)}H_{(12)}Cl_{(2)}N_{(2)}$

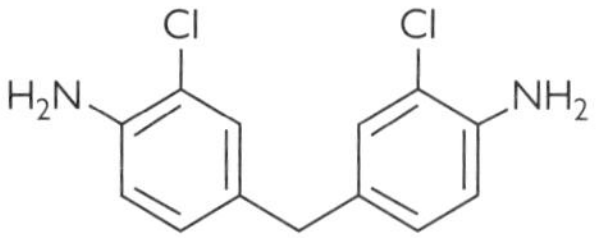


- *Occupational exposure limit*: WEL, 8 hours TWA of 0.005 mg/m$^3$
- *BMGV*: 15 μmol total 2,2′-dichloro-4,4-methylene dianiline (MbOCA)/mol creatinine in urine
- *Physical properties*: colourless to tan, odourless solid, slightly soluble in water, mp = 110°C

## Classification and labelling

Carc (1B), acute tox (4); H350, 302.

## Uses/occurrence

- MbOCA is used as a curing agent in the manufacture of polyurethane articles. Also used in glues and adhesives
- Workers exposed during manufacture of MbOCA or use it to manufacture plastic products

## Key health effects

- MbOCA is easily absorbed through the skin
- Bladder cancer following inhalation, skin absorption or ingestion via food, drink, or cigarettes
- Acute effects on the blood (formation of methaemoglobin)

## Measurement

- *Environmental monitoring*: MDHS 75/2 collection on pumped acid-coated filters, desorption and analysis by HPLC. Available at: https://www.hse.gov.uk/pubns/mdhs/pdfs/mdhs75-2.pdf
- *Biological monitoring*: total MbOCA in urine (end of shift) analysis by GC-MS

## HSE publications

HSE Research Report 828 (2010). *Occupational Exposure to MbOCA and Isocyanates in Polyurethane Manufacture*. Health and Safety Executive Book. Available At: http://www.hse.gov.uk/research/rrpdf/rr828.pdf

# Formaldehyde

## General substance information

- CAS No. 50–00–0. Formula HCHO

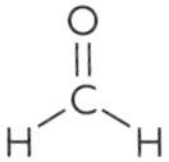

- *Occupational exposure limit*: WEL, 8 hours and 15 minutes TWA of 2.5 mg/m$^3$ (2 ppm)
- *Physical properties*: pungent colourless gas; soluble in water (formalin)

## Classification and labelling

Carc (1B), acute tox (3), skin corr (1B), skin sens (1), muta (2); H350, 331, 311, 301, 314, 317, 341.

## Uses/occurrence

- Main use in the production of resins, principally urea-formaldehyde and phenol-formaldehyde, which are used to make cores and moulds for foundries; formaldehyde is given off when resins are heated
- Formaldehyde-based resin are used as an adhesive for woods and carpets
- Formaldehyde has various other uses in agriculture and medicine where it is used as a disinfectant, fungicide, fumigant, and preservative (tissue in laboratories)
- Others exposed to formaldehyde include morticians in the embalming process and beauticians who apply hair dyes

## Key health effects

- Irritation of skin and upper respiratory tract
- Severe irritation of eyes
- Allergic contact dermatitis resulting from skin contact
- Suspected human carcinogen (nasopharyngeal cancer) (based on animal and human evidence)
- Little evidence that formaldehyde induces asthma
- Formaldehyde mixed with hydrochloric acid can generate bis (chloromethyl) ether, a potent carcinogen

## Measurement

- *MDHS 102* Aldehydes in air collected on to a chemical-coated glass fibre filter contained in a personal inhalable dust sampler, desorbed (into acetonitrile), analysed using HPLC Available at: https://www.hse.gov.uk/pubns/mdhs/pdfs/mdhs102.pdf

## Further information

HSE. *Formaldehyde—Its Safe Use in Foundries*. HSE Books, Sudbury. Available at: http://www.hse.gov.uk/pubns/iacl88.htm

Public Health England. Formaldehyde: health effects, incident management and toxicology 2017. Public Health England, London. Available at: https://www.gov.uk/government/publications/formaldehyde-properties-incident-management-and-toxicology

# Glutaraldehyde

## General substance information

- CAS No. 111–30–8. Formula $HCHO(CH_2)_3CHO$ (used in aqueous solution)

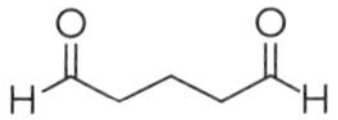


- *Occupational exposure limit*: WEL, 8 hours and STEL of 0.2 mg/$m^3$ (0.05 ppm)
- *Physical properties*: colourless oily liquid with pungent odour

## Classification and labelling

Acute tox (3), skin corr (1B), resp/skin sens (1), STOT SE (3); H331, 301, 314, 334, 317, 335.

## Uses/occurrence

- Used as a sterilizing agent in medicine, mainly in endoscopy and other surgical instruments which cannot be heat sterilized
- Fixative (tissues) in histology and pathology labs
- Used in leather tanning (leather softening and to improve resistance to water and moulds)
- Used as food preservatives
- Minor uses in the production of resins and dyes
- Used as a biocide in paper manufacturing and also in metal working fluids (MWF)
- Disinfect in animal housing (sprays)

## Key health effects

- Respiratory sensitization
- Skin sensitization
- Severe irritation of eyes
- Irritation of skin and upper respiratory tract

## Measurement

MDHS 102. Aldehydes in air Laboratory method using high performance liquid chromatography

# Isocyanates

## Definition

The most common aromatic diisocyanate are toluene 2,4-diisocyanate (TDI) and methylene bisphenyl isocyanate (MDI). Hexamethylene diisocyanate (HDI) is an example of an aliphatic di-isocyanate.

## General substance information

- CAS No. TDI, 584–84–9; MDI, 101–68–8. Formula TDI, $CH_3C_6H_3(NCO)_2$; MDI, $CH_2(C_6H_4NCO)_2$

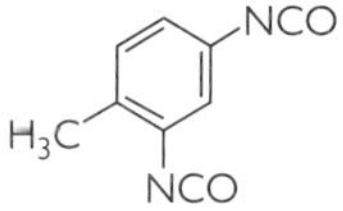


Toluene 2,4 diisocyanate (TDI)

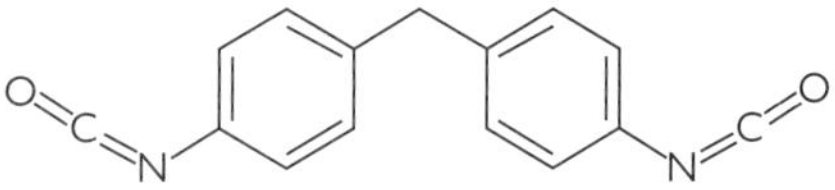


4,4'- Methylene diphenyl isocyanate (MDI)

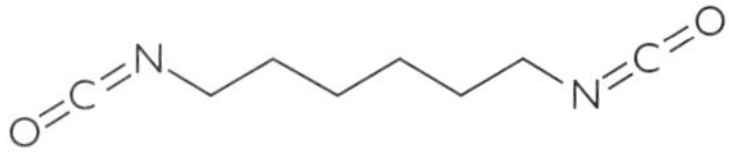


1,6-Hexamethylene diisocynate (HDI)

- *Occupational exposure limit*: WEL, 8 hours TWA of 0.02 mg/m$^3$ (total isocyanates as NCO); STEL of 0.07 mg/m$^3$
- *Physical properties:*
  - TDI: colourless to yellow solid, mp = 20–22°C, bp = 251°C
  - MDI: yellow solid, mp = 37°C, bp = 196°C

## Classification and labelling

- *TDI*: carc (2), acute tox (2), eye/skin irrit (2), resp/skin sens (1), STOT/SE (3); H351, 330, 319, 335, 315, 334, 317
- *MDI*: acute tox (4), eye/skin irrit (2), STOT/SE (3), resp/skin sens (1); H332, 319, 335, 315, 334, 317

## Uses/occurrence

- Used in the manufacture of polyurethane foams, paints ('one-pack', i.e. pre-reacted, or 'two pack', formed in situ by the addition of a catalyst)
- Motor vehicle coating; spraying produces the highest exposure
- Released when heating polyurethane products

## Key health effects

- Respiratory and skin sensitization (see ➔ p. 224, Occupational asthma and rhinitis)
- Irritation of eyes and respiratory tract

## Measurement

- *Environmental sampling*: *MDHS 25/4* P Organic isocyanates in air. Pumped sampling train with reagent-coated filters and absorbing solution, derivatization, HPLC. Available at: https://www.hse.gov.uk/pubns/mdhs/pdfs/mdhs25-4.pdf
- *Biological monitoring*: urine sample taken at the end of period of potential exposure (within 1 hour)

## Further information

Kate Jones. 2019. Biological monitoring for isocyanates. *Occupational Medicine*, 69(7), 515–517. Available at: https://academic.oup.com/occmed/article/69/7/515/5666202

HSE (2014). HSG276. *Isocyanate Paint Spraying*. HSE Books, Sudbury. Available at: https://www.hse.gov.uk/pUbns/priced/hsg276.pdf

HSE. *Guidance on Working with 2-Pack Isocyanate Paints*. HSE Books, Sudbury. Available at: https://www.hse.gov.uk/mvr/bodyshop/isocyanates.htm

# Methyl ethyl ketone

## General substance information

- CAS No. 78–93–3. Formula $C_2H_5COOH$. Also called butan-2-one

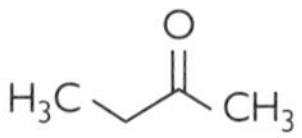

- *Occupational exposure limit*:
  - WEL, 8 hours TWA of 600 mg/m$^3$ (200 ppm)
  - STEL of 899 mg/m$^3$ (300 ppm)
  - BMGV of 70 μmol/l in urine
- *Physical properties*: colourless volatile liquid with a faint odour, moderately soluble in water, mp = −86°C, bp = 80°C

## Classification and labelling

Eye irrit (2), STOT/SE (2); H319, 336.

## Uses/occurrence

- Main use is in manufacturing and application of surface coatings
- Widely used as a solvent in the preparation of catalysts and resins (vinyl resin, acrylic resin, and phenolic resins)
- Used in the manufacture of coatings including paints, printing inks, lacquers, varnishes, stains, and associated cleaning materials
- Used in the manufacture of synthetic rubber
- Exposed workers include those working with glues, paints, coatings, and in printing plants

## Key health effects

- Can be absorbed through skin
- Irritation of eyes and respiratory tract
- Acute CNS effects, with unconsciousness at high exposure levels
- Prolonged or repeated skin contact with liquid causes de-fatting of skin
- Possible effects on reproduction (based on animal data)

## Measurement

- *Environmental monitoring*:
  - *MDHS 104* Pumped sorbent tubes, solvent or thermal desorption, analysis by GC
- MDHS 88. diffusive sorbent samplers, solvent desorption, analysis by GC *Biological monitoring*: MEK in urine (end of shift)

# n-Hexane

## General substance information

- CAS No. 110–54–3. Formula $CH_6(CH_2)_4CH_3$

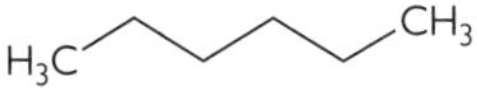


- *Occupational exposure limit*: WEL, 8 hours TWA of 72 mg/m3 (20 ppm)
- *Physical properties*: colourless volatile liquid insoluble in water, faint odour, mp = −95°C, bp = 69°C

## Classification and labelling

Repr (2), Asp tox (1), STOT/RE (2), skin irrit (2), STOT/SE (3); H361f, 304, 373, 315, 336.

## Uses/occurrence

- Produced from refining of crude oil
- Main use is as a solvent to extract edible oils from vegetables and seeds and polymerization processes, and as a starting material in the production of other organic chemicals
- Used in glues, e.g. shoemaking and leather products
- Used for cleaning and degreasing in various manufacturing processes
- Used in laboratories, e.g. solvent in liquid chromatography

## Key health effects

- Peripheral neuropathy, including subclinical effects such as electrophysiological changes in peripheral nerves
- Depression of CNS (e.g. drowsiness and vertigo)
- Suspected of damaging fertility

## Measurement

- *MDHS 96, MDHS 104, NIOSH 1500* Pumped sorbent tubes, solvent or thermal desorption, analysis by GC
- *MDHS 88* Diffusive sorbent samplers, solvent or thermal desorption, analysis by GC

# Pesticides

## General substance information

- Broad spectrum of biocidal agents used in agricultural and non-agricultural industries. WELs (Tables 2.4 and 2.5)
- *Biological monitoring value*: lindane, 35 nmol/l (10 μg/l) in whole blood

## Uses/occurrence

- Main categories are organophosphate, organochlorine, and carbamate pesticides
- Exposure occurs mainly in agriculture, although pesticide use is very widespread
- Exposure arises through preparation (decanting, mixing, spillage), application (spraying, coating, dipping), and through persons not directly engaged in application entering affected areas

## Key health effects (see also ➔ p. 840, Organophosphate poisoning)

- *Organochlorine* pesticides cause a range of neurological effects:
  - acute effects include headache, dizziness, nausea, vomiting, fatigue, convulsions, stimulated respiration, tremors, and ataxia
  - chronic effects include intermittent muscle twitching, muscle weakness, tremors, ataxia in coordination, slurred speech, visual impairment, memory loss, irritation, and depression
- *Organophosphate* pesticides act by inhibiting acetylcholinesterase activity, resulting in a range of neurological effects
- *Bipyridylium* herbicides (e.g. paraquat) may cause the below effects following ingestion:
  - severe inflammation of mouth, throat, and GI tract
  - effects in the lungs (dyspnoea, anoxia, progressive fibrosis)
  - necrotic damage to liver, kidneys, and myocardial muscle
  - extensive haemorrhage, coma, and death

See ➔ Chapter 39 for management of acute contamination and poisoning.

## Measurement

*MDHS 94/2* Pesticides in air and on surfaces. Inhalable dust/mists sample on to filter with sorbent tube analysis by GC-MS. For dermal exposure use swabs (number and sites stipulated in MDHS), analysis by GC-MS. Available at: https://www.hse.gov.uk/pubns/mdhs/pdfs/mdhs94-2.pdf

## Further information

HSE. *Guidance on Storing Pesticides for Farmers and Other Professional Users*. HSE Books, Sudbury. Available at: http://www.hse.gov.uk/pubns/ais16.pdf

HSE. *Pesticides*. HSE Books, Sudbury. Available at: https://www.hse.gov.uk/pesticides/

HSE. *Reporting Incidents Involving Pesticides*. HSE Books, Sudbury. Available at: https://www.hse.gov.uk/pesticides/enforcement/reporting-incidents.htm

HSE. *Sheep Dipping—Advice for Farmers and Others Involved in Dipping Sheep 2014*. HSE Books, Sudbury. Available at: https://www.hse.gov.uk/pubns/ais41.pdf

**Table 2.4** Classification and labelling of pesticides in EH40/2005 (as amended 2020)

| | CAS no. | Classification | H-statements |
|---|---|---|---|
| Captan | 133-06-2 | Carc (2), Acute tox (3), Eye dam (1), Skin sens (1) | H351, 331, 318, 317 |
| Chlopyrifos | 2921-88-2 | Acute tox (3) | H301 |
| Endosulfan | 115-29-7 | Acute tox (3), Eye irrit (2) | H311, 301, 319 |
| Malathion | 121-75-5 | Acute tox (4) | H302 |
| Paraquat dichloride | 1910-42-5 | Acute Tox. (2), STOT/RE (1), Eye irrit (2), STOT/SE (3), Skin irrit (2) | H330, 311, 301, 372, 319, 335, 315 |
| Phorate | 298-02-2 | Acute tox (1) | H310, 300 |
| Pichloram | 1918-02-1 | | |
| Pyrethrum | 8003-34-7 | | |
| Pyrethrin (I and II) | 121-21-1 121-29-9 | Acute tox (4) | H332, 312, 302 |
| Rotenone | 83-79-4 | Acute tox (3), Eye irrit (2), STOT/SE (3), Skin irrit (2) | H301, 319, 335, 315 |
| Sulfotep | 3689-24-5 | Acute tox (1) | H310, 300 |

**Table 2.5** WELs for pesticides in EH40/2005 (as amended 2020)

| | Type | WEL (mg/m3) | | |
|---|---|---|---|---|
| | | 8 hours | STEL | |
| Captan | OC | 5.0 | 15.0 | |
| Chlorpyrifos | OP | 0.2 | 0.6 | Sk |
| Endosulfan | OC | 0.1 | 0.3 | Sk |
| Malathion | OP | 10.0 | – | Sk |
| Paraquat dichloride (respirable dust) | Byp | 0.08 | – | |
| Phorate | OP | 0.05 | 0.2 | Sk |
| Picloram | | 10.0 | 20.0 | |
| Rotenone | Bot | 5.0 | 10.0 | |
| Sulfotep | OP | 0.1 | – | Sk |

Bot, botanical; Byp, bypiridylium; OC, organochlorine; OP, organophosphate; P, pyrethrin; Sk, can be absorbed through skin.

# Phenol

## General substance information

- CAS No. 108–95–2. Formula $C_6H_5OH$

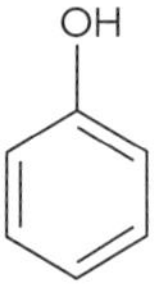

- *Occupational exposure limit*: WEL, 8 hours TWA of 2 ppm
- *Physical properties*: colourless or white crystalline solid, slightly soluble in water, mp – 43°C, bp = 182°C

## Classification and labelling

Muta (2), acute tox (3), skin corr (1B), STOT/RE (2); H341, 311, 301, 331, 373, 314.

## Uses/occurrence

- Main use is in the manufacture of phenolic resins and plastics
- Also used as intermediate in manufacturing nylon and epoxy resins
- Phenol has a range of other uses in the production of fertilizers, paints, rubber, textiles, drugs, paper, soap, and wood preservatives
- Also used as a disinfectant

## Key health effects

- Phenol can be absorbed through the skin
- Corrosive to eyes, skin, and respiratory tract
- Dermal exposure can lead to effects on the CNS (tremors, convulsions, nausea, circulatory failure, bowel cramps, and unconsciousness). Subsequent respiratory failure may result in death

See ➔ p. 844, Phenol poisoning for acute poisoning with phenols.

## Measurement

*MDHS 96 and MDHS 104* (Volatile organic compounds in air). Pumped sorbent tubes, solvent desorption, analysis by GC

## Further information

Public Health England. *Phenol*. Public Health England Publication, London. Available at: https://assets.publishing.service.gov.uk/government/uploads/system/uploads/attachment_data/file/562434/phenol_general_information.pdf

# Styrene

## General substance information

- CAS No. 100–42–5. Formula $C_6H_5CH=CH_2$

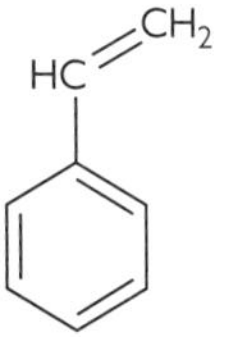

- *Occupational exposure limit*: WEL, 8 hours TWA of 430 mg/m$^3$ (100 ppm); STEL of 1,080 mg/m$^3$ (250 ppm)
- *Physical properties*: colourless liquid with oily odour, slightly soluble in water, mp = −31°C, bp = 145°C

## Classification and labelling

Acute tox (4), eye/skin irrit (2), STOT RE (1); H332, 319, 315, 372.

## Uses/occurrence

- Major use is in the production of polystyrene resins (used to make plastics, packaging, and insulation materials)
- Used in the production of styrene-butadiene rubber, styrene-acrylonitrile, and ABS polymers
- Styrene evaporates from resins, solvents, and surface coatings used in the manufacturing process for fibre-reinforced plastics

## Key health effects

- Acute CNS depression
- Eye irritation following exposure to liquid or vapour
- Skin irritation following repeated exposure to liquid
- Nasal irritation
- Repeated exposure can result in CNS effects and ototoxicity

## Measurement

- *MDHS 104*, *MDHS 96* Pumped sorbent tubes, solvent/thermal desorption, analysis by GC
- *MDHS 88* Diffusive sorbent samplers, solvent/thermal desorption, analysis by GC

## Further information

HSE (2018). *Styrene Control in Fibre-Reinforced Plastics Contact Moulding*. HSE Books, Sudbury. Available at: https://www.hse.gov.uk/pubns/ppis14.pdf

# Tetrachloroethylene

## General substance information

- CAS No. 127–18–4. Formula $Cl_2C{=}CCl_2$ also called perchloroethylene

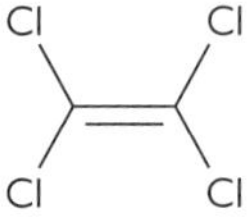


- *Occupational exposure limit*: WEL, 8 hours TWA of 138 mg/m$^3$ (20 ppm); STEL of 275 mg/m$^3$ (40 ppm)
- *Physical properties*: colourless liquid practically insoluble in water with an ether odour, mp = −22°C, bp = 121°C

## Classification and labelling

Carc (2); H351.

## Uses/occurrence

- Major use is as a dry-cleaning agent (dissolves greases and oils without damaging the fabric)
- Used as a cleaning/degreasing agent in the automotive and other industries
- Also used in paint removers, printing inks, glues, and polishes

## Key health effects

- Can be absorbed through skin
- Acute CNS effects (drowsiness, dizziness, with unconsciousness at high exposures; very high exposures may be fatal)
- Irritation of skin and respiratory tract
- Liver and kidney toxicity
- Evidence from animal studies indicates that tetrachloroethylene may cause cancer

## Measurement

- *MDHS 104*, *MDHS 96* Pumped sorbent tubes, solvent /thermal desorption, analysis by GC
- *MDHS 88* Diffusive sorbent samplers, solvent desorption analysis by GC

# Vinyl chloride

## General substance information

- CAS No. 75–01–4. Formula $H_2C{=}CHCl$ also called Vinyl chloride monomer (VCM)

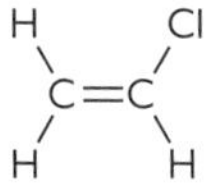


- *Occupational exposure limit*: WEL, 8 hours TWA of 1 ppm
- *Physical properties*: colourless gas with a sweet odour, slightly soluble in water, mp = −154°C, bp = −14°C

## Classification and labelling

Carc (1A); H350.

## Uses/occurrence

- Used as chemical intermediate in the production of polymers, mainly PVC for pipes, cable coatings, adhesives; and in furniture and kitchen ware

## Key health effects

- Liver cancer (angiosarcoma) (see ➔ p. 294, Hepatic angiosarcoma)
- Other chronic effects include liver and spleen toxicity, bone deterioration, circulatory disorders affecting feet and hands, and soft tissue lesions
- Acute CNS effects (e.g. dizziness and disorientation)
- *Note*: COSHH regulations require:
  - Individuals exposed to VCM in manufacture, production, reclamation, storage, discharge, transport, use, or polymerization need to be under medical surveillance (Schedule 6 of COSHH)
  - Continuous monitoring of VCM (Schedule 5 of COSHH)

## Measurement

- *MDHS 96* Pumped sorbent tubes, solvent desorption, GC
- *MDHS 88* Diffusive sorbent samplers, solvent desorption, GC

# Arsine

## General substance information

- CAS No. 7784–42–1. Formula $AsH_3$
- *Occupational exposure limit*: WEL, 8 hours TWA of 0.16 mg/m$^3$ (0.05 ppm)
- *Physical properties*: colourless gas, garlic-like odour but odourless at low concentrations, slightly soluble in water, mp = −117°C, bp = −63°C

## Classification and labelling

Acute tox (2), STOT/RE (2); H330, 373.

## Uses/occurrence

- Generated by the action of acid on arsenic
- Used as a doping agent in the semiconductor industry
- Minor use in the production of organic chemicals
- Arsine is produced commercially by the reaction of aluminium arsenide with water or hydrochloric acid
- Exposure when washing arsenic-contaminated slag during copper alloy production
- Accidental mixing of arsenic compounds and acids, e.g. when cleaning tanks/containers, hot dross (containing arsenic impurities) coming in contact with water

## Key health effects

- Haemolysis is the main acute effect leading to haemolytic anaemia, possible kidney damage, and jaundice
- Renal failure may subsequently occur, sometimes leading to death

## Measurement

*NIOSH method 6001* Sampling on a solid sorbent tube, analysis by AAS with graphite furnace. Available at: https://www.cdc.gov/niosh/docs/2003-154/pdfs/6001.pdf

# Carbon monoxide

## General substance information

- CAS No. 630–08–0. Formula CO
- *Occupational exposure limit*: WEL, 8 hours TWA of 35 $mg/m^3$ (30 ppm); STEL of 232 $mg/m^3$ (200 ppm)
- *Physical properties*: colourless odourless gas, sparingly soluble in water, mp = −199°C, bp = −92°C

## Classification and labelling

Acute tox (3), STOT/RE (1); H331, 372.

## Uses/occurrence

- Produced as a ubiquitous by-product of incomplete combustion, i.e. insufficient oxygen when burning carbon-based fuels, e.g. vehicle exhausts, coal burning plants, fuel burning furnaces, fork-lifts (diesel and liquefied petroleum gas)
- Used in the production of hydrogen, acetic acid, and hydrocarbons (Fischer–Tropsch process)
- Also used as an industrial reducing agent
- Exposed workers include those using petrol/diesel powered equipment/tools, working in enclose spaces (trench excavation), and garage workers

## Key health effects

Acute effects resulting from formation of carboxyhaemoglobin:

- Asphyxiation
- Effects on the developing foetus
- Cardiovascular effects (effects in subjects with pre-existing cardiovascular disease, exacerbation of exercise-induced angina, ventricular arrhythmia, tachycardia)
- CNS effects (headache, dizziness, impaired fine manual dexterity, impaired mental capacity, fatigue, visual disturbance)

### *Treatment*

See ➲ p. 832, Carbon monoxide poisoning for management of acute exposure.

## Measurement

- *NIOSH 6604* Pumped sampling into inert sample bag, electrochemical detector
- *OSHA ID-209* Air monitored using a direct-reading instrument with data logging facility
- *BMGV*: 30 ppm in end-tidal breath (post-shift)

# Hydrogen sulphide

## General substance information

- CAS No. 7783–06–04. Formula $H_2S$
- *Occupational exposure limit*: WEL, 8 hours TWA of 7 mg/m³ (5 ppm); STEL of 14 mg/m³ (10 ppm)
- *Physical properties*: colourless gas, odour of rotten eggs at low concentration but odourless at higher concentrations, mp = −86°C, bp = −61°C

## Classification and labelling

Acute tox (2); H330.

## Uses/occurrence

- Used as a digesting agent in paper production and in the production of sulphide ores
- Encountered as a product of the decay of organic matter (e.g. sewage works, animal rendering) and desulphurization processes in the metal, oil, and gas industries
- Exposed workers include those involved in manufacturing rayon textiles, petroleum and natural gas workers, farmers (manure storage pits), and waste water treatment workers

## Key health effects

- Irritation of eyes and upper respiratory tract
- Pulmonary oedema may occur with prolonged exposure
- CNS effects (headache, dizziness, staggering gait) may occur with high concentrations
- At higher concentrations, CNS effects can lead to paralysis of respiratory system, asphyxiation, and sometimes death

### *Treatment*

See ➔ p. 838, Hydrogen sulphide poisoning, for management of acute exposure.

## Measurement

*NIOSH 6013* Pumped sampling on to filter and sorbent tube, derivatization, ion chromatography

# Nitrogen dioxide

## General substance information

- CAS No. 10102–44–0. Formula $NO_2$
- *Occupational exposure limit*: none
- *Physical properties*: reddish brown gas with irritating odour

## Classification and labelling

Acute tox (2), skin corr (1B); H330, 314.

## Uses/occurrence

- Used in the production of nitric acid and nitrate fertilizers
- Produced as a by-product during metal degreasing with nitric acid and during the breakdown of silage in agriculture
- Also produced during combustion processes
- Road traffic is the main source of outdoor exposure to nitrogen dioxide. Important indoor sources (particularly in low-income countries) include tobacco smoke and fuel used for cooking and heating, e.g. wood, oil, kerosene, and coal-burning

## Key health effects

- Irritation of the upper respiratory tract resulting from brief exposure to high concentrations
- Lung damage in the form of emphysema may be caused by repeated exposure

## Measurement

*NIOSH 6014*. Nitrix oxide and Nitrogen dioxide. Pumped sampling on to sorbent tube, NO2 converted to nitrite, analysis by Absorption spectrophotometry.

## HSE publications

HSL (2009). RR757. Real-time Measurement of Nitrogen Monoxide in Tunnels and Its Oxidation Rate in Diluted Diesel Exhaust. Health and safety Executive (HSE). Available at: https://www.hse.gov.uk/research/rrpdf/rr757.pdf

# Ozone

## General substance information

- CAS No. 10028–15–6
- *Occupational exposure limit*: STEL of 0.2 ppm (0.4 mg/m$^3$)
- *Physical properties*: ozone is a liquid or gas, depending on temperature, appearing bluish in colour. The gas has a pleasant odour at low concentrations (<2 ppm); at higher concentrations the gas is pungent. Ozone is highly reactive and heavier than air

## Classification and labelling

Acute tox (1), skin corr (1B), eye dam (1), STOT RE (1); H330, 314, 318, 372.

## Uses/occurrence

- Ozone is generated by bombarding oxygen with UV light, e.g. during metal (in particular aluminium and stainless steel) arc welding and from photochemical oxidation of automobile exhaust gases
- Used as a disinfectant for air and water, and for bleaching textiles, oils, and waxes
- Ozone is produced near lamps which emit UV radiation, e.g. ink curing, projection xenon lamps
- Uses include water fumigant, bleaching and oxidizing agent
- Other workers exposed include fisheries workers treating storage water, pulp and paper mills workers, and waste water treatment plants

## Key health effects

- Respiratory tract and mucosal irritant
- Causes severe skin burns and serious eye damage
- High concentration leads to pulmonary oedema

## Measurement

- Static and portable direct reading instrument (e.g. with electrochemical sensors) and colorimetric detection tubes available
- OSHA ID-214. Air sample is collected using a sampling pump and a cassette containing nitrite-impregnated glass filter. Analysis by ion chromatography and UV_VIS detector. Available at: https://www.osha.gov/sites/default/files/methods/id214.pdf

## HSE publications

HSE. 2014. EH38. *Ozone Health Hazards and Precautionary Measures*. HSE Books, Sudbury. Available at: http://www.hse.gov.uk/pubns/priced/eh38.pdf

# Sulphur dioxide ($SO_2$)

## General substance information

- CAS No. 7446–09–5
- *Occupational exposure limit*: WEL, 8 hours TWA of 0.5 ppm (1.3 mg/$m^3$); STEL, 1 ppm (2.7 mg/m3)
- *Physical properties*: colourless gas with pungent odour; density twice than of air

## Classification and labelling

Acute tox (3), skin corr (1B); H331, 314.

## Uses/occurrence

- Used to manufacture sulphuric acid
- Formed when materials containing sulphur are burned
- Important air pollutant, especially in the vicinity (a by-product) of smelters and electrical power plants, burning soft coal, or high sulphur oil
- Also used in paper industries as a bleaching, disinfecting, and fumigating agent

## Key health effects

- *Acute*: mucous membrane irritant. Prolonged high exposures may lead to pulmonary oedema and death. May trigger asthmatic attacks in more susceptible individuals. Eye irritant, if prolonged may lead to corneal ulceration
- *Chronic*: chronic bronchitis and diminution in olfactory and gustatory senses

## Measurement

- *NIOSH 6004* Sample on impregnated cellulose filter containing potassium hydroxide. An acetate pre-filter is used to collect particulate sulphates. The impregnated filter is extracted with water and the extract is analysed by chromatography. Available at https://www.cdc.gov/niosh/docs/2003-154/pdfs/6004.pdf
- Direct reading instruments and colorimetric tubes are also available

# Oil mist (metal working fluids)

## General substance information

- Metal working fluids (MWFs) are neat oils or water-based fluids which include soluble oils and semisynthetic/synthetic fluids
- Water-based MWF may contain biological contaminants and their related biological by-products, e.g. endotoxins, exotoxins
- MWFs are used for lubrication, cooling, and removing metal particles when machining metals
- MWFs may contain oils, emulsifiers, corrosion inhibitors, extreme pressure additives, biocides, and other additives
- *Occupational exposure limit*: currently no classification
- *Physical properties*: variable composition and viscosity

## CLP classification and labelling

Currently no classification.

## Uses/occurrence

Exposure to MWFs occurs via inhalation, through direct contact with unprotected skin, and through cuts and abrasions. The cutting operation may generate a mist from the fluid, and splashes may result in dermal exposure. Exposure to microorganisms, including endotoxins, and antimicrobials, may also occur.

## Key health effects

- *Dermatitis*: irritant and allergic contact dermatitis have been widely reported in exposed workers (see ➲ p. 268, Dermatitis 1)
- *Cancer*: excess cancers of the larynx, rectum, pancreas, skin, scrotum, and bladder have been reported in exposed workers. However, high historical dermal and inhalation exposures have now been reduced because of improved control methods and the use of highly refined MWFs that are much reduced in carcinogenic substances (e.g. PAHs)
- *Respiratory conditions*: asthma, extrinsic allergic alveolitis, chronic bronchitis, and acute airway irritation have all been reported (see ➲ p. 224, Occupational asthma and rhinitis, ➲ p. 232, Hypersensitivity pneumonitis)

## Measurement

- *MDHS 84/2* Measurement of oil mist from mineral oil-based metalworking fluids Available at: https://www.hse.gov.uk/pubns/mdhs/pdfs/mdhs84-2.pdf
- *MDHS 95/3* Measurement of personal exposure of metalworking machine operators to airborne water-mix metalworking fluid. Available at: https://www.hse.gov.uk/pubns/mdhs/pdfs/mdhs95-3.pdf

## Further information

HSE (2006). *Outbreak of Respiratory Disease at Powertrain Ltd, Longbridge, Birmingham—emerging lessons*. HSE Books, Sudbury. Available at: https://www.hse.gov.uk/metalworking/experience/powertrain.pdf

HSE (2011). INDG365. *Working Safely with Metalworking Fluids. A Guide for Employees*. HSE Books, Sudbury. Available at: http://www.hse.gov.uk/pubns/indg365.pdf

HSE (2019). MW1. *Mist Control-Inhalation Risk*. HSE Books, Sudbury. Available at: https://www.hse.gov.uk/pubns/guidance/mw2.pdf

HSE (2019). MW2. *Control of Skin Risks During Machining*. HSE Books, Sudbury. Available at: http://www.ukla.org.uk/wp-content/uploads/UKLA-HSE-Good-Practice-Guide-for-Safe-Handling-and-Disposal-of-Metalworking-Fluids.pdf

HSE and UKLA (2018). *Good Practice Guide for Safe Handling and Disposal of Metalworking Fluids*. HSE Books, Sudbury. Available at: https://www.hse.gov.uk/pubns/guidance/mw1.pdf

# Chapter 3



# Biological hazards

# Human tissue and body fluids

## Sources of exposure/industries

Health care sector, public sanitation, research. See Table 3.1 for routes of exposure.

*Respiratory infections*

Those who undertake aerosol-generating procedures, e.g. post-mortem staff, physiotherapists (suction and expectoration), bronchoscopy staff, laboratory workers.

*Faecal–oral infections*

Sewage workers, laboratory staff.

## Factors affecting exposure and risk assessment

The risk of transmission is determined by:

- Dose or level of exposure, which depends on the details of the incident, including route of exposure and body fluid involved
- Source infectivity

Risk assessment for blood-borne viruses (BBV) exposure is described in detail on ➲ p. 856, Management of needle-stick and contamination incidents.

## Health effects

These are described for each organism: hepatitis B virus (HBV) (➲ p. 170); hepatitis C virus (HCV) (➲ p. 174); human immunodeficiency virus (HIV) (➲ p. 176); viral haemorrhagic fevers (VHF) (➲ p. 180); tuberculosis (TB) (➲ p. 188); severe acute respiratory syndrome (SARS) (➲ p. 196); influenza (➲ p. 200).

## Risk controls

- Adherence to standard infection control procedures, including hand hygiene, use of personal protective equipment (PPE), gloves for procedures that involve a risk of contamination, and double gloves for surgical procedures on patients known to be infected with BBV. Aprons, goggles, and masks are required where there is a risk of splashing; boots or overshoes are required if floor is contaminated. Other risk controls include:
  - use of safer sharps devices, avoidance of re-sheathing needles
  - correct disposal of sharps and infected waste
  - correct transport and receipt of specimens
  - filtering respiratory masks for aerosol-generating procedures
  - immunization against HBV, TB, influenza
  - appropriate decontamination procedures for spills
- Prompt management of sharps and contamination incidents (➲ p. 856, Management of needle-stick and contamination incidents)

## Relevant legislation

- An EU directive aimed at preventing sharps injuries in health care was issued in 2010. This was implemented in the UK as the Health and Safety (Sharp Instruments in Healthcare) Regulations 2013. For more information see: https://www.hse.gov.uk/pubns/hsis7.pdf.

**Table 3.1** Routes of exposure

| Route | Examples |
|---|---|
| Through non-intact skin or intact mucous membranes (blood-borne transmission) | • BBV<br>  • HBV<br>  • HCV<br>  • HIV<br>  • hepatitis D (HDV)<br>  • VHF<br>• Malaria |
| Inhalation (respiratory transmission) | • Tuberculosis<br>• Influenza<br>• SARS |
| Ingestion (faecal–oral transmission) | • Enteroviruses<br>• Typhoid |

## Human biological material associated with transmission of BBV

- Blood
- Blood-stained fluid
- Pleural fluid
- Pericardial fluid
- Peritoneal fluid
- Cerebrospinal fluid
- Synovial fluid
- Amniotic fluid
- Breast milk
- Semen
- Vaginal secretions
- Unfixed tissues and organs

## Occupations at increased risk from BBV

- Health care workers, in particular:
  - surgeons, theatre nurses
  - dentists
  - midwives
  - dialysis technicians
  - ambulance technicians
  - mortuary technicians
  - laboratory workers
  - chiropodists
  - acupuncturists
- Police and firefighters
- Prison workers
- Social workers
- Military personnel

There is a lower, but significant, risk among:

- Embalmers and crematorium workers
- Cleaners

## Specific guidance and further information

### *Guidance for clinical health care workers*

HSE. Blood-borne viruses in the workplace 2001. HSE Books, Sudbury. Available at: https://www.hse.gov.uk/pubns/indg342.pdf

HSE. Management and Operation of Microbiological Containment Laboratories 2019. HSE Books, Sudbury. *Available at:* https://www.hse.gov.uk/biosafety/management-containment-labs.pdf

HSE. *Managing Infection Risks When Handling the Deceased: Guidance for the Mortuary, Post-Mortem Room, and Funeral Premises, and During Exhumation. 2018*. HSE Books, Sudbury. Available at: https://www.hse.gov.uk/pubns/priced/hsg283.pdf Microbial pathogens (in laboratory settings)

# Microbial pathogens (in laboratory settings)

## Common sources

Exposure to dangerous pathogens through work occurs almost exclusively in the experimental or clinical laboratory setting, often in health care or veterinary science (see Table 3.2).

**Table 3.2** Classification of microbial pathogens (according to control of substances hazardous to health (COSHH) regulations)

| Hazard group | |
|---|---|
| HG 1 | Unlikely to cause human disease |
| HG 2 | Can cause human disease, and likely to be a hazard to employees, but unlikely to spread in the community and is treatable |
| HG 3 | A serious hazard to employees, and also likely to spread to the community, but is treatable |
| HG 4 | Can cause severe disease in humans, a serious hazard to employees and the community, and no treatment or prophylaxis available |

Afull list of specific agents and their classification is published.[1]

## Factors that affect the risk assessment

- Consequence of infection (serious human disease)
- *Potential for transmission*:
  - infect and harm employees
  - spread to the community
- Amenability to treatment

## Risk controls

These are defined in detail in guidance from the Health and Safety Commission (HSC) and Advisory Committee on Dangerous Pathogens (ACDP). In summary, risk controls include the following:

*Exposure controls*

- *Containment*: three levels of containment for Hazard Group 2–4 pathogens including:
  - separation from other activities
  - impervious bench (and floor) surfaces
  - −ve pressure ventilation
  - high-efficiency particulate absorption-filtered air intake and output
  - restriction to authorized personnel (e.g. access controls)
  - safety cabinet
  - dedicated equipment

1 HSE/ACDP (2021). *The Approved List of Biological Agents 4th edition*. Advisory Committee on Dangerous Pathogens. Health and Safety Executive (HSE), UK. Available at: http://www.hse.gov.uk/pubns/misc208.pdf

- observation window to allow monitoring from outside
- use of PPE including respiratory protective equipment (RPE)
- Emergency/incident planning (handling accidents)
- Vector control (rats mainly)
- Display biohazard warnings
- Safe decontamination and disinfection procedures
- Safe waste management
- Safe transport of pathogens
- *Good hygiene*
  - separation of eating areas for staff
  - hand washing routines
- Laboratory equipment servicing and testing

*Occupational health input*

- Immunization where available
- *Health surveillance*: in practice, this consists mainly of education to be vigilant and report symptoms, record of immunity
- Advise on individual susceptibility, e.g. pregnancy, immunosuppression

## Specific legislation and guidance

- Mainly outlined in general legislation (COSHH), Management of Health and Safety at Work Regulations (MHSWR) but with additional guidance:
  - Health and Safety Executive (HSE). 2019. *Biological Agents: Management and Operation of Microbiological Containment Laboratories*. HSE Books, Sudbury. Available at: https://www.hse.gov.uk/biosafety/management-containment-labs.pdf
- HSE. *Safe Working and the Prevention of Infection in Clinical Laboratories and Similar Facilities.* HSE Books, Sudbury. Available at: http://www.hse.gov.uk/pubns/priced/clinical-laboratories.pdf
- *Immunization Against Infectious Disease* (The Green Book). Public Health England, London. Available at: https://www.gov.uk/government/collections/immunisation-against-infectious-disease-the-green-book#the-green-book
- HSE. *Management and Operation of Microbiological Containment Laboratories*. HSE Books, Sudbury. Available at: https://www.hse.gov.uk/biosafety/management-containment-labs.pdf

# Genetically modified organisms

Genetic modification (GM) is the term given to deliberate manipulation of the genetic material (DNA or RNA) of organisms in a way that does not occur in nature. The aim of GM is to introduce new or altered characteristics into plants, animals, or most commonly, microorganisms (bacteria, viruses, and fungi). These modified attributes can be transferred subsequently between cells or organisms.

## Common sources/specific industries

- GM is carried out in laboratories, animal houses, and plant growth facilities (known as 'contained use')
- Those at risk of occupational exposure include:
  - laboratory workers
  - animal house workers
  - horticulturalists in experimental facilities

## Health effects

These mainly relate to genetically modified micro-organisms and include specific infections or the introduction of allergenic, toxic, or carcinogenic effects.

## Risk assessment and control

This is governed by primary legislation (genetically modified organisms (GMOs) (Contained Use) Regulations 2014). The regulations (see ➔ p. 122, References) give a framework for risk assessment (RA), risk reduction, monitoring, and review, requiring:

- Risk assessment of all activities involving GMOs
- Establishment of a GM safety committee to advise on RA
- Use of a four-level classification system based on the risk of the activity (this is determined by the control measures selected from the four levels of containment for microbial laboratories). See ➔ p. 120, Microbial pathogens (in laboratory settings), Table 3.2
- Notification of all premises to HSE before they are used for GM activities for the first time
- Notification of individual activities of Class 2 to Class 4 to the competent authority (administered by HSE)
- Maintenance of a public register of GM premises and activities

In addition, laboratories should follow good laboratory and containment practice.

## Relevant legislation

- The Genetically Modified Organisms (Contained Use) Regulations 2014. Available at: http://www.legislation.gov.uk/uksi/2014/1663/contents

## Further information and guidance

HSE. The Genetically Modified Organisms (Contained Use) Regulations 2014. HSE, Sudbury. Available at: https://www.hse.gov.uk/pubns/priced/l29.pdf

*Scientific Advisory Committee on Genetic Modification (SACGM) Compendium of Guidance*. Health and Safety Executive (HSE). Available at: https://www.hse.gov.uk/biosafety/gmo/acgm/acgmcomp/

# Animals and animal products

## Common sources and industries

Any industry that involves direct contact with animals (live or dead), their excreta, or products:

- Agriculture
- Veterinary medicine
- Meat processing (including abattoirs), packing, and distribution

## Potential health effects

### *Zoonoses*

These are a group of infections typically found in animals as the primary host, but which spread from animals to humans (see Table 3.3). Some can be transmitted from human to human. There are approximately 40 potential zoonoses in the UK and approximately 300,000 people in a variety of occupations are potentially exposed. Although most zoonoses are mild and self-limiting, some may cause long-term health effects.

**Table 3.3** Zoonoses

| Zoonotic infection | Animal host |
|---|---|
| Anthrax | Cows, sheep, others |
| Glanders | Horses, cats, dogs |
| *Streptococcus suis* | Pigs |
| Brucellosis | Cows, sheep, goats, pigs |
| Lyme disease | Deer |
| Chlamydia infections | Poultry, exotic birds, sheep |
| Q fever | Sheep, cows, goats |
| Orf | Sheep |

The common zoonoses are covered in ➲ Occupational infections, pp. 149–196.

### *Allergic (immune-mediated) disease*

Some organic antigens are animal products (e.g. rat urine) or found in association with animal products (e.g. bloom on bird feathers). See ➲ p. 126, Organic dusts and mists.

## Risk assessment

- *Route of exposure*:
  - high risk with skin contamination
  - inhalation of dusts and aerosols
  - ingestion

## Prevention/exposure control

- *Good husbandry practices for livestock*:
  - good standards of hygiene in young-stock housing
  - low stocking densities
  - avoid contaminating animal-drinking water with dung
  - keep animals as stress-free as possible

- *Education and awareness of zoonoses:*
  - warn employees and visitors about the risk of zoonoses and preventive measures
  - advise early consultation with a doctor and declaration of exposure to animals if suspicious symptoms occur
- *Identify those with individual susceptibility and restrict from exposure:*
  - pregnant women (avoid pregnant sheep)
  - immunocompromised people
- Immunizing and treating livestock
- Good occupational hygiene practices (Table 3.4)

**Table 3.4** Good occupational hygiene practices in agriculture and meat processing

| | |
|---|---|
| Safe working practices | • Avoid tools that cause cuts and injuries<br>• Safe use and disposal of sharps used to immunize/test animals<br>• Avoid mouth-to-mouth resuscitation on newborn animals<br>• Avoid handling birth fluids or placentae<br>• Control or eliminate rats<br>• Do not touch dead rats with unprotected skin |
| PPE | • Essential for birthing and handling infected stock, mouth, or rectal examinations: gauntlets/gloves, apron, boots<br>• Use face protection (mask and goggles) if there is a risk of splashing<br>• Use respirator if risk of exposure to aerosols (hosing down) or organic dust |
| Personal hygiene | • Good washing facilities, separate eating areas<br>• Wash hands and arms before eating or smoking<br>• Cover wounds with waterproof dressing<br>• Work wear should be retained and washed at the place of work (not taken home) |

## Relevant legislation

A number of diseases in animals, including brucellosis, anthrax, bovine tuberculosis, and bovine spongiform encephalopathy, are notifiable to the Animal and Plant Health Agency at the Department for Environment, Food, and Rural Affairs.

## Further information and guidance

Department for Environment, Food and Rural Affairs and Public Health England. *Zoonoses (Infections Acquired from Animals)*. Public Health England, London. Available at: https://www.gov.uk/government/collections/zoonotic-diseases-zoonoses-guidance-data-and-analysis/

HSE. *Common Zoonoses in Agriculture*. Available at: https://www.hse.gov.uk/agriculture/topics/zoonoses.htm

HSE/ACDP (1997). *Working Safely with Research Animals*. HSE Books, Sudbury. Available at: http://www.hse.gov.uk/pubns/priced/animal-research.pdf

HSE. *Zoonoses.*, Sudbury. Available at: http://www.hse.gov.uk/biosafety/diseases/zoonoses.htm

# Organic dusts and mists

These have the potential to cause occupational disease and are widespread in the workplace. The allergens are mainly high molecular weight proteins from plant and animal material and microorganisms.

## Common sources

*Organic dusts*

- *Animal proteins*:
  - urine and dander from farm or laboratory animals (e.g. cows, rats)
- *Plant proteins*:
  - natural rubber latex
  - grain dust
  - flour dust
  - wood dusts
  - colophony
- *Microbial*:
  - moulds and spores that grow in vegetable matter (e.g. hay, mushroom compost)
  - enzymes

*Organic mists*

- Proteinaceous mists from washing fish products, and surfaces or equipment contaminated with fish/animal proteins
- Bacterially infected metalworking fluids

## Specific industries

- Health care industry
- Rubber manufacturing
- Laboratories and animal houses/care facilities
- Farming
- Baking and flour milling
- Biological detergent manufacture
- Fish processing
- Engineering

## Health effects

- *Type I allergy (immunoglobulin E (IgE)-mediated)*:
  - occupational asthma
  - allergic rhinitis
  - contact urticaria
  - anaphylaxis
- Hypersensitivity pneumonitis

## Factors affecting the risk assessment

- Exposure
- Potency of the specific allergen
- Individual susceptibility (e.g. atopy, previous sensitization, cross-reactivity to similar allergens)

## Risk controls

- *Minimize exposure*: generic principles:
  - good animal husbandry, including avoidance of overcrowding
  - good hygiene: regular cleaning of animal cages and housing, wood workshops, bakeries
  - general and local ventilation
  - dust abatement techniques: avoid dry sweeping or compressed air lines for cleaning; instead use an industrial vacuum cleaner or wet clean
- Detailed guidance on the following specific biological allergens is available at: http://www.hse.gov.uk/asthma/index.htm
  - flour dust
  - grain dust
  - laboratory animals
  - natural rubber latex
  - wood dust
- *Use of PPE*: can be used if a significant risk exists after appropriate efforts at exposure control, e.g. for intermittent dusty tasks

Some advocate the use of RPE as a last resort in sensitized workers whose livelihood depends on working in 'at-risk' situations (e.g. farmers). If this approach is advised, it must be with extreme caution, and then only after all possible efforts have been made to reduce exposure. The individual must be monitored closely (health surveillance) for signs of deterioration.

## Health surveillance

All those who are exposed to a significant risk of allergic disease must have health surveillance as required by the MHSWR and COSHH.

- Regular symptoms questionnaire and lung function
- Follow-up positive symptoms with further investigation:
  - serial peak flow tests
  - skin prick tests
  - skin patch tests
  - total IgE and specific IgE for suspect agent (e.g. latex)
- Exclude if exposure cannot be controlled adequately or use PPE and monitor extremely closely

## Further information and guidance

HSE (2013). *Control of Exposure to Grain Dust*. HSE Books, Sudbury. Available at: https://www.hse.gov.uk/pubns/indg140.pdf

Chapter 4

# Mechanical and ergonomics hazards

# Ergonomics hazards: Overview

## Definitions

Ergonomics (or human factors) is the scientific discipline concerned with the understanding of interactions among humans and other elements of a system, and the profession that applies theory, principles, data, and methods to design in order to optimize human well-being and overall system performance (International Ergonomics Association).

Wilson and Corlett (2005) stated that ergonomics is concerned with interactions between people and the things they use and the environments in which they use them.

Ergonomics hazards to employees are ubiquitous, affecting almost every type of work. Poor work design can affect the physical and mental health of employees.

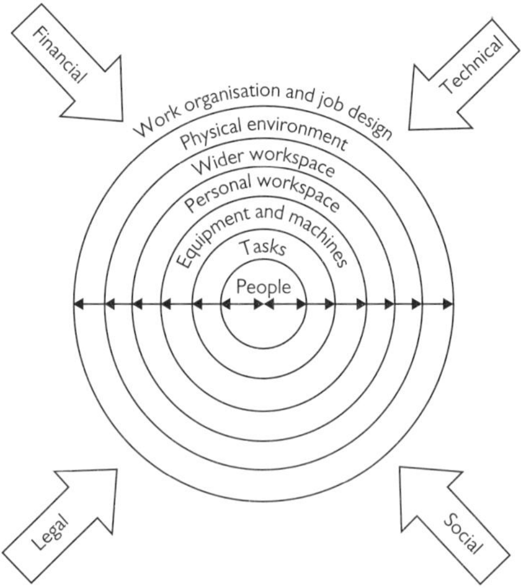


**Fig. 4.1** The ergonomic onion model.

From Wilson J and Corlett N 2005. Evaluation of Human Work, 3rd edition. Taylor & Francis.

## Specific ergonomics factors

The most important of these are covered separately in this chapter. Each layer of the Ergonomics Onion Model (see Fig 4.1) should be considered in the design of jobs and identification of potential issues. Ergonomics hazards often occur in combination with each other and are commonly addressed together in designing risk controls.

*People: individual factors*

- Physical ability
- Physiological ability
- Cognitive ability

- Anthropometrics
- Biomechanics
- Attitude and behaviour
- Risk perception
- Disabilities

*Tasks (physical or cognitive): interaction between people and the tasks they carry out*

- Loading (lifting and handling)
- *Posture*: awkward postures, reaching, static, or sustained postures
- Repetition, particularly at high speed
- Forceful exertions
- Task overload/under load
- Mental workload
- Poor system reliability

*Equipment and machines: interaction between people and the equipment they use*

- Poor design including lack of consideration of the user
- Equipment not suitable for the job
- Requires excessive force to operate
- Vibration
- Unintuitive to use
- Uncomfortable to use, e.g. forced into poor working postures
- Poor design of information, displays, and controls

*Workspace (design, layout, etc.)*

- Immediate workspace, e.g. desk and chair
- Wider workspace, e.g. access and egress
- Cramped

*Physical environment*

- Lighting
- *Thermal comfort*:
  - humidity
  - air temperature
  - radiant temperature
  - air velocity
- Noise
- Dust
- Radiation

*Organizational factors and job design*

- Long working hours
- Insufficient breaks
- Shift work
- Short deadlines
- Poor staffing levels, staff experience, and skill mix
- Lack of worker involvement in system design
- Control over work.
- Psychosocial factors
- Organizational structures
- Policies

### Adverse effects of poor ergonomics design

- Accidents
- Injuries
- Musculoskeletal disease (back, neck, and upper limb pain)
- Psychological morbidity (including stress)
- Critical incidents (including environmental disasters)
- Decreased efficiency and poor productivity
- Failure of complex systems
- Job dissatisfaction
- Low staff morale
- High job turnover

### Risk control

Ergonomic hazards should be controlled using the hierarchy of controls. Hazards should be avoided or eliminated by redesigning the issues identified in the ergonomics onion. Among others, redesign examples include automation, mechanizing the task, and the use of mechanical aids such as electric pallet trucks. If strategies at the top of the hierarchy of controls are not reasonably practicable other risk reduction strategies must be implemented, e.g. reduce the size of the load, job rotation or redesigning the work environment to avoid poor postures, etc.

The impact of any intervention must be considered in relation to the entire work system, i.e. implementing a control measure must not have an adverse impact on another aspect of the work system.

### Ergonomics risk management

Specific aspects of risk assessment and control are covered under each ergonomics hazard (see ➲ p. 136, Lifting and handling, ➲ p. 134, Posture, and ➲ p. 140, Repetitive work, and also ➲ p. 818, Carry out an ergonomics assessment and ➲ p. 816, Carry out a display screen equipment assessment).

### Implementing an ergonomics management system

Implementing an ergonomics management system to prevent health-related issues such as occupational musculoskeletal disorders and stress must take a holistic approach. Each 'layer' of the Ergonomics Onion Model should be considered in the design of the system. A participatory ergonomics approach should be used to ensure employees are consulted throughout.

### Relevant legislation

There is no specific legislation on ergonomics hazards, but some statutory instruments contain direction on ergonomics issues:

- Control of Major Accident Hazards Regulations 1999 (COMAH)
- Railways (Safety Critical Work) Regulations 1994
- The Manual Handling Operations Regulations 1992 (as amended)
- The Health and Safety (Display Screen Equipment) Regulations 1992
- Provision and Use of Work Equipment Regulations 1998 (PUWER)
- The Working Time Regulations 1998
- The Workplace (Health, Safety and Welfare) Regulations 1992
- The Control of Vibration at Work Regulations 2005

## Further information

Chartered Institute of Ergonomics and Human Factors. Warwickshire UK. Available at: http://www.ergonomics.org.uk

European Agency for Safety and Health at Work. Bilbao, Spain. Available at: https://osha.europa.eu/en

HSE. *Human Factors Guidance*. HSE Books, Sudbury. Available at: www.hse.gov.uk/humanfactors/index.htm

International Ergonomics Association. Available at: http://www.iea.cc

Wilson JR, Sharples S (eds.) (2015). *Evaluation of Human Work*, 4th edn. Taylor and Francis.

# Posture

It is likely that poor (non-neutral) posture is not an independent risk factor and works in combination with other risk factors (see the following sections).

## Definitions

Non-neutral means that the head, trunk, or limbs deviate from the normal anatomical (neutral) position.

## Specific industries

Adverse posture is widespread across many industries, affecting workers in office environments as well as heavy manual occupations. In particular:

- Display screen equipment users
- Food industry, meat handlers
- Assembly line workers

## Risk assessment

- *Non-neutral posture is associated with risk of health effects if it is:*
  - long duration: prolonged, constrained, or awkward position of the trunk or limbs (e.g. sustained stooping)
  - repetitive: repeated adverse posture (e.g. bending up and down)
  - forceful: handling heavy items, applying force such as hammering, or gripping items
- *Extreme deviation from the anatomical position increases risk:*
  - head or trunk: flexed or extended, especially 20°
  - upper limbs: extreme flexion or abduction of the shoulders (work with arms above shoulder height), elbows, or wrists

Following a suitable and sufficient risk assessment of the task, identified hazards must be reduced so far as reasonably practicable using the hierarchy of controls. The assessment tools listed in Table 4.1 can be used to assess posture:

**Table 4.1** Assessment tool for posture

| Risk assessment tool | Task |
|---|---|
| RULA: Rapid upper limb assessment | Upper limb tasks |
| REBA: Rapid entire body assessment | Whole-body handling tasks |

## Risk control

Risk reduction is mainly by the application of good ergonomics principles to the design of the task, working environment, and equipment. Common examples include:

- Appropriate seating that is adjustable to allow for anthropometric variations between operators
- Controls that are within reach to avoid overreaching or stretching
- Attention to the height at which tasks are carried out to minimize bending or stooping
- Task rotation, regular breaks, or variation in position to avoid prolonged constrained posture

## Potential health effects

- Low back pain
- Upper limb pain (neck, shoulders, elbow, forearm, wrist, hand)

## Further information and guidance

HSE (2004). *The Manual Handling Operations Regulations 1992. Guidance on Regulations*. HSE Books, Sudbury. Available at: https://www.hse.gov.uk/pubns/books/l23.htm

HSE. *Reducing Awkward Postures*. HSE Books, Sudbury. Available at: http://www.hse.gov.uk/msd/uld/art/posture.htm

HSE. *Upper Limb Disorders in the Workplace*. HSE Books, Sudbury. Available at: https://www.hse.gov.uk/pubns/books/hsg60.htm

Hignett S, McAtamney L (2000). Rapid entire body assessment (REBA). *Applied Ergonomics* 31(2):201–205.

McAtamney L, Corlett EN (1993). RULA: A survey method for the investigation of work-related upper limb disorders. *Applied Ergonomics* 24(2):91–99.

The Display Screen Equipment (DSE) Regulations. Available at: http://www.opsi.gov.uk/si/si1992/Uksl_19922792_En_1.htmHSE (2003).

Work with display screen equipment Health and Safety (Display Screen Equipment) Regulations 1992 as amended by the Health and Safety (Miscellaneous Amend https://www.hse.gov.uk/pubns/priced/l26.pdfments) Regulations 2002 Guidance on Regulations. HSE., UK. Available at: https://www.hse.gov.uk/pubns/priced/l26.pdf

# Lifting and handling

Manual lifting or handling of loads constitutes one of the most common and important ergonomics hazards. Handling, lifting, and carrying accounted for 20% of all Reporting of Injuries, Diseases, and Dangerous Occurrences Regulations reports in 2018/19 (HSE).

## Definitions

The term manual handling comprises any non-mechanized (or incompletely mechanized) manipulation of a load, including lifting, pushing, pulling, sliding, or carrying. Loads may be inanimate or living (people and animals).

## Specific industries

Manual handling is a ubiquitous exposure, which is common in a wide range of industries. However, of particular note are:

- Construction
- Factories
- Courier services
- Warehousing and logistics
- Heavy engineering
- Airport baggage handling
- Agriculture
- Health care (patient-handling)

## Workplace design hazards that may result in back pain

Adams et al. (2013) identified a number of factors that increase the risk of back pain in the workplace:

- Heavy loads
- Severe repetitive loading (particularly in bending and compression)
- Long reach distances
- Wrong work height
- Static or awkward postures
- Cramped workspace
- Unstable load
- Unsuitable hand holds
- Poor environmental conditions

Lifting more than 25 kg more than 15 times per 8-hour shift is a significant risk factor for back pain (Coenen et al. 2013).

## Risk assessment

Following a suitable and sufficient risk assessment of the task, identified hazards must be reduced so far as reasonably practicable using the hierarchy of controls. For ergonomic lifting and handling risk assessment tools types, see Table 4.2.

**Table 4.2** Risk assessment tools for lifting and handling

| Risk assessment tool | Job task |
|---|---|
| Manual handling assessment chart (MAC) lifting | Lifting tasks |
| MAC carry | Carrying tasks |
| MAC team handling | Team handling tasks |
| V-MAC | Repetitive handling or carrying with varying weights |
| Risk assessment of pushing and pulling (RAPP) | Pushing and pulling tasks |
| Quick exposure check (QEC) | Load handling tasks<br>Repetitive tasks |

## Risk controls

The following includes the most common examples of risk controls.

- Divide load into smaller units, or scale loads up, and switch to bulk handling systems
- Ensure loads are easy to grip and stable, and are not harmful (hot, chemicals, etc.), awkwardly stacked, or obstruct vision
- Arrange lifting environment free from obstacles and on level surface
- Design workplace to ensure an upright working posture when handling items, i.e. avoid lifting from the floor
- Design tasks to ensure staff are not required to twist, stoop, reach upwards, carry items for long distances, and repetitively handle loads. Also ensure loads are held close to body
- Avoid a work rate imposed by a process and ensure sufficient rest and recovery time
- Handling aids appropriate to the task. There are many examples for different purposes. Handling aids must be suitable for the task i.e., well maintained, appropriate wheels, handles, at the correct height, and brakes working if present. More common examples include:
  - hoists, cranes, and vehicles
  - powered pallet trucks and trolleys
  - scissor lifts or other height-adjustable surfaces
  - tracks, conveyors, chutes, and rollers
  - specialized equipment for 'live' loads (patients), e.g. hoists

## Health effects

- Low back pain
- Neck–shoulder pain
- Osteoarthritis of the hip

## Specific legislative requirements

The Manual Handling Operations Regulations 1992 (amended) give a framework for the generic risk assessment, risk control, and review cycle that is specifically relevant for hazards associated with manual handling.

## Further information and guidance

Adams MA, Bogduk N, Burton K, Dolan P (2013). *The Biomechanics of Back Pain*, 3rd edn. Elsevier, London.

Coenen P, Kingma I, Boot CRL, Twisk JWR, Bongers PM, Van Dieën JH (2013). Cumulative low back load at work as a risk factor of low back pain: A prospective cohort study. *Journal of Occupational Rehabilitation* 23(1):11–18.

HSE. *Guidance and Tools*. HSE Books, Sudbury. Available at: https://www.hse.gov.uk/msd/manual-handling/index.htm

HSE. *Lifting and Lowering Risk Filter*. HSE Books, Sudbury. Available at: https://www.hse.gov.uk/msd/manual-handling-risk-filters.htm

HSE (2016). *Manual Handling—Manual Handling Operations Regulations 1992—Guidance on Regulations*. Available at: https://www.hse.gov.uk/pubns/books/l23.htm

# Repetitive work

## Definition

Repetitive work includes activities that are physically repetitive or cognitively repetitive or monotonous. Physical and cognitive aspects of repetitiveness in work tasks often interact.

## Specific industries/tasks

- Packaging
- Assembly lines
- Textile/garment production (sewing machine operators, cutting room)
- Poultry processing (plucking, evisceration)
- Fruit pickers
- Computer data entry operators

## Health effects

*Musculoskeletal disorders*:
- Neck–shoulder pain
- Elbow, wrist pain
- Low back pain

## Risk assessment

Following a suitable and sufficient risk assessment of the task, identified hazards must be reduced so far as reasonably practicable using the hierarchy of controls. The risk arising for repetitive work can be assessed using tools (see Table 4.3). For risks factors to be considered for repetitive work, see Table 4.4.

**Table 4.3** Risk assessment tools for repetitive work

| Name | Tasks |
|---|---|
| ART | Repetitive upper limb tasks |
| QEC | Load handling tasks<br>Repetitive tasks |

## Risk controls

The following list is not exhaustive but includes the most common examples of risk controls.
- Worker participation in job design and organization
- Frequent rest breaks
- Task rotation
- Avoid forced pacing
- Job enrichment and variety
- Automation
- Mechanization
- Suitable workstation layout with good adjustability to ensure tools and equipment are within easy reach to minimize overreaching and awkward postures

**Table 4.4** Risk assessment for repetitive tasks

| Risk factor | ↑ Risk | ↓ Risk |
|---|---|---|
| Cycle time | Rapid | Slow |
| Grip strength | Tight grip | Loose grip |
| Recovery time | Short | Long |
| Synergism with posture | Awkward posture | Supported neutral posture |
| Psychosocial factors | Lack of control over work (e.g. forced pacing) | Able to determine speed of work |
| | Excessive workload | Able to intersperse repetitive tasks with other activities (both physical and cognitive) |

## Further information


HSE (2003). *The Law on VDUs: An Easy Guide*, HSG (90). HSE Books, Sudbury. Available at: https://www.hse.gov.uk/pubns/books/hsg90.htm

HSE (2003). *Work with Display Screen Equipment: Health and Safety (Display Screen Equipment) Regulations 1992 as amended by the Health and Safety (Miscellaneous Amendments) Regulations 2002*, L. (26). HSE Books, Sudbury. Available at: https://www.hse.gov.uk/pubns/books/l26.htm

HSE. *Assessment of Repetitive Tasks (ART) Tool*. HSE Books, Sudbury. Available at: www.hse.gov.uk/msd/uld/art/index.htm

HSE. (2002). *Upper Limb Disorders in the Workplace*. HSE Books, Sudbury. Available at: https://www.hse.gov.uk/pubns/books/hsg60.htm

# Mechanical hazards

In the operation of machines a person may be injured as a result of:
- Machine movement
- Being trapped between the machinery and materials
- Being struck by materials ejected from the machinery

## Identification of machinery hazards

It is useful to consider three factors:
- *The different phases of the machine's life (consider the tasks associated in each phase)*:
  - design and construction
  - installation
  - commissioning
  - operation
  - cleaning
  - maintenance
  - disposal
- The hazards that can cause an injury such as electrical, noise, heat/cold, vibration, and sudden release of pressure
- The circumstances giving rise to an injury

## Types of machinery hazards

For the different types and range of machines used, their hazards can be summarized as follows:
- *Traps*:
  - reciprocating traps due to vertical or horizontal motion of machines
  - shearing traps produced by a moving part traversing a fixed part, and *in-running nips* where limbs are drawn into a trap (e.g. where a moving belt or chain meets a roller or a tooth wheel)
- *Impact*: machinery parts, which can cause injuries by their speed or movement if the person gets in the way
- *Contact*: this may cause burns, lacerations, or injuries due to sharp, abrasive, hot, cold, or electrically live machine components
- *Entanglement*: limbs, hair, or clothing may become entangled with unguarded moving parts
- *Ejection*: machines may eject particles, metals, or actual parts of machines (e.g. grinding machines)
- *Injection*: machinery leaks may inject hydraulic fluid into the skin at high pressure

## Risk assessment

Following a suitable and sufficient risk assessment, risk controls must be implemented to reduce hazards. Consider the following (list is not exhaustive):
- Is the equipment fit for purpose?
- Who uses the equipment, how is it being used, and what is it being used for?
- Is the equipment being used as per the manufacturer's guidelines?
- Is the equipment being used as per its intended purpose?
- Worker interaction with equipment: reach, force required, repetition, postural constraints, accessibility, etc.
- Potential machinery hazards, e.g. traps, entanglement, ejection, etc.

- Is it suitable for use in the intended work conditions?
- Is it maintained in a safe condition?
- Some equipment should be regularly inspected to ensure it remains fit for use, e.g. power presses:
  - any inspection should be by a competent person
  - a record should be kept of the inspection

## Risk controls

- Mechanical hazards should be considered when purchasing equipment (how and where the worker could come into contact with such hazards)
- *Machinery should be fitted with suitable safety devices, e.g.*
  - machine guards
  - emergency stop buttons clearly marked and in easy reach to operate quickly in an emergency
  - interlocks to prevent operation if guards are removed
- Machinery should have appropriate warning signs
- Worker information, instruction, and training
- Safe systems of work including machine isolation before maintenance
- Personal protective equipment, e.g. safety goggles

## Relevant legislation and guidance

HSE (1999). *Simple Guide to the Provision and Use of Work Equipment Regulations 1998*, INDG 291. HSE Books, Sudbury. Available at: http://www.hse.gov.uk/pubns/indg291.pdf

HSE (2008). *Approved Code of Practice Safe Use of Work Equipment. Provision and Use of Work Equipment Regulations 1998*, L22. HSE Books, Sudbury. Available at: https://www.hse.gov.uk/pubns/books/l22.htm

# Chapter 5



# Psychosocial hazards

# Organizational psychosocial factors

## Definition

The term 'psychosocial hazard' is used to describe any factor that may cause distress or psychological harm either knowingly or unknowingly to the worker (see Table 5.1).

**Table 5.1** Psychosocial hazards—examples

| | |
|---|---|
| *Content of job*<br>Work overload, many deadlines, unrealistic deadlines, difficulty of work, time pressures, underloading (work too easy), safety critical work, continual vigilance | *Organization of work*<br>Shift work, long working hours, unsociable hours, zero-hour contracts, on-call working, unpredictable working hours, organizational restructuring, non-consulted changes, time-zone changes, payment structure encouraging working quickly or without breaks |
| *Workplace culture*<br>Communication, over-reliance on email working, expecting replies to emails 24/7, involvement in decision making, little feedback, insufficient resources, support, bullying/exclusionary practices, high level of effort not balanced by reward, e.g. status, remuneration | *Work role*<br>Clarity of job; conflict of interests and beliefs; lack of control over work and work methods (including shift patterns); carrying out repetitive, monotonous tasks; work demand perceived to be excessive |
| *Structure*<br>Over-promotion (self/others), under-promotion (self/others), redundancy threats, pay structure/inequalities, organizational injustices, and perceived unfairness | *Relationships*<br>Poor communication, harassment, bullying, verbal abuse, physical abuse/intimidation, poor management, and/or peer support |
| *Environment*<br>Noise, temperature, lighting, space, ergonomics, perceived hazard exposure, remote and isolated working, over-crowding, isolation | *Home–work interface*<br>Childcare issues, transport problems, commuting, relocation, housing issues, time-pressures |

## Health effects

- Stress
- Musculoskeletal disorders
- *Meta-analyses of the literature on stress show that many physical changes occur in stressed people, either directly or indirectly, and either with or without their awareness of it happening*:
  - cardiovascular problems (direct physiological)
  - some infections (direct physiological)
  - some immunosuppression (direct physiological)
  - mental health problems: anxiety, depression (direct psychological)

- cancers associated with behavioural responses resulting in increased use of drink, tobacco, and drugs (indirect behavioural and direct physiological)
- musculoskeletal problems (direct psychological)
- reduced pain tolerance/thresholds

## Other adverse effects

- Low morale and job satisfaction
- Low productivity
- Increase in industrial disputes
- Increased interpersonal conflicts
- Increased risk-taking
- Increased tolerance of poorer standards
- Increased accidents and injuries

## Risk controls

These primary interventions decrease adverse organizational factors:

*Workplace demands*

- Ensure employees are able to cope with the demands (physical and psychological) of their jobs
- Provide achievable demands relative to the hours of work
- Match employees' skills and abilities to the job demands
- Design jobs within the capabilities of employees
- Address employees' concerns about their work/environment

*Maintaining control*

- Employees can have a say about how they do their work
- Employees have control over the pace of work
- Employee initiative and skills are encouraged
- Employees encouraged to develop new skills and face challenges
- Employees can have a say when breaks are taken
- Employees are consulted over work issues whenever possible

*Workplace relationships*

- Employees not subjected to unacceptable behaviour (e.g. bullying)
- Promote positive working and ensure fairness
- Diversity and inclusivity among employees should be encouraged
- Avoid conflict and deal with unacceptable behaviour swiftly
- Employees share information relevant to their work
- Policies and procedures to address unacceptable behaviour swiftly
- Managers are able to deal with unacceptable behaviour
- Employees are able to report unacceptable behaviour safely

*Workplace roles*

- Ensure clarity of roles and tasks and avoid role conflicts
- Employees understand their role and responsibilities clearly
- Ensure different roles placed upon employees are compatible
- Check employees understand their roles and responsibilities
- Employees can raise concerns about role uncertainties or conflicts
- Ensure the ethics of what is done is congruent with employee beliefs

*Organizational change*

- Engage employees frequently when undergoing organizational change
- Ensure adequate employee consultation on changes
- Ensure all communications about any change is communicated clearly to employees
- Make employees aware of the impact and time frames of changes
- Employees have access to relevant support during changes

*Employee support*

- Employees receive adequate support from colleagues and superiors
- Policies and procedures to support employees
- Encourage managers to proactively support their staff
- Encourage employees to support their colleagues
- Employees know what support is available and how to access it
- Employees know how to use any resources to do their job
- Employees receive regular and constructive feedback
- Publicizing access and encourage use of employee assistance programmes

## Further information and guidance

HSE. Stress and mental health at work. HSE, Available at: https://www.hse.gov.uk/stress/index.htmHSE (2019). *Tackling Work-Related Stress Using the Management Standards Approach*. HSE, Sudbury. Available at: https://www.hse.gov.uk/pubns/wbk01.pdf

# Violence and aggression

## Definition

Any incident in which a person is abused, threatened, or assaulted in circumstances relating to their work, whether by colleagues, customers, or associates of the victim. This can include verbal abuse, threats, and physical attacks.

## Incidence

- The Crime Survey for England and Wales (2018/19) estimated that the number of violent incidents experienced by workers in England and Wales has doubled since 2009/10, with 694,000 violent incidents occurring at workplaces in 2017/18. Half of these incidents were threats and half were assaults
- 374,000 people experienced violence in UK workplaces in 2017/18
- *For most workers the risk of threats of violence or actual violence at work is around 3%. Groups at high risk of experiencing threats or actual violence include:*
  - protective services (e.g. police officers)
  - health care workers
  - prison staff
- There were 6017 Reporting of Injuries, Diseases, and Dangerous Occurrences Regulations (RIDDOR) reported injuries, including one fatality, due to workplace violence in 2019/20
- Violence from colleagues represents only 5% of workplace violent incidents; 65% of physical and verbal attacks come from strangers, and approximately 20% from clients or customers

## Risk factors

Workplace violence can occur in different environments, including health care, private residences, public spaces, and commercial premises. Those most at risk from violence in the workplace include those who:

- Provide (medical/health/social) care for others
- Provide front-line interaction with complainants
- Interact with active offenders/law breakers
- Deliver/collect goods
- Control/schedule services
- Represent authority
- Deliver education or instruction
- Transact cash or valuables

## Causes

Common causes of violence in workplaces include:

- Alcohol/drug intoxication
- People not receiving immediate attention that they demand
- Unhappiness resulting from unresolved grievances and issues
- Dissatisfaction with the (lack of) attention/treatment received
- Those committing acts of theft/robbery/burglary/criminal activity

## Behavioural markers of potential aggressors

- Previous history of violence
- Those who may have been in previous relationships with employees
- Severe mental health problems (e.g. psychoses, schizophrenia)
- Certain personality disorders (e.g. antisocial or psychopathic)
- Frustration (with the victim's organization)
- Emotional problems
- Those with behavioural issues (e.g. conduct disorder)
- Issues with substance abuse/misuse
- Social isolation with limited outlets
- Interpersonal problems
- Antagonistic relationships with others
- Obsessive behaviour (e.g. romantic, political, religious, racial)
- Stalkers who often present at their victim's workplace

## Risk control

Eliminating or reducing the potential for workplace violence should be a high priority for managers.

Organizations should not wait until violent events occur before preparing plans to combat violence and aggression and should train their staff to actively prevent violence. Training employees in de-escalation skills and providing a non-combative environment can help.

All organizations should have, and enforce, a zero-tolerance to violence policy, which is communicated to both employees and non-employees. Actions that can reduce workplace violence include:

- Employee training
- Publicizing/raise awareness of cases where aggression/violence was dealt with
- Communicating to employees that those found guilty of violence will be subject to disciplinary action
- Communicating to customers that legal action will be taken when required
- Effective security measures (e.g. security patrols, CCTV, controlled access measures)

See p. 388, Violence management policies, for specific guidance and examples of good practice.

## Further information and guidance

HSE (2020). *Violence at Work statistics*, 2020. Available at: https://www.hse.gov.uk/statistics/causinj/violence/work-related-violence-report.pdf

# Lone working

## Definition

Lone working can be defined as 'any situation or location in which someone works without a colleague nearby; or when someone is working out of sight or earshot of another colleague'.[1] This definition includes those who are not obviously lone workers, e.g. school teachers working in isolated classrooms and remote from the assistance of colleagues.

## Risk factors

Lone working of itself is not the issue—it is the lack of immediate assistance available to the worker. The main concerns are:

- Illness
- Accidents
- Personal safety (see also ➲ p. 146, Organizational psychosocial factors and ➲ p. 426, Violence management policies)

## Exposed occupations

Many employers have staff who work alone.

- *Those who work in the community, e.g.*
  - social workers
  - traffic wardens
  - district nurses
  - lorry, bus, and taxi drivers
  - delivery drivers
  - maintenance/repair staff
- *Those who work in single-occupancy premises, e.g.*
  - petrol stations
  - shops
  - those who work from home
- *Those who work in isolated areas of large buildings, e.g.*
  - reception staff
  - teachers
- *Those who work in premises outside routine office hours, e.g.*
  - cleaners
  - engineers
  - security staff

## Risk assessment

Factors to consider in a risk assessment include the following:

- *People*: both the employee and the people they might encounter
- Location
- Timing
- *Task*:
  - hazardous procedures
  - dealing with valuables or cash
  - dealing with difficult situations or people
  - enforcement activity (e.g. traffic wardens)
- Travel and accommodation

1 Health and Safety Executive. 2020. Published by TSO, London. https://www.hse.gov.uk/pubns/indg73.pdf

Where a risk assessment indicates inadequate control measures, lone working should not proceed. Consider working in pairs, or an alternative location/time for the task, etc. to eliminate or reduce risk.

## Control measures

- Employers of lone workers should have a lone-working policy
- Information, instruction, and training for lone workers and managers
- Access controls in buildings
- Internal alarm systems including panic buttons or fob-operated alarms are useful for premises (e.g. psychiatric hospitals)
- Lone-worker protection systems linked to a central control room (with or without a global positioning satellite technology) for mobile workers
- Personal attack alarm (although activation may inflame difficult situations)
- *Mobile phone*: check that it is fully charged, staff have any access PIN, has available credit, and that reception is adequate in that area
- Information sharing between public bodies regarding individuals with a history of violence towards staff
- *Visit log*: who is being visited, contact details, arrival/departure times, *but* this requires the cooperation of all staff to operate effectively
- *Lone worker details held in personal file including*:
    - make, model, and registration of any vehicle
    - next of kin
    - home and mobile phone numbers
    - establishment of an emergency procedure protocol if they 'go quiet' while out

Do not place undue reliance on lone-worker protection systems.

## Relevant legislation

- Under the Health and Safety at Work etc. Act 1974 employers have a duty to protect workers, and this would include lone workers
- Management of Health and Safety at Work Regulations 1999 requires that employers undertake a suitable and sufficient risk assessment of the risks to the health and safety of staff and others (regulation 3), which would include lone working

## Further information and guidance

Health and Safety at Work etc. Act (1974), Chapter 37.
HSE (1999). *Management of Health and Safety at Work Regulations (1999) Approved Code of Practice and Guidance*. Available at: https://www.hse.gov.uk/pubns/hsc13.pdf

# Shift and night work

## Definition

Night work is defined as at least 3 hours of work taking place between 23.00 and 06.00 hours (unless employers and employees adopt a different night-time period).

## Epidemiology

- Nearly 25% of workers have shift work that is not during the daytime
- Between one-quarter and one-third of shift workers are unable to tolerate the effects of their work schedules and have excessive sleepiness
- One-third of shift workers state that they sleep less than 6 hours per night on workdays, and 30% report that they only get a good night's sleep a few nights per month or less
- Shift work is only slightly more prevalent in men than women:
  - most common in personal protective services (45% men and 27% of women in the sector) and plant and machine operators (31% of men and 22% of women in the sector)
  - nurses are the most common group of female shift workers
  - uniformed services rely on permanent shift working more than any other sector

## Health effects

- Fatigue and chronic tiredness
- Sleep deficits
- Anxiety/depression
- Increased substance use (eating, smoking, drinking)
- *Functional gastrointestinal (GI) disorders*:
  - peptic ulcer
  - altered bowel habits
- Cardiovascular disease
- Neurological disorders
- Menstrual disorders
- Acute changes in cholesterol, uric acid, glucose, potassium, and lipids
- There is evidence of an association with miscarriage, preterm birth, and low birth weight, but it is not clear if the association is causal
- There is evidence of an association between long-term night shift work and certain cancers in some occupations, but it is not clear if the association is direct or indirect (see http://monographs.iarc.fr/ENG/Monographs/vol98/index.php) although circadian disruption is seen as a probable human carcinogen

## Complications of night work

Much research has gone into determining whether or not night working imposes extra health risks. Evidence is inconclusive, but it seems likely that circadian disruption, fatigue, and sleep deficit will be exacerbated by a 12-hour shift system. A consensus view is that shift work adversely affects worker productivity, performance, health, and quality of life, and that shift work also puts others at risk due to workplace or driving accidents. Other factors affecting health and safety should be considered, such as exposure to toxic materials or environmental risks, where occupational exposure limits appropriate for 8 hours would no longer be safe for 12 hours.

## Effects on function

Risk of accidental injury is 30% higher on night shifts than on morning shifts and is usually highest in the first 2–3 hours, with the risk increasing over successive nights. By the fourth night shift, there is a 1.3 times increased risk of accident than on the first night. The use of sedatives to aid sleep at unusual times may lengthen reaction times and exacerbate the risk of accidents. Although short/20-minute power naps help make up for the loss of sleep shift workers experience, they do not adequately repay the sleep deficit. In some cases, power naps are not long enough for people to reap the benefits of the deeper sleep stages they miss out on.

## Risk factors

Factors associated with adverse effects of night/shift work include:
- Incomplete/partial circadian adjustment
- Irregular food intake leading to stomach complaints
- Reduced quality of food intake due to 'convenience eating'
- Impairment of social or family life, and disrupted child care
- Increased time-pressures from completing activities that can only be undertaken during daylight/business hours

## Further reading

Cheng P, Drake C. (2019). Shift Work Disorder. *Neurol Clin.* 37(3), 563–577. doi:10.1016/j.ncl.2019.03.003. Epub 2019 May 7.PMID: 31256790.

Danielle Pacheco and Anis Rehman. 2020. *Shift Work Disorder—What it is, what causes it, and how it can be diagnosed and treated.* Sleep foundation. https://www.sleepfoundation.org/shift-work-disorder/what-shift-work-disorder/shift-work-disorder-symptoms

Torquati L, Mielke GI, Brown WJ, Burton NW, Kolbe-Alexander TL. (2019). Shift Work and Poor Mental Health: A Meta-Analysis of Longitudinal Studies. *Am J Public Health.* 109(11), e13–e20. doi:10.2105/AJPH.2019.305278. Epub 2019 Sep 19.PMID: 3153640.

► The ability to cope with changed sleep patterns varies considerably and should be considered when selecting night workers. Employees' lifestyle, domestic situation, and predilection to day/night life should be considered carefully.

## Relevant legislation

Workers who normally work at night (excluding those who only occasionally work at nights) are protected under the Working Time Regulations (see ➲ p. 608, Working Time Regulations 1998). This includes provision of health checks for night workers.

## Risk control

*Employees should*

- Drink caffeine in the first half of the shift only
- Take a short 15–20 minute 'power caffeine'
- Take small breaks at least every hour
- Take a main meal break between midnight and 01.00 hours
- Take a smaller food break between 03.00 and 04.00 hours
- Be aware of subjective sensations of inertia shortly after waking
- Avoid driving to/from work after prolonged periods of night shifts
- Eat healthily where possible
- Keep a regular exercise routine and remain active
- Design and define their own shifts whenever possible
- Take up flexible working patterns if permissible
- Advice is available for shift workers on how to cope with the demands of night working. The HSE offers tips on dealing with sleep problems, eating, physical fitness, and social contact. https://www.hse.gov.uk/humanfactors/topics/shift-workers.htm

*Employers should*

- Minimize use of permanent night shift working where possible
- Ensure safe travel to and from work at unusual hours
- Limit consecutive night shifts to no more than four
- If possible, allow 24 hours between two consecutive night shifts
- Some weekends (one in four) should be completely free of night shifts
- Consider making night shifts shorter than day shifts
- Avoid compressed working periods (of night shifts)
- The length of night shifts should be related to the tasks performed
- Forward rotation of shifts is preferable to continuous night shifts
- Morning shifts should start later rather than sooner
- Work schedules should be as regular as possible
- Allow opportunities to swap shifts and change handover times
- Avoid excessive short-term work schedule changes
- Forward notice should be given of changes in shift patterns
- Allow return to day work without penalty (especially older workers)
- Ensure availability of hot food and drinks, rest areas, and first aid
- Ensure catering options are equivalent with day-shift catering—night workers need the same access to training as other workers
- Allow access to union representation or daytime meetings
- Offer access to health checks for night workers

# Long working hours

## Definition

'Long hours' workers are those who work >48 hours/week.

## Epidemiology

- The average length of the European working week is decreasing. In the European member states, it has fallen from 40.5 hours in 1991 to 37 hours in 2019
- The proportion of the working population in Europe working longer than 48 hours has fallen from 15% in 2000 to <10% in 2019
- Long working hours are more common in men than women

## Health effects

- Generalized chronic fatigue, both physical and psychological
- Anxiety/depression

## Effects on function

- Poor performance
- ↑ *Risk of accident or injury*:
  - exponential increase with long hours: by the twelfth hour of work, risk is double that during the first 8 hours
  - not taking a regular break linearly ↑ the risk of injury: the risk of injury 1.5 hours after taking a break is twice that when resuming work immediately after the break

## Risk factors

A number of factors increase the likelihood of adverse effects from working longer hours:

- Female sex
- Older age
- Obesity
- Reduced sleep quality
- Poor diet
- Little exercise
- *Pre-existing poor health*: examples of medical conditions that may be adversely affected include asthma, depression, and diabetes. These need to be considered before selecting individuals for long working hours duties (although they are not an absolute contraindication to long hours)
- Complex or demanding domestic situations

## Relevant legislation

The European Working Time Directive enforces standards on working time (see ➲ p. 608, Working Time Regulations 1998).

## Further information and guidance

European Working Conditions Telephone Survey 2021. Available at: https://www.eurofound.europa.eu/surveys/2021/european-working-conditions-telephone-survey-2021

# Time zone changes

Crossing time zones is commonly associated with jobs that require frequent international travel.

## Health effects

Transmeridian displacement or dysrhythmia (jet lag) is a disturbance of the internal circadian rhythm (body clock) caused by crossing multiple international time zones. Crossing time zones when travelling east (travelling forward in time) is usually worse than when travelling west (backward in time). Temporary symptoms include:

- Tiredness
- Disorientation
- Lack of concentration
- Broken sleeping/night wakefulness
- Cognitive impairment
- Irritability
- GI upset

## Epidemiology of health effects

The impact of jet lag upon long-haul travellers is particularly high, with approximately 90–94% of travellers feeling some negative effects after flying. Some surveys have shown that 96% of experienced flight attendants continue to feel jet-lagged after long-haul flights.

## Risk factors

- Number of time zones crossed (≥5 time zones is of greater risk)
- Cabin pressure
- Being a person reliant on 'set routine'
- Pre-flight conditions (e.g. tiredness, stressed, nervous, drunk/hung-over)
- Excessive caffeine, alcohol, fruit juice
- Dehydration
- Poor fresh air supply/air quality
- Limited movement/stretching
- Flying at night time
- Older age

## Risk control

There are a number of preventive measures that travellers can take.

*Pre-flight*

- Ensure a good night's sleep before travel
- Be calm/not excitable
- Exercise the day before the flight

*Flight factors*

- Direction of flight (if possible)—may be a personal preference
- Daytime flights preferable to night time flights

*In-flight behaviour*

- Drink plenty of water or other non-alcoholic fluids
- *Using sleeping aids*:
  - pillows
  - neck-rests
  - blindfolds
  - earplugs
- Use of noise-cancelling headphones
- Remove footwear
- Exercise as much as possible
- Take walks at stop-overs if possible
- Shower if available (refreshing, and activates muscles and circulation)

## Management

Some research suggests that phototherapy and bright-light therapy can be useful in speeding up the circadian adaptation in those who are suffering ill effects. The efficacy of melatonin is uncertain.

# Section 2

# Occupational diseases

# Chapter 6

# Occupational infections

# Blood-borne viruses

An important group of occupational infections characterized by their blood-borne route of transmission.

The most common in the developed world are:

- Hepatitis B virus (HBV)
- Hepatitis C virus (HCV)
- Human immunodeficiency virus (HIV)

Others include:

- Hepatitis D virus (HDV)
- Viral haemorrhagic fevers (VHF), e.g. Ebola

## Sources of exposure/industries

Transmission can occur after exposure to infected biological material (see ➲ p. 816, Management of needlestick and contamination incidents and Chapter 3 Biological hazards).

## Epidemiology

Since 1997, when the surveillance system was introduced, 6,864 significant occupational exposures have been reported among health care workers (HCWs). Seventy per cent (4,830) were reported between 2004 and 2013 of which percutaneous needlestick injuries accounted for 71% and mucocutaneous exposures accounted for 29%. Among these were nine seroconversions (all were HCV).

## Factors affecting exposure and risk assessment

The risk of transmission is determined by:

- Details of incident including body fluid involved and exposure route
- Source patient infectivity

Risk assessment is described in detail in ➲ p. 856, Management of needlestick and contamination incidents.

### Biological material associated with transmission of blood-borne viruses (BBV)

- Blood
- Blood-stained fluid
- Pleural fluid
- Pericardial fluid
- Peritoneal fluid
- Cerebrospinal fluid
- Synovial fluid
- Amniotic fluid
- Breast milk
- Semen
- Vaginal secretions
- Unfixed tissues and organs

## Health effects

These are described separately for each virus: HBV, HCV, HIV, VHF (Hepatitis B; ➲ p. 170, Hepatitis C; ➲ p. 174, Human immunodeficiency virus; ➲ p. 176, Viral haemorrhagic virus).

### Occupations at risk from BBV

- *HCWs, in particular:**
  - surgeons
  - theatre nurses
  - dentists
  - midwives
  - anaesthetists
  - dialysis technicians
  - ambulance technicians
  - mortuary technicians
  - laboratory workers
  - chiropodists
  - acupuncture practitioners

*There is a lower, but significant, risk among:*
- embalmers
- crematorium workers
- cleaners
- police
- prison workers
- social workers
- military personnel
- sewage workers
- firefighters

* This list is not intended to be exhaustive.

## Risk controls

- Not all Control of Substances Hazardous to Health (COSHH) Regulations control measures will apply. Reducing exposure can only be achieved by changing ways of working and worker behaviour
- Adherence to standards of infection control precautions such as hand hygiene and use of personal protective equipment (PPE)
- Use gloves and double gloves where surgical procedures are performed on patients infected with BBV
- Use of aprons, goggles, and mask where there is a risk of splashing
- *Proper use of equipment*:
  - use of safer sharps devices
  - avoidance of re-sheathing needles
  - correct disposal of sharps
  - correct disposal of infected waste
  - correct transport of specimens
- Immunization against HBV
- Prompt management of sharps and contamination incidents in the workplace
- Supervision and training

## Relevant Regulations

- COSHH
- Management of Health and Safety at Work Regulations
- Provision and Use of Work Equipment Regulations
- Reporting of Incidents, Diseases and Dangerous Occurrences Regulations (RIDDOR)
- The Health Protection (Notification) Regulation 2010

## Specific guidance

- Biosafety—Resources. Available at: http://www.hse.gov.uk/biosafety/biologagents.pdf
- Guidance for Clinical Health Care Workers: Protection Against Infection with Blood-borne Viruses. Recommendations of the Expert Advisory Group on AIDS and The Advisory Group on Hepatitis. Available at: https://assets.publishing.service.gov.uk/government/uploads/system/uploads/attachment_data/file/382184/clinical_health_care_workers_infection_blood-borne_viruses.pdf
- Gloves should be worn for any procedures that involve a risk

## Further information

Eye of Needle Report National institute for Health Protection; 2020 https://www.gov.uk/government/publications/bloodborne-viruses-eye-of-the-needle

Infectious Diseases National institute for Health Protection. https://www.gov.uk/topic/health-protection/infectious-diseases

HSE. HSE Books, Sudbury. https://www.hse.gov.uk/biosafety/blood-borne-viruses/index.htm

HSE. HSE Books, Sudbury. https://www.hse.gov.uk/pUbns/priced/hsg283.pdf

HSE). HSE Books, Sudbury. https://www.hse.gov.uk/coshh/basics/index.htmNotifiable diseases and causative organisms: how to report

Notifiable diseases and causative organisms: how to report; PHE 2010

https://www.gov.uk/guidance/notifiable-diseases-and-causative-organisms-how-to-report

UK Health Security Agency 2021; https://assets.publishing.service.gov.uk/government/uploads/system/uploads/attachment_data/file/819197/Integrated_guidance_for_management_of_BBV_in_HCW.pdf

# Hepatitis B

## Epidemiology

- HBV is a DNA virus
- The World Health Organization (WHO) estimates that in 2016, 27 million people (10.5% of all people estimated to be living with hepatitis B) were aware of their infection, of which 4.5 million (16.7%) were on treatment. About 1% of persons living with HBV infection (2.7 million people) are also infected with HIV
- Endemic in many developing countries, where it affects up to 10% of the population; acquired mainly in childhood. The risk of vertical transmission is high up to 40%
- The epidemiology in westernized countries is quite different. In the UK, the prevalence rate is believed to be between 0.1% and 0.5%. Infection occurs mainly in young adulthood following sexual contact or intravenous drug misuse
- Occupational transmission to HCWs is well documented historically, but the incidence has reduced since the availability of vaccination A total of 590 occupational exposures were reported to the public health surveillance scheme 2004 to 2013, and no HBV seroconversion was reported

## Clinical features

- The HBV can survive outside the body for at least 7 days
- *Incubation period*: 40–160 days (30–180 days)
- *Acute illness*: malaise, fatigue, influenza-like symptoms, myalgia, nausea, vomiting, abdominal pain, and jaundice. About 30% of cases are asymptomatic
- Most patients clear the infection spontaneously
- 30–50% of children infected before the age of 6-years develop chronic infections. Less than 5% who are infected as adults will develop chronic infections and 20–30% of adults who are chronically infected will develop cirrhosis and/or liver cancer

## Causal exposures/industries

See ➲ p. 119.

## Clinical assessment and diagnosis

In the occupational setting, cases of HBV infection are usually diagnosed:

- When a HCW fails to respond to hepatitis B vaccine
- Following pre-placement assessment of fitness for exposure prone procedures (EPPs)
- Rarely, infection might be detected following an exposure incident

The main focus of investigation is to establish the degree of infectivity in order to assess the risk of transmission in the work setting. The occupational health (OH) professional should facilitate referral of active cases to a hepatologist for clinical management (if this has not already been done). Serological markers for HBV infection are shown in Table 6.1.

**Table 6.1** HBV serology

| Serological markers | Interpretation |
|---|---|
| Anti-HBc (core antibody) +ve *and* HbsAg (surface antigen) +ve | Current infection or infectious carrier |
| Anti-HBc +ve, HbsAg +ve, *and* HBeAg (e antigen) +ve | Current infection or infectious carrier with particularly high infectivity |
| Anti-HBc +ve *and* HBsAg –ve | Previous infection with natural immunity and non-infectious |

## Medical management and prognosis

- HBV is treatable with interferon-alpha, leading to reversal of the carrier state in 40% of cases
- Untreated, 20–25% of chronic cases infected as adults will develop chronic liver disease, of whom 15–25% will die

## Prevention/immunization

- *HBV is preventable by immunization:*[1]
  - recombinant vaccines provide protection in >90% of recipients
  - non-response to vaccine is associated with age >40 years and immune suppression
  - following immunization surface antibody levels (anti-Hbs) >100 IU/l are protective, but those at continuing risk of occupational exposure should have a single booster dose after 5 years. Poor responders (10–100 IU/l) require an immediate booster and a reinforcing dose at 5 years. Non-responders (<10 IU/l) should be tested for previous HBV infection, and if negative receive a second course
- Reduce exposure (see ➲ p. 166, Blood-borne viruses, risk controls)

## Fitness for work

- Modifications to work are required to prevent occupational transmission. EPPs may only be carried out by infectious carriers of HBV under specifically defined circumstances and with appropriate ongoing monitoring of viral load
- UK Advisory Panel for Occupational Health Registration (UKAPOHR) scheme registration is required for infected HCW performing EPP (see ➲ p. 166, Blood-borne viruses)

## Compensation

- Viral hepatitis (including HBV) is a prescribed disease (B8) for industrial injuries disablement benefit (IIDB) among those who have worked with human blood or blood products, or a source of viral hepatitis
- National Health Service (NHS) injury benefit (both temporary and permanent) would be payable to an NHS employee who lost remuneration because of HBV infection attributable to his or her NHS employment

1 Green Book Chapter 18, Hepatitis B; UK Health Security Agency 2020; https://assets.publishing.service.gov.uk/government/uploads/system/uploads/attachment_data/file/263311/Green_Book_Chapter_18_v2_0.pdf

## Relevant legislation

- Occupational acquired HBV infection (new case exposed to human blood or human blood products, or any source of HBV at work) is reportable to HSE under RIDDOR 2013
- Acute infectious hepatitis is notifiable under the Health Protection (Notification) Regulation 2010

## Further information

BBVs in healthcare workers: health clearance and management; UK Health Security Agency 2021; https://www.gov.uk/government/publications/bbvs-in-healthcare-workers-health-clearance-and-management

Occupational aspects of management of chronic fatigue; Faculty of Occupational Medicine & NHS Plus London 2020; http://www.nhshealthatwork.co.uk/images/library/files/Streamlining/Formatted_One-page_FINAL_Core_List_of_NHS_England_Imms_and_Vaccs_October_2019.pdf

Integrated guidance on health clearance; UK Health Security Agency 2021; https://assets.publishing.service.gov.uk/government/uploads/system/uploads/attachment_data/file/819197/Integrated_guidance_for_management_of_BBV_in_HCW.pdf

BBVs in healthcare workers: health clearance and management; UK Health Security Agency 2021; https://www.gov.uk/government/publications/bbvs-in-healthcare-workers-health-clearance-and-management

HSE. HSE Books, Sudbury. https://www.hse.gov.uk/biosafety/blood-borne-viruses/hepatitis-b.htm

https://www.who.int/news-room/fact-sheets/detail/hepatitis-b

SARS-CoV-2 variants of concern and variants under investigation in England; UK Health Security Agency 2021; https://assets.publishing.service.gov.uk/government/uploads/system/uploads/attachment_data/file/382184/clinical_health_care_workers_infection_blood-borne_viruses.pdf

# Hepatitis C

## Epidemiology

- Globally, an estimated 71 million people have chronic HCV infection. WHO estimates that in 2015 there were 1.75 million new HCV infections in the world
- Prevalence rate for chronic HCV in England is predicted to be around 0.5–1%
- Most common in men, 25- to 44-year age group
- In the UK, >90% of cases are caused by intravenous drug use and 5% by blood transfusion or exposure to blood products. In contrast with other BBVs, sexual transmission is rare (2% of cases)
- Fewer than 1% of cases are acquired occupationally
- A total of 23 HCV seroconversions in UK (19 HCW), with the last confirmed report in 2015 since Health Protection Agency (HPA) surveillance scheme started in 1996

## Clinical features

- Incubation period of 6–9 weeks
- Acute illness mild (malaise and jaundice)
- 80% asymptomatic
- Only 20–40% of cases clear the virus spontaneously after acute infection
- 80% go on to develop chronic infection

## Clinical assessment and diagnosis

- HCV antibodies (anti-HCV) are usually detectable 3 months after infection, but rarely may take up to 6 months to develop. The presence of anti-HCV indicates whether an individual has been infected, but does not distinguish between active and previous infection
- In the occupational setting, assessment of infectivity, on which advice about the likelihood of transmission to others is based, includes quantitative assessment of viral load (HCV RNA)
- New occupational cases should be referred to a hepatologist for clinical assessment (liver function tests (LFTs) ± liver biopsy) and treatment

## Prognosis

- Untreated, most chronic cases have a normal life expectancy
- 5–20% of chronic cases develop liver cirrhosis over 20 years, and a small proportion of these develop liver cancer
- Risk factors for more rapid progression to severe liver disease (once infected) include >40-year age group, male gender, alcohol consumption, co-infection with HIV or HBV, and immunosuppression
- Combination antiviral therapy is successful in clearing HCV in around 50% of cases (range 45–80% depending on genotype)

## Prevention

There is no vaccine or post-exposure prophylaxis (PEP) for HCV. The mainstay of prevention is avoiding exposure (see ➔ p. 166, Blood-borne viruses, risk controls).

## Medical management

- WHO recommends offering treatment (direct-acting antivirals (DAA)) to all individuals diagnosed with HCV infection who are 12-years of age or older, irrespective of disease stage
- National Institute for Health and Care Excellence (NICE) guidelines recommend sofosbuvir–velpatasvir–voxilaprevir to people who have had DAA (genotypes 1–6) and people with genotype 3 hepatitis C who have not had DAA before

## Fitness for work

Modifications to work are required to prevent occupational transmission. This is usually only required in the health care setting, where EPPs should not be carried out by infectious carriers of HCV (see ➔ Chapter 24, Fitness for exposure prone procedures).

## Compensation

- Viral hepatitis (including HCV) is a prescribed disease (B8) for IIDB in occupations exposed to human blood and body fluids
- HCWs who acquire HCV infection occupationally, and lose remuneration as a result, are eligible for temporary and permanent NHS injury benefit

## Relevant legislation and benefits

- Occupational acquired HCV infection (new case exposed to human blood or human blood products, or any other source of HCV at work) is reportable to HSE under RIDDOR 2013
- Acute infectious hepatitis (including HCV) is notifiable under the Health Protection (notification) Regulations 2010

## Further information

BBVs in healthcare workers: health clearance and management; UK Health Security Agency 2021: https://www.gov.uk/government/publications/bbvs-in-healthcare-workers-health-clearance-and-management

Hepatitis C Fact sheet World Health Organisation 2021; https://www.who.int/news-room/fact-sheets/detail/hepatitis-c

Hepatitis C Virus Health & Safety executive 2021; HSE https://www.hse.gov.uk/biosafety/blood-borne-viruses/hepatitis-c.htm

TA507 National Institute for Health & Care Excellence 2018; https://www.nice.org.uk/guidance/ta507/chapter/1-Recommendations

# Human immunodeficiency virus

## Epidemiology

- HIV is an RNA virus
- Worldwide, 37.9 million people were infected with HIV in 2018. In the UK 101,600 estimated adults had HIV in 2017 Overall, 87% of people living with HIV in the UK have an undetectable viral load and therefore not infectious
- >90% of HIV infection is sexually acquired; 2% is associated with injecting drug use
- Occupationally acquired HIV is rare (see Table 6.2). Five definite cases have been recorded historically in the UK. However, only one case of definite occupational transmission was documented in the UK due to a percutaneous exposure from a hollow bore needle in 1999 since the public health surveillance scheme started in 1996

## Clinical features

- *Seroconversion illness*: mild non-specific influenza-like symptoms and lymphadenopathy 2–4 weeks after infection
- Long asymptomatic phase (years) with gradually increasing immune suppression
- Acquired immune deficiency syndrome (AIDS) characterized by opportunistic infections

## Causal exposures/industries

*Health care work*

- Nurses and laboratory workers
- Surgeons
- Other doctors

## Clinical assessment and diagnosis

- Following acute infection, HIV antibodies become positive
- *The degree of immune suppression is assessed by measurement of CD4 count (normal range: 500–1500 × $10^6$ cells/mm$^3$)*:
  - bacterial infections, candida, and mycobacterial infections arise when CD4 < 500 (symptomatic phase)
  - AIDS is associated with CD4 < 200 × $10^6$ cells/mm$^3$, and infection with (e.g.) pneumocystis, toxoplasma, and cryptosporidia
- Infectivity is measured by HIV RNA viral load. Early in the illness, viral load can be several million copies/ml. This stabilizes during the chronic phase. HIV RNA is the best indicator of overall prognosis

## Medical management and prognosis

There is no cure for HIV infection. However, effective antiretroviral drugs (ARVs) can control the virus and help prevent onward transmission to other people. PEP use of ARVs (28-day course) drugs within 72 hours of exposure to prevent infection is recommended for both occupational and non-occupational exposures.

This is a rapidly changing field, with frequent introduction of new agents and combination regimens.

No available up-to-date world data for HIV
2004–2013—1,478 UK (excluding Scotland) exposures with no conversion
USA 1985–2013—58 confirmed conversions and 150 possible

## Fitness for work in HIV-infected employees

Modifications to work are sometimes appropriate:

- *To prevent occupational transmission to others*:
  - HIV-infected HCWs can undertake EPP if well controlled (viral load 200 copies/ml), but they need to be registered with the UKAPOHR
  - if a HCW's plasma viral load rises above 1,000 copies/ml, they should be restricted immediately from carrying out EPPs until their viral load returns to below 200 copies/ml
- *To accommodate impairment in function and to provide safe working environment*:
  - usually only necessary in the late symptomatic stages (AIDS)

  most HIV +ve employees in the clinical latent phase can work normally

### Adjustments to work in AIDS

- *If fatigue is a problem*: part-time or flexible work, or day physical work
- Restrict from activities where exposure to infection is a risk, e.g. care of patients who are sputum-positive for multidrug-resistant TB (MDR-TB)
- HIV-positive employees should not be given live vaccines (including bacillus Calmette–Guérin (BCG)) but can be immunized with recombinant or killed vaccines

## Compensation

- HIV is not a prescribed disease, but HIV acquired through discrete accidental exposure at work might be eligible as an industrial injury
- HCWs who acquire HIV infection occupationally, and lose remuneration as a result, are eligible for temporary and permanent NHS injury benefit

## Relevant legislation

- Any disease attributed to an occupational exposure to a biological agent is reportable under RIDDOR 2013
- It is automatically treated as a disability under the Equality Act 2010
- HIV is not a notifiable disease under the Health Protection (Notification) Regulations 2010

## Further information

Equity and excellence: Liberating the NHS; The Stationary Office 2010; https://assets.publishing.service.gov.uk/government/uploads/system/uploads/attachment_data/file/813168/HIV_annual_report_2018_-_Summary_key_messages_and_recommendations.pdf

UK Chief Medical Officers' Low Risk Drinking Guidelines; Department of Health 2016; https://assets.publishing.service.gov.uk/government/uploads/system/uploads/attachment_data/file/333018/Management_of_HIV_infected_Healthcare_Workers_guidance_January_2014.pdf

Health promotion for sexual and reproductive health and HIV Strategic action plan, 2016 to 2019 PHE https://assets.publishing.service.gov.uk/government/uploads/system/uploads/attachment_data/file/488090/SRHandHIVStrategicPlan_211215.pdf

*Notes from the Field:* Occupationally Acquired HIV Infection Among Health Care Workers — United States, 1985–2013; Centers for Disease Control & Prevention 2015. https://www.cdc.gov/mmwr/preview/mmwrhtml/mm6353a4.htm#:~:text=During%20that%20time%20frame%2C%2058,health%20care%20workers%20were%20reported

BBVs in healthcare workers: health clearance and management; UK Health Security Agency 2021 https://www.gov.uk/government/publications/bbvs-in-healthcare-workers-health-clearance-and-management

Bloodborne viruses: Eye of the needle; HSE 2020; https://www.gov.uk/government/publications/bloodborne-viruses-eye-of-the-needle

HIV/ AIDS Fact sheet World Health Organisation 2021; https://www.who.int/news-room/fact-sheets/detail/hiv-aids

## Fitness for work

- Modifications to work are required to prevent occupational transmission. EPPs may only be carried out by infectious carriers of HBV under specifically defined circumstances and with appropriate ongoing monitoring of viral load
- UKAPOHR scheme registration is required for infected HCW performing EPP (see ➔ p. 166, Blood-borne viruses)

## Compensation

- Viral hepatitis (including HBV) is a prescribed disease (B8) for IIDB among those who have worked with human blood or blood products, or a source of viral hepatitis
- NHS injury benefit (both temporary and permanent) would be payable to an NHS employee who lost remuneration because of HBV infection attributable to his or her NHS employment

## Relevant legislation

- Occupational acquired HIV infection (new case exposed to human blood or human blood products, or any other source of HIV at work) is reportable to HSE under RIDDOR 2013
- Acute infectious hepatitis is notifiable under the Health Protection (Notification) Regulation 2010

## Further information

SARS-CoV-2 variants of concern and variants under investigation in England Technical briefing 25; UK Health Security Agency 2021 https://assets.publishing.service.gov.uk/government/uploads/system/uploads/attachment_data/file/382184/clinical_health_care_workers_infection_blood-borne_viruses.pdf

https://www.gov.uk/government/publications/new-healthcare-workers-clearance-for-hepatitis-b-and-c-tb-hiv; Dept Health & Social Care 2007; https://www.gov.uk/government/publications/new-healthcare- workers-clearance-for-hepatitis-b-and-c-tb-hiv

Hepatitis B virus (HBV) Health & Safety Executive guidance 2020; https://www.hse.gov.uk/biosafety/blood-borne-viruses/hepatitis-b.htm

Hepatitis B Fact sheet WHO 2021; https://www.who.int/news-room/fact-sheets/detail/hepatitis-b

# Viral haemorrhagic fevers

These are a group of zoonotic infections caused by various families of viruses. They are all transmitted from primary wild animal hosts, none of which are natural residents in the UK. The diseases vary in severity and clinical picture. However, a number of VHFs are important in occupational medicine because of the following key features:

- High transmissibility from human to human
- High case fatality rate
- Difficulty in diagnosis in the early stages

**Table 6.2** Viral haemorrhagic fevers

| Disease | Virus family |
|---|---|
| • Lassa fever | • Arenavirus |
| • Marburg virus | • Filovirus |
| • Ebola virus | • Filovirus |
| • Crimean/Congo haemorrhagic fever | • Bunyavirus |

There are many more VHFs, but these are the most important with respect to occupational transmission.

## Epidemiology

- These diseases are endemic in parts of Africa, South America, and Asia with some present in parts of Europe. Primary cases in the UK are exceedingly rare, and can only arise from imported animals or laboratory sources
- Eight confirmed cases of Lassa fever have been imported (i.e. acquired abroad) to the UK since 1980, with no evidence of onward transmission from any of these cases. Four confirmed cases of Ebola were imported to the UK between 2014 and 2015. No cases of Marburg virus had been imported to the UK up to 2019
- There have been no cases of transmission to HCWs in the UK
- One case of Ebola virus and two cases of Marburg virus infection in the UK have resulted from laboratory accidents

## Clinical features

Some cases are mild or subclinical, while others can cause severe, life-threatening disease; some are high -consequence infectious diseases. The hallmarks of severe infection are:

- Fever
- Multisystem failure
- Bleeding in the terminal stages

## Causal exposures/industries

- Transmission in the UK is usually secondary (human to human rather than animal host to human). Infection occurs through exposure to blood and body fluids, and transmission to HCWs is well described in West Africa

- There is no evidence of transmission through the respiratory route
- VHFs have potential to be used in bioterrorism[1]

At-risk occupations include:

- Clinical HCWs caring for infected cases
- Laboratory workers handling viral material
- Mortuary staff handling infected bodies

## Clinical management and prognosis

Management is very specialized, and suspected cases must be notified and isolated in a high-security infectious diseases unit. Samples (with a full clinical and travel history) should be sent to Public Health England's (PHE's) Rare and Imported Pathogens Laboratory (RIPL). Treatment is with the antiviral agent ribavirin. The overall fatality of Lassa fever is 1%, although 15–20% of those who are hospitalized will die.

▶ There is no evidence to support the use of ribavirin as PEP.

## Prevention

- *Specialized guidance is available from the Advisory Committee on Dangerous Pathogens covering*:
  - risk assessment
  - isolation facilities
  - containment requirements
  - handling infected bodies
  - handling specimens
  - laboratory facilities
- There is no vaccine for VHFs

## Relevant legislation

- VHFs are notifiable (to Local Authority Proper Officers) under the Health Protection (Notification) Regulations 2010
- VHFs that are reliably attributable to occupation are reportable under RIDDOR
- An incident or accident that resulted in exposure to VHFs at work would be reportable as a dangerous occurrence under RIDDOR

## Further information and guidance

Public Health England (2018). *Viral Haemorrhagic Fevers: Origins, Reservoirs, Transmission and Guidelines*. Public Health England, London. Available at: https://www.gov.uk/guidance/viral-haemorrhagic-fevers-origins-reservoirs-transmission-and-guidelines

Public Health England (2020). *High Consequence Infectious Diseases (HCID)*. Public Health England, London. Available at: https://www.gov.uk/guidance/high-consequence-infectious-diseases-hcid

1 Public Health England (2013). *Deliberate and Accidental Releases: Investigation and Management*. Available at: https://www.gov.uk/government/collections/deliberate-and-accidental-releases-investigation-and-management

# Variant Creutzfeldt–Jakob disease

## Epidemiology

Creutzfeldt–Jakob disease (CJD) is one of a rare group of diseases, known as transmissible spongiform encephalopathies (TSEs), which affect the structure of the brain. TSEs cause dementia and a range of neurological symptoms including ataxia, myoclonus, chorea, or dystonia. TSEs are recognized in both animals and humans. In animals, the best-known TSE is bovine spongiform encephalopathy (BSE or 'mad cow disease'). In humans, there are four main types of CJD:

- Sporadic CJD
- Variant CJD
- Genetic CJD and other inherited prion diseases—autosomal dominant
- Iatrogenic CJD—through medical treatment, blood, or plasma products

Approximately 85% cases of CJD are sporadic with no known cause and 10–15% of cases are inherited. Variant CJD (vCJD) was first identified in 1996. It has affected younger patients (mean age 27 years vs 65 years) with a longer course (median of 14 vs 4.5 months). The epidemic of vCJD peaked in mid-2000 and caused 28 deaths in the UK. Total deaths from definite vCJD (confirmed) cases in the UK were 123 between 1995 and 2019. The number of cases in the UK is now declining and the last death reported in the UK was in 2016. It is strongly linked to exposure, probably through food, to a TSE of cattle called BSE. There is compelling scientific evidence that BSE and vCJD are caused by the same infectious agent, suggesting that BSE in cattle is the source of the human disease. All TSEs are caused by infectious proteins called prions.

## Clinical features

- *Initially psychiatric or behavioural symptoms*:
  - predominantly depression
  - less often, a schizophrenia-like psychosis
- Unusual sensory symptoms such as 'stickiness' of the skin
- Unsteadiness, difficulty walking, and involuntary movements
- Progressive dementia
- By the time of death usually 14 months later, patients become completely immobile and mute

## Causal exposures/industries

There is a *theoretical* risk of transmission through occupational exposure to infected tissues. Occupations at risk include:

- Abattoir workers
- Mortuary workers, neurosurgeons, and neuropathologists
- ▶▶ No occupationally acquired infections have been reported
- ▶▶ There are no reported cases of transmission to humans as a result of a surgical or dental procedure

## Clinical assessment and diagnosis

- The clinical presentation, progressive nature of the disease, and failure to find any other diagnosis are the hallmarks of vCJD
- Magnetic resonance imaging (MRI) brain scan may show a characteristic abnormality in the posterior thalamic region (pulvinar sign)
- Tonsillar biopsy and cerebrospinal fluid (CSF) tests may be helpful

- The brainwave pattern observed on electroencephalogram is usually abnormal, but waveforms characteristic of sporadic CJD do not occur
- Currently, the diagnosis of vCJD can only be confirmed following pathological examination of brain tissue, usually at post-mortem

## Treatment and prognosis

- vCJD is a progressive and ultimately fatal disease
- There is currently no proven treatment for the underlying process

## Risk control

Careful adherence to standard infection control procedures should prevent occupational exposure.

## Surveillance

The HPA, now part of PHE, and the National CJD Research and Surveillance Unit have set up a registry to find out more about the risk from exposures to CJD and other TSEs to health care and laboratory workers. In these occupational groups, percutaneous or mucocutaneous inoculation of tissues or blood from probable or confirmed cases of all types of human prion diseases including CJD or TSE infected animals or tissues must be reported to the registry. Details on how to report an exposure are available on the HPA website on the government archive (https://webarchive.nationalarchives.gov.uk/20140721221803/http://www.hpa.org.uk/Topics/InfectiousDiseases/InfectionsAZ/CreutzfeldtJakobDisease/RegistryForCJDAndTSEOccupationalExposures/)

The registry will provide long-term monitoring of the exposed workers. If you wish to report an occupational exposure to CJD/TSE please email: cjd@phe.gov.uk

## Further information and guidance

Department of Health and Social Care (2017). *Minimize Transmission Risk of CJD and vCJD in Healthcare Settings. Guidance from the ACDP TSE Risk Management Subgroup (formerly TSE Working Group)*. Available at: https://www.gov.uk/government/publications/guidance-from-the-acdp-tse-risk-management-subgroup-formerly-tse-working-group

HSE (2007). *BSE Occupational Guidance, Advisory Committee on Dangerous Pathogens*. Available at: http://www.hse.gov.uk/pubns/web22.pdf

Public Health England (2018). *Patients at Increased Risk of CJD: Background Information for Healthcare Staff*. PHE, London. Available at: https://assets.publishing.service.gov.uk/government/uploads/system/uploads/attachment_data/file/727300/Background_information_for_healthcare_staff.pdf

# Bovine spongiform encephalopathy

BSE is a transmissible prion disease of cattle.

## Epidemiology

A major problem with infection in UK cattle herds in the 1990s was associated with transmission to humans (as the human variant CJD) via the food chain. In theory, the disease can also be acquired occupationally, although occupational cases have not been described in the UK.

Statutory controls on animal feeding should have eliminated BSE in cattle born after 1 August 1996. Therefore, the incidence of the disease in cattle coming to slaughter should have decreased year-on-year to exceedingly low levels.

## Clinical features

See ➲ p. 182, Variant Creutzfeldt–Jakob disease.

## Causal exposures/industries

Transmission to humans could occur from exposure to the neural tissue of infected cattle through the percutaneous or mucocutaneous route (through breach of the skin or direct contact with non-intact skin or intact mucous membranes):

- Farmers
- Abattoir workers
- Meat processors

## Prevention

Prevention is through good hygiene practices in agriculture and meat processing (including abattoirs). This is covered in detail in ➲ p. 112, Animals and animal products (animals and animal products).

## Relevant legislation

- BSE in animals is notifiable to the Department for the Environment, Food, and Rural Affairs (DEFRA)
- Any infection reliably attributable to work would be notifiable to HSE under RIDDOR

## Further information and guidance

HSE (2007). *BSE Occupational Guidance, Advisory Committee on Dangerous Pathogens*. HSE Books, Sudbury. Available at: http://www.hse.gov.uk/pubns/web22.pdf

HSE. 2005; *Controlling the Risk of Exposure to Bovine Spongiform Encephalopathy (BSE)*. HSE Books, Sudbury. Available at: http://www.hse.gov.uk/biosafety/diseases/bovine.htm

# Meningococcal infection

These infections are a collection of systemic disorders caused by the bacterium *Neisseria meningitidis*. Humans are the only known reservoir for the organism.

Twelve types of *N. meningitides*, called serogroups, have been identified, six of which (A, B, C, W, X, and Y) can cause epidemics.

## Epidemiology

- Ten per cent of the population (and up to 25% of 15 to 19 year olds) carry *N. meningitidis* asymptomatically in the nasopharyx. It only causes disease in a small proportion. Rates of carriage are increased in closed populations such as military barracks and university halls of residence
- Most cases are sporadic, but <5% occur as clusters
- Strong seasonal variation; highest incidence in winter
- Most cases in the UK are caused by subtypes B and C
- Occupational cases are very rare

## Clinical features

- Early features are non-specific: fever, malaise, vomiting
- Characteristic petechial rash
- Progression from onset to death can be extremely rapid (few hours)
- Septicaemia (can be complicated by multiorgan failure)
- Meningitis

## Causal exposures/industries

- *Transmission is through very close contact*: inhaling respiratory secretions from the mouth or kissing
- *HCWs (documented case in ambulance technician)*: *only* if very close contact with aerosolized respiratory secretions
- *University students*: first-year college students who live in halls of residence have a higher risk of disease than non-college students of a similar age. OH professionals who provide services to universities may be asked to advise
- Occupational travellers to endemic countries (sub-Saharan Africa, Middle East)

## Clinical assessment

Confirmation of disease requires either:

- Isolation of the organism from a normally sterile body site (usually CSF or blood) or
- DNA detection by polymerase chain reaction (PCR) assay (from CSF, serum, plasma, ethylenediamine tetra-acetic acid-coagulated whole blood, or joint fluids)

## Treatment and prognosis

- Penicillin or third-generation cephalosporins intravenously (IV). In view of the risk of rapid progression, GPs are guided to treat with a bolus of IV benzylpenicillin (1.2 g intramuscular (IM)/IV) prior to admission if the diagnosis is suspected. Intensive support is needed for severe cases. 90% recover, 10% fatal

## Prevention

*Post-exposure Chemo prophylaxis*

- Ciprofloxacin 500 mg single oral dose (unlicensed indication) or rifampicin 600 mg bd for 2 days for:
  - HCWs who have taken part in resuscitation, endotracheal intubation, suctioning, or post-mortem without wearing appropriate respiratory protection
  - students who are prolonged close contacts of cases

*Vaccination*

- MenACWY conjugate vaccine is offered to new university entrants up to their 25th birthday, lab workers regularly exposed to meningitis, and occupational travellers, where indicated by advisory sources (see ➔ p. 451)
- Subgroup B vaccination (4C MenB, Bexsero®) has been part of the infant programme since September 2015. Meningitis B vaccine is now available

*Education*

OH departments may be involved in informing HCWs/students/occupational travellers to report suspicious symptoms early. Occupational travellers should be advised about disease transmission and activities that may put them at higher risk (i.e. they should be advised to practice good hand hygiene and to avoid activities that promote exchange of respiratory secretions, such as sharing drinks and eating utensils. Overcrowded and confined spaces should also be avoided where possible).

## Compensation

A HCW who contracted meningococcal infection at work, and lost pay as a result, would be eligible for NHS injury benefit.

## Relevant legislation

- Meningococcal septicaemia is notifiable (to Local Authority Proper Officers) under the Health Protection (Notification) Regulations 2010
- Meningococcal infection that is readily attributable to work is reportable to HSE under RIDDOR

## Further information and guidance

Guidance for public health management of meningococcal disease in the UK PHE 2019; 🔗 https://assets.publishing.service.gov.uk/government/uploads/system/uploads/attachment_data/file/829326/PHE_meningo_disease_guideline.pdf

Equity and excellence: Liberating the NHS 2010; The Stationary Office; 🔗 https://assets.publishing.service.gov.uk/government/uploads/system/uploads/attachment_data/file/582511/MenACWY_HEI_Guidelines.pdf

Managing risks in Internationalisation: Security related issues; Universities UK London 2021; 🔗 http://www.universitiesuk.ac.uk/Publications/Pages/Publication-218.aspx

Meningitis Fact sheet WHO 2021; 🔗 https://www.who.int/news-room/fact-sheets/detail/meningococcal-meningitis

HSE. HSE Books, Sudbury. 🔗 https://www.hse.gov.uk/pUbns/priced/hsg283.pdfHealthcare Personnel Vaccination Recommendations CDC Atlanta 2017; 🔗 https://www.immunize.org/catg.d/p2017.pdf

# Tuberculosis

## Epidemiology

Tuberculosis (TB) is an infection caused by a bacterium belonging to the *Mycobacterium* complex which includes *M. tuberculosis*, *M. africanum*, and *M. bovis*.

TB notifications declined in the UK until the mid-1980s. Subsequently, there have been small increases in annual incidence. The number of people with TB in England fell from a peak of 8,280 in 2011 to 4,655 in 2018 (a reduction of 44%). People born outside the UK accounted for 72% of notifications in 2018.

## Clinical features

TB can affect many body sites; therefore, the range of presenting symptoms may be wide and non-specific. TB may be asymptomatic (latent).

- Consider TB in anyone with intermittent fever and weight loss
- *Symptoms*:
  - chronic cough
  - night sweats
  - haemoptysis

## Causal exposures/industries

Transmission is by inhalation of droplets following close personal contact with a sputum-positive case. At-risk occupations include:

- HCWs having contact with patients or clinical specimens, especially if involved in aerosol-generating procedures (bronchoscopy, nebulization)
- Veterinary staff who handle animal species that are susceptible to TB
- Staff of prisons, old people's homes, and hostels for the homeless or refugees
- Low-risk professionals are aircraft crew, schoolteachers, and childcare workers

## Individual susceptibility

- Contacts, including people from the same household sharing kitchen facilities, boy- or girlfriend, and frequent visitors to the home of the index case. A contact at work may be close enough to be equivalent to a household contact; therefore, a risk assessment is imperative
- Those who have lived in, who travel to, or receive visitors from places where TB is 'common' (incidence >40 per 100,000 per year)
- Immunocompromised people such as HIV infection, children, and elderly, homeless, drug or alcohol dependency
- Hostel dwellers and those living in poor or crowded housing

## Clinical assessment and diagnosis

- *Diagnosis of latent TB*: tuberculin skin test (TST), i.e. Mantoux or interferon-gamma testing if available locally. Those with a positive TST or gamma-interferon test should be assessed for active infection and if not actively infected they should be considered for treatment of latent TB
- *Respiratory TB*: chest X-ray (CXR), multiple sputum samples, or bronchial washings for microscopy and culture
- *Non-respiratory TB*: biopsy for culture or needle aspiration for cytology, computed tomography(CT)/MRI/ultrasound/echocardiogram depending on suspected site. CXR to exclude coexisting respiratory TB

## Treatment and prognosis

Sputum +ve respiratory TB is usually rendered non-infectious after a 2-week treatment with quadruple therapy. However, individuals with MDR-TB may be intermittently sputum +ve for long periods. British HIV Association Guidelines should be consulted when caring for any patient who is or might be co-infected with HIV. All TB should be managed by a specialist, usually a respiratory physician.

## Management of occupational risk

*Occupational risk can be reduced by*:

- A risk assessment for staff working at an increased risk of TB infection
- Provision of educational material, TB awareness at induction, and follow-up health awareness training
- Screening new staff working in a high-risk occupation or with vulnerable people
- Provision of BCG vaccination for high-risk occupational
- Provide contacting tracing advice or programme—contact tracing for aircraft crew, schools, and childcare is provided in NICE guidelines

## Health care workers

New HCWs should be screened according to the NICE guidelines and clinical algorithm and should not work with patients or handle clinical specimens until screening is complete.

*Assessment for HCWs should include*:

- Symptoms and signs enquiry
- Documentary evidence of a BCG scar checked by an OH professional
- TST or interferon-gamma result within the last 5 years, if available

All staff should be reminded to report symptoms suggestive of TB promptly to their OH department. HIV positive staff are at increased risk of TB and may require modifications to their work. A tuberculin or interferon-gamma negative HCW who declines BCG vaccination should have the risks explained and supplemented by written advice,

- with a positive TST or gamma-interferon test should be assessed for active infection and if not actively infected they should be considered for treatment of latent TB
- *Respiratory TB*: CXR, multiple sputum samples, or bronchial washings for microscopy and culture
- *Non-respiratory TB*: biopsy for culture or needle aspiration for cytology, CT/MRI/ultrasound/echocardiogram depending on suspected site. CXR to exclude coexisting respiratory TB

### *Personal protective equipment*

HCWs caring for people with TB need not use PPE unless MDR-TB is suspected, or aerosol or cough-inducing procedures are being performed. For the latter, filtering respirator masks (FFP3) are required.

## Compensation

- Occupationally acquired TB is prescribed (B5) for IIDB
- HCWs who acquire TB infection occupationally, and lose remuneration as a result, are eligible for temporary and permanent NHS injury benefit

## Relevant legislation and guidance

- Occupationally acquired TB is RIDDOR reportable
- TB is notifiable under the Health Protection (Notification) Regulations 2010

## Further information

Tuberculosis NICE guideline 2016; https://www.nice.org.uk/guidance/ng33/resources/tuberculosis-pdf-1837390683589

The English Indices of Deprivation 2019; Ministries of Housing, Communities & Local Government; https://assets.publishing.service.gov.uk/government/uploads/system/uploads/attachment_data/file/411156/NKS_-_TB_and_Occupational_Health_-_280714_edited_by_CT_4_-_AR_-_010814.pdf

SARS-CoV-2 variants of concern and variants under investigation in England UK Health Security Agency 2021; https://assets.publishing.service.gov.uk/government/uploads/system/uploads/attachment_data/file/821335/Tuberculosis_in_England_executive_summary_2019.pdf

Tuberculosis Fact sheet WHO 2021; https://www.who.int/news-room/fact-sheets/detail/tuberculosis

Global Tuberculosis Report WHO 2019; https://apps.who.int/iris/bitstream/handle/10665/329368/9789241565714-eng.pdf?ua=1

NICE guideline. *Clinical Diagnosis and Management of Tuberculosis, and Measures for its Prevention and Control*. Available at: http://guidance.nice.org.uk/CG117/Guidance

# Legionnaires' disease

Legionnaires' disease is an uncommon bacterial infection caused by the bacterium *Legionella pneumophila*. The organism is found living naturally in environmental water sources. The term Legionnaires' disease refers to severe pneumonia and systemic infection caused by this organism which was first identified in 1977 and is recognized as a common cause of community-acquired pneumonia and a rare cause of hospital-acquired pneumonia.

## Epidemiology

Most cases are sporadic (single), but outbreaks can occur. The first recognized cases of the disease occurred in 1976 in Philadelphia among attendees of an American Legion convention held at the Bellevue-Stratford Hotel. Out of a total of more than 2,000 attendees 182 attendees contracted the disease and 29 of them died. There are approximately 300–400 reported cases in England annually, of which 30–50% are acquired abroad.

## Clinical features

- Incubation 2–19 days (median 6–7 days)
- Influenza-like illness with fatigue, myalgia, fever, headache, and dry cough
- Diarrhoea and confusion
- Atypical pneumonia

## Causal exposures/industries

Transmission is by inhalation of infected aerosols. It can also occur when contaminated water is aspirated. In workplaces, *L. pneumophila* is found in air-conditioning units, cooling towers, and showers. Any occupation working in air-conditioned buildings might be affected. Occupational travellers who stay in hotels can be exposed to infected droplets in showers. It typically does not spread directly between people and most people who are exposed do not become infected.

## Individual susceptibility

Mainly susceptible individuals are affected by the multisystem disease. Risk factors are:

- Age >50 years
- Men are three times more likely than women to be affected
- Smoking
- Underlying chronic disease
- Immunosuppressive treatment

## Clinical assessment

- The disease is not always clinically suspected because its symptoms are non-specific, and the routinely available diagnostic laboratory tests do not offer the desired sensitivity. Tests are:
- Rapid urine antigen test
- Culture of respiratory secretions
- Serology

## Treatment and prognosis

*Legionella* spp. multiply within the cell, so any effective treatment must have excellent intracellular penetration. Current treatments of choice are the respiratory tract quinolones (levofloxacin, moxifloxacin, gemifloxacin) or newer macrolides (azithromycin, clarithromycin, roxithromycin). The antibiotics used most frequently have been levofloxacin, doxycycline, and azithromycin. Most cases recover, but 10–15% are fatal (higher in susceptible groups).

## Prevention

There is no vaccine. Prevention is through treating water systems, and detailed specific guidance is available from HSE (see relevant legislation and guidance). Disease notification systems provide the basis for initiating investigations and limiting the scale and recurrence of outbreaks.

## Relevant legislation and guidance

Legionnaires' disease is notifiable (to local authority proper officers) under the Health Protection (Notification) Regulations (2010)

Legionellosis that is readily attributable to work is reportable to HSE under RIDDOR

HSE (2013). *Approved Code of Practice and Guidance. Legionnaires' Disease: The Control of Legionella Bacteria in Water Systems*. HSE Books, Sudbury. Available at: http://www.hse.gov.uk/pubns/priced/l8.pdf

## Further information and guidance

Public Health England (2019). *Legionnaires' Disease: Guidance, Data, and Analysis. The Symptoms, Diagnosis, Management, Surveillance and Epidemiology of Legionnaires' Disease*. Available at: https://www.gov.uk/government/collections/legionnaires-disease-guidance-data-and-analysis

# Tetanus

Tetanus is caused by a neurotoxin produced by *Clostridium tetani*, an anaerobic spore-forming bacillus. *C. tetani* is present in the gastrointestinal (GI) tract of horses and other animals. It is widespread in the environment, including soil, where it can survive for long periods. Transmission from human to human does not occur. The incubation period of the disease is usually between 3 and 21 days but it may range to several months.

## Epidemiology

Tetanus infection in humans is rare. Seven cases of clinical tetanus were identified in England between January and December 2018. Three tetanus-related deaths were recorded during this period. Most cases are non-occupational.

## Clinical features

- Localized muscle spasm
  - generalized tetany (trismus (lockjaw), tonic contractions, and spasms)
  - cephalic tetanus (after a head or neck injury, involving primarily the musculature supplied by the cranial nerves)

## Causal exposures/industries

Transmission is through non-intact skin following contamination with soil or other infected material. Spores can be introduced into the body, often through a puncture wound but also through trivial, unnoticed wounds, chronic ulcers, and drug injection. Outdoor workers who might sustain skin cuts or abrasions are at risk:

- Forestry workers
- Farm workers
- Veterinary practitioners
- Construction workers
- Microbiology laboratory workers must be protected by immunization

## Clinical assessment

Usually a clinical diagnosis, but the following confirmatory tests may help:

- Tetanus toxin in serum using a bioassay
- Isolation of *C. tetani* from the wound by PCR and culture
- Tetanus toxin antibodies in serum
- However, a negative laboratory test does not rule out a case

## Treatment and prognosis

- Intravenous (IV) human tetanus immune globulin (TIG)
- Wound debridement is clinically beneficial and wound samples provide diagnostic material for isolation of *C. tetani* or detection of toxin by PCR
- Antimicrobials, e.g. intravenous benzylpenicillin or metronidazole
- Supportive care
- 29% fatality rate

## Prevention

- Active immunization
- PEP by human TIG
- Management of tetanus-prone wounds—cover cuts and abrasions if working with soil or outdoors

## Relevant legislation

- Tetanus is notifiable (to Local Authority Proper Officers) under the Health Protection (Notification) Regulations 2010
- Tetanus that is readily attributable to work is reportable to HSE under RIDDOR

## Further information and guidance

Tetanus Guidance on the management of suspected tetanus cases and on the assessment and management of tetanusprone PHE 2019; wounds https://assets.publishing.service.gov.uk/government/uploads/system/uploads/attachment_data/file/820628/Tetanus_information_for_health_professionals_2019.pdf

Tetanus Fact sheet WHO 2018; https://www.who.int/news-room/fact-sheets/detail/tetanus

Public Health England. *Tetanus Supplementary Data Tables England 2018*. Public Health England, London.

# Coronaviruses (severe acute respiratory syndrome and COVID-19)

## COVID-19 (SARS-CoV-2)

The first human cases of COVID-19 (SARS-CoV-2) were first reported in Wuhan City, China, in December 2019. The full genetic sequence of SARS-CoV-2 shows that it has an ecological origin in bat populations. It was declared a pandemic and 'global health emergency' by the WHO in March 2020.

### Clinical features

The incubation period is approximately 2–14 days.

**Symptoms include:**
- Fever ≥38°C
- Cough, difficulty in breathing, and shortness of breath
- New loss of taste or smell
- *Non-specific symptoms*:
  - malaise
  - headache
  - myalgia
- Profuse watery diarrhoea

### Individual susceptibility

- Immunosuppressive treatment such as for cancer treatment or autoimmune disorders
- Chronic conditions, e.g. lung and heart conditions, diabetes
- Older age (over 70 years)
- Pregnant women
- Obesity
- Black and Asian ethnicity

Priority groups for coronavirus (COVID-19) vaccination: advice from the JCVI, 2 December 2020; Dept. Health & Social Care. https://www.gov.uk/government/publications/priority-groups-forcoronavirus-covid-19-vaccination-advice-from-the-jcvi-2-december2020

Covid-19 Medical Risk assessment, Association of Local authority Medical advisers Nov 2021; https://alama.org.uk/covid-19-medical-risk-assessment/

### Routes of transmission

- Droplets of infected body fluids through coughs or sneezing landing on mucocutaneous surfaces of a person is in close contact (within 2 months)
- Contact from contaminated surfaces or objects
- Airborne is still questionable

## Causal exposures/industries

At-risk occupations include:

- HCWs in clinical contact with COVID-19 patients especially if involved in aerosol-generating procedures (intubation, bronchoscopy, nebulization)
- Workers in laboratories where the virus is stored
- Caring for, living with, or direct contact with infected person, e.g. social care workers, prisons services, old people's homes, hostels for the homeless or refugees
- Occupational travellers to high-risk areas

## Clinical assessment and diagnosis

Direct virus detection tests (current infection) from swabs of the inside of the nose and throat: nucleic acid amplification tests, e.g. PCR.
Antibody tests (past infection) using a blood sample.
https://www.finddx.org/wp-content/uploads/2020/04/FIND_COVID-19_GUIDE-24.03.2020.pdf

COVID-19: guidance for sampling and for diagnostic laboratories; Public Health England 2021; https://www.gov.uk/government/publications/testing-for-wuhan-novel-cov-2019-ncov

## Health surveillance

- Maintain a list of all staff who have had contact with COVID-19
- All staff should be vigilant for symptoms of SARS in the 14 days following exposure and must self-isolate
- Inform public health (emergency line) of any contacts and their details to ensure contact tracing

## Risk controls in the health care industry

- Infection control measures to include hygiene measures and suitable PPE
- Aerosol-generating procedures (nebulizers, bronchoscopy) constitute a particular risk; use of PPE include FFP3 masks
- https://assets.publishing.service.gov.uk/government/uploads/system/uploads/attachment_data/file/879221/Coronavirus__COVID-19__-_personal_protective_equipment__PPE__plan.pdf
- Isolation and social distancing
- Barrier nursing; the patient should be admitted to a designated isolation unit. Visitors should be kept to a minimum

## Immunization

For UK population the following vaccines are approved. Health care and social care workers are prioritized.

- *Pfizer BioNTech COVID-19 mRNA Vaccine BNT162b2*: The dose of Pfizer BioNTech COVID-19 vaccine is 30 μg contained in 0.3 ml of the diluted vaccine. After dilution each multidose vial contains five doses of 0.3 ml. The vaccine should be administered in two doses, a minimum of 21 days apart.

- *AstraZeneca COVID-19 vaccine*: The dose of AstraZeneca COVID-19 vaccine is 0.5 ml. The vaccine should be administered in two doses, a minimum of 28 days apart:
  - https://www.gov.uk/government/publications/covid-19-the-green-book-chapter-14a
  - https://www.england.nhs.uk/coronavirus/wp-content/uploads/sites/52/2020/12/C0956-Patient-Group-Direction-for-COVID-19-mRNA-vaccine-BNT162b2-Pfizer-BioNTech-11-December-2020.pdf

## Compensation

HCWs who acquire COVID-19 infection occupationally, and lose remuneration as a result, are eligible for Temporary and Permanent NHS Injury Benefit

## Relevant legislation and guidance

COVID-19 is notifiable (to Local Authority Proper Officers) under the Health Protection (Notification) Regulations 2010

COVID-19 is RIDDOR reportable as a dangerous occurrence, disease, or fatality

## Further information

Covid-19 updates; Centers for Disease Control & Prevention CDC 2021; https://www.cdc.gov/coronavirus/2019-ncov/index.html

Who is at high risk from coronavirus (COVID-19); National Health Service 2021; https://www.nhs.uk/conditions/coronavirus-covid-19/people-at-higher-risk/whos-at-higher-risk-from-coronavirus/

Coronaviris disease 2019 Situation report-98 World Health Organisation 2021 https://www.who.int/docs/default-source/coronaviruse/situation-reports/20200423-sitrep-94-covid-19.pdf?sfvrsn=b8304bf0

Middle East respiratory syndrome coronavirus (MERS-CoV); World Health Organisation 2019; https://www.who.int/news-room/fact-sheets/detail/middle-east-respiratory-syndrome-coronavirus-(mers-cov)

# Influenza

Influenza is a virus that is found in animals and humans. There are two main types of influenza viruses that cause illness in humans: type A and type B. Majority of outbreaks are caused by influenza A.

An important characteristic of the organism is the propensity to undergo minor or major changes in antigenic profile (antigenic drift or shift, respectively).

## Epidemiology

*Seasonal influenza*

Seasonal influenza infection shows strong seasonal variation with highest incidence in the winter (December–March in the northern hemisphere). A very small proportion of cases of seasonal influenza are acquired occupationally.

*Epidemic influenza*

Normal seasonal activity crosses threshold into severe 'epidemic' activity unpredictably.

*Pandemic influenza*

Pandemics, with high rates of transmission worldwide, have occurred when new strains emerge which have high transmissibility against a background of absent herd resistance. Previous pandemics in 1918–1919, 1957, and 1968 resulted in high global mortality (40–50 million in 1918–1919). Recent pandemic involved zoonotic flu such as avian influenza (H5N1 strain) and swine flu (H1N1) that emerged in Mexico in 2009. Severe illness and death did occur in a small proportion of cases, particularly among susceptible groups, e.g. pregnant women.

## Clinical features

- Fever >38°C
- Headache, myalgia, severe malaise
- Complications include pneumonia

## Causal exposures/industries

Most occupations do not have a greater risk than the general population. The following groups are at increased risk:

- HCWs who:
  - look after infected patients
  - handle influenza organisms in the laboratory
- Teachers and care workers in institutions
- Animal handlers

## Individual susceptibility

The working age population is at increased risk if they have chronic disease or immune suppressed (e.g. diabetes mellitus, renal failure, cancer, chronic respiratory illness, HIV, or using immunosuppressing medication).

## Clinical assessment

- Serology
- Near patient test can be useful for instant diagnosis

## Treatment and prognosis

Treatment is with anti-viral agents (oseltamivir, zanamivir, or amantadine). Prognosis varies according to the strain and the level of herd immunity.

## Prevention

*Influenza immunization*

- The Chief Medical Officer has recommended annual immunization against seasonal influenza for fit HCWs (i.e. in the absence of specific medical indications). As well as protecting HCWs from occupational transmission, there is reasonable evidence that immunization reduces mortality in their elderly patients
- Many OH providers offer influenza immunization to staff outside the health care sector, even in the absence of increased occupational risk. This is usually justified on the basis that it might reduce sickness absence, although the evidence base for this assumption is incomplete.

*Preventing exposure*

In the health care industry, exposure to staff is minimized by:

- Observing infection control procedures
- Use of PPE

## Pandemic planning

OH professionals who provide services to health care or emergency services (fire, police, and ambulance) have a major role in advising about pandemic preparedness.

## Relevant legislation

If occupationally acquired at work, it is RIDDOR reportable

Influenza is not a notifiable disease to PHE under the Health Protection (Notification) Regulations 2010 BUT microbiology laboratories are required to report all serologically confirmed cases

## Further information

- https://assets.publishing.service.gov.uk/government/uploads/system/uploads/attachment_data/file/831861/Schools_guidance_ILI_Outbreaks_Sep19.pdf
- https://www.hse.gov.uk/biosafety/diseases/pandflu.htm
- http://www.euro.who.int/en/health-topics/communicable-diseases/influenza/news/news/2020/01/increase-in-bird-flu-outbreaks-whoeurope-advice-for-handling-dead-or-sick-birds
- https://www.ncbi.nlm.nih.gov/pmc/articles/PMC5006982/

# Anthrax

Anthrax is a rare zoonosis caused by *Bacillus anthracis*, a spore-forming Gram +ve bacterium that can survive in soil for long periods.

## Epidemiology

Anthrax occurs mainly in herbivores and is transmitted to humans from infected animal products, but not human-to-human spread. Thirty confirmed cases were notified in England and Wales 1981–2013 (most were occupational). None was notified between 2014 and 2019.

## Clinical features

There are three clinical forms of anthrax depending on the route of exposure. In 95% of naturally acquired human cases, the infection is cutaneous. Occupationally acquired anthrax is usually cutaneous. Inhalational anthrax in non-endemic areas raises the possibility of bioterrorism. Since 2009, large outbreaks of injectional anthrax have occurred in drug users from infected heroin.

- *Cutaneous anthrax*: skin lesion appears days or weeks after exposure, usually on the head, neck, arms, or hands. The lesion is surrounded by oedema and develops into a characteristic painless ulcer with a black centre (eschar). Cutaneous anthrax can be complicated by septicaemia
- *Gastrointestinal anthrax*: acquired by consuming undercooked infected meat

*Inhalational anthrax*: much rarer than cutaneous anthrax but has a higher mortality. Characterized by Influenza-like Illness; onset up to 48 hours after exposure

## Causal exposures/industries

- Laboratory staff handling anthrax spores or infected material
- Workers handling infected hides, e.g. leather tanners
- Workers handling infected animals, e.g. abattoir workers, veterinary practitioners
- Postal workers (deliberate release) (see ➲ p. 872, Biological weapons)

## Clinical assessment and diagnosis

*Suspected cases should be investigated in liaison with the Rare and imported pathogens laboratory*

RIPL[1] which offers diagnostic services for rare pathogenic organisms. Investigation includes:

- Detailed exposure history
- Serology
- Blood cultures
- Swab of lesion fluid for stain and culture
- *Biopsy lesion*: PCR for *B. anthracis* DNA
- For inhalational anthrax, CXR, CT scan of thorax, and LFTs

## Prognosis

Without treatment, the risk of death from skin anthrax is 24%. For intestinal infection, the risk of death is 25 to 75%, while respiratory anthrax has a mortality of 50 to 80%, even with treatment.

1 Rare and imported pathogens laboratory (RIPL); PHE 2016; https://www.gov.uk/government/collections/rare-and-imported-pathogens-laboratory-ripl

## Prevention

Inactivated acellular vaccine is available from PHE. It is given in a series of five doses over 18 months. Vaccination only offered to occupational groups at high risk of exposure. Vaccine is not indicated in the public unless exposed.

## Medical management

Consult PHE's most recently updated guidelines for treatment and immediately contact the local hospital infection control team. Cutaneous anthrax is treatable with oral antibiotics; ciprofloxacin is the drug of choice. Management of inhalational anthrax is very specialized, involving IV ciprofloxacin plus two other antibiotics.

## Post-exposure prophylaxis

Following exposure, antibiotic treatment ± vaccination is indicated.

- *Antibiotics for 60 days*:
  - initial 3 days: oral ciprofloxacin 500 mg bd
  - remaining 57 days: oral ciprofloxacin 500 mg bd OR oral doxycycline 100 mg bd
- *Immunization*:
  - three doses at 0, 3, and 6 weeks after exposure
  - given with vaccine, duration of antibiotics can be ↓ to 4 weeks
  - further doses at 6 months and 1 year, if continuing exposure
  - PEP not required for contacts unless exposed to original source

## Compensation

- In the UK anthrax is a prescribed disease (B1) for IIDB in workers who have contact with anthrax spores, including contact with infected animals, or those involved in handling, loading, unloading, or transport of a type susceptible to infection with anthrax or of the products or residues of such animals
- HCWs are eligible for NHS Injury Benefit if they contract anthrax at work and lose pay as a result

## Relevant legislation

- Anthrax is notifiable (to Local Authority Proper Officers) under the Health Protection (Notification) Regulations 2010
- Anthrax that is readily attributable to exposure to *B. anthracis* at work is notifiable to HSE under RIDDOR
- An exposure in the workplace would be notifiable to HSE under RIDDOR as a dangerous occurrence

## Further information and guidance

Center for Disease Control & Prevention (2020). Emergency Preparedness and Response. Available at: https:// www.cdc.gov/ anthrax/ bioterrorism/ preparedness.html

Public Health England (2013). *Deliberate and Accidental Releases*. Available at: https://www.gov.uk/government/collections/deliberate-and-accidental-releases-investigation-and-management

Public Health England (2017). *Anthrax: The Green Book, Chapter 13*. PHE, London. Available at: https://www.gov.uk/government/publications/anthrax-the-green-book-chapter-13

Summary table Chap. 3. ➔ *Biological Hazards*.

# Glanders

Glanders is a zoonotic infection caused by the bacterium *Burkholderia mallei*. It is essentially a disease of equine species including horses, donkeys, and mules. It is rarely found in dogs, cats, and goats.

## Epidemiology

Glanders has been eradicated from the UK and most of Europe, North America, and Australia through surveillance and destruction of affected animals and import restrictions. However, it remains endemic in Africa, Asia, the Middle East, and Central and South America.

## Clinical features

The incubation period is 10–14 days, but long latency (up to 30 years) has been described. Presentation depends on the route of infection, which can be through non-intact skin or mucous membranes, inhalation, and potentially ingestion. Once infected, it can affect any organ system and result in non-specific symptoms and can be either acute or chronic, impeding rapid diagnosis.

- *Acute infection*:
  - skin infection, with ulceration and local lymphadenopathy
  - mucosal upper respiratory tract infection, with bloody nasal discharge
  - pneumonia, with pleural effusion and lung abscess
  - septicaemia
- *Chronic infection*: with abscess formation in skin, muscle, liver, and spleen

## Causal exposures/industries

Glanders does not occur in the environment. It can only be acquired through prolonged contact with infected animals whereby only a small number of organisms are required to establish infection, although the infectivity of secretions is extremely low. Realistically, the only occupational cases in the West are likely to be laboratory workers:

- Laboratory workers handling *B. mallei*
- Veterinary practitioners
- Horse handlers, grooms, and breeders

## Treatment and prognosis

Glanders can be treated with antibiotics. Historically, treatment was with sulphonamides, but newer antibiotics including co-trimoxazole may be effective (the disease disappeared before these could be evaluated). Untreated, it is rapidly fatal in >90% of cases (particularly if acquired through the inhalational route).

## Prevention

There is currently no vaccine for glanders. The lack of a vaccine for the bacterium with its high rate of infectivity by aerosols as well as its high mortality rate in humans makes the disease a potential candidate for bioterrorism (see ➔ p. 872, Biological weapons), although no incidents have occurred to date.

## Compensation

Glanders is a prescribed disease for IIDB in workers who have contact with equine animals or their carcasses.

## Relevant legislation

- Glanders is a notifiable disease in the UK, although it has not been reported here since 1928
- Glanders that is readily attributable to work would be reportable to HSE under RIDDOR

## Further information and guidance

DEFRA and Animal and Plant Health Agency (2018). *Glanders and Farcy: How to Spot and Report the Diseases*. Update 2021; Available at: https://www.gov.uk/guidance/glanders-and-farcy

# Leptospirosis

Leptospirosis is a zoonotic disease caused by a spirochaete bacterium of the genus *Leptospira*. There are many different pathogenic varieties that use different animal hosts. Common carriers in the UK are rats (*Leptospira ictohaemhorrhagica*), cattle (*Leptospira hardjo*), and pigs. Person to person transfer is rare, if it occurs at all.

## Epidemiology

Leptospirosis is uncommon. Between 71 and 87 cases per year have been notified in the UK over the past 5 years. Most of these are acquired during leisure activities or overseas. Between 2014 and 2019, a total of 395 cases were notified in the UK, including 54 of occupational origin.

The most frequent occupational exposures are working in rivers, floodwater, or other surface water; followed by agricultural workers. The most frequent animal exposure is to dogs. History of travel outside UK is important.

## Clinical features

- Incubation most commonly 7–14 days (range 2–30 days)
- Biphasic clinical illness

*Acute bacteraemic phase*

Bacteria are disseminated to every organ system. Characterized by influenza-like symptoms, headache, chills, and myalgia. Most cases are mild and resolve without treatment, but rarely severe illness occurs (Weil's disease) characterized by jaundice, renal impairment, and bleeding. If it also causes bleeding into the lungs, then it is known as severe pulmonary haemorrhage syndrome.

*Immune phase*

It is usually severe and can be complicated by multiorgan failure or meningitis.

## Causal exposures/industries

Transmission is by direct or indirect contact with infected animal urine or by water or soil contaminated with animal urine. This usually occurs through intact mucous membranes of the eyes, mouth or nose, or non-intact skin:

- Farm and fish workers
- Sewerage workers
- Dog handlers
- Abattoir workers
- Veterinary practitioners
- Mine workers
- Military personnel

## Clinical assessment and diagnosis

Diagnosis is typically by looking for antibodies against the bacterium or finding its DNA in the blood. Serological tests are available through the National Leptospira Service.[1]

## Treatment and prognosis

Oral penicillin or doxycycline, IV antibiotics, and intensive support are required for severe cases. Prognosis is good if the diagnosis is made early and appropriate treatment started. Emergency and Intensive Care Units in rural areas should be aware of the possibility of leptospirosis in febrile icteric illnesses. Weil's disease and severe pulmonary haemorrhage syndrome result in death rates greater than 10% and 50%, respectively, even with treatment.

## Prevention

- There is no vaccine for humans
- Prophylactic doxycycline (200 mg weekly) can be given for high-risk occupational tasks
- Reduce rodent populations by avoiding rubbish accumulation and culling
- Infected farm animals can be immunized and treated
- PPE (especially waterproof gloves and footwear) for jobs that entail splashing or immersion in rivers, puddles, or sewage
- Advise workers of risk and symptoms; information cards are often used for this purpose
- Cover cuts and abrasions with waterproof dressings. Wash new cuts thoroughly if acquired near potentially contaminated water
- Employees at risk can be issued with HSE pocket card

## Compensation

Leptospirosis is prescribed (B3) for IIDB for those who work in places which might be infested by rats, field mice, voles, or other small mammals, in dog kennels or the care or handling of dogs, or in contact with bovine animals or their meat products, or pigs or their meat products.

## Relevant legislation

- Since 2010, leptospirosis is no longer notifiable under public health legislation
- Leptospirosis that is reliably attributable to work is reportable to HSE under RIDDOR

## Further information and guidance

Leptospirosis Fact sheet Centres for Disease Control & Prevention 2018; https://www.cdc.gov/leptospirosis/exposure/index.html

Leptospirosis update 2020 World Health Organisation, Geneva; https://www.who.int/zoonoses/diseases/Leptospirosissurveillance.pdf

Zoonoses Report PHE London 2018; https://assets.publishing.service.gov.uk/government/uploads/system/uploads/attachment_data/file/765111/UK_Zoonoses_report_2017.pdf

Infections at work leaflets; Health & safety Executive London 2019 https://www.hse.gov.uk/pubns/infection.pdfPublic Health England (2018). *Leptospirosis: The Characteristics, Diagnosis and Epidemiology of Infections Caused by Spirochaetes of the Genus Leptospira (Leptospires)*. Available at: https://www.gov.uk/guidance/leptospirosis

Guidance on National leptospirosis service; PHE 2018; https://www.gov.uk/guidance/leptospira-reference-unit-services

# *Streptococcus suis*

*Streptococcus suis* is a zoonotic infection, of which 35 subtypes have been identified. The organism is an important pathogen in pigs but can occur in cattle and other animals.

## Epidemiology

*Streptococcus suis* is endemic in most pig-rearing countries of the world including the UK. The organism is carried in the tonsils of pigs, and pig-to-pig spread is mainly by nose-to-nose contact or by aerosol over short distances. Transmission to humans is rare, but it is probably under-diagnosed or rarely reported. Only a few hundred human cases have been reported worldwide, and the annual incidence in England and Wales is around two cases. Annual UK confirmed cases in humans from 2008 to 2017 ranged from one to seven.

## Clinical features

Incubation period is a few hours to several days. Symptoms usually starts as flu-like initially, but they often progress to severe febrile illness, with systemic disease:

- Meningitis
- Septicaemia
- Endocarditis
- Deafness

The disease may progress to toxic shock syndrome, which often leads to multiple organ failure and subsequently death.

## Causal exposures/industries

Transmission is through non-intact skin from infected pig products, although overall the risk of infection is low. It is also possible that the bacteria may spread in the air and be inhaled, but very close contact with pigs or pig products is needed. However, there have been no reported cases of transmission through inhalation. Person to person spread is not known in this disease. Occupations at risk are:

- Abattoir workers
- Butchers
- Meat processing plant workers
- Farmers
- Veterinary practitioners

## Individual susceptibility

Immunosuppressed (particularly asplenic) individuals are at increased risk.

## Medical management

Anyone with flu-like symptoms who may have been in contact with infected pigs or their products should seek immediate medical attention. Penicillin is the treatment of choice and is effective if given early.

## Prevention

- There is no human vaccine
- The mainstay of prevention is to follow good occupational hygiene practice in slaughterhouses and butchers. Thorough washing of hands and arms before and after touching pig products is essential
- Exposed workers must be educated about good occupational hygiene practice and should report suspicious symptoms (febrile illness) immediately, declaring their exposure to the treating doctor. Any employee who knows they are immunosuppressed and who works with pigs should inform their manager
- Skin cuts and abrasions should be covered with waterproof plasters.
- A suitable disinfectant should be used

## Compensation

*Streptococcus suis* is a prescribed disease (B9) for IIDB among those who are in contact with pigs infected by *S. suis* or with infected carcasses, pig products, or residues.

## Relevant legislation

- *S. suis* is *not* reportable under public health legislation
- *S. suis* that is readily attributable to work is reportable to HSE under RIDDOR

## Further information and guidance

HSE. *Zoonoses: Guidance on Protecting Farmers and Farm Workers From Zoonoses*. July 2021; Available at: https://www.hse.gov.uk/agriculture/zoonoses-data-sheets/streptococcus-suis.pdf

Zoonoses Report UK PHE London 2018; https://assets.publishing.service.gov.uk/government/uploads/system/uploads/attachment_data/file/765111/UK_Zoonoses_report_2017.pdf

Leaflets; Infections at Work HSE London 2021; https://www.hse.gov.uk/pubns/infection.pdf

Dutkiewicz J, Sroka J, Zając V, Wasiński B, Cisak E, Sawczyn A, Kloc A, Wójcik-Fatla A (2017).*Streptococcus suis*: A re-emerging pathogen associated with occupational exposure to pigs or pork products. Part I—Epidemiology. *Annals of Agricultural and Environmental Medicine* 24(4): 683–695.

# Brucellosis

Brucellosis (also known as undulant or Mediterranean fever) is a highly transmissible bacterial infection, acquired from infected cattle, sheep, goats, and their products.

A group of zoonoses caused by the bacterial species *Brucella*:

- *Brucella melitensis*: sheep and goats (not found in the UK)
- *Brucella abortus*: cattle and camels
- *Brucella suis*: pigs
- *Brucella ovis*: sheep, goats
- *Brucella ceti and Brucella pinipedalis*: marine mammals

The main source of non-occupational brucellosis is unpasteurized milk products.

## Epidemiology

Brucellosis is a rare disease in the UK as it is a non-endemic country. Sixty-six cases were reported in England and Wales between 2014 and 2019. About ten cases per year are seen in the UK and are almost always acquired abroad mainly in a Mediterranean or Middle Eastern country (the disease is still endemic in Africa, the Middle East, Asia, and South America). There is likely to be under-reporting of laboratory-acquired occupational infection.

## Clinical features

- 2–8 weeks incubation
- *Non-specific ILI*:
  - fever and malaise
  - arthralgia
  - can affect any organ system

## Causal exposures/industries

The main source of non-occupational brucellosis is eating or drinking unpasteurized milk products contaminated with brucellosis. Occupational transmission is through direct contact with infected animals leading to bacteria entering through non-intact skin or mucous membranes, inhalation, or ingestion. Direct skin exposure occurs in occupations that handle raw meat and unpasteurized dairy products. Respiratory exposure is through washing down farm or slaughterhouse buildings or in laboratories through inhalation of *Brucella* organisms.

- Farm workers
- Abattoir workers
- Meat packers (raw products)
- Veterinary practitioners
- Animal laboratory workers
- Laboratory workers handling *Brucella* species or infected material

The risk of getting brucellosis from an infected animal is low for most types of contact. Direct contact during animal birth including contact with body fluids and products of conception is associated with a higher risk. However, *Brucella* is a potential candidate for bioterrorism in view of its high infectivity on inhalation (see ➲ p. 867).

## Clinical assessment

Diagnosis is by serology and culture of blood and body fluids in liaison with the Brucella Reference Unit[1] which provides a brucella serodiagnosis service and tests are performed weekly.

## Treatment and prognosis

- Treatment is with antibiotics, usually combination of tetracycline-streptomycin or tetracycline-rifampicin
- Brucellosis is rarely fatal, but it can cause prolonged debilitating illness

## Prevention

- There is no human vaccine
- Prevention is through good occupational hygiene practice in slaughterhouses and farms, including handwashing and wearing respiratory protection for aerosol-generating procedures

## Compensation

Brucellosis is a prescribed disease (B7) for IIDB in those who handle animals infected by *Brucella*, or their carcasses or their untreated products, or laboratory specimens containing *Brucella*.

## Relevant legislation

- Brucellosis is notifiable (to Local Authority Proper Officers) under the Health Protection (Notification) Regulations 2010
- Brucellosis that is readily attributable to work is reportable to HSE under RIDDOR

## Further information and guidance

Zoonosis- Agriculture HSE 2019; https://www.hse.gov.uk/agriculture/zoonoses-data-sheets/brucellosis.pdf

HSE (2021). The approved list of biological agents-4TH EDITION. Available at https://www.hse.gov.uk/pubns/misc208.pdf

HSE. *Zoonoses: Guidance on Protecting Farmers and Farm Workers From Zoonoses*. HSE Books, Sudbury. Available at: https://www.hse.gov.uk/agriculture/topics/zoonoses.htm

Public Health England (2017). *Brucella Reference Unit (BRU): Managing Laboratory Exposure. Guidance*. PHE, London. Available at: https://www.gov.uk/government/publications/brucella-reference-unit-bru-managing-laboratory-exposure

Public Health England (2017). *Brucellosis: Veterinary Exposure. Guidance*. PHE, London. Available at: https://www.gov.uk/government/publications/brucellosis-veterinary-exposure

Public Health England (2019). *Brucella: Laboratory and Clinical Services. Guidance*. PHE, London. Available at: https://www.gov.uk/guidance/bru-reference-services

1 Public Health England (2019). Update 2020 *Brucella Reference Unit (BRU) Liverpool*. Open Government Licence Available at: https://www.gov.uk/government/collections/brucella-reference-unit-bru

# Lyme disease

Lyme disease is a bacterial infection of birds and mammals caused by the spirochaete *Borrelia burgdorferi*. It is spread to humans from the animal reservoir (commonly deer) by a tick vector (*Ixodes* species).

## Epidemiology

In the UK in 2015, 2016, and 2017, confirmed cases were 1,262, 1,308 and 1,750, respectively. Factors contributing to the rise in case numbers include increased awareness, access to diagnostics, more sensitive diagnostic methods, and complete reporting of cases.

Majority of UK cases are acquired through countryside recreational activities.

Most cases are non-occupational. Infections tend to be seasonal, with over half of all cases occurring between July and September coinciding with tick activity and with its peak feeding period of late spring and early summer.

## Clinical features

Erythema migrans, a spreading rash, is the most common manifestation and often the only symptom. However, untreated cases can develop the following complications:

- Transverse myelitis
- Cranial nerve palsies
- Meningitis
- Arthritis
- Encephalitis (rare)
- Post-viral syndrome

## Causal exposures/industries

- Forestry workers
- Gamekeepers
- Farmers

## Clinical assessment

- Do not discount the possibility of Lyme disease in the absence of a history of tick bite as many sufferers cannot recollect a tick bite
- Diagnosis is by serology, but antibodies are often not detectable within the first few weeks of appearance of the rash

## Treatment and prognosis

Treatment is with antibiotics (doxycycline or amoxycillin). The rash responds promptly but established neurological symptoms can be slow to improve.

## Prevention

- There is no vaccine
- *The mainstay of prevention is tick avoidance*:
  - cover skin if working in infested areas
  - use insect repellents
  - daily skin checks (particularly skin folds, axillae, and groins) and removal of ticks. The risk of transmission is low in the first 24 hours, and so risk is greatly reduced by vigilant tick removal
  - education among at-risk groups to report rashes and seek early treatment

## Compensation

Lyme disease is prescribed (B14) for IIDB in those who are exposed to deer or other mammals of a type liable to harbour ticks carrying *Borrelia* bacteria.

## Relevant legislation

- Lyme disease is NOT reportable by clinicians under public health legislation but, since 2010, Public Health Laboratory Service; PHLS microbiology laboratories are required to report all serologically confirmed cases to the Health Protection Agency
- Lyme disease that is reliably attributable to work is reportable to HSE under RIDDOR

## Further information and guidance

Lyme disease A-Z series NHS 2021; https://www.nhs.uk/conditions/lyme-disease/

Zoonoses report UK PHE London 2017; https://assets.publishing.service.gov.uk/government/uploads/system/uploads/attachment_data/file/765111/UK_Zoonoses_report_2017.pdf

Lyme disease Centers for Disease Control & Prevention 2021; https://www.cdc.gov/lyme/index.html

Lyme disease services; Diagnostic and advisory services for Lyme disease PHE London 2018 https://www.gov.uk/guidance/lyme-borreliosis-service

Lyme Disease Health & Safety Executive. HSE Books, Sudbury. Available at: https://www.hse.gov.uk/agriculture/zoonoses-data-sheets/lyme-disease.pdf

Health & Safety Executive. *Zoonoses: Guidance on Protecting Farmers and Farm Workers From Zoonoses*. 2021 HSE Books, Sudbury. Available at: https://www.hse.gov.uk/agriculture/topics/zoonoses.htm

Public Health England (2018). *Lyme Disease: Resources and Guidance. The Characteristics, Diagnosis, Management, Surveillance and Epidemiology of Lyme Disease*. HSE Books, Sudbury. Available at: https://www.gov.uk/government/collections/lyme-disease-guidance-data-and-analysis

Public Health England (2020). *Common Animal-Associated Infections Quarterly Reports: 2019*. HSE Books, Sudbury. Available at: https://www.gov.uk/government/publications/common-animal-associated-infections-quarterly-reports-2019

# Zoonotic Chlamydia infections

Chlamydiosis is a bacterial zoonosis caused by the organism *Chlamydia psittaci*. There are two main types: avian chlamydiosis (psittacosis or ornithosis) and ovine chlamydiosis. Human-to-human spread is rare.

## Epidemiology

Most cases of chlamydiosis are non-occupational, occurring in pet owners.

## Clinical features

Incubation 1–2 weeks.

*Avian chlamydiosis*

- Fever, cough, myalgia
- Delirium in severe cases
- Pericarditis, myocarditis, endocarditis
- Atypical pneumonia
- Hepatitis

*Ovine chlamydiosis*

Abortion/stillbirth

## Causal exposures

*Avian chlamydiosis*

*Chlamydia psittaci* is excreted in the faeces and nasal discharges of infected birds. A range of bird species are susceptible. The most important sources for occupational transmission are ducks and other poultry, pigeons, and psittacines (exotic birds, e.g. parrots, cockatiels, macaws). The organism is resistant to dessication and can remain infectious for months. Transmission to humans is by inhalation of dust containing excreta of infected birds or by direct handling of birds, plumage, and tissues.

*Ovine chlamydiosis (Chlamydia abortus)*

A mild flu-like disease usually, but in pregnant women it can cause abortion/stillbirth. Characteristic symptoms in pregnancy include:

- Systemic illness with disseminated intravascular coagulation, renal complications, and hepatic complications
- Transmission is through handling infected sheep placentas at lambing. Clothing soiled with sheep products of conception are also infectious

## Industries

- Pet shop workers
- Poultry farm workers
- Feather-processing workers
- Abattoir workers
- Poultry meat inspectors
- Pigeons nesting in buildings that are used as workplaces can lead to exposure in a wide range of occupations
- Sheep farm workers
- Veterinary practitioners

## Individual susceptibility

Pregnant women are at risk of ovine chlamydiosis and must avoid contact with pregnant sheep.

## Clinical assessment and treatment

Diagnosis is by serology and treatment is with tetracycline.

## Prevention

*Avian chlamydiosis*

The mainstay of prevention is good animal husbandry, and avoidance of build-up of bird excreta in any area where people are at work.

- Screen breeding stock and treat with medicated seed
- Good flock husbandry (avoidance of overcrowding and stress among caged birds)
- Avoid dry sweeping of bird excreta
- Good general ventilation where birds are housed
- Local exhaust ventilation for de-feathering and evisceration tasks
- *PPE*: respirator with protection factor of at least 20 for dust-generating tasks

*Ovine chlamydiosis*

- Vaccinate breeding ewes
- *PPE*: waterproof overalls and gloves for lambing
- *Segregation and decontamination of soiled PPE*: must not be taken home to be washed

## Compensation

Chlamydiosis is prescribed (B10(a) Avian, B10(b) Ovine) for IIDB.

## Relevant legislation

- Chlamydiosis is NOT reportable under public health legislation, but microbiology laboratories are required to report *Chlamydophila psittaci* confirmed cases
- Chlamydiosis that is reliably attributable to work is reportable to HSE under RIDDOR

## Further information and guidance

HSE. *Zoonoses: Guidance on Protecting Farmers and Farm Workers From Zoonoses*. HSE Books, Sudbury. 2021 Available at: https://www.hse.gov.uk/agriculture/topics/zoonoses.htm

Public Health England (2017). *Psittacosis: Information for Clinicians on the Characteristics, Diagnosis and Epidemiology of Infections Caused by Chlamydia psittaci. Guidance*. Available at: https://www.gov.uk/guidance/psittacosis

Public Health England (2020). *Common Animal-Associated Infections Quarterly Reports: 2019*. PHE, London. Available at: https://www.gov.uk/government/publications/common-animal-associated-infections-quarterly-reports-2019

# Q fever

Q fever is a highly infectious zoonosis caused by the bacterium *Coxiella burnetii*. Exposure to just one *Coxiella burnetii* bacterium can cause Q fever. The organism is widespread in animals, but the most common sources of transmission to humans are cattle, sheep, and goats. Human-to-human spread does not generally occur.

*Coxiella burnetii* survives in the environment for many months as an infectious spore-like form that is resistant to heat, drying, and disinfection.

## Epidemiology

It is difficult to estimate the true incidence of Q fever, as cases are often mild and may go unreported. Therefore the 50–100 cases per year reported in the UK are probably an underestimate. There were 158 confirmed cases between 2014 and 2019 in England and Wales. The peak incidence in the UK is in the spring, associated with the lambing season.

## Clinical features

- *Incubation period*: 7–30 days
- *Acute infection*: 50% experience an acute influenza-like illness with pneumonia. Symptoms are often mild and only 5% need hospital treatment
- *Chronic infection*: develops in a small proportion up to 18 months after the acute event. Complicated by endocarditis. Chronic infection has a high fatality rate if untreated

## Causal exposures/industries

*Coxiella burnetii* bacterium is found in the waste products (urine or faeces) of infected animals. It can also be found in the milk of infected animals. The bacteria can live for weeks in the environment. Transmission is through inhalation of infected dusts or aerosols comprising infected animal products. Direct transmission can occur through non-intact skin. The most common source of infected material is the placenta and other products of conception at lambing:

- Sheep farmers
- Abattoir workers
- Meat packers (raw)
- Veterinary practitioners

## Individual susceptibility

*Pregnant women*: infection can have an adverse effect on the developing foetus including premature birth or abortion and low birth weight

Those with chronic diseases are most at risk (chronic renal disease, cancer, prosthetic heart valve, immunocompromised, and transplant recipients).

## Treatment and prognosis

Treatment of acute Q fever is with antibiotics (doxycycline or tetracycline) for 7–14 days. The prognosis for patients with acute Q fever is very good, with most patients recovering fully within a few weeks to months. Chronic disease is difficult to treat, and 50% relapse despite combination therapy. Therefore, antibiotics for chronic cases must be continued for 3 years. The prognosis for patients with chronic Q fever is poorer, with up to 10% of patients dying even with appropriate treatment.

## Prevention

- There is no vaccine available in the UK for the prevention of Q fever, although there is a vaccine used in Australia to protect humans in certain occupations like those in the sheep industry
- Mainstay of prevention is minimizing exposure to animal products, including good animal husbandry and hygiene. Use of PPE (gloves, waterproof overalls) at lambing reduces skin exposure (see ➲ p. 124, Animals and animal products)

## Compensation

Q fever is a prescribed disease (B11) for IIDB among those who are in contact with infected animals, their remains, or untreated products.

## Relevant legislation

- Q fever is NOT reportable under public health legislation, but microbiology laboratories are required to report all serologically confirmed cases
- Q fever that is readily attributable to work is reportable to HSE under the RIDDOR

## Further information and guidance

DEFRA, HSE, and PHE (2015). Pregnant women advised to avoid animals that are giving birth. Press release. Available at: https://www.gov.uk/government/news/pregnant-women-advised-to-avoid-animals-that-are-giving-birth--2

HSE. *Q Fever. Guidance*. 2018; HSE Books, Sudbury. Available at: http://www.hse.gov.uk/agriculture/zoonoses-data-sheets/q-fever.pdfZoonoses-Agriculture " Health & Safety Executive London 2017 https://www.hse.gov.uk/agriculture/zoonoses-data-sheets/q-fever.pdf

Q Fever- Information for farmers; PHE London 2017; https://assets.publishing.service.gov.uk/government/uploads/system/uploads/attachment_data/file/487806/Q_fever_information_for_farmers_2015.pdf

Health A-Z Q Fever; 2021; https://www.nhs.uk/conditions/q-fever/

Q fever infections in humans: sources, transmission, treatment; PHE London 2008; https://www.gov.uk/guidance/q-fever

# Enteric zoonoses

A number of organisms colonize the GI tract of farm and domestic animals and can be transmitted to humans.

## Causal exposures/industries

Infection occurs after contact with animal dung, usually after putting hands or fingers in the mouth without washing. It is spread via consumption of undercooked and infected meat and meat products, contaminated water, or contaminated hands (faecal).

High risk occupations:

- Farm workers
- Veterinary practitioners
- Abattoir workers
- Meat processing plant workers and butchers
- Workers in the leisure industry (water sports or outdoor activities)
- Sewage and waste-water workers

## Clinical features

These are similar for a number of organisms.

### *Escherichia coli 0157:H7 (E. coli 0157:H7)*

Shiga toxin-producing *Escherichia coli* (STEC) are a group of zoonotic bacteria associated with human disease. In the UK, STEC serogroup O157:H7 is the most common type and around 700 cases of STEC O157:H7 are reported annually in England. Healthy ruminants, particularly cattle, sheep, deer, goats, pets, and wild birds are the main reservoir of infection harbouring the organism in their guts. STEC has a very low infectious dose as few organisms are required to infect humans. Transmission to humans occurs through:

- Consumption of contaminated food or water
- Direct or indirect contact with infected animals or their environment
- Person to person spread

Each transmission route can cause sporadic infection as well as outbreaks. It produces a toxin that causes illness in humans ranging from diarrhoea to renal failure. Can be fatal in humans (but rarely). There is no specific treatment. A definite diagnosis is based on culture of *E. coli 0157:H7* from the patient's sample of stool on special culturing plates that then are tested with antiserum (antibodies) that react only with *E. coli 0157:H7*. Most *E. coli 0157:H7* infections resolve spontaneously and require no treatment. However, supportive treatment is quickly required if the patient becomes dehydrated, anaemic, or develops haemolytic uraemic syndrome (HUS) or thrombotic thrombocytopenic purpura (TTP). Most of *E. coli 0157:H7* infections have excellent outcomes. If complications such as severe dehydration, anaemia, HUS, or TTP develop, the outcomes can decline from good to poor quickly.

### *Salmonella*

Salmonellosis is caused by *Salmonella* bacteria, and is characterized by fever, diarrhoea, vomiting, and abdominal pain. As well as the more familiar food-borne transmission to humans, infection can be acquired directly from farm animals that carry the organism as it contaminates their enclosures, fur, feathers, and the groundwater. The animals that have been known to spread salmonella include poultry, goats, cattle, sheep, and pigs. These animals can appear clean and healthy and still transmit the bacteria. An important mode of transmission is hand-to-hand contact in farm workers. Treatment is with oral ciprofloxacin.

*Cryptosporidium*

There are two main species of cryptosporidium that cause infection in humans—*Cryptosporidium hominis* and *Cryptosporidium parvum*. The organism is carried by calves, sheep, lambs, deer, and goats. Human-to-human transmission is possible. It presents as an influenza-like illness with diarrhoea and abdominal pain. Most people with cryptosporidiosis do not need any specific medication or treatment. Some studies have shown that medicines such as nitazoxanide may help clear symptoms more quickly in some people. However, this medicine is not routinely used in the UK. More importantly fluid therapy should be started to prevent or treat any dehydration until symptoms clear.

## Prevention

Risk controls are outlined in detail on ➔ p. 124, Animals and animal products. *Salmonella* is treatable in herds using medicated feed.

## Relevant legislation

Enteric zoonoses (enteric fever, food poisoning, infectious bloody diarrhoea, HUS) are notifiable diseases to PHE under the Health Protection (Notification) Regulations 2010

Any infection that is readily attributable to work is reportable to HSE under RIDDOR

## Further information and guidance

HSE. *Zoonoses: Guidance on Protecting Farmers and Farm Workers From Zoonoses*. 2021 HSE Books, Sudbury. Available at: https://www.hse.gov.uk/agriculture/topics/zoonoses.htm

Public Health England (2017). *Cryptosporidiosis: Guidance, Data and Analysis*. PHE, London. Available at: https://www.gov.uk/government/collections/cryptosporidiosis-guidance-data-and-analysis

Public Health England (2018). *Shiga Toxin-Producing Escherichia Coli: Guidance, Data and Analysis*. PHE, London. Available at: https://www.gov.uk/government/collections/vero-cytotoxin-producing-escherichia-coli-vtec-guidance-data-and-analysis

Zoonoses- Agriculture HSE London 2021; https://www.hse.gov.uk/agriculture/zoonoses-data-sheets/salmonella.pdf

Salmonella: guidance, data and analysis UK Health Security Agency 2021;
https://www.gov.uk/government/collections/salmonella-guidance-data-and-analysis

Notifiable diseases and causative organisms: how to report; PHE 2021 https://www.gov.uk/guidance/notifiable-diseases-and-causative-organisms-how-to-report

# Zoonotic skin infections

## Causal exposures/industries

Transmitted by direct skin contact with infected animal lesions:

- Shepherds
- Farmers
- Veterinary practitioners
- Abattoir workers
- Meat inspectors

## Orf

Orf is a viral zoonosis caused by the parapoxvirus. It causes contagious pustular dermatitis (ecthyma contagiosum or 'scabby mouth') in sheep (mainly lambs) and goats. The virus is spread by handling infected sheep or goats, infected carcasses, or contaminated material. Handling infected animals near their mouth is thought to increase the risk of orf. Human-to-human transmission is extremely rare.

*Epidemiology*

The frequency of orf in the general population is extremely low. Virtually all cases are occupational. Because the disorder is mostly trivial in humans, and is not a notifiable disease, PHE do not collect information on the number of human cases of orf. From 2008 to 2017 there was an annual average of 42 government laboratory-confirmed cases of orf in animals.

*Clinical features, diagnosis, and treatment*

- 1-week incubation period
- Rapidly developing red papule, typically on the finger; usually up to 5 cm in diameter, and can ulcerate
- Can be complicated by fever, lymphadenopathy, erythema multiforme, and (rarely) bullous pemphigoid
- Diagnosis is usually based on the history of contact with infected animal and the presence of a typical clinical lesion. Confirmation of the clinical diagnosis is by electron microscopy of a lesion biopsy
- Self-limiting; usually clears up within 3–6 weeks. It may be useful to cover the lesion with a sterile (hygienic) dressing and immobilize the finger to help reduce discomfort. Rarely, the lesion may not go away, and a minor surgical procedure may be required to remove it. Infection usually confers immunity
- Antibiotics for 2° bacterial infection when the lesion is not healing and may be associated with a high fever and severe pain

*Individual susceptibility*

Immunocompromised (particularly haematological malignancy) may develop large fungating granuloma or tumour-like lesion.

*Prevention*

Good hygienic practices when handling or rearing sheep and goats: wearing protective gloves, good hand hygiene, and vaccinating animals at risk.

## Ringworm

Ringworm is a dermatophyte (fungal) infection.

*Clinical features, diagnosis, and treatment*

- Characteristic annular plaque with raised edge and central clearing
- Scaling and pruritis common
- Diagnosis by microscopy and culture of skin scales
- Treatment with topical antifungals
- Oral griseofulvin only for severe cases
- Treat secondary bacterial infection with antibiotics

## Others

- *Viral warts (papillomavirus) in butchers and fishermen*: it is estimated that up to 23% of people who frequently handle meat, fish, and poultry will develop warts on their hands
- *Erysipeloid (erysipelothrix) in fish processors*: it is a rare skin condition caused by the bacterium *Erysipelothrix rhusiopathiae*. The bacteria are introduced accidentally from infected animals through pre-existing skin wounds. Human erysipeloid, rare in the UK, is largely an occupational disease of slaughterhouse and agricultural workers, and those in the meat-handling and fishing industries. It does not spread from person to person. Antibiotic treatment is available, but most cases will get better within 2–4 weeks without treatment. Rarely infection leads to a severe, possibly life-threatening disease
- *Cutaneous granulomata (*Mycobacterium marinum*) in tropical fish dealers*: skin lesions may be single but are often multiple. Typically, clusters of superficial nodules or papules. They may be painful or painless and may become fluctuant. A prolonged course of antibiotic is curative in most superficial cases, but adjunctive surgical intervention is sometimes indicated in extensive and deep infections

## Prevention of zoonotic dermatoses

- Live vaccine for affected flocks
- Use PPE (gloves) when examining the mouths of sheep and lambs
- See ➲ p. 124, Animals and animal products, for specific guidance

## Compensation

Orf is prescribed (B12) for IIDB in those who have contact with sheep or goats, or with the carcasses of sheep or goats.

## Relevant legislation

Any infection clearly attributable to work is reportable under RIDDOR

## Further information and guidance

DEFRA and Public Health England (2017). *HM Government UK Zoonoses Report 2017*. PHE, London. 2018. Available at: https://www.gov.uk/government/publications/zoonoses-uk-annual-reports

HSE. *Erysepeloid*. HSE Books, Sudbury. 2021. Available at: http://www.hse.gov.uk/agriculture/zoonoses-data-sheets/erysipeloid.pdf

HSE. *Orf*. HSE Books, Sudbury. 2021. Available at: http://www.hse.gov.uk/agriculture/zoonoses-data-sheets/orf.pdfHSE. *Zoonoses: Guidance on Protecting Farmers and Farm Workers From Zoonoses*. 2021 HSE Books, Sudbury. Available at: https://www.hse.gov.uk/agriculture/topics/zoonoses.htm

# Chapter 7

# Respiratory and cardiovascular disorders

# Occupational asthma and rhinitis

Occupational asthma and rhinitis are caused by immunological sensitization to agents in the workplace. Once an individual is sensitized, symptoms can occur after very low-level re-exposure.

## Epidemiology

- Around 9–15% of asthma in adults of working age is occupational
- The number of new cases of occupational asthma in the UK has been falling over the past 10 year
- The estimated rate of occupational asthma is 45–75 cases per 100,000 workers per year (based on a European population-based study)

## Clinical features and aetiology

- *Asthma*: wheeze, chest tightness, dyspnoea. Classically, symptoms are worse at work or soon after work, and better at weekends or during holidays. This pattern can be lost in the later stages of the disease. Late reactions can occur at night or early morning after a day at work
- *Rhinitis and conjunctivitis*: rhinorrhoea, nasal stuffiness, itching of the eyes/nose, and sneezing. These are often associated with asthma and may precede chest symptoms
- When the individual is sensitized, symptoms can be precipitated by non-specific irritation (e.g. cigarette smoke or cold air)

## Causal exposures/industries

See Table 7.1. Allergens can be divided broadly into:

- High molecular weight proteins (e.g. animal and plant proteins)
- Low molecular weight substances that act as haptens (e.g. isocyanates, acid anhydrides)

## Individual susceptibility

- Atopy
- Cigarette smoking

💣 Atopy is common (30% of the population); it is not usually appropriate to screen out atopics from exposure to sensitizing agents at pre-employment.

## Clinical assessment and diagnosis of occupational asthma

- Initial investigation with lung function tests ($FEV_1$, forced vital capacity (FVC), and peak flow) to explore the diagnosis of asthma (reversible airways obstruction)
- *Exposure assessment (pattern of exposure and specific allergens and relationship to symptoms, use of respiratory protective equipment)*:
  - a full history should include current and previous exposures
  - be aware of the possibility of late reactions
  - the lack of a clear temporal relationship to work does not exclude the diagnosis of occupational asthma

**Table 7.1** Causal exposures/industries

| Exposure | Industry/uses |
|---|---|
| Isocyanates | Car body shops |
| Flour, grain dust | Bakeries, agriculture |
| Acid anhydrides | Manufacturing, use of epoxy resins/varnishes |
| Rosin flux | Electronics (soldering) |
| Proteolytic enzymes | Manufacture of biological washing powders |
| Animal proteins (urine/dander) | Laboratory animal research |
| Platinum salts | Platinum industry |
| Antibiotics, cimetidine, ispaghula | Pharmaceutical manufacturing |
| Glutaraldehyde, natural rubber latex | Health care |
| Wood dust | Construction, forestry, carpentry |
| Persulphate salts or henna | Hairdressing |
| Fish proteins, soya bean, tea dust | Fish preparation, food industry |
| Reactive dyes | Cosmetic and rubber manufacture |
| Metal working fluids | Manufacturing |

## Serial peak flow recording (see ➔ p. 800, Serial peak flow testing)

- *Bronchial provocation challenge tests*:
  - should be carried out in a specialist centre (contact your local consultant respiratory physician for advice)
  - individuals can be sensitized to more than one asthmagen
- Specific immunoglobulin E (IgE), skin prick testing (if specific test reagents are available)

## Prognosis

Symptoms usually resolve after removal from exposure, but the practical constraints of exposure control can be a real threat to employment.

💣 Where exposure cannot be controlled completely, individuals are sometimes allowed to continue working while wearing personal protective equipment (PPE). However, they must be informed about risk and have frequent health surveillance.

## Compensation

Occupationally acquired asthma and allergic rhinitis are both prescribed for Industrial Injuries Disablement Benefit (IIDB) (D7 and D4, respectively) in those who are exposed to a known sensitizing agent at work.

## Health surveillance

Individuals who are exposed to respiratory sensitizers must undergo health surveillance (MHSWR and Control of Substances Hazardous to Health (COSHH) Regulations). The surveillance programme depends on the likelihood of sensitization and is outlined in specific guidance from HSE.[1]

## Relevant legislation and guidance

- Occupational asthma is reportable under Reporting of Injuries, Diseases, and Dangerous Occurrences Regulations (RIDDOR). Asthmagen? *Critical Assessments of the Evidence for Agents Implicated in Occupational Asthma*
- *Occupational Asthma: A Guide for Occupational Physicians and Occupational Health Physicians*. British Occupational Health Research Foundation'. London 2010 ☞ http://www.bohrf.org.uk/downloads/asthlop.pdf

1 *MS 25. Medical Aspects of Occupational Asthma*. HSE, Sudbury.

# Latex allergy

Latex allergy may manifest as:

- A type I immediate hypersensitivity reaction due to a reaction to natural rubber latex (NRL) proteins
- More commonly as a type IV delayed hypersensitivity reaction in response to the chemical additives in latex products

## Epidemiology

During the past 20 years, latex allergy has become a major occupational hazard in the rubber processing and health care industries. In the health care industry the use of disposable powdered NRL gloves, many dusted with corn starch to aid donning, increased exponentially after 1987 until the mid-1990s. However, the apparent prevalence of latex allergy has been steadily decreasing since 1998. The prevalence of type I allergy (based on skin-prick testing) in health care workers (HCWs) is currently estimated to be up to 12%. Around 1% of the general population are sensitized to NRL, but not all sensitized individuals develop symptoms.

## Clinical features

- *Type I*: urticaria, rhinitis, conjunctivitis, occasionally asthma, or very rarely anaphylaxis. Onset is usually within 20 minutes of exposure
- *Type IV*: dermatitis, characterized by a red, itchy, scaly rash often localized to the area of use, i.e. wrists and forearms with glove use, but may spread to other areas. Onset is usually >12 hours after exposure

## Causal exposures/industries

- HCWs
- Individuals exposed to NRL regularly, e.g. food handlers, hairdressers, and construction workers
- Latex product manufacturing workers

## Individual susceptibility

- Patients with spina bifida and congenital genitourinary abnormalities
- A history of certain food allergies such as banana, avocado, kiwi, and chestnut
- Individuals with atopic allergic disease may be at increased risk

## Clinical assessment and diagnosis

- The clinical history is essential in establishing the diagnosis of type 1 allergy:
  - supporting tests include a positive skin prick test to latex allergens and a serological test for specific IgE, not all individuals with a positive skin or serological test manifest allergic disease
  - consider referring the individual for specialist advice and a latex challenge or use test
- Type IV allergy is diagnosed by a positive patch testing

## Prognosis

Reducing exposure to latex may lead to a reduction in type 1 allergic symptoms in sensitized individuals.

## Management

*Latex policy*

All health care organizations should have a latex policy outlining the hazards of NRL, how to identify and manage individuals with NRL allergy, and how to reduce exposure in the workplace. Organizations should be moving towards a latex-free environment.

*Adjustments to work*

If NRL allergy is diagnosed, a risk assessment of the individual's workplace must be made to ensure a safe working environment. If the individual has a history of severe type I allergy or anaphylaxis, they must work in a latex-free environment. Redeployment may be necessary. They should be advised to wear a medic alert bracelet, carry an epipen, and inform health care providers of their NRL allergy.

For non-life-threatening allergies the following are recommended:

- Avoid contact with NRL gloves or products
- Avoid areas where there is a risk of inhalation of powder from NRL gloves worn by others
- Substitute to other glove materials where appropriate, e.g. nitrile, polyvinyl chloride, or neoprene
- If use of NRL gloves is necessary, they should be single-use disposable gloves and be low protein (<50 μg/g) and powder free

## Relevant legislation

Employers and employees need to comply with the COSHH Regulations 2002 (as amended) (see ➲ p. 566, Control of Substances Hazardous to Health). This includes assessing and reducing risks and providing health surveillance in appropriate cases (see ➲ p. 462, Skin surveillance and ➲ p. 464, Respiratory health surveillance)

## Further information and guidance

HSE (1998). *Medical Aspects of Occupational Skin Disease*, MS24. HSE Books, Sudbury.

HSE. *Latex Allergy*. HSE Books, Sudbury. 2021 Available at: http://www.hse.gov.uk/skin/employ/latex.htm

NHS. *Latex Allergy: Occupational Aspects of Management*. NHS, England. London 2008, Available at: http://www.nhsplus.nhs.uk/providers/images/library/files/guidelines/Latex_allergy_guidelines.pdf

# Byssinosis

## Epidemiology and pathogenesis

This disease has been associated historically with exposure to cotton dust. It is thought that the disease is caused by an endotoxin, which is produced by bacteria within raw cotton, but the precise pathology is unclear. Byssinosis is rare, having largely been eliminated by good exposure controls in the textile industry. In the UK, the disease was most common in Lancashire and Northern Ireland; both are areas that have local textile mills. The condition is more prevalent in developing countries with large textile industries (e.g. India and China) where poor control of exposure may result in extremely high exposures, in some cases >100 mg/m$^3$.

## Clinical features

- Wheezing and chest tightness
- Typically, worse after a break from work (Mondays), improving with return to exposure (better towards the end of the working week)
- Temporal relationship can be obscured after prolonged exposure

## Causal exposures/industries

- Raw cotton, flax, or hemp
- Development of byssinosis within 10 years of exposure is rare; usually symptoms are associated with >20 years of exposure
- Textile and rope-making industry

## Individual susceptibility

Cigarette smokers develop more severe disease.

## Clinical assessment and treatment

- *Lung function*: cross-shift decline in $FEV_1$
- There are no specific radiological abnormalities associated with byssinosis
- Treatment is with bronchodilators and antihistamines

## Prevention

Exposure controls include enclosure of carding operations and steaming of raw cotton to reduce particle formation.

## Compensation

Byssinosis is a prescribed disease (D2) for IIDB in those who work with raw cotton or flax.

## Relevant legislation

- Byssinosis is reportable under RIDDOR

# Organic dust toxic syndrome

The syndrome known as organic dust toxic syndrome (ODTS) is an acute inflammatory disorder of the lower respiratory system. Precise pathology is unclear but is thought to be caused by a toxic reaction to organic dusts. It occurs in the absence of immunological sensitization.

## Epidemiology

ODTS is primarily a disorder of agricultural workers. It does not feature in routinely collected statistics, but surveys of farming populations suggest a prevalence of around 6%.

## Clinical features

- Fever, chills, malaise, dry cough, dyspnoea
- *Acute onset*: 4–6 hours after exposure
- Brief duration (<36 hours)
- Transient decrease in lung function ($FEV_1$, FVC, and PEF)

## Causal exposures/industries

- Mouldy grain and vegetable material
- Agricultural workers
- Clusters of cases are typically associated with very heavy exposures (e.g. emptying silos)

## Differential diagnosis and clinical assessment

ODTS shares many features with acute hypersensitivity pneumonitis (farmer's lung (farmer's hypersensitivity pneumonitis, FHP)), including exposure, a similar clinical presentation, and the presence of neutrophils in alveolar lavage fluid. However, the prognosis and treatment are different and differentiation is important. ODTS is distinguished from FHP by:

- Short duration of symptoms
- Benign natural history, with absence of progressive lung damage
- Absence of immunological hypersensitivity
- Absence of lung infiltrates on chest X-ray (CXR)
- Absence of hypoxaemia

## Treatment and prognosis

- Self-limiting
- No specific medical intervention required

## Prevention

- Reduction of exposure to mouldy organic material (see ➲ p. 126, Organic dusts and mists)
- PPE for high exposure activities
- Because of the link to heavy exposures, education of farm workers is particularly important

# Hypersensitivity pneumonitis

Also known as extrinsic allergic alveolitis (EAA), this inflammatory disorder of the lower respiratory system results from an immunological reaction to specific allergens (particularly thermophilic *Actinomycetes* and *Aspergillus* spp.) in mouldy organic material. The classical pathological feature is lymphocytic interstitial pneumonitis. Pathogenesis is not fully understood, but it is likely to result from a type III (immune complex) or type IV (cell-mediated) reaction. It is not an IgE-mediated (type I) allergic condition.

## Epidemiology

- In the UK, an average of 47 cases of allergic alveolitis per year (2006–2010) were reported to the Surveillance of Work-related and Occupational Respiratory Disease (SWORD) reporting scheme by respiratory and occupational physicians. There have been fewer than five cases per year assessed for IIDB over the same period. These figures are likely to be an underestimate of the number of new cases
- Data from death certificates in the UK show attribution of death to occupational allergic alveolitis of <10 cases per year
- The most prevalent form is FHP or farmer's lung, but a number of other forms are recognized, each with a specific causal antigen (Table 7.2). Up to 5% of farmers report symptoms. HSE has reported a recent increase of cases related to metal working and wash fluids in the engineering sector. There is some evidence of EAA in association with exposure to hard metals (nickel)

**Table 7.2** Forms of EAA, causal antigens, and source

| Disorder | Antigen | Antigen source |
|---|---|---|
| Farmer's lung (FHP) | Thermophyllic actinomycetes including *Saccharopolyspora rectivergula*<br>*Aspergillus* species | Mouldy hay, grain, straw |
| Bird fancier's lung | Avian proteins | Bird excreta and bloom |
| Mushroom workers lung | *Aspergillus fumigatus*, *Aspergillus umbrosis* | Mushroom compost |
| Bagassosis | *Thermoactinomyces sacchari* | Bagasse (fibrous residue of sugar cane) |
| Malt workers lung | *Aspergillus clavatus* | Mouldy barley in whisky distilling |
| Ventilation pneumonitis | Thermophilic actinomycetes species | Water reservoirs in air-conditioning systems |

This list is not intended to be exhaustive.

## Clinical features

*Acute form*

- Fever, chills, cough, dyspnoea, myalgia, headache
- *Onset*: 4–8 hours after exposure to antigen
- Resolution after 1–3 days

*Subacute/chronic form*

- Gradual onset of dyspnoea over months or years
- Recurrent acute attacks may be distinguished in some cases
- Chronic productive cough

## Causal exposures/industries

- Agricultural workers
- Forestry workers
- Mushroom workers
- Bird handlers
- Sugar cane processors
- Distillery workers

## Clinical assessment

- ↑ Erythrocyte sedimentation rate and neutrophil count (peripheral blood eosinophilia does not occur)
- Lung function (↓$FEV_1$, FVC, typically with restrictive pattern, although mild obstructive changes may occur)
- Impaired gas transfer (↓ transfer factor for carbon monoxide); hypoxia may occur
- CXR shows diffuse pulmonary infiltrates (acute) or upper- and mid-zone interstitial fibrosis (chronic); 20% of CXRs in acute cases are normal
- Serum precipitins to causal allergens

## Treatment and prognosis

- Low-dose oral steroids
- Avoidance of exposure
- Prognosis is highly variable. Can be progressive, with lung fibrosis. If fibrosis develops, the main functional consequences for work are reduced stamina and physical capability

## Prevention

- Reduction of exposure to mouldy organic material (see ➔ p. 126, Organic dust and mists)
- PPE for high exposure activities

## Compensation

EAA is prescribed for IIDB (B6) in those who are exposed to moulds, fungal spores, or heterologous proteins.

## Relevant legislation

The Control of Substances Hazardous to Health Regulations 2002 (as amended)

# Humidifier fever

Humidifier fever is a self-limiting illness that is associated with exposure to humidified air from air-conditioning systems. The pathophysiology is incompletely understood. However, the disorder is distinct from hypersensitivity pneumonitis (HP) (ventilation pneumonitis), which can result from the same exposure. It is currently thought that humidifier fever is caused by either a direct effect of organisms in contaminated humidifier reservoirs or a product of such organisms (e.g. endotoxin).

## Epidemiology

Because of the self-limiting nature of this condition, prevalence estimates are neither readily available nor likely to be accurate.

## Clinical features

- Usually non-specific, e.g. fever, chills, myalgia
- Dyspnoea and wheezing can occur
- *Onset*: 6–8 hours after exposure
- Rapid and complete recovery
- Usually occurs after a break from work (e.g. on Mondays)

## Differential diagnosis

- Can develop mild hypoxia, ↓ gas transfer, and audible crackles at the lung bases
- Distinguished from HP by an invariably normal CXR
- Serum precipitins to organisms that are present in humidifier fluid are often positive. However, these do not bear any relation to disease activity and are only useful as a marker of exposure. The presence of serum precipitins cannot help to distinguish from HP, as they are positive in both disorders

## Treatment and prognosis

Self-limiting; medical intervention is not indicated.

## Causal exposures

- Recirculated air from air-conditioning units, particularly where the aim is to achieve high humidity
- Long list of possible causative organisms in humidifier fluid include many species of bacteria, fungi, and protozoa
- Ubiquitous exposure in many office environments
- Highest risk in textile industry where high humidity is desirable as this makes fibres pliable and easier to work

## Prevention

Guidance on the selection, maintenance, and cleaning of humidifiers and air-conditioning systems to minimize the risk of humidifier fever and other disorders is available from HSE.

# Metal fume fever

This benign disease results from deposition of fine metal particulates in the alveoli. The precise pathological mechanism is unknown. No epidemiological information is available, as the mild symptoms are often overlooked and tolerated by metal workers.

## Causal exposures and industries

- Primarily caused by zinc oxide fume generated by cutting, welding, or brazing galvanized steel
- *Similar effects can be caused by other metal fumes. However, although these metals have been implicated, there is little evidence in the literature. Moreover, the nature of work activities is such that exposure is often to a mixture of metal oxides*:
  - iron
  - copper
  - aluminium
  - tin
  - magnesium
- *Found in a wide range of jobs involving metal working*:
  - welders
  - oxy-fuel gas cutters
- *Typically, in heavy engineering industries*:
  - shipbuilding
  - foundries
  - scrap metal industry
  - demolition
  - motor vehicle repair

## Factors affecting exposure

Exposure is increased by:

- increasing thickness of metal in cutting operations
- speed of metal cutting and arcing (welding) time
- automated cutting
- poor ventilation

## Clinical features

- Influenza-like illness with fever, chills, headache, and myalgia
- Dyspnoea and cough
- Metallic taste in the mouth
- Tolerance over the working week, with recurrence after break from exposure ('Monday fever')
- *Onset*: 4–12 hours after exposure
- Benign illness, self-limiting after 1–2 days

⚠ Must not be confused with exposure to cadmium fume, which can cause a severe toxic reaction in lungs and kidneys.

## Prevention

- It is difficult to avoid metal cutting completely in demolition and shipbuilding
- Alternative cutting methods (thermal and non-thermal) are available. However, they are not suitable for all purposes and all have associated hazards to health. Specialized advice on use of cutting tools is required
- Using the correct nozzle for cutting
- Turning off the torch during pauses in activity
- Fume capture methods including local exhaust ventilation
- Use of appropriate respiratory protective equipment
- Training and information, including advice on hygiene (hand washing and avoiding eating or smoking in the work area) and other risk controls

## Further information

*Oxy-Fuel Cutting: Control of Fume, Gases and Noise*. HSE 668/30. Health & Safety Executive 2011, Available at: http://www.hse.gov.uk/fod/infodocs/668_30.pdf#search=%22metal%20fume%20%22

# Chronic obstructive pulmonary disease

This is a group of chronic lung disorders comprising chronic bronchitis and emphysema. They are characterized by irreversible airflow limitation, with impairment of lung function and debility in severe cases.

## Epidemiology

- The main risk factor is smoking
- Population studies have estimated the burden of chronic obstructive pulmonary disease (COPD) that is attributable to occupational causes, with a population attributable risk per cent of 15% (median).[1] This equates to around 4,000 deaths per year
- A total of 145 cases of chronic bronchitis and emphysema were prescribed for IIDB during 2010

## Clinical features

- Exertional dyspnoea
- Wheeze
- Chronic productive cough for >3 months of the year

## Causal exposures/industries

An increased risk of COPD has been associated with the following:
- *Mineral dusts*:
  - coal mining
  - manmade vitreous fibres
  - oil mists
  - cement (construction)
  - silica
- *Organic dusts*:
  - *farming*: animal confinement (especially pigs), grain dust
  - flour mill work and baking
  - cotton textile work
  - wood (paper milling)
- *Chemicals*:
  - cadmium
  - welding fumes
  - vanadium
  - polycyclic aromatic hydrocarbons
  - isocyanates

## Clinical assessment

- *Lung function declines progressively*: $FEV_1$ <80% of predicted values, $FEV_1$/FVC <70% (obstructive pattern). The pattern of lung function in occupational cases can be complicated by dual pathology (e.g. pneumoconiosis) and restrictive patterns may be seen in coal miners and silica-exposed workers
- CXR is not necessary for diagnosis

1 HSE (2011). *Chronic Obstructive Pulmonary Disease (COPD): COPD in Great Britain*. HSE Books Sudbury. Available at: http://www.hse.gov.uk/statistics/causdis/copd/copd.pdf

## Treatment and prognosis

- Removal from occupational exposure
- Advise smoking cessation
- Inhaled bronchodilators
- Inhaled corticosteroids
- Oral corticosteroids and antibiotics for acute infective exacerbations
- Supportive treatment for advanced disease
- Prognosis is variable; severe disease can result in respiratory failure

## Prevention

See ➜ p. 126, Organic dust and mists, ➜ p. 244, Coal worker's pneumoconiosis for preventive measures and exposure control.

## Compensation

- Chronic bronchitis and emphysema have recently been added to the list of prescribed diseases for IIDB (D1), but only for coal miners who have spent >20 years working underground. $FEV_1$ must be reduced by 1 L to qualify for benefit
- Emphysema is prescribed for IIDB (C18) for those exposed to cadmium fumes for a cumulative period of ≥20 years

## Relevant legislation and further information

See ➜ p. 244, Coal worker's pneumoconiosis, for legislation and guidance relevant to dust control in the mining industry

# Asbestos-related diseases

A number of medical conditions are related to asbestos exposure:

- Asbestosis
- *Pleural disorders*:
  - mesothelioma
  - diffuse pleural thickening
  - benign pleural effusion
  - pleural plaques
- Lung cancer
- Laryngeal cancer

Details of epidemiology, clinical features, and management are covered under each condition (asbestosis, lung cancer, pleural disorders, and laryngeal cancer). Aspects that are common to all asbestos-related disease (exposure, prevention, compensation, and legislation) are covered here.

## Causal exposures/industries

- Historically, asbestos has been widely used for fire protection and insulation. In the past (before the danger of asbestos was recognized) controls were poor and exposures in some industries were very high.
  - *dockyards*: shipbuilders, ship breakers, and fitters
  - railway engineering
  - asbestos textile industry
  - construction
  - plumbing
  - pipe lagging and thermal insulation/pipe fitters
  - asbestos mining and distribution
  - engineering (brake linings and clutch faces)
- Currently, exposure mainly occurs during the demolition or renovation of old buildings (asbestos insulation, lagging, and roof tiles)

## Prevention

- Mainly by elimination (replacement of asbestos with other materials)
- *UK legislation*:
  - prohibits import, supply, and use of most asbestos products
  - defines exposure limits for asbestos
  - controls the identification and removal of asbestos in buildings

## Health surveillance

- Employees who are currently exposed to asbestos above a defined action level must undergo regular health surveillance (2-yearly lung function) by a doctor who has been appointed by HSE. CXRs are not required as part of health surveillance
- Individuals who have been exposed previously need not undergo surveillance. However, it is important to:
  - document previous exposure carefully, including historical hygiene measurements where available. It is appropriate to inform the GP with the individual's consent, so that the exposure is noted in the event of future asbestos-related disease
  - counsel the individual about the risk of asbestos-related disease and the availability of compensation

Counsel the individual about smoking cessation, as the risk of lung cancer from smoking and asbestos is multiplicative.

## Compensation

It can be difficult to clarify the source and extent of exposure after >20-year latency. It is essential to take an exhaustive occupational history to ensure that affected patients have appropriate access to benefits.

*Industrial Injuries Disablement Benefit*

Some asbestos-related disorders prescribed are:

- Asbestosis (D1)
- Mesothelioma (D3)
- Primary carcinoma of the lung ± accompanying evidence of asbestosis (D8, D8A)
- Diffuse pleural thickening (D9).

Specific details of prescription according to exposure activities are outlined in the List of Prescribed Diseases.[1] Surviving next of kin can claim up to 6 months posthumously.

*War Pensions Scheme*

Those who develop asbestos-related disease as a result of exposure while working in HM Forces may be eligible for compensation.

*Civil compensation*

If an employee can prove negligence on the part of the employer, they may be successful in seeking compensation through the civil courts. Claims must be declared within 3 years of the diagnosis of asbestos-related disease, including pleural plaques.

## Relevant legislation

- Asbestosis is reportable under RIDDOR 2013. Exposure to asbestos is reportable under RIDDOR when a work activity causes the accidental release or escape of asbestos fibres into the air in a quantity sufficient to cause damage to the health of any person.
- Control of Asbestos Regulations 2012
- Asbestos (Licensing) Regulations 1983
- Asbestos (Prohibitions) (Amendment) Regulations 1999

## Further information

Department of Work and Pensions (DWP). *Appendix 1: List of Diseases Covered by Industrial Injuries Disablement Benefit*. Technical Guidance DWP, London 2022. Available at: https://www.gov.uk/government/publications/industrial-injuries-disablement-benefits-technical-guidance/industrial-injuries-disablement-benefits-technical-guidance

HSE Web Community Platform. *Asbestos Health and Safety*. HSE Books, Sudbury 2021. Available at: http://www.hse.gov.uk/asbestos/index.htm

1 DWP. *Appendix 1: List of Diseases Covered by Industrial Injuries Disablement Benefit.* Available at: http://www.dwp.gov.uk/advisers/db1/appendix/appendix1.asp

# The pneumoconioses

Pneumoconioses are a group of chronic lung diseases caused by long-term exposure to respirable particles (<5 μm diameter) of mineral dust (see Table 7.3).

## Epidemiology

In the UK, an average of 167 cases of pneumoconiosis per year (2005–2010) were reported to the SWORD reporting scheme by respiratory and occupational physicians. This is likely to be an underestimate of the number of new cases.

## Pathophysiology

The classical features of pneumoconiosis are as follows:

- Deposition of mineral dust in the alveoli
- Mineral particles are phagocytosed by alveolar macrophages
- Localized inflammatory reaction leads to long-term changes in the histology of the lung:
  - fibrotic reaction in the surrounding lung parenchyma, with reticulin formation and collagen deposition
  - necrosis and cavitation of the fibrotic nodules can occur in the later stages of the disease
  - progressive disease leads to coalescence of fibrotic areas into large parenchymal masses (progressive massive fibrosis (PMF))
- Gas diffusion is affected, leading to ↓ transfer factor
- Lung volumes are ↓ ($FEV_1$ and FVC), classically a restrictive pattern

**Table 7.3** The pneumoconiosis

| Disease | Exposure | Cross reference |
|---|---|---|
| Coal worker's pneumoconiosis | Coal dust | ➲ p. 244, Coal worker's pneumoconiosis |
| Asbestosis | Asbestos fibres | ➲ p. 246, Asbestosis |
| Silicosis | Quartz (crystalline silica) | ➲ p. 248, Silicosis |
| Kaolin pneumoconiosis | Kaolin (china clay) | ➲ p. 251, Kaolin pneumoconiosis |
| BeryllIiosis | Beryllium | ➲ p. 250, Berylliosis |
| Stannosis | Tin ore | ➲ p. 252, The 'simple' pneumoconiosis |
| Siderosis | Iron oxide | ➲ p. 252, The 'simple' pneumoconiosis |
| Baritosis | Barium sulphate | ➲ p. 252, The 'simple' pneumoconiosis |
| Bauxite worker's lung, Shaver's disease | Aluminium | |

## Radiological features

CXR shows small nodular opacities in the lung parenchyma. Distribution depends on the specific disease but tends to affect the upper lobes first.

- PMF is associated with large areas of confluent shadowing, usually starting in the upper zones
- The International Labour Organization (ILO) has devised a classification system for the CXR features of all pneumoconioses.[1] This classification is used to determine severity of disease for compensation purposes, and is based on the size, shape, and distribution of the opacities:
    - size: small round opacities *p* (up to 1.5 mm), *q* (1.5–3 mm), or *r* (3–10 mm). Irregular small opacities are classified by width as *s*, *t*, or *u* (same sizes as for small, rounded opacities)
    - profusion (frequency) of small opacities is classified on a four-point major category scale (0–3), with each major category divided into three, giving a 12-point scale between 0/– and 3/+
    - large opacities are defined as any opacity >1 cm that is present in a film. Large opacities are classified as category A (for one or more large opacities not exceeding a combined diameter of 5 cm), category B (large opacities with combined diameter >5 cm, but not exceeding the equivalent of the right upper zone), or category C (larger than B)

## Natural history

Natural history, clinical features, and radiological appearance vary according to the specific mineral exposure. Some conditions always follow a benign course (stannosis, siderosis), others are often aggressive (asbestosis), and coal worker's pneumoconiosis (CWP) can follow either a benign or a progressive pattern.

## Management

There is usually no specific treatment. Management is to remove from exposure and treatment of advanced disease is supportive.

## Compensation

Pneumoconiosis is prescribed for IIDB (D1) in those who have been exposed to the appropriate mineral at work. In general, pneumoconiosis would have to be at least ILO category 2 on CXR for an employee to be eligible for benefits.

1 International Labour Office (ILO) (2011). *Guidelines for the Use of the ILO International Classification of Radiographs of Pneumoconioses*, rev edn. ℘ http://www.ilo.org/safework/info/publications/WCMS_168260/lang–en/index.htm

# Coal worker's pneumoconiosis

CWP is a form of pneumoconiosis caused by exposure to coal dust, characterized pathologically by collections of coal-laden macrophages in the lung parenchyma, surrounded by fibrosis and localized emphysema.

## Epidemiology

- The onset of CWP lags behind exposure by >10 years, and so incidence and mortality reflect past exposures and working conditions
- *Mortality is declining in developed countries*:
  - new cases are uncommon in the UK because of improved dust control and the decline in coal mining
  - cases are still common in China and there is a low, but significant incidence in India
- *In the UK*:
  - more than 65% of new cases occur in those who have reached retirement age (>65 years), although in the past miners would develop symptoms in their thirties and forties
  - published incidence data are based on claims for IIDB. Compensation is well established in the industry. An average of 251 cases/year prescribed for IIDB 2005–2010

## Clinical features

Severity of disease varies according to local conditions, including composition of the coal (proportional content of silica and other minerals) and its surrounding strata. It is also related to total cumulative respirable dust exposure.

## Simple CWP

- Often asymptomatic
- Minor impairment in ventilatory capacity is difficult to distinguish from the effects of cigarette smoking

## Complicated CWP

- *PMF*: development of large or confluent solid fibrotic nodules in the lung parenchyma. Cavitation and necrosis can occur in larger lesions, leading to expectoration of tarry black sputum (melanoptysis). Local emphysema can develop
- Dyspnoea and productive cough

## Comorbidity

It is accepted that COPD develops in parallel with fibrosis in coal miners. They are also at risk of silicosis. It can be difficult to distinguish silicosis other than at autopsy, as the radiological features are similar.

## Causal exposures/industries

- *Coal mining*: the dustiest jobs give rise to the highest risk (face work, roof bolting, drilling holes for shot placement)
- Coal trimming and transportation

## Individual susceptibility

A rare complication of CWP is described in miners who are rheumatoid factor +ve. Large cavitating parenchymal nodules develop at relatively low dust exposure levels (Caplan's syndrome).

## Diagnosis

- History of chronic exposure to coal dust
- *Lung function*:
  - simple CWP: normal $FEV_1$ and FVC, but transfer factor can be reduced
  - PMF: ↓ $FEV_1$ and FVC with restrictive pattern, or obstruction if widespread emphysema has developed, transfer factor ↓
- *X-ray findings*: nodular opacities, predominantly in the upper zones (see ➲ p. 216, The pneumoconiosis, for ILO classification of radiographic changes)

## Prognosis

- Simple CWP is benign in most cases
- Prognosis in complicated CWP is variable. Severe disease can be debilitating. Life expectancy can be normal, but some develop life-limiting cor pulmonale
- There is no increased risk of lung cancer or emphysema with CWP
- The effect of exposure to cigarette smoke is additive

## Prevention

Exposure controls in the mining industry including ventilation, dust reduction measures, and use of PPE.

## Health surveillance

Miners must undergo regular CXRs at 4-yearly intervals. Those in whom early signs of CWP are detected should be removed from exposure.

## Compensation

CWP is prescribed (D1) for IIDB (see ➲ p. 242, Coal worker's pneumoconiosis) in those who have been exposed chronically to coal dust in mining or above ground.

## Relevant legislation

- The Control of Substances Hazardous to Health Regulations 2002 (as amended)
- The Coal Mines (Control of Inhalable Dust) Regulations 2007. Available at: http://www.legislation.gov.uk/uksi/2007/1894/contents/

# Asbestosis

This disease is characterized by chronic pulmonary interstitial fibrosis, resulting from exposure to asbestos (in particular amphibole fibres).

## Epidemiology

- The disease develops after a long latent period of 25–40 years following exposure
- There is a clear dose–response relationship, and asbestosis tends to occur in those who have been exposed heavily
- *In Great Britain*:
  - although exposures have improved, the incidence is still increasing due to historical exposure. Claims for IIDB rose from 405 in 1999 to 1,015 in 2010
  - industries most commonly cited in IIDB claims are construction, extraction, energy, water supply industry, and manufacturing
  - 189 deaths due to asbestosis were recorded in 2009[1]

## Clinical features

- Gradual onset of dyspnoea and cough
- Basal crepitations on auscultation
- Finger clubbing in 40% of cases

## Individual susceptibility

Smoking is associated with ↑ severity and rate of deterioration of asbestosis.

## Clinical assessment and diagnosis

- Lung function typically shows ↓ $FEV_1$ and FVC with a restrictive pattern, although obstructive or mixed patterns can occur
- ↓ Transfer factor
- *Radiographic investigations*:
  - CXR shows fine nodular shadowing predominantly in the lower zones. Other hallmarks of asbestos exposure (pleural plaques) may be present
  - because CXR is relatively insensitive for early disease, high-resolution CT scanning is often used to confirm the diagnosis
- Lung biopsy is the gold standard for diagnosis, showing interstitial fibrosis and asbestos bodies

## Treatment and prognosis

- No specific intervention can halt the disease
- Patients should be advised to stop smoking
- Treatment is supportive in the later stages
- Up to 40% of patients progress after removal from exposure
- The correlation between CXR findings, lung function, and clinical progression is poor
- The risk of lung cancer is increased

1 Based on death certifi cates, where asbestosis was the main cause of death.

## Other aspects

For causal exposures/industries, prevention, compensation, legislation, and further sources of information, see ➔ p. 240, Asbestos-related diseases.

## Further information

HSE (2022). Asbestos-related disease statistics, Great Britain 2022. Available at: https://www.hse.gov.uk/statistics/causdis/asbestos-related-disease.pdf

# Silicosis

This is a pneumoconiosis associated with exposure to respirable crystalline silica. Silica is encountered mainly as crystalline quartz, a component of igneous rocks.

## Epidemiology

- There is a long latent period between exposure to silica and onset of disease
- The risk of disease varies according to level of exposure
- Silicosis is now rare because of substitution and controls in mining

## Clinical features

There are three recognized types of silicosis:

- *Acute*: early onset of dyspnoea and dry cough within a few months of heavy exposure to fine dusts (e.g. sand-blasting). CXR shows patchy small airway consolidation (appearance similar to pulmonary oedema). Progression over 1–2 years, with respiratory failure
- *Subacute*: gradual onset of dyspnoea and dry cough over years after moderate exposure. CXR shows upper- and mid-zone nodular fibrosis, with classical feature of 'egg-shell' calcification of the hilar lymph nodes. PMF can occur, with coalescence of the fibrotic nodules. Restrictive pattern of impaired lung function
- *Chronic*: slow development of nodules on CXR over many years after low-level exposure

Silicosis is associated with larger nodules on CXR and more rapid progression than CWP with which it may coexist. However, with the exception of eggshell calcification, silicosis can be difficult to distinguish from CWP clinically and radiologically in dual exposed cases.

↑ Risk of infection with tuberculosis (thought to be due to impairment of phagocytosis in the lung). Characterized by cavitation on CXR.

## Causal exposures/industries

- *Mining*: silica is often contained in surrounding strata in coal and other mineral mines. Tunnel drillers/blasters, roof bolters, transportation crew are at highest risk (although face workers and others are also exposed)
- *Quarries*: workers who blast, cut, and transport stone
- *Stone-working*:
  - stone-masonry (granite dressing and grinding)
  - flint-knapping
- *Heavy engineering and manufacture*:
  - shot blasting
  - preparation and use of grinding wheels/stones (historically, cutlers)
  - use of compressed airlines to clean off silica-containing material
- *Foundries*:
  - sand-moulding
  - shot-blasting
  - compressed air cleaning of moulded items
  - fettling
- Ceramics and pottery making
- Brick making

## Prognosis and treatment

- No specific intervention halts progression
- Remove from further exposure
- Regular examination of sputum for tubercle bacilli; confirmed infection is treated with standard anti-tuberculous chemotherapy
- 10–30% of silicosis cases progress after removal from exposure

## Health surveillance

Health surveillance (respiratory questionnaire, lung function tests, and CXR) is required for those who are exposed above a defined threshold exposure (despite control measures).

## Prevention

Control of exposure is through substitution with low-silica sand for moulding and shot-blasting, dust control measures (ventilation, suppression), and use of RPE. See ➲ p. 59 for workplace exposure limit (WEL).

## Compensation

Silicosis is prescribed (D1) for IIDB (see ➲ p. 243, The pneumoconiosis) in those who have been mining, quarrying, or working with silica rock or dust (sand).

## Relevant legislation

The Control of Substances Hazardous to Health Regulations 2002 (as amended)

## Further information

HSE (2013). *Control of exposure to Silica dust. Leaflet INDG463*. Available at: https://www.hse.gov.uk/pubns/indg463.pdf

HSE (2004). *Silica, Construction Information Sheet No 36 Revision 1*. HSE Books, Sudbury. Available at: http://www.hse.gov.uk/pubns/cis36.pdf

# Berylliosis

Beryl is a hard crystalline ore (aluminium beryllium silicate), found in the strata of mines dug for other purposes. Beryllium is an extremely hard metal, producing useful alloys when mixed with copper and other metals. The metal, oxide, and soluble salts are all extremely toxic.

## Epidemiology

Berylliosis is extremely rare (because of elimination from industrial use).

## Causal exposures/industries

- Because of its extreme toxicity, the previous widespread use in fluorescent light tubes and the ceramic industry has been eliminated
- However, it is still used in the nuclear industry and in the production of X-ray tubes

## Clinical features

There are two main forms of disease.

*Acute*

- Follows inhalational exposure to high levels of the dust of soluble beryllium compounds
- Severe bronchoalveolitis with tissue necrosis
- High fatality rate within a few days
- Progression to subacute phase, with tissue scarring, in the survivors

*Subacute/chronic*

- Only a proportion of those exposed (<5%) develop the disease
- Florid non-caseating granulomata heal by fibrosis, with disruption of the normal lung architecture
- Progression to diffuse interstitial fibrosis, leading to respiratory failure, is usual
- CXR shows fine nodular shadowing and hilar lymphadenopathy
- Lung function tests show a restrictive deficit
- ↓ Transfer factor

Differential diagnosis is from sarcoidosis, which has similar clinical and CXR features.

## Treatment and prognosis

Treatment is with high-dose oral corticosteroids. Treatment can be tailed off but needs to be prolonged for many months in chronic cases. Relapse can follow early cessation of therapy.

## Prevention

Prevention is by elimination, or by containment, ventilation (with filtering of discharged air), and fastidious use of PPE.

## Compensation

Chronic beryllium disease is prescribed for IIDB (C17) in those who are exposed to beryllium and its compounds.

# Kaolin pneumoconiosis

Kaolin (china clay) is a multilayered particulate containing aluminium hydroxide and silicon oxide. Formed from the action of water on granite and commonly contaminated by silica-containing compounds.

## Epidemiology

- Historically, this was variable in different kaolin mining regions because of differing levels of contamination and extraction methods
- Generally, low incidence in the exposed populations gave rise to a belief that contaminating silica was responsible for lung disease in kaolin workers
- It is now accepted that kaolin itself can cause pneumoconiosis

## Clinical features

- Asymptomatic, or mild exertional dyspnoea
- Mild ↓ FVC
- CXR shows small nodular opacities consistent with interstitial fibrosis
- PMF can occur
- No specific treatment

## Causal exposures/industries

China clay mining.

## Prevention

Prevention is by dust abatement measures.

# The 'simple' pneumoconioses

These disorders are all relatively uncommon.

## Exposures

- *Siderosis*:
  - exposure to iron ore (haematite)
  - iron ore mining
  - welding (mild steel)
  - classic finding of red lungs at autopsy
- *Stannosis*: exposure to tin ore
- *Fuller's earth pneumoconiosis*:
  - occurs in workers who extract clay material
  - traditional use of fuller's earth to clean wool
  - results from exposure to a mixture of silicates of sodium, potassium, aluminium, and magnesium
- *Baritosis*: exposure to barites in mining, processing, or handling
- *Gypsum pneumoconiosis*: exposure in open-cast or deep mining, and production of plasterboard

## Clinical features

- Asymptomatic
- Benign course
- Normal lung function
- Small, rounded opacities on CXR (appearance similar to CWP)

## Prevention

Prevention is by dust suppression and ventilation and use of PPE.

# Lung cancer

## Epidemiology

- Lung cancer is the second most common cancer in the UK and leading cause of cancer mortality worldwide
- 90% of lung cancers are related to smoking
- The proportion of lung cancer deaths attributed to occupational carcinogen exposure (including all established (International Agency for Research on Cancer (IARC) Group 1) and probable (IARC Group 2A) human carcinogens) in the UK has been estimated at 14.5% (attributable fraction in men 23.2% and in women 5.7%)
- 200 awards of IIDB for new cases of lung cancer associated with asbestos exposure or asbestosis were made in the UK in 2018
- The interaction between smoking and both asbestos and nickel are multiplicative (or between additive and multiplicative)

## Clinical features

Clinical presentation is very variable and some patients present with metastatic features rather than the effects of local disease. The most common features are:

- Unexplained haemoptysis
- Cough
- Dyspnoea
- Chest pain
- Weight loss
- Fatigue
- Appetite loss

## Causal exposures and industries at risk

**Table 7.4** Occupational Lung Carcinogens identified by IARC

| Occupational causes of lung cancer | ***Sufficient*** evidence of carcinogenicity in humans | ***Limited*** evidence of carcinogenicity in humans |
|---|---|---|
| Exposures | Silica dust, Asbestos (all forms), Arsenic, Beryllium, Bis(chloromethyl ether BCME, Cadmium, Chromium (VI) compounds, Coal tar pitch, Diesel exhaust fumes, Nickel compounds, Second-hand tobacco smoke, X-ray and gamma radiation, Radon, Soot | Acid mists, Benzene*, Cobalt metal with tungsten carbide, Creosotes, diazinon, Hydrazine |
| Occupations | Acheson process, Aluminium production, Coal gasification, Coke production, Iron/Steel founding, Painting, Rubber production, Welding fumes | Bitumen application, printing processes, Carbon electrode manufacture, Frying, Insecticide (non-arsenical) spraying and application |

## Clinical assessment and medical management

- Investigation and staging involve CXR, CT, bronchoscopy, and biopsy
- Treatments may include one or more of chemotherapy, radiotherapy, surgery, chemoradiotherapy (chemotherapy with radiotherapy), immunotherapy, and symptom control treatment

Biological therapies have improved survival outcomes of advanced stage non-small cell lung cancer

## Prognosis

- Survival depends on factors such as the type of cancer, stage, and comorbidities
- Overall, 5-year survival is around 10%

## Health surveillance

No valid clinical occupational health surveillance techniques have been proven to reduce morbidity or mortality from lung cancer in occupational groups.

Nevertheless, under the COSHH regulations employers are required to maintain an individual 'health record' for every employee potentially exposed to known or suspected carcinogens. This record may be limited to basic demographic and exposure data. However, where Schedule 6 of COSHH may apply formal periodic medical assessment may be required.

## Prevention

Prevention in the workplace is through exposure control.

## Compensation

Primary carcinoma of the lung is prescribed for IIDB in those who have:

- Worked underground in a tin mine, exposed to BCME, or zinc, calcium, or strontium chromates (D10)
- Worked with asbestos in defined circumstances (D8)
- Been exposed to crystalline silica in defined industries (D11)
- Worked before 1950 in the refining of nickel (C22(b))
- Been exposed to fumes, dust, or vapour of arsenic or arsenic-containing compounds (C4)

## Relevant legislation

An employer who is notified of a current employee diagnosed with a cancer attributed to an occupational exposure is required to report this to the HSE under RIDDOR 2013

COSHH Regulations 2002 (as amended)

## Further information

HSE. *Index of Data Tables*. HSE Books, Sudbury 2021. Available at: http://www.hse.gov.uk/statistics/tables/index.htm

HSE. *The Burden of Occupational Cancer in Great Britain, HSE Research Report RR931*. HSE Books, Sudbury 2021. Available at: https://www.hse.gov.uk/research/rrhtm/rr800.htm; IARC https://monographs.iarc.fr/agents-classified-by-the-iarc/

# Pleural disorders

## Benign pleural disorders

*Pleural plaques*

These are the most common sequelae of asbestos exposure, occurring in up to 50% of an exposed population:

- Can occur after low-level exposure
- Discrete areas of pleural thickening ± calcification
- Latent period of 20–30 years after exposure
- No evidence that the plaque lesions are pre-malignant
- Usually asymptomatic; rarely mild dyspnoea if sufficiently extensive to restrict expansion of the underlying lung
- Lung function usually normal

*Diffuse pleural thickening*

- Dose-related, usually after heavier exposures
- Extensive poorly circumscribed areas of adhesion in the parietal pleura and fibrosis in the visceral pleura
- Often symptomatic (chest pain and exertional dyspnoea), and can be associated with restrictive lung function tests
- CXR shows extensive shadowing (>25% of chest wall affected) ± obliteration of the costophrenic angles
- Surgical treatment is difficult and the results are often unsatisfactory
- Important differential diagnosis is mesothelioma; investigation (biopsy) is required in an attempt to exclude malignancy

*Benign pleural effusion*

- Dose-related, usually after heavier exposures
- Usually develops within 10 years of exposure
- Typically asymptomatic
- Pleural aspiration and biopsy to exclude malignancy
- No evidence of progression to mesothelioma

## Mesothelioma

Mesothelioma is a diffuse malignant tumour that arises in the pleural, peritoneal, or (rarely) pericardial lining.

*Epidemiology*

- Asbestos exposure is the single major cause (>90% mesotheliomas)
- Any asbestos type can cause the disease, but the risk is highest with amphibole fibres
- Long latency between exposure and disease of 15–60 (mean 40) years

► Unlike asbestosis, there is no dose–response relationship. There is no threshold below which there is no risk, but the risk is very small at low exposure levels. Mesothelioma has occurred in workers' spouses who have washed contaminated work clothes.

*In Great Britain*

- Applications for IIDB have risen steadily in the past 10 year (640 in 1996 to 1895 in 2010) and continue to rise
- Deaths due to mesothelioma have steadily from 153 in 1968 to 2,321 in the year 2009.[1] It has been estimated that annual deaths will peak in the year 2016, with 2,100 per annum. The highest mortality occurs in geographical areas where shipbuilding or railway engineering were common (Dumbartonshire and Clyde; Tyne and Wear; Portsmouth, Southampton, and Plymouth; and Eastleigh, Doncaster, and Crewe, respectively)

*Clinical features*

- Usually presents with pleural effusion
- Chest wall pain and dyspnoea
- Rarely presents with ascites, pericardial effusion, or encasement syndromes
- CXR (or CT) shows:
  - pleural effusion
  - pleural mass or thickening ± free fluid
  - local invasion of chest wall, heart, or mediastinum
  - concomitant pleural plaques or pulmonary fibrosis (minority)

*Treatment and prognosis*

- Surgical intervention (pleurectomy) is offered in some cases
- *Palliative treatment*: drain effusions, pleurodesis
- Typically, fatal over 1–2 years

## Other aspects

Causal exposures/industries, prevention, compensation, legislation, and further sources of information are covered in ➔ p. 240, Asbestos-related diseases.

1 Mesothelioma age standardized death rates per million by region, time period, and sex.

# Nasal disorders

## Sinonasal cancer (SNC)

Cancer of the nasal passages has been noted to have an occupational association since early descriptions in nickel workers in the 1920s, furniture makers in the 1960s, and workers in the boot and shoe manufacturing industry in the 1970s.

*Epidemiology*

- SNC is rare with about 400 cases diagnosed per year in the UK of which a third is attributable to occupation. There are less than 150 deaths per year from SNC and nasal cavity is most affected. Squamous cell carcinoma is the commonest histological type, but the rarer Nasal Adenocarcinoma and hardwood have one of the strongest (500-fold risk) occupational associations ever recorded
- <6 cases per year are awarded IIDB due to cancer of the nasal cavity

*Causal exposures/industries*

- *Leather and wood dust in*:
  - boot and shoe manufacture
  - furniture and cabinet making
- Isopropyl alcohol manufacture
- Nickel/chromium compounds
- Formaldehyde
- Organic solvents

*Clinical features*

- Blood-stained nasal discharge
- Unilateral nasal stuffiness/obstruction
- Facial pain
- Facial numbness

*Treatment*

- Usually an Multi-Disciplinary Team (MDT). Commonest intervention is an endoscopic skull base surgery followed by radiotherapy

*Compensation*

Primary cancer of the nose or paranasal sinuses is prescribed for IIDB:

- In those who worked before 1950 in the refining of nickel (exposure to oxides, sulphides, or water-soluble compounds of nickel) (C22 (a))
- In those working in the repair and manufacture of wooden goods or footwear; or exposed to wood dust during the machine processing of wood (D6 (a–d))

## Other nasal disorders

- Chronic rhinosinusitis (CRS) is also associated with paper metal and organic dusts, mould and damp, animal and cleaning work. CRS typically presents with nasal blockage or discharge (+/− facial pain and anosmia) for >3 months. Can be allergic and accompanied by nasal polyps. Chronic hypertrophic rhinitis, nasal mucosal atrophy, and nasal polyps have been associated with woodworking
- Nasal septal ulceration associated with long-term exposure to chromates (work with dyes, tanning agents, and chromium-plating tanks)

## Prevention

Prevention is through exposure control:

- enclosure with exhaust ventilation
- portable tools with dust extraction
- use of respiratory PPE
- portable tools with dust extraction
- use of respiratory PPE

## Further information

HSE. *COSHH and Woodworkers*. HSE Books, Sudbury. Available at: https://www.hse.gov.uk/coshh/industry/woodworking.htm

## Further information

HSE (2022). ). Wood dust: Controlling the risks. Information Sheet No 23 (revision 3). Available at: https://www.hse.gov.uk/pubns/wis23.pdf

HSE (2007). *COSHH and the Woodworking Industries*. Available at: http://www.hse.gov.uk/pubns/wis6.pdf

# Laryngeal cancer

Laryngeal cancer has been associated with some carcinogens that are used in occupational settings. There were 1,830 registrations for laryngeal cancer in 2017 (0.6% of all cancer registrations). It is the commonest head and neck cancer and strongly associated with alcohol and smoking.

## Causal exposures/industries

- Asbestos (see ➲ p. 240, Asbestos-related diseases, for list of industries)
- Mustard gas (also carcinoma of the pharynx)
- Nickel and nickel compounds (nickel refining)
- Strong inorganic acid mists (e.g. sulphuric acid) (these are used widely in industry)
- Rubber industry and polycyclic aromatic hydrocarbons
- Textile industry
- Isopropyl alcohol manufacture

## Clinical features and management

- Hoarse voice (commonest), dysphagia, throat/neck lump, breathlessness, and persistent cough
- *Surgical treatment*: 5-year survival for Stage 1 disease is 90% tailing off to 60% for stage 3

## Prevention

Generic exposure control measures.

## Relevant legislation

- See ➲ p. 240, Asbestos-related diseases

# Occupational voice disorder

## Epidemiology

- US statistics suggest that 25% of employees critically rely on their voice for their work. Occupations such as teachers, tour guides, Islamic officials, clergymen, sport coaches, drill instructors, radio broadcasters, street vendors, singers, theatre performers, to name a few are at higher risk of heavy vocal demands
- Voice disorders are common in the general population, with more than 50,000 GP referrals to ear, nose, and throat (ENT) clinics annually on account of dysphonia and is estimated to affect one in 13 adults annually
- In some occupations having common respiratory symptoms can impair ability to undertake the task requirements of the job but does not mean that the job causes the voice disorder

## Clinical features

Voice disorders, whether caused or impacting on occupation, present with the same symptoms, i.e. aphonia, hoarseness, dry throat, repeated clearing of the throat, weak voice, vocal fatigue, breathiness, and a lack of vocal projection.

## Occupational causes

Development of voice disorders is often multifactorial and non-occupational risk factors include age, gender, allergies, respiratory disease, alcohol abuse, smoking, hydration stress, and gastroesophageal reflux disease. The following general features of work increase the risk of voice disorders:

- Excessive voice use, e.g. frequently shouting
- Poor upper body posture
- Work in contaminated environments (such as those involving exposure to dusts, vapours, and fumes)

Dissatisfaction and occupational stress are also associated with increase in voice disorders. The literature contains many studies linking voice disorders to specific occupations, but most are cross-sectional and do not prove causation. Teachers are over-represented in outpatient attendances for voice disorders.

This is no evidence that voice disorders are *caused* by teaching as it may indicate that if there is a voice condition then the job of teaching is more difficult and prompts access for medical advice.

## Prevention

Prevention involves:

- Work design, e.g. ensuring shorter scripts for call centre workers
- *Workplace design*:
  - reduce ambient noise to prevent the need to talk-over colleagues in offices
  - classroom design
  - adequate humidity and ventilation
- *Education and information*: individuals who rely on their voice for their job need to be provided with advice on prevention:
  - avoid shouting and highly charged explosive speech
  - ensure adequate hydration
  - use aids such as microphones

## Clinical assessment and diagnosis

An individual who has had a hoarse voice for longer than 2–3 weeks should be referred to a multidisciplinary service to primarily exclude malignancy. Usually an ENT specialist will carry out an initial assessment, but once malignancy is excluded, follow up is with a speech therapist. The cornerstone of management is education about:

- Vocal hygiene
- Exercises
- Advice on breathing

## Compensation/legal aspects

Civil litigation has been pursued and been successful in some jobs, e.g. call centre workers, but a review by the Industrial Injuries Advisory Committee found insufficient evidence for inclusion as an industrial injury.

## Further information

Williams N, Carding P (2005). *Occupational Voice Loss*. Taylor & Francis, Boca Raton.

# Coronary heart disease

Little is known about occupational risks for coronary heart disease (CHD), except for established links with certain toxins (including carbon disulphide ($CS_2$) nitro-glycerine, and carbon monoxide (CO)), extreme heat and cold, exposure to tobacco smoke, depression, and occupational stress (50% increased risk of CHD). Other occupational hazards potentially related to CHD include noise exposure at work, shift work (linked to disruption of circadian rhythms with a 40% increased risk of CHD), and physical activity at work (either too much or too little). While in general more physical activity results in less heart disease, heavy lifting (in occupational and nonoccupational settings) has been associated with increased risk of heart attack.

## Individual susceptibility

- In the UK, one in five men and one in seven women die from CHD. As of 2017 CHD has a prevalence of 6% among men and 3% among women. Non-occupational risk factors include age, gender, smoking, poor nutrition, social deprivation, physical inactivity, and obesity
- Twin studies proved that the heredity grade of CHD was over 50%
- Numerous genetic variants are associated with an increased susceptibility to CHD
- Screening of common causal variants is an efficient way to predict the individual risk of developing CHD
- Adiponectin has both anti-atherogenic and anti-inflammatory properties with significantly decreased levels seen in patients with CHD. This suggests that adiponectin might exert favourable protection effects against CHD

## Clinical assessment

The investigation of CHD is the same whether occupational risk factors are suspected or not. However, where chemical exposures are implicated, an exposure history is indicated.

## Possible causal exposures/industries

- *Some industrially used chemicals are known cardiotoxins. Both acute and long-term exposures can result in damage to the cardiovascular system:*
  - metals
  - pesticides (2.2 times more likely to have CHD than workers without this exposure)
  - historically, $CS_2$ was heavily used in the viscose rayon industry and high levels affect cardiovascular system.
  - painters may be exposed to methylene chloride ($CH_2Cl_2$) in confined spaces. Metabolism of $CH_2Cl_2$ leads to production of carbon monoxide and thus angina
- *Non-chemical exposures at work:*
  - mentally stressful work with lack of control and effort-reward imbalance
  - low social support at work; injustice or insufficient opportunities for personal development; or job insecurity
  - shift work; or long working week
  - exposure to noise

## Health surveillance

No health surveillance is currently recommended in the UK for workers exposed to job strain or shift work.

## Prevention

- Promoting healthy lifestyles in the workplace and getting staff back into work after a heart problem
- Staff well-being strategies to help introduce lifestyle changes, such as being physically active, giving up smoking, and eating a balanced diet, as lifestyle choices have a direct link to CHD
- *PHE has called to action local authorities, clinical commissioning groups, general practice, pharmacists, and community settings to:*
  - use the NHS Health Check to support early diagnosis and management
  - implement NHS England's RightCare CHD prevention pathway
  - use existing data to make the case for action
  - make positive behavioural changes for preventing CHD
  - raise public awareness of CHD risk factors and opportunistic detection
- For chemical exposures, minimize workplace exposures such as working in well-ventilated areas, utilizing protective equipment such as gloves, eyewear, or respirators, and washing hands or skin encountering hazardous agents
  - Exposure to noise

## Health surveillance

No health surveillance is currently recommended in the UK for workers exposed to job strain or shift work.

## Prevention

- Promoting healthy lifestyles in the workplace and getting staff back into work after a heart problem
- Staff well-being strategies to help introduce lifestyle changes, such as being physically active, giving up smoking, and eating a balanced diet, as lifestyle choices have a direct link to CHD
- *PHE has called to action local authorities, clinical commissioning groups, general practice, pharmacists, and community settings to:*
  - use the NHS Health Check to support early diagnosis and management
  - implement NHS England's RightCare CHD prevention pathway
  - use existing data to make the case for action

# Chapter 8

# Skin disorders

# Dermatitis 1

## Epidemiology

Prevalence data[1] suggest that approximately 16,000 people in the UK have skin problems that are caused or made worse by work. Occupational dermatitis (OD) makes up the greatest proportion of these. Data come from two main sources:

- *Voluntary reporting schemes for dermatologists and occupational physicians (EPIDERM and OPRA)*: the incidence of OD is falling steadily.[2] Of 982 new cases of occupational skin disease reported in 2018, 842 (86%) were due to contact dermatitis. However, this is likely to be an underestimate as mild cases might not present to a dermatologist and many workplaces do not have access to Occupational Health (OH)
- *Industrial Injuries Disablement Benefit (IIBD)*: There has been a considerable reduction in awards in Great Britain in recent years. The annual average of 43 cases over the last 10 years (2009–2018) has reduced to an annual average of 20 cases over the latter 3 years (2016–2018).[3] These are, however, a small proportion of the most severe OD

## Classification

Dermatitis is skin inflammation and can be caused by endogenous eczema or contact from an external irritant or allergen.

### *Endogenous eczema*

An inherited disorder often associated with other atopic conditions such as rhinitis. Not primarily caused by work but may be exacerbated by exposures at work.

### *Acquired occupational contact dermatitis*

- *Irritant contact dermatitis (IrCD)*: skin inflammation from direct contact with environmental irritants, e.g. chemicals, friction, or cold. Reversible impairment of the barrier properties and local inflammation of skin is dose related for mild (chronic) irritants
- *Allergic contact dermatitis (ACD)*: has an immune-mediated mechanism due to a type IV (cell-mediated) reaction. Sensitization can occur within 7–10 days of exposure; usually develops after months or years. Once sensitized, the individual can react to very low-level exposures

Data from EPIDERM for 1996–2018 show that the breakdown of cases of contact dermatitis was approximately 44% irritant, 37% allergic, with the remainder mixed or unspecified.[3] These reported figures likely reflect that ACD is reported more in occupational settings, underestimating the true incidence of occupational IrCD.

## Clinical features

The clinical appearance of dermatitis derives from oedema of the epidermis and inflammatory infiltration in the dermis. Typically, onset is slow and >24 hours after exposure. There may be a temporal relationship to work, with improvement during holidays. IrCD is classically confined to

1 Labour Force Survey 2016/17, 2017/18, and 2018/19. Office for National Statistics, London

2 The Health and Occupation Reporting Network (THOR) scheme.

3 HSE. HSE Books, Sudbury. 2021 Available at: http://www.hse.gov.uk/statistics/

areas of contact, usually the face and hands. With ACD, involvement of eyelids and spread to secondary sites, not directly exposed, is common. Colour pictures of OD available at Health and Safety Executive (HSE) website: https://www.hse.gov.uk/skin/imagelibrary.htm

*Acute features*

- Erythema
- Oedema/papulation
- Pruritis
- Vesiculation
- Exudation/crusting
- Excoriations

*Chronic features*

- Cracking/fissuring
- Dryness/scaling
- Lichenification

*Complications*

2° bacterial infection

## Causal exposures/industries

*Exposures*

Causal exposures often occur in combination. The causal agents most commonly reported during 2014–2018[4] were:

- Soaps and cleaners
- Wet work
- Preservatives
- Personal Protective Equipment (PPE)
- Rubber chemicals and materials
- Nickel
- Fragrances and cosmetics
- Bleaches and sterilizers
- Resins and acrylics

Other causal exposures such as mechanical trauma, radiation, and ultraviolet (UV) light may also occur.

*Occupational irritants*: common irritants include alkalis such as soaps/detergents; acids; hydrocarbons such as oils and petroleum; solvents such as isopropyl alcohol; wet work; and mechanical trauma.

*Occupational allergens*: common allergens include carbamate mix and thiuram mix used in rubber accelerators, epoxy resin in production of plastics and glues, formaldehyde, and nickel.

*Jobs*

Dermatitis can occur in any job, but is particularly common in:

- Health care workers (HCWs)
- Cleaners
- Florists
- Beauticians
- Hairdressing and barbers

4 HSE. HSE Books, Sudbury. Available at: http://www.hse.gov.uk/statistics/

- Agriculture
- Chemical manufacture
- Engineering and machine operatives
- Printing
- Catering roles

## Individual susceptibility

- The response of normal skin to physical and mechanical damage and to irritant agents varies widely in the population
- The risk of sensitization ↑ if the barrier integrity of skin is impaired, e.g. pre-existing skin conditions which lead to ↑ antigen presentation
- Risk of irritation and sensitization ↑ in those with a history of atopy

## Compensation

Non-infective dermatitis is prescribed for IIDB (D5) in workers whose skin is exposed to irritants. Dermatitis and skin ulceration (C30) is prescribed in those exposed to chromic acid, chromates, or dichromates.

## Relevant legislation and further information

- OD is reportable under Reporting of Injuries, Diseases, and Dangerous Occurrences Regulations (RIDDOR). Dermatitis is reportable when associated with work-related exposure to any chemical or biological irritant or sensitising agent. This includes any chemical with the warning 'may cause sensitisation by skin contact', or 'irritating to the skin'.
- HSE (2021). Work related skin disease statistics in Great Britain , 2021. Available at: https://www.hse.gov.uk/statistics/causdis/dermatitis/skin.pdf

# Dermatitis 2: Management

## Clinical investigation and treatment

*Differential diagnosis*

Distinguishing IrCD and ACD clinically, from history and examination, can be very difficult or even impossible. Clues include exposure to a known irritant or sensitizing agent. Exposure to a previously unknown sensitizer should also be considered. Careful enquiry into exposures at home and work is important but does not always identify the cause. While a history of childhood eczema indicates endogenous dermatitis, exacerbation by irritants or sensitizers at work should still be considered.

▶▶ *Skin patch testing* is essential in making a diagnosis. This should include common allergens, medicaments, and agents that are present at work. Patch testing is a specialized procedure and should be carried out by an experienced dermatologist, particularly when investigating rare or possible new sensitizers, as standardized skin patch test reagents may not be available commercially. Care is needed in the standardization of tests in this context, and the interpretation of results. The occupational health team has an important role in:

- Providing dermatologist with a list of possible workplace exposures
- Ensuring that samples of products, excipients, and other potential causative agents are supplied to the investigating clinic

*Treatment*

The treatment of OD is the same as for endogenous eczema—topical emollients and topical steroids.

## Occupational health input

*Advise the employer about primary prevention*

- Substitution of known sensitizing agents with suitable alternatives
- Engineering controls (e.g. enclose computerized cutting operations to reduce contact between cutting oils and the skin of operators)
- Use of PPE (gloves).

⚠ Some components of gloves (typically carbamates and thiurams used as preservatives and accelerants) can themselves cause sensitization.

- Education about the risks and good hand care (see Box 8.1)Manage individual cases
- Facilitate careful clinical investigation and diagnosis
- Reinforce education about good hand care (see Box 8.1)
- Advise about adjustments to work to reduce direct skin contact with irritants or allergens

*Epidemiological surveys*

Sometimes it can be difficult to determine if a single case of dermatitis is occupational. It is useful to ascertain whether there is a higher incidence of dermatitis among the population of employees who have similar dermal exposures. Surveys are also useful for investigating unexplained clusters of cases. It is important to undertake epidemiological investigations ethically and to involve the employees' representatives.

**Box 8.1 Good hand care: steps to ↓ risk of irritant dermatitis**

- Limit wet work—ensure hands are not wet for >2 hours/day or >20 times each day. For potent irritants ↓ these exposure limits
- Avoid wearing gloves for >4 hours/day
- Use tools that avoid wet work or contact with irritants
- Wash hands in warm (not cold or hot) water and dry thoroughly
- Use protective gloves from the start of wet work
- Minimize glove use—induces dermatitis by occluding skin surface
- If protective gloves will be used for >10 minutes wear cotton gloves underneath
- Keep gloves intact and dry inside
- Avoid introducing irritants into the gloves
- Do not wear rings at work—they trap water and contaminants
- Use lipid-rich moisturizing creams at and after work

*Health surveillance*

Skin surveillance is required under the Control of Substances Hazardous to Health Regulations where a significant risk of dermatitis remains after control measures have been introduced. The detail of skin surveillance programmes is covered on ➔ p. 462, Skin surveillance.

OH has a role in:

- Advising employers about the need for and format of surveillance
- Training competent persons
- Follow-up of cases identified by routine surveillance

## Prognosis

- Because IrCD is dose related, it is usually possible to manage by attention to exposure controls outlined here
- ACD can be much more difficult to manage:
  - once an individual is sensitized, they react to very low levels of exposure; elimination of the allergen is not always possible
  - redeployment is sometimes required as a last resort if symptoms cannot be controlled by other means, but the risks of dermatitis need to be weighed carefully against the (often greater) health risks of losing employment completely
  - if the allergen is common in the environment outside work, symptom control is more difficult to achieve

## Further information and guidance

*British Association of Dermatologists Guidelines for Management of Contact Dermatitis* (2017).British Journal of Dermatology. Available at: http://www.bad.org.uk/shared/get-file.ashx?id=4375&itemtype=document

HSE (2004). *Medical Aspects of Occupational Skin Disease*. Guidance Note MS24, 2nd edn. HSE Books, Sudbury. Available at: http://hse.gov.uk/pubns/ms24.pdf

HSE (2015). *Managing Skin Exposures at Work*. HSE Books, Sudbury. Available at: https://www.hse.gov.uk/pubns/priced/hsg262.pdf

HSE (2019). *Skin at Work*. HSE Books, Sudbury. Available at: http://www.hse.gov.uk/skin/index.htm

National Guidelines (2011). *Concise Guidance to Good Practice: Diagnosis, Management, and Prevention of Occupational Contact Dermatitis*. Royal College of Physicians London 2011, Available at: http://www.bad.org.uk/library-media%5Cdocuments%5CRCP-BAD-BOHRF-FOM-HWDU%20Contact%20dermatitis.pdf

# Contact urticaria

## Epidemiology

Data from the specialist physicians reporting schemes[1] show that the annual incidence of reported new cases of occupational contact urticaria has declined from an annual average of 95 cases (1998–2007) to an average of 36 cases per year from 2008 to 2017.

## Clinical features

- *Wheal and flare*: 'nettle rash', itchy skin lumps with erythema:
  - rapid onset within 20 minutes of exposure
  - subsides within hours of exposure (<24)
- *Associated systemic features*: wheeze, Gingival Index symptoms, anaphylaxis

## Allergic contact urticaria

A classical type I (immunoglobulin E (IgE)-mediated) hypersensitivity reaction that occurs when a previously sensitized individual is re-exposed.

*Causal exposures/industries*

- *Exposures*:
  - latex (see ➲ p. 228, Latex allergy)
  - protein allergens, e.g. animal products
  - foods, spices, herbs, food additives (benzoic acid, cinnamic acid)
  - resins
  - disinfectants
- *Industries*:
  - health care
  - rubber manufacture
  - veterinary practitioners
  - food handlers
  - horticulture

*Investigation*

- Skin-prick testing
- Total and specific IgE

*Management*

- Allergen avoidance

## Non-allergic contact urticaria

Typically causes mild local reactions without systemic features. Local release of histamines and bradykinins in response to direct stimulus.

*Causal exposures*

- Certain arthropods, jellyfish, algae
- Nettles and certain seaweeds
- Benzoic acid, ascorbic acid

1 Under The Health and Occupation Reporting Network (THOR) scheme (see ➲ Chapter 34, Routine health statistics).

2 HSE website for colour pictures of urticaria. HSE Books, Sudbury. Available at: http://www.hse.gov.uk/skin/imagelibrary.htm

# Skin cancers

## Epidemiology

- Skin neoplasia is the second most commonly reported form of occupational skin disease[1]
- Skin cancers accounted for 7% of all reported cases in 2018[1]
- Consultant dermatologists reported an annual average of 380 cases of skin cancer from 1998 to 2018, with a decline in cases in the latter decade. Just 67 cases were reported in 2018. This may be attributable to systematic reporting changes rather than a true decline[2]

## Types

- Squamous cell carcinoma
- Basal cell carcinoma
- Melanoma

## Causal exposures/industries

- *Ultraviolet A and Ultraviolet B radiation*: any occupation where work is predominantly outdoors, e.g. agricultural and construction workers
- Ionizing radiation
- *Pulmonary Arterial Hypertensions*: historically an important cause of skin cancer. Now rare because of good hygiene controls
- Arsenic and arsenicals

## Clinical features and management

- Skin nodule; itching or colour change in existing naevi
- Surgical excision

## Prevention

- Education and protection against the sun for outside workers
- Reducing exposure to tar, pitch, and mineral oils through substitution and engineering controls
- Control of ionizing radiation (see ➔ p. 26, Ionizing radiation 4: exposure control)

## Compensation

Primary carcinoma of the skin is prescribed for IIDB (C21) in those who are exposed to arsenic or arsenic compounds, tar, pitch, bitumen, mineral oil (including paraffin), or soot.

## Relevant legislation

- *RIDDOR*: skin cancer attributed to an occupational exposure is reportable
- *EU Directive Optical Radiation*: health surveillance required for exposed workers likely to have health effects

1 HSE (2019). *Skin at Work*. HSE Books, Sudbury. Available at: http://www.hse.gov.uk/skin/index.htm

2 HSE (2019). *Occupational Cancer Statistics in Great Britain*. HSE Books, Sudbury. Available at: https://www.hse.gov.uk/statistics/causdis/cancer.pdf

# Skin pigmentation disorders

## Epidemiology

Occupational pigmentary changes predominantly consist of chemically induced hypo-/depigmentation. Occupational leukoderma/vitiligo is rare in developed countries but more common in developing countries. The most common exogenous hyperpigmentation is post-inflammatory. Darker skin types are more prone to exogenous pigmentary changes.

## Altered skin colour

*Causal exposures*

- Silver and silver salts produce blue-grey skin pigmentation: *argyria*
- Trinitrotoluene causes orange staining of skin
- *A number of other chemicals can cause skin staining*:
  - potassium permanganate
  - fluorescein, etc.

## Hyperpigmentation

The most common exogenous hyperpigmentation is post-inflammatory.

*Causal exposures*

- Pitch, tars; associated with photosensitivity
- Mercury compounds
- Arsenic and arsenicals

## Hypopigmentation (vitiligo)

Can be localized or generalized and is indistinguishable from naturally occurring vitiligo.

*Causal exposures*

- Hydroquinones
- Phenols
- Catechols

*Industries*

- Production workers (antioxidants, glues, dyes, rubber, stabilizers)
- Beauticians, hairdressers
- Health workers
- Farmers

*Screening*

Using a Woods lamp, loss of melanin can be detected before it is apparent in white skin. This method is useful for detection of occupational vitiligo in exposed workers.

## Compensation

Vitiligo is prescribed for IIDB (C25) in those exposed to paratertiarybutylphenol, paratertiarybutylcatechol, para-amylphenol, hydroquinone, monobenzyl, ether of hydroquinone, or mono-butyl ether of hydroquinone.

# Folliculitis and acne

## Epidemiology

Data from the specialist physicians reporting schemes[1] show that reported new cases of occupational folliculitis and acne are declining. The annual average fell from 16 cases per year (1998–2007) to two cases per year (2008–2017), with no new cases reported since 2011.

## Clinical features

*Oil folliculitis*

- Papules and pustular lesions
- Discolouration of the hair follicles
- Comedone formation with marked inflammatory component
- Typically on thighs and forearms

*Coal tar acne*

- Comedone formation
- Photosensitivity
- Skin pigmentation

## Causal exposures

***Oil folliculitis***: cutting oils, lubricants
***Coal tar acne***: coal tar and products used in roofing/civil engineering

## Prevention

The incidence of oil acne has reduced drastically due to better exposure controls, ↓ use of cutting oils, use of safer products, better hygiene.

## Chloracne

Chloracne is a systemic disease with prominent skin involvement.

*Clinical features*

- Pale comedones and cysts (unlike the inflamed lesions of oil acne)
- *Typically on the face*: cheeks, forehead, and neck
- Less commonly on the trunk, limbs, and genitalia

*Causal exposures*

- Chlorinated naphthalenes (used as a synthetic insulating wax)
- Polychlorinated biphenyls (PCBs), e.g. chlorinated dibenzodioxins, dibenzofurans (heat insulator in electric transformers and capacitors)

*Prevention*

The use of PCBs has been greatly restricted in the UK.

## Compensation

Folliculitis/acne are prescribed for IIDB: D5 non-infective dermatitis. Chloracne is now prescribed for IIDB schedule as C33.

1 Under The Health and Occupation Reporting Network (THOR) scheme (see ➜ Chapter 34, Routine health statistics).

# Photodermatitis

Some occupational exposures contain photosensitising agents and can give rise to photodermatitis through interaction with UV light.

## Classification

The reaction can be phototoxic (more frequent) and/ or photoallergic:

- *Phototoxic reactions*: result from direct tissue damage caused by light activation of the photosensitizing agent
- *Photoallergic reactions*:
  - a cell-mediated immune response in which the antigen is the light-activated photosensitizing agent
  - only occurs in previously sensitized individuals
- *Phytophotodermatitis*: a phototoxic reaction from the interaction of UV radiation and photosensitising compounds of some plants

## Clinical features

- *Phototoxic reactions*: generally similar to bad sunburn.
- *Photoallergic reactions*: generally present as eczema, confined to sun-exposed areas of skin in contact with responsible chemical.
- *Phytophotodermatitis*: patchy, streaky phototoxic erythema typically erupts 24 hours after cutaneous exposure to plants containing furocoumarins and sunlight l secondary hyperpigmentation.

## Causal exposures

*Polycyclic aromatic hydrocarbons*

- Coal tar
- Pitch
- Creosote
- *Industries*:
  - gas production
  - coke oven work
  - roofing
  - production of graphite from pitch

*Plants (phytophotodermatitis)*

- *Umbelliferae*:
  - giant hogweed
  - celery, parsnip, parsley etc.
- *Rutaceae*:
  - Citrus spp
  - Bergamot lime
- Some lichens
- Gardeners and grounds men are at risk when handling plants, but particularly when using lawn strimmers

*Others*

- Methylene blue causes dermatitis through a phototoxic reaction

# Scleroderma

Occupational scleroderma is rare.

## Causal exposures

*Inhalation of vinyl chloride monomer (VCM)*

Scleroderma-like changes have been reported in association with exposure to the following:

- Pesticides
- Epoxy resins
- Perchlorethylene and trichloroethylene
- Silica

## Clinical features

Thickened shiny skin on the fingers.

*VCM disease*

Occurs as part of a syndrome which includes the following:

- *Acro-osteolysis*: resorption of the terminal phalanges on X-ray
- *Raynaud's phenomenon*: digital vascular spasm giving rise to blanching in cold conditions
- *Associated features of VCM exposure include*:
  - hepatic fibrosis
  - angiosarcoma of the liver

## Prevention

VCM disease has been virtually eliminated by good hygiene controls (enclosure) in the polyvinyl chloride (PVC) manufacturing industry.

## Compensation

Sclerodermatous thickening of the skin of the hands is prescribed for IIDB C24 (c) in those who are exposed to VCM in the manufacture of PVC.

# Occupational skin infections

Occupation can be a risk factor for skin infection because of either association with environmental conditions that favour microbial overgrowth or exposure to specific organisms.

## Epidemiology

Data from the specialist physicians reporting schemes[1] show that new cases of infective skin disease due to occupation have been declining. The annual average fell from 38 cases per year (1998–2007) to three cases per year (2008–2017), with only four cases reported since 2011.

## Saturation diving

Divers who live for prolonged periods in dive chambers are susceptible to infections of the skin and ear because of the persistently warm humid conditions. *Pseudomonas species* are a particular problem. Prevention of otitis externa requires meticulous aural toilet.

## Zoonotic skin infections

These are a hazard for agricultural workers, veterinary practitioners, abattoir, and fish-processing workers. They include orf, herpes simplex, anthrax, scabies, and Lyme disease.

## Multi-resistant *Staphylococcus aureus*

Persistent carriage of MRSA has been described in HCWs, mainly as nasal colonization on repeated swabbing, and is mostly asymptomatic. While it usually clears with topical antibiotic treatment for the nose and chlorhexidine body washes, true infections (e.g. of skin lesions) are potentially serious and difficult to treat.

▶ Those at increased risk of methicillin-resistant *Staphylococcus aureus* (MRSA) carriage include HCWs with hand eczema or persistent respiratory tract infection (e.g. sinusitis or bronchiectasis).

▶ OH staff and HCWs should be familiar with local policy to reduce the risk of transmission of MRSA.

💣 There is no definitive guidance on exclusion of HCWs at risk of MRSA colonization or infection, or who are chronically colonized. Decisions to restrict from work where there is a high risk of acquiring or transmitting infection to patients (e.g. care of surgical wounds) should be made on an individual basis, based on local risk assessment. There is little hard evidence to guide such decisions, and the risk of legal challenge in the event of loss of employment is significant.

## Compensation

Certain occupational zoonoses that affect skin are prescribed for IIDB: B1(a) anthrax-cutaneous, b2 glanders, and b12 orf.

## Relevant legislation

- Erysipelas is reportable under RIDDOR 2013

1 Under The Health and Occupation Reporting Network (THOR) scheme (see ➲ Chapter 34, Routine health statistics).

# Chapter 9

# Musculoskeletal disorders

# Low back pain

## Epidemiology

- Musculoskeletal disorders are the second most common cause of work-related ill health (prevalence 498,000 workers in 2018/19) resulting into loss of 6.9 million working days (29% of all working days lost attributable to work-related illnesses) in the UK. Around 40% of them were due to back pain (around 200,000 employees)
- Musculoskeletal disorders were the second most common (21%) disabling condition entitled for Personal Independence Payment
- Lower back pain (LBP) has a lifetime prevalence of 60 to 70% in industrialized countries, 1-year prevalence of 15 to 45%, and annual incidence of 5%
- Prevalence highest in the third decade. It increases until the age group of 60 to 65 years and then declines
- LBP was the highest-ranking condition for disability (years lived with disability) in the Global Burden of Disease study 2000–2016
- There has been a reduction in the prevalence and incidence of work-related back pain since 2001/02

## Causal exposures/industries

- *Exposures*:
  - physical (lifting/forceful movement, awkward posture, e.g. bending, twisting, whole-body vibration, or a combination of these)
  - psychosocial (high demand, low control, low job satisfaction)
- *Industries*: exposures are ubiquitous, but LBP is most common in transport and logistics, constructions, agriculture, and clinical health care

## Features and investigation

- Pain radiating to the thigh is common (>40% of cases)
- In most cases, pathology is not defined (non-specific or mechanical LBP). <10% of cases have identifiable pathology, e.g. nerve root compression. <1% of cases have serious spinal pathology
- *Clinical diagnosis*: X-rays and magnetic resonance imaging are not useful in most cases; indicated to distinguish cases of serious spinal pathology. This is mainly done based on clinical markers (red flags; see Box 9.1)
- Conceptual models of LBP recognize the importance of psychological and social factors (bio-psychosocial theme)

## Prevention

Ergonomic risk controls (covered on ➲ p. 10, Vibration 1: whole-body vibration; ➲ p. 136, Lifting and handling; ➲ p. 134, Posture).

## Prognosis

- *Natural history*: most episodes of mechanical LBP are self-limiting:
  - more than 50% of episodes resolve completely within 4 weeks, but up to 20% have some symptoms for a year
  - there is a marked tendency to recurrence; 70% of those with back pain go on to experience three or more attacks
  - 20% of those with LBP develop chronic symptoms
- 50% patients with nerve root pain recover within 6 weeks

- Timescale for return to work (RTW): two-third of patients return within a week; three-fourth within a fortnight and around 84% within a month[1]
- Probability of RTW varies with the length of sickness absence. The longer a patient is off the lower the chance of their return.
- Clinical examination and investigations are poor predictors of disability
- Outcome is strongly influenced by individual psychological, workplace, and cultural factors (see Box 9.1; ➔ p. 286, Work-related upper limb disorders 1)

**Box 9.1 Red flags indicate possible of serious spinal pathology**

Thoracic pain, fever, weight loss, bladder or bowel dysfunction, carcinoma, other illness, progressive neurological deficit, disturbed gait, saddle anaesthesia, age <20 years or >55 years, structural deformity, violent trauma, systemic steroid therapy, IV drug use, and HIV.

***Yellow, blue, and black flags are risk factors for chronicity and disability***

*Yellow flags are psychological and behavioural*
- A negative attitude that back pain is harmful or severely disabling
- Fear avoidance behaviour and reduced activity levels
- Expectation that passive, rather than active, treatment will be beneficial
- A tendency to depression, low morale, and social withdrawal
- Social or financial problems

*Blue flags are occupational psychological factors*
- Poor job satisfaction
- Blaming working conditions
- Adverse job characteristics (heavy work, poor relationships)

*Black flags are organizational and social factors*
- Health benefits or insurance
- Litigation
- Sickness policies

## Management

- Refer those with red flags for urgent clinical assessment
- *Rehabilitation comprises:*
  - encouragement to stay active; early physical therapy; reassurance
  - advise early RTW; risk reduction by job adjustments and job redesign
  - rarely, restriction from work or redeployment
- Early rehabilitation and job redesign to reduce employment costs and litigation

## Relevant legislations

HSE (2016). *Manual Handling Operations Regulations 1992, as amended by the Health and Safety (Miscellaneous Amendments) Regulations 2002*. HSE Books, Sudbury. Available at: https://www.hse.gov.uk/pubns/indg143.pdf

HSE (2009). *Work with Display Screen Equipment: Health and Safety (Display Screen Equipment) Regulations 1992 as Amended by the Health and Safety (Miscellaneous Amendments) Regulations 2002*. HSE Books, Sudbury. Available at: http://www.hse.gov.uk/pubns/priced/l26.pdf

## Further information and guidance

Clinical Standards Advisory Group (1994). *Back Pain and Epidemiology Review: The Epidemiology and Cost of Back Pain*. Her Majesty's Stationery Office, London. Available at: https://www.sciencedirect.com/science/article/abs/pii/0277953695001646

Department of Work and Pensions (DWP) (2020). *Personal Independence Payment: Official Statistics*. DWP, London. Available at: https://assets.publishing.service.gov.uk/government/uploads/system/uploads/attachment_data/file/873332/pip-statistics-to-january-2020.pdf

HSE. *Back Pain*. HSE Books, 2021 Sudbury. Available at: https://www.hse.gov.uk/msd/backpain

HSE (2019). *Work Related Musculoskeletal Disorder Statistics (WRMSDs) in Great Britain, 2019*. HSE Books, Sudbury. Available at: https://www.hse.gov.uk/statistics/causdis/msd.pdf

National Institute for Health and Care Excellence (NICE (2009). Last review 2020 *Low Back Pain and Sciatica in Over 16s. Assessment and Management*. NICE, London. Available at: https://www.nice.org.uk/guidance/NG59

Waddell G (2004). *The Back Pain Revolution*, 2nd edn. Churchill Livingstone, Edinburgh, UK.

Waddell G, Burton AK (2001). *Occupational Health Guidelines for the Management of Low Back Pain at Work: Evidence Review*. Occupational Medicine, London. Available at: https://academic.oup.com/occmed/article/51/2/124/1404175

World Health Organisation, WHO (2013). *Chapter 6.24 Low Back Pain. Priority Medicines for Europe and the World Update Report, 2013*. WHO, Geneva. Available at: https://www.who.int/medicines/areas/priority_medicines/Ch6_24LBP.pdf

World Health Organisation, WHO (2016). *Health Statistics and Information Systems. Disease Burden and Mortality Estimates. Disease Burden 2000–2016*. WHO, Geneva. Available at: https://www.who.int/medicines/areas/priority_medicines/Ch6_24LBP.pdf

# Work-related upper limb disorders 1

## Epidemiology

- Upper limb and neck pain are common. In some surveys, up to 17–20% of people complain of neck–shoulder pain and 20% of hand–wrist pain during the past 7 days
- Many have pain in the absence of clearly defined clinical pathology, but distinct disorders (e.g. epicondylitis, carpal tunnel syndrome (CTS)) each affect 1–3% of older subjects. Such symptoms are often attributed to work
- Estimated incidence of work-attributed upper limb and neck complaints in Britain of 280/100,000 adults/year
- *Prevalence*: in the year 2018/19, 41% of the estimated 0.5 million work-related musculoskeletal disorders were due to upper limb and neck problems leading to loss of around 2.8 million working days

## Clinical features

According to NIOSH, some 165 ICD disease codes should be considered under the umbrella definition of 'work-related upper limb disorders'. Classification is contentious and complex. The surveillance criteria for nine of the more common upper limb disorders (ULDs), as agreed at a UK expert workshop, are listed here (see Table 9.1).

## Clinical assessment and diagnosis

- Diagnosis is based on history and clinical examination
- Median nerve conduction is used if CTS is suspected
- Table 9.1 provides a short guide on diagnostic criteria
- Assessment should cover comorbid non-occupational factors, e.g. trauma, diabetes, rheumatoid arthritis, acromegaly, hypothyroidism

## Medical management

- *For all disorders*: non-steroid anti-inflammatory agents, analgesics
- *Shoulder disorders*: physical therapy, corticosteroid injection, exercise, manipulation under anaesthesia, arthroscopic interventions
- *Neck disorders*: soft cervical collar, physical therapy (heat pad, exercises, ultrasound/short-wave diathermy, massage, transcutaneous electrical nerve stimulation, manipulation, acupuncture)
- *Elbow disorders*: corticosteroid injection, pulsed ultrasound, wrist splint (to prevent wrist dorsiflexion), physiotherapy
- *Tenosynovitis/peritendinitis*: local heat, corticosteroid injection, splinting, surgical decompression of the first extensor compartment +/− tenosynovectomy (chronic cases)
- *CTS*: splinting, local corticosteroid injection, surgical release

## Prognosis

- Acute florid tenosynovitis tends to settle quickly if thoroughly rested
- Frozen shoulder can last for 12–24 months and is resistant to treatment
- Epicondylitis is said to resolve in 8–12 months, but often lasts longer
- Symptoms of CTS can improve if the causal factor is removed, but otherwise tend to become chronic

**Table 9.1** Diagnostic criteria for ULDs proposed by an HSE-convened expert workshop

| Disorder | Diagnostic criteria |
|---|---|
| Rotator cuff tendinitis | Pain in deltoid region + pain on resisted active movement (abduction—supraspinatus; external rotation—infraspinatus; internal rotation—subscapularis) |
| Bicipital tendinitis | Anterior shoulder pain + pain on resisted active flexion or supination of forearm |
| Shoulder capsulitis (frozen shoulder) | Pain in deltoid area + equal restriction of active and passive glenohumeral movement with capsular pattern (external rotation > abduction > internal rotation) |
| Lateral epicondylitis | Epicondylar pain + epicondylar tenderness + pain on resisted extension of the wrist |
| Medial epicondylitis | Epicondylar pain + epicondylar tenderness + pain on resisted flexion of the wrist |
| De Quervain's disease of the wrist | Pain over radial styloid + tender swelling of first extensor compartment + either pain reproduced by resisted thumb extension or positive Finkelstein's test |
| Tenosynovitis of wrist | Pain on movement localized to the tendon sheaths in the wrist + reproduction of pain by resisted active movement |
| Carpal tunnel syndrome | Pain or paraesthesia or sensory loss in the median nerve distribution + one of: Tinel's test positive, Phalen's test positive, nocturnal exacerbation of symptoms, motor loss with wasting of abductor pollicis brevis, slowed nerve conduction |
| Non-specific diffuse forearm pain | Pain in the forearm in the absence of a specific diagnosis or pathology |

- According to one systematic review only a half of new shoulder episodes end in complete recovery within 6 months
- In general, ULDs tend to persist if causal or aggravating factors remain in place. Persistence is more frequent if 'yellow flag' (see Box 9.1) –ve psychological factors are also present

## Further information and guidance

HSE (2019). *Work Related Musculoskeletal Disorder Statistics (WRMSDs) in Great Britain, 2019*. HSE Books, Sudbury. Available at: https://www.hse.gov.uk/statistics/causdis/msd.pdf

# Work-related upper limb disorders 2

## Causal exposures and industries

- ULDs may be caused (or aggravated) by undesirable permutations of force, repetition, duration, and posture, with insufficient recovery time (see Table 9.2) (see also ➔ p. 136, Lifting and handling, ➔ p. 134, Posture, ➔ p. 140, Repetitive work)
- Occupations in which high rates of ULD have been reported include packing, assembly, and food processing
- Psychological risk factors (e.g. low mood, somatizing tendency, job dissatisfaction, negative perceptions about the work environment) are also associated with disease reporting and 'yellow flag' risk factors for persistence.

⚠ All the ULDs labelled as 'work-related' also have non-occupational risk factors. The clinical pattern may be indistinguishable in occupationally and non-occupationally related cases, making attribution problematic in the individual case.

## Prevention

Depending on the risk assessment and context, preventive measures at work may include:

- *Automation, better design of tools, equipment, and work layout*: to make the work easier, the posture better, the forces lower, etc.
- *Environmental measurements*: optimization of temperature, lighting
- *Advice and training*: to promote risk awareness and better working practices. Promoting stretching and exercises during breaks
- *An induction period*: new employees to start out at a slower pace
- *Job rotation/job enlargement*: respite from repetitive work
- *Rest breaks*: to allow recovery time
- *A rehabilitation programme*: to ease affected workers back into productive work
- *Redeployment*: as a last resort in recalcitrant cases

## Relevant legislation and guidance

There are no specific regulations about managing the risks of ULDs, but employers have legal duties under these regulations:

- The Health and Safety at Work Act 1974
- The Management of Health and Safety at Work Regulations 1999
- Work with display screen equipment: Health and Safety (Display Screen Equipment) Regulations 1992
- The Control of Vibration at Work Regulations 2005

HSE provides useful advice on good practice and prevention:

- Managing ULDs in the workplace (INDG171rev3)
- ULDs in the workplace (HSG60)
- Working with visual display units (INDG36)
- Aching arms (or RSI) in small businesses (INDG171rev1)
- The Assessment of Repetitive Tasks tool. Available at: http://www.hse.gov.uk/pubns/indg438.pdf
- A task rotation worksheet. Available at: http://www.hse.gov.uk/msd/uld/art/resources.htm

**Table 9.2** Associations between mechanical factors and ULDs

| Anatomic site | Strong evidence of effect | Some evidence of effect | Insufficient evidence of effect |
|---|---|---|---|
| **Neck and neck/shoulder** | | | |
| Repetition | | + | |
| Force | | + | |
| Posture | + | | |
| Vibration | | | + |
| **Shoulder** | | | |
| Posture | | + | |
| Force | | | + |
| Repetition | | + | |
| Vibration | | | + |
| **Elbow** | | | |
| Repetition | | | + |
| Force | | + | |
| Posture | | | + |
| Several of these three exposures | + | | |
| **Tendonitis of the hand/wrist** | | | |
| Repetition | | + | |
| Force | | + | |
| Posture | | + | |
| Several of these exposures | + | | |
| **Carpal tunnel syndrome** | | | |
| Repetition | +/− | +/− | |
| Force | | + | |
| Posture | | | + |
| Vibration | | + | |
| Several of these exposures | + | | |

Source: NIOSH Publication No. 97–141 (1997).

# Osteoarthritis of the hip and knee

## Epidemiology

- Prevalence of hip and knee osteoarthritis (OA) rises with age
- Prevalence in England among adults aged 45 years and over (2012): hip OA (11%; M > F) and knee OA (18.2%; F > M)[1]
- In the National Joint Registry (2003–2018), OA was quoted as the sole indication for 966,771 (88.5%) of primary hip replacements and 1,148,855 (96.2%) of primary knee replacements[2]

## Clinical features (Hip)

- Pain around the hip (in the groin, buttock, or lateral to the joint), with radiation to the knee in some patients; worse with exercise
- Stiffness of the hip after immobility (e.g. on getting up in the morning and after prolonged sitting)
- Limitation of hip movement, especially internal rotation and flexion
- In severe cases there may be fixed flexion of the joint

## Clinical features (knee)

- Knee and anterior joint pain during standing or walking, going up and down the stairs, difficulty with kneeling and squatting
- Stiffness which may improve with movement
- Night pain, reduced function, and restricted movement when worse
- Sensation of knee giving way; falls. Sometimes locking
- *Signs*: crepitus, effusion, cysts, stiffness, muscle wasting, bony enlargement, and varus/valgus deformity

## Occupational causes

- Hip OA is associated with prolonged standing, heavy physical work, and lifting. Relevant industries: farming, construction, and heavy labour industries
- Repetitive kneeling, squatting, heavy lifting, and climbing increases predisposition to knee OA. Relevant industries include mining, forestry, farming, carpet and floor layer, and construction

## Individual susceptibility

- General risk factors include genetic factors, obesity, weight bearing, joint injury, occupational usage, recreational usage, joint laxity, muscle weakness, and joint malalignment. Women > Men
- Developmental deformities of the hip (congenital dislocation, Perthes disease, slipped femoral epiphysis) can predispose to OA
- Other risk factors include inflammatory joint disease, acromegaly neuropathic conditions such as diabetes

## Clinical assessment and diagnosis

- History of relevant symptoms and associated disability
- *Clinical examination*: to confirm diagnosis and identify limitation of movement and deformities
- *Knee OA*: primarily clinical diagnosis. X-ray features may not correlate symptoms. Arthroscopy if history of mechanical locking

1 Arthritis Research UK and Public Health England birmingham-oa-1.pdf (versusarthritis.org)

2 National Joint Registry https://reports.njrcentre.org.uk/

- *Hip OA*: to look for narrowing of the joint space, osteophytes, and subchondral thickening of bone with cyst formation
- *Additional tests*: may be required to exclude other types of arthritis

## Prognosis

- Tends to progress, but at a variable rate. Spontaneous improvement can happen as OA is a process of repair and regeneration
- *Hip OA*: progressive; may need replacement within 5 years
- *Knee OA*: structural changes non-reversible but symptoms can stabilize or improve in two-third of patients; one-third however, progresses

## Medical management

- *Hip OA*: analgesics; reduction of weight bearing and exacerbating factors; support from walking aid. Hip replacement eventually
- *Knee OA*: analgesics; reduction of weight bearing and exacerbating factors; knees strengthening exercises; swimming and cycling; physiotherapy and weight loss. Arthroscopy and newer techniques for young patients. Replacements for progressive disabling OA

## Occupational health management

- *Before operation*: encourage weight loss; education; moral support. Ergonomic workplace assessment; job adjustment; limitation of standing, walking, climbing, kneeling, squatting; sedentary role
- *Following replacement surgery*:
  - 80–100% patients manage to return to original work. Individual assessment help. Some patients may require permanent relocation
  - Opportunity for a rehabilitated return, motivation, necessity facilitates RTW
  - Post-operative symptoms such as pain, stiffness, and restrictions, age >60, high BMI, physical demand of job, sickness absence, and inconsistent advice from HCWs impeded RTW
- *Timescale of RTW following surgery*: sedentary/admin role: within 4–6 weeks; job involving standing, lifting, and walking (light manual work) 8–12 weeks and heavy manual work 12–26 weeks; failure to RTW by 6 months may indicate poorer prospect of return

## Compensation under Industrial Injuries Disablement Benefit (IDDB)

- *Hip OA*: prescribed disease (A13) for IDDB in people who have worked in agriculture as a farmer or farm worker for at least 10 years
- *Knee OA*: prescribed disease (A14) in coal miners with at least 10 years of service underground and carpet fitters with at least 20 years of service

## Further information and guidance

National Joint Registry for England, Wales and Northern Ireland and the Isles of Man 16th Annual report 2019. Hemel Hempstead 2019, Available at: https://reports.njrcentre.org.uk/Portals/0/PDFdownloads/NJR%2016th%20Annual%20Report%202019.pdf

Public Health England (PHE). *Musculoskeletal Conditions*. PHE, London 2021. Available at: https://fingertips.phe.org.uk/profile/msk/data

# Bursitis

The beat conditions are a group of disorders that comprise bursitis or subcutaneous cellulitis overlying pressure points in the palm, elbow, or knee.

## Clinical features

- *Beat hand*: bruising or tenderness in the palm
- *Beat elbow/knee*: painful localized swelling, with inflammation, and sometimes effusion in the bursa
  - Olecranon bursitis: 'student's elbow'
  - Prepatellar bursitis: 'housemaid's knee'
  - Infrapatellar bursitis: 'clergyman's knee'

## Causal exposures/industries

Repeated local trauma/sustained exposure to friction, pressure, or impact—linked to prolonged kneeling, squatting, and heavy physical work.

- *Prolonged use of hammers, picks, or shovels*:
  - miners
  - road workers
- *Regular elbow trauma/pressure*:
  - mechanics
  - gardeners
  - plumbers
  - roofers
- *Prolonged kneeling*:
  - carpet fitters/tillers
  - joiners/carpenters
  - painters
  - gardeners

## Treatment and prognosis

- Usually self-limiting
- *Reduced activity/minimize ongoing trauma*: rest, ice, simple analgesia may be helpful to alleviate symptoms
- Occasionally require antibiotics (if infected) or local steroid injection

## Prevention

The mainstay of prevention is in improving the ergonomics of physical tasks. Solutions might include attention to working posture, tool redesign, task rotation, frequent rest breaks (see ➔ p. 130, Ergonomics hazards: Overview), and appropriate use of personal protective equipment (e.g. kneeling pads, padded clothing).

## Compensation

Bursitis or subcutaneous cellulitis is prescribed for Industrial Injuries Disablement Benefit (A5, A6, A7) in manual workers who sustain severe or prolonged pressure or friction over the hand, knee, or elbow.

# Chapter 10

# Gastrointestinal and urinary tract disorders

# Hepatic angiosarcoma

## Epidemiology

Primary hepatic angiosarcoma (HAS) is a rare liver tumour, accounting for 0.1 to 2% of all primary liver malignancies. Historically, 25% of cases were associated with occupational exposures or medicinal carcinogens but today most cases have no known aetiology.

## Clinical features

- Mainly non-specific symptoms of liver disease, resulting in late diagnoses. Nine per cent present with manifestations secondary to metastasis
- Common symptoms include abdominal pain, fatigue, weight loss, anorexia
- Examination findings include hepatomegaly, jaundice, ascites, hepatic bruits, oesophageal varices, acute liver failure, fulminant liver failure with encephalopathy and coagulopathy

## Causal exposure/industries

- Vinyl chloride monomer (VCM), used in the manufacture of plastic. In 1974, it was shown to increase the risk of HAS 10- to 15-fold, with a latency period of 9–35 years. With worldwide regulations on its emission, cases have reduced
- Arsenic, found in contaminated drinking water and pesticides, or used in Fowler's solution to treat asthma, psoriasis, and other conditions
- Thorotrast, used as a radioactive contrast between 1928 and 1955. Its widespread use ceased in the 1950s

## Clinical assessment/diagnosis

- Thrombocytopenia, anaemia, leucocytosis on full blood count
- Abnormal liver function tests (LFTs), hypercalcaemia
- Contrast-enhanced ultrasound
- *Hepatic angiography*: vascular lakes with central areas of hypovascularity and peripheral contrast staining
- Computerized tomography/magnetic resonance imaging (CT/MRI) scan:
    - CT scan may show a multifocal tumour with hypo-attenuation; hyper-attenuation to liver suggests haemorrhage into the tumour
    - angiosarcoma is hypo-intense to normal liver on T1-weighted MRI images
- *Liver biopsy*: histology variable within a tumour. Vascular spaces, lined with tumour cells, may or may not be obvious. Risk of haemorrhage and death

## Prognosis

Poor, due to diagnostic challenges, rapid progression, and early metastatic nature. Median survival is approximately 6 months, with only 3% of patients living >2 years.

Hepatic failure and haemoperitoneum are the main causes of death followed by metastatic disease and infection.

## Health surveillance

- Long latent interval between exposure and presentation
- LFTs (alanine aminotransferase (ALT), aspartate aminotransferase) identify hepatic impairment in VCM-exposed workers
- Hepatic ultrasound has been used to identify pre-symptomatic angiosarcoma

## Medical management

Radical surgery with resection is the only curative treatment. Adjuvant chemotherapy with surgery gives the highest chance of cure, with a median survival of approximately 17 months.

Treatment with radiotherapy has been abandoned due to radioresistance.

Liver transplant is contraindicated due to high recurrence rates and poor survival post-transplant; the median survival after transplant is <7 months.

## Prevention

Prevent by limiting exposure to VCM.

## Compensation

Angiosarcoma of the liver is a prescribed disease (C24) for Industrial Injuries Disablement Benefit (IIDB) in those exposed to VCM in the manufacture of polyvinyl chloride (PVC).

## Relevant legislation

- *Control of Substances Hazardous to Health (COSHH) Regulation Schedule 5*: monitor employee breathing zone VCM exposure
- *COSHH Schedule 6*: annual health surveillance by a HSE appointed doctor
- *Reporting of Injuries, Diseases and Dangerous Occurrences Regulations 2013*. Angiosarcoma of the liver is a reportable disease amongst those exposed to VCM

# Hepatic cirrhosis

## Epidemiology

Cirrhosis is a complication of liver disease that involves loss of liver cells and irreversible scarring of the liver. Alcohol and viral hepatitis B and C are common causes of cirrhosis. The global age-standardized prevalence of liver cirrhosis due to alcohol has increased by 16.1%, compared with hepatitis B virus (HBV) (11.9%), hepatitis C virus (HCV) (14.2%), and others (9.9%). Around 50% of patients diagnosed with liver cancer, ranked fifth among all cancers, have liver cirrhosis. A small proportion of cirrhosis may be due to occupational exposure such as halogenated hydrocarbons.

## Clinical features

- *Stage 1*: jaundice, pruritis, fatigue, weakness, loss of appetite, bleeding/bruising
- *Stage 2*: portal hypertension, oesophageal varices
- *Stage 3*: ascites, liver failure
- *Stage 4*: hepatocellular cancer, hepatic encephalopathy, end-stage liver disease

## Causal exposures/industries

- *HBV*:
  - health care workers (HCWs)
- *HCV*:
  - HCWs
- *Alcohol*:
  - transport industry
  - publicans and bar staff
- *Organic solvents*:
  - carbon tetrachloride
  - 1,1,1-trichloroethane

## Clinical assessment/diagnosis

- Liver function tests (LFTs)
- Full blood count and clotting studies
- Hepatitis B surface antigen
- Hepatitis C antibody
- Hepatic ultrasound, CT scan, MRI
- Liver biopsy

## Prognosis

Depends on the cause and disease stage. In patients who have not developed any major complications, the average survival rate is more than 12 years. Once complications such as hepatic encephalopathy supervene, the prognosis is generally poor. Liver transplant is usually required with life expectancy of more than 5 years. Those who are unsuitable for transplantation, life expectancy may be less than 6 months.

## Health surveillance

- Biological monitoring of solvent-exposed workers using urinary metabolites or exhaled breath sampling may be indicated dependent on the risk assessment
- Most patients with cirrhosis, particularly hepatitis B and C, are screened for liver cancer each year or every 6 months with ultrasound examination of the liver and measurements of cancer-produced proteins in the blood, for example, alpha fetoprotein

## Medical management

- See ➲ p. 170, Hepatitis B; ➲ p. 174, Hepatitis C
- Abstinence from alcohol in alcoholic cirrhosis
- *Liver transplant*:
  - post-transplant, 22 to 55% of patients return to some form of active employment
  - age at transplant, pre-transplant employment status, male gender, and functional status are independent predictors of employment post-transplant
  - work ability is impaired by physical fatigue and depression
  - job modifications pre- and post-transplant with education of employers about liver disease and transplant can help maintain work when the patient later becomes decompensated and requires transplant. At this point, partial disability benefits, instead of full disability benefits, may offer the opportunity to retain a job to return to after transplant
  - transplant recipients may choose to stay on disability income for fear of losing financial security and health care access. It is important to remove the barriers that require transplant recipients to choose between health care coverage and work

## Prevention

Preventing exposure to human blood and body fluids—see ➲ p. 118, Human tissue and body fluids.

HCWs and others at risk of hepatitis B should be immunized and their immune status confirmed by measuring hepatitis B surface antibody levels.

## Compensation

Liver fibrosis is a prescribed disease for IIDB in those who have been exposed to VCM in the manufacture of PVC (C24d). Cirrhosis is prescribed in those who have been exposed to chlorinated naphthalenes (C13).

# Acute hepatotoxicity

A number of chemicals are recognized as causing acute hepatotoxicity. Acute liver injury has decreased in high-income countries, given the improvement in health and safety in workplaces achieved over the recent years.

Unpredictable routes of exposure such as breakdown, cleaning and maintenance of machinery, and accidental leakage still occur and new causes of occupational liver diseases will potentially come to light, such as liver silicosis, particulate matter air pollution, and increasing use of nanomaterials.

## Epidemiology

*Common causes of hepatic insult*

- Alcohol
- Metabolic syndrome
- Drug reactions

## Clinical features

- Fatigue
- Weight loss
- Right upper quadrant abdominal pain
- Anorexia
- Nausea
- Jaundice
- Pruritis
- Hepatic encephalopathy

## Causal exposures/industries

- *Chemical industry including*:
  - carbon tetrachloride (CCl4)
  - chlorinated naphthalenes
  - dimethylformamide/dimethylacetamide
  - methylene dianiline
  - polychlorinated biphenyls
  - phosphorus
  - trichloroethylene
- *Painting*:
  - 2-nitropropane
  - xylene
- *Dry cleaning*:
  - perchloroethylene
  - *Pesticides*:
  - *Rocket fuel/munition*:
  - dimethyl nitrosamine

## Mechanism of hepatotoxicity

Exposure may result from inhalation (the most important portal of entry) percutaneous absorption, or accidental ingestion.

Acute chemical hepatotoxicity may manifest itself in three different ways

- *Steatosis (fatty liver)*:
  - steatohepatitis if hepatic inflammation present
  - seen with exposure to dimethylformamide

- *Acute hepatocellular injury (necrosis)*:
  - direct toxicity
  - idiosyncratic reaction (e.g. halothane)
- *Cholestasis (impaired bile flow)*: seen with exposure to methylenedianiline and paraquat

## Clinical assessment and diagnosis

- Clinical examination looking for stigmata of chronic liver disease or alcohol misuse
- *Ratio of liver enzymes*:
  - alkaline phosphatase
  - ALT
  - gamma glutamyl transpeptidase
  - total bilirubin
- *Carbohydrate deficient transferrin*: in suspected alcohol misuse
- Full blood count
- *Clotting screen*: prothrombin time
- Hepatitis B surface antigen and core antibody
- Hepatitis C antibodies
- *Liver ultrasound +/− biopsy*: findings are dependent on the nature of the hepatic insult

## Prognosis

Dependent on the degree of hepatic injury but some cases will progress to cirrhosis.

## Health surveillance

Biological monitoring may be indicated for some agents (e.g. solvents).

## Medical management

- Withdraw from exposure to hepatotoxin
- *Lifestyle changes*:
  - abstinence from alcohol
  - weight loss if obese
- Review workplace risk assessment—further controls may be required

## Compensation

Liver toxicity is prescribed for IIDB in those who are exposed to carbon tetrachloride (C26(a)) or trichloromethane (C27).

# Gastrointestinal cancers

A number of occupational exposures have been identified as suspected causes of gastrointestinal (GI) cancers.

## Oesophageal cancer

*Epidemiology*

Oesophageal cancer accounts for 3% of all cancers.

*Clinical features*

- Dysphagia
- Upper abdominal pain
- Reflux
- Dyspepsia
- Weight loss
- Anaemia
- Vomiting

*Causal exposures and industries*

- X-radiation, gamma radiation [IARC Cat 1]
- Dry cleaning [IARC Cat 2]
- Rubber production [IARC Cat 2]

*Clinical assessment, diagnosis, and treatment*

Upper GI endoscopy, imaging, laparoscopy, and biopsy may be used for diagnosis and staging of oesophageal cancer. Oesophagectomy is the most common treatment if the cancer has not spread. Chemotherapy and/or radiotherapy may be used as an adjunct/neoadjunct to surgery, or for more advanced cancer, where surgery is not indicated.

## Gastric cancer

*Epidemiology*

Gastric cancer accounts for 2% of all cancers.

- Adenocarcinoma is the most common gastric cancer
- Gastric cancer is much more common in Asia (Japan and China) than in Europe
- The annual incidence of gastric cancer is falling
- Men are at twice the risk of gastric cancer as women

*Clinical features*

- Upper abdominal mass
- Dysphagia
- Upper abdominal pain
- Reflux
- Dyspepsia
- Weight loss
- Haematemesis

*Causal exposures and industries*

- Asbestos (all forms) [IARC Cat 2]
- Lead compounds, inorganic [IARC Cat 2]
- X-radiation, gamma radiation [IARC Cat 1]
- Rubber production [IARC Cat 1]

Other suspected associations include crystalline silica, chromium (VI) com pounds, and painting and decorating

## Clinical assessment, diagnosis, and treatment

Investigation of gastric cancer includes endoscopy and biopsy. CT scan may be used to identify metastases. Treatment depends on the stage, and may include surgery, radiotherapy, chemotherapy, or targeted cancer drugs.

## Colorectal cancer

*Epidemiology*

Colon cancer is the third most common cancer.

*Clinical features*

- Unexplained weight loss
- Unexplained abdominal pain
- Unexplained rectal bleeding
- Iron deficiency anaemia
- Change in bowel habit

*Causal exposures and industries*

- X-radiation, gamma radiation [IARC Cat 1]
- Asbestos (all forms) [IARC Cat 2]
- Night shift work [IARC Cat 2]

*Clinical assessment, diagnosis, and treatment*

Investigation of colonic cancer can include digital rectal examination, flexible sigmoidoscopy, colonoscopy, blood carcinoembryonic antigen levels, and/or CT colonoscopy. The outcome of these investigations, alongside tissue biopsy, assist in the staging of colonic cancer. Treatment of colonic cancer may include partial colectomy.

## Epidemiology

Gastric cancer survival is improving and has almost tripled in the last 40 years in the UK. When diagnosed at its earliest stage, 88% survive.

## Prognosis

**Table 10.1** Prognosis for gastrointestinal cancers (Cancer Research UK)

| Cancer | 5-year Survival | | |
|---|---|---|---|
| | Male (%) | Female (%) | Combined (%) |
| Oesophageal | 15 | 15 | 15 |
| Gastric | 19 | 18 | 19 |
| Colorectal | 59 | 58 | 59 |

Cancer Research UK., London 2021, https://www.cancerresearchuk.org/health-professional/cancer-statistics-for-the-uk

## Health surveillance

No valid occupational health surveillance techniques have been proven to reduce morbidity or mortality from GI cancers in occupational groups.

Nevertheless, under the COSHH regulations, employers are required to maintain an individual 'health record' for every employee potentially exposed to known or suspected carcinogens. This may be limited to basic demographic and exposure data.

## Prevention

Prevention of occupationally related GI cancer relies on control of exposure to carcinogens.

## Relevant legislation

COSHH Regulations 2002 (as amended)

# Renal failure

## Acute kidney injury

*Occupational exposures that can cause acute kidney injury*

*Acute kidney injury (AKI) can be caused by:*

- Cadmium (see ➲ p. 72, Cadmium)
- Mercury (see ➲ p. 83, Mercury)
- Lead
- Organic solvents
- Occupationally acquired infections (e.g. leptospirosis)
- Acute heat stress

*Clinical features of AKI*

- Oliguria or anuria
- Nocturia
- Ankle oedema
- Fluid retention
- Impaired appetite
- Tremor
- Fatigue
- Hypertension

## Clinical assessment of renal failure

- Urinalysis
- Urea, electrolytes, and creatinine
- Blood lipids
- Full blood count
- Renal ultrasound
- Intravenous pyelogram (IVP)

## Health surveillance

Health surveillance for nephropathy is only likely to be undertaken in chronic exposure to cadmium and mercury. Cadmium workers should wear appropriate protective equipment and have regular biological monitoring of blood and urinary cadmium levels, with retinol binding protein if levels are persistently elevated. Mercury workers should wear appropriate protective equipment and have biological monitoring of urinary mercury by random sampling.

## Compensation

Kidney toxicity is prescribed (C26(b)) for IIDB in those who are exposed to carbon tetrachloride.

# Bladder cancer

## Epidemiology

- Bladder cancer is the tenth most common cancer in the UK, causing 3% of all cancers (men > women)
- About 5 to 10% of bladder cancer in Europe may be due to occupational exposures
- Smoking is the major risk factor and may account for up to 80% of cases. Where smokers are exposed to carcinogens, it is not possible to distinguish between occupational and non-occupational causes
- Bladder cancer is most common in the elderly and rare under age 40. Therefore, bladder cancer occurring at a young age is a red flag for possible occupational aetiology

## Clinical features

- Unexplained visible or microscopic haematuria
- Dysuria
- Persistent unexplained urinary tract infection

## Causal exposures and industries at risk

**Table 10.2** Occupational bladder carcinogens identified by IARC

| Occupational causes of lung cancer | *Sufficient* evidence of carcinogenicity in humans | *Limited* evidence of carcinogenicity in humans |
|---|---|---|
| Exposures | Polycyclic aromatic hydrocarbons (including: benzidine; 2-naphthylamine; ortho-toluidine; auramine; magenta), arsenic and inorganic arsenic compounds, 2,2′-dichloro-4,4′-methylene dianiline (MBoCA), X-radiation, gamma-radiation | Coal tar pitch, engine exhaust (diesel), tetrachloroethylene, soot |
| Occupations | Dye production (auramine, magenta), painting, rubber production industry, aluminium production | Printing processes, textile manufacturing, hairdressers and barbers, dry cleaning |

## Clinical assessment and diagnosis

- Physical examination
- Abdominal ultrasound; IVP or intravenous urogram; cystoscopy
- *Disease staging*: tumour biopsy, CT urogram, chest X-ray, bone scan

## Prognosis

- A 5-year survival is 54% but is dependent on tumour staging

## Health surveillance

- No valid occupational health surveillance techniques have been proven to reduce morbidity or mortality from bladder cancer in occupational groups
- Nevertheless, under the COSHH regulations, employers are required to maintain an individual 'health record' for every employee potentially exposed to known or suspected carcinogens. This is typically limited to basic demographic and exposure data. However, where Schedule 6 of COSHH may apply (marked * previously), formal periodic medical assessment is required
- Workers should remain subject to follow-up after exposure ceases

## Medical management

- Some 50% of patients undergo surgery as part of primary treatment. Chemotherapy and radiotherapy are also used. All treatments may be used for either curative or palliative effect. Once diagnosed, patients with superficial bladder cancer are followed up with regular cystoscopy at 3- to 6-month intervals

## Prevention

- Improved control of chemical exposures has reduced the incidence of occupational bladder cancer
- Most agents associated with bladder cancer are now banned in the UK (Schedule 2 COSHH, e.g. benzidine)
- Substitution of carcinogenic agents with less hazardous agents

## Compensation

- *Primary neoplasm of the epithelial lining of the urinary tract is a prescribed disease (C23) for IIDB in those involved in the following processes:*
  - manufacture and use of specified aromatic amines
  - 4,4′-Methylene bis-2-choroaniline manufacture for more than 12 months
  - coal tar pitch volatiles produced in aluminium smelting involving the Soderberg process for more than 5 years

## Relevant legislation

- An employer advised of an employee exposed to bladder carcinogens and diagnosed with bladder cancer is required to report the condition under RIDDOR 2013
- COSHH Regulations 2002 (as amended)

# Chapter 11

# Eye disorders

# Eye injuries

## Epidemiology

Occupational eye injuries are common. Men suffer >80% of eye injuries with young men at highest risk. Those using power tools in engineering, construction, and farming are at particular risk.

## Causes

*Trauma (majority blunt)*

Leading to:

- *Foreign body*: note: subtarsal
- Corneal abrasion and foreign body
- Intra-ocular foreign body with complications of infection, retinal detachment, and metal toxicity
- Globe perforation
- *Contusion/blunt injury*:
  - ➲ Hyphaema, ➲ Lens dislocation, ➲ Retinal tear, ➲ Commotio retinae ➲ Globe rupture

*Non-ionizing radiation*

- *Ultraviolet (UV) radiation B (UVB)*: 280–315 nm

*Arc welding*: 'arc eye' or 'welder's flash' especially in bystanders

- Infra-Red; *IR*: note: cataracts in furnace workers and glass blowers
- Lasers
- High-intensity discharge lamps (HIDL)

*Chemicals*

- Acids
- Alkalis, especially penetrating as digest tissue

## Industries/occupations at greatest risk

- Construction
- Agriculture
- Metalworking, especially welding, grinding, shot blasting
- Woodworking
- Transport

## Prevention

- Safe systems of work
- Machinery guards, interlocks
- Dust suppression
- *Enforce use of appropriate eye protection*: goggles, glasses, masks
- Information, instruction, and training

## Clinical assessment and diagnosis

- *Visual inspection*: evert eyelids to identify subtarsal foreign body
- Fundoscopy
- Slit-lamp microscopy
- *Fluorescein staining for suspected corneal abrasions*: fluoresce under blue light
- *Test visual acuity (VA)*: near and distance vision
- X-ray globe to identify retained foreign body

## Medical management

- *Chemical exposures*: copiously irrigate eye thoroughly using normal saline or sterile water. Exposure to strong alkali or acid can be sight threatening (see ➲ p. 831 General principles, Management of chemical exposures to the eye)
- It is important that appropriate first aid facilities including eye-wash stations are present in high-risk work areas. Note: use of chelation agent diphoterine except for hydrofluoric acid burns. Its hypertonic solution can cause reverse flow of contaminated tissue.
- Low threshold for referral to specialist eye unit with slit lamp facility. Use of eye shield, cf. eye patch for transport to hospital

## Relevant legislation

Any injury likely to lead to permanent loss of sight or reduction in sight in one or both eyes in reportable under RIDDOR 2013.

In UK, criteria for being registered blind is VA 3/60 or worse or 6/60 with visual field impairment

Definition of partially sighted in UK is person who is substantially and permanently handicapped by defective vision

## Relevant adaptions at work

Enlarged computer screens and text-to-speech software. (see ➲ Chaps 1 Physical hazards & ➲ 3 Ergonomics)
*Burns Open* (April 2018), 2(2):104–105.

# Conjunctivitis and keratitis

Conjunctivitis may be due to exposure to physical, chemical, or biological agents (e.g. bacteria, viruses). Contact lens wearers at risk of acanthamoeba keratitis.

## Epidemiology

Data from an American workers compensation scheme found:
- Annual incidence of allergic conjunctivitis, 731/100,000 workers
- Annual incidence of keratitis, 723/100,000 workers

## Clinical features

- Severe photophobia
- Lacrimation
- Conjunctival injection
- Headache

## Causal industries and exposures

- *Arc welding*: intense UV-B light from the arc
- Inappropriate use of UV-C lights instead of the required UV-A lights in electric fly killers used in food industry and commercial kitchens: such incidents may affect several workers who develop keratitis and facial erythema. Diagnosis is often delayed by several months
- Acid mists

Hydrogen sulphide ($H_2S$) conjunctivitis occurs at 750 ppm H2S (see ➲ p. 110, Hydrogen sulphide and ➲ p. 838, Hydrogen sulphide poisoning)
- Vanadium pentoxide
- Some organic solvents

*Allergens*, e.g. laboratory animals such as rats and mice, in association with rhinitis: *rhinoconjunctivitis*
- *Ophthalmology*: exposure when examining infected patients may lead to the clinician developing bacterial or viral conjunctivitis
- Sharing microscopes, e.g. in electronics factories, may lead to outbreaks of infectious conjunctivitis

## Diagnosis

*Welder's flash*

History of unprotected eye exposure to arc welding
- *Symptoms develop 6–12 hours post-exposure*:
  - severe photophobia
  - lacrimation
  - headache
- The typical patient is an apprentice who, through ignorance or carelessness, is close to a welder when an arc is struck

*Allergic conjunctivitis*

Based on history of exposure to allergen and specific IgE.

*Infectious conjunctivitis*

Diagnosis by swabs for microscopy, culture, and sensitivity.

## Prognosis

*Welder's flash*: full recovery.

## Health surveillance

None appropriate.

## Medical management

- 'Arc eye' (kerato-conjunctivitis) is treated with topical local anaesthetic drops and a mydriatic
- Bacterial conjunctivitis is treated with topical antibiotics
- There is no consensus as to whether ophthalmologists should work when suffering from conjunctivitis, given the potential to cross-infect patients

## Relevant legislation

An injury at work that caused conjunctivitis and was associated with 7 days' work loss or temporary loss of sight would be reportable under RIDDOR

# Cataract

## Epidemiology

- Worldwide, cataract is the most common cause of blindness
- A number of occupational exposures contribute to this burden
- Penetrating eye injuries are most common in young men and may lead to traumatic cataract

## Causes

- *Non-ionizing radiation*:
  - UV-B (cortical cataract)
  - IR
  - X-ray—interventional radiologists
- Lasers (medical, industrial)
- Electrocution
- Penetrating eye injuries
- Inorganic lead
- Chemicals, e.g. trinitrotoluene, ethylene oxide, methyl isocyanate

## Industries at risk

- Metal foundries
- Arc welding
- Glass blowing
- Printing with use of HIDL

## Investigations

In the event of a disease cluster, an occupational hygiene survey may be undertaken to monitor workplace exposures.

## Health surveillance

There is no regulatory requirement for health surveillance other than those under Ionising Radiation Regulations.

## Medical management and prevention

- *Engineering controls*:
  - interlocks
  - shielding
- *Administrative controls*:
  - information, instruction, and training
  - access controls
- *Personal protective equipment*:
  - safety goggles

## Compensation

Cataract is a prescribed disease (A2) for Industrial Injuries Disablement Benefit in those who have frequent or prolonged exposure to radiation from red-hot or white-hot material.

## Relevant legislation

Any injury likely to lead to permanent loss of sight or reduction in sight in one or both eyes in reportable under RIDDOR 2013

# Retinal burns

## Epidemiology

Retinal burns may occur in the workplace because of the use of high-power lasers (the acronym laser stands for light amplification by the stimulated emission of radiation) or, less commonly, arc welding equipment. Intense exposure to solar radiation (e.g. on snowfields) may also lead to retinal burns.

Lasers are very widely used (e.g. consumer electronics, telecommunications, engineering). However, estimates suggest there are <15 occupational laser injuries per year worldwide, mostly due to exposure to powerful Q-switched industrial or military lasers (see ➲ p.32, Non-ionizing radiation 3: laser).

Lasers can cause photomechanical and photochemical eye injuries as well as retinal burns. Most laser incidents involve macular damage.

## Clinical features

- Blurred vision
- Usually painless

## Causal exposures/industries

- *Research*: nuclear physics
- *Military*: weapon systems
- *Health care*: ophthalmology

## Clinical assessment and diagnosis

- VA and visual fields
- Fundoscopy
- Retinal photography
- Fluorescein angiography

## Prognosis

- Retinal damage due to lasers is permanent
- Outcome depends on the location and size of the burn
- Foveal burns may have a severe effect on VA

## Health surveillance

In the UK, no HSE currently recommended.

## Medical management

Refer on to for specialist ophthalmologist assessment.

## Relevant legislation

- Maximum permissible exposure values for lasers are specified by the International Commission on Non-ionizing Radiation Protection and are set at levels where no harm is likely to occur. Risk assessments under the Management of Health and Safety at Work Regulations 1999 should also consider non-beam hazards such as the use of high-voltage power sources
- The Private and Voluntary Health Care (England) Regulations 2001 govern the use of lasers in the private health sector in England

# Refractive errors

## Myopia

- Corrected by concave lens or surgery

## Hypermetropia

- Corrected by convex lens or surgery

## Astigmatism

- Corrected by cylindrical lens or surgery

## Compound astigmatism

- Combination of myopia or hypermetropia with astigmatism

## Surgical correction of refractive errors

- *Lower refractive errors*: laser-based techniques
- *Higher refractive errors*: lens-based techniques
- *Myopic ablation profile*: flattens central cornea
- *Hypermetropic ablation profile*: central cornea steepened

## Kerato-refractive techniques

- PRK photorefractive keratectomy
- Lasix laser in-situ keratomileusis
- Lasek laser epithelial keratomileusis

## Other techniques include

- Phakic intra-ocular lens
- Refractive lens exchange
- Both procedures are used for larger refractive errors

## Monovision concept

- One eye corrected for distance, other for near sight, either by lens or surgery

# Chapter 12

# Neurological disorders

# Brain cancer

## Epidemiology

Primary brain cancers are relatively rare with an annual incidence in UK adults of 7/100,000 population.

- Although relatively rare, 1° brain tumour is the ninth most common tumour in people of working age
- Most adult 1° brain tumours are supratentorial and are gliomas (85%) primary from lung, breast, bowel, or melanoma
- The incidence of 1° brain tumour increases with increasing age
- *Metastatic brain tumour is much more common than 1° brain tumour*:
  - up to 40% of adult cancer sufferers develop brain metastases

## Clinical features

Patients with a primary brain tumour may present with:

- Headache
- Seizure
- *Focal neurological deficits*:
  - diplopia
  - dysphasia
  - hemiparesis
  - hemisensory deficits
- *Non-focal neurological deficits*:
  - confusion/memory problems
  - visual symptoms
  - ataxia
- *Personality change. Non-focal neurological deficits*:
  - confusion/memory problems
  - visual symptoms
  - ataxia
- grading 1–4 (1 and 2 usually benign)

## Causal exposures/industries

Few occupational risk factors for primary brain tumour have been identified.

- Some studies suggest an increased risk in the petroleum industry

## Clinical assessment and diagnosis

- CT scan with contrast or MRI scan/EEG
- Tumour excision or biopsy will permit histological diagnosis

## Prognosis

Survival for those adults with malignant brain tumour remains poor with 64% mortality in 12 months and 88% mortality by 5 years.

## Medical management (Multidisciplinary teams)

- Surgical excision or biopsy, with/without subsequent local radiotherapy
- Corticosteroids to reduce brain swelling
- Chemotherapy such as vincristine, lomustine, carmustine (BCNU), temozolomide, and procarbazine
- During the immediate phase of diagnosis and management most patients will not be fit for work

## Legislation/guidance

- DVLA. Assessing fitness to drive—a guide for medical professionals. Reference MIS828. DVLA, Swansea. Available at: https://www.gov.uk/guidance/neurological-disorders-assessing-fitness-to-drive#history

# Acute narcosis

Acute narcosis occurs in those workers exposed to solvent vapour or to gases with narcotic action.

## Epidemiology

There is little information regarding the incidence of acute narcosis in the workplace in the UK.

## Clinical features

The features of acute narcosis are those of anaesthesia. If sufficiently heavily exposed, workers will go through the four stages of anaesthesia unless exposure ceases. This is characterized by 'intoxication' leading through stupor to anaesthesia (lack of sensation of pain), then death by respiratory arrest.

Signs and symptoms of narcosis include:

- Euphoria
- Disinhibition
- Aggression
- Dizziness
- Ataxia
- Loss of consciousness
- Apnoea
- Death

## Causal exposures

Exposure to narcotic agents may occur during normal work or following spills or accidents. Rarely, volatile substance abuse may present in the workplace with narcosis.

- *Organic solvents*:
  - glues and adhesives
  - polishes
  - paint or varnish
  - degreasants (e.g. trichloroethylene)
  - printing inks
  - dry cleaning fluids (e.g. perchloroethylene)
- Nitrogen dioxide
- Nitrogen (air divers below 30 m)
- Vinyl chloride monomer

## Clinical assessment and diagnosis

The diagnosis may be made by workmates or the emergency services responding to a reported collapse. History of exposure to narcotic agents such as organic solvents (especially in confined spaces) should alert you to the diagnosis. The features of intoxication can impair self-rescue and awareness during an exposure incident.

## Prognosis

Most make a full recovery. Those workers who suffer hypoxia may sustain long-term damage (e.g. cognitive impairment).

## Emergency medical management

See ➲ p. 830, General principles and contact details for specialist advice, Immediate management of poisoning in the workplace)

- The affected worker, if conscious, may appear drunk
- *If it is safe to do so:*
  - withdraw from exposure
  - remove contaminated clothing
- If respiratory depression is present, administer oxygen

## Relevant legislation

Acute narcosis leading to unconsciousness is reportable under RIDDOR 2013.

# Parkinsonism

Parkinsonism is the term for a group of movement disorders, the best known of which is Parkinson's disease (PD). Degeneration of the dopaminergic neurons of the substantia nigra occurs in PD. The neuropathological hallmark of PD is the presence of Lewy bodies, although this is not unique to PD.

## PD epidemiology

- *Peak age at disease onset*: 65 years
- *Incidence*: 17/100,000 population/year
- *Prevalence*: 1 in 1,000 of population
- *Prevalence*: 1 in 100 of population aged >65 years
- No figures exist regarding the number of cases of PD that may be due to occupational exposures

## PD clinical features

- Tremor
- Rigidity
- Bradykinesia (slow movements)—essential for diagnosis
- Postural instability
- Half of patients show unilateral onset
- Expressionless face
- Shuffling gait
- Cognitive impairment later in illness
- Speech becomes soft and indistinct as disease progresses
- Drooling
- Sleep problems
- 'On–off' phenomenon

## Causal exposures

- Repeated head trauma
- *Pesticides*: no single agent identified as causal
- *Manganese*: parkinsonism, not PD
- Carbon disulphide (CS2)
- 1-Methyl-4-phenyl-1,2,3,6-tetrahydropyridine, very rare

## Industries at risk

- Contact sport especially boxing
- Farming
- Manganese mining, smelting
- Industrial chemistry

## Individual susceptibility

- Tobacco smoking halves the risk of PD
- Familial forms of PD are recognized

## Clinical assessment and diagnosis

- On clinical features and response to L-dopa-containing drugs
- Based on the UK Parkinson's Disease Society Brain Bank Clinical Diagnostic Criteria (the presence of bradykinesia plus one of rigidity, rest tremor, or postural instability)
- Exclude vascular parkinsonism (stepwise progression) or drug-induced parkinsonism

## Prognosis

Progressive deterioration in neurological and cognitive function occurs over several years. Working life may be curtailed by disease progression. The main functional consequences are reduced mobility, dexterity, and stamina.

## Medical management

- *Optimize drug regime*: levodopa (first line for primary motor symptoms), dopamine agonists, and Monoamine Oxidase Type B Inhibitors (MAO-B inhibitors)
- Patients do best when cared for by a neurologist with an interest in movement disorders, reviewed every 6–12 months
- Physical therapy is important, all patients should be seen by physiotherapy
- Support from a specialist PD nurse is helpful for patients and their families
- Depression is common and may go unrecognized

## Compensation

Central nervous system toxicity characterized by parkinsonism is prescribed (C2) for Industrial Injuries Disablement Benefit (IIDB) in those who are exposed to the fumes, dust, or vapour of manganese, or a compound of manganese, or a substance containing manganese.

# Compression neuropathies

Compression neuropathies may occur in jobs where local pressure, high force, or repetition leads to peripheral nerve entrapment. They include the following:

- *Carpal tunnel syndrome (CTS)*: compression of the median nerve within the carpal tunnel at the wrist
- *Cubital tunnel syndrome*: compression of the ulnar nerve at the medial humeral epicondyle or more distally as it goes between the two heads of flexor carpi ulnaris in the forearm
- *Guyon's canal syndrome*: compression of the ulnar nerve at the wrist
- *Radial tunnel syndrome*: compression of the posterior interosseous branch of the radial nerve in the forearm without motor symptoms. Where motor weakness occurs, it is termed posterior interosseous nerve syndrome

## Epidemiology

- CTS is the most common entrapment neuropathy in the upper limb; cubital tunnel syndrome is the second most common
- Radial tunnel syndrome is uncommon
- Twin studies suggest that genetic factors may explain up to half of CTS cases among women
- Prevalence estimates of CTS vary widely, reflecting differing case definitions between studies
- Occupational exposures are only one among a number of risk factors for these conditions. There is an association with hypothyroidism, diabetes, RA & pregnancy

## Clinical features

*Carpal tunnel syndrome*

- Tingling or burning of the thumb, index, middle fingers, and lateral border of the ring finger
- Pain in the hand and wrist, sometimes spreading up the forearm
- Symptoms often worse at night
- Symptomatic relief by shaking the affected limb in the air—'flick sign'
- Thenar wasting
- ↓ Grip strength

## Cubital tunnel syndrome/Guyon's canal syndrome

- Tingling of the little and ring fingers and medial border of the hand
- ↓ Grip strength

## Radial tunnel syndrome

- May be confused with lateral epicondylitis (tennis elbow)
- Maximal tenderness approximately 4 cm below the lateral epicondyle
- Forearm pain without objective weakness
- Pain ↑ by extending the middle finger against resistance

## Causal exposures

- Awkward posture
- High force
- Frequent repetition
- Hand-transmitted vibration

## Individual susceptibility for CTS

- Female gender
- Pregnancy
- Diabetes mellitus
- Obesity
- Hypothyroidism
- RA
- Acromegaly

## Clinical assessment and diagnosis

- A good history is central to the diagnosis of CTS
- *Tinel's test*: pain on percussing the median nerve in the carpal tunnel
- *Phalen's test*: pain reproduced by holding the forearm upright and flexing the wrist for 1 minute
- Nerve conduction studies may be helpful in confirming the diagnosis
- Neither a negative Tinel's test nor normal nerve conduction studies excludes CTS

## Prognosis

- Following surgery to divide the flexor retinaculum, most CTS sufferers will make an excellent recovery
- Time to return to normal work following open or endoscopic CTS surgery is about 7–14 days for sedentary work and 42–70 days for heavy work. Where workplace modifications are available, return to work can be earlier
- Dependent on underlying cause, CTS may develop in the other wrist
- An important differential diagnosis of CTS is hand–arm vibration syndrome (HAVS). Surgery for CTS in a worker with HAVS and symptoms consistent with CTS is unlikely to give complete resolution of CTS symptoms because of digital nerve damage

## Health surveillance

None appropriate.

## Medical management

- Clinical care includes physiotherapy, splinting, and surgical decompression
- Workplace interventions should focus on occupational risk factors
- Task redesign may be required because of ↓ grip strength and dexterity; the advice of an ergonomist may be required

## Prevention

- Task rotation and ↑ automation may be indicated
- Consider tool redesign

## Compensation

CTS is prescribed (A12) for IIDB in those who are exposed to hand-transmitted vibration or repeated palmar flexion and dorsiflexion of the wrist (for at least 20 hours per week for a period or periods amounting in aggregate to at least 12 months in the 24 months prior to the onset of symptoms).

## Relevant legislation

- CTS that is reliably attributable to work is reportable under RIDDOR

# Peripheral neuropathy

Peripheral neuropathies may occur because of occupational exposure to physical agents, neurotoxic chemicals, or zoonoses (e.g. Lyme disease). Physical factors include local pressure leading to compression of a peripheral nerve. Peripheral neuropathy may affect the sensory, motor, or autonomic nerves. A mixed sensory–motor neuropathy is usual, but some agents such as inorganic lead may cause a pure motor neuropathy.

## Epidemiology

Most peripheral neuropathy is not due to occupation—common causes of peripheral neuropathy include diabetes mellitus and connective tissue diseases.

## Clinical features

*Sensory neuropathy*

- Altered sensation (paraesthesia) or anaesthesia
- Patient may describe a *glove and stocking* pattern of altered sensation (as if wearing gloves and stockings)
- Typically, the feet are affected first; with continued exposure the neuropathy may ascend the legs before affecting the hands and arms
- ↓ Vibration perception
- ↓ Thermal sensation
- ↓ Proprioception
- Loss of reflexes
- *Neuropathic pain*: burning pain (worse at night)
- *Allodynia*: non-painful stimuli (e.g. light touch) are perceived as painful
- *Altered skin appearance*: skin becomes shiny, with loss of hair

## Motor neuropathy

- Muscle wasting
- Paralysis
- Fasciculation
- Cramps

## Autonomic neuropathy

Symptoms depend on affected organ:

- Postural hypotension
- Loss of sweating
- Diarrhoea or constipation
- Incontinence (faecal or urinary)

## Causal exposures

- Radiation
- Lead
- Mercury
- Arsenic
- Thallium
- Tellurium (rare)
- Methyl bromide ($CH_3Br$)
- Acrylamide monomer

- *Organic solvents*:
  - n-hexane
  - methyl n-butyl ketone
- *Organophosphates*:
  - tri-orthocresyl phosphate (TOCP)
  - organophosphate insecticides (see ➔ p. 102, Pesticides; ➔ p. 328, Organophosphate poisoning)

## Clinical assessment and diagnosis

- A good history is important in the diagnosis of occupationally acquired peripheral neuropathy
- Neurological examination
- Nerve conduction studies to confirm the diagnosis
- Electromyography to distinguish between muscle and nerve disease
- Nerve biopsy, if taken, may show demyelination, but an axonopathy is more usual in occupational toxic neuropathy. Some agents may cause axonopathy and demyelination

## Prognosis

- After withdrawal from exposure some patients continue to deteriorate for several months
- Over many months, recovery generally occurs (assuming the neurons have survived) but may be incomplete

## Health surveillance

Depends on the agent implicated. For lead, see ➔ p. 472, Inorganic lead.

## Medical management

- Substitute a less hazardous agent in the workplace
- Withdraw the worker from further exposure to the neurotoxin

## Compensation

Peripheral neuropathy is a prescribed disease (C29) for IIDB in those exposed to n-hexane or methyl n-butyl ketone

## Relevant legislation

- Lyme disease in work involving tick exposure is reportable under RIDDOR

# Organophosphate poisoning

Organophosphates (OPs) are used widely as insecticides.

## Epidemiology

- Most cases of acute OP poisoning occur in developing countries
- Worldwide, there are 3 million poisonings from OPs

## Clinical features

Three patterns of illness are associated with OP poisoning.

## Acute OP poisoning

Acute poisoning presents with the symptoms of cholinergic toxicity due to inhibition of acetylcholinesterase (AChE), leading to a failure to break down acetylcholine post-synaptically. 'Ageing' of the enzyme may occur, resulting in irreversible inhibition. Main clinical features of OP poisoning:

- Bronchospasm
- Diarrhoea
- Meiosis (constricted pupils)
- Nausea and vomiting
- Excess lacrimation, salivation, or bronchorrhea
- Urinary or faecal incontinence.

Other effects include:

- *Psychomotor effects*: increasing confusion, anxiety, sleep problems
- *Cardiac arrhythmia*: bradycardia (dizziness, fainting) or tachycardia
- Tremor, muscle fasciculation
- Sweating
- Seizures
- Coma and refractory hypotension (poor prognosis)
- Death (respiratory paralysis or cardiac arrhythmias)

## Intermediate syndrome

- Develops ~12–96 hours after exposure
- Proximal muscle weakness
- Cranial nerve palsies
- Respiratory muscle paralysis
- Death due to respiratory paralysis

## OP-induced delayed neuropathy(OPIDN)

- OPIDN occurs with OPs that inhibit neuropathy target esterase, e.g. TOCP. Nowadays this is only seen following severe OP poisoning
- Gradual onset over several days after acute OP poisoning
- Paraesthesia
- *Distal muscle-wasting*: feet > hands
- Ataxia
- Spasticity

Chronic OP poisoning in the absence of previous acute poisoning is a condition that some attribute to exposure to OPs, e.g. in sheep dipping or aviation. The symptoms reported are similar to chronic fatigue syndrome. However, a causal association with OPs remains unproven.

TOCP is the commonest reported neurotoxin.

## Causal exposures/industries

The main route of exposure is dermal.

- *Agriculture*:
  - pesticide applicators
  - cotton growers
  - market gardening
  - sheep dippers
  - crop-dusting pilots, pesticide loaders
- Agrochemical manufacture
- Terrorism, chemical warfare (sarin, tabun, VX) (see ➲ p. 870, Chemical weapons)

## Clinical assessment and diagnosis

- 5 ml of blood in EDTA tube for measurement of both red cell and plasma cholinesterase in suspected poisoning
- Therapeutic trial IV atropine
- Nerve conduction tests in suspected OPIDN

► AChE level within the normal range does not exclude poisoning.
► The emergency treatment of OP poisoning is covered in ➲ p. 840, Organophosphate poisoning.

## Prognosis

- *Acute poisoning*: resolves over 3–4 days
- *Intermediate syndrome*: resolves over 14 days
- *OPIDN*: depends on severity. Recovery takes place over 6–12 months, but deficits are lifelong if severe.

## Health surveillance

- Pre-exposure red cell and plasma AChE level
- Monthly AChE testing during use of OPs
- Absolute level of AChE is less important than change in level
- Multiple exposures may lead to cumulative depression of cholinesterase levels and presentation with acute poisoning after apparently low-level exposure
- If AChE ↓ 30% from pre-exposure level, examine worker and consider suspension from OP exposure

## Relevant legislation/guidance

BMJ Best Practice OP poisoning. Available at: https://bestpractice.bmj.com/topics/en-gb/852/treatment-algorithm#patientGroup-1-0HSE. *Biological Monitoring of Workers Exposed to Organo-Phosphorus Pesticides*. MS 17. 3rd Edition 2000 HSE Books, Sudbury

Reporting exposure to biocides available at https://www.hse.gov.uk/biocides/reporting.htm

# Hand–arm vibration syndrome

The term 'hand–arm vibration syndrome' has been used to collectively define the disorders thought to be associated with exposure to hand-transmitted vibration. The disorders are categorized into vascular (also known as vibration white finger), sensorineural, and musculoskeletal.

## Clinical features

- *Vascular component*: cold-induced episodic finger blanching, meeting the diagnostic criteria for Raynaud's phenomenon, which include
  - defined episodes of
  - clearly demarcated
  - blanching and/or cyanosis
  - initially affecting distal parts of digits (only rarely affecting the thumbs, and usually when there has been specific exposure of the thumb to vibration)
  - affects the areas most in contact with vibrating parts
  - associated with numbness during the attack
  - may be preceded by feeling of coldness
  - and in recovery phase with pain and paresthesiae (known as hot-aches) and often (but not always) a reactive hyperaemia
- Vibration-induced sensorineural disease is a peripheral sensory neuropathy
- There is a range of opinion regarding the role of vibration in the development of CTS. Although the association with 'use of vibrating tools' has been identified, that may reflect the effect of other factors such as grip and posture as well as/instead of vibration
- Effects on hand function (weakness of grip, poor manual dexterity) that may have a neuropathic or myopathic origin
- Dupuytren's contracture also appears to be common in workers exposed to hand-transmitted vibration
- Those using vibratory tools commonly describe cramps of the digits, hand, and forearms

## Epidemiology

HAVS is common. According to one population survey, there are more than 220,000 cases in the UK and new cases reported to the Health Service Executive (HSE) in the UK exceeded 800 for each year from 2015 to 2018 inclusive. In the same period over 300 cases per year of CTS were reported in those with regular exposure to vibration. Claims assessed among ex-miners from British Coal exceeded 90,000.

## Causal exposures and industries

See ➲ p. 12, Hand-transmitted vibration.

## Clinical assessment and diagnosis

Diagnosis relies on obtaining a careful clinical history in a worker with symptoms post-dating substantial exposure. For the vascular component a diagnosis of Raynaud's phenomenon is required, followed by a judgement that other causes are not likely. Episodic attacks of vascular HAVS (vascular component (VWF)) are seldom witnessed, and cold challenge tests have not been shown to have sufficient sensitivity or specificity.

Diagnosis of the sensory component relies on a history of paresthesiae, often initially associated with tool use, assessment of sensory function, and exclusion of other causes of the reported symptoms. Standardized tests of vibration and temperature sensation may be used.

Vascular and sensory effects are graded separately, according to two three-point scales proposed in 1986 by an expert Stockholm Workshop, and subsequently revised by Lawson et al. (see ➲ p. 806, Clinical assessment of HAVS).

## Medical and occupational health management

General management of HAVS is aimed at avoiding further deterioration of the symptoms, achieved by reduction of further exposure if possible.

- Management of the vascular attacks is primarily aimed at avoidance of local cold exposure and maintenance of core body temperature. Hence the wearing of thermal gloves, warm clothing and hats, avoidance of draughts, and exposure to cold, wet, windy conditions are likely to be helpful. Use of medications is not widely advocated, although calcium-channel blockers may offer some relief. Slow-release medication is recommended to avoid side effects
- Management of the loss of sensation is aimed at ensuring lack of secondary damage and avoidance of progression

## Prognosis

- Until the 1960s the VWF was considered irreversible, but more recent studies show vascular symptoms can improve on withdrawal from exposure, albeit slowly, over several years. Workers with advanced disease are less likely to recover
- The neurological effects do not improve with time, reflecting the damage to nerve endings and small nerve fibres. Stage 3SN disease can be seriously disabling, in terms of impaired hand function, and is the most important avoidable morbidity (the aim should be to prevent progression from early- to late-stage 2SN)

## Prevention

See ➲ p. 12, Hand-transmitted vibration.

## Health surveillance

- In UK, the HSE offer guidance in their document L140
- Under UK legislation, this is required for workers who remain regularly exposed above the EAV A(8) of 2.5 $m/s^2$ despite controls, or others who are, or are likely to be exposed to vibration and where there is a risk to health
- *The aims are*:
  - to aid early detection of symptoms of HAVS
  - and offer advice about further vibration exposure
  - to provide a check of workplace control measures
- The main element is periodic enquiry about symptoms
- Employers are required to maintain health records symptom, being distinct from confidential medical records

## Compensation

- In the UK, HAVS is prescribed for IIDB A11, broadly equivalent to stage 2 v and/ or 3 sn in those who have undertaken a scheduled occupation.[1] CTS is prescribed as disease A12 among those who have been using vibratory tools at the time of onset of symptoms
- *Common law claims are required to meet the diagnostic criteria identified at the Court of Appeal in Montracon vs Whalley, being*
  - relevant exposure to vibration
  - symptoms compatible with the condition, and
  - exclusion of other causes of those symptoms
- Many other European countries compensate VWF on a similar basis

## Relevant legislation

Under the RIDDOR regulations, employers are required to notify to the enforcing authority (HSE or local authority) newly diagnosed cases of HAVS or CTS, in those regularly exposed to vibration cases, and cases where there has been significant worsening of symptoms

1 Social Security (Industrial Injuries) (Prescribed Diseases) Regulations 1985, Schedule 1: http://www.dwp.gov.uk/docs/a4-3851.pdf

# Noise-induced hearing loss

Hearing loss due to occupational noise exposure is, in theory, preventable, but noise-induced hearing loss (NIHL) remains common.

## Epidemiology

- Hearing loss affects 2% of adults of working age in Britain
- Prevalence varies from 1% among 4% aged 16–24 years to 8% among those aged 55–64 years
- HSE estimates that 2 million people in Great Britain have deafness due to occupational noise exposure

## Clinical features

- Reduced auditory acuity
- Tinnitus
- Increasing social isolation as hearing decreases

## Causal industries

- Extractive industries
- Food industry and agriculture
- Entertainment industry
- Armed forces and security services
- Construction industry
- Metal working
- Aviation

## Individual susceptibility

Large variation. Some individuals appear to be especially sensitive to the adverse effects of noise exposure. Others, despite significant noise exposure, have apparently normal hearing.

## Clinical assessment and diagnosis

Noise exposure history (both occupational and hobby exposures):

- DIY
- Music
- Motor sport
- Hunting/target shooting

## Medical history seeking risk factors for hearing loss

- Meningitis
- *Congenital infections*: rubella, cytomegalovirus
- Head injury (fracture of base of skull)
- Ototoxic medication including aminoglycosides (e.g. gentamicin), quinine, salicylates, furosemide
- *Industrial ototoxins*: carbon monoxide, hydrogen cyanide, solvents, heavy metals
- *Ménière's disease*: tinnitus, deafness, vertigo
- Family history of deafness
- Otitis media
- Otosclerosis
- Perforated tympanic membrane

## Examination

- *Examine external ear*: scars (previous surgery)
- *Otoscopy*:
- *Tuning fork testing (512 Hz tuning fork)*:
    - Rinne's test:
        - air conduction (AC) > bone conduction (BC) (Rinne positive) in sensorineural loss or normal hearing
        - bone conduction > air conduction (Rinne negative) in conductive hearing loss (e.g. otosclerosis)
    - Weber's test: lateralizes to affected ear in conductive loss
- *Pure tone AC audiometry*: classical pattern in NIHL is a 4-kHz dip with recovery although peak loss can be anywhere between 3 and 6 kHz (➔ p. 466, Classification of hearing loss and ➔ p. 470, Patterns of hearing loss). Note: screening AC audiometry not diagnostic
- Results of previous audiometry testing should be available when conducting on-going health surveillance
- Auditory evoked response
- Auditory fitness for duty. Due to legal challenges, speech-in-noise testing using a practical assessment of comprehension of speech with standard background noises is used within some security organizations

## Prognosis

NIHL does not progress after withdrawal from exposure. However, the combination of established NIHL and age-related hearing loss (presbyacusis) means that even after withdrawal from exposure, the affected worker's hearing will continue to decline.

## Health surveillance

- Pre-placement audiometry (identifies existing losses) (➔ p. 802)
- Annual testing for first 2 years of employment
- Three-yearly testing after first 2 years if no deterioration

## Medical management

NIHL suggests that the hearing conservation programme has not protected worker's hearing. Exclude other causes of hearing loss.

## Acoustic shock

Note: call centre operators.

## Compensation

NIHL is prescribed (A10) for IIDB for those involved in specified activities. Hearing loss must be at least 50 dB in each ear to qualify.

## Relevant legislation/guidance

HMSO (2005). *The Control of Noise at Work Regulations*. Stationery Office, London. Available at: http://www.legislation.gov.uk/uksi/2005/1643/contents/made

HSE paper. *Current Practice for Health Surveillance for Noise RR966*. 2013, HSE Books, Sudbury

# Chapter 13

# Psychiatric disorders

# Psychoses due to occupational exposures

## Epidemiology

Organic psychosis due to occupational exposures is thankfully unusual, but its very rarity means that the diagnosis may be missed. Historically, exposures in certain industries put workers at risk of organic psychoses or psychiatric effects:

- Mirror silvering (mercury)
- Manganese mining
- Cold vulcanization of rubber ($CS_2$)
- Manufacture of organoleads (tetraethyl lead) for leaded petrol. Note: Outlawed for cars in UK in 2000

## Clinical features

*Manganese madness*

A syndrome of hallucinations, nervousness, insomnia, emotional lability (especially inappropriate laughter), compulsive behaviour, and altered libido.

*Organolead*

Insomnia, anxiety, emotional lability, delusions, and mania. If exposure is severe, death due to encephalopathy may occur.

*Methylmercury (from food intake)*

Depression, emotional lability (including inappropriate laughter), and increased response to stimuli (erethism). Neurological deficits, including coarse tremor, dysarthria, ataxia, visual field losses, and peripheral neuropathy, may coexist.

*Carbon disulphide*

Irritability, agitation, hallucinations, and bipolar illness.

## Causal exposures/industries

- Organic lead (tetraethyl lead, triethyl lead)
- Methylmercury (from action of microbes in inorganic Hg)
- *Manganese*: chronic exposure in manganese mining
- Aluminium (concern about amyloid deposition causing neurodevelopmental toxicity and Alzheimer's)
- Tin (triethyl tin, trimethyl tin)
- *Organic solvents*: e.g. in glues, paints, degreasants
  - carbon disulphide ($CS_2$)
  - styrene: boat building
  - lacquers, varnishes: furniture making
  - microelectronics industry

## Individual susceptibility

*Manganese*: adverse effects generally present in susceptible individuals after 6 months' exposure. The young appear more susceptible.

## Clinical assessment and diagnosis

A history of exposure to any of these agents should alert the treating doctor to the possibility of an organic cause for the patient's illness. Manganese intoxication may present with both psychiatric symptoms and parkinsonian features (see ➔ p. 322, Parkinsonism).

## Prognosis

The psychiatric effects of manganese may be reversible if identified early and exposure ceases.

## Health surveillance

See ➲ p. 474, Organic lead for details of organic lead surveillance.

## Medical management

Withdraw from exposure.

## Compensation

Central nervous system toxicity characterized by tremor and neuropsychiatric disease is prescribed (C5(a)) for Industrial Injuries Disablement Benefit in those who have been exposed to mercury for >10 years.

## Relevant legislation

Control of Lead at Work Regulations 2002 Approved Code of Practice

# Stress 1: Recognition and assessment

## Definition

The emotional and physiological state of disequilibrium that pertains when the perceived demands of life exceed one's perceived ability to cope. Although anxiety is beneficial up to the plateau of optimal functioning beyond this level of anxiety performance deteriorates. (Yerkes–Dodson curve plotting performance vs tension/arousal/anxiety.)

Stress is:

- Natural response to range of challenges or life events
- In some individuals may be a risk factor for poor mental ill health
- Severe type is listed in ICD-11, as post-traumatic stress disorder (PTSD), complex PTSD, prolonged grief disorder, and adjustment disorder (AD)
- In Diagnostic and Statistical Manual of Mental Disorders (DSM-V), as disorders which are precipitated by specific stressful and potentially traumatic events are included in a new diagnostic category, 'Trauma and Stress-Related Disorders', which includes both ADs and PTSD

## Epidemiology

- 12.8 million days lost within UK with cost of £5.2 billion due to reported work-related stress, anxiety, or depression in 2018/19. See Health and Safety Executive (HSE): http://www.hse.gov.uk/statistics/overall/hssh1819.pdf
- Individual, local, organizational, and cultural factors affect the level of reported stress
- Increased reporting stress cases since 2015

## Clinical features

**Individual symptoms**

- Reduced self-confidence
- Feelings of tension and nervousness
- Self-doubt
- Indecisiveness
- Increased irritability
- Fluctuations of mood
- Sleep difficulties
- Poor concentration
- 'Burn-out' from prolonged and excessive stress

**Behavioural changes**

- Increased irritability
- Impulsive behaviour
- Social withdrawal
- Less able to relax at home
- Working more than usual
- Increased use of caffeine, cigarettes or alcohol, addictive drugs, or other substances

⚠ Remember stress is not a defined illness and all these symptoms are non-specific

*Adjustment disorders*

- Mainly anxiety ± depressive symptoms
- Temporal association with an apparent stressor
- Significant impairment of social and occupational functioning is required to establish the diagnosis

## Causal exposures/industries

**The Management Standards**
HSE describes a system to identify risk factors at work (see ➲ p. 146, Organizational psychosocial factors)

- Demand
- Change
- Relationships
- Control
- Role
- Support

Perceived job insecurity and lack of management engagement are powerful aggravating factors.

Workers in several sectors report higher levels of stress, but that does not mean these sectors are more stressful:

- Secondary school teachers
- Health care workers
- Call centre operatives
- Emergency service workers (police in particular)

Sector-specific guidance on risk management is available on the HSE website. http://www.hse.gov.uk/stress/information.htm

## Individual susceptibility

- Previous history of work-related stress
- Coexisting non-work-related stress (e.g. domestic upheavals)
- Previous history of mental health problems
- High alcohol intake
- Excessive personal expectations, type A personality

## Diagnostic assessment

- *Exclusion of psychiatric disorder*: e.g. major depressive illness, generalized anxiety disorder, obsessive–compulsive disorder
- *Identification of potential occupational stressors*: including interpersonal conflict, bullying, harassment, or grievances, by risk assessment
- Identification of non-work stressors
- *Identify current coping strategies*: are they helpful, can they be influenced by individual mentors or training?
- 'PTSD' has very specific diagnostic criteria and the term should not be used if these are not met

## Prognosis

- In general, excellent
- Early intervention critical to successful outcome (see ➲ p. 344, Stress 2: Interventions/risk controls)

## Time off work

- Except in burnout time away from work can be detrimental to recovery of the employee unless the condition interferes significantly with performance at work. As far as possible, with adequate support and adjustments, it is advisable to keep the employee with moderate stress symptoms at work
- If time off work is needed, there should be clarity about reason for absence, return to work process, and how progress will be monitored

## Relevant legislation and guidance

- HSE. Stress at Work Sudbury Available at: https://www.hse.gov.uk/stress/
- HSE (2019). *Tackling Work-Related Stress Using Management Standards Approach* (1WBK01 (2019)). HSE Books, Sudbury. Available at: http://www.hse.gov.uk/stress/standards/
- National Institute for Clinical Excellence (NICE) QS 147 (2017)
- *Protection from Harassment Act 1997*. NICE, London
- http://www.hse.gov.uk/risk/risk-assessment-and-policy-template.doc

# Stress 2: Interventions/risk controls

## Primary (preventing stress in the workforce)

See ➲ p. 146, Organizational psychosocial factors, Risk controls.

- Stressor identification and risk assessment
- Attention to job design
- Skills and leadership training at all levels in the organization
- Flexible working as part of work–life balance programme

## Secondary (preventing recurrence or exacerbation in an individual with work-related stress)

- Attentive and compassionate management
- Cognitive behavioural therapy (CBT)
- Mindfulness-based stress reduction
- Change management
- Assertiveness training
- Time management
- Interpersonal skills training

## Interventions for the individual with work-related stress

Psychological support through occupational health (OH) and employee support programme:

- Confidential self-referral service available to all employees
- Access to clinical psychology
- Therapy techniques aimed at problem solving
- Highly focused individualized approach
- Emphasis on therapeutic benefits of work

*Including round-table discussions*

- Involving employee, OH +/− treating psychologist, patient's manager, and human resources taking a shared problem-solving approach to deal with stress issues. Particularly useful if patient is off work and where interpersonal conflict has complicated the situation
- Enabling early agreement on a graduated rehabilitation programme back to work, establishing job definition, hours and days of work, etc.
- Educating managers on nature of stress-related difficulties and ensuring their commitment to the rehabilitation programme, including preparation of the rest of the team for the employee's return from sickness absence

## Further information and guidance

Calnan M, Wainwright D (2002). *Work Stress: The Making of a Modern Epidemic.* Open University Press, London. Available at: http://www.hse.gov.uk/stress/index.htm.

HSE (2001). *Tackling Work-Related Stress: A Manager's Guide to Improving and Maintaining Employee Health and Wellbeing.* HSE, Sudbury.HSE (2009). *How to Tackle Work Related Stress.* HSE, Sudbury. Available at: http://www.hse.gov.uk/pubns/indg430.pdf.

# Post-traumatic stress disorder 1: Diagnosis and risk factors

## Effects of severe stress

Extremely disturbing events can have marked and sustained emotional effects. Warfare has provided most evidence and generated many diagnoses, including soldier's heart, neurasthenia, and shell shock. The Vietnam War led to PTSD entering the DSM-III (American Psychiatric Association, 1980). The current revision is the DSM-V (American Psychiatric Association, 2013), although the nosology used most frequently in the UK is ICD-11 (World Health Authority (WHO), 2020).[1]

## Epidemiology

- *Prevalence*: rates vary considerably across nations. Epidemiological studies in the UK general population are rare and most data derive from the USA
  - lifetime prevalence for adult general population 6.1–9.2% US and Canada, and 3.9% globally
- *Incidence*: the risk of developing PTSD after a traumatic event 8.1% for ♂, 20.4% for ♀. Younger urban populations report higher incidence (up to 30.2% for ♀ and 13% for ♂)
- *Selected samples*:
  - 6.2% of UK-armed forces deployed to Iraq and Afghanistan
  - 28% of health care workers who have been physically assaulted

## Diagnosis and assessment

⚠ Do not use the term PTSD loosely.

- *ICD-10 Criteria*
  - Victim must have been exposed to a stressful event or situation (either short- or long-lasting) of an exceptionally threatening or catastrophic nature, which is likely to cause pervasive distress in almost anyone
  - Symptoms must include persistent reliving of the stressor, fear and avoidance of circumstances resembling/associated with the stressor, and hyperarousal
- *DSM-V Criteria*:
  - Identifies the trigger as exposure to actual or threatened death, serious injury, or sexual violation. This can be from directly experiencing/witnessing the event, or from learning of it occurring to somebody close. Also cites cumulative exposure as a trigger, particularly relevant to occupational groups such as police, first responders, and military personnel
  - Symptoms are separated into four distinct diagnostic clusters—re-experiencing, avoidance, negative cognitions, mood, and arousal

1 ICD-11 (https://icd.who.int).

*Acute, chronic, and delayed PTSD*

- *ICD-10*: onset follows the trauma with a latency, ranging from a few weeks to months (but rarely exceeds 6 months)
- *DSM-V*: requires only that the disturbance continues for >1 month and removes the distinction between acute and chronic PTSD
- Delayed onset is uncommon; delayed reporting is more common

*Assessment*

- Victims may be reluctant to admit to symptoms for fear of being perceived as weak (especially military and emergency services)
- Victims may find it too disturbing to talk about the event
- Insensitive and premature assessment may lead to re-traumatization

### In addition to clinical interview and mental state examination, there are standardized psychiatric measures

- *Clinician Administered PTSD Scale for DSM-V (CAPS-5)*: highly structured interview used to diagnose PTSD and measure lifetime and current symptom severity and functional impairment
- *Impact of Event Scale–Revised (IES–R)*: a 22-item self-report scale, which assesses frequency of the core symptoms (not diagnostic)
- *Davidson Trauma Scale (DTS)*: a 17-item self-report scale that provides a measure of the severity and frequency of each symptom

## Risk factors for PTSD

No single event will cause PTSD in all exposed individuals. Risk factors include the following:

- *Pre-trauma factors*:
  - premorbid psychological vulnerability
  - previous and/or familial psychiatric history
  - lower education and sociocultural status
  - genetic predisposition, ↑ concordance in monozygotes
  - female gender
  - younger age
- *Trauma and peritraumatic factors*:
  - severity: generally, there is a dose–response curve
  - physical injury: the meaning of an injury is as important as its objective severity
  - level of threat: (perceived) threat of serious injury or to life
  - dissociation: depersonalization, derealization
  - extended or repeated exposure: hostages, prisoners of war, emergency services/first responders
- *Post-trauma factors*: include adverse reactions of others (criticism, rejection, blame), 2° life stressors, lack of support

## Occupations at risk

Sectors likely to expose employees to work-related trauma:

- Military/police/emergency services
- Offshore oil and gas industry
- Heavy industry/construction
- Train drivers
- Non-governmental organizations

# Post-traumatic stress disorder 2: Management

## Early intervention

- *Psychological first aid is a widely agreed paradigm for helping individuals and communities in the acute phase after major calamity, including*:
  - attending to basic needs for food, safety, etc.
  - outreach and dissemination of information
  - facilitating peer, family, and community support
  - emphasis that their experience is 'a normal reaction to an abnormal situation'
- *Active monitoring*: most individuals do not develop PTSD; thus, do not subject all victims to psychiatric treatment or even counselling. Instead, monitor progress and provide treatment for those whose symptoms last >1 month
- *Psychological debriefing for preventing PTSD*:
  - compulsory psychologically focused debriefing is not recommended
  - single session debriefs are neutral or occasionally harmful
- *Workplace support*:
  - crisis management plan providing appropriate information and support, and encouraging an early return to work
  - health surveillance for affected workers

## Formal treatments

PTSD often occurs in the context of comorbidity, especially depression, anxiety, and alcohol abuse. The National Institute for Clinical Excellence (NICE) guidelines endorse the following treatments:

- *Individual trauma-focused CBTs*:
  - cognitive processing therapy
  - cognitive therapy for PTSD
  - narrative exposure therapy
  - prolonged exposure therapy
- *Eye movement desensitization and reprocessing*
- *Pharmacotherapy*:
  - venlafaxine and sertraline for general use
  - antipsychotics in combination with psychological therapies for specialist use
  - some evidence of prazosin in reducing nightmares and improving sleep but only under specialist supervision
- Medication is appropriate if the patient has not responded to, or is unwilling and/or unable to engage in, psychological therapies
- Patients should be advised of side effects and discontinuation/withdrawal symptoms
- A hypnotic may be used in the short term for sleep problems although should be used with caution
- Antidepressants are preferred for chronic sleep difficulties to avoid dependence
- Propranolol and hydrocortisone may have psychoprophylactic properties, but routine use *cannot* be justified

## Prognosis

- Most spontaneous recovery is within the first few weeks
- There may be a re-emergence of symptoms 12 months after the event—the anniversary reaction
- If persistent or recurrent after 12 months, symptoms may run a lengthy chronic course

## PTSD and the law

- *Civil proceedings*: concerns about feigning and exaggeration of PTSD symptoms are common, but evidence suggests that this is not a widespread problem. Symptoms tend not to remit after claim settlement; conversely, prolonged litigation can impair recovery
- *Criminal proceedings*: a PTSD diagnosis may be used to mitigate sentencing or explain the conduct of the accused. However, merely suffering from PTSD does not indicate a causal connection
- *False vs genuine claimants*: PTSD is a self-reported diagnosis; rigorous assessment is essential and should include:
  - clinical interview
  - standardized measures (e.g. performance validity tests)
  - collateral data (e.g. GP and hospital records, police reports)
  - information from others (e.g. spouse)
- *Distinguishing false from genuine symptoms*: genuine claimants display consistent accounts across different settings and at different times. Caution should be exercised when individuals describe their symptoms and experiences in pseudo-technical language that may suggest coaching. In most genuine cases, descriptions of dramatic events are accompanied by appropriate emotional displays (e.g. distress, disgust, anxiety). Reporting of symptoms (e.g. hallucinations and delusions), rarely associated with PTSD, should raise suspicion, as should the reporting of unremitting symptoms: PTSD is a phasic condition with spells of remission and relapse. Genuine claimants do not tend to be uncooperative or suspicious of the examiner, and many minimize their suffering and distress, rather than blame all their difficulties on PTSD.

## Further information

McManus S, Bebbington P, Jenkins R, Brugha T (eds.) (2016). *Mental Health and Wellbeing in England: Adult Psychiatric Morbidity Survey 2014*. NHS Digital, Leeds.

Meze G (2006). Post-traumatic stress disorder and the law. *Psychiatry* 5:243–247.

NICE (2018). *Post-Traumatic Stress Disorder* (NICE Guideline No 116). NICE, London. Available at: https://www.nice.org.uk/guidance/ng116.

Stevelink Sam, Jones M, Hull L, Pernet D, MacCrimmon S, Goodwin L . (2018). Mental health outcomes at the end of the British involvement in the Iraq and Afghanistan conflicts: A cohort study. *British Journal of Psychiatry* 213(6):690–697.

# Chapter 14

# Reproductive disorders

# Impaired fertility

Infertility is defined as a failure to conceive after 12 months of having regular unprotected sex.

- Many factors which can lead to delayed time to pregnancy are not due to reduced fecundity
- Occupational factors which may interfere with reproduction by reducing the opportunity for sexual intercourse, e.g. shift working, long working hours, prolonged absences from home, or chronic stress
- Relatively few occupational exposures have been associated with impaired fertility and usually only in the most exposed. Improved workplace control measures mean that some exposures, such as non-scavenged anaesthetic gases, are only of historical interest
- Some studies have linked environmental oestrogens (polychlorinated biphenyls, phthalates, dioxin, etc.) to recent reductions in male sperm counts

## Epidemiology

- Infertility now affects 15% of couples in developed countries and has almost doubled in the last 20 years
- The ratio of ♀ to ♂ causes of infertility is approximately 2:1 and in 25% of cases a cause cannot be found
- One difficulty in identifying occupational risk factors is that only a proportion of workers are seeking to conceive at any given time. Therefore, detecting reproductive hazards can be difficult
- As sensitive pregnancy tests have become available, it has become apparent that a significant proportion of conceptions do not lead to successful pregnancy

## Clinical factors

*Males*

- *Azoospermia*: no detectable spermatozoa
- Low sperm count
- Reduced or absent libido

*Females*

- Anovulation
- Reduced or absent libido
- Implantation failure
- Abortion

## Causal exposures

The following have been associated with reduced fecundity in those exposed in an occupational setting. Evidence is usually based on cross-sectional surveys and case–control studies.

- *Metals*: lead, mercury, chromium
- *Pesticides*: dibromochloropropane, carbaryl
- *Organic solvents*: carbon disulphide, glycol ethers
- Anaesthetic gases
- Sex hormones
- Ionizing and non-ionizing radiation
- Heat stress

## Industries at risk

- Chemical industry
- Lead smelting
- Farming
- Industrial painting

## Clinical assessment and diagnosis

- *Reproductive history*: establish whether either partner has previously had children to distinguish primary infertility from secondary infertility
- Confirm that the couple are sexually active (shift work, overseas postings, etc.) and that the woman is menstruating
- The occupational history should focus on work with known reproductive hazards, considering likely exposure intensity
- It may be difficult to establish whether workplace factors are responsible for delayed conception, although in 5% an improved sperm count on exposure reduction would support an occupational aetiology
- ♂ Semen analyses should be done on two samples
- ♀ Menstruation suggests ovulation, but check mid-luteal (day 21 of a 28-day cycle) serum progesterone
- Blood test for anti-Mullerian hormone to check for ovarian reserve can be taken anytime in the cycle
- Referral to an infertility clinic for further investigation
- Hysterosalpingogram or diagnostic laparoscopy
- Ultrasound to confirm ovulation may be useful

## Prognosis

Depends on cause. Withdrawal from exposure may allow recovery in some cases.

## Health surveillance

None.

## Medical management

- Women contemplating pregnancy may seek advice from an occupational health professional
- Many couples finding it difficult to conceive will do so within 12-months of presentation without intervention
- Age and family history of early menopause may dictate early investigation
- Assisted reproduction may be necessary in some cases

## Relevant legislation

- HSE (2002). *Control of Lead at Work Regulations. Approved Code of Practice and Guidance*, L132, 3rd edn. HSE Books, Sudbury.
- HSE (2017). *Ionizing Radiation Regulations 2017. Approved Code of Practice and Guidance*, L121, 2nd edn. HSE Books, Sudbury.

# Adverse pregnancy outcomes

Adverse pregnancy outcomes include:
- Spontaneous abortion
- Low birth weight (<2,500 g)
- Pre-term delivery (<37-week gestation)
- Birth defects

## Epidemiology

- Over half of pregnant women are in paid employment
- Between 10 and 20% of pregnancies end in a spontaneous miscarriage
- 60% of congenital malformations have no identified cause
- Attention has focused on maternal factors, but paternal pre-conceptual exposures may be relevant. Further studies are required
- Many studies have examined occupations and occupational exposures and pregnancy outcomes

## Causal exposures

*Chemical hazards*
- *Metals*:
  - lead
  - mercury
- Organic solvents
- Pesticides?

*Physical hazards*
- Lifting
- Heavy physical work
- Prolonged standing
- Ionizing radiation
- Heat
- Physical violence
- Biological hazards

*Infections*
- Rubella
- Toxoplasma
- *Chlamydia psittaci* (enzootic abortion)
- *Coxiella burnetti* (Q fever)
- Parvovirus B19 (fifth disease)
- Measles

## Industries at risk

Several industries have been associated with adverse pregnancy outcomes, but the evidence is inconsistent. Industries implicated include:
- Agriculture
- Health care
- Painting
- Printing
- Firefighting
- *Security services (risk of violence)*:
  - police
  - prison service

## Health surveillance

None appropriate.

## Medical management

The issue of adverse pregnancy outcomes may arise when an employee is pregnant, and the question is asked whether it is safe for her to continue her current role. This is a difficult area as an anxious worker's fears may be realized even where there is no association between her work and adverse pregnancy outcomes. For many work exposures, there is insufficient evidence to offer definitive advice regarding the likely risks.

HSE advises against a number of work activities during pregnancy:

- Diving
- Work at pressure
- Lead work
- Preparation of cytotoxic drugs

Evidence-based guidelines on 'Physical and shift work in pregnancy' found consistent evidence for some adverse pregnancy outcomes in relation to prolonged standing, heavy lifting, and prolonged hours (>40 hours), but the risk was low. On precautionary grounds, they advised employers should reduce pregnant workers' exposure to prolonged standing, heavy physical work, and lifting.

Measures to control exposures should be taken for women potentially exposed to ionizing radiation or hazardous chemicals. If adequate control cannot be achieved, the pregnant worker should be allocated alternative duties or, if this is not possible, should be suspended from work. Note that as pregnancy progresses, the hazards may change (e.g. ergonomic factors in office workers) and the risk assessment should be kept under regular review (see ➲ p. 559, New and expectant mothers and ➲ p. 591, Employment law).

## Relevant legislation and guidance


- HSE (1999). *Management of Health and Safety at Work Regulations 1999*. HSE Books, Sudbury. Available at: http://www.hse.gov.uk/pubns/books/l21.htm
- HSE (2002). *New and Expectant Mothers at Work*, 2nd edn. HSE Books, Sudbury.
- NHS Plus, Royal College of Physicians, Faculty of Occupational Medicine (2009). *Physical and Shift Work in Pregnancy: Occupational Aspects of Management. A National Guideline*. RCP, London.

# Gynaecomastia

- Gynaecomastia is the most common benign breast condition in men
- Breast enlargement may be painless or associated with discomfort
- Galactorrhoea may also occur

## Epidemiology

- The most common causes of gynaecomastia are puberty, obesity, drugs, including anabolic steroid abuse, and medication for HIV
- Rarely, gynaecomastia in ♂ may be due to breast cancer
- Gynaecomastia is present in up to a third of adolescents ♂.

## Clinical features

Gynaecomastia may be bilateral or unilateral.

## Causal exposures

- *Gynaecomastia*:
  - female sex hormone manufacture
  - anabolic steroids (bodybuilders)
- *Pseudo-gynaecomastia*:
  - obesity
  - work requiring repetitive force on chest (rare)

## Industries at risk

- Pharmaceutical industry
- Sex hormone manufacture
- Professional sports especially 'power' sports where misuse of anabolic steroids may be prevalent

## Clinical assessment and diagnosis

Palpable gynaecomastia is common in otherwise healthy males but the palpable breast tissue is generally <5 cm in diameter.

## Prognosis

Most cases settle with withdrawal from exposure.

## Health surveillance

Periodic medical examination is indicated where pharmaceutical workers may be exposed to sex hormones despite workplace control measures.

## Medical management

- If occupationally acquired, withdraw from exposure
- If gynaecomastia fails to settle following withdrawal from exposure to drugs, surgery may be necessary

# Chapter 15

# Haematological disorders

# Bone marrow aplasia

Bone marrow aplasia refers to haematologic conditions that are caused by a marked reduction and/or defect in the pluripotent stem cells, or the failure of the bone marrow to support haematopoiesis. Aplastic anaemia is a bone marrow failure syndrome characterized by bone marrow aplasia and peripheral blood pancytopenia.

## Causal exposures/industries

- *Ionizing radiation*: acute (usually accidental) exposure to a dose of ionizing radiation above ~0.2 Sv produces marrow hypoplasia/aplasia as a deterministic (dose-related) effect
  - nuclear industry
  - medical radiography and nuclear medicine
  - industrial radiography
- *Benzene*: chronic exposure above ~50 ppm produces a range of haematotoxic effects including marrow suppression
  - rubber and shoe industries
  - plastics production
  - explosives production
  - motor vehicle repair

## Clinical features

The clinical features vary according to the severity of stem cell suppression, and the cell lines that are affected (erythrocytes, leucocytes, and platelets), but include combinations of:

- *Anaemia*:
  - fatigue
  - dyspnoea
- *Neutropenia/lymphopenia*: incidence of bacterial infections
- *Thrombocytopenia*:
  - petechiae and ecchymoses
  - gingival bleeding
  - risk of serious bleeds, e.g. renal or GI

### *Radiation exposure*

- Following acute exposures, the peripheral blood lymphocyte count falls within 24–48 hours (because of rapid cell death). Other cell lines are not destroyed immediately. Although unable to divide, damaged neutrophils and platelets can survive for up to 2–3 weeks, and red cells for up to 100 days. Therefore, there is a delay of 1–3 weeks before pancytopenia develops because of failure of replacement from marrow stem cells
- Treatment for victims of serious exposures is intensive multisystem support, transfusions of red cells and platelets, and management of acute infection with appropriate antibiotics. In severe cases, erythropoietin and colony-stimulating factors (e.g. granulocyte-colony stimulating factor, granulocyte-macrophage colony-stimulating factor) are used to facilitate stem cell function. Bone marrow transplantation is possible, but the success rate is very low

- *Prognosis depends on the dose*:
  - dose of ≥1 Sv has a fatality rate of at least 10%; at <1 Sv recovery from a nadir in peripheral blood counts at 4–6 weeks is usual. Normal blood counts re-established 2–3 months after the exposure incident
  - dose of 3–4 Sv has a 50% fatality rate at 30 days post-exposure

## Prevention

Prevention is through fastidious regulatory control of exposure including control of the working environment and work practices, and workplace exposure limits (see ➲ p. 26, Ionizing radiation 4: exposure control; ➲ p. 576, Ionizing Radiation Regulations 1999).

## Health surveillance

- *Ionizing radiation*: 'classified' workers under the Ionizing Radiation Regulations (personal exposure >6 mSv or 3/10ths of any other exposure limit) require baseline medical assessment plus periodic reviews (usually annual) of dosimetry results and sickness absence records (see ➲ p. 576, Ionizing Radiation Regulations)
- *Benzene*: appropriate health surveillance for benzene would be a health record with health checks at regular intervals including urine sampling for benzene, as described in the Control of Substances Hazardous to Health Regulations. Routine periodic screening of haematological indices is probably inappropriate with adequate risk controls

# Anaemia

Anaemia can be caused by several (acute or chronic) occupational exposures, and by some different mechanisms including impairment of haem synthesis, marrow suppression, and haemolysis. Marrow suppression and haemolysis are covered separately in ➲ p. 358, Bone marrow aplasia and ➲ p. 363, Haemolysis.

## Impaired haemoglobin synthesis

*Exposures/industries*

- Lead is the classical occupational exposure associated with impaired haemoglobin synthesis
- *Industries*:
  - lead smelting
  - battery manufacture
  - demolition
  - glass making

## Mechanism

Lead, through its high affinity for binding to sulphydryl groups, inhibits important enzymes in the haem synthesis pathway (see Fig. 15.1).

## Clinical features

- Mild anaemia, which may play little or no part in the fatigue that is commonly associated with lead poisoning
- Hypertension, renal impairment, immunotoxicity, and toxicity to the reproductive organs. The neurological and behavioural effects of lead are believed to be irreversible
- Associated features include palsies due to peripheral neuropathy, arthralgia, and (rarely) confusion due to encephalopathy
- The characteristic finding on investigation is basophilic stippling of erythrocytes on a peripheral blood film
- Suspension level for male lead workers under the Control of Lead at Work Regulations is 60 μg/100 ml and for female workers of reproductive capacity 30 μg/100 ml
- Treatment includes removal from the source of lead and, for people who have significantly high blood lead levels or who have symptoms of poisoning, chelation therapy

## Prevention

Prevention is by substitution and exposure control (see ➲ p. 572, Control of Lead at Work Regulations 2002).

## Health surveillance

Statutory surveillance includes baseline and periodic screening (intervals are specified by individual susceptibility (e.g. women and young people) and exposure level). For health surveillance for inorganic lead, see ➲ p. 472, Inorganic lead.

## Compensation

Anaemia with haemoglobin ≤9 g/dl and a blood film showing punctate basophilia is prescribed (C1(a)) for Industrial Injuries Disablement Benefit (IIDB) in those who are exposed to lead.

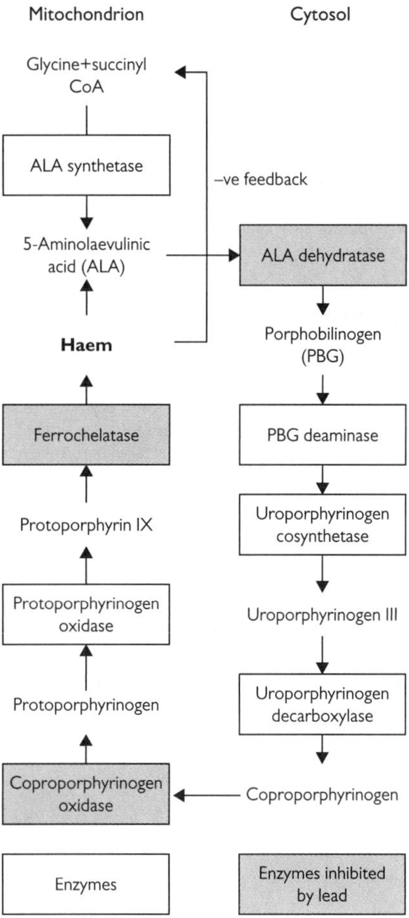


**Fig. 15.1** Haem synthesis.

# Methaemoglobinaemia

Methaemoglobinaemia arises when ferrous ($Fe^{2+}$) haemoglobin is oxidized to ferric ($Fe^{3+}$) haemoglobin, which makes it unable to transport oxygen effectively, resulting in tissue hypoxia. Occupational cases are uncommon, but preventable, with improved provisions for health and safety at workplaces and reduction in the use of known causative chemical agents.

## Causative agents

- Ferricyanide
- Bivalent copper
- Chromates
- Chlorates
- Quinones
- Dyes with a high oxidation reduction potential
- Nitrite, often used as a preservative, is one of the most common methaemoglobin-forming agents
- Aniline dye derivatives

## Clinical features

- Cyanosis unresponsive to oxygen therapy
- Dyspnoea
- Headaches and dizziness
- Muscle weakness
- Peripheral blood film shows mild anaemia and erythrocyte abnormalities (Heinz bodies and punctate polychromasia)
- High methaemoglobin concentration in arterial blood (key diagnostic feature)

## Individual susceptibility

Hereditary methaemoglobin reductase deficiency.

## Treatment

Acute treatment is with methylene blue (methylthioninium chloride), administered by slow IV infusion. Management of acute poisoning is covered in detail on ➲ p. 846, Methaemoglobinaemia (acute treatment).

⚠ Methylthioninium chloride may cause brisk haemolysis in those with glucose-6-phosphate dehydrogenase (G6PD) deficiency.

# Haemolysis

Haemolysis is the process of premature red-blood-cell destruction.

## Clinical features and treatment

- *Acute*:
  - anaemia, haemoglobinuria, leucocytosis, jaundice, methemoglobinemia, hepatic dysfunction, anuric renal failure, cerebral anoxia
  - exchange blood transfusion is lifesaving in severe cases
- *Chronic*:
  - intense focal headache, nausea, low-grade fever, paraesthesia, haemolysis, anaemia, hepatic and renal impairments, and characteristic finger-nail changes (Mee's lines)
  - reticulocytosis due to red cell production is the hallmark of haemolysis

## Exposures

- *Arsine gas*:
  - industries: microelectronics industry (semiconductor manufacture), metal smelting, plating, galvanizing, and soldering
  - effects occur with acute poisoning at exposures >3 ppm for several hours, or >20 ppm for <1 hour
  - chronic low-level exposure can cause anaemia with mild bilirubin
  - diagnosis is based on history of exposure and urinary arsenic
- *Naphthalene*:
  - industries: manufacture of plastics and dyestuffs, mothballs, biocides for the wood industry
  - individuals with G6PD deficiency are particularly susceptible
- *Rare occupational exposures associated with haemolysis include*:
  - potassium chlorate
  - pyrogallic acid
  - stibine gas
  - phenylhydrazine
  - aniline
  - ethylene oxide
  - formaldehyde
  - lead

## Prevention

Prevention is by substitution and exposure control.

# Haematological malignancies

## Leukaemias

Represents 2.5% of all cancers. Main subtypes are 33% acute myeloid leukaemia (AML), 33% chronic lymphoid leukaemia (CLL), 10% chronic myeloid (CML), 10% acute lymphoid leukaemia (ALL).

*Exposures*

IARC have classified the following as leukaemogenic:

- *Ionizing radiation*: (excluding CLL)—radiologists, technologists, nuclear workers, aircraft crews, underground miners
- *Benzene*: (AML, ALL, CLL)—petroleum refining, boot and shoe manufacture, and repair, rubber industry
- *Ethylene oxide*: chemical industry, sterilizing agent (hospitals, spice fumigation)
- *Formaldehyde*: pathologists, medical laboratory technicians, plastics, textile industry
- *1,3-Butadiene*: (CML, CLL)—chemical and rubber industries

Other classed as probable leukaemogenic:

- *Non-arsenical pesticides*: pest control and agricultural workers, flour and grain mill workers
- Other statistically significant risk of leukaemia:
  - among workers highly exposed to extremely low-frequency electromagnetic fields (ELF EMF)
  - workers in livestock farming, workers in slaughterhouses, butchers, cooks involved in the processing of animal meat products, possibly due to exposure to infectious agents
  - some studies link leukaemia to exposure to asbestos. However, more research is needed to support this causal link

*Clinical features*

Presents with a combination of anaemia, bleeding, and infection.

*Compensation*

Acute non-lymphatic leukaemia is prescribed (C7) for IIDB in those who are exposed to benzene.

## Lymphoproliferative disorders

*Exposures*

- Ionizing radiation (non-Hodgkin lymphoma (NHL) and myeloma (MM))
- Benzene (NHL, MM)
- Dioxin (NHL)
- Ethylene oxide (NHL, MM)

*Clinical features*

Presents with anaemia or local mass.

## Treatment and prognosis of haematological malignancies

Treatment includes chemotherapy, radiotherapy, monoclonal antibodies, and stem cell transplantation. The 5-year survival rate for all subtypes of leukaemia is 61.4% (AML 28.3%, ALL 68.6%, CML 69.2%, CLL 85.1%), 68% NHL, 50% MM.

## Prevention

Prevention is through exposure control. See ➔ p. 576, Ionizing Radiation Regulations 2017.

# Chapter 16

# Medically unexplained occupational disorders

# Post-conflict illness in military personnel

In the aftermath of every major conflict over the past century, some returning personnel have complained of ill health. Some have symptoms of physical origin, others psychiatric disorder including post-traumatic stress disorder (PTSD). However, there is a third group characterized by vague and non-specific symptoms, for which (despite extensive investigation) no cause is found. Different names have been ascribed to this third group including Agent Orange syndrome, multisymptom illness, and Gulf War illness/syndrome (GWI). These syndromes share many common features. There are also similarities with other medically unexplained symptoms including chronic fatigue syndrome, multiple chemical sensitivity syndrome, and neurasthenia.

## Gulf War illness (preferred term by US Department of Veteran Affairs)

Gulf War illness affecting the veterans of the Arabian Gulf Conflict of 1991 has been extensively investigated, with over $300 million of funds from the US and UK governments. Reported prevalence estimates are between 25 and 34%. Despite extensive study into possible links with vaccinations, depleted uranium exposure, oil well fires, and exposure to pesticides or other chemical agents; no definitive cause has been found. Research is hampered by the absence of agreed case definition for the illness. Symptoms described include mood-cognitive, musculoskeletal GI, respiratory, dermatological, and fatigue groups; however, there is no unique symptom cluster differentiates from other conditions.

However, the following lessons have emerged and are pertinent to other post-deployment conditions:

- In general, military populations are healthier than civilians—the healthy warrior effect
- More than two decades after deployment, some Gulf War veterans still suffer ill health. However, the same symptoms and groupings are seen in non-Gulf Veterans control groups. Many veterans remain ill, and few have experienced recovery in more than 25 years. A 2001–2016 longitudinal follow-up study shows that the increased burden of GWI in veterans relative to non-veterans is not resolving or worsening as the veterans age
- Gulf veterans are two or three times more likely to have symptom complexes including multifocal pain, fatigue, cognitive or memory problems, and psychological distress. There is a strong association with mental health problems; however it does not explain the higher prevalence of the condition
- Although there is a raised incidence of PTSD (and other psychiatric diagnoses) in Gulf War veterans as in other conflicts, it is not elevated to the degree that could explain the overall increase in ill health. Common symptoms include tiredness, headaches, lack of concentration, memory loss, and numbness
- Thorough medical examination including physical, physiological, and psychological testing have revealed no major abnormalities
- Reported health is worse the lower the rank and after retirement

- In contrast to control groups, Gulf War veterans report more of every hazard and recall exposure to more of these over times. Those who are in good health recall fewer exposures
- There is no evidence of an excess of malignancy, birth defects, or increased mortality
- Longitudinal studies have shown inconsistent findings with regards to symptom change over time
- More likely to screen positive for GWI if also deployed in later conflicts, younger age (at baseline), racial/ethnic minorities, and women
- Aging complicates issue as it becomes less clear whether symptoms secondary to comorbid illness/aging

Prevention is more likely with risk communication strategies, collection of routine exposure data, and commissioning research.

## Management of post-conflict illness

- A detailed history, examination, and investigation should be taken to detect the presence of any organic disease. Treatment should be appropriate to the findings, and any patient with a known clinical disorder should be referred promptly to the appropriate 2° care consultant
- Enquiries about stress-related symptoms should be handled with care to avoid any impression that the individual's symptoms are being dismissed as psychological. However, it is worthwhile exploring patient's beliefs regarding the aetiology of the condition
- *If necessary, a follow-up appointment should be used to*:
  - discuss investigation results
  - give the physician an opportunity to review the literature
  - counsel the patient over any subjective concerns

Within the UK, the Veterans and Reserves Mental Health Programme (VRMHP) provides assessment and treatment advice for veterans (who have deployed since 1982) and reserves (who have been deployed overseas since 1 January 2003 as a reservist (covering the 1991 and 2003 Gulf Conflicts and subsequent operations in Iraq and Afghanistan)) and believes that their deployment may have affected their mental health.

## Further information and guidance

Support for War Veterans; The Veterans and Reserves Mental Health programme; Ministry of Defense and Veterans UK 2018; London; On VRMHP: Available at: https://www.gov.uk/guidance/support-for-war-veterans

# Sick building syndrome

The term sick building syndrome (SBS) was first used in the mid-1980s to describe an ill-defined collection of symptoms that are typically reported by workers located in the same building. Despite substantial research, the cause of the syndrome has not been fully explained.

## Epidemiology

- More common in women
- More common at lower end of the organizational hierarchy

## Reported symptoms

Usually mild, but can lead to significant impairment of performance and productivity but seldom direct sickness absence:

- Fatigue
- Headache
- Dizziness
- Nausea
- Eye soreness and dryness
- Upper respiratory tract (nose, throat) symptoms
- Skin rash/redness
- Generalized pruritis
- Rate of respiratory infections

## Possible causative factors

Many causal factors have been proposed. Among the factors listed here, some have been associated with SBS in epidemiological studies. Most have a plausible link to some of the common symptoms, but none have been proven to be the cause of the syndrome at low-level exposure.

*Physical and environmental factors*

- *Humidity*: either excessively high (encouraging mould formation) or excessively low (leading to drying of the mucous membranes)
- Excessively high temperature
- *Air conditioning*: associated with microbial contamination, exotoxins produced by contaminating organisms, biocides
- Poor lighting
- Nuisance dusts
- Video display units
- Open plan office (with >10 workstations)
- Poor office design and maintenance

*Chemicals*

- Formaldehyde is ubiquitous in office environments due to 'off-gassing' from furniture, carpet adhesive, and other fixtures made of particle board
- *Volatile organic compounds*: many are known irritants at high exposure levels. Some have low odour thresholds, thus contributing to the perception of poor air quality (irrespective of actual health effects)
- Nitrogen dioxide
- *Cigarette smoke*: passive smoking may have been a factor in the past but smoking in public buildings is no longer permissible by law in the UK

*Bio-aerosols*

Airborne particles comprising or contaminated with bacteria, fungi, or mites.

*Psychosocial factors*

- Low control over work
- Insufficient or excessive demands
- Low job satisfaction
- Poor support

The syndrome is likely to have a multifactorial aetiology with contributions from more than one of the factors listed here. Mechanisms are unclear but might include allergic (immune-mediated) or non-allergic (non-specific inflammatory or directly toxic) reactions.

## Management

- *Optimize physical environment*:
  - attention to standards of lighting, temperature, humidity
  - allow adequate personal space to work
  - regular cleaning to minimize nuisance dust
- *Address known risk factors for stress (see* *➔ p. 146, Organizational psychosocial factors**)*:
  - promote good industrial relations and communication
  - increase control (demand ratio where possible)
- Investigate specific issues, e.g. odours

## Further information and guidance

HSE (1995). *How to Deal with Sick Building Syndrome*, HSG132. HSE Books, Sudbury.

# Karoshi: Death from overwork

The concept of '*karoshi*' or death from overwork originates in Japan and refers to sudden death in workers believed to have been caused by very long working hours. The major medical causes are stroke and heart attack, i.e. acute myocardial infarction (AMI).

The family of a worker whose death has been accepted for by the Labour Standards Bureau (part of Japan's Ministry of Health, Labour and Welfare [MHLW]) as being due to karoshi is eligible for compensation. Suicide deemed to be from overwork (karojisatsu) is also eligible for compensation as is non-fatal cardiovascular or cerebrovascular disease that is considered to be secondary to overwork. A cultural disposition to working very long hours also leads to increased psychological burden of work demands that contributes to mortality from suicide.

While similar postulations exist in other East Asian countries (China—*guolaosi*; South Korea—*gwarosa*) Karoshi is not a concept widely recognized in the West. However, there are overlaps between the beliefs that sudden death may be due to overwork and the increasing body of research that describes associations between long hours of work and stroke as well as coronary artery disease.

## Mechanisms

Mechanisms described in research include increased cardiovascular disease (CVD) secondary to long working hours (reduced time for recovery from cardiovascular stress), insufficient sleep (potential specific effect on the onset of AMI), physical inactivity, type A personality, and job stress. Associations have been reported between stress and CVD including AMI, angina, and left ventricular dysfunction. Biologically changes in the autonomic nervous system may lead to increased sympathetic nervous system activity to such a critical level to induce onset of CVD. Stroke (commoner than heart attack in Karoshi) is also believed to result from repetitive triggering of the stress response. Like with CVD, behavioural mechanisms, such as physical inactivity, might also link long working hours and stroke. It has also been suggested that individuals who work long hours are more likely to ignore symptoms of disease.

## Epidemiology

A 2018 ILO report notes that 45% of Eastern Asia workers worked more than 48 hours per week compared with 10.4% in Western Europe and 16% in Northern America.

The MHLW compensated 96–133 deaths (of 251–338 recognized cases) from *karoshi* each year between 2012 and 2016. Some authors estimate that up to 10,000 deaths in the 20- to 59-year-old age group may be due to *karoshi*. Robust estimates of incidence are lacking. Two Japanese case-control studies have shown increased odds ratios for AMI in workers working >11 hours/days or >60 hours/weeks, respectively.

## Relevant legislation and prevention

In an effort to prevent Karoshi, the Japanese government issued guidance in 2002 that employees should not work more than 45 hours overtime per month, introduced medical examinations for all workers, and offered doctor consultations for those who are overworked. In 2014 the government went further and promulgated an act on 'Promotion of Preventive Measures against Karoshi and other Overwork-Related Health Disorders' legislating for inquiries into work-related deaths and illness, increasing awareness and research, and mandating annual reports to the National Diet (Japan's bicameral legislature). Korea and Taiwan have followed suit in recognizing cardiovascular and cerebrovascular disease due to heavy workloads as occupational diseases.

Overall, prevention must be aimed at reducing long working hours, stress prevention/mitigation, and management of vascular risk factors.

Section 3

# Occupational health practice

# Chapter 17

# Operational issues

# General principles of occupational health services

## Aims

Occupational medicine is a preventative medicine practiced in the workplace, promoting health and fostering wellness within the workforce. Although services must be reactive to unforeseen problems, the aim is to proactively prevent work-related ill-health wherever possible.

Occupational health (OH) is concerned with the interaction between work and health and is concerned with the health and welfare of four (overlapping) groups:

- The workforce as a group or population
- *Individual* workers or prospective employees
- The employer's customers or clients (product or service safety)
- The local population (environmental issues)

► The population perspective is central to understanding OH practice.

## Status of occupational health advice

In health and safety law, the ultimate responsibility for protecting the health and welfare of employees and the public rests with the employer. Managers may choose whether to take and how to implement OH advice. Therefore, rather than *instructing* the employer, the OH professional seeks to *influence* key decision-makers (management and trade unions) regarding health and safety issues. This is best achieved by developing strong and trusted relationships with employers. The approach will be most effective if the OH professional is well respected by all parties.

💣 OH professionals should remain impartial (preserving good relationships even if managers ignore advice) but should ensure that the responsibility for accepting risk has been taken at an appropriate level in the organization.

### Impartiality

OH professionals advise *both* employee(s) and the employer. This fundamental difference between occupational medicine and other specialties, in which the health professional is primarily responsible for providing care, is often misunderstood. In an environment where employer, employees, and their representatives may be adversarial, the OH professional must remain impartial to be effective.

This dual responsibility must be understood and respected by all. Its importance in effective OH practice cannot be overemphasized.

## Trade unions

- Trade union support can be crucial in developing OH services
- Trade unions have a legitimate interest in their members' welfare
- The principles of medical confidentiality hold whether or not a union representative is involved in issues concerning individual members

Traditionally, OH activities have been classified under two main headings:

- The effect of work on health
- The effect of health on work

## The effect of work on health: Preventing work-related illness

Occupational illness is prevented by a proactive cycle of risk assessment, risk reduction, and review.

- The classical occupational diseases of the industrial age are becoming less common in the developed world due to improved health and safety practice, increasing mechanization, and reduced exposure to hazards. However, these diseases remain in developing countries
- Work-related illnesses still represent a significant proportion of morbidity in developed countries
- Sir Austin Bradford Hill established a checklist of criteria for suggesting likely work causation (strength of association, consistency, specificity, temporality, biological gradient, plausibility, coherence, experiment, and analogy)
- The workplace is often one of the number of interacting factors. Many musculoskeletal or mental health problems are multifactorial and may have a substantial psychosocial component. It can be difficult to disentangle the contribution of workplace and non-work factors
- Occupational demands may aggravate or sustain existing illness

## The effect of health on work: Fitness for work

The important underpinning principle is that most work is 'healthy' and is a positive aspect of overall health and well-being.

Advice about fitness for work can be divided conceptually as follows.

*Context*

- Pre-employment or pre-placement
- *Intra-employment*:
  - following an episode of ill health
  - following a change to job or exposures
  - following/during long-term sickness absence
  - to inform the management of short-term sickness absence

*Timescale*

- *Short-term*: temporary rehabilitation programme with the finite endpoint of achieving a return to *normal* work (hours and tasks)
- *Long-term*: permanent adjustments to hours or tasks

Context and timescale are not mutually exclusive but are important dimensions in a conceptual framework for fitness for work. This framework emphasizes the important hierarchy of advice; the broad aims of which are:

- To maximize the potential for maintaining gainful employment
- To minimize any health risks to the employee
- To view ill-health retirement as a last resort after all options for maintaining employment have been explored

# The occupational health team

## Roles and overlap

- Occupational health is a multidisciplinary specialty
- Each professional group has different expertise and may have different approaches influenced by background and training
- However, there is substantial commonality of experience between professional groups, and potential overlap between roles
- There is no fixed or typical configuration for an OH team
- Provided role definitions are clear, overlaps and gaps are managed sensitively, and many different models can be successful

### The occupational health team

The make-up of the OH team is likely to be influenced by:

- The model of service delivery (see ➲ p. 382, Models of OH services)
- The service requirements of client organization(s)
- Prevailing hazards, and the knowledge to assess them
- Availability of manpower in the various OH professions
- Local, historical, or industry precedent
- Individual personalities and attributes
- Legal requirements
- The prevailing OH market

## Occupational physician

- In a small OH service the occupational physician (OHP) may act as part-time medical support to a nurse-led service
- In other services the OHP may be the service manager, with overall responsibility for OH and sometimes other business functions (e.g. safety)
- An OHP's clinical work includes sickness absence assessments, health surveillance, and giving advice on adjustments and rehabilitation for ill, injured, or disabled workers
- In the broader clinical context, workplace visits, advice on risk management, attendance at safety meetings, meetings with managers and trade unions, and policy writing may be undertaken
- Some OHPs have a managerial function. They manage an OH service, provide clinical governance, set overall strategy, policy, and procedures for others to follow. This role may cross national boundaries and involve the management of health professionals from varying backgrounds, working to different policies
- All OHPs should have input to audit and quality assurance

## Occupational health nurse

- Occupational health nurses (OHNs) may work in isolation in single-handed services, or within a larger occupational health service (OHS)
- Trained OHNs, often called occupational health advisers, may be involved in an extended range of professional activities, including pre-employment and sickness absence assessments, health surveillance (e.g. screening audiometry, skin inspections), drug and alcohol screening, workplace monitoring (e.g. noise, chemicals), advisory role in risk management, health promotion, counselling, and first aid training

- Some OHNs have a managerial role and lead OH departments
- Some nurses in industry may have had no formal training in OH and can be professionally isolated. Such nurses may fill a limited role, providing a treatment room service, immunizations, and basic (non-statutory) health and pre-employment screening

## Occupational hygienist

- Specialists in assessing and monitoring workplace exposures. Their role is described in detail in ➲ p. 632, Role and function of occupational hygienists
- Relatively few organizations employ a full-time occupational hygienist
- Many hygienists work in consultancies or as independent contractors

## Counsellor

- Many OHSs provide in-house staff counselling or have contracted with an employee assistance programme that employs counsellors and occupational psychologists
- While some counsellors may be qualified psychologists, this is not an occupational requirement

## Ergonomist

- Specializes in fitting the task to the human and may be involved in assessing and advising on processes, products, and work systems
- Ideally an ergonomist's advice should be sought at the process or plant design stage in an effort to design out potential problems
- As with occupational hygienists, ergonomists are generally found in large organizations or working on a consultancy basis

## Case manager

- Case managers are employed by some OH services to manage sickness absence and rehabilitation. They can come from various health professional backgrounds
- Their role focuses on identifying and overcoming, in conjunction with the ill or injured employee and their employer, barriers to an early, sustained return to work
- Their approach to sickness absence follows a non-medical model

## Other occupational health team members

- Health and safety adviser or manager
- Fire safety specialist
- Manual handling adviser
- Physical therapist
- Health promotion specialist
- Business/finance adviser
- Clerical administrative and technical support (including specialist medical secretaries and information technology support)
- Screening technicians (non-medically qualified)
- Environment specialists

The Council for Work and Health is a UK-based organization that has members from the many diverse professions and organizations representing those with an interest in supporting work and health.

# Models of OH services

Models of OH provision are influenced by many changing factors, including legal requirements, the economy, the nature of risks, and political priorities (see Table 17.1).

- In 1998 the World Health Organization defined the purpose of OH services as the 'promotion of health and maintenance of workability'
- In Scotland the Healthy Working Lives and Health Works strategies 'maximize the functional capacity (physical, mental, social, spiritual) of the working age population', and help the unemployed find work
- In the Netherlands, the political initiative to move the responsibility for sickness absence benefits to employers led to models that were focused on the evaluation and control of sickness absence. In the UK it has been proposed that employers should commission a functional capacity assessment after 4 weeks' sickness absence

## Factors that influence OHS models

- *Legal*: in some countries the model may be prescribed (e.g. Germany, Italy, Austria)
- *Risks and type of industry*: treatment and primary care will be included in countries or locations with poor access to health services. The services that are needed by an office population in a large city will require a different skill mix to those in a steel foundry or shipyard
- *Priorities of the service purchaser*: these may include health surveillance, sickness absence control and rehabilitation, and workplace health promotion depending on priorities and profitability
- *Resources and manpower availability*: in some countries the discipline of OH nursing is not well developed or recognized; in others there may be few OH physicians
- *Extent of multidisciplinary working*: services may be monodisciplinary (e.g. a doctor or nurse working independently) or, more commonly, two disciplines when a team consists of OH physicians and nurses
- *Internal services*: OH professionals are employed by the enterprise
- *External contracted services*: the enterprise buys in services from a commercial provider or local group service
- *Government-funded services*: for small and medium enterprises, self-employed, home workers, microenterprises, the unemployed, e.g. in Scotland

## Rationale for occupational health models

OH delivery requires a multidisciplinary effort, with close cooperation between health and safety, occupational hygiene, ergonomics or other specialists, human resources, and legal advisers. Where the OH professionals are not an integral part of a multidisciplinary team, it will be necessary to liaise with these other disciplines. OH services, which do not have close operational links with other professionals, are more likely to undertake inappropriate health checks and health surveillance. Much OH provision is determined by the perceptions of the enterprise or employing organization. An organization that has financial problems is more likely to focus on the control of sickness absence, while a profitable organization (with low absence) may invest more in health improvement.

**Table 17.1** Advantages and disadvantages of the different models

| Model | Advantages | Disadvantages |
|---|---|---|
| Single OHP or OHN | Autonomy | Difficult to maintain clinical competence and establish clinical governance |
| OHP and OHN | Team work<br>Appropriate use of resources | May do more health examinations than necessary<br>Issues about adequacy of the risk assessment process |
| In-house OH service | Understanding of the organization's needs<br>Knowledge of other members of the extended OH team | Can become institutionalized and inward looking; loss of independence (actual or perceived) |
| Group OH service: providing services to a number of enterprises | May have critical mass of resource and experience of different sectors<br>More likely to have quality assurance processes if in a contracting situation with large commercial enterprises | May experience shareholder pressure for profit maximization, which can distort advice given to organizations<br>May not be multidisciplinary and have blind spots in provision |
| Multidisciplinary service | Potentially the best model, if well integrated and there is good teamwork<br>Should be able to give the most appropriate advice to a client organization, i.e. advice not subject to the bias of a dominant professional group | Difficult for small and medium size enterprises (SMEs), microenterprises, and home workers to access such services unless provided within the public sector |

## Current and future developments

Recent years have seen the decline of large within-company models and a growth of alternative models including contracted-in services. Many countries have strategies to address the lack of access to competent OH advice for many workers and employers in the SME sector (<250 employees). Across the world, OH services for this sector are very variable and are generally inadequate. This has led to parallel developments in the countries of the UK. In Scotland, the Healthy Working Lives service provides free OH, safety, and rehabilitation telephone advice to the employed and unemployed, access to a workplace visit and advice, and third-level access to OH advice. The 2017 Improving Lives, Health, Work and Disability strategy seeks to promote access to OH for all UK workers.

One of the most highly developed models of OH provision is in Finland, which has a network of regional centres and high levels of coverage of the workforce.

# Managing occupational health records 1: Electronic record systems and security

## Electronic records

Most OHSs are now computerized. Their security is critical to the continued success of the OH service.

- Although IT security can be viewed in the narrow sense of hardware theft, protecting data is equally important and key to service reputation and trust.
- Just as access to written OH records should be restricted, so data on an IT system must be protected. This is particularly important where the OH service uses an organization-wide IT system
- Medical information is deemed to be special category data under the General Data Protection Regulation 2018 and the Data Protection Act 2018, and particular care is required to protect it
- Staff should be trained on information security and how to report any security breaches
- Data security should be audited, and any breaches or suspected breaches of security investigated
- Where management reports are e-mailed, these should be encrypted (this is NHS policy) and sent in portable document format (pdf) to reduce the likelihood of the report being altered without the originator's permission

## Physical security

- Threats to the physical security of computer hardware may arise from theft, fire, flood, power surges, or accidental damage
- All IT hardware (monitors, printers, CPUs) should be security marked and kept on an asset register
- An uninterruptible power supply should be provided
- Building security should be at a level proportionate to local crime levels and the likely impact of loss of IT equipment on the OH service. This may include the provision of alarm systems, floodlighting, security patrols, etc.
- Particular care is needed when dealing with portable data storage devices such as data pens, detachable hard drives, lap tops and note books, or personal digital assistant. Such devices are easily lost or stolen, and their contents should be protected using high quality encryption

## Software security

- Loss, corruption, theft, or unauthorized access to data should be guarded against
- Data should be backed up to a remote server on a daily basis or saved on a detachable hard drive and stored in a fireproof safe. Small operations may be able to use CDs or other IT storage media to back up files. Ideally, these should be stored in a separate building
- Data backups should be checked for integrity in case the backup data is itself corrupt

- All data should be password protected and the passwords should be regularly updated
- Passwords should not be written down, nor should computer user names or passwords be shared
- All computers should be locked when not in use
- Computer users should log off any network application after use. This is especially important where the computer is shared with others
- Computer monitor privacy screen filters should be used to keep confidential data secure and prevent others viewing the screen's contents, e.g. clinic appointment lists
- Networked IT systems should have varying access levels, defined by operational need, with data only accessible to those with valid reason to use
- IT systems should provide an audit trail to identify unauthorized access or attempts to access sensitive OH data. (Often the greatest threat to data security comes from within an organization)
- IT support staff, whether in-house or contracted to an OH department, should be asked to sign a confidentiality agreement
- Increasingly, smart cards (an identification card which carries an integrated computer circuit capable of holding personal data) are being employed to record health and safety data. Such cards require several layers of security to restrict access to data and to prevent unauthorized changes to existing electronic records
- Systems that allow remote working via the Internet should employ the highest possible security

⚠ E-mail systems, where used for medical communications, should be secure and encrypted. Beware of similar e-mail addresses lest the wrong person receives the e-mail.

*Computer viruses*

- All IT systems should employ virus protection software to prevent computer viruses from compromising system operations
- Virus software must be kept up to date
- IT systems that connect to the Internet are especially vulnerable to infection with computer viruses, and this can lead to service loss for extended periods
- Unauthorized use or installation of pirated software may compromise IT security by introducing viruses and should be forbidden

## IT policy

It is advisable for OH departments to have a written IT policy that covers the use of computer technology. This should cover the security issues outlined here as well as access to and use of stored data, and compliance with data protection legislation.

# Managing occupational health records 2: Security, transfer, and archiving of records

There are both legal and ethical issues around the security, transfer, and archiving of medical records. The General Medical Council (GMC), the Faculty of Occupational Medicine, the British Medical Association (BMA), and the Department of Health (DH) have all issued guidance on confidentiality. Concerns around confidentiality are a recurring issue in occupational medicine. OH professionals need to be aware of the many ways in which confidentiality may be compromised.

## Security of OH records

- All contacts between an employee and an OH service should be recorded in the employee's OH record
- The medical records should be securely stored in a lockable cabinet or room or on a secure IT system
- Access to OH records should be restricted to OH staff
- All OH staff should sign a confidentiality agreement
- It is unethical and also unlawful to allow access to OH records to non-OH staff, such as personnel managers and company lawyers without consent of the employee

## Transfer of OH records

- Companies may outsource OH services, change OH provider, or go out of business. Independent occupational physicians may retire or change jobs. In all these cases, OH records will need to be transferred to an individual or organization that is in a position to maintain them for the appropriate period (this may be 50 years after the last entry in the records in some cases, e.g. ionizing radiation records) or 40 years afterwards (e.g. asbestos, lead, and COSHH health records). It is only the basic health record with identifying details and reports of health surveillance procedures in terms of fit/unfit/fit with adjustments that need to be kept for these long periods and it is the employer's duty to do so. Clinical records of health surveillance are confidential to OH and do not need to be kept for as long, unless with good reason e.g. possible legal action, research
- The Faculty of Occupational Medicine publication *Guidance on Ethics for Occupational Health Practice* provides guidance on the transfer of OH records
- When it is proposed that OH records are to be transferred, employees should be informed and given the opportunity to request that their OH notes be archived, rather than transferred
- Where an organization closes, it may be appropriate to issue the OH records to the individual or (with their consent) their GP. In some situations, statutory records may be offered to the Health and Safety Executive (HSE) for retention

## Archiving

- Employees leave, are dismissed, or retire, and over time the number of inactive OH records held by an OH service will increase. Inactive files occupy valuable storage space. They can make it difficult for administration staff to locate current OH notes. As a result, all OH services need to have in place a standard operating procedure for archiving OH records. It should also be noted that the General Data Protection Regulation provides that personal data should not be kept longer than is necessary. OH services should fix a date when records will be reviewed and, if no longer required, deleted. NHS Digital recommends that as a general rule OH records should be retained as long as the employee is employed and for 6 years thereafter, or until their 75th birthday, whichever comes first
- Archives may be held on or off site, but it is important that archiving medical records does not compromise medical confidentiality
- Readily accessible records detailing the location of all archived notes should be maintained. The location of records should be tracked to avoid the loss or misfiling of records
- OH notes may need to be abstracted at a later date from an archive for a number of reasons, e.g. legal action, audit, or re-employment
- Data protection legislation requires destruction of records no longer required

## Relevant legislation and guidance


- British Medical Association. (Updated July 21) *Confidentiality and Disclosure of Health Information Toolkit*. BMA, London. Available at: http://bma.org.uk/practical-support-at-work/ethics/confidentiality-tool-kit
- Department of Health (2003). *Confidentiality: NHS Code of Practice*. DOH, London. Available at: http://www.dh.gov.uk/en/Publicationsandstatistics/Publications/PublicationsPolicyAndGuidance/DH_4069253
- Faculty of Occupational Medicine (2018). *Ethics Guidance for Occupational Health Practice*, 8th edn. FOM, London.
- GMC. *Confidentiality 2017: Disclosing information for Insurance, Employment and Similar Purposes*. Available at: http://www.gmc-uk.org/Confidentiality_disclosing_info_insurance_2009.pdf_27493823.pdf. GMC London.

# Quality and audit in occupational health practice 1: General principles

OH practice is naturally embedded within enterprises or is supplied under contract. It faces scrutiny by purchasers, users, and enforcing authorities, who all wish to see evidence of compliance with standards. Standards can be derived from a number of sources such as:

- The purchaser of services (e.g. contract specifications)
- The professional body (e.g. good OH practice guidelines)
- The statutory enforcing authority (e.g. standards for legal compliance)

Organizations strive constantly to improve the efficiency of their operation and also that of their suppliers of services. OH professionals must be able to show benefit, constantly seek to justify and improve what they do, and demonstrate the use of evidence-based best practice guidelines.

## Quality

*Definitions*

- 'The degree and standard of excellence'
- 'Fitness for a purpose' (Juran—multiple publications during 1980s)[1]

*Customer-driven quality*

This is a useful approach which ensures that the OH service meets the needs of its customers. It first requires that the customers are defined. There are many who could be considered as customers or stakeholders, and they all have different (real or perceived) needs:

- Service purchaser
- Patients or clients
- Legislative bodies
- Trade unions
- Other health care professionals
- Insurance companies
- Pension fund trustees

The aim is to build a complex provider–client relationship, through which the needs of the many stakeholders can be addressed. This should not be an entirely reactive process. Many of the stakeholders and customers of OH services may be ignorant of the range of services available, and each will have a different perspective. The art of OH service practice is to meet the needs of the individual client (or patient), while at the same time taking into account the needs of the organization in which they work. To be successful, the OH professional must engage in a continuing educational dialogue with the various stakeholders of the service.

*Quality improvement*

Excellence in OH practice is not an endpoint but is a continually moving target. Therefore, the pursuit of excellence requires continuous improvement. Juran suggested that up to 40% of all activity involved correcting individual or system failures. Quality principles provide a mechanism for continual improvement, which requires:

1 Joseph Juran—early proponent of benchmarking and quality costing.

- Awareness of the need for improvement
- A willingness to improve
- A product or service
- Measurements

*Quality assurance*

Quality assurance encompasses all the planned and systematic activities needed to demonstrate that the OH service is meeting all its defined standards and customer requirements. It includes processes:

- To eliminate faults
- Maintain consistent performance

## Audit

The systematic evaluation of the quality and effectiveness of OH service is a professional obligation. Audit is the process of observing the practice and comparing it against a defined standard. It may also be a high-level process used to undertake a needs assessment of an organization or review of an OH service.

- How many of your employees are sick?
- Who gets sick and why are they sick?
- How many accidents occur and what are the causes?
- Why do they retire?
- What do your people die from?
- What do you do?
- Do you have a mission statement?
- Do you have goals?
- Do you have specific objectives for this year?

Audit can be of the structure of an OH service, its processes, or its outcomes. An audit will compare practice against the standard as a means of establishing whether the standard is met or, if not, informing the need for change in either the standard or the practice—the audit cycle (see Fig. 17.1). Audit is an essential part of professional practice and is the tool that monitors and supports quality assurance and quality improvement.

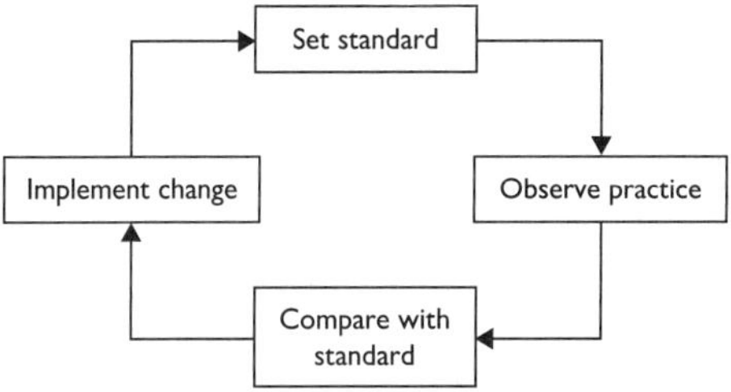


**Fig. 17.1** The audit cycle

# Quality and audit in occupational health practice 2: Systems and tools

## Quality systems

A quality system requires that the OH service:
- Defines its processes
- Ensures that all staff know and understand these
- Ensures that the processes meet the needs of the customer
- Reviews standards and procedures regularly
- Improves continuously
- Audits all the above regularly

## Measurements

Measurements are important in OH practice. However, many organizations and individuals collect data of little relevance to health improvement, such as the numbers of people seen and other activity analysis. The data that any OHS or OH professional should strive to gather are given in Table 17.2. Outcomes are always more important than process measurements.

An effective OHS will be able to demonstrate positive change in some or all of the following:
- Attitudes, knowledge, or behaviour
- Health status or self-rated health
- Morbidity
- Mortality
- OH process and practice
- Effects on work organizations

## External quality standards

Internationally recognized quality systems have developed to support the assessment and maintenance of quality in industry. Many organizations routinely require that their suppliers of services operate a quality system including external audit of their service.

**Table 17.2** Data collection in OH

| Outcome | Source |
|---|---|
| Morbidity | Sickness absence by location, occupation, function |
| Mortality | In service, pensioners |
| Occupational disease | Sickness absence by cause |
| Accidents and incidents | Reported accident statistics |
| Health | Health survey data |
| Stress | Employee Assistance Programme data |
| Litigation | Analysis of compensation claims |

Examples of external standards can be:

- *Specific*: e.g. the UK Faculty of Occupational Medicine 'Safe Effective Quality of Occupational Health Services' and a German system for occupational physician practice
- *Generic*: industry standards such as ISO 9000 and the European Foundation For Quality Management. These require that holders of their quality standard systematically apply all the principles described here

Holders of a recognized quality standard will usually have some advantage with potential customers over their competitors who do not. However, possession of a quality standard will not necessarily ensure that the OH service is delivering the highest standards of OH and safety or clinical service—that still requires professional excellence and leadership.

## National audit

A series of national audits of NHS OHSs have been carried out by the Health and Work Development Unit of the Royal College of Physicians. This work is also relevant to other (non-NHS) providers. At present audit cycles are ongoing in two topics: screening for depression in employees who are on long-term sickness absence, and the management of back pain.

## Clinical governance

Clinical governance is defined as management's responsibility for clinical performance. This requires that managers of a service ensure that the highest standards of clinical performance are maintained by the consistent development and use of:

- Evidence-based guidelines (or consensus-based in the absence of evidence)
- Appropriate and ethical standard procedures
- Continuing professional development of clinical staff
- Peer review of clinical performance
- Monitoring of clinical outcomes

Quality systems can encompass clinical governance processes. However, if the system does not apply to individual clinical performance, then separate procedures for ensuring clinical governance must be in place for the individual clinician or larger clinical team.

## Further information

Guidelines in occupational health:

Royal College of Physicians. (2012). *Back Pain Management Audit*. Available at: http://www.rcplondon.ac.uk/resources/back-pain-management-audit. RCP London.

Royal College of Physicians. *Depression Screening Audit*. (2008). Available at: http://www.rcplondon.ac.uk/resources/depression-screening-audit-2008. RCP London.

Royal College of Physicians. (2009). *Depression Detection and Management of Staff on Long-term Sickness Audit*. Available at: http://www.rcplondon.ac.uk/resources/depression-detection-and-management-staff-long-term-sickness-audit. RCP London.

## Guidelines, governance, and quality

The development of clinical guidelines relevant to OH practice plays an important role in driving up clinical quality in the specialty. Guidelines form the link between scientific evidence (or professional consensus in the absence of clear evidence) and agreed standards for care. Clinical standards provide a framework for assuring:

- Consistency of practice across OH providers
- A baseline for continuous improvement in quality through repeated cycles of audit (see ➲ p. 388, Quality and audit)

## Guideline development methodology

A number of guideline methodologies have been used to develop guidelines in clinical medicine. These vary in complexity, but they have a common aim to use standardized tools to:

- Categorize evidence (peer reviewed papers, reviews, or grey literature) in terms of quality
- Summarize the implications for practice

► One of the main problems with the application of these methods in OH is the relative lack of evidence from experimental studies (randomized controlled trials being the gold standard). Much of the published research in OH is based on cross-sectional surveys and observational studies, so will score at the lower end of the quality rating scales within most of the agreed methodologies in Table 17.3. Nevertheless, a consistency of approach enables the reasonable justification of guidelines and the practice standards that are derived from them.

**Table 17.3** Common methods for guideline development

| Method | Web reference |
|---|---|
| Scottish Intercollegiate Guideline Network (SIGN) | http://www.sign.ac.uk/ |
| National Clinical Guideline Centre (NCGC) | http://www.ncgc.ac.uk/Guidelines/Methodology/ |
| Grading of Recommendations Assessment, Development and Evaluation (GRADE) | http://www.gradeworkinggroup.org/index.htm |

## Guideline development groups

The most important points to note when setting up a guideline development groups (GDG) are:

- *Ensure all relevant stakeholders are included*:
  - professional groups from OH practice (including a representative from a primary care background if relevant)
  - experts in the particular field (e.g. dermatology or microbiology)
  - users of a service (employers, employees, or their representatives)
  - patient representatives (patients who have personal experience of the condition in question)
  - enforcing or regulatory agencies (HSE, DH)

- Training will be required if GDG members will be appraising evidence
- Consider contracting out the systematic review and/or evidence appraisal to an experienced research unit
- A clear dissemination and implementation plan for any output is essential from early in the process
- The budget for a guideline should be split; 50% for development and 50% for dissemination and implementation

## Sources of occupational health guidance

The main sources of guidelines that are relevant for OH practice are outlined in Table 17.4

**Table 17.4** Main sources of guidelines that are relevant for OH practice

| Source | Web reference |
|---|---|
| Cochrane collaboration: Occupational Health and Safety Review Group | http://osh.cochrane.org/ |
| National Institute for Health and Clinical Excellence (NICE) | http://www.nice.org.uk |
| NHS Health at Work Network | https://www.nhshealthatwork.co.uk |
| Various other bodies including: | |
| • Department of Health | http://www.dh.gov.uk |
| • NHS Employers | http://www.nhsemployers.org |
| • Health Protection Agency | http://www.hpa.org.uk |
| • Health and Safety Executive | http://www.hse.gov.uk |

## Further information

Although not specific for OH, the following are useful general evidence-based resources:

National Institute for Clinical Excellence (NICE) (2012). *NICE Clinical Pathways Section*. NICE, London. Available at: http://pathways.nice.org.uk/

# Chapter 18

# Ethics

# Ethical principles in clinical occupational health practice

## Role

Occupational health (OH) advice may be provided by a wide range of health care practitioners and other specialists (such as safety professionals, ergonomists, and hygienists) concerned with the interaction of work and health. While practitioners should ensure compliance with general ethical principles, recommended by their professional registration organizations, by its nature the OH role has additional ethical considerations driven by:

- Having a largely preventive or rehabilitative role rather than the traditional therapeutic role with a treatment focus
- A need to maintain an objective and impartial position between various groups, including the employee (and his/her GP), the employer, and others (other employees, unions, local population)

## Principles

The underlying ethical principles of medical practice (bioethics) for all Health Care Professionals (HCPs) including OH practitioners are as follows:

- *Respect for autonomy*: competent adults may make decisions for themselves irrespective of the consequences to themselves
- *Non-maleficence*: the doctor shall do no harm
- *Beneficence*: the doctor shall do good and act in the best interests of the patient
- *Distributive justice*: how rights and responsibilities are equitably and fairly distributed

In the UK and Europe respect for autonomy is the predominant principle. These ethical principles are further specified by ethical rules such as truthfulness, respect for privacy, fidelity, and confidentiality. These principles place active, relevant responsibilities on OH practitioners, which should be implemented even if not specifically required by law, rules, or contract.

## Rules

Occupational physicians are bound by 'the duties of a doctor' and *Good Medical Practice*, published by the General Medical Council (GMC).[1] The Faculty of Occupational Medicine (FOM) has produced a specific version *Good Occupational Medical Practice*[2] is recognised by the GMC as an authoritative source of guidance and is used by other OH professionals and lay people. Occupational physicians are required, inter alia, to do the following:

- *Revalidate in accordance with the requirements of the GMC*:
  - audit their work and demonstrate improvements in practice
  - evidence-based working must be at the heart of their activities
  - seek the views of their customers and clients and incorporate them
  - have an effective complaints procedure in place
  - ensure appropriate arrangements for clinical governance in their work
  - support specialist training

1 General Medical Council (GMC). *Regulating Doctors, Ensuring Good Medical Practice*. (2020). GMC, London. Available at: http://www.gmc-uk.org/index.asp

2 Faculty of Occupational Medicine (2010). *Good Occupational Medical Practice*. FOM, London.

## Ethical guidance

*United Kingdom*

- Other HCPs publish ethical guidance such as the Nursing and Midwifery Council and the Royal College of Nursing
- British Medical Association (2003). *Medical Ethics Today*, 2nd edn. BMJ Books, London. Ethical guidance for all doctors is also published in the UK by the British Medical Association. Third edition likely to be published in February 2022
- Faculty of Occupational Medicine (2018). *Guidance on Ethics for Occupational Health Practice*, 8th edn. FOM, London. ISBN 9781527232402
- Nursing and Midwifery Council (2018). The Code of Professional Standards of practice and behaviour for nurses, midwives and nursing associates NMC, London. Available at: http:// www.nmc.org.uk/ globalassets/sitedocuments/nmc-publications/nmc-code.pdf
- Other non-health-care professionals such as the Institute of Occupational Safety and Health also produce ethical guidance
- Royal College of Nursing (2005). *Confidentiality*. RCN, London. Available at: http://www.rcn.org.uk/publications/pdf/ confidentiality.pdf

*International*

- International Commission on Occupational Health ICOH (2014). *International Code of Ethics for Occupational Health Professionals*. 3rd edition.

# Confidentiality, consent, and communication

## General principles

The principles of communication in OH may be different from other doctor–patient relationships. Explain this to clients when first referred.

- The OH practitioner is impartial and aims to give objective advice to both employer and employee
- Personal information is kept confidential. Information is only disclosed if justified and then only with the employee's consent
- Any disclosure is the minimum required for the purpose, even if wider consent is available

## Legal requirements

In addition to the ethical requirement, confidentiality is ensured by:

- General Data Protection Regulation 2018
- Human Rights Act 1998
- Common law
- Access to Medical Reports Act 1988. This gives additional rights to individuals where an OH professional requests medical information from a doctor who has provided the individual with clinical care. This is covered more fully on ➔ p. 580, Access to Medical Reports Act 1988

► Breaches of confidentiality may lead to action in the courts by the GMC or by the Information Commissioner.

## Consent

In the setting of OH practice, consent may be required for any interaction with the client, including but limited to:

- Preventative or therapeutic interventions (e.g. immunizations)
- Assessment of risk to the employee or others (e.g. drug screening, assessment of immunity to infectious diseases)
- Health surveillance and biological monitoring
- Disclosure of confidential information held by the OH department
- Acquisition of confidential information by the OH department

For consent to be ethically valid, it must be freely given by a competent individual who knows:

- What action is proposed (including the content of proposed disclosure of information)
- By whom
- To whom
- The benefits and adverse consequences of giving/withholding consent

Consent may be:

- *Given explicitly*: either in writing or orally, and recorded in the contemporaneous medical record
- *Implied*: only used in obvious circumstances such as a patient offering his/her arm for the taking of a previously explained blood specimen. Consent is freely given if no external pressure is put on the individual to agree or decline a particular course of action

- The fact that there are consequences to a particular decision does not render the consent ethically invalid
- The fact that an individual has to agree to an examination in order to gain a particular benefit (e.g. gain a pilot's license or obtain an ill-health retirement pension) does not invalidate the consent

Consent is valid only for the purpose for which it was given. It may be withdrawn at any stage at which the change has practical effect (e.g. consent to disclosure cannot be withdrawn after disclosure has occurred).

## Withholding consent

*For assessment or treatment*

If consent for risk assessment, health screening, or interventions is withheld, the consequences must be explained to the individual and recorded in the OH record. These will depend on the situation but might include refusal to give health clearance for particular activities or jobs. The consequences of refusal to participate in screening programmes should be agreed in advance with employees' representatives.

*Disclosing confidential information without consent*

Rarely, confidential information may be disclosed without consent. Some examples include:

- Overriding public interest (avoiding serious harm to third parties)
- Statutory requirement (terrorism, notifiable disease, GMC or other statutory Regulator, road traffic accident, Driver and Vehicle Licensing Agency)
- By order of a court

However, occupational physicians who disclose information without consent may be required to justify their decisions. It is prudent to seek advice from senior colleagues, medical defence insurer, or lawyers before taking such action. Individuals must be informed about what information will be disclosed and to whom, and the possible consequences.

## Communicating the output from OH assessments

It is essential that the individual is informed of the content of any reports that are generated by the OH department and agree to their release. This applies even if the report does not contain sensitive or confidential medical information. A copy of the report should be offered to the individual, and their right of access to it should be explained clearly.

## Further information

*GMC guidance on confidentiality*

GMC (2017). *Confidentiality: Guidance for Doctors*. Confidentiality: disclosing information for employment, insurance and similar purposes. Available at: https://www.gmc-uk.org/ethical guidance/ethical-guidance-for-doctors/confidentiality—disclosing-information-for-employment insurance-and-similar-purposes

Faculty of Occupational Medicine (2018). *Guidance on Ethics for Occupational Physicians*, 8th edn. FOM, London

# Ethics in business and medico-legal work

## Business ethics

Globalization has increased diversity in the workplace and companies increasingly operate their own ethical codes and values. Practitioners should follow sound principles of business ethics where these do not conflict with their duties as a registered professional.

- OH practitioners remain as registered practitioners and are subject to the rules of their relevant national regulator (e.g. the GMC, NMC, etc.); the lack of a therapeutic relationship in many activities does not absolve practitioners working in business of their biomedical ethical responsibilities
- OH practitioners have a duty to promote health and well-being in the workplace regardless of geography
- Commercial pressures can impact, but do not justify breaches of ethical or legal rules
- OH practitioners must not contract for work outside their own or their organization's competence
- Competitors must not be denigrated, and information gleaned by OH staff through their work should not be used for personal advantage
- Care must be taken that contracts or agreements for services do not contain unethical provisions such as a requirement to release confidential medical information to the employer
- When services are being transferred, the OH and safety of client organizations and their workforces must take primacy over commercial considerations

## Medico-legal work

OH professionals may be required to give evidence:

- As a factual witness, e.g. on some aspect of OH procedure or their personal input in a case. A factual witness does not give an opinion, just a statement of the facts or events as they occurred
- *As an expert witness*: an expert witness gives an educated or expert opinion on a question, e.g. the relationship between a workplace exposure and a particular health effect:
  - the expert witness is responsible to the court, not to the party who has funded the report
  - independence and expert knowledge are paramount
  - never stray outside your area of expertise
  - expect to be challenged on your views; be prepared to produce evidence to justify your position
- Legal report writing and giving evidence in court requires particular skills; ensure you have the appropriate training. The Expert Witness Institute provides training programmes for doctors (http://www.ewi.org.uk)

# Chapter 19

# Policies

# Writing a policy

The purpose of any policy is to set out how an organization plans to conduct that aspect of its business in compliance with relevant legislation and current best practice. Behind the organizational policy may lie one or more operational procedures/protocols which document how the policy will be delivered. Well-written, up-to-date, occupational health (OH) policies and procedures are one element of good clinical governance (see Fig. 19.1).

► To be effective, these policies must have support at the highest level of the organization.

A comprehensive policy sets out organizational intention, and explicit arrangements (who does what and when) with respect to the management of any given organizational risk.

**An effective policy should**

- Define the purpose of the policy
- Define responsibilities from the top of the organization down the management tree
- Identify a director or senior manager responsible for that policy
- Describe the responsibilities of managers and supervisors
- Describe the responsibilities of employees
- Describe the responsibilities of other parties where relevant, e.g.
  - OH and well-being service
  - human resources (HR)
  - health and safety department
  - training and education department
- Describe arrangements for
  - monitoring and review of the policy
  - monitoring of the effectiveness of the policy
- Allocate appropriate resources
- Ensure the organization has access to competent advice
- Set a date for policy review

## Relevant legislation and guidance


- HSE (2003). *Management of Health and Safety at Work Regulations 1999. Approved Code of Practice and Guidance*, L21, 2nd edn. HSE Books, Sudbury
- HSE. *Safety Management*, HSG65. (2021). HSE Books, Sudbury
- TSO (2003). *Health and Safety at Work, Etc. Act 1974*. Chapter 37. TSO, Norwich

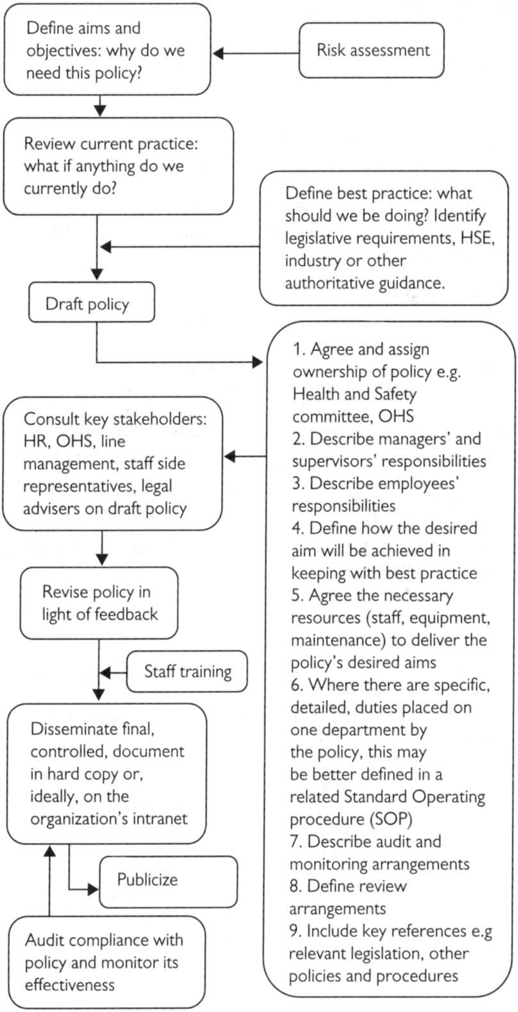


**Fig. 19.1** Flow chart showing the key steps in drafting a policy

# Health and safety policies

The purpose of a health and safety policy is to set out how an organization plans to conduct its business in compliance with health and safety law. It expresses commitment to sustained improvement in the management of health and safety risk.

► All employers with more than five workers are required by the Health and Safety at Work etc. Act 1974 to have a written health and safety policy, and to communicate it to employees. Under the Health and Safety Information for Employees Regulations 1989, employers must display a health and safety poster or provide leaflets with health and safety information for the workers.

## Health and safety policy

► To be effective, a health and safety policy must have support at the highest level of the organization.

The prevailing culture should give supervisors and staff a clear message that health and safety is an important organizational priority. A comprehensive health and safety policy sets out organizational intention, and explicit arrangements (who does what and when) with respect to the management of health and safety risk. The policy should specify the owner of the policy, the scope, definitions/glossary, relevant reference documents including legislation, regulations, and other internal policies, e.g. Control of Substances Hazardous to Health Regulation (COSHH), First Aid, Noise. Many large organizations will require that draft policies are subject to Equality assessment prior to implementation.

**A health and safety policy should**

- Be signed (and dated) by the chief executive
- Define responsibilities from the top of the organization down the management tree
- Identify a director/senior manager responsible for health and safety
- Describe the responsibilities of managers and supervisors
- Describe the responsibilities of employees
- Encourage the involvement of safety representatives
- *Define how health and safety issues will be communicated effectively*:
  - at board level: health and safety on the agenda of all meetings
  - to all staff: toolbox talks/team briefing, newsletters, and circulars
- *Describe arrangements for*:
  - monitoring and review of health and safety performance
  - monitoring of the effectiveness of the policy
- Allocate appropriate resources to health and safety
- Ensure the organization has access to competent health and safety advice
- Commit the organization to review and revise the policy regularly and set a date for policy review

## Principles of health and safety management: 'Five steps'

The Health and Safety Executive (HSE) describes five steps to effective health and safety management.

1. *Produce a health and safety policy*
2. *Develop a safety culture through control, competence, cooperation, and communication*

- *Control*:
  - senior managers should lead by example
  - a senior manager should chair the health and safety committee
  - allocate and communicate health and safety responsibilities
  - company organizational chart
  - clear job descriptions
  - allocate appropriate resources (time, staff, finance)
  - identify especially hazardous tasks or jobs, and ensure that these workers receive appropriate additional training
  - monitor health and safety performance against agreed standards
- *Competence*:
  - recruit and train competent staff
  - provide or obtain specialist advice where required
- *Cooperation*:
  - work with safety representatives and trade unions
  - liaise with contractors to manage health and safety
  - consult with staff on health and safety issues
- *Communication*:
  - provide information, instruction, and training to staff, including short-term or agency workers
  - make health and safety a priority issue

3. *Planning and standard setting*
4. *Measure health and safety performance*
5. *Review and revise health and safety policy*

## Relevant legislation and guidance

*Information from the HSE*


- HSE (1997). *Successful Health and Safety Management*, HSG65. HSE Books, Sudbury
- HSE (2003). *Management of Health and Safety at Work Regulations 1999. Approved Code of Practice and Guidance*, L21, 2nd edn. HSE Books, Sudbury
- HSE. *Do You Have Any Information on How to Compile a Health and Safety Policy?* (2021). HSE Books, Sudbury. Available at: http://www.hse.gov.uk/contact/faqs/policy.htm
- HSE. *Health and Safety Made Simple: The Basics for Your Business*. HSE Books, Sudbury. (2021). Available at: http://www.hse.gov.uk/simple-health-safety/write.htm
- TSO *Health and Safety at Work Etc. Act 1974*, Chapter 37. (2003). TSO, Norwich

# Sickness absence policies

All employers should have a written policy, agreed between management and staff representatives, describing how the organization will manage absence attributed to sickness.

► Well-managed organizations record and monitor sickness absence and other causes of non-attendance and act on it at all levels—individual workers, departments, and work sites.

## Purpose

To inform employees and managers about how the organization manages sickness absence.

## Main requirements

The sickness absence policy should:

- Give a working definition of sickness absence
- Describe the arrangements for recording and analysing absence rates in the organization (see ➔ p. 438, Sickness absence: general principles)
- Define the roles and responsibilities of senior managers, line manager, HR advisers, occupational health service (OHS), and the employee in absence management
- Outline employees' rights to sick pay. Discretionary sick pay (not statutory sick pay) may be withdrawn if the employer has information that the employee could do some work, but does not return to work despite appropriate adjustments (check employee's contract allows this)
- Enable the employer to seek a medical report with the employee's consent if there is no OHS
- *Describe the practical arrangements to support 'return to work'*:
  - how and when to seek OH advice
  - rehabilitation plans should be mutually agreed between employee and employer, including any temporary adjustments to duties or hours of work
  - pay arrangements during 'phasing-in' periods should be explicit
  - monitoring and review of rehabilitation programmes should be planned in advance
- Define training in sickness absence management for managers

## Managers' roles

*Senior managers*

Overall responsibility for absence management strategy, ensuring fair and consistent implementation.

*Line managers*

Day-to-day absence management is a fundamental part of a line manager's role. The line manager should:

- Monitor their team's attendance records, compare with absence levels in other teams/departments, and manage individual cases proactively
- Maintain contact with those employees on sickness absence and consider any work modifications/adjustments suggested by health professional in Fit Notes to hasten employee rehabilitation
- Hold a brief informal *return to work interview* with all employees following *any* sickness absence. This is a supportive fact-finding approach separate from any disciplinary process in poor attenders

- *Refer to the OHS for medical input. Late referral to OH is associated with a poor prognosis for return to work. Therefore, early referral, depending on the cause of absence, should be encouraged. Ideally, a referral form or letter should include:*
  - employee's details
  - job description
  - sickness absence record for last 12 months (causes and duration)
  - workplace adjustments/modifications already in place
  - specific queries to be addressed
  - confirmation that employee has given informed consent to referral

## Role of the HR team

HR representatives may have special expertise in managing absence. Their primary role is to advise managers on the correct and equitable implementation of absence policies and associated procedures. They play an important part in helping to resolve disputes or poor relationships between employee(s) and managers. HR representatives can be valuable in overcoming barriers to implementation of OH advice.

## Role of the OHS

The OH professional aims to ensure that for all absence referrals:
- Medical reasons for absence are assessed fully, while protecting the confidentiality of sensitive information
- Both employer and employee receive impartial objective advice
- Advice about adjustments to work are provided, wherever appropriate, which are justifiable and practicable

## Employees' responsibilities

Clarify employees' responsibilities in the event of sickness absence.
- When to inform the employer if they are ill
- Whom to inform—usually their line manager
- Requirement to maintain contact while off sick
- When to provide a self-certification of absence
- When to provide a doctor's Statement of Fitness for Work

## Further information

ACAS. Available at: ☞ https://www.acas.org.uk/article/4199/Managing-staff-absence-A-step-by-step-guideFit *for Work: The Complete Guide to Managing Sickness Absence and Rehabilitation*. (2005). Engineering Employer's Federation, London. ISBN 1903461715.

HSE (2004). *Managing Sickness Absence and Return to Work. An Employers' and Managers' Guide*, HSG249. HSE Books, Sudbury. Federation, London. Available at: ☞ http://www.cipd.co.uk/default.cipd. See absence management section

National Institute for Health and Clinical Excellence (2012). *Management of Long-Term Sickness and Incapacity for Work*, PH19. NICE, London. Available at: ☞ http://guidance.nice.org.uk/PH19

National Institute for Health and Clinical Excellence (2019). *Workplace Health; Long-Term Sickness Absence and Capability to Work*, NG146. NICE, London. Available at: ☞ https://www.nice.org.uk/guidance/ng146

# Wellness/well-being policies

## Purpose

Workplace well-being aims to take a holistic approach to wellness at work by preventing occupational illness and accidents while enhancing well-being in the workplace, but also addressing the physical and social factors that influence health such as:

- Poor nutrition
- Lack of exercise
- Work/home conflicts

There are clear economic benefits for those employers achieving effective health promoting workplaces. These include reduced sickness absence rates, improved morale, and a better public image.

▶ The National Institute for Health and Clinical Excellence (NICE) has produced evidence-based guidance for employers including:

- Promoting physical activity in the workplace (PH 13)
- Workplace interventions to promote smoking cessation (PH 5)
- Promoting mental well-being at work (PH 22)
- Healthy workplaces (QS 147)

## Workplace wellness/well-being

There are several aspects to a workplace wellness programme, including physical, social, and health initiatives. Research supported by National Health Service (NHS) England and NHS Improvement has shown that effective workplace well-being interventions require some key enablers—leadership and management involvement, data collection, communication, and establishing a healthy working environment.

*A healthy physical environment*

- Enhance the physical environment with better lighting, noise abatement, and action to reduce the risks of violence to staff
- *Develop a travel plan:*
    - encourage walking or cycling to work (provide bike lockers, shower facilities)
    - allow home working
    - encourage the use of stairs
    - promote walking to meetings nearby
- Organize lunchtime walking groups, allow exercise groups to use rooms for yoga or aerobics, and offer discounted membership to gyms
- Participation in national or corporate challenges to increase physical activity among employees
- Workplace smoking controls including developing a smoking policy

*A healthy social environment*

- Promote an open organizational culture
- Meet stress/mental health policy
- Employee assistance programme (EAP) or a staff counselling service

- *Family-friendly work policies, e.g.*
  - home working
  - flexitime
- Staff 'climate' surveys to assess employee satisfaction

*Health initiatives*

- *Health education, e.g. on*: safe drinking, time management, maintaining a healthy work–life balance
- Smoking cessation clinics
- Offering healthy eating options in the staff canteen and fruit as a snack
- Promote exercise/weight management
- Executive health checks

Effective workplace well-being approaches actively engage employees and managers to identify priorities.

## Workplace well-being in the UK

The UK government's white paper *Choosing Health* has highlighted priority areas for lifestyle change in the interests of improving the public health. Key areas include healthy eating, stopping smoking, sensible alcohol drinking, and exercise. The importance of OH professionals in promoting healthy behaviours within the workplace is explicit in the document.

- The Healthy Workplace Initiative is sponsored by the Department of Health and the HSE and aims to promote workplace health in England and Wales
- A similar initiative in Scotland is called Healthy Working Lives
- The NHS has developed a diagnostic tool and staff health and well-being framework for its own workforce in England

## Main requirements

- To be successful, a workplace wellness policy must involve all workers
- The policy must have the active support of senior managers
- The organizational culture should encourage employee participation
- The draft policy should be discussed and agreed by a working group of managers and staff before being circulated to staff for comment and feedback
- The final policy should commit the organization to integrating workplace well-being into its management systems
- The policy should affirm that all wellness initiatives are to be project managed and so require a needs analysis, priority setting, project implementation, continuous monitoring, and audit
- HR policies should reflect the well-being objective by embracing wellness issues, e.g. encouraging work–life balance
- The wellness policy should include the provision of a fully integrated OH and safety service

## Further information

*Creating a Healthy Workplace* (2006). *A Guide for Occupational Safety and Health Professionals and Employers*. Faculty of Occupational Medicine and Faculty of Public Health Medicine, London.

European Network for Workplace Health Promotion (ENWHP). Regularly updated website. Available at: http://www.enwhp.org

*Fitness for Work; The Medical Aspects* (2019). 6th edn. Chapter 5. Health promotion in the workplace. ISBN 978-0-19-880865-7.

HSE. *Management Standards for Work Related Stress*. HSE. (2017). HSE Books, Sudbury. Available at: http://www.hse.gov.uk/stress/

National Institute for Health and Clinical Excellence (2012). *Promoting Mental Wellbeing at Work*. NICE, London. Available at: http://guidance.nice.org.uk/PH22

National Institute for Health and Clinical Excellence (2012). *Promoting Physical Activity in the Workplace*. NICE, London. Available at: http://www.nice.org.uk/PH13

National Institute for Health and Clinical Excellence (2012). *Workplace Interventions to Promote Smoking Cessation*. NICE, London. Available at: http://www.nice.org.uk/PH5

*NHS Staff Health and Wellbeing Framework and Diagnostic Tool*. (2021) Available at: https://www.nhsemployers.org/retention-and-staff-experience/health-and-wellbeing/developing-your-health-and-wellbeing-strategy/health-and-wellbeing-framework

# Immunization policies

Immunizations may be carried out by OH departments:

- To protect workers against preventable infections
- To protect patients/colleagues (in health care setting) against infection
- For employees who are required to travel abroad

## OH department policies

If immunization programmes are offered, a written immunization policy should be developed. As a minimum, the policy should outline:

- The list of immunizations that are given
- The broad indications for immunization including staff groups who will normally be immunized and others according to a risk assessment
- Who will give immunizations, and arrangements for their training
- *Arrangements for record keeping/advising worker of vaccination status*:
  - arrangements for storage and disposal of vaccines
  - include arrangements for monitoring and recording of the cold chain, e.g. refrigerator temperatures
  - safeguards to protect vaccines in the event of refrigerator power failure
- Arrangements for recalls (e.g. for scheduled doses and boosters)
- *Arrangements for reporting adverse events related to immunization*:
  - report to in-house adverse event monitoring system
  - report to Committee on Safety of Medicines via 'yellow card' scheme (reports can be made electronically to Medicines and Healthcare Products Regulatory Agency (MHRA))
- Arrangements for communication of fitness for work/necessary restrictions in light of outcome of immunization to the employer
- Arrangements for those who decline immunization or fail to attend
- Arrangements for monitoring including audit of immunization policy

## Vaccination procedures

These are usually outlined in a separate document or as an appendix to the main immunization policy. Checklists should include:

- Clinical governance arrangements to be followed
- Gaining and recording employees' consent
- Protocol for the safe administration of vaccines
- Recording immunizations in OH records and communicating information to general practitioners (GPs) (with employee's consent)
- Management of adverse events including anaphylaxis (see ➔ p. 814, Management of anaphylaxis)

## Patient group directions(PGDs)

OH nurses usually carry out immunizations under generic instruction from OH physicians. By law (Statutory Instrument 2000 No. 1917), vaccines that are given in this way must be the subject of written PGDs.

> The legal definition of a PGD is:
>
> a written instruction for the supply and/or administration of a licensed medicine (or medicines) in an identified clinical situation, signed by a doctor or dentist and a pharmacist.

- *PGDs should be developed by*:
  - a senior OH physician
  - a senior OH nurse
  - a senior pharmacist
  - the clinical governance leads
  - as a matter of good practice, local drugs and therapeutics committees, and area prescribing committees should also be involved
- *Each vaccine should have a separate PGD, which should include*:
  - name of the body to which the PGD applies
  - dates of commencement and expiry of PGD
  - description of vaccine
  - class of registered health professionals who may administer vaccine
  - signature of a doctor and a pharmacist
  - signature by appropriate health organization
  - indications for vaccine
  - patients who should be excluded
  - description of circumstances when advice should be sought
  - dose, route, and schedule of administration
  - potential adverse reactions and actions to be taken
  - records to be kept for audit purposes

## Minimum training requirements

OH nurses who are giving immunizations must receive appropriate training. A set of national standards, defined by the Health Protection Agency, outline the basic training requirements including:

- Professional qualifications
- Specified training content, duration of baseline training and frequency of updates, post-training assessment
- Access to national immunization policies
- Inclusion of training in formal audit of immunization programmes
- Content of training for trainers

## Further information and guidance

Department of Health and Social Care (2021). Immunization against Infectious Disease. —*'The Green Book'*. DoH, London. Available at: http://www.dh.gov.uk/en/Publicationsandstatistics/Publications/PublicationsPolicyAnd Guidance/DH_07991

Public Health England (2018). National Minimum Standards and Core Curriculum for Immunisation Training for Registered Healthcare Practitioners. Available at https://assets.publishing.service.gov.uk/government/uploads/system/uploads/attachment_data/file/679824/Training_standards_and_core_curriculum_immunisation.pdf

National Prescribing Centre: Guidance and Framework of Competencies for the Use of PGDs (2009). Available at: http://www.npc.nhs.uk/non_medical/resources/patient_group_directions.pdf

Nursing and Midwifery Council (2008). *Standards for Medicines Management*. NMC, London. Available at: http://www.nmc-uk.org/Documents/Standards/nmcStandardsForMedicinesManagementBooklet.pdf

# Mental health policies

## Purpose

To assist the organization in fulfilling its responsibilities to maintain the mental health and well-being of employees at work.

## Development

Must have support from senior management, ideally at board level. Set up a steering group, chaired by a senior manager and include representatives from:

- Management
- HR
- OH
- Safety
- Union(s) or other employee representatives

## Framework

In October 2017, Thriving at Work, a review of mental health and employers, provided a series of policy recommendations to support employers in improving mental health approaches.

Physical hazard model (see ➔ p. 146, Organizational psychosocial factors; ➔ p. 344, Stress 2: interventions/risk control).

A mental health policy should describe local arrangements for the prevention and management of mental ill health under the following headings:

*Assessment of risk*

- *Discussion between interested parties*:
  - satisfy HSE's requirement to consult
  - structured discussion around six key areas (HSE Management Standards)
  - give picture of current work situation
  - identify processes which may cause stress
  - facilitate practical recommendations, especially from employees
- Staff satisfaction surveys
- Sickness absence rates
- Employee turnover
- Business trends

***Prevention/risk reduction***

*Primary*

- Supportive management culture
- Reporting outcome of risk assessment and resulting action plan to directors/board
- Effective leadership and management skills
- *Appropriate management systems*:
  - resource and project management
  - process management
  - interdependency and infrastructure management
- Change management
- Communication

- *HR-related policies and procedures*:
  - appraisal and training
  - work–life balance
  - flexible working, including home working
  - bullying and harassment
  - violence at work
  - shift work
  - alcohol and drugs
- *Ergonomics*: job design, and so on
- *Awareness of available support interventions*

*Secondary*

- Mental health first aid or similar training
- Effective sickness absence policy
- Early referral of cases to OH; option of self-referral to OH
- Easy access to appropriate psychological treatment
- *General health promotion*:
  - regular exercise programme/relaxation regime
  - smoking cessation support
  - healthy eating/sensible alcohol consumption

*Tertiary*

An effective rehabilitation policy has a joint approach towards individual case management through round-table discussions (see ➔ p. 344, Stress 2: interventions/risk control), where:

- *OH advise on*:
  - functional capacity
  - temporary or permanent nature of disability
  - types of reasonable adjustments
- *Management consider*:
  - business requirements
  - health and safety issues
  - training requirements
  - preparation of colleagues for return of employee's return to work
- HR coordinates programme

*Monitoring and auditing policy*

- Trends in employee satisfaction and engagement
- Action plans for effecting appropriate interventions to address recognized difficulties
- Compliance with and effectiveness of the policy in managing employees' mental ill health

## Further information and guidance

HSE. *Work-Related Stress—Together We Can Tackle It.* (2021). HSE Books, Sudbury. Available at: http://www.hse.gov.uk/stress

*Mental Health First Aid*. Regularly updated website. Available at: http://mhfa.org.uk/en/

*Thriving at Work: The Stevenson/Farmer Review of Mental Health and Employers.(2019)* Available at: https://www.gov.uk/government/publications/thriving-at-work-a-review-of-mental-health-and-employers

# Substance abuse policies

## Epidemiology of substance abuse

Alcohol and drug misuse is common in the UK, with alcohol misuse being most common, with major societal costs.

Drug misuse is more common in younger people: NHS Digital statistics for 2016/7 suggest one in 12 adults (8.5%) aged 16–59 had taken an illicit drug in the last year. Statistics for alcohol abuse are much higher but are difficult to determine accurately.

## Why have a policy?

Substance misuse has important implications for personal health, work performance (particularly if safety critical), protecting business probity, and complying with customer requirements. A policy forms the framework for managing alcohol and drug misuse, ensuring clarity, consistency, fairness, and legal compliance (see Tables 19.1 and 19.2 ➲ p. 796, Methods for alcohol and drug screening).

**Table 19.1** The main substance abuse policy components

| | |
|---|---|
| Purpose | Safe working arrangements, employee support |
| Roles and responsibilities | Management leadership, employee cooperation |
| Application | Applies to managers, employees, and contractors |
| Procedures | Communicated and understood by all |
| Discipline | Possible job termination for policy breach |
| Support | Managed as 'sickness' when worker seeks help |
| Testing | Defined testing reasons and chain of custody for quality assurance |

**Table 19.2** Legal obligations

| | |
|---|---|
| Health and Safety at Work Act 1974 | Employers have a duty to protect employees and others involved in their business. Employees have duty to cooperate in health and safety matters |
| Transport and Works Act 1974 | Bans safety critical railway operations while under the influence of alcohol or drugs |
| Work in Compressed Air Regulations 1996 | Prohibits working in compressed air while under the influence of alcohol or drugs |
| Road Traffic Act 1984 | Employers must assure safe driving arrangements. Employees must not drive under the influence of alcohol or drugs |
| Misuse of Drugs Act 1971 | Employers must not allow the use, possession, or production of any controlled substance, including cannabis on their premises |

## Policy components

A supportive approach should be taken, encouraging those with health problems to seek help. Principles should be aligned with the employer's values, the law, good employment, and medical practice.

## Ethical considerations

These cover the right to personal privacy and the confidential management of sensitive personal information.

- International organizations need to respect legal and cultural differences between the countries in which they operate
- Employees should be fully advised on testing procedures and their rights
- Observe reasonable standards of enquiry and respect privacy in searching personal belongings and so on
- OH staff undertaking tests must avoid giving medical advice to individuals, to avoid confusing their testing and OH roles
- Disciplinary action following substance misuse testing should not involve OH staff: this could compromise employee relationships

## Roles and competencies

- Managers are responsible for the implementation of the policy
- Medical Review Officer is a physician with specialist knowledge and training in specimen collection, chain of custody, analytical procedures, and alternative explanations for positive analytical results
- OH practitioners may advise on policy and test arrangements. They have a separate role in advising employers and managers in support and rehabilitation arrangements and assessing fitness for work

## Treatment and rehabilitation

Workers who volunteer a substance misuse problem may receive advice and support to seek treatment and rehabilitation. Subject to their cooperation, many organizations will maintain their employment.

## Further information

BMA (2016). Alcohol, drugs and the workplace—The role of medical professionals. Available at https://www.bAlcohol, drugs and the workplace—The role of medical professionals.

# Travel policies 1: General travel policy

- International travel is now a common feature of employment. Employees who travel on company business should be assessed, screened, prepared, and cared for during and after their trip. The risk of travel-related illness or injury requires consideration of a number of factors, including individual, occupational, destination, and organizational related factors.

## Travel policy

A corporate travel policy will depend on the potential hazards associated with the overseas work, and the organizational approach to international health and safety. Any policy should include both individual and organizational risk assessments and risk mitigation measures.

Such a policy should include the following:

*Risk assessment*

This risk assessment should be at both an individual and organizational level. This will include evaluation of work activity, location, security situation, health care facilities, endemic disease, and environment insurance (medical care).

- Comprehensive cover, appropriate to the individual and destination(s)
- Include insurance for emergency medical evacuation for remote areas
- Use insurers that provide remote access to health resource information and identify and source medical assistance if required

*Security*

- Awareness and understanding of local security issues are vital
- Include 24-hour contact for emergency advice
- Give advice on personal behaviours that affect individual's risk
- Consider specific safety and security courses for certain environments
- Road traffic accidents are a common cause of morbidity and mortality due to poor vehicle maintenance, driving skills, and roads

*Crisis management*

- Situations abroad can change rapidly (disease outbreaks, natural disasters civil unrest)
- Monitor events worldwide
- Include contingency plans to deal with emergency events

*Fitness to travel or work abroad*

- The aim is to ensure that the individual is fit to travel and work abroad with any risk to themselves or others
- How this is done will vary
- For certain industries, there may be best practice guidance
- For those with pre-existing conditions, consider the effect of travel, environment, endemic diseases, adequacy of local medical facilities, and availability of medication/medical equipment

*Travel health*

- Provision of immunizations, malaria prophylaxis, and other preventive health advice should be started at least 4–6 weeks in advance of travel
- Detailed destination-specific recommendations must be obtained from up-to-date online resources from national or international authorities such as the UK National Travel Health Network and Centre, the US Centers for Disease Control and Prevention, or World Health Organization
- These resources are also essential for highlighting disease outbreaks
- Maintain documented mandated immunizations (e.g. yellow fever or polio) to avoid entry denial, forced quarantine, or vaccination at borders

*Psychological stressors*

Stressors include:

- Complex and long travel itineraries
- High expectations by the business
- Jet lag
- Cultural adaptation/adjustment
- Family separation

Recognize the challenges and legitimize mitigating behaviours:

- Encourage adequate rest before meetings
- Consider providing access to an EAP

*Personal guidance*

- Ensure traveller is aware of potential health challenges that may be encountered
- Confirm traveller understands strategies to preserve health during trip
- Highlight potential ↑ risk behaviours during travel for business traveller
- Pay particular attention to alcohol, drug use, and sexual behaviours
- Give traveller a simple guide of essential health tips

*Venous thromboembolism (VTE)*

- VTE can occur as a result of long periods of immobility associated with any form of travel.
- For a flight >4 hours, in healthy individuals, the risk is estimated to be one in 6,000
- Those at increased risk include older travellers, pregnant women, those with a previous history of VTE or recent surgery, those with certain blood clotting disorders, malignancy, certain heart conditions, and those taking oestrogen-containing medicines
- Advice on maintaining mobility and exercising during travel
- Discourage tranquillizing medication—may affect mobility during flights
- Those at increased risk may benefit from the use of properly fitted compression socks; low-molecular-weight heparin therapy may also be recommended

*Circadian desynchrony (jet lag)*

- Starts to have an effect after three time zones (➔ p. 160, Time zone changes)
- Resulting fatigue affects concentration and decision-making
- Allow time to acclimatize on arrival at destination in travel plans

*Traveller's diarrhoea (TD)*

- The most common travellers' health problem
- Attack rates range from 30 to 70%, depending on destination and season
- Bacterial pathogens thought to account for up to 80–90% of TD
- Following advice on food and water hygiene may help but should be prepared to manage the symptoms. Usually resolves spontaneously, aim of treatment is to avoid dehydration, reduce the severity and duration, and reduce impact on travel plans
- Standby antibiotics such as azithromycin can be considered for those at high risk of severe illness or those visiting high-risk areas where access to medical care is limited

*Malaria*

- Malaria is a significant risk factor for travellers to endemic areas particularly in sub-Saharan Africa
- *Promote ABCD*: awareness; bite prevention; chemoprophylaxis; prompt diagnosis and treatment

► Business appears well informed regarding malaria risk but complies poorly with preventive measures.

*Travel medical kits*

- Content should be tailored to the individual, the destination, and travel plans; from simple over-the-counter painkillers, insect repellents, and skin dressings to more comprehensive kits with prescription-only medication and other pre-hospital care supplies
- Instructions should be clear and comprehensive

*Post-trip precautions*

- Asymptomatic short-term travellers rarely need a post-travel medical examination
- Screening may be relevant for certain exposures (e.g. schistosomiasis)
- Early reporting of post-travel fever or illness is essential
- ► Need to complete the full course of malaria prophylaxis, if prescribed
- EAP to be available for problems related to the stressors of travel

## Further information

National Travel Health Network and Centre (UK). Regularly updated web resource London. Available at: https://travelhealthpro.org.uk/

Travax (Scotland). Regularly updated Web resource Scotland. Available at: http://www.travax.nhs.uk/Centers for Disease Control and Prevention (CDC) Travelers Health (USA) Available at: http://www.cdc.gov/travel/

*World Health Organization (WHO) International Travel and Health*. WHO, Geneva. Regularly updated web resource. WHO. Available at: http://www.who.int/ith/en/

# Travel policies 2: Expatriate policy

## Definition of the expatriate worker

An employee who resides in another country for occupational purposes but returns to their original country upon completion of the assignment.

## Expatriate policies

Policies should include general travel advice (➲ p. 418, Travel policy 1: general travel policies). However, prolonged residence requires extra considerations. Therefore, expatriate worker policies should also include the following sections:

*Selection process*

- Avoid pressing workers to accept postings, e.g. for career progression
- Encourage spouse to be involved in decision-making, as family problems are a common reason for expatriate posting failure
- Those with pre-existing health conditions may wish to research the suitability of an assignment before applying

*Pre-posting orientation*

Family orientation visits are helpful before acceptance of posting. The employee and their family should consider lifestyle factors that will be affected by the move, including environmental, cultural, and social changes, medical care, family adjustments, security, and schooling.

*Fitness for duty*

*Literature on pre-travel fitness assessments for overseas workers is limited. The use of general traveller risk assessment and health questionnaires will be sufficient for most situations, with a medical examination where appropriate.*

- *Fitness for overseas assignments should contain the following elements*:
  - a detailed medical history
  - detailed occupational history
  - evaluation of physical capacity if duties have specific fitness requirements.
- Psychological suitability for assignment is difficult to predict. Future mental health problems are associated with a number of risk factors such as previous history of psychological problems, depressed mood, family history of mental ill-health, physical ill-health, and work stress
- Where pre-existing health concerns are identified, careful planning is required
- Health resources at location: detailed evaluation of local and regional health care resources
- Include national, private, and if available, in-house health facilities
- Guidance on identified limitations of available health care
- Define how to assist expatriates identify/access routine health care
- Avoid single providers wherever possible as options allow choice

*Emergencies and medical evacuations (medivacs)*

- Define emergency procedures to deal with illness or injury that may exceed the scope of local health care resources
- Include all management that need to authorize release of corporate resources or finance for management of the severely ill or injured

- Identify in-country 'liaison physician' to assess and communicate the patient's condition to local management and/or corporate medical staff
- Understand evacuation alternatives and time delays for each option. In certain postings, consider a contract with air ambulance providers

*Medication supply*

- Understand potential limitations in supply of prescribed drugs
- Encourage routine prescription-filling during scheduled home leaves
- Advise holding a minimum of a 3-month supply of medication
- Where appropriate, communicate concerns related to counterfeit medicine supply in destination country or region
- Identify providers that will fill and ship personal prescriptions overseas
- Some countries may require a formal doctor's prescription when carrying some medications or may prohibit use of certain medications in some administrations.

*Medical insurance*

- Insurance should cover expatriate to provide, as far as practicable, equivalent level of care to that in home country
- Include medical evacuation insurance where appropriate
- Ensure there is clarity on elective procedures, chronic disease management, obstetric care (locally, at a regional referral centre, country of residence)
- Ensure that excluded conditions are explicit, so that expatriates can mitigate potential gaps in care while on home leave
- Communicate processes for use of medical insurance and policy on reimbursement of any excess payments

## Other issues

*Employee assistance programme*

- ► Expatriates have been shown to have a consistently higher incidence of mental health problems
- Mental health problems are one of the principal causes of assignment attrition
- EAPs offer a valuable resource
- Local EAP provider is preferable but cultural factors may preclude this—home country resource as a default
- OH department follow-up should be arranged as appropriate

*Rotational assignments*

- Complicated risk group because of swinging cultural exposures
- Often very extensive travel involved
- On-site behaviours may be negatively affected by poor perception of risk, including unrealistic beliefs about ready accessibility to home country health care

*Post-assignment*

- Recognize the *reverse culture shock* of return to home country
- Consider medical screening for specific exposures such as schistosomiasis
- Consider OH follow-up for those who have significant illness, injury
- Reiterate availability of the EAP service to returning expatriates

*In-patriates*

Expatriates from another country who are on a temporary business-related posting to the host country corporate office location:

- Need to understand scope of/access to local health care provision
- Need to be appraised of cultural issues
- Recognize potential of employee importing illness not normally seen in host population, leading to difficulty/delay in diagnosis (e.g. malaria)
- EAP provision is essential for this group and families

# Violence management policies

## Purpose

To assist the organization in protecting its staff from abuse, threats, or violence. (See also ➔ p. 150, Violence and aggression.) Policy documents should cover the following:

## Arrangements for risk assessment and control

- Management responsibility for assessing the risk of violence in every workplace and for each job or group of jobs
- Examples of good practice in risk reduction can usefully be given in an appendix as pre written examples

## Promoting a culture where abuse is not permitted

Give a clear message that aggression towards staff is not appropriate, and offenders will be prosecuted, i.e. a 'zero tolerance' approach.

## Training for employees

All staff should be given basic information about violence and instructions for managing difficult behaviour including how to raise the alarm:

- Understand the mindset of the hostile or potentially violent person
- There may be a need to 'communicate' their grievance to someone
- Provide the hostile person with a verbal outlet
- Use 'active listening'
- Avoid confrontation/'fight back'
- Build trust with the hostile individual and provide help if needed
- Allow a total airing of the grievance without comment or judgment
- Preserve the individual's dignity, as fear of embarrassment will prevent hostile individuals from abandoning plans for violence
- Allow hostile people to suggest solutions for a win–win resolution

Staff who are working in high-risk areas should have detailed training including predicting and avoiding anger and aggression, effusion techniques and using control and restraint as a last resort

## Management of staff who have been abused

- Debriefing by a manager to explore distress when staff are ready
- Information about routes to crisis organizations and helplines will allow employees to choose a source appropriate for their needs
- Specialist counselling (including therapeutic techniques) may be needed if employees are severely traumatized
- Affected individuals often need help and support to seek redress from attackers. Involvement of the police can be helpful
- Where necessary, offer access to legal advice regarding civil claims or compensation from the Criminal Injuries Compensation Board

## Employees' responsibilities

- Employees must try, wherever possible, to defuse violent situations
- Report violent or aggressive incidents

## Arrangements for reporting incidents

The adverse event recording system must be clear to all employees.

**Table 19.3** Examples of practical risk management

| Increased risk of violence | Risk control |
|---|---|
| Any jobs that involve public interface, especially if controlling or enforcing (e.g. traffic wardens) | Wide counters, barriers, security cameras, restricted access to work in areas for members of the public |
| Client group with risk factors for aggression: particularly, health care (ambulance workers, accident and emergency staff, mental health workers), custodial services (prison and probation officers) | Assessment of individual client's potential for violent behaviour should be a routine part of the care or service plan |
| Boredom, frustration, anxiety | Environmental factors: avoid long waits for services, provide comfortable waiting rooms, basic refreshments, children's play areas. Inform clients about delays and explain the reason |
| Control and restraint tend to escalate violence | Restraint techniques should be used only in extremes, as a last resort |
| Alcohol and drugs | Prohibit alcohol and drug use at high-risk events. Recognize intoxicated behaviours |
| Cash transactions | Avoid keeping large quantities of cash in work premises |
| Lone or night working | Avoid isolation. Have a means for lone workers to summon assistance. Pair-up staff for visits to high-risk clients. Ensure good lighting outside premises and in car parks |

## Monitoring and review

- Regular monitoring of incidents, and link to review of risk assessments
- Staff surveys and exit interviews of staff who resign help to define the size and nature of the problem, and under-reporting of incidents

## Further information and guidance

NICE (2005). *Violence: The Short-Term Management of Disturbed/Violent Behaviour in Psychiatric In-Patient Settings and Emergency Departments*, NICE Clinical Guideline 25. NICE, London.

NICE (2015). *Violence and Aggression: Short-Term Management in Mental Health, Health and Community Settings*, NG 10. NICE, London. Available at: https://www.nice.org.uk/guidance/ng10

Special rules apply to the restraint or treatment of patients with acute mental illness. Further information is available in the Code of Practice (Revised 2008). Mental Health Act 1983.

The NHS Security Management Service gives sector-specific advice for health care. NHS, England. Regularly updated web resource. Available at: http://www.nhsbsa.nhs.uk/SecurityManagement.aspx

Useful links (including some industry-specific guidance) are available via the HSE website. Available at: http://www.hse.gov.uk/violence/information.htm

Chapter 20

# Sickness absence, rehabilitation, and retirement

# Improving health and well-being through work

## Health and unemployment

There is good research evidence to suggest that unemployment is associated with poor health.

- *Those who are out of work have an increased risk of*:
  - mortality from cardiovascular disease, cancers, suicide, accidents, and violence
  - morbidity from depression, ischaemic heart disease, and other conditions
  - experiencing inequality in health and social opportunities
- In general, getting people back to work after illness or with disability is likely to benefit their long-term health
- However, it is clear that it is 'good work' rather than any employment that is health promoting
- Long-term absence from work due to sickness has a poor prognosis. The likelihood of returning to work is below 50% after 6 months of absence

## Barriers to work and rehabilitation

- Cultural beliefs about the right of sick people to be excused from work, and failure to recognize that work is beneficial for most people
- Pressure on general practitioners (GPs) from patients or relatives to certificate absence from work, and difficulty for GPs in declining to certificate
- Poor access to occupational health (OH) advice for many employees because of a shortage of OH professionals and other factors
- Fit note completion often fails to propose work adjustments
- Employers' reluctance to arrange adjustments to work ('all or nothing' mentality), or poor understanding about positive effects for business
- Lack of practical affordable support for rehabilitation

## Overcoming barriers to rehabilitation in the UK

The drive to improve return to work and rehabilitation has been helped by changes in legislation, primarily the Equality Act. However, cultural attitudes are slow to change. Pro-active and coordinated effort is required from political and social drivers and a range of stakeholders. The 'Improving Lives: Health, Work and Disability' consultation and Command Paper has outlined a Government strategy to enable 1 million additional people with disability or long-term conditions to access work. A comprehensive description of solutions is beyond the scope of the handbook, but some broad approaches, current leads, and stakeholders are outlined here for reference.

### *Broad approaches*

- *Preventing ill health and injury in the workplace*:
  - general measures to improve the public health
  - maximizing opportunities to support health promotion at work
  - managing specific risks to health and safety at work
- Encouraging all doctors to consider return to work as part of the clinical management plan, including introduction of the 'fit-note' (revised Med 3 suggesting what work can be done by an employee, rather than automatically certificating off all work) and promoting work as a clinical outcome

- Supporting employers to make adjustments to work
- Improving access to OH advice
- *Improving the consistency and quality of OH advice* (➔ p. 388, Quality and audit in occupational practice 1: general principles; ➔ p. 390, quality and audit in occupational practice 2: systems and tools):
  - audit in OH practice
  - evidence-based guidelines on OH issues
  - accreditation for quality and governance
- Providing work rehabilitation schemes for those who are off work long term due to ill health, particularly using a case management approach
- Promoting good human resources (HR) practice

*Government lead*

The White Paper 'Choosing Health'[1] shows leadership in tackling the barriers to retaining, regaining, or accessing work. Work from a number of initiatives underpin this lead, including:

- *The Health, Work, and Well-being Unit established in 2005, and jointly sponsored by the Department for Work and Pensions (DWP), the Health and Safety Executive (HSE), the Department of Health (DH), and the Scottish Government and the Welsh Assembly Government. The unit:*
  - promotes the link between good work and health
  - collates and adds to the evidence base
  - drives change in this area
- *The National Director for Health and Work undertook reviews, which outline relevant recommendations for improving health through work and for promoting early rehabilitation to work:*
  - on the health of the working age population (2008, government response—Improving Health and Work—Changing Lives)
  - on sickness absence, jointly with the Director General of the British Chambers of Commerce (2011, government response awaited)
  - consultation exercises on 'Improving Lives, Health, Work and Disability' and 'Health is Everyone's business' have informed policy proposals

*Other stakeholders*

- OH professionals and service providers
- GPs and other health professionals, e.g. doctors in secondary care
- Faculty and Society of Occupational Medicine, Royal Colleges
- Employers and employers' organizations, e.g. Confederation of British Industry (CBI), UK manufacturers' organization (EEF), NHS employers
- Employees and their representatives (e.g. trade unions), self-employed
- HR professionals
- Insurance companies
- Local authorities
- Voluntary sector organizations

Table 20.1 lists the most important initiatives from the UK government and other stakeholders. It is not an exhaustive list, and it is important to recognize different stakeholders may hold differing interests and perspectives.

1 Department of Health (2004). *Choosing Health: Making Healthier Choices Easier*. Public Health White Paper. Department of Health, London.

**Table 20.1** Supporting prevention, rehabilitation, and healthy working in the UK

| Driver | Strategy or initiative | Description | Web reference |
|---|---|---|---|
| National Director for Health and Work and Director General British Chambers of Commerce | Health and Work: an independent review of sickness absence | Review of the sickness absence system in Great Britain to help combat the costs and impact of sickness absence | http://www.dwp.gov.uk/policy/welfare-reform/sickness-absence-review/ |
| HSE | Health and Safety made simple 2011 | Web-based guidance for employers on simplifying compliance with health and safety law | http://www.hse.gov.uk/simple-health-safety/ |
| DWP | Good for Everyone. The next steps in the Government's plans for reform of the health and safety system in Britain 2011 | Sets out a new start for health and safety regulation for businesses. Focus on deregulation for well-performing employers and making poorly performing employers bear the costs of inspection and rectification of non-compliance | http://www.dwp.gov.uk/docs/good-health-and-safety.pdf |
| Work and Health Unit | Improving lives, the future of work, health, and disability 2017 | Describes a 10-year strategy to improve employment access for those with disability | https://www.gov.uk/government/publications/improving-lives-the-future-of-work-health-and-disability |
| Work and Health Unit | Health is everyone's business proposals to reduce ill-health related job loss | Consultation of improving access to occupational health advice | https://www.gov.uk/government/consultations/health-is-everyones-business-proposals-to-reduce-ill-health-related-job-loss |
| HSE | The Health and Safety of Great Britain//Be part of the strategy 2009 | Sets out the HSE Board's strategy for the health and safety system, recognizing the role of stakeholders in maintaining and improving health and safety standards | http://www.hse.gov.uk/strategy/strategy09.pdf |

| Driver | Strategy or initiative | Description | Web reference |
|---|---|---|---|
| DH and DWP | Improving Health and Work: changing lives 2008 | The Government's response to Working for a Healthier Tomorrow | http://www.dwp.gov.uk/docs/hwwb-improving-health-and-work-changing-lives.pdf |
| National Director for Health and Work | Working for a Healthier Tomorrow 2008 | Report on the health of the working age population, presented to the Secretary of State for Health and the Secretary of State for Work and Pensions | http://www.dwp.gov.uk/docs/hwwb-working-for-a-healthier-tomorrow.pdf |
| DWP | Information for professionals and advisers | Various educational tools including desk-aids and web-based learning packages for doctors. Aimed at promoting good practice in relation to managing return to work after sickness or with disability | http://www.dwp.gov.uk/healthcare-professional/guidance/ |
| DH | NHS Plus | A network of NHS OH departments that provide OH advice to SMEs | https://nhshealthatwork.co.uk |
| DH | NHS Health at Work Network | Network of NHS OH providers, working in partnership with NHS Plus and NHS Employers to promote collaborative working and exemplary provision of OH services to NHS staff | https://nhshealthatwork.co.uk |
| HSE partnership | Workplace Health Connect | A free occupational health and safety advisory service for SMEs | http://www.workplacehealthconnect.co.uk/ |

Note: It is also important to be mindful of the impact of broader societal and social changes and their impacts on strategic intents.

## Further information

Advice for employers and employees on returning to healthy work.

Advising patients about work: An evidence-based approach for GPs and other health professionals. (2013) DWP, TSO London. Available at: http://www.dwp.gov.uk/docs/hwwb-health-work-gp-leaflet.pdf

DWP. *Health and Well-being Unit—Resources*. Regularly updated web resources. Available at: http://www.dwp.gov.uk/health-work-and-well-being/resources/

Healthy Working Lives. Regularly updated web resources. DHSC London. Available at: http://www.healthyworkinglives.com/

Healthy Working UK. *Fit note guide*. Regularly updated web resources. DHSC London. Available at: http://www.healthyworkinguk.co.uk/

Healthy Working Wales. Regularly updated web resource. Available at: http://www.healthyworkingwales.com/splash_wales/en.html

# Sickness benefits

In the UK, state benefits are payable to those who cannot work due to illness. The process is summarized in Fig. 20.1.

## Statutory Sick Pay (SSP) or equivalent

- Payable by employer for spells of incapacity <28 weeks
- *Certificated according to fitness for own occupation*:
  - <7 days, self-certificate SC1, SC2, or employers own form
  - >7 days, Med 3 (Statement of Fitness for Work) provided by GP or hospital doctor for out-patients or Med 10 provided by hospital doctor for hospital in-patients. Includes advice on rehabilitation

## State benefits[1]

*Employment and Support Allowance (ESA)*

- Entitlement depends on National Insurance (NI) contributions
- Those who have not paid sufficient NI may qualify for income-based ESA depending on income and capital
- State benefits are subject to an assessment of work capability

*Work Capability Assessment (WCA)*

- Eligible when SSP ended, self-employed, or unemployed
- Assessment by a health professional +/− medical assessment
- *Carried out during the first 13 weeks after application*:
  - assessment of limited capability for work: the focus is on what work activities the patient *can* carry out. The applicant has access to a personal adviser, training, and condition management and is expected to move towards a return to work
  - assessment of limited capability for work-related activity: for the most severely affected, who are not expected to prepare for work
- GP no longer required to certificate if ESA awarded
- *The WCA assesses*:
  - the impact of health on daily life
  - the patient's view of the future from a health and work perspective
  - activities the patient enjoys or would like to develop to help them move into work
  - the support the patient feels they need to move into work
- *Following WCA, support for those who are capable of work-related activities*:
  - condition management programme
  - expert health advice
  - workshops on health topics, e.g. coping with pain, positive mood management, motivational support, preparing for work
  - formal-independent reviews of WCA have highlighted controversy in relation to the nature of the assessment and its perceived fairness for benefit applicants

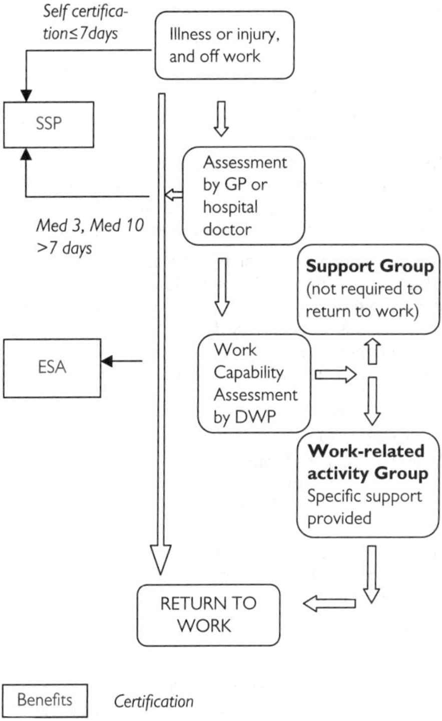


**Fig. 20.1** Summary of the process for assessing eligibility for benefits in relation to fitness for work 1 (as above)

## Further information and guidance

For GPs. DWP Web resources regularly updated. Available at: http://www.dwp.gov.uk/docs/esa-gp-leaflet.pdf; also available at: http://www.dwp.gov.uk/docs/gp-benefit-guide.pdf; also available at: http://www.dwp.gov.uk/docs/fitnote-gp-guide.pdf

For Occupational Health. Available at: http://www.dwp.gov.uk/docs/fitnote-occupational-health-guide.pdf

# Sickness absence: General principles

## Definition and size of the problem

Sickness absence is defined as any absence from work attributed to illness or injury and accepted as such by the employer. It gives rise to significant costs for all organizations. The Office of National Statistics published data in 2019 estimating 141.4 million working days lost due to sickness or injury in 2018 (4.4 days per worker). Although surveys often show higher rates of absence in the public sector, evidence from HSE suggests that differences between the public and private sectors are small and may be partly explained by under-reporting in small private sector organizations.

Estimates of the proportion of sickness absence actually due to non-medical reasons vary widely (~10% up to 30%) and should be viewed with great caution. Determining what proportion of sickness absence is not genuine is, for obvious reasons, very difficult.

Unplanned absence may be a better, more encompassing, term as sickness absence often hides other non-illness or injury causes of lost time.

## Risk factors for sickness absence

Absence rates tend to be higher:

- Among women compared with men
- In older workers (total days of absence), although young workers have more spells of short-term absence
- In larger compared with smaller organizations
- In the public sector compared to private industry (but note that the public sector employs more women and older workers and comprises mostly large organizations)

## Patterns of sickness absence

- *Short-term*:
  - frequent short-term absence is most commonly due to minor unrelated self-limiting illness or injury, although it can indicate chronic underlying ill health
  - however, it can mask non-medical absence
- *Long-term*: almost invariably due to significant medium- to long-term ill health
- Because of this general difference in the nature of short- and long-term absence, the broad approach to management also differs. (See ➔ p. 404, Short-term sickness absence; ➔ p. 406, Long-term sickness absence)

## Measurement of sickness absence

Simply counting hours or days lost as a proportion of total days worked by all staff (*crude absence rate*) may be misleading and does not show whether the main issue is short- or long-term absence.

- *Frequency rate*: shows the mean number of absences per worker as a percentage

  (No. spells of absence in the period/No. employees) × 100

- *Lost time rate*: measures the mean number of working days lost as a percentage of total working days

(Total no. working days lost due to absence in a year/working day in year × total no. employees) × 100

The lost time rate can be calculated across the company or for specific business units or by trade/profession, thus highlighting 'hotspots' of poor attendance. This calculation can also be made for lost hours rather than lost days—useful for employers with a large number of part-time staff.

However, other causes of non-attendance often mean true absence rates are higher (e.g. lateness, carers, or bereavement leave, 'special leave', and so on).

*Bradford score*

$$S^2 \times D$$

where $S$ is the number of spells of absence and $D$ is the number of days of absence in a given time period (e.g. rolling 52-week interval).

The Bradford score is calculated for each worker individually. It highlights the disruption caused by repeated short-term absence by weighting the number of episodes (or spells) of absence. For example,

- Twelve 1-day absences: 12 × 12 × 12 = 1,728
- One 12-day absence: 1 × 1 × 12 = 12
- Three 1-day absences: 3 × 3 × 3 = 27
- One 3-day absence: 1 × 1 × 3 = 3

The Bradford score has been used to set a threshold for case management so that consistency in approach between employees can be demonstrated. The threshold score can be based on the extreme of the distribution (upper 5–10% of all scores) rather than an absolute total score, avoiding the perception of a 'safe score' among employees. This measure tends to be used in organizations where most staff work in shifts and short-term absence is more disruptive than long-term absence.

# Short-term sickness absence

► Frequent short-term term absence is usually regarded as a management issue. The input from OH professionals generally have a different focus compared with long-term absence.

There is no accepted definition of short-term sickness absence—the National Institute for Health and Clinical Excellence (NICE) define it as any absence of less than 28 days and recurrent short-term absence as more than one episode of short-term absence, each episode lasting less than 28 days.

## Factors that affect short-term absence

*Medical*

- Self-limiting illness
- *Poor control of chronic medical conditions*:
  - inadequate treatment
  - poor self-management
  - side-effects of treatment
- *Substance misuse*:
  - alcohol misuse
  - drug misuse
- Epidemics

*Organizational*

- Sick pay
- Personnel policies
- *Poor working conditions*:
  - long or unsociable hours
  - boring or unpleasant work
  - poor training or supervision
  - shift work
- *Interpersonal difficulties in the workplace*:
  - between manager or colleagues

  Note: suspect bullying if absences mirror the supervisor's shifts
- Poor labour relations
- Poor holiday arrangements
- Change, e.g. redundancies

*Psychosocial and cultural*

- Retirement age
- Local unemployment
- *Domestic factors*:
  - childcare
  - elderly relatives
  - sick or disabled relatives
  - intimate partner violence: the British Crime Survey found that 20% of employed female victims and 6% of employed male victims took time off work and 2% of both sexes lost their job as a result
- *Poor work motivation*:
  - young people
  - temporary workers
- *Social and cultural factors*:
  - sporting events
  - appointments with hairdressers, tradesmen, etc.

- holidays
- cultural, e.g. a widespread belief that employees are entitled to a level of sick leave, to be used as additional holiday

## Flag categorization

Another way of segmenting obstacles to return to work may be to use a flag system:

- *Red Flags*: confirmed medical pathology
- *Orange Flags*: psychological disorders
- *Yellow Flags*: individual factors impacting on perception, mood, or beliefs
- *Blue Flags*: organizational issues and policies
- *Black Flags*: societal and social factors

## Role of occupational health

When an employee with repeated short-term absence is referred, the main purpose is to ensure that medical issues are properly taken into account by the employer in managing the absence pattern. The role of OH is to identify medical reasons why the employee's absence pattern might deviate from the average for the organization and to advise the employee on measures that could improve any underlying condition.

- In the absence of medical factors, the OH practitioner should give a clear message that no underlying chronic or recurrent illness explains the excess absence. This is the case when absences are a collection of minor self-limiting illness that are no more likely to occur in the referred employee than in any other. It can be helpful to add that there is no medical intervention that would have an important impact on the pattern of absence
- If an underlying health problem makes the employee more susceptible to short-term absence, the OH practitioner should communicate the susceptibility (but not necessarily the diagnosis) clearly. It is helpful to comment on the likely future pattern of absence (taking into account any medical intervention), and how much excess absence might reasonably be expected
- In the case of recurrent short-term sickness absence due to a single medical condition then the same approach as NICE recommends for the management of long-term sickness absence (NICE PH19) is appropriate (see ➔ p. 442, Long-term sickness absence)

*Interacting psychosocial factors*

- The division between medical and psychosocial is rather more blurred than implied by the checklist here. Factors such as difficulties at home and work often impact on well-being even if they do not cause a well-defined 'illness'
- The OH adviser should facilitate the raising of any workplace issues that might be influencing absence, so that these can be addressed
- It can also be helpful to highlight any major domestic problems so that the manager and HR can at least take these into account, offering support or adaptations where this is appropriate. However, this must be done sensitively, and with the employee's consent

## Further information

NICE (2019) Workplace health: long term sickness absence and capability to work. Available at: https://www.nice.org.uk/guidance/ng146/resources/workplace-health-longterm-sickness-absence-and-capability-to-work-pdf-66141783176389

# Long-term sickness absence

Absences >28 days are usually due to significant illness/injury. OH input aims to enable rehabilitation where possible: ill-health retirement is a last resort. The most common causes of long-term absence are:

- Mental illness (stress, anxiety/depression)
- Musculoskeletal disorders (low back pain, osteoarthritis)

## NICE guidance on sickness absence management (PH19)

NICE guidance on sickness absence management advises early contact with absent employees, ideally at 2–6 weeks' absence, and suggests a tiered response.

*Initial enquiries*

Employers should task someone impartial to make initial enquiries to:

- Identify reasons for sickness and barriers to returning to work
- Discuss return to work options and agree any action needed
- If necessary, appoint a case worker to contact the worker, agree management plan, and coordinate interventions

*Detailed assessment*

*If needed*, arrange assessment by a relevant specialist—may include:

- Specialist advice on diagnosis and treatment
- Use of a screening tool
- A combined interview and work assessment
- Develop a return-to-work plan, and if needed, interventions

*Level of interventions (if needed)*

In addition to usual treatment consider:

- 'Light' interventions for workers likely to return to work
- 'Intensive' interventions for those unlikely to return to work (e.g. cognitive behavioural therapy or physiotherapy)

## Occupational health assessment

*Process* frequent and active case management, clinical assessment +/− discussion with manager, or HR +/− workplace visit.

*Purpose*

- Establish the nature of the underlying medical condition
- In a minority of cases it is useful to obtain a report from the GP, hospital doctor, or other specialist (physiotherapist or psychologist)
- *Facilitate optimal medical management*:
  - some employers provide treatment or fund private health care
  - careful communication with the GP essential, as is written consent from employee. If medical intervention is arranged, inform GP
- Carry out a functional assessment. This is crucial to the OH management of long-term absence, as it informs rehabilitation (see Box 20.1)
- Identify precipitating or exacerbating factors at work
- Explore and address psychosocial factors (see Box 20.2). Facilitation of self-directed goal-setting and use of positively influencing consultation skills (e.g. motivational interviewing) by the OH team can be helpful

*Output*

Written report to management +/− HR detailing:

- Prognosis for work including likely duration of absence and likelihood of recurrent absence in the future
- *Need for adjustments to work, where relevant*:
  - to facilitate rehabilitation. Agree a rehabilitation programme with employer/employee. It is sometimes helpful to share the rehabilitation plan with the GP (with the employee's consent)
  - to reduce the risk of recurrence
- Outline the plan for review (clinical +/− workplace)
- Do not disclose medical details to the employer, except where:
  - required by law (e.g. RIDDOR), but obtain employee's consent
  - disclosure (with consent) to facilitate the employer's/coworkers' understanding of impact of condition, e.g. if an insulin-dependent diabetic is at high risk of hypoglycaemic attacks, informed intervention by colleagues is important
  - the minimum necessary information should be disclosed. The worker must know what will be disclosed and to whom
- Advise manager if the Equality Act is likely to apply. Only an employment tribunal can decide if the definition of disability is actually fulfilled

Identify and try to resolve disparity between sources of medical advice. In the event of unresolved disparity, the employer can take their occupational physician's advice if their expertise is the most appropriate.

**Box 20.1 Functional assessment**

Record symptoms (severity and duration), but the emphasis should be on *functional capacity*. A useful checklist includes:

- *Generic capabilities*: duration of sitting, standing, walking, reading/concentrating. Ability to bend, lift/carry, reach up. *'Down time'*: time spent in bed during the day
- *Day-to-day activities*: washing/dressing, cooking, housework, gardening, driving, shopping, computer use, sport, and social activity
- *Work activities*: enquiry tailored to specific job tasks

⚠ This is not intended to be a complete list.

**Box 20.2 Psychosocial factors (Yellow Flags)**

Successful return to work dependent on employee's motivation/beliefs about health/work—belief that they will never again be fit for work means they are unlikely to return to work, irrespective of medical condition. Useful to assess such beliefs at an early stage.

## Further information

NICE (2019) Workplace health: long term sickness absence and capability to work. Available at: https://www.nice.org.uk/guidance/ng146/resources/workplace-health-longterm-sickness-absence-and-capability-to-work-pdf-66141783176389

## The 'Fit Note' and 'Fit for Work' service

The Fit Note was introduced in 2010 following recommendations in Dame Carol Black's 2008 review. It enables GPs to identify adjustments that may enable a return to work. Following review in the 'Improving Lives; work, health, and disability' consultation in 2017, changes are being considered including wider promotion of a more detailed Allied Health Professionals report.

In 2014 a 'Fit for Work' service was established to offer advice to employees, health care professionals, and employers to improve return to work. Unfortunately referral rates were significantly below forecasts and expectations and the service was closed in 2018, with online advice support still available.

## Evidence-based recovery times

Increasingly, evidence-based guideline material is being used to promote consistency of medical advice in the assessment of fitness for work. Many of the Royal Colleges of Medicine and other Health Care Professional organizations now publish guidance on average recovery times. A good example is the resource provided by the Royal College of Surgeons which may be found at: https://www.rcseng.ac.uk/patient-care/recovering-from-surgery/

Another example is provided by the Royal College of Obstetricians and Gynaecologists (2012). *Return to Fitness: Recovering Well*. Available at: http://www.rcog.org.uk/recovering-well/

**Talking work—advice for GPs**

In 2018 the Council for Work and Health was commissioned by the Work and Health Unit to research and develop a resource for GPs to help support completion of Fit Notes and encourage use of work modifications. The resource is freely available for use by employers, employees, and other health professionals.

Council for Work and Health 2018 Talking Work Resource. Available at: https://www.councilforworkandhealth.org.uk/wp-content/uploads/2019/01/Work-Modifications-Guide.pdf

# Rehabilitation and disability services

A range of facilitative services are available for disabled people who are trying to maintain or regain employment:

- These are provided by a variety of organizations including charitable trusts and government-funded departments
- These resources can be accessed by employees themselves, but OH departments can usefully signpost routes of contact
- The services include provision of financial support for employers of disabled people, and provision of sheltered employment opportunities for those who are out of work because of disability
- The Vocational Rehabilitation Association consists of professional practitioners with a wide range of training and skills to support rehabilitation to work

## Jobcentre plus

This government agency is part of the DWP. It aims to support people of working age, who are on state benefits, in overcoming barriers to gainful employment. Further information is available at: http://www.dwp.gov.uk/jobcentreplus/; also at : http://www.direct.gov.uk/en/Employment/Jobseekers/ContactJobcentrePlus/DG_186347

*Access to work scheme*

Gives advice and grants towards additional employment costs. For new employees, the grant is up to 100% of the approved costs. For existing employees, the grant is up to 100% of the approved costs up to £10,000 depending on the size of the organization. Larger employers are expected to share a proportion of the costs. Available at: http://www.direct.gov.uk/en/DisabledPeople/Employmentsupport/WorkSchemesAndProgrammes/DG_4000347

The range of services includes the following:

- Support at interview
- Special equipment, e.g. induction loops for hearing impaired individuals
- Adaptations to premises (e.g. improving wheelchair access)
- Help with travel costs if disabled employees cannot use public transport

*Work Choice*: special advice and support for disabled people to find or stay in work and whose needs cannot be met by other Jobcentre plus services.

*Residential training*: for disabled adults.

## Adaptations for disabled drivers

A network of independent regional mobility centres in the UK, offering advice and assessment for drivers with medical problems. Available at: http://www.mobility-centres.org.uk/

## Information technology and disability

Ability Net is a charitable organization that provides free information and advice, individual assessment of technology needs, the supply of assistive technology with free support, a programme of awareness education, and consultancy for employers on system and workstation adaptations and web accessibility. Available at: http://www.abilitynet.org.uk/

## Disability in education/ universities

Under the Equality Act 2010, universities and other educational establishments are required to make adjustments for disabled students. Many universities have well-defined resources for supporting disabled students, and these are often a source of useful information. Available at: http://www.cam.ac.uk/cambuniv/disability/university/trainingdb/

## Charities and organizations that support disabled people in work

- *The Shaw Trust*. Available at: http://www.shaw-trust.org.uk/
- *Remploy*. Available at: http://www.remploy.co.uk/
- *Scope*. Available at: http://www.scope.org.uk/

# Ill-health retirement

Ill-health retirement (IHR) is not a decision to take lightly. However, if an individual will never again be fit for his/her designated post, no suitable alternative employment is available, and he/she fulfils pension scheme criteria, further delay in recommending ill-health retirement is undesirable and unethical. Factors to consider in assessing whether an individual is eligible include the following.

## Medical factors

- *Diagnosis*: seek medical reports and/or interview and examine the applicant in person. Seek consent for up-to-date medical reports from the individual's doctors:
  - a GP's report is helpful in giving an overview of an employee's health including psychosocial factors
  - a specialist can best address issues around prognosis and treatment options
  - in cases of doubt, an independent medical report for occupational purposes may be helpful, and some pensions boards require independent reports as a matter of routine
- *Duration of illness*: a reasonable period should have elapsed to allow for appropriate treatment to be instituted and its effect assessed. As a general guide, it should be possible to make a decision after 6–9 months of incapacity
- *Treatment*: has a range of treatment options been explored? This does not mean all available treatments, but several options should be explored before concluding that a condition is permanent. Treatment outcomes should be carefully considered in relation to their impact on functional capacity
- *Permanence*: usually interpreted as meaning that the illness will persist until the normal retirement age. Some schemes require that the condition should be permanent before IHR will be approved. Others apply the less stringent criterion that the condition is expected to persist for the 'foreseeable future'. However, 'foreseeable future' can be difficult to define, and discussion with the other doctors advising within a particular pension scheme is desirable in order to maintain consistency. Permanence is easier to demonstrate in those close to normal retirement age
- *Comorbidity*: where an individual has several conditions, these may make the difference between the employee coping with his/her designated post and being unfit
- *Ageing*: an employee with a fixed deficit (e.g. polio) may find that, although the condition itself has not changed, he/she is no longer able to cope with work owing to age-related loss of physiological reserve. However, be absolutely sure that you can demonstrate a clear deterioration in a function that is a recognized feature of the disease. Work modification should always be considered
- *Sickness absence*: a pattern of increasing sickness absence (frequency, duration) may indicate that an employee is no longer able to offer regular effective service. In that case, IHR may be appropriate if the condition is permanent. An individual applying for IHR is, by definition, unfit for work and should be on sick leave

- *Reasonable adjustments*: (see ➔ p. 446, Rehabilitation and disability services). IHR is a last resort, only after adjustments and redeployment have been carefully considered
- *Limited life expectancy*: terminally ill employees may have their application fast-tracked by the pension scheme. Depending on scheme rules, it may be financially advantageous to some employees to remain in employment until death (death in service) rather than seek IHR. Some schemes offer an enhanced lump sum and commuted pension if an individual, usually without dependents, has limited life expectancy

## Non-medical factors

- *Organizational pressures*: requests to retire on health grounds may increase at times of reorganization or downsizing for one of two reasons:
  - IHR may be financially more attractive than redundancy to some long-serving staff
  - some staff may genuinely be unfit but have been 'carried' by colleagues. Restructuring may reveal such problems
- *Operational pressures*: managers may try to remove incompetent staff by persuading them to retire on health grounds; this pressure should be resisted
- *Financial pressures*: once occupational sick pay has ceased, both employer and employee may be keen to seek IHR rapidly. Financial pressures are not in themselves a reason to advise IHR

## Pension scheme membership

- Retirement is distinguished from termination of employment on medical grounds by the payment of a 'pension'

➔ Do not assume that an employee is a pension scheme member: check.

## Scheme rules

- *Pension scheme rules*: these vary, and it is imperative to be aware of the relevant scheme's rules before offering an opinion
- *Length of service*: many schemes will not award a pension to members with short service (<2 years); instead contributions are refunded
- *Approved doctors*: some schemes will only accept a recommendation for IHR from a qualified occupational physician. Others restrict this role to doctors on an approved list, e.g. an organization's chief medical adviser
- *Added years*: some schemes offer 'added years' of reckonable service where a member is retired on health grounds. This increases the value of the final pension, but can have unintended consequences where employees select the financially optimum time for ill health retirement
- *Higher/lower tier*: some schemes have two tiers—retirees unfit for their job but fit for other work (*lower-tier* retiral) receive a smaller pension than those permanently unfit for all employment (*higher-tier*)

Chapter 21

# Principles of risk assessment and risk management

# Introduction and terminology

## Need and context

Decisions in occupational health (OH) often entail a choice between two or more options, the comparative merits of which are not immediately obvious. The decision may be for an individual (e.g. whether to ground a pilot because of a health problem), for the whole of a workforce (e.g. whether to immunize health care workers against smallpox), or at a societal level (e.g. whether to permit the use of a pesticide). Risk management is the process by which decisions of this sort are made, following an assessment of the risks and benefits associated with each option. Depending on the nature of the decision, the process of risk assessment and management may be more or less formalized.

## Terminology

In the context of risk management, several terms have a more precise meaning than when they are used in everyday language.

### *Hazard*

A hazard is the potential to cause harm or adverse effect. For example, mesothelioma may arise from exposure to the hazard of asbestos, and physical trauma from a fall is a hazard of working at heights.

### *Risk*

Risk is the probability that a hazard will be realized, given the nature and extent of a person's exposure to an agent or circumstance. For example, the risk of mesothelioma from asbestos depends on the type of fibre and the amount that it is inhaled. There is no risk of mesothelioma from the handling of intact asbestos products if no fibres are inhaled.

A risk in an individual corresponds to an excess rate of the adverse outcome in a population of exposed people. Thus, populations of asbestos workers have an elevated rate of mesothelioma.

### *Uncertainty*

Often there is uncertainty about the existence of a hazard (e.g. there was much debate about whether radiofrequency radiation from mobile phones was a hazard with risk of brain cancer), or about the levels of risk associated with exposures to a hazardous agent or circumstance (e.g. how much the risk of leukaemia is increased by low levels of exposure to benzene). In managing risks, it is important to take account of uncertainties in the assessment of hazards and associated risks.

# Conceptual model

A number of similar models are used in OH practice to summarize and guide the process of assessing and managing risks in the workplace and the environment. One example is given in Fig. 21.1.

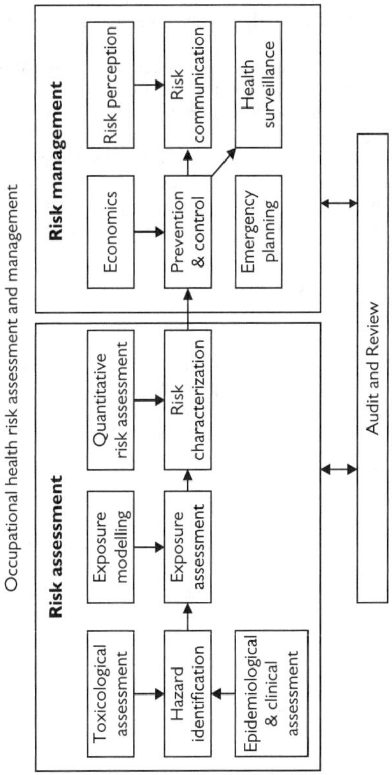


**Fig. 21.1** Health and safety management

S. Sadhra and K.G. Rampal, Occupational Health: Risk assessment and management. Copyright (1999). By permission of Blackwell Publishing.

# General principles

## Risk assessment

Assessing the risks and benefits from a possible course of action requires evaluation of relevant scientific evidence. There are four main elements to this. Typically, these elements are described in relation to potential adverse effects, but beneficial effects can be considered analogously.

- *Hazard identification*: what are the potential adverse effects of the agent or circumstance?
- *Hazard characterization*: how does the probability of these hazards vary according to the nature and extent of exposure?
- *Exposure assessment*: what are the nature and extent of the exposures that will occur if the course of action is followed?
- *Estimation of risk*: what is the likely probability of each hazard if the course of action is followed? For each risk estimate there should be an evaluation of the associated scientific uncertainty (might the true risk be much larger or smaller than the figure estimated, and if so, how likely is this?)

## HSE's 5 steps to risk assessment

HSE advises:

- *Step 1*: Identify hazards
- *Step 2*: Decide who might be harmed and how
- *Step 3*: Evaluate risks and decide on precautions
- *Step 4*: Record your findings and implement them
- *Step 5*: Review your risk assessment and update if necessary

## Risk management

Risk management entails the application of value judgements to decide between possible courses of action, given the estimated risks and benefits associated with each option. Value judgements should reflect the interests of all people who could be materially affected by the decision, with greatest weight being given to the interests of those who will be most affected.

Who makes the decision will depend on the number of people affected. If the important risks and benefits involve only one person, then ideally that individual should decide which option to follow. If more than one person will be affected and their interests conflict, then the decision may require societal input (e.g. through an elected government or the judiciary). For example, governments set exposure limits on hazardous substances in the workplace, taking into account the interests of both workers and employers.

## Frameworks for the assessment and management of risks

Where complex, but similar risk management decisions must be made on a regular basis (e.g. in the regulation of toxic chemicals in the workplace), a generic framework may be established within which risks are assessed and managed. This has the advantage of transparency (it is easier for affected parties to understand the basis on which decisions are made) and promotes internal consistency of decisions. For example, the framework for regulation of pesticides in the EU specifies standard requirements for scientific data and the approaches that should be used to determine whether potential risks will be acceptable.

## The precautionary principle

As defined in 1992, the precautionary principle stated that 'where there are threats of serious or irreversible damage, lack of full scientific certainty shall not be used as a reason for postponing cost-effective measures to prevent environmental degradation'. It has since been extended to encompass hazards to health as well as to the environment. Essentially, it is an affirmation that decisions in risk management should take appropriate account of scientific uncertainty.

# Sources of scientific evidence and uncertainty

## Sources of scientific evidence on hazard and risk

Information about hazard and risk may come from various sources:

- *Extrapolation from accepted scientific theory*: e.g. in assessing the health risks from static magnetic fields, account is taken of the relevant principles of biophysics
- *Experiments in vitro*: e.g. tests for mutagenicity in bacteria
- *Toxicological experiments in live animals*: these can be more informative, but are relatively expensive and must be justifiable in relation to the impact on animal welfare
- *Studies investigating risk in humans*: these may be experimental (e.g. randomized controlled trials) or observational (e.g. cohort and case-control studies). They have the advantage of avoiding the uncertainties of extrapolation between species but are limited by the practical and ethical constraints on research in humans. Moreover, they can only be conducted after human exposure to a potentially hazardous agent has occurred
- *Studies to assess patterns of exposure that may result from a risk management decision*: depending on the nature of the exposure, these may use methods of occupational hygiene, ergonomics, microbiology, psychology, or other scientific disciplines

## Reasons for scientific uncertainty

Scientific uncertainty in the assessment of risks may occur for various reasons.

- Doubts about the validity of accepted scientific theory and of its extrapolation to the exposure of interest
- Possible differences in susceptibility to a hazard between humans and the animal species in which toxicology has been investigated, sometimes taken into account by application of an 'assessment factor' ('safety factor')
- Possible differences between individuals in susceptibility to a hazard (e.g. because of differences in genetic constitution, sex, age, coincident disease, and medication, or aspects of lifestyle and environment). Again, an assessment factor may be used to allow for this
- Deficiencies in the design or execution of studies
- Statistical uncertainties when results are based on finite samples of observations that may be unrepresentative by chance. Confidence intervals can be used to help gauge the potential for error of this type

# Risk communication and perception

## Risk communication

Good communication of risk is important for two main reasons:

- People who take decisions in risk management ('risk managers') need to understand the likely risks and benefits of each possible course of action. This information must be conveyed to them by the scientists who have assessed the risks and benefits
- Where decisions in risk management are made at a societal level, the people affected need to understand the basis on which decisions are made and to have an opportunity for informed contribution to the decision making (e.g. through consultation processes or lobbying of politicians)

► Conveying a clear assessment of risk is not easy, especially when the target audience is not scientifically trained. Language should be tailored to the audience, and it may help to draw analogies with other risks that are more familiar (e.g. how risk compares with that of a road traffic accident or from living with a smoker)

- It is best to avoid referring to a situation as 'safe', since nothing in life can ever be guaranteed as totally free of risk. The term 'at risk' is also unhelpful without some indication of the level of risk implied

## Perceptions of risk

The value judgements that are applied in risk management will depend on people's perceptions of hazards, risks, and uncertainties. A number of factors influence perceptions.

- *The nature of the hazard*: this encompasses not only the gravity of the hazard (e.g. is it life-threatening?), but also its nature (e.g. cancer may generate more fear than heart disease even though the risk of fatality is similar)
- The risk of the hazard being realized
- *The timeframe within which the risk will apply*: is it transient (e.g. the risk of acute injury from undertaking a dangerous activity), prolonged (e.g. the risk of cancer from ionizing radiation), or delayed (e.g. the risk of cancer from taking up smoking)?
- *Whether the risk is offset by an obvious personal benefit*: e.g. there is more public concern about risks from mobile phone masts than from mobile phones themselves, although the latter give higher exposures to radiofrequency radiation
- Whether the risk is voluntary or imposed
- *The familiarity of the risk*: risks that are well understood (e.g. of road traffic accidents) are less threatening
- *Risk experience*: e.g. someone who has lost a relative to cancer is likely to be more worried about contracting the disease themselves than someone who has had no personal experience of it

# Chapter 22

# Health surveillance

# Health surveillance: General principles

## General principles

- *Health surveillance should only be introduced where the risk assessment indicates that it is required (Regulation 6, Management of Health and Safety at Work Regulations 1999) or it meets the criteria listed in the associated Approved Code of Practice:*
  - an identifiable disease or adverse effect is associated with the work activity
  - appropriate methods are available to identify such ill effects
  - it is reasonably likely that the adverse effect will occur given the prevailing work conditions
  - health surveillance will offer additional protection to the workforce's health
- Health surveillance should be supported by a health surveillance policy agreed between management and the employees or their representatives
- The health surveillance policy should document the roles and responsibilities of the line manager, employee, occupational health (OH) service, and human resources department
- The health surveillance policy should clearly state how results are to be handled and records stored
- Where an employee's continued fitness for work may be affected by the outcome of health surveillance, an agreed policy on redeployment should be in place
- Informed consent to participate in the health surveillance programme should be sought from each employee at the outset
- The consequences of refusal to participate in health surveillance where this is legally required for work with an agent/process should be made explicit

## Frequency of health surveillance

- An initial assessment of fitness is required prior to exposure commencing. This provides a baseline against which subsequent changes can be compared. In addition, it identifies those workers with pre-existing deficits not attributable to that employment
- Thereafter, the risk assessment dictates the frequency of workers' health surveillance unless published guidance stipulates a greater frequency of checks

## Quality assurance

- All staff involved in health surveillance should be appropriately trained and understand the purpose of the surveillance programme
- Equipment used for health surveillance should be well maintained, regularly calibrated, and fit for purpose
- Any samples taken for health surveillance, e.g. biological monitoring should be analysed in a laboratory that participates in a recognized quality assurance programme
- Any abnormal results should be checked and repeated before further action is taken

## Results

The results of health surveillance should be fed back to the worker and a decision made on his/her continuing fitness for work. If a predetermined action level is exceeded, the employer should investigate the reasons for this and review the efficacy of control measures.

Grouped, anonymized, results of health surveillance should be fed back to staff and the health and safety committee. No personally identifiable data should be disclosed except to the individual employee unless consent has been given for such release.

The health surveillance programme should be regularly audited, and any adverse trends investigated and acted on.

## Health records

- An entry documenting the individual's fitness status (fit/fit with restrictions/unfit) for work with the relevant agent should be made in the worker's health record and be sent to their employer. This record must be retained for the required statutory period (normally 40 years)
- The clinical surveillance records should be retained by the OH health service for an appropriate period after considering General Data Protection Regulation compliance (may vary according to circumstance)

## Relevant legislation

Faculty of Occupational Medicine (2018). *Ethics Guidance for Occupational Health Practice*, 8th edn. FOM, London

General Data Protection Regulation (2018). UK Government TSO London. Described in: https://www.gov.uk/government/publications/guide-to-the-general-data-protection-regulation

HSE (2000). *Management of Health and Safety at Work Regulations 1999*, Approved Code of Practice and Guidance, 2nd edn, L21. HSE Books, Sudbury

HSE (2005). *The Control of Substances Hazardous to Health Regulations 2002* (as amended), Approved Code of Practice and Guidance, L5. HSE Books, Sudbury

# Skin surveillance

Skin surveillance is appropriate where there is a recognized risk of occupational skin disease as defined in Control of Substances Hazardous to Health Regulation (COSHH) 2002, Regulation 11. This decision may be based on previous experience, Manufacturer's Safety Data Sheets, or industry advice. Following the introduction of new agents suspected of causing skin problems, skin surveillance may be instituted.

Value of skin surveillance is contested by some occupational physicians. An National Health Service Plus systematic review failed to find any published evidence regarding skin surveillance for occupational hand dermatitis.

## Frequency of inspection

Frequency of skin inspection depends on the agents in use. Monthly skin inspection may be usual in some hazardous work environments or annual questionnaires used in others.

## Methods

- Annual hand dermatitis screening questionnaire to identify those workers who need to be seen by an OH professional for assessment is often used to triage

⚠ Such questionnaires should be validated against direct skin inspection in that workforce: some questionnaire validation studies have shown disappointing agreement levels with direct skin inspection.

- *Regular skin inspection of 'at-risk' staff by an OH nurse or a responsible person. Those deemed 'at-risk' may be based on*:
  - occupational exposure, e.g. hairdressers
  - occupational exposure and a history of hand dermatitis
- Vinyl chloride workers must be subject to skin surveillance under the supervision of an HSE appointed doctor or employment medical adviser (EMA)
- *Patent fuel manufacture from pitch*: workers are subject to skin surveillance under the supervision of an HSE appointed doctor or EMA

## Results

- Individuals with skin problems should be referred to a medical practitioner for further assessment
- A health record should be kept as required by COSHH
- *Further tests may include*:
  - patch testing
  - skin-prick testing for urticaria
  - blood tests for immunoglobulin E and Radioallergosorbent test immunology
  - skin biopsy (skin cancer)

## Relevant legislation and guidance

HSE (1998). *Medical Aspects of Occupational Skin Disease*. Guidance Note MS24. 2nd edn. HSE Books, Sudbury. Available at: http://www.hse.gov.uk/pubns/ms24.pdf

# Respiratory health surveillance

Respiratory health surveillance is required under COSHH, Regulation 11, for employees who are exposed to known respiratory sensitizers (asthmagens). The purpose is to identify cases of occupational asthma (OA) as early as possible. A list of asthmagens for which surveillance is likely to be required is given in ➲ p. 225, Occupational asthma and rhinitis.

## Methods

*Screening methods*

- Questionnaire (baseline and follow-up) based on a symptoms' checklist. Enquiry covers exposure in the proposed job, previous history of exposure to asthmagens, asthma, or work-related respiratory symptoms, and any changes to exposure or symptoms, during follow-up (see Box 22.1)
- *Spirometry*: forced expiratory volume in 1 s and FVC
- *Education*: an important part of screening is to inform employees about the nature and level of the risk to their health and to counsel them about early reporting of symptoms. Explanation should be given about the possibility of late symptoms

*Format and frequency*

This depends on the level, duration, and frequency of exposure (and therefore the risk of sensitization). Two levels of health surveillance are defined in HSE guidance.

- *Low level*: where there is only suggestive evidence of a hazard or a low likelihood of exposure:
  - baseline questionnaire and spirometry
  - annual follow-up questionnaire
- *High level*: where there is strong evidence of a hazard and it is not possible to exclude a risk of sensitization:
  - baseline questionnaire and spirometry
  - follow-up of newly exposed employees is by questionnaire (+ spirometry if the risk of sensitization is significant) after 6 weeks and 12 weeks, respectively; the interval can fall to annually thereafter in the absence of positive findings

*Responsible person*

Questionnaires may be administered by a responsible person (usually a line manager) who has been trained appropriately by an OH doctor or nurse. Positive questionnaire responses must be referred to a competent OH professional for further investigation.

## Investigation and management of potential cases

This is usually carried out by an occupational physician.

- *Investigation aims to distinguish the following*:
  - work related from non-work-related disease—usually possible from a detailed history and lung function, but may need further investigation by serial peak expiratory flow rate (PEFR) testing (see ➲ p. 800, Serial peak flow testing)

**Box 22.1 Example questions for baseline questionnaire***

1. Do you believe that your chest has suffered as a result of previous employment?
2. Have you ever left a job because of your chest?
3. Do you have or have you ever had (do not include isolated colds, sore throats, or flu):
   a) Recurring soreness or watering of your eyes?
   b) Recurring blocked or running nose?
   c) Bouts of coughing?
   d) Chest tightness?
   e) Wheezing?
   f) Breathlessness?
   g) Any persistent of history of chest problems?

**Example questions for follow-up questionnaire***

Since you last answered our questionnaire

1. Has your job changed?
2. Have you had any of the following symptoms? (list three, a to g)

* Adapted from HSE sample questionnaire (see web reference in Further information and guidance).

- true immunological sensitization (OA) from non-specific irritation of pre-existing reversible airways disease—it is often impossible to distinguish these on history or PEFR testing alone. Exposure to a known sensitizing agent might give rise to a presumptive diagnosis of OA. However, the gold standard investigation is specific broncho-provocation challenge testing (see ➲ p. 224, Occupational asthma and rhinitis)
- *Management of OA*: confirmed cases should be restricted from exposure or exposure controlled to the level where symptoms are not detectable. Frequent follow-up should occur if exposure continues

## Other surveillance

- Employers should monitor trends in sickness absence to detect any excess absence that might be due to allergic respiratory disease
- *Useful information can be gained from exit interviews*: employees with OA and rhinitis often select themselves out of work with the allergen

## Further information and guidance

Bohrf Asthma Review. (2010,2011). Available at: http://www.bohrf.org.uk/downloads/OA_Guide-1.pdf

HSE (1998). Health Surveillance for Occupational Asthma. In: *Medical Aspects of Occupational Asthma*, MS25. HSE Books, Sudbury. Available at: http://www.hse.gov.uk/asthma/employers.htm#health

Sample baseline and follow-up questionnaires. (1998). Available at: http://www.hse.gov.uk/asthma/samplequest2.pdf; also available at: http://www.hse.gov.uk/asthma/samplequest3.pdf

# Health surveillance for noise-induced hearing loss

Screening for hearing loss is required under the Control of Noise at Work Regulations 2005 (➲ p. 566, Control of Noise at Work Regulations 2005). Audiometric health surveillance is recommended by HSE for workers exposed above the Upper Exposure action level (85 DB) defined in the Noise at Work Regulation, and for other workers identified as at risk or vulnerable. The method of screening is by audiometry (➲ p. 802, Screening audiometry).

## Purpose of hearing loss classification

There are a number of hearing loss classification systems developed for the purposes of:

- Determining compensation in civil litigation
- Determining disability benefits
- Monitoring hearing in audiometric surveillance programmes

One method of classifying occupational hearing loss which is employed in the UK is that published in Appendix 5 of the HSE publication *Controlling Noise at Work 2005*.

► Whether or not such a classification scheme is employed all audiograms should be reviewed by a competent health professional.

## Method of classification using revised HSE scheme

- The results of audiometry are summed across 1, 2, 3, 4, and 6 kHz frequencies in each ear separately
- Audiograms are classified using the information in Table 22.1
- Table 22.2 is used to determine whether the hearing loss exceeds the warning or referral levels for that age band
- Where the sum for either ear is greater than or equal to the warning level for the worker's age and gender, he/she is graded category 2 (mild hearing impairment)
- Where the sum for either ear is greater than or equal to the referral level for the worker's age and gender, he/she is graded category 3 (poor hearing). Such individuals should be referred to a doctor
- Where the previous test took place within 3 years and ↑ in hearing threshold of 30 dB or greater is found (as the sum of 3, 4, and 6 kHz), the worker is graded category 4 (rapid hearing loss) and should be referred to an occupational physician or GP
- To assess unilateral hearing loss, take the sum of the hearing level at 1, 2, 3, and 4 kHz for both ears. If the difference between the ears is >40 dB, notify the worker and refer for medical advice
- Where referral is indicated, an occupational physician should review the worker and consider the need for further assessment by an ear, nose, and throat (ENT) surgeon

## Actions following audiometry

- Offer all workers advice on the use of hearing protection and the health effects of noise
- Workers in category 2 should be notified of the presence, and implications of any hearing loss and the advice recorded in the OH notes
- Give workers a copy of their audiogram
- Workers in category 4 may need audiometry more frequently

**Table 22.1** The HSE categorization scheme

| Category | Calculation | Action |
|---|---|---|
| 1 *Acceptable hearing ability*<br>Hearing within normal limits | Sum of hearing levels at 1, 2, 3, 4, and 6 kHz | None |
| 2 *Mild hearing impairment*<br>Hearing within 20th percentile, i.e. hearing level normally experienced by one person in five. May indicate developing NIHL | Sum of hearing levels at 1, 2, 3, 4, and 6 kHz. Compare value with figure given for appropriate age band and gender in Table 22.2 | Warning |
| 3 *Poor hearing*<br>Hearing within 5th percentile, i.e. hearing level normally experienced by one person in 20. Suggests significant NIHL | Sum of hearing levels at 1, 2, 3, 4, and 6 kHz. Compare value with figure given for appropriate age band and gender in Table 22.2 | Referral |
| 5 *Rapid hearing loss*<br>Reduction in hearing loss of 30 dB or more within 3 years or less. Such a change could be caused by noise exposure or disease | Sum of hearing levels at 3, 4, and 6 kHz | Referral |

**Table 22.2** Classification of audiograms into warning and referral levels

| Age | Sum of hearing levels 1, 2, 3, 4, and 6 kHz | | | |
|---|---|---|---|---|
| | Males | | Females | |
| | Warning level | Referral level | Warning level | Referral level |
| 18–24 | 51 | 95 | 46 | 78 |
| 25–29 | 67 | 113 | 55 | 91 |
| 30–34 | 82 | 132 | 63 | 105 |
| 35–39 | 100 | 154 | 71 | 119 |
| 40–44 | 121 | 183 | 80 | 134 |
| 45–49 | 142 | 211 | 93 | 153 |
| 50–54 | 165 | 240 | 111 | 176 |
| 55–59 | 190 | 269 | 131 | 204 |
| 60–64 | 217 | 296 | 157 | 235 |
| 65 | 235 | 311 | 175 | 255 |



## Relevant guidance/legislation

HSE (2005). *Controlling Noise at Work, Guidance on the Control of Noise at Work Regulations 2005*, L108. HSE Books, Sudbury. Available at: http://www.hse.gov.uk/pubns/indg362.pdf

# Patterns of hearing loss

The audiogram varies with the age of the individual, the degree of noise exposure, and any coexisting auditory conditions.

## Normal audiogram

Fig. 22.1 shows a normal audiogram of a young person with a hearing threshold of approximately 0 dBHL. In older workers, the hearing threshold may be poorer than this, although in most normal individuals it will remain above 20 dBHL.

## Noise-induced hearing loss

- Typically, noise-induced hearing loss will produce a notch lying between 3 and 6 kHz with recovery (see Fig. 22.2). This dip is usually most prominent at 4 kHz
- In older workers with coexisting presbyacusis (age-related hearing loss) the audiogram may not show recovery at higher frequencies
- Firearms use can lead to hearing loss. Initially this loss may be unilateral, but with continued exposure the hearing loss will affect both ears although asymmetry may be evident

## Otosclerosis

- This conductive hearing loss (Fig. 22.3) is due to an autosomal dominant disorder that causes progressive conductive deafness due to a localized disorder of bone metabolism
- Family history may be positive
- In women, this disease may first present during or following pregnancy
- Typically, the audiogram shows hearing loss more marked at low frequencies than at high frequencies
- Carhart's notch may be observed with a dip at 2 kHz

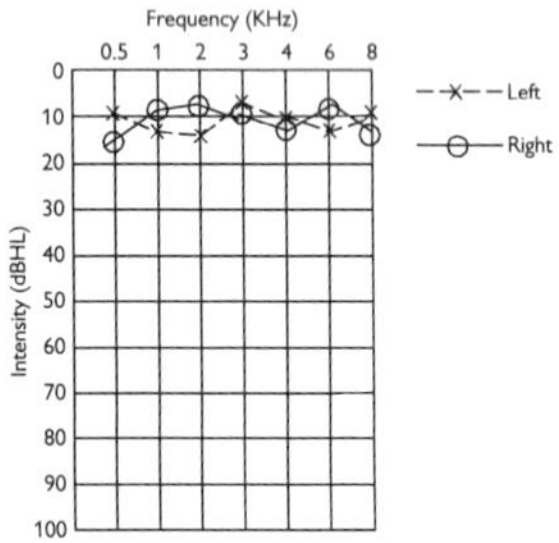


**Fig. 22.1** Normal audiogram: X, left; O, right

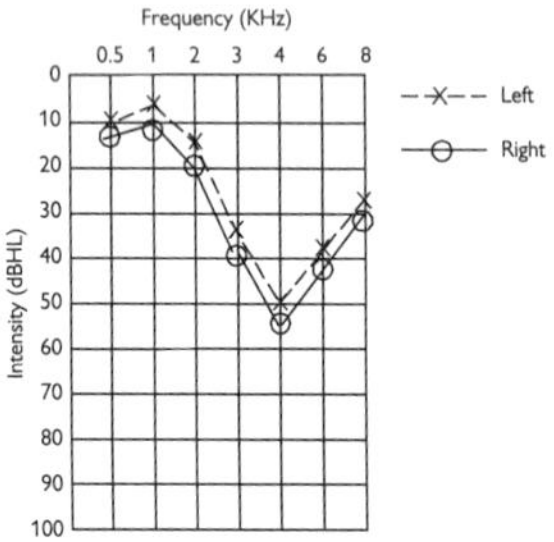


**Fig. 22.2** Noise-induced hearing loss: X, left; O, right

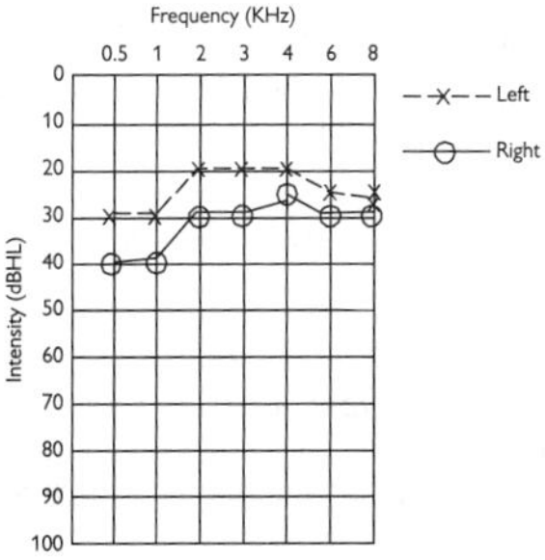


**Fig. 22.3** Otosclerosis: X, left; O, right

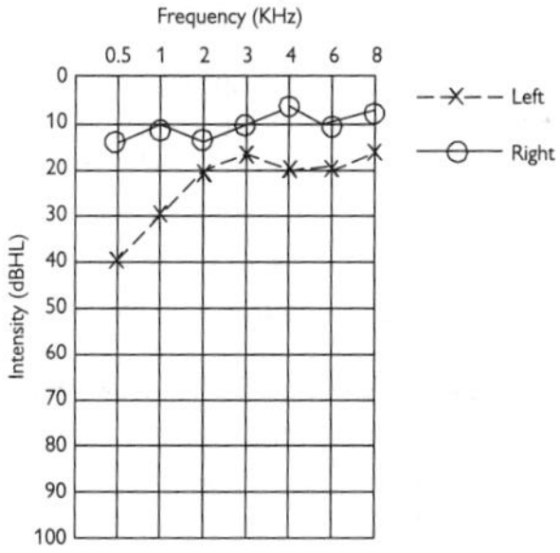


**Fig. 22.4** Méniére's disease: X, left; O, right

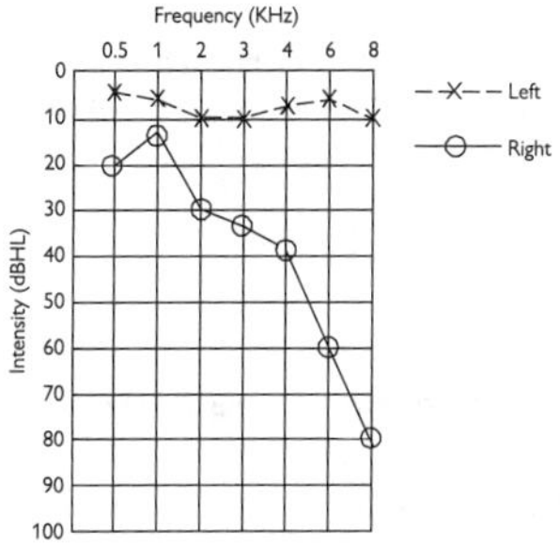


**Fig. 22.5** Acoustic neuroma: X, left; O, right

## Ménière's disease

This condition (Fig. 22.4) produces a low-tone hearing loss often accompanied by tinnitus.

## Acoustic neuroma

- A schwannoma of the vestibulocochlear nerve. It presents with unilateral hearing loss (Fig. 22.5), tinnitus, and sometimes vertigo
- Workers with unilateral hearing loss and associated tinnitus should be referred for ENT investigations to exclude an acoustic neuroma: the diagnostic yield of such investigations is, however, low

# Inorganic lead

Workers exposed to inorganic lead should be subject to health surveillance where breathing zone sampling indicates that the 8-hour time-weighted average concentration (TWA) is greater than half the lead in air standard of 0.15 $mg/m^3$.

▶ Only HSE Employment Medical Advisers/HSE appointed doctors should carry out such health surveillance.

## Frequency of health surveillance

An initial medical assessment of fitness for lead work is required together with a baseline blood lead and haemoglobin prior to commencement of work with lead. Consideration should be given to factors that may increase lead absorption:

- Nail biting
- Smoking
- Poor personal hygiene

Thereafter, the work activity and/or blood lead level dictates the frequency of workers' health surveillance. As a minimum this means an annual clinical review including:

- Physical examination
- Review of medical records
- Review of blood lead levels
- *Other relevant tests*:
    - haemoglobin
    - zinc protoporphyrin (levels in unexposed workers are usually <2 μg/g haemoglobin)

However, for women of reproductive capacity or young people health surveillance should take place at 3-monthly intervals.

**Table 22.3** Maximum intervals for blood lead monitoring by blood lead levels

| Blood lead | Maximum interval for surveillance |
|---|---|
| <30 μg/dl | 12 months |
| 30≤40 μg/dl | 6 months |
| 40≤60 μg/dl | 3 months |
| 60 μg/dl | At doctor's discretion, but not >3 months |

## Samples

A 5-ml blood sample should be collected in an ethylenediamine tetra-acetic acid tube. The timing of sampling is not critical. A laboratory participating in the joint HSE/UK National External Quality Assessment Service programme should carry out atomic absorption spectroscopy to determine blood lead levels.

## Results

- Results of blood lead monitoring should be fed back to worker and a decision made on their continuing fitness for work with inorganic lead
- If an action level is exceeded the employer should investigate the reasons for this and review the efficacy of control measures. Aim is to prevent the worker's blood lead level reaching the suspension level
- Where the relevant suspension level is reached, the appointed doctor must decide whether to certify that the employee is no longer fit to work with lead

The Control of Lead at Work Regulations 2002 indicates the following action and suspension levels (Box 22.2)

### Box 22.2 Actions required for given blood lead level

| | Action level | Suspension level |
|---|---|---|
| Adult (not of reproductive capacity) | 50 μg/dl | 60 μg/dl |
| Young person | 40 μg/dl | 50 μg/dl |
| Woman of reproductive capacity* | 25 μg/dl | 30 μg/dl |

*A woman of reproductive capacity is a woman medically and physically capable of conceiving. This includes any woman on hormonal contraceptives.

- Background blood lead levels in the general population are usually <10 μg/dl
- ▶ Pregnant workers should be suspended from work involving significant exposure to lead
- ▶▶ Where a worker's blood lead level reaches the suspension level, the blood lead should be rechecked as a matter of urgency

## Health records

An entry documenting the individual's fitness for work with inorganic lead should be made in his/her health record and be sent to his/her employer. The medical surveillance records should be retained for 40 years.

## Relevant legislation


- HSE (2000). *Management of Health and Safety at Work Regulations 1999, Approved Code of Practice and Guidance*, L21, 2nd edn. HSE Books, Sudbury
- HSE (2002). *Control of Lead at Work Regulations 2002, Approved Code of Practice and Guidance*, L132. HSE Books, Sudbury 🖰 http://www.hse.gov.uk/pubns/priced/l132.pdf

# Organic lead

Workers exposed to lead alkyls (e.g. tetraethyl lead, tetramethyl lead) should be subject to health surveillance where breathing zone sampling indicates that the 8-hour TWA is greater than half the lead in air standard of 0.10 mg/m3 or there is a risk of dermal absorption of lead alkyls. Most exposure to organolead occurs in the manufacture or use of lead alkyls employed as anti-knock agents in leaded petrol.

▶ Only HSE EMAs/HSE appointed doctors should carry out such health surveillance.

## Frequency of health surveillance

An initial medical assessment of fitness for lead work is required together with baseline urinary lead prior to work with lead commencing. Those with a recent history of psychiatric illness should not work with organic leads to avoid confusion between organic lead poisoning and a relapse of pre-existing mental illness. Consideration should be given to factors that may increase lead absorption:

- Nail-biting
- Smoking
- Poor personal hygiene

Thereafter, the work activity and/or urine lead level dictates the frequency of workers' health surveillance. As a minimum this means an annual clinical review including:

- Physical examination
- Review of medical records
- Review of urinary lead
- Annual blood lead

## Samples

A 25-ml urine sample should be collected at the end of the shift at the end of the working week. Analysis is by atomic absorption spectrophotometry to determine urinary lead levels.

## Results

The results of lead monitoring should be fed back to the worker and a decision made on his/her continuing fitness for work with organic lead. Where the relevant suspension level is reached and is confirmed by repeat testing, the appointed doctor will certify that the employee is no longer fit to work with organic lead. The Lead at Work Regulations 2002 indicate the following suspension levels (Box 22.3).

- ▶ Pregnant workers should be suspended from work involving significant exposure to lead
- ▶▶ Where a worker's urinary lead level reaches the suspension level, the urinary lead should be rechecked as a matter of urgency

## Health records

An entry documenting the individual's fitness for work with organic lead should be made in his/her health record and be sent to his/her employer. The medical surveillance records should be retained for an appropriate period.

**Box 22.3 Suspension levels for urinary lead**

| | Suspension level |
|---|---|
| Adult (not of reproductive capacity) | 110 μg Pb/g creatinine |
| Young person (aged 16 or 17) | 110 μg Pb/g creatinine |
| Woman of reproductive capacity* | 25 μg Pb/g creatinine |

* A woman of reproductive capacity is a woman medically and physically capable of conceiving. This includes any woman taking hormonal contraceptives.

## Relevant legislation

HSE (2000). *Management of Health and Safety at Work Regulations 1999*. Approved Code of Practice and Guidance, L21, 2nd edn. HSE Books, Sudbury

HSE (2002). *Control of Lead at Work Regulations 2002*. Approved Code of Practice and Guidance, L132. HSE Books, Sudbury. Available at: http://www.hse.gov.uk/pubns/priced/l132.pdf

# Surveillance for hand–arm vibration syndrome

The health surveillance requirements for hand–arm vibration syndrome (HAVS) are described in the Control of Vibration at Work Regulations 2005.

## Main requirements

Health surveillance should be provided for vibration-exposed employees who:

- Are likely to be regularly exposed above the exposure action value of 2.5 $m/s^2$ A(8)
- Are likely to be exposed occasionally above the exposure action value and where the risk assessment identifies that the frequency and severity of exposure may pose a risk to health
- Have a diagnosis of HAVS (even when exposed below the exposure action value)

## Process and methods

The HSE recommends a tiered approach to health surveillance for HAVS. Further information and example questionnaires are available through the HSE website (http://www.hse.gov.uk/vibration/hav).

- *Tier 1—initial baseline assessment*: a short questionnaire to be used for people moving into a job involving exposure to vibration. Questionnaire responses determine whether the individual is referred for health assessment (tier 3)
- *Tier 2—annual (screening) questionnaire*: a short questionnaire to be used annually for individuals exposed to vibration, to determine whether they need to be referred to tier 3
- *Tier 3—assessment by qualified person*: this involves a HAVS health assessment by a qualified person, e.g. an OH nurse. A clinical questionnaire asks about relevant symptoms and limited clinical examination is recommended. If the assessment shows that the individual has HAVS, he/she should be referred to tier 4
- *Tier 4—formal diagnosis*: at this stage a formal diagnosis is made by a doctor qualified in OH. The reported history of symptoms is considered to be the most useful diagnostic information. Information from tiers 1–4 is also used to make decisions on fitness for work
- *Tier 5—standardized tests (optional)*: this stage is optional and involves referral for certain specialized tests for individuals who have signs and symptoms of HAVS

Tests include:

- *Vascular tests*:
  - finger rewarming after cold provocation test
  - finger systolic blood pressure test
- *Sensorineural*:
  - vibrotactile perception threshold
  - thermal (temperature) perception threshold

Symptoms related to carpal tunnel syndrome may need to be investigated by nerve conduction tests (see p. 324, Compression neuropathies)

- Specialist training is required to carry out clinical assessments for HAVS. The Faculty of Occupational Medicine (UK) has developed a syllabus for approved training in health surveillance for HAVS
- As part of the health surveillance programme a record-keeping system is needed for results of reports of symptoms and medical examinations

## Related legislation

Occupational cases of HAVS and carpal tunnel syndrome are reportable to HSE under RIDDOR 2013

## Further information

HSE (2019). *Hand–Arm Vibration: The Control of Vibration at Work Regulations 2005*. L140, 2nd ed. HSE Books, Sudbury Available at https://www.hse.gov.uk/pubns/priced/l140.pdf.

HSE. *Health Surveillance—Guidance for Occupational Health Professionals*. (2005). HSE Books, Sudbury. Available at: http://www.hse.gov.uk/vibration/hav,

Section 4

# Fitness for work

# Chapter 23

# Generic fitness for work issues and specific disorders

# General principles of fitness for work assessments

## Purpose

The purpose of undertaking fitness for work assessments is to try to achieve the best possible job–person fit. Knowledge of workplace hazards and job demands should inform the assessment. The objective should be to be inclusive and, where practicable, to make reasonable adjustments to accommodate those with disabilities. Such assessments may be carried out pre-placement, prior to promotion or job transfer, or following sickness absence or work-related injury. Other reasons for carrying out a fitness for work assessment include:

- *Legislative compliance*: for example, medical assessments under the Control of Asbestos Regulations 2012, Diving at Work Regulations 1997
- *Infection control*:
  - food industry (product safety)
  - health services (patient safety)
- *Baseline data for health surveillance*: e.g. audiometry, spirometry

Routine periodic medicals, unless subject to rigorous assessment, may generate activity but fail to achieve any useful purpose. Employers may be under the mistaken impression that a 'rigorous' medical will reduce or eliminate sickness absence.

- *Identification of vulnerable individuals requiring additional duty of care*:
  - individuals with disability which may increase risk of injury or require additional protection
  - measures to support those with fluctuating conditions

The rationale for the fitness assessment should be clear to all parties, as should the procedures to be followed where an individual is deemed unfit following assessment.

## Key information

- Knowledge of workplace hazards and task demands
- Special requirements, e.g. emergency response duties, working in isolation, driving
- Current job description
- The assessor should be familiar with the workplace or should specifically visit the workplace to ensure appropriate knowledge of the job. This is especially important where the post makes unusual demands of employees
- Any legislative fitness standards should be observed
- Company or industry sector guidance, where available, is helpful in identifying relative and absolute medical contraindications to work

## Reports to employer

- The employer should be informed in writing of the individual's fitness for his/her designated post
- Any restrictions on fitness should be clearly stated

- Identify any adjustments the employer may wish to consider under the Equality Act 2010
- No information regarding underlying medical conditions should be disclosed except with the employee's consent and where disclosure is necessary for health and safety reasons or for the employer to comply with legislation

## Record keeping

- Clear legible contemporaneous notes should be kept (see ➲ p. 786, Recording an occupational health consultation)
- Entries in the employee's occupational health (OH) record should be signed and dated
- Health questionnaires and records of any medical assessment should be filed in the employee's medical record
- All OH files should be securely stored in the OH department. It is illegal and unethical for sensitive health records to be stored where others may have access to them (see ➲ p. 386, Managing occupational health records 2: Security, transfer, and the archiving of records ➲ p. 398, Confidentiality, consent, and communication, ➲ p. 614, General Data Protection Regulations 2016 and Data Protection Act 2018).

## Relevant legislation and guidance

Equality Act (2010).

Faculty of Occupational Medicine (2019). Hobson J and Smedley J. Fitness for Work: The Medical Aspects, 6th edn. Oxford University Press, Oxford

Faculty of Occupational Medicine (2018). *Ethics Guidance for Occupational Health Practice*, 8th edn. Faculty of Occupational Medicine, London

# Occupational history

## Purpose

- Identify occupational risk factors for disease
- Understand job demands
- Advise on fitness for work
- Inform efforts at rehabilitation or redeployment

► It is not sufficient to ask: 'What is your job?' although even that may be overlooked by some doctors. Job names vary and may mislead. It is much more useful to know what an employee actually does at work or has done in his/her previous main job. This should be followed by enquiry about the main workplace hazards, the likely intensity and route of any exposures, and any control measures in place (including personal protective equipment).

Ask about concurrent jobs (paid or unpaid) as otherwise these may not be declared. This includes second jobs, evening or weekend work, participation in family businesses such as farms or shops, and moonlighting, i.e. work not declared for tax purposes.

Some jobs place workers at high risk of certain occupational diseases. For example, spray painters are at risk of occupational asthma (due to isocyanates in 'two-pack' paints). Such a work history should prompt the physician to consider whether the patient may have that disease.

### Key questions

- What do you do at your work?
- Do you have another job?
- Does anyone else at work have this problem?
- Does it get better away from work?

*and sometimes*:

- Have you ever worked with …?
- What are your hobbies?

## Diseases of long latency

Some diseases such as bladder cancer or pneumoconiosis have a long latent interval between exposure and presentation. To establish an occupational cause in that situation requires a lifetime occupational history. Sometimes it is more efficient to ask if the patient has ever worked with the suspected agent, e.g. for mesothelioma ask about asbestos exposure.

## Hobbies

Pastimes can lead to significant non-occupational exposures especially in those whose hobby occupies many hours per week. Prolonged exposure may be compounded by a lack of health and safety knowledge and inadequate control measures. As a result, hobbies may cause illness often confused with occupational illness.

# Pre-placement assessment

## Purpose

The purpose of a pre-placement health assessment is to establish a prospective employee's fitness for employment including his/her ability to offer regular effective attendance. Consider relevant previous and current health problems and significant workplace risks.

## Process

⚠ Prospective employees should be advised *not* to submit their resignation to their current employer until their fitness is confirmed (including results of drug screen where relevant; see Fig. 23.1).

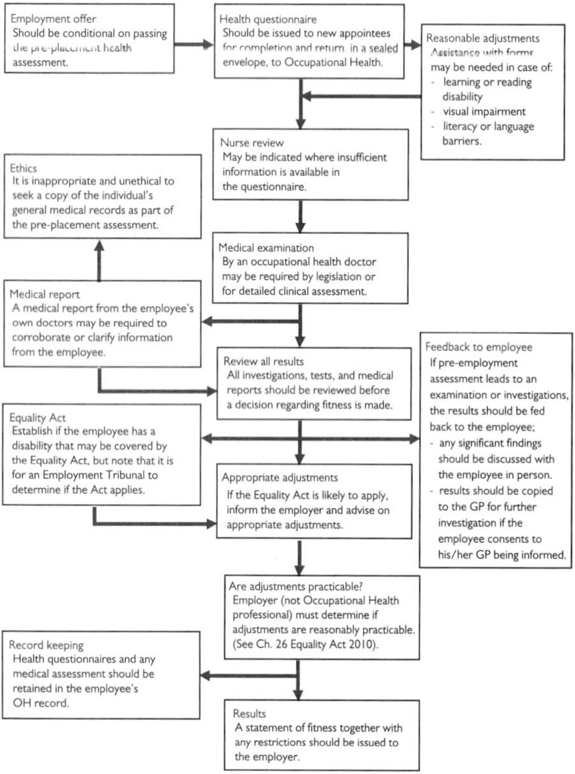


**Fig. 23.1** Flow chart showing the process for pre-placement assessment

- The Equality Act 2010 requires that only the successful applicant should be offered a pre-placement assessment. It is crucial that assessment is undertaken *after* selection or outcome should not be known to employer at the time of selection. Thus, the term pre-placement is often used rather than the previously common term 'pre-employment assessment'

Where there is high turnover (e.g. service industries), a rapid access scheme (same-day clinical assessment, where indicated, by rapid screening questionnaires) reduces costs, while managing the associated risk.

## Key information

- Current job description including special job requirements
- Knowledge of workplace risks and task demands
- Sickness absence record for last 2 years
- Any legislative fitness standards
- Industry sector guidance, where available

## Clinical investigations

Depending on the post, these may include tests listed in Table 23.1.

## Legislation and guidance

- Faculty of Occupational Medicine (2019). *Fitness for Work*, 6th edn. Oxford University Press, Oxford
- Equality Act 2010. Available at: http://www.legislation.gov.uk/ukpga/2010/15/contents
- Faculty of Occupational Medicine (2018). *Ethics Guidance for Occupational Health Practitioners*, 8th edn. Faculty of Occupational Medicine, London

**Table 23.1** Clinical investigations*

| Test | Example |
|---|---|
| Spirometry | Animal house technicians |
| CXR | Commercial divers |
| Audiometry | Call centre workers, pipe fitters |
| Visual acuity and visual fields | Occupational drivers |
| Colour vision | Seafarers, electricians |
| Exercise test | Firefighters |
| Full blood count | Divers, lead workers |
| Immunity to infectious diseases (rubella, varicella, hepatitis B) | Health care workers (see ➔ p. 494, Fitness for exposure prone procedures 1; see ➔ p. 496, Fitness for exposure prone procedures 2) |
| Drug screening | Safety critical jobs |

* This list is not exhaustive.

# Psychosocial factors and fitness for work

Psychosocial factors have been recognized increasingly over the past 10 years as having an important impact on work capacity and the risk of work-related ill health.

The factors listed here increase the risk of occurrence or recurrence of psychological morbidity and musculoskeletal disorders. However, they should also be taken into consideration when advising about fitness for work, likelihood of absence, and adjustments required, thus facilitating rehabilitation and reducing risk.

## Personal psychosocial factors

- *Personality type*: type A personality, and perfectionist and obsessional traits
- *Pre-existing psychiatric morbidity*:
  - depression and anxiety
  - psychotic disorders
- Health beliefs
- Somatizing tendency
- Conflicting family responsibilities
- Poor work–life balance

## Workplace psychosocial factors

These factors and their control are covered in detail on ➔ p. 146, Organizational psychosocial factors. However, the most important are:

- Job demands
- Excessive or insufficient workload
- *Control over work*:
  - lack of control over the volume or rate of work, or achievement of targets
  - low decision latitude
- *Monotonous or repetitive work*: intellectual demands mismatched with the individual's ability or professional background
- Low job satisfaction
- Low perceived value by service users or colleagues
- *Poor relationships with others*:
  - Managers, colleagues, or customers
- Bullying and harassment
- Perceived unfairness

## Control of psychosocial hazards at work

- Organizational psychosocial hazards (see ➔ p. 146, Organizational psychosocial factors)
- Violence and aggression (see ➔ p. 150, Violence and aggression), violence policies (see ➔ p. 426, Violence management policies)
- Low back pain (see ➔ p. 282, Low back pain), work-related upper limb disorders (see ➔ pp. 286, 288, Work-related upper limb disorders 2)
- Stress (see ➔ p. 344, Stress 2: Interventions/risk controls)
- Depression and fitness for work (see ➔ p. 496, Depression)

# Ageing and fitness for work

## Epidemiology and workforce demographics

- The demographics of populations are changing. The proportion of the UK population who are in the 50- to 64-year age group is increasing
- Changes in UK pension arrangements are likely to increase retirement age, with more individuals working beyond the age of 65 years
- It is predicted that within the next 25 years, 30% of the workforce in Europe will be >50 years old

## Physiological changes with age

- There is some evidence that certain physiological and cognitive parameters change with ↑ age

*Physical*

- ↓ Cardiovascular capacity (measured by $VO_2$ max)
- ↓ Musculoskeletal capacity.
- ↓ *Heat tolerance*: unclear whether this is simply a function of age, or whether it reflects a higher incidence of cardiovascular disease
- Sleep disturbance

There is wide individual variation in the baseline level and rate of decline of physiological parameters. A physically fit 50-year-old can have a greater physical capacity than an unfit 20-year-old

*Cognitive*

- ↓ Precision
- ↓ Speed of perception and cognitive processing
- ↑ Control of language
- ↑ Ability to process complex information in difficult situations

## Overall function in ageing workers

There is good evidence that job performance does *not* weaken markedly with age; indeed, it can improve.

'Workability' is a concept that assumes that overall performance derives from a portfolio of skills and attributes. The relative contribution of various attributes changes with age; overall performance is preserved. Motivation, loyalty, and experience all generally improve with age, and these factors tend to compensate for physiological decline. If better use is made of enhanced attributes in older workers (e.g. using their experience to train and mentor others), their work potential is maximized.

## Sickness absence

Long-term absence is more common in older employees as a group because of the higher incidence of serious or degenerative diseases. However, short-term absence is lower in this group because of a combination of factors including lack of immediate dependents (e.g. time off to look after children) and higher levels of motivation.

⚠ As with overall function, there is a wide individual variation in absence-taking, and generalization is unwise in decision-making about individuals.

## Risks for older workers

The following factors are associated with ↓ work ability and ↑ risk of ill health, and it is particularly important to be aware of them in older workers:

- Role conflict
- Fear of error
- Poor control over work
- Lack of professional development
- Lack of feedback and appreciation
- High speed of decision-making

## Interventions to manage an ageing workforce

There is little direct evidence of benefit from the scientific literature because of a lack of intervention studies. However, these adjustments are based on enhancing 'workability' as described here.

- *Careful management of change*:
  - tailored retraining for new technology
  - flexible career development initiatives for older workers
- Train supervisors to be aware of age management
- *Apply age ergonomics*:
  - special attention to ergonomics solutions for manual handling tasks and avoiding *extremely* heavy physical work
  - adaptations to man–machine interfaces for long-sightedness (clear controls, large visual displays) and slower reaction times
  - avoiding *extremely* hot working environments
- Health promotion and facilitation of exercise programmes to promote general physical fitness. This is clearly a matter of personal choice for employees, but the effect of physical fitness on overall work capacity with increasing age is often not appreciated
- Adopt a generally positive approach and supportive culture for older employees; value their experienced input

## Relevant legislation

- The Equality Act 2010 (➲ p. 596, ➲ p. 598, Disability Discrimination 1, ➲ p. 606, Age discrimination) puts an onus on employers not to discriminate in employment on the grounds of age. Because of the wide variation in fitness in older people, it will be necessary to carry out a careful individual assessment of capacity and make adjustments where these are practicable.

# Obesity

*Definition:* 'A disorder in which excess fat has accumulated to an extent that health may be adversely affected' (Royal College of Physicians).

## Epidemiology

According to the World Health Organization (WHO) there is an epidemic of obesity. The Health Survey for England in 2017 estimated that obesity (body mass index > 30 kg/m²) affects nearly 29% of adults, with a further 35.6% being overweight.

## Risk factors

Predisposing factors for obesity include:
- Age (obesity rises with age)
- Gender (females > males)
- Social class (risk increases with lower social class)
- Genetic
- Marital status (married > single)

It can be precipitated by:
- Smoking cessation (e.g. by substituting food for cigarettes)
- Physical inactivity (e.g. due to ill health, work, and family pressures)
- Increased dietary calorie intake (e.g. holidays, psychological distress)
- Rarely, sympatho-adrenal or other endocrine disorders
- Drugs, e.g. anti-epileptics, anti-psychotics, anti-depressants, and insulin

## Classification

WHO classifies weight as in (Table 23.2).

►► Waist circumference is important because abdominal fat deposition dictates risk of medical complications. Risk is increased with increasing waist circumference:
- Europeans/Caucasians: men >102 cm, women >88 cm
- South Asians: men >90 cm, women >80 cm

## Clinical features

Obesity is important because it is associated with an increased risk of:
- Type 2 diabetes
- Cardiovascular disease (hypertension, angina, myocardial infarction, cerebrovascular accidents)
- Respiratory complications, e.g. sleep apnoea
- Cancers, e.g. of breast, colon, uterus, kidney, and oesophagus
- Other conditions, e.g. gout, varicose veins, gallstones, fatty liver, menorrhagia

**Table 23.2** WHO classification of weight

| | BMI (Caucasians) kg/m² | BMI (South Asians) kg/m² |
|---|---|---|
| Overweight | 25.0–29.9 | >23.0 |
| Obese (class 1) | 30.0–34.9 | >25.0 |
| Obese (class 2) | 35.0–39.9 | |
| Obese (class 3) (morbid obesity) | >40 | |

## Sickness absence

Obesity is a predictor of:

- Short-term sickness absence in men and women
- Long-term sickness absence in men and women

Overweight is a predictor of:

- Short-term absence on men
- Long-term absence on women

Obesity can accelerate physical disorders (e.g. osteoarthritis of the knees). In terms of work limitations, the effects of obesity are estimated to be the equivalent of the worker being 20 years older.

## Other potential occupational issues

- Increased travel costs due to the need to use two seats (air, rail travel)
- Impaired fit of personal protective equipment, e.g. face masks, clothing
- Costs of adapted furniture
- Special arrangements for evacuation during emergencies
- Inability to mount an emergency response

## Prevention

The workplace is an important opportunity for the prevention of overweight and obesity. See ➲ p. 404, Health and safety policies.

## Clinical management

- Dietary advice
- Physical activity management

National Institute for Health and Clinical Excellence (NICE) (Scottish Intercollegiate Guidelines Network in Scotland) have produced guidelines on the use of drugs and surgery.

- *Orlistat, lipase inhibitor*: improves weight loss if taken with a low-fat diet
- *Surgical interventions*:
  - laparoscopic banding (least invasive)
  - gastric bypass (effective weight loss, but significant complications)

## Compensation/legal aspects

Obesity is recognized as a clinical condition and appears in ICD-10. It is associated with frequent reports of disability both in mobility and activities of daily living and may be covered by the Equalities Act 2010. Any adjustments/adaptations should be consistent with the medical advice on the importance of physical activity.

## Further information

Nerys W (2008). *Managing Obesity in the Workplace*. Radcliffe Publishing, Oxford.

# Cognitive impairment and fitness for work

## Causes of cognitive impairment

- Dementia
- Pseudo-dementia in those with severe depression
- Space-occupying lesions, e.g. subdural haematoma
- Brain injury
- Alcohol or substance misuse
- Hypothyroidism
- Vitamin $B_{12}$ or folate deficiency
- Vasculitis

## Epidemiology

- Alzheimer's disease (AD) and vascular dementia are the most common forms of dementia
- There are 850,000 people estimated to be living with dementia in the UK
- Five per cent of people over the age of 65 years have dementia, rising to 20% over the age of 80 years
- Evidence that work is a risk factor for AD is conflicting. Some evidence that blue-collar work more at risk, but this may be confounded by premorbid ability and/or socio-economic status
- Exposures to organic solvents, lead, mercury, aluminium, or pesticides have all been implicated, but the evidence is inconclusive

## Symptoms and practical problems at work

- *Impairment of*:
  - memory
  - reasoning
  - personality
  - communication (word finding difficulties)
- Workers may be referred to the OH service owing to concerns regarding their memory, decision-making, time-keeping, communication, interpersonal relationships, attendance, or overall performance
- Initial signs and symptoms of cognitive impairment are subtle and may go unrecognized, or be misdiagnosed as stress or depression
- Poor insight can make management challenging

## Clinical assessment and diagnosis

*History*

It is helpful if managers give specific examples of workplace difficulties as this may alert the assessing physician to the possibility of cognitive impairment. If suspected, then explore the following:

- The employee's perceptions of their difficulties
- Family history of dementia
- *Past medical history*: history of head injury, brain tumour, etc.
- Drug/alcohol history
- Educational history
- Occupational history (exposure to occupational neurotoxins)

- ⚠ *Consider treatable causes of dementia*:
  - pseudo-dementia in those with severe depression
  - space-occupying lesions
  - alcohol misuse
  - hypothyroidism
  - vitamin $B_{12}$ or folate deficiency
  - vasculitis

*Investigation*

- If cognitive difficulties are suspected then tests to screen for cognitive impairment such as the Addenbrooke's Cognitive Examination – Revised or the widely used but less sensitive Mini-Mental State Examination (MMSE)[1] may be helpful. An MMSE score of <29–30 in a person of working age is unusual (anxiety may compromise performance). An MMSE score <24 indicates significant cognitive difficulties
- Referral to a psychologist for formal cognitive assessment

## Prognosis

- Prognosis depends on cause and the outcome of treatment
- The prognosis of dementia is one of declining cognitive function, and employment cannot usually be sustained in the medium term
- *Workplace adjustments*:
  - highly structured/routine work
  - regular supportive supervision
  - predictable workload
- *Factors that reduce the feasibility of remaining at work*:
  - highly variable work pattern
  - high decision latitude
  - multitasking
  - time pressures
  - cognitively demanding work
  - behavioural problems
- Caution should be exercised in assessing workers in safety critical posts or key decision-makers

## Medical management

- Identify reasonably practicable workplace adjustments
- If, despite adjustments, the worker is unable to cope with his/her current post, he/she may be eligible for ill-health retirement (if the condition is progressive and untreatable)

## Relevant legislation

- The Equality Act 2010

1 Folstein MF, Folstein SE, McHugh PR (1975). 'Mini-mental State': A practical method for grading the cognitive state of patients for the clinician. *Psychiatry Resolutions*, 12:189–198.

# Depression

*Types*: The most common type of depression is unipolar depression; bipolar disorder (manic depression) affects around 1%.

## Epidemiology

- *Major depressive episode*: annual prevalence 7.1% (males 5.3%, females 8.7%)
- *Mixed anxiety and depression*: point prevalence 7.8% (males 6%, females 9.8%)
- *Lifetime risk of depression*: males 14.7%, females 26.1%
- More common in people living alone, in poor physical health, not employed, and claimants of Employment and Support Allowance
- Often comorbid with anxiety disorders, substance misuse, and long-term physical conditions

## Causation

*Predisposing factors*

- Genetic (>×2 increased risk if first degree relative affected)
- Adverse childhood experiences
- Previous history of depression
- Underlying physical illness

*Precipitating factors*

- Major adverse life events
- Physical illness, e.g. onset, worsening of symptoms
- Drug therapy, e.g. corticosteroids
- Work-related difficulties, especially bullying

*Perpetuating factors*

- Lack of confiding relationship with partner
- Misuse of alcohol or drugs
- Combination of work and domestic problems
- Isolation and lack of adequate support

## Diagnostic assessment

- *Classification*:
  - DSM-IV (American Psychological Association): 'Major depressive disorder'
  - ICD10 (WHO): 'Depressive episode'/'Recurrent depressive disorder'
  - both sets of criteria require impairment of social, *occupational*, or other important areas of functioning

## Clinical treatment

- *Psychological*:
  - cognitive behavioural therapy (CBT): linking thoughts, feeling, and behaviours to challenge negative patterns of thinking
- *Pharmacological*:
  - Selective Serotonin Reuptake Inhibitors (SSRIs) most commonly used, e.g. fluoxetine, sertraline, citalopram
  - other drugs include, e.g. mirtazapine, venlafaxine, agomelatine
  - maintain treatment for at least 6 months from point of maximum recovery (2 years if recurrent depression)
- Relapse rate of major depression: 60% in 5 years if untreated

## OH input

Facilitate early referral for psychiatric assessment/psychological treatment.

*Fitness for work*

- *Performance*:
  - poor motivation
  - reduced concentration and poor decision-making
  - lack of confidence
  - impaired communication, withdrawal, and/or irritability
  - lack of energy
  - antidepressant medication
- *Sickness absence*:
  - significant impairment of performance
  - non-compliance with medication
  - side effects of medication
  - premature reduction of dose

*Fitness to attend disciplinary hearing*

- Legal fitness to plead criteria relate mainly to capacity. Main question is whether the employee understands the allegations and their significance—can they take part in the decision-making process?
- Useful guide to cognitive ability is the employee's own correspondence with the employer
- Understandable that employee is likely to feel anxious and preoccupied, and to eat and sleep badly around the time of any hearing; but postponement of the hearing can only protract and intensify this natural reaction
- Speedy resolution helps to prevent chronicity and secondary morbidity, and can help both parties move on
- Location of the hearing is important; the workplace might be too aversive and a meeting in the employee's home would be intrusive. Therefore, a neutral location, e.g. hotel suite, might be more acceptable

*Time off work*

See ➔ p. 340, Stress 1: Recognition and assessment; ➔ p. 344, Stress 2: Interventions/risk control.

*Rehabilitation and reasonable adjustments at work*

- 'Round-table' discussions can be helpful:
  - shared problem-solving approach
  - OH, Human Resources (HR), employee, manager +/− treating psychiatrist/psychologist
  - realistic goal setting, job definition, and work routine
  - agreed hours and d of work, and how these change over time
  - manager's involvement
  - preparation of work colleagues for employee's return

## Further information

World Health Organization (2022). Mental Health at work. Information sheet. WHO, Geneva. Available at: https://www.who.int/news-room/fact-sheets/detail/mental-health-at-work

Henderson M et al. (2011). Work and common psychiatric disorders. *Journal of the Royal Society of Medicine*, 104:198–207. DOI 10.1258/jrsm.2011.

# Chronic fatigue syndrome/ myalgic encephalomyelitis

There is a broad range of disability among patients with chronic fatigue syndrome (CFS). Some at the mild end of the spectrum manage to work normally, while others will need protracted adjustments to work.

- Intervention studies have shown that ~30–60% of CFS/myalgic encephalomyelitis (CFS/ME) patients do not return to work after treatment. Between 25 and 42% of CFS/ME patients are on disability benefits
- Work status is an important predictor of recovery. CFS/ME patients who are out of work have a poor overall prognosis compared with those who manage to maintain some employment (even after adjustment for severity)
- Low likelihood of a good treatment outcome in CFS/ME predicted by:
  - severe symptoms
  - psychiatric comorbidity
  - long duration of symptoms

The prediction of return to work might be assumed for practical purposes to reflect these factors, although, because few studies look at work outcomes, there is little direct evidence on this question.

## Medical management of CFS/ME

The approach to clinical management follows a bio-psychosocial model. It is recognized that outcome is greatly influenced by psychosocial factors including illness beliefs, personal experience, personality, and coping skills. Treatment includes:

- A multidisciplinary approach to rehabilitation, including the input of physicians, pain specialists, psychologists, dieticians, physiotherapists, and sometimes alternative therapists
- Medical control of symptoms (e.g. treating pain and sleep disturbance)
- Management of comorbid conditions (e.g. depression)
- Of the specific treatment modalities, CBT and graded exercise therapy (GET) have been shown to be effective for CFS/ME, although GET is not popular among patients
- Employers or insurance companies will sometimes fund or facilitate treatment by multidisciplinary clinical teams. This is particularly helpful in view of the scarcity of National Health Service resources in this area

## Adjustments to work in CFS/ME

It may be difficult for an employer to implement or sustain prolonged adjustments to work. Therefore, it is important that there is close liaison between treating physicians and allied specialists, OH advisers, managers, and HR advisers in supporting a return to work. In CFS/ME it is best if a work rehabilitation can be coordinated as part of an overall graded activity programme.

- A protracted phasing up of working hours with a low baseline (e.g. 2–3 hours, 2–3 days/week) and very gradual increase may be necessary. It may take many months (or even more than a year in some cases) to reach premorbid working hours

- If a long commute to work exacerbates fatigue, home working or a change of work site should be considered. Alternatively, working hours can be tailored to avoid peak traffic times
- Frequent rest breaks should be built in to the work schedule
- Reduction in heavy physical work or repetitive work is sometimes appropriate
- Permanently reduced hours of work may be required for those unable to return to their previous contracted hours

Tolerance of a higher level of sickness absence by the employer might be reasonably expected if there are frequent exacerbations of symptoms.

## Overlap with other conditions

There is considerable overlap between CFS/ME and a number of other conditions for which the precise pathology and aetiology are unknown, including fibromyalgia and irritable bowel syndrome. For example, 20–70% of patients with fibromyalgia meet the diagnostic definition for CFS/ME, and 35–70% of patients with CFS/ME could also be defined as having fibromyalgia.

## Relevant legislation

The Equality Act 2010 would apply to individuals with CFS/ME and employers would be expected to make reasonable adjustments to work.

## Further information and guidance

NHS Plus/Department of Health (2006). Occupational aspects of the management of chronic fatigue syndrome: A National Guideline, related leaflets for employers and employees. Available at: https://www.nhshealthatwork.co.uk/images/library/files/Clinical%20excellence/CFS_full_guideline.pdf

# Diabetes mellitus

## Terminology and diagnostic criteria

- Type 1 usually develops in childhood and adolescence
- Type 2 predominantly occurs in adults and accounts for 90% of cases

### WHO criteria for diagnosis

Depends on symptoms of diabetes (polydypsia, polyuria, and weight loss) plus:

- a random venous plasma glucose >11.1 mmol/l *or*
- a fasting plasma glucose concentration >7.0 mmol/l (whole blood > 6.1 mmol/l) *or*
- plasma glucose concentration >11.1 mmol/l 2 hours after 75 g anhydrous glucose in an oral glucose tolerance test

If asymptomatic the diagnosis requires at least one additional glucose test result on another day.

## General OH considerations

Fitness to work should be based on an individual risk assessment taking into account the nature of the work, the health status of the worker, and how well their diabetes is controlled. A report from the individual's specialist or general practitioner (GP) may be useful. Employers must make reasonable adjustments to employee's duties as required by the Equality Act 2010.

From an occupational aspect, the most important clinical complications of diabetes are:

- *Hypoglycaemia*: premonitory warning signs include hunger, sweating, and dizziness, but these may be reduced or absent. Risk factors for hypoglycaemia are:
  - treatment with insulin or sulphonylureas
  - poor compliance with medication or diet
  - excessive exercise
  - alcohol
  - renal failure
  - intensification of treatment
- *Impaired visual acuity*: proliferative retinopathy, maculopathy, and pan-retinal laser photocoagulation may bring individuals below Driver Vehicle Licensing Association (DVLA) standards for Group 1 driving
- *Neuropathy*: this may lead to a reduction in fine motor skills, reduced positional awareness, and postural hypotension. Sensory loss leads to an increased risk of accidental damage to peripheral tissues

## Sickness absence

Studies of sickness absence in employees with diabetes show increases in absence rates (estimates between 50 and 100% increase compared with non-diabetics). However, the better controlled the diabetes, the less likely the person is to take sick leave.

## Shiftwork

In theory, timing of insulin and meals can be difficult with rotating shifts. However, modern insulin treatments have made shift work less problematic than previously and most diabetics cope well.

## Safety critical jobs

In the UK, people on insulin may be restricted in some employments, requiring adjustments or removal, e.g. airline pilot, the armed forces. The jobs for which there is a blanket ban are frequently reviewed and the latest list is available from Diabetes UK. Since October 2011, insulin-treated diabetics have been able to apply for a group-2 driving license, subject to strict DVLA qualifying criteria.

A careful risk assessment needs to be done to assess the suitability of people with insulin-treated diabetes for employment where there may be a risk of injury or harm to the individual or the public, e.g. firefighting. Suitability for such employment should be regularly reviewed by an OH professional in consultation with a diabetes specialist; and should be based on the following criteria:

- Be fit for task and may require Equality Act 2010 considerations of adjustments
- Be under regular (at least annual) specialist review and their diabetic control must be stable
- Be well-motivated and be able to self-monitor their glucose levels at least bd
- Have understanding of hypoglycaemic symptoms
- Be able to demonstrate good awareness of the risks of hypoglycaemia

## Further information and guidance

Diabetes, UK. Meet our new Peer Support Network. Available at: http://www.diabetes.org.uk/ (Online resources to enable access to Peer support)

DVLA (2022). Assessing fitness to drive -guide for medical professionals. Available at https://assets.publishing.service.gov.uk/government/uploads/system/uploads/attachment_data/file/1084397/assessing-fitness-to-drive-may-2022.pdf

# Epilepsy

Defined by the International League Against Epilepsy as two or more epileptic seizures unprovoked by any immediate identifiable cause.

## Epidemiology

Depends on definition, but the most commonly quoted statistics are:

- *Prevalence*: 5–10 active cases per 1,000 population
- *Incidence*: 50 (range 40–70) first fits per 100,000 population/year

## Clinical classification of seizures

### *Partial seizures*

- Simple partial seizures (no loss of consciousness)
- *Complex partial seizures*:
  - with impairment of consciousness at onset
  - simple partial onset followed by impairment of consciousness
  - partial seizures evolving to generalized tonic–clonic seizures

### *Generalized seizures*

Convulsive or non-convulsive with bilateral discharges involving subcortical structures:

- Absence
- Myoclonic
- Clonic
- Tonic
- Tonic–clonic
- Atonic

### *Unclassified epileptic seizures*

Usually used when an adequate description is not available.

## Treatment and prognosis

### *Treatment*

Treatment is with anticonvulsants. Chronic stable treatment rarely affects performance significantly. Acute drug overdosage can cause serious impairment but is rapidly reversible.

### *Prognosis*

The risk of further seizures depends on the clinical situation:

- *First seizure* (see Fig. 23.2):
  - 67% have a second seizure within 12 months
  - if seizure-free for 6 months, 30% have a further seizure within 12 months
- *Established epilepsy* (more than one seizure):
  - most patients who achieve remission (seizure-free for 5 years) do so within the first 2 years; >95% remain seizure-free for 10 years
  - approximately 20–30% will have further seizures despite treatment
  - the risk of further seizures ↑ with ↑ duration of poor control and ↑ frequency, combination of partial and tonic–clonic seizures, structural cerebral lesions, and impairment of cerebral function

## Fitness for work

### *General issues*

Advice about fitness for work should consider the risk to the individual and to others (e.g. passengers). ⚠ Never base risk assessment on the label of epilepsy, but on individual clinical and job details.

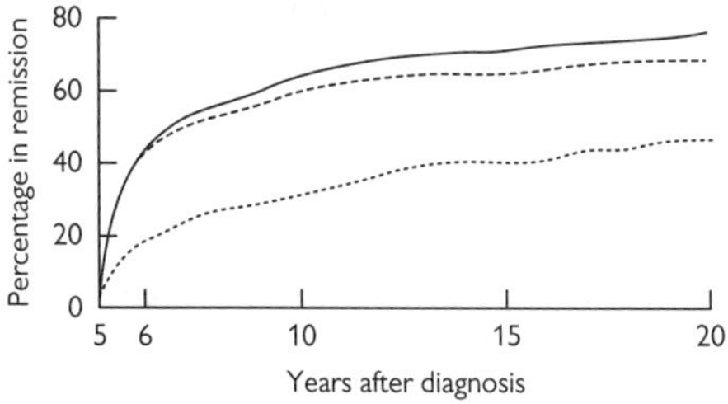


**Fig. 23.2** Actuarial percentage recurrences after first seizure and after 6, 12, and 18 months without seizures.

From Hart YM, Sander JW, Johnson AL, and Shorvon SD (1990). National general practice study of epilepsy. *Lancet*, 8726:1271–1274. Reproduced by kind permission of Elsevier.

*Specific issues*

- *High-risk activities*: restrict those with epilepsy from:
  - lone working
  - working at heights
  - swimming or working unprotected near water
  - working with dangerous or unguarded machinery, or fire
  - carrying out or assisting at surgical procedures
  - sole care of dependent (e.g. ventilated or unconscious) patients
  - sole manual handling of patients, e.g. carrying infants
  - usually excluded: aircrew, armed forces, police, firefighters
- *Driving*: see DVLA guidance, but in general:
  - group 1: restrict until seizure-free for 1 year (+/− treatment), unless seizures only occur during sleep, and the last seizure was >3 years ago
  - group 2: restrict until seizure-free *off* treatment for 10 years (5 years if seizure due to substance abuse and abuse is controlled)
  - advise not to drive during and 6 months after treatment withdrawal
  - provoked seizures (e.g. eclampsia) will be advised on an individual case basis by the DVLA
- Jobs that are associated with sleep disturbance or fatigue (e.g. shift work) are not contraindicated, but can exacerbate epilepsy
- Visual display equipment is associated with an extremely low risk of seizure provocation, and it is usually inappropriate to restrict

## Disclosure

Individuals are often reluctant to disclose a diagnosis of epilepsy; 50% do not declare it at pre-employment assessment. It can be useful to inform the line manager, but only with the individual's consent.

## Adjustments to work

Diagnosis of epilepsy likely be considered a disability under the Equality Act 2010 Where practical, employer must provide adjustments/redeployment as indicated by a risk assessment.

## Further information and guidance

DVLA (2022). Assessing fitness to drive-guide for medical professionals. Available at https://assets.publishing.service.gov.uk/government/uploads/system/uploads/attachment_data/file/1084397/assessing-fitness-to-drive-may-2022.pdf

# Alcohol misuse and fitness for work

- An increasing use of alcohol (especially among women) means that more workers are likely to present with alcohol misuse or alcoholism
- People who are alcohol dependent may not accept that a problem exists, making management challenging
- Initial signs and symptoms of alcohol misuse may go unrecognized or be 'overlooked' by well-intentioned colleagues
- ► Binge drinking is defined as consuming, in one episode, 8–10 U for men and 6–8 U for women
- A unit of alcohol is 10 ml, by volume, of pure alcohol
- The UK Chief Medical Officer's Guidance on sensible drinking has suggested that no more than 14 U per week on a regular basis is a sensible limit

## Epidemiology

- Twenty-four per cent of adults in England and Scotland regularly drink above the CMOs low-risk guidelines
- In 2017, 20% of the population reported no alcohol use
- Alcohol-related mortality rate in England was 46.5/100,000 in 2018 (nearly 25,000 deaths)
- Road deaths involving at least one driver over the drink drive limit rose between 2009 and 2017 to reach an estimated 290
- Five per cent of road casualties in 2009 involved someone driving 'over the limit'

## 'Soft' signs of substance misuse

- Variable work performance
- ↑ Accidents
- ↑Errors
- ↑ Complaints
- ↑ Absenteeism, especially around weekends and holidays
- Poor time-keeping

## Clinical assessment and diagnosis

Workers may be referred to the OH service because of ↑ sickness absence, ↓ performance, work attendance while intoxicated, or alcohol consumption at work. Not all will have alcoholism.

It is helpful when referring an employee to the OH service if the manager gives examples of workplace difficulties. This may alert the occupational physician to the possibility of alcohol misuse. If suspected, then explore the following:

- The employee's perceptions of their difficulties
- Medical history, focusing on illnesses associated with alcohol misuse:
  - dyspepsia
  - jaundice
  - cirrhosis
  - cardiac arrhythmia
  - peripheral neuropathy
  - hypertension
- Alcohol history

- Family history of alcohol misuse
- Accidents or assaults
- Money problems due to alcohol misuse
- Legal problems, e.g. drink driving convictions
- Clinical examination, seeking the stigmata of alcoholism
- Use the Alcohol Use Disorders Identification Test to establish severity of misuse
- If cognitive difficulties are suspected, arrange a cognitive assessment

## Prognosis

- The prognosis for a worker with alcoholism is guarded
- Some problem drinkers aim for 'controlled drinking'. In practice, this is rarely achieved and may indicate a failure to acknowledge the problem
- *Special caution should be exercised in assessing workers in safety critical posts, such as vocational drivers, or key decision-makers*
  - see also ➲ p. 508, Fitness to drive 1; ➲ p. 510, Fitness to drive 2
  - see also ➲ p. 540, Fitness for safety critical work

## Alcohol testing

Where supported by an alcohol policy, pre-employment, with cause, or random breath or blood alcohol testing may be undertaken.

## Medical management

- Identify a treatment provider, usually via the GP
- In-patient care for assisted alcohol withdrawal is not usually required, but may be required in those:
  - consuming >30 U/day
  - with significant comorbidities
  - history of seizures or delirium tremens
- Agree a contract with the worker for regular follow-up including, where obtainable, regular reports from treatment agency
- A sustained period of abstinence is required before any return to work
- Once at work, monitor time-keeping, performance, and absences
- Prolonged OH service follow-up (up to 12 months) may be appropriate

## Relevant guidance and legislation

- The Equality Act 2010
- Faculty of Occupational Medicine (2006). *Guidance on alcohol and drug misuse in the workplace*. FOM, London

## Further information and guidance

NICE (2012). *Alcohol Dependence and Harmful Alcohol Use*. NICE Clinical Guidance CG115. Available at: http://www.nice.org.uk/CG115

See also ➲ p. 416, Substance abuse policies.

# Chapter 24

# Fitness for specific work

# Fitness to drive 1

The Driver and Vehicle Licensing Agency (DVLA) is responsible for licensing drivers in the UK.

- Group 1 drivers are licensed to drive cars and motorbikes
- Group 2 drivers are licensed to drive buses and lorries (passenger-carrying vehicle (PCV) and large goods vehicle (LGV))

Ultimately, it is for the DVLA's medical advisers to determine, on behalf of the Secretary of State for Transport, an individual's fitness to drive. However, if driving is a special requirement of a job, employers need also to make their own assessment of fitness to drive.

## Driving for employment purposes

Decisions about fitness for vocational driving may be challenged under the Equality Act. Therefore occupational health (OH) professionals should carry out a risk assessment and be prepared to justify their advice. Examples where Group 2 standards may also be applied are as follows:

- Driving in hazardous areas such as quarries or construction sites
- *Driving emergency response vehicles (ambulances, police cars, fire engines)*:
    - the National Health Service (NHS) employing authority determines whether Group 2 standards shall apply to their ambulance drivers
- Carrying passengers (see p. 510, Fitness to drive 2)

The Medical Commission on Accident Prevention (now discontinued) recommended that Group 2 fitness standards be applied to taxi drivers, by their local authority, prior to licensing. More than half of local authorities follow this advice

- Driving large vehicles (see p. 510, Fitness to drive 2)

## General principles

- It is the duty of the license holder to notify the DVLA of any medical condition, or change to a medical condition, which may affect his/her fitness to drive
- Drivers need not notify the DVLA if their medical condition is not expected to last >3 months, but they should be guided by medical advice and refrain from driving if advised to do so
- Any person suffering from a medical condition that is likely to cause sudden incapacity should not drive
- Any person who is unable to control his/her vehicle safely should not drive

## Assessment frequency

- A Group 1 license is valid until age 70, and thereafter is renewable every 3 years
- License applications must be accompanied by a self-declaration of fitness

## Specific medical conditions

The DVLA publishes extensive guidance on fitness to drive in respect of a range of important medical conditions (see p. 509, Legislation and guidance).

## Ethical issues

- Where an employee is medically unfit to drive, the OH doctor should confirm that the employee understands that his/her condition may impair his/her fitness to drive
- The doctor should advise the employee verbally, and in writing, of his/her legal duty to notify the DVLA if he/she is medically unfit to drive. This advice should be recorded in the medical records
- If an employee who is medically unfit to drive refuses to notify the DVLA, then the doctor should offer to arrange a second medical opinion on the understanding that the employee does not drive pending reassessment
- The General Medical Council (GMC) advises that a doctor should make every reasonable effort to persuade an individual who is unfit to drive not to do so
- If an individual continues to drive despite the advice, then the DVLA medical adviser should be informed in confidence (having first advised the employee in writing of the intention to do so)

⚠ Always check current GMC guidance before notifying the DVLA in this situation.

## Adjustments to driving work

- An OH professional should advise reasonable adjustments to the job (including adaptations to vehicles) if this would enable an employee, whose ability to drive is impaired by a medical condition, to work
- Such adjustments would be a matter of good practice for all employees. However, the employer has a legal obligation if the Equality Act applies
- Disabled drivers and their advisers can access expert advice and driving assessment through the forum of mobility centres. Available at: http://www.mobility-centres.org.uk

## Legislation and guidance

- DVLA (2022). Assessing fitness to drive -guide for medical professionals. Available at https://assets.publishing.service.gov.uk/government/uploads/system/uploads/attachment_data/file/1084397/assessing-fitness-to-drive-may-2022.pdf
- General Medical Council Guidance for Doctors. Confidentiality: Protecting and Providing Information (Updated 2018) FAQs #17. GMC, London. Available at: http://www.gmc-uk.org/index.asp

# Fitness to drive 2

## LGV/PCV drivers

The DVLA sets the fitness standards for UK drivers including drivers of LGVs or PCVs with more than eight seats.

*General principles*

The fitness standards for HGV or PCV drivers (Group 2 drivers) are more stringent than these for Group 1 drivers. The reasons for this are the higher annual mileages driven by occupational drivers and the potentially greater consequences of an accident involving an HGV or PCV.

*Assessment frequency*

A Group 2 license is usually issued at age 21 and is valid until age 45 unless medical fitness changes. Thereafter, it is subject to review every 5 years or shorter periods depending on medical conditions until age 65. After age 65, licenses are renewable annually.

*Specific issues*

- It is the duty of the license holder to notify the DVLA of any medical condition that may affect his/her fitness to drive
- Any person suffering from a medical condition likely to cause sudden incapacity should not drive
- Any person unable to control his/her vehicle safely should not drive
- A registered medical practitioner must complete a medical report using Form D4

*Medical assessment*

- Height
- Weight
- Smoking history
- Alcohol consumption
- Current medication
- Corrected visual acuity >6/9 in the better eye and >6/12 in the other eye with uncorrected visual acuity being >3/60 in each eye
- Visual fields intact
- *Medical history*:
    - epilepsy
    - other neurological conditions
    - diabetes
    - psychiatric illness
    - cardiovascular disease
    - blood pressure
    - musculoskeletal disease sufficient to interfere with vehicle control

The final decision regarding fitness for Group 2 driving lies with the DVLA's medical adviser and not the examining doctor.

## Forklift truck operators

*Task demands*

Operation of a forklift truck, whether in a factory, on a farm, or on a building site, can be associated with the following hazards:

- Proximity to other vehicles and people
- Noisy environments
- Relatively confined spaces
- Frequent reversing and manoeuvring

*General principles*

- There are no regulations governing fitness to operate forklifts on private ground. HSE has published useful guidance (see ➔ p. 509, Legislation and guidance)
- If the forklift is to be operated on the public highway, the operator must meet current DVLA standards on fitness to drive
- Operators should usually be age 17 or over. Construction workers must be age 18. Agricultural workers should be over school-leaving age
- The fitness required is only that sufficient for the task to be carried out safely and efficiently. Individuals with a disability should be assessed bearing in mind good employment practices and disability legislation

*Fitness requirements*

Include good eyesight, adequate hearing, and reasonable head/neck mobility. The ability to look over the shoulder is important; no condition that predisposes to sudden loss of consciousness.

*Assessment frequency*

- Assess at pre-employment
- Assess at 5-yearly intervals from age 40
- Over age 65 review annually
- An operator with a medical condition should be reviewed more frequently if this is indicated

*Specific issues*

- Visual acuity should be 6/12 (corrected) with adequate visual fields
- Hearing should be sufficient to understand instructions and warnings
- Alcohol/drug addiction renders a worker unfit to operate a lift truck
- Careful assessment is necessary where there is a history of psychosis
- Poorly controlled angina or conditions predisposing to loss of consciousness (arrhythmias, transient ischaemic attack) are a bar to work with lift trucks
- Epilepsy is acceptable where the criteria for a car license are met
- Diabetes is permitted subject to good glycaemic control. Loss of awareness of hypoglycaemia will cause a diabetic to be considered unfit for this task
- Musculoskeletal problems should not significantly impair the driver's ability to look up, sideways, or over the shoulder

## Legislation and guidance

- A guide to vehicle licensing requirements including definitions of license categories and vehicles is given at: http://direct.gov.uk/
- HSE (2000). *Safety in Working with Lift Trucks*, HS(G)6. HSE, London. Available at: http://www.hse.gov.uk/pubns/priced/hsg6.pdf

# Fitness for professional diving

## Purpose

To establish whether a worker is fit to undertake diving at work and to identify, at an early stage, diving-related illnesses such as dysbaric osteonecrosis. Difficulties may arise when individuals undertake diving activity for hire or reward and do so out with (and in breach of) regulations (see ➲ p. 578, Diving at Work Regulations 1997).

## General principles

- Statutory medical assessments can only be carried out by a Health and Safety Executive (HSE) approved medical examiner of divers The examiner has to satisfy the HSE that they have the required knowledge of diving medicine to carry out this work. Usually, this knowledge is acquired by attending a 5-day diving medicine course
- The initial medical assessment involves the prospective diver completing a medical questionnaire, which is then validated by his/her general practitioner (GP). The approved medical examiner then reviews this and advises whether the individual has a medical condition that would disqualify him/her from diving without a full assessment
- Prior to commencing diver training the prospective diver should undergo a full diving medical examination. The results of this are recorded on form MA2 which includes the certificate of fitness to dive. The white copy of MA2 is given to the diver and the pink lower copy should be retained by the medical examiner for 7 years
- Where a diver is found unfit to dive, he/she has the right to appeal this decision to HSE within 28 days

## Assessment frequency

- *The medical certificate is valid for any period stipulated by the examining doctor up to a maximum of 12 months*
    - where a diver is medically unfit for work for >14 days *or* suffers a neurological, cardiorespiratory, or ear disorder, his/her fitness to dive must be reassessed by an approved examiner

## Specific issues

- Female divers should not dive when pregnant
- Chest X-ray and long-bone views are only required where clinically indicated
- The British Thoracic Society has issued guidelines on respiratory aspects of fitness for diving
- Extensive guidance on diving fitness standards is provided in the HSE publication MA1 which is available on the HSE website. The underlying principle is that the diver should not be at increased risk of a diving accident because of an existing medical condition

**Table 24.1** Investigations required at diving medical

| Initial examination | Annual review |
|---|---|
| Exercise testing (step test) | Exercise testing (step test) |
| Resting electrocardiogram (ECG) | Resting ECG (5 yearly from age 40) |
| Urinalysis | Urinalysis |
| Spirometry | Spirometry |
| Audiometry | |
| Full blood count | |

## Relevant legislation and guidance


- Diving at Work Regulations 1997 available at Diving at Work Regulations 1997 Legislation.gov.uk
- HSE. *The Medical Examination and Assessment of Divers*, MA1. HSE Books, London. Available at: ✆ http://www.hse.gov.uk/diving/ma1.pdf
- British Thoracic Society (2003). Guidelines on respiratory aspects of fitness for diving. *Thorax* 58:3–13. 2003 London

# Fitness for work in food handlers

## Definition of a food handler

A food handler manufactures, prepares, or transports food, and may come into direct contact with the food or with machines handling unwrapped food. This definition includes engineers, cleaners, and those visiting the premises. The definition also includes those preparing or serving food in canteens and shops.

## Health screening

Fitness for work is assessed by health screening. The screening process aims to exclude individuals with medical conditions who may pose a risk of microbiological or general contamination of food products. The assessment should also identify conditions that may be caused or exacerbated by work or jeopardize employee safety. Therefore, it should identify the following:

- Those suffering from, or carriers of, infectious disease which can be transmitted to the product, e.g. norovirus infection of the gastrointestinal (GI) tract
- Those suffering from conditions such as an infected wound or skin condition, which can transmit pathogens
- Those suffering from conditions (e.g. respiratory/musculoskeletal) which may be exacerbated by work or make work unsafe (allergies/ blackouts)

## Screening process

A questionnaire is completed before starting work, by visitors, or existing employees returning from absence from work. Examples of questions are shown in Box 24.1. Those with no positive answers can start work; those with a positive response must be assessed by a competent OH professional. Questionnaires are confidential and must be handled as sensitive information under the Data Protection Act.

► By law, all food handlers must receive training in food hygiene.

## Legislation and guidance

- NHS Plus, Royal College of Physicians, Faculty of Occupational Medicine (2008). *Infected Food Handlers: Occupational Aspects of Management. A National Guideline*. RCP, London. Available at: http://www.nhsplus.nhs.uk/providers/clinicaleffectiveness-guidelines-evidencebased.asp
- *Food Handlers: Fitness to Work*. Food Standards Agency. 2009 London. Available at: http://www.food.gov.uk/multimedia/pdfs/publication/fitnesstoworkguide09v2.pdf

**Box 24.1 Examples of questions to be included on a food handler's questionnaire[1]**

- In the last 2 weeks, have you had any of the following?
  - A skin infection
  - Diarrhoea and/or vomiting
  - An infection involving the ears, eyes, or gums
  - Contact with anyone who may have had typhoid or paratyphoid fever
- Have you ever had any of the following?
  - Typhoid or paratyphoid fever
  - Asthma or any other chest condition
  - Recurring skin disorders
  - Allergic reactions (including to nuts)
  - Persistent back, neck, arm, or wrist problems
  - Deafness or defective vision
  - Blackouts or dizzy spells

1 Harker C. (2001). *Occup Med* 51: 332–335 with kind permission from Oxford University Press.

# Fitness for air passenger travel 1: The physics and physiology of air travel

Many employees are required to fly as part of their job. This can cover a large spectrum from frequent to infrequent flying, and short to long-haul flight. The main issues to consider when advising about air travel are summarized here.

## Relative hypoxia

- Most passenger aircraft are pressurized to between 4,000 and 8,000 feet at their cruising altitude. This 20–30% reduction in atmospheric pressure results in a reduction of the partial pressure of oxygen inspired
- Due to the sigmoid nature of the oxygen dissociation curve of blood, this only results in about a 10% fall in oxyhaemoglobin saturation in healthy people (Fig. 24.1)
- However, those with significant lung disease and a degree of hypoxia (at sea level pressures) will operate on the steeper section of the curve (Fig. 24.1). They are at risk of significant desaturation. The risk varies between patients, particularly depending on hypoxic drive
- As a rough guide, in-flight oxygen is likely to be needed if the individual's oxygen saturation ($SaO_2$) at sea level is less than 90%

## Pressure change

The reduction in ambient pressure also results in an increase in volume of any gas trapped in a body cavity:

*PV* = constant (Boyle's law).

Gas expansion in an aircraft cabin can be of the order of 20–40%. This is demonstrated by the need to 'clear the (middle) ears' when ascending or descending. Other closed and semi-closed cavities will be similarly affected.

⚠ In ascending to altitude, passengers are effectively decompressing in a similar way to an ascending diver. Therefore, travellers who have been on diving holidays should carefully plan their last days of diving to reduce the risk of decompression illness during their flight home. The accepted general advice is not to fly within 24 hours of scuba diving.

## Low humidity

The air conditioning of cabin air results in low humidity and can lead to modest drying of mucous membranes. There is no evidence that even the longest flight would contribute to passengers becoming dehydrated.

## Seated immobility

- Air travel leads to long periods of sitting with limited posture changes. Flights longer than 4 hours are considered a risk factor for developing deep vein thrombosis (DVT)
- Travellers with pre-existing risk factors (e.g. recent surgery, known clotting disorders, malignancy, etc.) should seek medical advice. Preventative strategies range from leg exercises/stockings to medication (e.g. aspirin, heparin)

## Noise and motion

Noise (engine noise, cabin ventilation systems, and airflow over the external surfaces) is not a hazard to hearing but may be a factor in travel fatigue. Studies have shown that 0.5% of passengers have vomited and 8.4% experience nausea in flight, especially in turbulence.

## Stress

New environments, time pressures, and delays can increase stress in vulnerable people. Fear of flying is common and can normally be dismissed, but desensitization is available for the few who are severely affected.

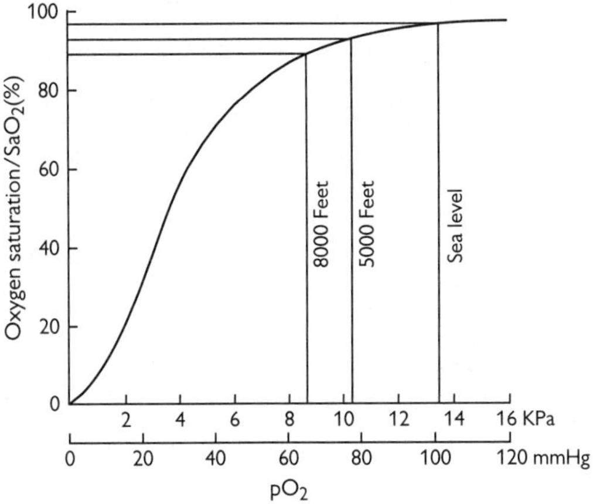


**Fig. 24.1** Effect of cabin pressure on oxygen saturation in a healthy passenger. Those with cardiovascular and respiratory disease where $SaO_2$ is below 90% may operate on the steeper part of the curve with significant desaturation at altitude

# Fitness for air passenger travel 2: Specific medical conditions

Medical conditions that need assessment prior to flight can be divided:

- Stable chronic (e.g. chronic obstructive pulmonary disease (COPD))
- Chronic with recent change (myocardial infarction and angina)
- Acute (e.g. illness, injury, surgery)

The physiological challenges of air travel outlined on the previous page need to be taken into account in the assessment of fitness to fly.

Most large airlines have medical advisers who advise on fitness to fly. Usually, a few weeks in advance, the passenger and his/her doctor are asked to complete a Medical Information Form. This allows the airline to assess the risks of travel and/or any special facilities needed (e.g. stretcher, oxygen, escort).

Extensive guidance is available from government, regulators, and airlines (see ➔ p. 519, Further information and guidance). Most guidance is pragmatic and often not evidence based, and specific rules can vary between carriers. The most important examples are given here.

## Cardiovascular and respiratory disease

- Broadly, if a passenger can walk 50 m without dyspnoea, the relative hypoxia at altitude will not become a health threat.
- Recent cardiovascular event should result in caution because of the relative hypoxia and risk of further acute event. As a general guide, do not allow air travel if myocardial infarct within 10 days if uncomplicated (3–4 weeks with complications), coronary angioplasty within 3–5 days, cerebrovascular accident within 3 days
- *Pneumothorax*: passengers with pneumothorax should not fly for 6 weeks

## Diabetes

- Crossing time zones and disruption of sleep/meal patterns can risk destabilizing control
- Diabetic passengers should be advised to stay on home time for medication until arrival
- Modern (basal bolus) regimes make problems less likely with good education, and medication should be carried in hand baggage because of low temperatures in the aircraft hold. Sharps (e.g. needles) must be declared for security reasons

## Pregnancy

Most carriers will allow travel up to the 36th week for single pregnancies and the 32nd week for multiple pregnancies.

## Infectious disease

- It is an international health regulation that individuals should not fly during the infectious phase of a contagious disease
- The main risk is the proximity of others (rather than spread via the cabin air, which is filtered) and acute worsening of the condition

## Other

- *Recent surgery*: advise against flying within 10 days, because of risk of trapped gas (eye, abdomen) and DVT
- *ENT conditions*: those affecting Eustachian tube patency can cause tympanic membrane rupture
- *Anaemia*: risk of severe hypoxia if haemoglobin is <7.5 g/dl
- *Psychiatric*: patients with acute psychotic illness require an escort and available sedation
- *Fractures*: restrict flying for 24–48 hours
- The best advice is for passengers to contact their carrier in plenty of time to discuss medical issues to avoid being denied boarding or experiencing complications in flight

## On-board facilities for dealing with medical emergencies

All cabin staff are trained in first aid including defibrillation when automatic external defibrillators are carried. Aircraft are required to carry extensive first aid and medical packs, which include drugs to treat the commonly occurring ailments. Many airlines also subscribe to air-to-ground medical services which can advise crew and medical attendants.

## Further information and guidance

*British Lung Foundation Leaflet on Flying with a Lung Condition*. Regularly updated on line resource. Available at: http://www.lunguk.org/you-and-your-lungs/living-with-a-lung-condition/air-travel

British Thoracic Society Guidelines (2011). *Air Travel Guidelines*. Available at: http://www.brit-thoracic.org.uk/guidelines/air-travel-guideline.aspx

Federal Aviation Administration. *Passenger Health and Safety Guidance*. (2020). Available at: http://www.faa.gov/passengers/fly_safe/health/

*UK Civil Aviation Authority*. Regularly updated on line resource. Available at: https://www.caa.co.uk/Passengers/Before-you-fly/Am-I-fit-to-fly-/

# Fitness for work in professional pilots: Commercial pilots/aircrew

## Regulation/standards

- The international standards for the medical fitness of aircrew are maintained and updated by the International Civil Aviation Organization (ICAO)
- In the UK, the European Aviation Safety Agency (EASA) currently define standards for airworthiness, operations, and licensing compliant with the ICAO standards. A number of private or sport flying regulations remain under UK Civil Aviation Authority (CAA) oversight
- These regulatory provisions cannot cover every aeromedical situation. Therefore, to facilitate flexibility, 'accredited medical conclusion' (a decision by one or more medical experts), operational limitations, and relevant pilot skill and experience can be taken into account if the licensing authority believes that this would not jeopardize flight safety. However, this flexibility standard has resulted in different national regulators around the world applying different standards

## Medical assessment of pilots

*Process*

- Professional Aircrew are medically examined annually under the age of 40 years, and 6-monthly thereafter if undertaking single pilot operations (annually for two crew operations up to 60 years and 6 monthly from 60 to 65 years)
- A health declaration is completed, and a physical examination performed. Clinical tests focus on visual performance, ECG, and audiogram when required
- Any pilot not meeting the medical standard is referred to the regulatory authority, who defines what further investigation/evidence is required in order to assess fitness to fly against the EASA regulations
- A medical certificate to fly may be suspended at any time if there is a risk to flight safety

*Principles*

Fitness for aircrew is based on two broad principles: the physical and mental capability to fly/operate the aircraft, and the risk of an acute incapacitating event while flying (which could lead to a fatal accident).

*Functional capability*

- *Visual acuity*: good vision is required for long distance (to taxi, take off, and land the aircraft under visual conditions), intermediate (reading and operating cockpit instruments), and near distance (reading maps/flight plans, etc.)
- *Colour vision*: acceptable colour discrimination is required to identify signal lights from air traffic control, and other aircraft, vehicles, buildings, etc.
- *Visual field*: a normal visual field is required to maintain an adequate look-out to identify and avoid other aircraft
- Good hearing is required for communicating with and understanding instructions from air traffic control and other members of the flight crew, sometimes on a noisy flight deck

- Physical operation of aircraft controls and switches, and ability to assist passengers in the event of emergency
- *Psychological stability*: cognitive functions are important in dealing with complex aircraft and air traffic environments. There has been a real focus on the mental health of aircrew in recent years. While accidents attributed to untreated depressive illness, alcohol, substance misuse, and the suicidal intent of one or more of the crew are rare, the consequences are potentially devastating. Much is being done to identify those at risk and treat any illness where appropriate

*Incapacitation risk*

- Over the last four decades in the UK and elsewhere, and latterly within the European member states, an annual medical incapacitation risk limit of 1% has been applied in two-pilot public transport operations. This is known as the '1% rule', and assumes a target all-cause fatal accident rate for large public transport aircraft of 1 per 107 flying hours, not more than 10% of which should be due to one system failure (e.g. pilot failure), and not more than 10% of system failures should be due to a subsystem failure (e.g. medical incapacitation)
- This gives a target fatal accident rate due to aircrew medical incapacitation of one accident per 109 hours. This is almost unachievable in single-pilot operations
- The times during which the aircraft is closest to the ground (i.e. take-off and initial climb, and approach and landing) are the accident-critical phases. At the time the 1% rule was formulated, it was considered that in-flight incapacitation of one of the pilots would result in a fatal accident in about one in 1,000 such events. Therefore, in order to achieve the target medical cause fatal accident rate of one accident per 109 hours, neither pilot should have a risk of medical incapacitation greater than one in 106 hours, i.e. approximately 1% in 1 year. Note that the maximum DVLA Group 2 (LGV) driving risk is 2%

However, since its development there have been important changes to airline operations. Flights have become longer and aircraft more automated, so a higher risk might be tolerable while maintaining flight safety. Some states accept risks of 2% per annum, although this has not been accepted universally.

## Cabin crew

From 2014, cabin crew medical status has come under EASA regulation. All cabin crew must undergo a medical review every 5 years (or more frequently if risk dictates). The initial medical consists of a health declaration and physical examination by a medical examiner authorized by the UK CAA. Subsequent medical reviews may involve only a health declaration.

## Further information

EASA. Regularly updated on line resource. Available at: https://www.easa.europa.eu/

ICAO. Regularly updated on lie resource. Available at: http://www.icao.int/Pages/default.aspxpilots/aircrew

UK CAA. Regularly updated on lie resource. Available at: https://www.caa.co.uk/Commercial-industry/Pilot-licences/Medical/EASA-Part-MED-requirements/

UK CAA. Regularly updated on lie resource. Available at: https://www.caa.co.uk/Commercial-industry/Airlines/Cabin-crew/

# Fitness for military service

## Recruits

*Principles of screening*

- Recruits to the armed forces must undergo intensive training, which is physically arduous and mentally taxing. They need to be of robust constitution, free from disease and injury. Given the investment placed in individuals in military training, those who are likely to be lost from training on medical grounds need to be screened out
- On completion of training, personnel may operate in locations remote from medical care, and in situations where illness or injury of one individual may have profound and immediate effects on units
- Opportunities for flexibility of employment are very limited, and to remain in the military most individuals will need to be fit for unrestricted active service (i.e. at sea or on operations)
- This isolation means that medical follow-up of existing conditions can be impossible, and medication may not be available
- An initial engagement in the military can be for many years, and so any chronic effects from past conditions or injuries must be considered
- These all mitigate towards setting a high initial standard of fitness for the military. This standard needs to be generic since many different centres are providing recruitment medicals. The minimum standards apply across all three services, but certain branches of the military, notably aircrew and divers, have higher requirements (see ➔ p. 523)

*Screening process*

- In the UK, initial medicals will normally be carried out by uniformed or civilian medical officers on contract to Ministry of Defense (MOD), and where appropriate a full history will also be obtained from the recruit's GP. Specialist referral may be necessary
- Candidate is assessed using a grading system, physique, upper limbs, lower limbs (or 'locomotion', as this includes the back), hearing (right), hearing (left), eyesight right (corrected/uncorrected), eyesight left (corrected/uncorrected), mental function stability (emotional), and compared with a predetermined profile for his/her chosen specialization
- If successful, following the medical examination, the candidate will be required to complete a fitness assessment

## In service

- Many countries maintain a separate military health system. In the UK this is limited to responsibilities for primary care (including OH, community mental health, and rehabilitation) and operational medical care. Secondary care is the responsibility of the NHS, although some cases may be fast tracked to obtain an early return to service
- Decisions on fitness for work are the prerogative of service medical officers and MOD civilian medical practitioners. NHS GPs may only treat military personnel as temporary residents and can only certify them as unfit to travel rather than unfit to work
- A detailed system of Medical Employability Standards (MESs) describing capability in each environment has now been introduced

- Where individuals fall below standards in the long term (normally >12 months), they will be required to appear before a medical board to assess functional capacity. The relevant service personnel departments will subsequently decide if they can continue to serve under specified restrictions. If long-term employment is not available, they will be medically retired

## Specific medical conditions affecting fitness for entry to UK Armed Services

- Personnel with a history of anxiety may not do well in the armed forces, and so equal weight must be given to mental fitness. Repeated self-harm, mood disorders, and ongoing medication will normally be a bar to entry
- Chronic medical conditions such as asthma, epilepsy, eczema, and migraine are usually incompatible with service
- Orthopaedic conditions or injuries, particularly affecting the lower limbs, are likely to prejudice new entry training
- There are specific eyesight requirements for individual branches and services, as well as an overall minimum generic standard. If in doubt, a proper opthalmological evaluation is essential
- Conditions requiring regular medication, specific diets, and allergies will normally be unacceptable for service because of operational constraints affecting supply, catering, etc.
- Many conditions such as cardiological murmurs will require formal specialist evaluation
- Further information is available from Armed Forces Careers Offices

## Military pilots

In the UK and many countries, civilian aviation authorities have no jurisdiction over aircraft on the military register. Furthermore, the high medical standards set for commercial aircrew in order to ensure flight and passenger safety are not always enough to satisfy the demands of military flying. Therefore, a separate system of standards and regulatory systems exists. These are additional to the considerations that apply to any military recruit outlined here.

*Standards*

- In view of joint operations with other air forces, some joint standardization is also necessary
- These standards will be reflected in a system of medical grading which should only be applied by those specifically trained and familiar with the requirement
- There may be an additional requirement imposed for aptitude testing, and cognitive testing may form part of a separate non-medical assessment. May include ability to tolerate high G forces where appropriate

**Table 24.2** Medical standards for military pilots

| The following are relevant in the assessment of medical standards for military pilots: | |
|---|---|
| • Flight safety | • Risk of incapacitation |
| • Aviation environment | • Hypoxia, hypobaria, acceleration, extremes of temperature, noise, vibration |
| • Mission accomplishment | • Ability to complete task |
| • Operational efficiency | • Ability to perform task repeatedly |
| • Cost effectiveness | • Is outcome worth investment |
| • Escape and evasion | • Ability to survive if shot down |
| • Nuclear biological chemical | • Ability to operate warfare environment |
| • War role | |

## Relevant legislation

- The Armed Services are currently exempt from the disability provisions of The Equality Act 2010, although the principles of the legislation are usually followed, wherever possible, on a voluntary basis

# Fitness for work in health care

## Definition

Health care workers (HCWs) are those whose work involves medical management of patients, and wider aspects of their health and social care. Health care work is one of the most common occupations in the UK, including almost 2 million employees in the public (NHS) and private sectors.

Three groups of HCW have been defined for practical purposes:

- *Clinical and other staff*: including those in primary care and students, who have regular clinical contact with patients. This includes doctors, dentists, nurses; paramedical professionals such as occupational therapists, physiotherapists, radiographers; ambulance workers, etc.
- *Laboratory and other staff* (including mortuary staff): who have direct contact with potentially infectious clinical specimens and may additionally be exposed to pathogens in the laboratory. This includes those in academic (or commercial research) laboratories who handle clinical specimens. They do not normally have direct contact with patients
- *Non-clinical ancillary staff*: who may have social contact with patients, but not usually of a prolonged or close nature. This group includes receptionists, ward clerks, administrative staff working in hospitals and primary care, and maintenance staff such as engineers, gardeners, cleaners, etc.

## Specific hazards and occupational disorders in health care (list not exhaustive)

- Infection (see ➲ p. 117, Biological hazards and ➲p. 163, Occupational infections, for individual hazards and diseases)
- Violence (see ➲ p. 150, Violence and aggression)
- *Musculoskeletal disorders*: low back (see ➲ p. 282, Low back pain) and neck/shoulder pain
- Stress (see ➲ p. 340, Stress 1: Recognition and assessment; ➲ p. 344, Stress 2: Interventions/risk controls); the NHS refers to stress as mental ill health, e.g. stress at home or work related, anxiety/depression, diagnosed mental health conditions
- Latex allergy (see ➲ p. 228, Latex allergy)
- Dermatitis (see ➲ p. 268, Dermatitis 1; ➲ p. 272, Dermatitis 2)
- Radiation (see ➲ p. 22, Ionizing radiation 2: Principles of radiation protection)
- Cytotoxic drugs

## Fitness assessment

Health care work covers a very wide range of duties. HCWs often change role, and robust arrangements should be made to identify internal job changes, with reassessment of fitness where appropriate. Standard health clearance[1] for new HCW includes checks for tuberculosis disease/immunity, hepatitis B virus (HBV), immunization with post-immunization testing of immunity, and the offer of human immunodeficiency virus (HIV) and hepatitis C virus (HCV) tests.

Immunity from vaccine-preventable infections is advisable (see Table 24.3).

NB It is important to check current guidance as changes regularly.

1 Department of Health (2007). *Health Clearance for Tuberculosis, Hepatitis B, Hepatitis C and HIV: New Healthcare Workers*. DH, London.

**Table 24.3** Immunization requirements for HCWs

| Recommended routine assessment of immunity and immunization | Clinical (1) | Laboratory (2) | Non-clinical (3) |
|---|---|---|---|
| History of routine childhood immunization: diphtheria, polio, tetanus (DPT); mumps, measles, rubella (MMR); tuberculosis (bacillus Calmette–Guérin (BCG))<br>*or* positive measles, rubella antibodies, and Mantoux test if no satisfactory history of immunity<br>*and* immunization of non-immune | + | +<br>For polio, only boost those handling faecal specimens; diphtheria special arrangements to boost those handling organisms | DPT and MMR<br>BCG not routinely recommended |
| History of infection with varicella (chicken pox)<br>*or* positive varicella antibodies if history unsatisfactory<br>*and* immunization of non-immune | + | + | + |
| History of immunization against hepatitis B<br>*and* immunization, followed by check of serology in non-immune | + | + | +<br>If exposed to blood or body fluids |
| History of immunization against hepatitis A and typhoid<br>*and* immunization of non-immune | | Only if handling specific organisms | Only if exposed to sewage, e.g. drainage engineers |
| Influenza: offer of annual immunization | + | Only if handling organisms | |
| Cholera, meningococcus ACW 135Y, smallpox, tick-borne encephalitis, yellow fever, rabies, Japanese encephalitis, anthrax | | Only if handling specific organisms | |

Detailed guidance: Department of Health. Chapter 12. In: *Immunisation against Infectious Disease*. Available at: ➚ http://www.dh.gov.uk/health/category/publications/reports-publications/

Note: In June 2019 pertussis immunization was added—all those working with the pregnant and children are to be offered pertussis which is now a combined vaccine (polio-Diph, Tet and Pertussis) where no physical evidence of vaccination is presented. Refusal means blood testing non-immune status and no vaccine means risk assessment and potential for moving staff to non-child/pregnant work. ➚ https://www.gov.uk/government/publications/pertussis-occupational-vaccination-of-healthcare-workers/pertussis-occupational-vaccination-of-healthcare-workers

## Special fitness requirements

- Fitness for exposure prone procedures (see ➲ p. 530, Fitness for exposure prone procedures 1; ➲ p. 532, Fitness for exposure prone procedures 2)
- Fitness to work with children and vulnerable patients (see ➲ p. 534, Fitness to work with children)

## Transfer of information about fitness for work

Transfer of OH records or conclusions about fitness for work (including immunization status) should only be done with the employee's consent. Smart cards (transferable electronic record) are increasingly used for some staff groups, e.g. junior doctors and medical students. Very few use smart cards, many organizations are using the Employee Staff Record system with employee consent to move between Trusts where OH places information on that record.

## Specialist skills for professionals who care for HCWs

It is recognized that OH and other health professionals who provide care and support to health care practitioners need particular skills, including the management of alcohol and substance abuse, mental health specialists, etc. The Faculty of Occupational Medicine and Royal College of Psychiatrists have published guidance on competencies for OH Physicians and psychiatrists, respectively.

# Fitness for exposure prone procedures 1

## Definition of EPPs

Exposure prone procedures (EPPs) are health care procedures where there is a risk that injury to the HCW may result in the exposure of the patient's open tissues to the blood of the worker (bleed-back). Procedures include those where the worker's gloved hands may be in contact with sharp instruments, needle tips, and sharp tissues (spicules of bone or teeth) inside a patient's open body cavity, wound, or confined anatomical space where the hands or fingertips may not be completely visible at all times.

## Categorization of EPPs

EPPs are classified according to the likelihood that infection would be transmitted from an infected HCW to the patient.

*Category 1*

Procedures where the hands and fingertips of the worker are usually visible and outside of the body most of the time and the possibility of injury to the worker's gloved hands from sharp instruments and/or tissues is slight. This means that the risk of the HCW bleeding into the patient's open tissues should be remote.

*Category 2*

Procedures where the fingertips may not be visible at all times but injury to the worker's gloved hands from sharp instruments and/or tissues is unlikely. If injury occurs it is likely to be noticed and acted upon quickly to avoid the HCW's blood contaminating the patient's open tissues.

*Category 3*

Procedures where the fingertips are out of sight for a significant part of the procedure, or during certain stages, and in which there is a distinct risk of injury to the worker's gloved hands from sharp instruments and/or tissues. In such circumstances it is possible that exposure of the patient's open tissues to the HCW's blood may go unnoticed or would not be noticed immediately.

## Transmission from infected HCW to patients following EPPs

- HBV transmission from Hepatitis B e antigen (HBeAg) positive HCW is well documented. Several transmissions from HBeAg negative HCW prompted the use of HBV viral load testing in determining fitness for EPPs
- *HCV*: five reported incidents of transmission to 15 patients in the UK, and at least four other incidents worldwide
- *HIV*: three reported incidents with eight possible transmissions worldwide. None in the UK, despite 28 notification exercises in 7,000 patients up to the year 2003. The risk of transmission to patients is very low

## Duties of health care workers

HCWs who carry out EPPs and believe they have been exposed to blood-borne viruses (BBV) have a duty to seek professional advice on whether they should be tested. HCWs who know they are infected *must* seek and follow confidential OH and expert medical advice.

## Duties of employers

Employers in the health care sector must:

- Ensure that staff are aware of the guidance on BBV and EPPs
- Make every effort to arrange occupational adjustments, re-training, or (as a last resort) ill-health retirement for infected employees
- Promote a climate which encourages confidential disclosure
- Arrange for HCW to have access to a Consultant Occupational Physician (and or specialist nurse)

NB: It is important to check current guidance as regularly updated.

**Table 24.4** Summary of testing protocol to assess fitness for EPPs

| Initial screening (minimum documentation of fitness for EPPs) | Periodic annual screening |
|---|---|
| All HCW undertaking EPPs<br>Hepatitis B surface antigen (HBsAg) −ve<br>*or*<br>HBsAg +ve, *but* HBeAg −ve *and* HBV DNA <$10^3$ copies/ml | Annual HBsAg if non-responder to vaccine (persistent anti-HBs <10 IU/l) and not naturally immune (anti-HBc −ve)<br>Annual HBV DNA (must remain below $10^3$ geq/ml) |
| New HCW<br>Anti-HCV −ve<br>*or*<br>Anti-HCV +ve and HCV RNA −ve<br>*and*<br>Anti-HIV −ve | |

## Routine assessment of fitness for EPPs

Laboratory tests (summary in Table 24.4)

- *In new HCW:*[1]
    - HBsAg (and, if −ve, HBeAg with viral load testing (HBV DNA) in those who are HBeAg +ve)
    - *and* HCV antibody (and, if +ve, HCV RNA)
    - *and* HIV antibody
- *Must be carried out on an identified validated sample, i.e.:*
    - blood sample taken in an OH department
    - photographic proof of identity provided
    - sample not delivered to laboratory by HCW
- Must be carried out in an accredited laboratory. Only two specific laboratories are designated by Department of Health (DH) for HBV DNA testing (see HSC 2000/020 under Further reading and guidance (➔ p. 532, Exposure prone procedures 2))

1 *New* HCW are defined as those who are new to the NHS, those who are starting a post or training involving EPPs for the first time, and those who are returning to the NHS, and many have been exposed to BBV while they were away. All locum and agency-recruited HCW performing EPPs should be treated as *new* HCW.

# Fitness for exposure prone procedures 2

## Restrictions from work involving EPPs

Box 24.1 summarizes the current UK guidance on initial restriction of the practice of HCWs who are infected with BBV, and the specific circumstances under which HCWs can be allowed to return to EPPs following appropriate treatment.

### Box 24.2 UK guidance on initial restriction of the practice of HCWs who are infected with BBV

*Restrict from work involving EPPs*

HCW with the following serological markers of infection:
- HBeAg +ve
- HBsAg +ve, but HBeAg –ve *unless* viral load (HBV DNA) <$10^3$ geq/ml
- Hepatitis C antibody (anti-HCV) +ve *and* HCV RNA +ve
- HIV antibody +ve (⚠ this guidance is subject to current public consultation—see following bullet points)

*Fitness for EPPs following treatment for BBV infection*

HBV and HCV infected HCWs can recommence EPPs under specified circumstances following successful antiviral treatment.
- If HBV DNA levels are <$10^3$ copies/ml during continuous antiviral treatment or 12 months after treatment ceases:
  - during treatment, monitoring HBV DNA at 3-monthly intervals by a designated hepatologist is mandatory
  - and they must cease EPPs immediately if treatment stops
  - sharps injuries to an infected HCW during EPP must be reported, and the patient offered counselling and post-exposure treatment with HB immune globulin, according to a risk assessment
  - an infected HCW must cease EPPs if HBV DNA rises >$10^3$ geq/ml either during or after treatment
- If HCV RNA is negative 6 months *after* cessation of therapy, a further check on HCV RNA should be carried out 6 months later. HCV-infected HCW may not carry out EPPs *during* treatment
- Currently HIV-infected HCW who are on antiviral treatment cannot resume EPPs

⚠ However, a public consultation is in progress regarding a change in policy to allow EPPs if viral load remains consistently <200 copies/ml on combination antiretroviral treatment subject to explicitly defined 3-monthly monitoring and follow-up by a consultant occupational physician and HIV specialist.

## Patient notification exercises

- *Notification of patients who are known to have been exposed to a risk of infection from an infected HCW is necessary*:
  - to inform the patient about the nature and magnitude of risk
  - to enable treatment and prevention of onward transmission
  - to inform existing estimates of the risks of nosocomial transmission

- Newly identified cases of infected HCW who have carried out EPPs should be discussed with the local Director of Public Health, who will decide on the need to notify patients
- *In the presence of an index case of transmission from the HCW to a patient, a patient notification exercises will be required in the case of:*
  - HBV
  - HCV
  - HIV
- *In the absence of proven transmission*:
  - HBV or HCV: there is no automatic requirement for a patient notification exercise, but anonymized case-specific advice must be sought from UK Advisory Panel (UKAP; see below, Specific advisory bodies)
  - HIV: in the absence of known transmission, notification will be confined to patients who have undergone Category 3 EPPs by the infected HCW[1]

## Specific advisory bodies

Advice about restrictions to work and the need for notification exercises for new cases of BBV-infected HCW is available from the UK Advisory Panel for HCWs infected with BBV (UKAP).

## Further legislation and guidance

Department of Health (1996). *Protecting Health Care Workers and Patients from Hepatitis B, Addendum to HSG(93)40*. DH, London. Available at: http://www.dh.gov.uk/assetRoot/04/08/06/26/04080626.pdf

Department of Health (2002). *Hepatitis C Infected Health Care Workers*. DH, London. Available at: http://www.dh.gov.uk/en/Publicationsandstatistics/Publications/PublicationsPolicyAndGuidance/DH_4010554

Public Health England (2017). Integrated guidance on the management of healthcare workers infected with bloodborne viruses (HIV, hepatitis B and / or hepatitis C). Available at: https://www.gov.uk/government/collections/bloodborne-viruses-bbvs-inhealthcare-workers

UK Advisory Panel for health care workers infected with blood-borne viruses. Regularly updated UK Gov.UK London. Available at: http://www.hpa.org.uk/Topics/InfectiousDiseases/InfectionsAZ/BloodborneVirusesAndOccupational Exposure/UKAP/

1 Department of Health (2005). *HIV-Infected Health Care Workers, Guidance on Management and Patient Notification*. DH, London.

# Fitness to work with children

## General considerations

Considerable psychological and emotional demands are placed on people who work with children. Some jobs involve the worker acting in loco parentis, or supervision of potentially hazardous sports, such as swimming. Workers need to be able to relate to children and be able to maintain control without loss of temper or physical violence.

## Hazards associated with working with children

- Voice trauma
- Communicable diseases
- Ergonomic (bending, manual handling, sitting on small chairs)
- Physical or verbal assault from children or parents

## Criminal record

Individuals whose work will involve contact with children should have their records checked by the Criminal Records Bureau. This will undertake a level of disclosure appropriate to the post applied for. Available at: http://www.homeoffice.gov.uk/agencies-public-bodies/crb/

## Statutory requirements

The Education (Health Standards) (England) Regulations 2003 state that employers and training providers must ensure that a person has the health and physical fitness to teach. If it appears to an employer that a teacher may no longer have the health or physical capacity to carry out a relevant activity, the employer must follow the procedures under the 2003 regulations.

## Occupational health assessment

The decision on fitness should be made following an individual risk assessment based on:

- The nature of the work
- The age group of the children
- The health status of the worker

*General factors*

- Ability to undertake the duties of the post (adjusted if necessary), without constituting a health or safety risk to the children
- Ability to communicate effectively with children, parents, and colleagues
- Ability to deal with an emergency situation and administration of first aid
- Any adverse effect the job may have on the individual's health
- Individuals whose responsibility includes driving children should meet the DVLA driving standards
- A history of paedophilia or voyeurism (e.g. child pornography websites) precludes working with children

Any decision to find an individual unfit should be made only if the individual has been fully investigated by their GP or specialist and has been given appropriate treatment. Such decisions are often difficult and may be contentious; therefore discussion with a more experienced colleague may be helpful.

**The following specific conditions would need careful consideration in consultation with a specialist:**

- Specific psychiatric conditions
- *Schizophrenia*
  - poorly controlled bipolar affective disorder
  - persistent or recurrent severe depression resistant to treatment
  - anxiety disorder with uncontrolled panic attacks
  - eating disorders associated with self-injury
  - Fabricated or Induced Illness (previously known as Munchausen's syndrome and Munchausen's syndrome by proxy)
  - profound personality disorder
  - drug or alcohol dependency
- Individuals with epilepsy (see ➔ p. 502, Epilepsy), or impairment of vision or hearing must have a full risk assessment
- Individuals with active tuberculosis should not work with children until they are non-infectious

## Protection of employees

- Consider testing female staff of childbearing age for rubella antibodies and offer immunization well in advance of pregnancy if non-immune
- Consider hepatitis B vaccine if working with children with learning difficulties or behavioural problems, due to the risk of biting or scratching

## Legislation and guidance

- The Equality Act 2010
- The Education (Health Standards) (England) Regulations 2003
- Fitness to Teach. Occupational health guidelines for the training and employment of teachers. Department of Education and Employment

# Fitness for work in confined spaces (or with respirators)

## Task demands

Confined spaces can be found in many workplaces. Hazards in confined spaces include:

- Difficult access/egress
- A non-respirable atmosphere
- Low oxygen levels
- Toxic gas
- An explosive atmosphere

One means of controlling some of these risks is a full-face respirator or, in some circumstances, an escape set.

## General principles

- The worker should not be suffering from a medical condition that would be aggravated by wearing a respirator
- Any illness should not pose an unacceptable risk to the health or safety of the individual or other workers. Examples of conditions which may cause problems include:
  - cardiac disease
  - COPD
  - musculoskeletal problems
- A doctor should carry out a pre-placement medical assessment focusing on fitness to use a respirator
- Test lung function using spirometry to identify individuals with impaired lung function as this might compromise their ability to tolerate a respirator or to escape in an emergency
- Getting the prospective worker to use the relevant respirator is a useful exercise to see if he/she has any difficulties

## Assessment frequency

- Every 2 years for workers over age 18
- Following illness or injury if it is believed the operator may be unfit

## Specific issues

- *Vision should be adequate*: 6/6 corrected vision in the better eye without visual field deficit
- *Asthma*: some asthmatics cannot tolerate a respirator
- *Claustrophobia*: is a contraindication to work in confined spaces
- *Respirator fit*: should be tested[1] ideally by a Fit2Fit accredited fit tester. Factors that influence respirator fit:
  - facial deformity, e.g. retrognathia
  - beard
  - other personal protective equipment

1 HSE. *Fit Testing of Respiratory Protective Equipment Face Pieces*, HSE operational circular OC282/28. Available at: http://www.hse.gov.uk/foi/internalops/fod/oc/200–299/282_28.pdf

## Legislation and guidance


- *Confined Spaces Regulations 1997. Approved Code of Practice, Regulations and Guidance*. L101, HSE Books, Norwich 1997. ISBN 071761405.
- Faculty of Occupational Medicine (2019). Hobson J and Smedley J. Fitness for Work: The Medical Aspects, 6th edn. Oxford University Press, Oxford
- British Safety Industry Federation Fit2Fit RPE fit testers accreditation scheme. Available at: http://www.fit2fit.org/

# Fitness for seafaring

## Task demands

- Seafaring is a diverse occupation that encompasses those operating in near-coastal waters and those sailing in distant waters. The latter group may be at sea for many weeks in remote locations far from medical assistance
- *Broadly speaking, there are three categories of crew*:
  - deck crew (cargo handling, watch keeping)
  - engineers and radio operators
  - support staff (caterers, stewards, entertainment staff, etc.)
- Fitness standards and task demands vary by occupation, but in any event, crew must be fit to undertake emergency response procedures (e.g. abandon ship, firefighting)
- MSN 1887 (M) and 1883 (F) provide guidance on the application of the regulations in seafarers and fishermen and MSN 1886 (M & F) contains the relevant statutory standards with the rationale for fitness standards for specific conditions. Further detail can be found in the Approved Doctors' Manual

## General principles

- The seafarer should not be suffering from a medical condition that would be aggravated by being at sea
- Any illness should not pose an unacceptable risk to the health or safety of the individual, other crew, or the vessel
- A doctor approved by the Maritime and Coastguard Agency (MCA) carries out seafarer medical assessments
- The doctor assesses the individual's fitness against occupational demands and the medical and eyesight standards
- Following assessment the doctor issues a medical fitness certificate (form ENG1) for category 1 or 2. An ENG3 form Notice of Failure/Restriction is issued for categories 2, 3, or 4
- If the ENG3 form runs for longer than 3/12 the seafarer may appeal against the examining doctor's decision

## Assessment frequency

- Every 2 years for seafarers over age 18
- Annually for seafarers aged less than 18 years old
- Where, as a result of illness or injury, it is believed that the seafarer may no longer be fit

### Fitness categories

- *Category 1*: Fit for sea service, with no restrictions
- *Category 2*: Fit for sea service but *with restrictions* (e.g. UK near-coastal waters only)
- *Category 3*: Temporarily unfit for sea service
- *Category 4*: Permanently unfit for sea service

## Specific issues

- *Vision*: deck crew must have 6/6 corrected vision in the better eye and 6/12 vision in the other eye without visual field deficits. Engineering crew must reach at least 6/18 in each eye
- *Colour vision*: deck crew must have normal colour vision assessed using Ishihara test plates to undertake watch keeping. Where an individual fails this test, he/she may be tested using the Colour Assessment and Diagnosis test at an MCA approved centre. Different supplementary testing is used for engineering crew

## Legislation and guidance

- Merchant Shipping (Maritime Labour Convention) (Medical Examination) Regulations 2010 as amended
- Merchant Shipping (Work in Fishing) (Medical Certification) Regulations 2018
- Merchant Shipping Notices MSN1886 (M & F), 1887 (M), and 1883 (F)

# Fitness for safety critical work

## Definition

Safety critical work is any task that (in the event of failure) may lead to an accident, or otherwise compromise the safety of:

- People (employees, clients or service users, the public)
- Plant or premises
- The environment

## Safety critical work

- Regular vehicle driving, particularly passenger vehicles, e.g. train drivers, pilots
- Work at heights
- Work in confined spaces
- Work with, or near, electrical or mechanical equipment, including those in customer's houses
- Managing safety critical control systems, e.g. plant control rooms, air traffic controllers, nuclear industry
- Working on railway premises or infrastructure; this includes drivers, guards, and signalmen
- Work on construction sites, e.g. banks men, tower crane operators

## Task demands and fitness standards

Safety critical jobs depend on the employee being competent to undertake the required task and being fit to do so.

- Fitness standards for safety critical work vary by industry. Some are statutory and others advisory (see ➔ p. 510, Fitness to drive 2; ➔ p. 512, Fitness for professional diving; ➔ p. 520, Fitness for work in professional pilots)
- Doctors who advise about fitness for safety critical work must have special knowledge of both task demands and statutory or industry fitness standards

## General principles

- A useful rule of thumb is 'Would this person be able to drive an LGV/PCV under DVLA rules?'
- A disease or disability may affect fitness for safety critical posts where the condition is a fixed disability (e.g. loss of a limb) or a progressive condition that may compromise fitness in the future, such as multiple sclerosis
- Pharmacological treatment of a condition may compromise fitness for safety critical posts, e.g. by leading to increased drowsiness (these effects may be temporary)
- *Broadly speaking, conditions that may compromise fitness for safety critical posts are those that:*
  - lead to sudden incapacity/altered consciousness (e.g. epilepsy, diabetes)
  - affect mobility (e.g. rheumatoid arthritis)
  - affect balance (e.g. Ménière's disease)
  - affect cognition (e.g. dementia, brain damage)
  - affect risk perception (e.g. mental handicap)

  - affect behaviour (e.g. psychosis, personality disorder, substance misuse)
  - affect communication (e.g. deafness, visual impairment, speech problems, abnormal colour vision)
- Review of the job description, task analysis, a workplace visit, and discussion with experienced supervisors will assist in determining the demands of a safety critical post
- When assessing an individual's fitness for a safety critical post it may be difficult to obtain sufficient information to make an informed decision based solely on a health questionnaire. In such cases a consultation for a detailed medical history and examination will be necessary
- Useful additional information regarding the medical condition may be obtained from the individual's GP or specialist, especially when dealing with an employee suffering from a rare condition
- In cases of doubt, discussion with a senior OH physician may be helpful
- In some cases a supervised workplace assessment may be necessary to establish an individual's fitness for the task

## Specific issues

Health and safety reasons may genuinely preclude an individual with a disability from undertaking a safety critical task. However, before concluding an employee is unfit, an employer should consider whether any reasonable workplace adjustments would allow the employee to undertake safety critical work. The employer should carefully document their reasoning in case it is subsequently challenged at an employment tribunal under the Equality Act 2010.

## Assessment frequency

This will vary by industry sector. Generally, annual review is the minimum assessment interval, but longer intervals may be stipulated where dealing with young fit workers without pre-existing disease. Where an employee suffers from a progressive medical condition, more frequent review of fitness by the physician may be indicated.

## Legislation and guidance

BMA (2016). Alcohol, drugs and the workplace—The role of medical professionals. Available at https://www.bAlcohol, drugs and the workplace—The role of medical professionals

Section 5

# Occupational health law

Chapter 25

# UK health and safety legislation

# Health and safety regulation in the UK

## Background

Health and safety legislation in the UK developed in a piecemeal fashion from the early nineteenth century onwards. This had the unfortunate consequence of some sectors being heavily regulated by many separate pieces of legislation, while others were effectively unregulated.

In 1970, the Robens Commission was set up to review the UK's workplace health and safety laws. Their report led to:

- The Health and Safety at Work etc. Act of 1974 (HSW)
- The establishment of the Health and Safety Executive (HSE)
- Brexit
- After the UK leaves the EU, the existing legislation and case law will continue in force (with minor amendments) until repealed by Parliament or overruled by the Supreme Court or the Court of Appeal

## Health and Safety Executive

- Exists to protect the health and safety of workers (including the self-employed) and the public from hazards arising from work
- *Governing board of up to 12 persons, appointed by the Secretary of State for Work and Pensions in consultation with key stakeholders*:
  - employers' organizations
  - employee organizations—trade unions
  - local authorities
- Proposes health and safety legislation and associated guidance to government ministers
- Responsible for enforcement of health and safety legislation in conjunction with local authorities
- Undertakes reactive and planned inspection of workplaces
- Funds research into health and safety issues in support of regulation

## HSE strategy 2016

*Helping Great Britain work well in 2016*

See https://www.hse.gov.uk/strategy/assets/docs/hse-helping-great-britain-work-well-strategy-2016.pdf

This document sets out a new plan to engage employers and employees in continuing to improve health and safety. The key features are:

- Acting together to promote broader ownership of health and safety (H&S)
- Tackling ill health
- Managing risk well
- Supporting small employers
- Keeping pace with change
- Sharing our success

## Local authorities

- *Statutory responsibility for health and safety inspection and enforcement in*:
  - shops
  - offices
  - leisure
  - residential homes
  - hotels and restaurants
  - distribution (wholesale and retail) including petrol stations
- Links with HSE through the Health and Safety Executive/Local Authorities Enforcement Liaison Committee (HELA) to ensure conformity of approach by Local Authorities across the UK (see ➔ p. 548, Health and safety inspectors)

## Relevant legislation

- Legislation.gov.uk (2003). *Health and Safety at Work etc. Act 1974*, Chapter 37. TSO, Norwich. Available at: http://www.legislation.gov.uk/ukpga/1974/37
- The Legislative Reform (Health and Safety Executive) Order 2008. Available at: http://www.legislation.gov.uk/uksi/2008/960/contents/made

## Further information

*The Health and Safety System in Great Britain*. Regularly updated on line resource HSE UK. Available at: http://www.hse.gov.uk/ pubns/ohsingb.pdf

# Health and safety inspectors

Enforcement of workplace health and safety law in the UK is the responsibility of HSE inspectors and their equivalents in local authority environmental health departments.

## HSE inspectors

HSE inspectors are normally graduates from a range of industry backgrounds. On appointment, they receive extensive additional training in health and safety and the relevant law. Currently, inspectors are organized into several directorates.

- Field Operations Directorate (FOD) is the largest grouping of inspectors and covers a number of sectors excluding railways (the rail industry is the responsibility of the Office of the Rail and Road): the regional offices also house the occupational physicians and nurses who work with FOD
- *Office for Nuclear Regulation*: an agency of the HSE that regulates the nuclear industry
- *Hazardous Installations Directorate covers health and safety in the following sectors*:
  - petrochemical industry
  - explosives industry
  - mines
  - diving
  - sites where genetically modified organisms or biological agents are handled
  - transport of hazardous agents

## Role of HSE inspectors

The role of HSE inspectors includes:

- *Inspection of workplaces*: this may lead to:
  - advice to the employer
  - improvement notice
  - prohibition notice
  - prosecution
- Accident investigation
- Liaison with local authorities
- Advice to the public
- Information gathering

Where an HSE inspector gives a costs recovery notice in writing of a material breach of health and safety legislation the organization must pay a fee for the time spent by the inspector in inspecting and preparing paper work. This fee for intervention is payable to the HSE. An appeal can be made to an independent disputes panel.

## Local authority inspectors

Local authority inspectors are generally environmental health officers (EHOs). Some inspectors, in larger authorities, specialize in a specific area such as health and safety. In contrast, EHOs in smaller authorities may also be responsible for dealing with food hygiene, noise pollution, and other statutory duties placed on local authorities.

## Powers of inspectors

- Statutory right of entry to work places (without notice)
- Right to interview staff and supervisors and to take written statements (which cannot be used as evidence in a prosecution of the individual)
- Right to take samples and photographs
- Right to seize dangerous equipment
- *Enforcement*: inspectors can take enforcement action against employers, the self-employed, or employees where the prevailing standards of health and safety management are unacceptable. They can issue either an improvement notice or a prohibition notice. In serious cases they may also pursue a prosecution through the criminal courts

### *Improvement notice*

This notice requires an organization to address a named health and safety breach within a specified period. An employer may appeal to an employment tribunal against an improvement notice. In this case, the notice is suspended pending the decision of the tribunal.

### *Prohibition notice*

Issued by an inspector where there is thought to be a risk of illness or injury. Work must stop until the breach is addressed. Generally, a prohibition notice takes immediate effect unless stopping a process immediately will be dangerous. In that situation a prohibition notice will be delayed until the process is complete. No suspension occurs if an appeal against a prohibition notice is made to an employment tribunal.

## Relevant legislation

- HM Govt. (2003). Health and Safety at Work, etc., Act 1974, Chapter 37. TSO, Norwich. Available at: http://www.legislation.gov.uk/ukpga/1974/37

# Regulations, approved codes of practice, and guidance

The HSW Act laid down the framework for subsequent health and safety legislation in the UK. The Act has been supplemented by various regulations that relate to particular topics (e.g. manual handling at work). Regulations set out general principles and are supported by more detailed codes of practice.

## Regulations

The Secretary of State, on the recommendation of the HSE, makes new regulations under the umbrella of the HSW Act. When the UK was a Member State of the EU new regulations were enacted in response to EC directives. Any proposed new regulation under the HSW Act must be laid before parliament for a period of 40 days. Thereafter, it becomes law, provided that no objections are raised during this period.

## Approved codes of practice

Approved Codes of Practice (ACOPs) have a special status within the UK regulatory framework. The HSE approve ACOPs after agreement by the relevant Secretary of State. Failure to comply with an ACOP can be held to be evidence of a breach of the HSW Act, or a breach of the specific regulations to which the ACOP relates.

In principle, an employer can choose not to follow an ACOP. However, in the event of challenge by an inspector, defendants must demonstrate that they have complied with regulations in an equivalent manner to that recommended by the ACOP.

- In practice, it is easier for employers to comply with an ACOP than to justify their own approach
- As an ACOP can be readily updated, this allows health and safety standards to be kept up to date

## Guidance

The HSE regularly issue guidance on health and safety matters and on the implementation of health and safety regulations. Unlike ACOPs, employers are not compelled to follow guidance notes. However, compliance with regulations must still be achieved.

## Relevant legislation

- HM Govt. (2003). *Health and Safety at Work, etc., Act 1974*, Chapter 37. TSO, Norwich. Available at: http://www.legislation.gov.uk/ukpga/1974/37

# Safety committees and safety representatives

The Safety Representatives and Safety Committees Regulations 1977 cover the prescribed functions of union-appointed safety representatives.

Representatives of employee safety are the equivalent of union-appointed 'safety reps' in non-unionized workplaces. Their more limited role is defined in the Health and Safety (Consultation with Employees) Regulations 1996.

Separate regulations, the Offshore Installations (Safety Representatives and Safety Committees) Regulations 1989, apply to workers on offshore installations.

*Safety representatives*

- Represent employees' interests on matters of workplace health and safety
- Are immune from prosecution for their actions as safety reps
- Must be given paid time off work to act as safety reps, and to attend training relevant to their role and responsibilities. If an employer fails to give paid time off, the safety representatives can complain to an employment tribunal

*Representatives of employee safety*

Although the role of representatives of employee safety is more limited than that of safety reps, it is open to the employer to give them a wider remit. Their role, as defined in legislation, is:

- To represent workers' interests to the employer
- To approach the employer about workplace hazards/dangerous occurrences
- To approach the employer about issues affecting the workers they represent

## Purpose

- Under the HSW Act, employers are required to consult with safety representatives to ensure health and safety at work
- Workplaces with safety committees have lower accident rates than workplaces where managers only are responsible for health and safety

## Main requirements of the Safety Representatives and Safety Committees Regulations 1977

A union may appoint a person to represent its members at a work site.

*Role of the safety representative*

- To investigate complaints on health and safety or workplace welfare issues
- To represent employees in meetings with the employer about health and safety issues
- To undertake workplace inspections (Regulation 5), usually at 3-monthly intervals
- To investigate workplace accidents and dangerous occurrences (Regulation 6)
- To raise health and safety or welfare issues with the employer

- To consult with HSE/LA inspectors regarding workplace health and safety
- To attend safety committee meetings as a safety representative

*Role of employers*

- Discuss with safety reps any changes that may affect health and safety
- Communicate to safety reps the results of any risk assessments
- Discuss emergency and worksite evacuation plans with safety reps
- Provide any health and safety information to safety reps that is necessary for them to fulfil their role (excludes individual health data)
- If requested by two safety representatives, an employer must set up a safety committee within 3 months

## Legislation and guidance


- HM Govt. (1977). *Safety Representatives and Safety Committees Regulations 1977*. UK Government, UK. Available at: http://www.legislation.gov.uk/uksi/1977/500/contents/made
- HM Govt. (1996). *Health and Safety (Consultation with Employees) Regulations 1996*. National Archives, London. Available at: http://www.legislation.gov.uk/uksi/1996/1513/contents/made
- HSE (2008). *Consulting Workers on Health and Safety. Safety Representatives and Safety Committees Regulations 1977 (as amended)*; and HSE (2008). *Health and Safety (Consultation with Employees) Regulations 1996 (as amended) Approved Code of Practice and Guidance*, L146. HSE Books, Sudbury

# Health and Safety at Work etc. Act 1974

## Purpose

The purpose of this Act is to secure the health, safety, and welfare of workers, and others affected by work activities. It is termed an enabling act, as it empowers the Secretary of State to create regulations under the Act. The Health and Safety Committee and HSE were set up as result of this Act and merged in 2008 as the HSE (see ➲ p. 554, UK Health and safety regulation).

## Application

The Act applies to all workers except those employed as domestic servants.

## Definitions

'So far as is reasonably practicable' is a key phrase in UK health and safety legislation, which requires an employer to assess the risk posed by a hazard against the costs of addressing it: the greater the risk, the greater the effort that should be employed to address it. If prosecuted, the burden of proof lies with the employer to demonstrate that it was not reasonable to do more to control a risk.

- Limited financial resources are not a justification for failing to do all that is 'reasonably practicable'

## Main provisions

- *Section 2*:
  - places a *duty on employers* (including self-employed) to ensure, so far as is reasonably practicable, the health, safety, and welfare of employees
  - the provision and maintenance of safe plant and procedures (systems of work)
  - requires that employers maintain a written health and safety policy
  - provides for the election of workers' safety representatives and, if requested, for the creation of a safety committee
- *Section 3*: creates a general duty of care on employers (and the self-employed) towards those who are not in their employ, but who may be affected by their work activities
- *Section 4*: places a *duty on those who control premises* to ensure:
  - they are maintained
  - they do not pose a health and safety risk to people (other than employees) who may work there
- *Section 5*: places a general *duty on those who control premises* to prevent and control harmful/offensive releases into the environment
- *Section 6*: a *duty on manufacturers, importers, and suppliers* to:
  - ensure, so far as is reasonably practicable, that any work equipment or agents for use at work do not pose a risk to health and safety
  - arrange appropriate testing, unless information is already available
  - provide information to ensure that the equipment or substance is used safely, and for its intended purpose
- *Section 7*: places a general *duty on employees* with regard to ensuring the health and safety of themselves and others:
  - this section places a duty on employees to cooperate with employers to comply with health and safety legislation

- *Section 8*: requires that no person shall interfere with any measures provided to protect health, safety, and welfare
- *Section 9*: employers are forbidden from charging employees for anything done in respect of the HSW Act (e.g. health and safety training or provision of personal protective equipment (PPE))

## Relevant legislation


- HM Govt. (1974). *Health and Safety at Work, etc., Act 1974*, Chapter 37. TSO, Norwich. Available at: http://www.legislation.gov.uk/ukpga/1974/37

# Management of Health and Safety at Work Regulations 1999

## Purpose

The Management of Health and Safety at Work Regulations are generally referred to as the 'Management Regulations'. They provide an overarching framework for the management of health and safety at work. More specific regulations give additional detail regarding the assessment and control of key hazards. Generally, compliance with these more specific regulations will fulfil the requirements of the Management Regulations. The Management Approved Code of Practice was withdrawn by the HSE in 2013 and replaced with Guidance.

## Exemptions

- *These regulations do not apply to:*
  - the captain and crew of sea-going vessels, except where the ship is in harbour, e.g. for ship repair
  - domestic staff in private homes

## Main requirements

- Every employer is required to undertake a suitable and sufficient risk assessment of the risks to the health and safety of employees and others (Reg. 3)
- Regulation 3 places a similar duty on the self-employed
- Where a number of different employers share premises, they must cooperate to produce an overall risk assessment (Reg. 11)
- Organizations with more than five employees should record risk assessment findings
- *Regulation 4 covers the application of preventative measures. The principles of prevention are:*
  - avoid risks
  - evaluate unavoidable risks
  - control risks at source
  - fit the workplace to the human
  - update work practices as technology improves
  - substitute with less hazardous agents/processes
  - have a comprehensive workplace health and safety policy
  - measures that protect everyone should be preferred over those that protect the individual
  - provide information, instruction, and training (Reg. 13)
- *Employers and the self-employed must have in place effective health and safety arrangements (Reg. 5). This covers:*
  - planning
  - organization
  - control
  - monitoring
  - review

- Employers must provide health surveillance, where appropriate (Reg. 6). This mirrors the requirements of other regulations including Control of Substance Hazardous to Health regulations (COSHH) see ➲ p. 566, Control of Substances Hazardous to Health Regulations 2002 and ➲ p. 572, Control of Lead at Work Regulations 2002
- Employers must have competent assistance to manage health and safety (Reg. 7)
- Employers must have procedures to deal with dangerous situations (Reg. 8)
- Links must be established with the emergency services for situations such as fire, bomb threats, or other dangerous occurrences (Reg. 9)
- Employers must provide information to staff regarding the results of any risk assessment, control measures in place, and emergency procedures (Reg. 10)
- Where a child below minimum school-leaving age is employed, special attention must be paid to health and safety risks (Reg. 19). There is a duty to communicate the results of the risk assessment to the child's parents (see ➲ p. 558, Young people at work)
- Employees must cooperate with health and safety measures
- Special measures are required to control any risk that may affect the health of a new or expectant mother, or her baby (see ➲ p. 559, New and expectant mothers)

## Corporate manslaughter

If an individual, including a health professional, is guilty of gross negligence that causes the death of another they can be convicted of the crime of gross negligence manslaughter.

A corporation can be convicted of corporate manslaughter under the Corporate Manslaughter and Corporate Homicide Act 2007 where the senior management of the organization has acted in such a way as to amount to a gross breach of a relevant duty of care causing a person's death.

Individual managers or employees cannot be convicted of corporate manslaughter, though they can be prosecuted for health and safety offences or gross negligence manslaughter.

## Penalties

In 2016 new Sentencing Council guidelines for health and safety offences were adopted, considerably increasing the fines imposed by the courts for such offences.

## Legislation and guidance

- HSE (2000). *Management of Health and Safety at Work Regulations 1999 L21*. HSE Books, Sudbury. Available at: http://www.legislation.gov.uk/uksi/1999/3242/contents/

# Young people at work

## Purpose

The Management of Health and Safety at Work Regulations 1999 contains measures intended to protect the health and safety of young people at work.

## Application

Young people are recognized as being at particular risk in the workplace by virtue of their lack of work experience, in some cases compounded by psychological or physical immaturity. The guidance associated with the regulations gives a number of examples where the young worker may be at special risk. The risks of some work activities are deemed unacceptable and young people are prohibited from such work (e.g. lead glazing). The regulations do not apply to short-term employment in domestic service or to non-harmful work in a family business.

# Definitions

- A *young worker* is someone aged less than 18 years of age
- The *minimum school leaving age* (MSLA) is age 16 or just before
- A child is someone below the MSLA

## Main requirements

- Employers should, when undertaking a risk assessment, pay particular attention to vulnerable groups of workers including young people
- Employers must carry out the assessment before the young person starts work
- Where a risk assessment identifies a process or agent that may affect the health of the young worker, the employer should inform the employee and explain how they intend to protect health
- When dealing with children under school-leaving age, the employer must communicate the risk assessment findings and control measures to their parents
- Where, despite controls, significant risks remain, a young person under MSLA cannot be employed to do that work

## Legislation and guidance

- *Management of Health and Safety at Work Regulations 1999*. UK Government, TSO, Norwich. Available at: http://www.legislation.gov.uk/uksi/1999/3242/contents/made
- HSE. *Young People at Work. A Guide for Employers*, HS(G)165 (2000). HSE Books, Sudbury. ISBN 0717618897

# New and expectant mothers

## Purpose

The Management of Health and Safety at Work Regulations 1999 contain measures intended to protect the health and safety of pregnant workers and their unborn children, and also breastfeeding mothers, and their children.

## Application

The guidance to the regulations gives a number of examples where occupational exposures may be harmful to the worker or her child. These include work with lead, mercury, diving, underground mining, hyperbaric work, ionizing radiation, biological agents, carcinogens, and mutagens.

## Definitions

- A *new or expectant mother* is a woman who is pregnant, has given birth in the preceding 6 months (delivered a living child or suffered a stillbirth after 24 weeks pregnancy), or is breastfeeding
- Note that there is no limit on the duration of breast-feeding. It is for the nursing mother to determine for how long she wishes to breastfeed. The employer must then apply the regulations to protect her and her child's health

## Main requirements

- Employers should, when undertaking a risk assessment, pay particular attention to vulnerable groups of workers including pregnant workers and breastfeeding mothers
- Where a general risk assessment identifies a process or agent that may affect the health of this group of workers, the employer should inform all female employees of childbearing age and explain how they intend to protect workers' health
- If a female employee informs an employer in writing that she is pregnant the employer must perform an individual risk assessment
- *If the risk assessment indicates that, despite appropriate controls, a significant risk to health remains, the employer has to take other measures to protect the worker's health*:
  - first, consider adjusting the work conditions or working hours
  - if this is not possible, the employer should offer suitable alternative work
  - if this is not possible give paid leave
- The risks to health during pregnancy may change and so employers must regularly review their risk assessment
- Employers must provide suitable facilities for pregnant workers and breastfeeding mothers to rest
- There is currently no requirement for employers to provide a suitable place for breastfeeding women to express or store breastmilk. However, enlightened employers will wish to make suitable provision. Toilets would not be deemed suitable for this purpose

## Legislation and guidance


- HSE (1999). *New and Expectant Mothers. Management of Health and Safety at Work Regulations 1999*. HSE Books, Sudbury. Available at: http://www.hse.gov.uk/pubns/indg373hp.pdf
- HSE (2002). *New and Expectant Mothers at Work. A Guide for Employers*, HSG122. HSE Books, Sudbury

# Workplace (Health, Safety and Welfare) Regulations 1992

## Purpose

These regulations expand on the duties placed on employers by the HSW Act. While the welfare requirements may seem detailed, they are largely based on common sense.

## Application

All workplaces are covered with the exception of transport (Reg. 13 applies to planes, trains, and road vehicles if stationary in a workplace), mines and quarries, oil rigs, or building sites (Reg. 3). Work on farms or forests away from main buildings and temporary work sites such as carnivals have more limited requirements covering provision for sanitation, washing, and drinking water 'so far as is reasonably practicable'.

## Definitions

- *Workplace* means any place of work including shops, offices, factories, schools, and hospitals. The definition includes private roadways, corridors, and temporary workplaces (excluding building sites)
- *Domestic premises*: a private dwelling where the regulations do not apply

## Main requirements

- *The employer must maintain the workplace*:
  - keep it clean (Reg. 5)
  - well ventilated (Reg. 6)
  - dispose of waste (Reg. 9)
- *Any indoor workplace should have a reasonable temperature (usually no lower than 16 C Medically unexplained disorders, but 13 C Psychiatric disorders if work is physically demanding) (Reg. 7). No maximum temperature is given; instead the regulations refer to 'reasonably comfortable' temperatures*:
  - this does not apply where it conflicts with food safety or is impractical, e.g. vehicle loading bays
  - thermometers should be provided
  - measures to prevent excessive solar gain should be taken
  - heating systems should be maintained so they do not produce noxious fumes, e.g. carbon monoxide
  - where temperatures cannot be maintained at comfortable levels, task rotation should be employed
- Every workplace shall have suitable lighting including emergency lighting if necessary (Reg. 8)
- Room dimensions must be sufficient for health, safety, and welfare purposes (Reg. 10). This does not apply to sales kiosks or parking attendants' cabins where space is limited. The minimum space per person is 11 $m^3$ (maximum ceiling height for calculation is 3 m)
- Seating should be fit for the task and the person doing the task (Reg. 11)
- Floors, paths, and roadways should be well maintained (Reg. 12)
- Guard rails, fences, or covers must be provided where there is a risk of falls from height or into a tank or pit (Reg. 13)

- Windows and transparent doors, gates, and walls must be made of safety materials, e.g. polycarbonate, annealed glass, or safety glass (Reg. 14)
- *Windows*:
  - should be capable of being opened and cleaned safely (Reg. 16)
  - should not pose a hazard once open (Reg. 15)
- Workplaces should be organized so that pedestrians and vehicles can move around the site safely (Reg. 17), ideally by separating people and vehicles
- Doors and gates must be suitably constructed and operate safely (Reg. 18)
- Escalators and moving walkways must operate safely and have an emergency stop button (Reg. 19)
- Provide suitable and sufficient toilets and washing facilities (Regs 20 and 21)
- Potable water should be readily available (Reg. 22)
- *Provide facilities for*:
  - changing clothes (Reg. 24)
  - storage for work clothing and the worker's own clothing (Reg. 23)
- Provide suitable canteen and rest areas (Reg. 25). Facilities for making a hot drink should be available. Pregnant workers or nursing mothers should be provided with somewhere to rest and, if necessary, to lie down

## Legislation and guidance


- *Workplace (Health, Safety and Welfare) Regulations 1992*. HSE TSO Norwich. Available at: http://www.legislation.gov.uk/uksi/1992/3004/contents/made
- HSE (1996). *Workplace (Health, Safety and Welfare) Regulations 1992. Approved Code of Practice and Guidance*, L24. HSE Books, Sudbury

# Health and Safety (Display Screen Equipment) Regulations 1992

## Purpose

The Health and Safety (Display Screen Equipment) Regulations 1992, as amended by the Health and Safety (Miscellaneous Amendments) Regulations 2002, implement an EC directive on minimum health and safety standards for display screen equipment (DSE) and its use.

## Application

DSE includes:

- Computer monitors (also termed visual display units (VDUs))
- Microfiche readers
- Laptop or notebook computers (depends on usage)

It excludes:

- DSE equipment intended for short-duration public use, e.g. bank automated teller machine
- Laptops/notebooks used for short periods
- DSE on board a means of transport
- Calculators
- Cash registers
- Medical/scientific instruments used for short periods, e.g. heart monitors

The regulations cover DSE users and do not apply to infrequent users of VDUs or to the general public.

## Definitions

**Who is a DSE user?**

Someone who fulfils most of the following:

- Depends on DSE to do their job
- Has no discretion as to use
- Uses DSE for >1 hour
- Uses DSE daily

## Main requirements

- *Risk assessment* (Reg. 2) (see ➔ p. 816, Carry out a display screen equipment assessment). This may involve a generic assessment for a group of workers doing similar tasks and a user questionnaire completed by each user:
  - *Workstation minimum requirements* (Reg. 3): cover the workstation including hardware, software, working environment, and the user interface. Specific requirements are described in Annex A of the Guidance on Regulations:
    - Equipment
    - Environment
    - Tasks and software should be designed using good ergonomic practice with an effective equipment–user interface, and software should be fit for purpose

  - Work schedules (Reg. 4): there is no specific guidance on break timing and frequency. In general, short frequent breaks away from the workstation are preferable. Users should have some discretion as to how they manage their work
- *Vision and vision testing* (Reg. 5): users may request an eye and eyesight test at the employer's expense. An optometrist or a registered medial practitioner must carry out the test. Some employers offer vision screening prior to sight testing. The user is not obliged to accept such screening and may proceed directly to sight testing
- *Employers must pay for spectacles, where these are required solely for DSE use ('special' corrective appliances)*:
  - the employer is only required to provide corrective appliances that are fit for purpose and not designer spectacle frames
  - an employer may specify which professional undertakes sight tests and dispenses spectacles
- *Information, instruction, and training* (Regs 6 and 7): users should receive health and safety training regarding DSE workstations and their safe use

## Legislation and guidance

- Work with display screen equipment. *Health and Safety (Display Screen Equipment) Regulations 1992 as amended by the Health and Safety (Miscellaneous Amendments) Regulations 2002*. Guidance on Regulations L26, 2nd edn. Available at: http://www.legislation.gov.uk/uksi/1992/2792/contents/made; also available at: http://www.hse.gov.uk/pubns/indg36.pdf
- *Guidance on Eye Examinations for VDU Users: Association of Optometrists*. Regularly updated on line resource College of Optometrists London. Available at: http://www.aop.org.uk/uploads/uploaded_files/guidance_on_Eye_Examinations_for_vdu_users.pdf
- *E03: Examining Patients Who Work with Visual Display Screen Equipment*. College of Optometrists Guidelines for Professional Conduct, 2011. Regularly updated on line resource College of Optometrists London. Available at: http://www.college-optometrists.org/en/utilities/document-summary.cfm/docid/570D3F84–5B24–4DBF-B7145510CBBC5B15

# Provision and Use of Work Equipment Regulations 1998

## Purpose

The aim of the regulations is to ensure that the use of work equipment does not affect worker's health and safety.

## Application

The regulations apply to all work sites covered by the HSW Act. It covers the provision and use of all work equipment including lifting equipment, although additional regulations govern lifting operations and lifting equipment (LOLER 1998). Provision and Use of Work Equipment Regulations 1998 applies to employers, the self-employed, and persons controlling equipment such as plant hirers (Reg. 3). Domestic work in a private house is excluded from the regulations.

## Definitions

- Work equipment means any tools, machinery, appliances, apparatus, or installations (e.g. a production line) provided for use at work (Reg. 2). This is true even if the employee provides the tools, as occurs in garages
- The definition excludes privately owned cars but does include vehicles not in private ownership when they are off public roads, e.g. within a factory

## Main requirements

- The regulations cover the management of the provision and use of work equipment. They also deal with features of the equipment itself, such as the provision of emergency stop buttons, guards, and safety markings
- Employers must ensure that equipment is suitable for its intended use (Reg. 4), and that it is only used for those activities for which it is intended
- High-risk equipment must be regularly inspected (Reg. 6) and maintained (Reg. 5) by competent persons. Records should be kept of maintenance to high-risk equipment such as fairground rides
- Information, instruction, and training must be provided to equipment users (Regs 8 and 9). Special attention should be paid to the training of young people
- Any equipment should conform to European Community requirements and be CE marked[1]
- Equipment should have suitable guards on dangerous parts (Reg. 11)
- Measures to protect workers and others from objects falling or being ejected from equipment. Controls should protect against equipment failure, fire, explosion, overheating, or discharge of substances from equipment (Reg. 12)
- Workers must be protected from very hot or cold parts of a machine or articles produced by the machine (Reg. 13)

1 CE Marking indicates that a product conforms to EU product safety rules.

- Equipment should have appropriate controls including emergency stop controls (Regs 14–16)
- Any controls should be clearly visible and located in safe areas, and there should be a safe system of operation
- Audible or visible warnings should be in place, where employees may be at risk if the machine starts unexpectedly while they are in a danger area, e.g. inside a paper-making machine (Reg. 17)
- Control systems should 'fail to safe' in the event of malfunction (Reg. 18)
- Any power source should be capable of being isolated for maintenance, or where operating conditions are unsafe. This may require interlocks and isolating devices to be fitted (Reg. 19)
- Equipment should be stable and secure, e.g. ladders should be properly footed
- Adequate lighting must be provided where equipment is operated. This may require additional lighting, especially during construction or maintenance
- Equipment should be designed such that maintenance operations do not place workers at risk (Reg. 22)
- Any work equipment must be clearly marked with any necessary health and safety warnings. Any warnings (reversing alarms, 'power on' lights, etc.) must be clear and unambiguous (Regs 23 and 24)
- *Additional rules cover the use of mobile equipment, in particular its movement (Regs 25–30)*:
    - the use of roll-over protection (rather than a cab) on mobile equipment such as forklift trucks will often require the use of restraining devices
    - mobile equipment should be designed so that it is safe to move, and does not place the operator or others at risk
    - drive shafts or power take-offs should be guarded and have a slip-clutch to prevent catastrophic equipment failure if the shaft seizes

## Legislation and guidance


- HSE (1998). *Provision and Use of Work Equipment Regulations 1998. Approved Code of Practice and Guidance*, L22. HSE Books, Sudbury, Available at: http://www.opsi.gov.uk/si/si1998/19982306.htm
- HSE (1998). *Lifting Operations and Lifting Equipment Regulations 1998. Approved Code of Practice and Guidance*, L113. HSE Books, Sudbury. Available at: http://www.opsi.gov.uk/si/si1998/19982307.htm

# Control of Substances Hazardous to Health Regulations 2002

## Purpose

The regulations are intended to protect workers from risks posed by chemical hazards in the workplace. The Regulations and ACOP specify how chemical hazards should be assessed, controlled, and monitored (including health surveillance).

## Application

These regulations apply to employers and the self-employed. They cover most hazardous substances excluding the following, for which specific regulations apply:

- Asbestos
- Lead
- Radioactive agents
- Substances being used in medical treatment
- Substances hazardous because of flammable/explosive properties

## Definitions

- *Substance*: a natural or artificial substance whether a solid, liquid, gas, dust, fibre, mist, smoke, or vapour. This term includes microorganisms. It encompasses individual agents and mixtures which are impurities, intermediates, by-products, wastes, or final products
- *Workplace*: any place where work is being carried out, including domestic premises and the public highway
- *'So far as is reasonably practicable'*: financial factors may be taken into account when determining whether risk controls are reasonably practicable. Note that the level of risk outweighs the financial resources of the organization in determining practicability. The greater the health risk, the greater the expectation of effort and expense
- *Biological agents are categorized under COSHH as follows:*
    - Group 1: unlikely to cause human illness
    - Group 2: can cause human disease. Usually effective treatment or prophylaxis is available
    - Group 3: can cause severe human illness and may be a serious hazard to employee's health
    - Group 4: causes severe human disease. Usually no effective treatment is available for such agents

## Main requirements

- The duties placed on employers under COSHH also apply to the self-employed (Reg. 3), except for the duty to undertake workplace monitoring and health surveillance
- The use of substances listed in Schedule 2 are either restricted or prohibited, as they are deemed too hazardous to health (Reg. 4)
- Employers are required to carry out a risk assessment before exposing employees to a hazardous substance (Reg. 6). If an organization has more than five employees, this risk assessment must be recorded

- Employers must prevent or control exposure to hazardous substances (Reg. 7). This includes substitution of a less hazardous agent, reformulation of an agent (e.g. using a paste instead of a powder), process re-engineering, industrial hygiene controls, and administrative control measures. Appendix 1 of COSHH guidance provides further information on the control of carcinogens and mutagens. Schedule 3 lists additional provisions for biological agents
- Employers must ensure that employees use control measures provided, and employees have a duty to do so (Reg. 8). If an employee finds a defect in a control measure, he/she must inform the employer
- Control measures must be maintained, examined, and tested regularly (Reg. 9). Suitable records of such tests must be retained for at least 5 years. All control measures should be regularly inspected. For most processes (except those in Schedule 4), regular inspection means weekly visual checks, and examination and testing every 14 months
- Where a risk assessment indicates that workplace monitoring is needed to confirm the effectiveness of control measures, an employer must comply (Reg. 10). Processes and agents listed in Schedule 5 must have specified workplace monitoring. Suitable records of employee monitoring should be maintained for 40 years
- *Health surveillance (Reg. 11)* (see ➲ p. 460, Chapter 22 Health surveillance: general principles) *is required where the worker is exposed to an agent or process listed in Schedule 6 or exposure to a hazardous substance is such that*:
  - an identifiable disease is related to exposure
  - there is a reasonable likelihood of the illness occurring
  - valid methods exist to detect the disease
- Health records must be kept for 40 years after the last entry. A health record (which should not include confidential clinical information) is distinct from medical records of health surveillance maintained by health professionals
- Information, instruction, and training should be provided for employees who may be exposed to hazardous substances (Reg. 12)
- Regulation 13 requires employers to make plans to deal with emergencies such as spills, fires, or leaks. These requirements may overlap with other regulations relating to major accident hazards (➲ p. 624, Control of Major Accident Hazards Regulations 1999)

## Legislation and guidance


- HSE (2002). *Control of Substances Hazardous to Health Regulations 2002 (as amended). Approved Code of Practice and Guidance,* 5th edn, L5. HSE Books, Sudbury. Available at: http://www.legislation.gov.uk/uksi/2002/2677/contents/made
- HSE (2005). *Workplace Exposure Limits: Containing the List of Workplace Exposure Limits for Use with the Control of Substances Hazardous To Health Regulations 2002* (as amended), EH40. HSE Books, Sudbury
- COSHH (2002). HSE Books, Sudbury. Available at: www.coshh-essentials.org.uk

# Reporting of Injuries, Diseases, and Dangerous Occurrences Regulations 2013

## Purpose

To ensure that injuries, accidents, and dangerous injuries arising from work are reported to the relevant enforcing authority (HSE or local authority). They provide a single set of reporting rules applicable to all work. A 2° benefit is that Reporting Injuries Diseases, Dangerous Occurrence Regulations (RIDDOR) provides information on trends for workplace accidents and some occupational illnesses. In reality, significant under-reporting across all sectors compromises the system.

## Application

- Regulations apply to Great Britain including the offshore oil industry
- Separate regulations apply to Northern Ireland
- Injuries arising directly from medical treatment are excluded

## Definitions

- *Enforcing authority*: either HSE or the local authority
- *Over-7-day injury*: a worker is unfit for his/her normal work for 7 days excluding the day of the incident
- *Responsible person*: the employer, the person in control of the workplace, or the individual, if self-employed
- *Accident*: includes as 'an act of non-consensual violence done to a person at work' and excludes injuries to professional sportsmen in the normal course of play

## Main requirements

*Reportable injuries, diseases, and dangerous occurrences*

All injuries can be reported online to HSE, but a telephone service remains for reporting fatal and major injuries only. The following must be reported by the responsible person to the enforcing authority:

- Death due to an accident
- *Specified injury*:
  - a fracture other than to fingers, thumbs and toes;
  - amputation of an arm, hand, finger, thumb, leg, foot or toe;
  - permanent loss of sight or reduction of sight;
  - crush injuries leading to internal organ damage;
  - serious burns (covering more than 10% of the body, or damaging the eyes, respiratory system or other vital organs);
  - scalpings (separation of the skin from the head) which require hospital treatment;
  - unconsciousness caused by head injury or asphyxia;
  - any other injury arising from working in an enclosed space, which leads to hypothermia, heat-induced illness or requires resuscitation or admittance to hospital for more than 24 hours;
  - Over seven day injuries to workers ie the person is unable to perform their normal work duties for more than seven consecutive days (not counting the day of the accident).
  - acute illness requiring medical treatment due to exposure to a biological agent, its toxin, or infected material; this covers needle-stick

injuries where the exposure is to blood or body fluids infected with agents such as hepatitis B, C, or human immunodeficiency virus
- From April 2012 over-7-day injuries (excluding day of incident) must be reported within 15 days. A record (e.g. accident book) of over-3-day injuries must still be maintained despite the move from reporting of over-3-day injuries to over-7-day injuries
- *Reportable diseases*: an employer must notify the relevant authority using Form F2508A where one of their workers develops a prescribed occupational disease. The 2013 Regulations reduce the numbers of work-related diseases reportable to: carpal tunnel syndrome, cramp in the hand or forearm, occupational dermatitis, hand–arm vibration syndrome (HAVS), occupational asthma, tendonitis or tenosynovitis in the hand or forearm, any cancer attributed to an occupational exposure to a known human carcinogen or mutagen (including ionizing radiation), any disease attributed to an occupational exposure to a biological agent. This applies where the employer is notified in writing by a doctor that the employee has a disease listed in the regulations and that the disease is work related
- Any dangerous occurrence listed in Schedule 2 of the regulations. This covers injuries such as the collapse of a crane, failure of a pressure vessel, or a fire or explosion leading to plant shutdown for >24 hours

*Other provisions*
- Death is reportable whether the affected individual is an employee or a member of the public
- There is no duty on anyone to report to the HSE the death of a self-employed person who dies on his or her own premises
- Injuries sustained in 'hazing' (initiation ceremonies) would be reportable if the new worker was forced to take part in such an event
- Injuries to members of the public, where they are taken to hospital, are reportable even where no treatment is administered (Reg. 3)
- Regulation 6 requires that, where a worker (but not a member of the public) dies as a result of an accident within 12 months, the responsible person must inform the enforcing authority
- Gas Safe registered gas fitters[2] are required to report dangerous gas fittings or installations to HSE
- Gas suppliers must notify HSE when they learn of an incident involving gas they supply which causes injury or death (Reg. 11)
- Regulation 12 places a duty on the responsible person to keep a record of any report for 3 years after the incident
- Where an employer was unaware of an incident, they can use this as a defence if subsequently prosecuted for failing to report it. The employer would have to demonstrate they had taken reasonable steps to have such injuries reported

## Legislation and guidance

- *Reporting of Injuries, Diseases and Dangerous Occurrences Regulations 2013*. UK Government. TSO Norwich. Available at: https://www.legislation.gov.uk/uksi/2013/1471/contents/made
- *RIDDOR Reporting Online*. HSE Regularly updated on line resource. Available at: http://www.hse.gov.uk/riddor/report.htm

2 Gas Safe Register.

# First Aid at Work Regulations 1981

## Purpose

To describe the first aid provision that employers must make in workplaces.

## Application

Apply to all employers in the UK, except where other regulations apply (Reg. 7) in offshore oil, diving, and merchant shipping. The armed forces are exempt.

## Definitions

First aid means the provision of immediately necessary care to ill or injured people and, where necessary, calling an ambulance. It does not include the administration of drugs to treat an illness (e.g. paracetamol for headache), except aspirin for a suspected heart attack.

## Main requirements

- *Employers must assess likely first aid needs (Reg. 3) having considered*:
  - workplace risks such as machinery, chemicals
  - high-risk areas, e.g. laboratories
  - staff numbers
  - shift work and out-of-hours work
  - accident history
  - location of workplace, e.g. remote forests
  - lone workers
  - trainees on work experience
  - needs of any disabled or young persons employed
  - workers who travel
  - general public[1]
  - multiple buildings on a single site, e.g. universities
  - arrangements for workers on shared sites, e.g. construction sites
  - availability of first-aiders due to holidays and sickness
  - staff with language/reading difficulties
- *The minimum first aid provision is*:
  - a first aid container stocked with the recommended contents
  - an appointed person to take charge of first aid arrangements
  - information for workers on first aid provision (Reg. 4)

► The self-employed must undertake a risk assessment and make suitable first aid provision (Reg. 5).

- Employers must provide suitable and sufficient first aid materials in an easily identifiable first aid container. First aid kits may be issued to lone workers, those in remote locations, or those who travel at work
- *First aid rooms*:
  - should be provided if the risk assessment identifies a need
  - should have a couch, desk, chair, phone, sink with hot/cold water, soap and paper towels, adequate heating and lighting
  - should be clearly identified, with a notice identifying first aiders, their locations, and how to contact them
  - should be easily accessible, clean, and ready for use

1 Employers are not required to make first aid provision for the public but many in the retail and hospitality industries will wish to do so.

- *First aiders*:
  - select on aptitude; should hold a valid first aid certificate
  - first aid certificates are valid for 3 years
  - the number of first aiders is determined by the risk assessment
- *Record keeping*: an accident book should be maintained to record injuries including the date, time, and location of any incident, the name and job of the injured/ill person, details of the injury or illness, what first aid was administered, disposal of the casualty (e.g. return to work, sent to hospital), and the name and signature of the first aider

## Other regulations and guidance

The Offshore Installations and Pipeline Works (First-Aid) Regulations 1989 address the provision of first aid on offshore oil installations. The National Health Service does not provide medical cover to oil platforms and so operators must make their own arrangements for nursing cover onboard (rig medics) and for land-based medical support (topside medical cover). The oil industry has produced guidance on suitable first aid and medical equipment on offshore platforms.

The Diving at Work Regulations 1997 require the diving contractor to provide first aid during a diving project (see ➲ p. 578, Diving at Work Regulations 1997).

## Legislation/guidance


- HSE (2016). Health care and first aid on offshore installations and pipeline works. Offshore Installations and Pipeline Works (First-Aid) Regulations 1989. L123 3rd ed. Available at: https://www.hse.gov.uk/pubns/priced/l123.pdf
- *The Health and Safety (First-Aid) Regulations 1981*. HSE UK. Available at: http://www.legislation.gov.uk/uksi/1981/917/contents/made

# Control of Lead at Work Regulations 2002

## Purpose

Lead regulations were first introduced in the early twentieth century in an effort to protect workers' health. Historically, lead toxicity was an important occupational disease in the UK. It still causes much morbidity in developing countries (lead as a hazard is covered in ➔ p. 80, Lead).

## Application

Control of Lead at Work applies to all work that exposes workers to lead in any form in which it may be absorbed by:

- Inhalation
- Dermal absorption
- Ingestion

## Definitions

- *'Lead exposure is significant' means that one of the following applies*:
  - exposure exceeds half the occupational exposure limit for lead
  - there is a substantial risk of ingesting lead
  - skin contact with dermally absorbed lead may occur (lead alkyls, lead naphthenate)
- Where exposure is significant, all regulations apply, and in particular the need for hygiene surveys and health surveillance
- 'Woman of reproductive capacity' is a woman medically capable of conceiving

## Main requirements

*Risk assessment (Reg. 5)*

- The employer must assess the risks to workers and others, who may be affected by lead, record their findings, retain the record for 5 years, and review the assessment as necessary
- This complements the duty placed on employers by the Management of Health and Safety at Work Regulations to undertake suitable and sufficient risk assessments using competent personnel

*Prevention and control (Reg. 6)*

Employers must prevent or control exposure to lead, *so far as is reasonably practicable*, without resort to PPE. In other words, respiratory protective equipment (RPE) should be the last, not the first, means of control. The hierarchical principles of occupational hygiene apply (see ➔ p. 670, Control hierarchy: source, transmission, and the individual):

- *Substitution*:
  - lead-free compounds
  - low-solubility lead compounds
  - use pastes, emulsions, or liquid formulations
- *Engineering controls*:
  - enclose work processes
  - low-temperature processes <500°C to ↓ lead fume
  - local exhaust ventilation (LEV)
  - wet processes
  - design plant for easy cleaning

- *Administrative controls*:
  - maintenance and testing of controls
  - provide suitable washing facilities
  - ensure washing facilities are used at breaks/meals
  - provide 'clean' canteen/rest facilities (Reg. 7)
  - enforce 'clean' and 'dirty' areas
  - ban smoking, drinking, eating in lead-contaminated areas (Reg. 7)
  - identify areas where smoking, eating, or drinking is/is not permitted
- *PPE*:
  - suitable protective clothing; impermeable coveralls/gloves are required for work with organolead
  - RPE
  - Provide suitable storage for PPE

*Maintenance and testing of control measures (Reg. 8)*

LEV maintenance:

- LEV should be visually inspected once a week and fully tested every 14 months
- All control measures must be maintained
- Keep records of maintenance and testing

*Hygiene surveys (Reg. 9)*

Breathing zone sampling should be carried out every 3 months. The exception is where work practices are unchanged and on the two previous consecutive occasions the lead in air concentration was $<0.10$ mg/m$^3$. In that case testing every 12 months is permitted.

*Medical surveillance*

Special rules apply for young persons (aged 16 or 17) and women of reproductive capacity. These are covered in ➔ p. 460, Health Surveillance: general principles; ➔ p. 472, Inorganic lead; and ➔ p. 474, Organic lead.

*Information, instruction, and training (Reg. 11)*

Training and communication should include:

- Risks to health of lead exposure
- Control measures and precautions
- Results of lead in air monitoring
- Grouped anonymized health surveillance results; communicating this information is very important as it allows the employer and employees to confirm that controls are adequate

## Legislation


- HSE (2002). *Control of Lead at Work Regulations 2002*, 3rd edn. HSE Books, Sudbury
- HSE (2002). *Approved Code of Practice and Guidance*, L132, 3rd edn. HSE Books, Sudbury. Available at: http://www.legislation.gov.uk/uksi/2002/2676/contents/made

# Control of Asbestos Regulations 2012

## Purpose

To protect workers and the public from exposure to asbestos.

## Application

The Control of Asbestos Regulations (CAR) 2012 replaces the CAR 2006 and covers most work with asbestos in the UK. Most of the requirements of the 2006 regulations are unchanged but the 2012 Regulations introduces a third category of work; notifiable non-licensed work (NNLW) in addition to the existing categories of licensed work and non-licensed work with asbestos.

- *NNLW requires*:
  - notification to HSE before work commences
  - medical examinations every 3 years
  - health records
  - compliance with risk assessment
  - control of exposure
  - training

## Definitions

- The *control limit* for asbestos is 0.1 fibre/cm$^3$ over any 4-hour period
- Exposure must not exceed 0.6 fibres/cm$^3$ in any 10-minute period

## Main requirements

- Asbestos work is licensable where it is not sporadic and low intensity (SALI) or the risk assessment shows the *control limit* will be exceeded or work on asbestos coating, or work on asbestos insulation board or insulation where the risk assessment shows work is not SALI; the *control limit* will be exceeded; work is not short duration (short duration means all work is less than 2 hours/no-one will work >1 hour)
- *Non-licensed work is not notifiable where exposure is SALI and less than the control limit and involves*:
  - short, non-continuous maintenance where only non-friable materials are handled
  - removal without deterioration of non-degraded materials in which the asbestos fibres are firmly linked in a matrix
- No asbestos work is of low intensity if exposure is >0.6 fibres/cm$^3$ over 10 minutes
- Employers must manage asbestos in non-domestic premises
- Assess, by survey, whether buildings contain asbestos
- Assess the risk from any asbestos so identified

There are two levels of survey:

- *Management survey*: this is the standard survey to identify any material that might contain asbestos and assess its condition. Such a survey may employ a mix of:
  - sampling to identify asbestos
  - the presumption that material contains asbestos and is managed as such

- *Refurbishment and demolition survey*: suspect materials are sampled and analysed with a view to asbestos removal. The condition of the asbestos is not generally assessed. This approach is employed where demolition or major rebuilding is planned
- *Before commencing work that might lead to exposure to asbestos, the employer must*:
  - identify the presence and type of asbestos
  - assess risks, identify control measures, and record findings
  - draw up a site-specific plan of how the work is to be done (method statement)
  - notify HSE of the planned work
- Any employer undertaking asbestos work (this covers work with asbestos, ancillary work, or supervision), except where exempt under Reg. 3(2) must have an HSE asbestos licence
- Employers must give employees information, instruction, training, and maintain training records
- Where possible, exposure to asbestos should be prevented or, if not feasible, reduced to as low a level as practicable
- Control measures must be used and maintained. Employees must report defects in controls
- Employers must make arrangements to deal with emergencies arising during asbestos work and with unplanned releases of asbestos
- Employers must prevent or reduce the spread of asbestos by using enclosures, restricting access, using decontamination procedures (preliminary and final), and waste removal
- Good housekeeping with clear procedures for cleaning
- Before re-occupation the site must be certified clear
- Areas where exposure may exceed the action level must be signed as a designated asbestos area. If exposure may exceed the control limit, the area must be signed as a respirator zone
- Those undertaking air sampling or laboratory analysis must be accredited to ISO 17025 by the United Kingdom Accreditation Service
- *Medical surveillance* by an HSE-appointed doctor including respiratory questionnaire, respiratory examination, and spirometry is required before licensable work begins and every 2 years thereafter (see MS31). Employers must retain the health record for 40 years
- *Medical examinations* are required for NNLW every 3 years and must include a chest examination and be carried out by a registered medical practitioner
- Asbestos waste must be disposed of in suitable labelled containers, and transported in an enclosed vehicle to a licensed disposal site

## Legislation and guidance


- *Guidance for Appointed Doctors* (2018). HSE Books Sudbury Available at: http://www.hse.gov.uk/pubns/ms31.pdf
- *The Control of Asbestos Regulations 2012* (2012). UK Government TSO Norwich. Available at: http://www.legislation.gov.uk/uksi/2012/632/contents/made

# Ionizing Radiation Regulations 2017

## Purpose

The Ionizing Radiation Regulations (IRR) provides the framework for the management of hazards arising from ionizing radiation (naturally occurring or man-made) in the workplace. The objective is to reduce, so far as is reasonably practicable, occupational exposure to radiation.

## Application

These regulations apply in the UK and cover three areas of work:

- Practice, which means work involving the production, use, storage or transport of radioactive substances, or operation of electrical equipment that emits ionizing radiation
- Work where the concentration of radon gas exceeds 300 Bq/m$^3$ when averaged over a year
- Work with naturally occurring radionuclides where employees are likely to receive >1 mSv in a year, e.g. naturally occurring radioactive material deposited in pipework in the oil industry
- The regulations apply to both employers and the self-employed

## Main requirements

- Employers who wish to use radiation in their practice must seek authorization from HSE, unless they comply fully with the conditions stated in one of HSE's generic authorizations (Reg. 7)
- Radiation employers must undertake a risk assessment prior to commencing work with radiation (Reg. 8) and record their findings
- Employers must take all steps required to reduce radiation exposure.
- The employer may employ dose constraints[1] when assessing the risk to carers of patients, when the patient is receiving radiopharmaceuticals

*Risk controls*

- Any PPE provided must be fit for purpose and comply with the Personal Protective Equipment Regulations 2002
- Any PPE or engineering controls should be maintained and examined regularly (Reg. 11)
- The employer must prepare local rules for radiation use (Reg. 18)
- The employer must designate controlled areas where the external dose rate exceeds 7.5 μSv/h over a working day or employees are likely to receive >6 mSv in 1 year
- Monitoring of designated areas is required to assess likely radiation exposures
- Employers are required to account for all sources held by them

*Competent advice and training*

Radiation employers must:

- Consult with a recognized radiation protection adviser for advice on compliance with the IRR regulations
- Provide information, instruction, and training to all relevant staff (Reg. 15)

1 *Dose constraint*: the upper limit of exposure likely to be received by a non-professional carer whe supporting a relative or friend receiving medical treatment with a radiopharmaceutical.

*Monitoring and classification of workers*

Dose limits are as follows;

- 20 mSv for workers >18 years
- 6 mSv for workers aged 16–18 years
- 1 mSv for members of the public
- Employees shall be designated as 'classified' workers under the IRR (Reg. 21) if personal exposure is likely to be >6 mSv, or three-tenths of any other exposure limit
- An approved dosimetry service (ADS) must be appointed by the employer to undertake exposure monitoring of employees
- An employer must investigate when personal annual exposure to radiation exceeds 15 mSv. The results of such investigations should be retained for 2 years

*Medical assessments*

- Must be undertaken by a doctor appointed by the HSE who is known as an 'Appointed doctor'
- *Prospective classified workers must be examined prior to commencing work with radiation (Reg. 25). Caution should be exercised when assessing:*
  - skin problems which might increase the dose received when exposed to unsealed sources
  - mental health problems that might affect safety behaviour
  - fitness to wear PPE
- Periodic reviews (usually annual) involve review of dosimetry results and sickness absence records. Medical examination may be required at the doctor's discretion
- Health records must be kept for 30 years after the last entry

*Accidents and overexposures*

- Where a radiation accident occurs, the ADS should be contacted, and arrangements made to determine employees' radiation exposure as soon as possible
- Where an overexposure occurs the employer must investigate the circumstances, having notified the affected individual and HSE of the suspected overexposure

## Legislation and guidance

HSE. *Ionizing Radiation Regulations 2017. Approved Code of Practice and Guidance*, L121. HSE Books, Sudbury. Available at: https://www.legislation.gov.uk/uksi/2017/1075/contents/made

# Diving at Work Regulations 1997

⚠ Assessment of fitness to dive at work is the remit of an HSE approved medical examiner of divers (AMED). Where such an assessment is required, the diver should be referred to such a doctor.

## Purpose

To regulate diving operations at work.

## Application

The Diving at Work Regulations apply to all diving at work, but different codes of practice apply to the five industry sectors and give sector-specific information on the management of health and safety in diving operations.

The ACOPs cover:

- Commercial diving inland/inshore
- Commercial diving offshore
- Media diving
- Scientific and archaeological diving
- Recreational diving projects

▶ Hyperbaric treatment at a hospital is excluded from the regulations.

## Definitions

- *Diver*: a person who dives at work
- *Diving operation*: that portion of a diving project which can be safely supervised by one diving supervisor
- *Diving project*: the overall job, which may be a single dive or series of dives
- *Diving contractor*: each diving project can have only one diving contractor (Reg. 5), usually the divers' employer. Most of the duties under these regulations fall on the diving contractor

## Main requirements

- The ACOP relevant to a diving project is usually obvious. However, any diving project using a closed diving bell or saturation diving automatically falls under the commercial diving projects offshore ACOP, irrespective of dive location
- The dive contractor must ensure that the diving project is safely run, and that risk assessments are undertaken
- A project plan must be prepared for each diving project (Reg. 6)
- All staff involved in a diving operation must be competent
- A diving supervisor must be appointed in writing
- All equipment and plant must be suitable and well maintained (Reg. 6)
- Only one diving supervisor can supervise a diving operation at a time (Reg. 9), and there must be well-documented handovers between supervisors
- *All divers must possess*:
  - an HSE approved qualification to dive (Reg. 12)
  - a valid medical certificate of fitness to dive issued by an AMED

## Legislation and guidance


- *Diving at Work Regulations (SI 1997 No2776)*. (1997) Stationery Office, Norwich. Available at: http://www.legislation.gov.uk/uksi/1997/2776/contents/made
- HSE *Commercial Diving Projects Inland/Inshore, Approved Code of Practice*, L104. (1998). HSE Books, Sudbury
- HSE (2014). Commercial diving projects inland/inshore Diving at Work Regulations 1997. Approved Code of Practice and guidance. L104 (2nd ed). Available at: https://www.hse.gov.uk/pubns/priced/l104.pdf
- HSE (2014). Media diving projects. Diving at Work Regulations 1997. Approved Code of Practice and guidance. L106 (2nd ed.). Available at: https://www.hse.gov.uk/pubns/books/l106.htm
- HSE (2014). Scientific and archaeological diving projects Diving at Work Regulations 1997. Approved Code of Practice and guidance. L107 (2nd ed.). Available at: https://www.hse.gov.uk/pubns/books/l107.htm
- HSE (2014). Recreational diving projects Diving at Work Regulations 1997. Approved Code of Practice and guidance. L105 (2nd Ed.). Available at: https://www.hse.gov.uk/pubns/books/l105.htm

# Work in Compressed Air Regulations 1996

## Purpose

These regulations govern the conduct of construction works in compressed air.

## Application

Applies to all construction work under pressures >0.15 bar, except where the Diving Operations at Work Regulations apply.

## Definitions

*Dysbaric illness*

- *Barotrauma*: usually affects sinuses, ears, or lungs
- Dysbaric osteonecrosis (see Table 25.1)
- Decompression illness

**Table 25.1** Radiological surveys to detect dysbaric osteonecrosis

| Pressure | X-rays | Frequency |
|---|---|---|
| <1.0 bar | Not required | None |
| >1.0 bar | AP of both shoulders and hips including proximal third of shafts together with AP and lateral views of distal two thirds of both femurs and proximal third of both tibia including knees | Within 3 months of commencement<br>Annually while work continues and 1 year after exposure ceases |
| >2.0 bar | As above | >than annual |

## Main requirements

- The compressed air contractor must have a safe system of work in compressed air (Reg. 7)
- *The contractor must appoint competent personnel as the*:
  - person in charge
  - compressor attendant
  - lock attendant
- For work at >1 bar the contractor must appoint a medical lock attendant
- *The contractor must notify in writing 14 days before and on suspension/completion of compressed air work (Reg. 6)*:
  - HSE
  - local hospital casualty department
  - emergency services (fire, ambulance)
  - local hyperbaric facilities
- The contractor must provide suitable equipment, fit for use at pressure

*Medical adviser and examinations*

- A contract medical adviser (Reg. 9) shall be appointed. This person may also be the HSE-appointed doctor
- *The contract medical adviser's role includes*:
  - planning for compressed air work including health surveillance (Reg. 10)
  - treatment of dysbarism
  - record keeping (retain for 40 years)
  - occupational medical advice
- No-one can work in compressed air unless passed fit by the appointed doctor (Reg. 16)
- *Medical surveillance requires*:
  - full medical examination of fitness for work at pressure at entry
  - review every 3 months (<1.0 bar) or every month (>1.0 bar)
  - full medical assessment for every 12 months
- medical assessment following illness of >3 days
- medical assessment after any dysbaric illness
- *The content of the full medical examination and review are described in Appendix 7 of the regulations. The initial assessment includes detailed history and examination, spirometry, and audiometry*:
  - for work at pressures >1.0 bar, an exercise step-test, initial chest X-ray, and full blood count are also required
  - the employer shall maintain a health and exposure record for 40 years, including employee's and employer's details, appointed doctor's details, health surveillance results, exposure record, and training record

*Treatment*

- The contractor must provide treatment facilities for dysbaric illness (Reg. 12)
- Provision for emergencies, including fires, must be made
- Decompression from >1.0 bar normally employs the Blackpool tables. Rates of decompression illness associated with these tables exist and can be used to benchmark decompression illness rates on a project
- All workers must be provided with a badge to alert others to their work in compressed air should they be incapacitated owing to dysbarism

*Training*

Employees and other workers must receive information, instruction, and training (Reg. 15) as to safe operating procedures, hazards of compressed air work, and health surveillance.

## Legislation and guidance


- *Construction (Design and Management) Regulations 2007*. UK Government TSO Norwich. Available at: http://www.legislation.gov.uk/uksi/2007/320/contents/made
- *Reporting of Injuries, Disease and Dangerous Occurrences Regulations 2013*. UK Government TSO Norwich. Available at: http://www.hse.gov.uk/riddor/report.htm
- *The Work in Compressed Air Regulations 1996*. UK Government TSO Norwich. Available at: http://www.legislation.gov.uk/uksi/1996/1656/contents/made

# Control of Noise at Work Regulations 2005

## Purpose

The aim of the regulations is to ensure that workers are protected from the risks to health caused by noise. The noise regulations implement the EU directive 2003/10/EC on the minimum health and safety requirements regarding the exposure of workers to the risks arising from physical agents (noise).

## Application

- The regulations apply to employers, the self-employed, and trainees
- The regulations do not apply to the master and crew of a merchant ship during normal shipboard activities
- Members of the public are not covered where they are exposed to noise through their own activities (e.g. DIY) or where they have made a conscious decision to enter a noisy place (e.g. a nightclub)

## Definitions

- *For daily or weekly exposure*:
  - lower exposure action value (EAV) is 80 dB(A)
  - upper EAV is 85 dB(A)
  - exposure limit value (ELV) is 87 dB(A)
- *For peak sound pressure*:
  - lower EAV is 135 dB(C)
  - upper EAV is 137 dB(C)
  - ELV is 140 dB(C)

## Main requirements

- Employers must undertake a 'suitable and sufficient' risk assessment (Reg. 5) of the risks of noise exposure and identify control measures
- Employers must ensure that the risk from noise exposure is either eliminated at source or, where this is not possible, reduce exposure to as low a level as is reasonably practicable (Reg. 6)
- Where employees are likely to be exposed at, or above, the lower EAV, the employer must provide hearing protectors on request
- Any area where employees are likely to be exposed at, or above, the upper EAV must be signed as a hearing protection zone and, where possible, demarcated
- Where the upper EAV is likely to be exceeded, the employer must eliminate exposure at source or reduce exposure to a level as low as is reasonably practicable (excludes hearing protection)
- Workers must not be exposed to noise above an ELV.
- Where an ELV is exceeded, after allowing for any noise attenuation afforded by hearing protectors, the employer must take immediate action to reduce exposure. This may include stopping the work
- Hearing protectors must be provided in a hearing protection zone (Reg. 7)
- Employers must enforce the use of hearing protectors where they are required (Reg. 8)

- Any noise control equipment must be used and maintained (Reg. 8).
- Employees have a duty to use personal hearing protectors provided in compliance with Reg. 7 and other noise control measures provided
- Employees should report promptly, any defects in noise control measures, including hearing protectors, to their employer
- Where the risk assessment indicates a risk to workers' health because of noise exposure, suitable health surveillance must be provided (Reg. 9)
- Appendix 5 of the guidance gives detailed information on audiometric testing and Part 6 of the guidance gives more information on health surveillance for noise-induced hearing loss
- *Where, following health surveillance, hearing damage due to noise is found the employer shall ensure that:*
  - a suitably qualified person notifies the employee
  - the noise risk assessment is reviewed
  - the employer considers redeploying the worker to a non-exposed job
- Employees must cooperate with health surveillance and attend appointments
- The employer must pay the employee when attending health surveillance and meet any associated costs (Reg. 9)
- Where employees are likely to be exposed above the lower action value, the employer must provide suitable information, instruction, and training (Reg. 10). This should cover the risks of noise exposure, the results of any risk assessment, and the measures in place to control noise
- Employees should be advised of the availability of hearing protectors and how to obtain them
- Workers should be told how to detect and report hearing damage
- Employees should be given an explanation of the reasons for health surveillance and informed of the grouped results of any health surveillance

## Legislation and guidance

- HSE (2021). Controlling noise at work. The Control of Noise at Work Regulations 2005. L108, 3RD Ed. Available at : https://www.hse.gov.uk/pubns/priced/l108.pdf
- *The Control of Noise at Work Regulations 2005*. Available at: http://www.legislation.gov.uk/uksi/2005/1643/contents/made
- See also ➲ p. 4, Noise 1: legal requirements, and risk assessment; ➲ p. 6, Noise 2: instrumentation and determination of $L_{EP,d}$; ➲ p. 302, Noise induced hearing loss; ➲ p. 486, Classification of hearing loss; ➲ p. 470, Patterns of hearing loss; ➲ p. 802, Screening audiometry; ➲ p. 812, Carry out a noise assessment.

# Control of Vibration at Work Regulations 2005

## Purpose

To protect against risks to both health and safety from hand-transmitted vibration. This includes risk of HAVS and carpal tunnel syndrome in exposed workers and situations where vibration may affect the ability to handle controls safely.

## Application

- Duties apply to both employers and self-employed persons
- The specific regulation dealing with compliance with exposure limits will not apply to agricultural and forestry until 2014 for work equipment provided to employees before July 2007
- The regulations do not apply to the master or crew of a merchant ship during normal shipboard activities

## Definitions

- Hand-transmitted vibration is the vibration which enters the body through the hands, e.g. tools used in construction, agriculture, and mining
- *Daily personal exposure or A(8)*: average vibration over a working day of 8 hours
- Daily ELV is 5 $m/s^2$ A(8)
- Daily EAV is 2.5 $m/s^2$ A(8)

## Main requirements

Part 1 of the guidance on regulations deals with the legal duties of employers:

- The ELV is the maximum amount of vibration to which an employee may be exposed in any single day. The EAV is the daily exposure to vibration above which action needs to be taken to reduce exposure (Reg. 4)
- An employer who carries out work which is liable to expose employees to risk of vibration is required to assess the risk to the health and safety of employees and identify measures needed to prevent or adequately control exposure (Reg. 5)
- *The risk assessment should take into consideration the following*:
  - the type of vibration, and its magnitude, and duration
  - the effect of vibration on employees whose health is at particular risk from exposure to vibration
  - information from manufacturers of equipment used
  - work conditions, e.g. temperature
  - information from health surveillance
- Significant findings of the assessment should be recorded together with measures taken to minimize risks
- Action must be taken to eliminate risks from vibration exposure completely wherever it is reasonably practicable to do so (Reg. 6). Hence there is a need to consider alternative processes, choice of work equipment, and/or better working methods

- Health surveillance (Reg. 7) to be provided for:
  - employees likely to be exposed above the EAV *or*
  - where the risk assessment indicates individuals may be at risk, e.g. those more sensitive to vibration
- A health record must be kept for each employee who undergoes health surveillance. This should contain information on the outcome of the health surveillance and the individual's fitness to continue to work with vibration exposure
- Where as a result of health surveillance an employee is found to have a disease from exposure to vibration, the employer must ensure that a qualified person informs the employee. The employer should also review the risk assessment and the health of other employees
- Employers should ensure that employees understand the level of risk they may be exposed to, how it is caused, possible health effects, safe work practices, and how to detect and report signs of injury (Reg. 8)
- Parts 2–5 of the guide to the regulations provide practical information for employers on carrying out risk assessment, estimating exposure, controlling risks, and arranging health surveillance, and the duties of machinery manufacturers and suppliers. Part 6 provides technical guidance on exposure measurement and Part 7 provides guidance on health surveillance

## Legislation and guidance


- HSE (2019). *Hand-arm vibration. The Control of Vibration at Work Regulations 2005*. Guidance on Regulations. L140, 2nd ed. Available at: https://www.hse.gov.uk/pubns/priced/l140.pdf
- HSE. *The Control of Vibration at Work Regulations 2005*. HSE Books, Sudbury. (2005) Available at: http://www.legislation.gov.uk/uksi/2005/1093/contents/made
- HSE (2012). Hand-arm vibration at work. A brief guide. Leaflet INDG175 (rev3). Available at: https://www.hse.gov.uk/pubns/indg175.pdf
- HSE (2014). Hand-arm vibration. A guide for employees. INDG296 (rev2). Available at: https://www.hse.gov.uk/pubns/indg296.pdf

- See also ➔ p. 10, Vibration 2: hand-transmitted vibration, ➔ p. 476, Surveillance for hand–arm vibration syndrome; and ➔ p. 806, Clinical assessment of hand–arm vibration syndrome

# Food Safety and Hygiene (England) Regulations 2013

## Purpose

The Food Hygiene (England) Regulations 2006 were introduced to ensure food hygiene regulations in England met EU directives. Similar regulations apply in Wales, Northern Ireland, and Scotland. They apply to anyone who owns, manages, or works in a food business. They cover primary producers, large manufacturers and restaurants, as well as small mobile catering vans or fast-food outlets.

## Main provisions

In summary the regulations require:

- Food businesses to register all premises with the local authority. New premises must be registered 28 days before food production begins
- Meat, egg, fish, or dairy producers must have their premises approved by the local authority
- Food safety management should be *based* on the principles of Hazard Analysis and Critical Control Points (HACCP)
- Food premises to be clean and well maintained
- Food premises to have adequate handwashing and toilet facilities
- Raw materials to be free from contamination
- Water used to be of drinking quality
- Measures to avoid contamination during transport
- Food handlers to be trained in hygiene procedures and to report conditions such as diarrhoea or vomiting to their manager
- Foods that need temperature control must be hot at or above 63°C, or cold at or below 8°C

## HACCP

In order to manage the potential risks to food in a complex business, a management system is required. HACCP is an internationally recognized system used to identify hazards and control risks along the production line. The business must:

- Identify hazards such as contamination with bacteria or foreign bodies (e.g. glass)
- Look for critical points where the contamination can take place
- Implement control measures at these points
- Check that control methods work
- Put in place procedures to review these points regularly
- In a small business the system will be simpler but will (for example) involve regular checks of refrigerator temperatures

## Further information and guidance

Food Safety and Hygiene (England) Regulations 2013 https://www.legislation.gov.uk/uksi/2013/2996/contents/made

HM Govt (2006). Food Hygiene (England) Regulations 2006. UK Government TSO Norwich. Available at: http://www.legislation.gov.uk/uksi/2006/14/contents/made

See also ➔ p. 514, Fitness for work in food handlers.

# Registration, Evaluation, Authorization, and Restriction of Chemicals (REACH)

## Purpose

REACH is a single, unified framework for the regulation of chemical substances throughout the EU. Its purpose is to:

- Provide a high level of protection for human health and the environment
- Improve the competitiveness of the EU chemical industry
- Promote the development of test methods other than animal testing

## Application

- REACH was launched in 2007 and applies to manufacturers or importers (M/I) that supply chemical substances to the EU market in quantities greater than 1 ton per year. A substance cannot be manufactured or imported into the EU without prior registration. Registration is due to be completed in 2018
- REACH applies to chemical substances, mixtures, and (with qualifications) substances released from preparations or articles. However, REACH assessment is conducted only in relation to a single substance regardless of potential coexposure to other substances whether added intentionally or occurring as waste products
- The European Chemicals Agency (ECHA) is responsible for the implementation of REACH within the EU. After Brexit EU REACH was amended by UK legislation to create UK REACH which imposes a similar regime to EU REACH. GB companies need to register with the HSE, which enforces the regulations.

## Definitions

Key definitions of relevance to occupational health in REACH are:

- *Chemical safety assessment (CSA)*: determination of risk presented by a substance
- *Chemical safety report (CSR)*: documentation of the CSA
- *Derived no-effect level (DNEL)*: level of exposure below which no adverse effects are expected to occur
- *Exposure scenario*: set of conditions defining the use of a substance through its life cycle
- *Risk characterization*: estimation of the incidence and severity of adverse effects due to actual or predicted exposure
- *Substance of very high concern (SVHC)*: substances that are carcinogenic, mutagenic, persistent bioaccumulative and toxic (PBT), very persistent and very bioaccumulative (vPvB), or otherwise SVHC assessed on a case-by-case basis
- *Technical dossier*: description of intrinsic properties, classification, and guidance on safe use of a substance

## Main requirements

### *Registration*

GB manufacturers/importers of chemicals registered pre-Brexit in the EU must also register with the HSE during a transitional period which varies with the nature of the substance.

*Main M/I and related responsibilities*

- Submission of a technical dossier (>1 ton/year) and CSA (>10 tons/years). CSA is to include calculation of the DNEL
- If a substance is 'dangerous' (under REACH Article 10a), PBT, or vPvB, CSA is also to include exposure scenarios, exposure assessment, and risk characterization. These are to incorporate the effect of existing or planned Risk Management Measures (RMM)
- M/I is to convey information on the safe use and necessary RMM to downstream users (DU). DU have a responsibility to apply the necessary RMM
- CSA to be documented in the CSR
- M/I may pool data through a substance information exchange forum and apply for joint registration though a lead registrant

*Evaluation*

ECHA and member states' (MS) competent authorities are responsible for the examination of dossiers for completeness, testing proposals in relation to health effects and substance evaluation, i.e. need for further information.

*Authorization*

Specific conditions may apply to authorization of SVHC with consideration of the following; the suitability of alternative substances or technologies, a study of the feasibility of substitution, socio-economic analysis to assess overall risk/benefit and the effectiveness of existing RMM.

*Restriction*

Provision for a limitation on use or complete prohibition of substances that present an unacceptable risk at a community-wide level. Companies based in GB may need to comply both with UK REACH and EU REACH if trading with EU States.

EU REACH continues to apply in Northern Ireland.

UK REACH covers imports to GB from Northern Ireland.

## Further information

European Chemical s Agency (ECHA) provides information on chemical substances and legislation (REACH, CLP) which is regularly updated. Available at: https://echa.europa.eu/about-us

# Chapter 26

# Employment law

# Employment law

This is, of necessity, an abridged account of detailed and complex legislation. The interested reader is referred to more detailed texts.

## Employment law

- Employment law in the UK is a mixture of civil law, concerned with compensation, and criminal law, concerned with punishment. Some employment law is in the form of case law, and some in the form of statute law, setting standards for the behaviour of employers in terms of equality, data protection, and health and safety at work (see Table 26.1)
- The courts of law, in deciding cases brought before them, create precedents which may be applied in future similar disputes. Decisions of higher courts, like the Supreme Court and Court of Appeal, are binding on lower courts. Much of the civil law is made by the judges in this way, without recourse to parliament. We call this judge-made law the common law
- Statutes are Acts of Parliament; that is the House of Commons, the House of Lords, and the Queen. The Scottish Parliament and the Welsh Assembly have limited powers to create legislation for Scotland and Wales. Northern Ireland has its own parliament. Statute law takes precedence over case law, but the courts in interpreting the meaning of statutes also create precedents
- Statutory instruments, or statutory regulations, are delegated legislation made by a government minister by virtue of the authority given to them in a statute. They do not need to be debated in parliament, unless an MP questions them. Delegated legislation is used to provide detailed provisions which parliament has insufficient time to create. The statute lays down the principle, which is then expanded in regulations

## Employment tribunals (EmTs)

- EmTs are specialist employment courts which deal with unfair dismissal, redundancy payments, and laws against discrimination at work
- They sit in several large towns and are composed of a legally qualified judge who sometimes sits with two lay members, one representing employers and the other employees
- They can award money compensation and make recommendations, but have no power to force an employer to reinstate an employee
- The law that the EmTs administer is laid down in a number of statutes and regulations, which have been interpreted by the courts

## Employment rights

The legal rights of those who work for another depend on the status of the 'employee'. Employers attempt to exclude workers from statutory rights by classifying them as self-employed or employing them on 'zero hours' contracts where there is no ongoing obligation to give work. Courts have protected some workers by holding that some of these contracts do not represent the true state of affairs. Some statutory rights, like unfair dismissal, are conferred only on 'employees' under the direct control of the employer, others, like the right to holiday pay, also on 'workers' who undertake to perform work personally but are not necessarily classified as employees. This is a very complex area and subject to ongoing judicial and legislative review.

## Enforcement of the civil law of compensation

- The enforcement of the civil law is not a matter for the Health and Safety Executive (HSE), the local authorities, or the police. A civil action is brought by the person claiming a remedy: the claimant
- In England and Wales actions for damages for personal injury must be brought in the County Court or the High Court
- In Scotland actions for damages for personal injury are brought in the Sheriff Court or the Court of Session
- Appeals against a refusal of social security benefits must be taken to a first-tier tribunal
- Complaints that an employer has unfairly dismissed an employee or unlawfully discriminated against them because of a protected characteristic under the Equality Act 2010 must be taken to an EmT

**Table 26.1** The main differences between civil law and criminal law

| | Civil law | Criminal law |
|---|---|---|
| Main purpose | Compensation | Punishment |
| Source of law | Statute or case (common) law | Mainly statute law |
| Prosecuting authority | None—civil action by claimant | Crown Prosecution Service[1]<br>Procurator Fiscal[2]<br>HSE<br>Local authority |
| Insurance | Employers' Liability Insurance | None |

[1]England and Wales.

[2]Scotland.

# Compensation

## State benefits

- A system of no-fault compensation for occupational injuries and diseases, originally named Workmen's Compensation, now the Industrial Injuries Disablement Benefits (IIDB) Scheme, has existed in the UK since 1897
- Financed through taxation; administered by the State (now the Department of Work and Pensions (DWP))
- The scheme covers all employed earners, but not the self-employed
- *A disablement pension is payable to a person who has*:
  - suffered a personal injury caused by accident arising out of and in the course of employment, *or*
  - contracted a prescribed disease, i.e. one designated by the Secretary of State as a special risk for a particular occupation
- The Industrial Injuries Advisory Council advises the Secretary of State regarding the diseases that should be considered for prescription under the scheme, and generally on its operation.
- Prescription will be recommended when epidemiological evidence shows that a particular job is associated with a doubling of risk of the disease (compared with a member of the general public).
- *A list of prescribed diseases is found in the Social Security (Prescribed Diseases) Regulations 1985. Regularly updated by statutory instrument. Prescribed diseases are divided into*:
  - conditions due to physical agents (e.g. tenosynovitis for manual labour or frequent repetitive movements of the hand or wrist)
  - conditions due to biological agents (e.g. anthrax for work involving contact with animal products or residues)
  - conditions due to chemical agents (e.g. lead poisoning for work involving exposure to lead), *and*
  - miscellaneous conditions (e.g. asthma for work involving exposure to any of a long list of agents including isocyanates)

## Claims for IIDB

- Claims for IIDB must be made to the DWP, where assessment is made by a civil servant aided by medical evidence from the DWP's doctors. Appeal to a tribunal consisting of a legally qualified judge and two doctors
- A tax-free pension is payable to those who qualify for benefit only where the disability is assessed as at least 14% (except noise-induced hearing loss (>20%) and pneumoconiosis, byssinosis, or diffuse mesothelioma (no level))
- Lump sum payments and death benefits have been abolished
- A reduced earnings allowance to compensate for incapability to follow the regular occupation is payable to those injured by an accident or the onset of a prescribed disease before 1 October 1990
- Those who are 100%
- Disabled and need constant care are also entitled to a constant attendance allowance or an exceptionally severe disablement allowance

## Civil compensation

Compensation can be obtained through a civil action in tort. A tort (from the Latin for twisted) is a civil wrong, which gives rise to an action for damages. The equivalent in Scotland is a delict. Liability is based on fault

- A successful claimant must deduct from the damages awarded all social security benefits received over 5 years, to reimburse the DWP
- Legal aid is now available in only a few cases. Most claimants finance their actions through a conditional fee agreement with the lawyer, under which the lawyer is paid only if successful
- An action must normally be brought within 3 years of the damage. Therefore, it is important to advise an individual when an occupational disease is diagnosed, and to make a written record of this advice in the medical records. Where the claimant is unaware of the damage (as where an illness has a long latency period), he/she has 3 years from the date he/she discovers the illness or ought reasonably to have discovered it to make a claim
- In the field of industrial injury or disease the claimant alleges negligence by the employer
- Negligence is defined as a failure to take reasonable care to prevent foreseeable harm

The Enterprise and Regulatory Reform Act 2013 abolished the civil action for breach of statutory duty which was based on breach of the statutory regulations, such as the Control of Substances Hazardous to Health Regulations 2002. Now, employees must prove negligence in order to be successful in a claim for compensation.

- Since the numbers of prosecutions brought by the enforcing authorities are relatively few, a civil action is a more likely sanction for breach of health and safety laws
- The Health and Safety at Work Act 1974 does not give rise to a civil action. It lays down a framework for the criminal law of health and safety at work. The common law of negligence already provides a civil action for damages for negligence
- Damages are awarded for loss of earnings and also for pain and suffering and loss of amenity
- The employer is vicariously liable for the wrongdoing of its employees in the course of employment
- The Employers' Liability (Compulsory Insurance) Act 1969 imposes an obligation on employers to take out insurance against a claim by an employee for an industrial injury

## Relevant legislation

- Social Security (Industrial Injuries) (Prescribed Diseases) Regulations 1985, as amended
- Social Security Act 1998

## Further information

DWP. Available at: http://www.dwp.gov.uk for information about welfare benefits. Department or Welfare and Pensions, London. Regularly updated web resource.

Kloss D (2020). *Occupational Health Law*, 6th edn, Chapter 6. Wiley-Blackwell, Oxford.

# Equality Act 2010

## The protected characteristics

- *This Act, most of which came into force in England and Wales and Scotland on 1 October 2010, repeals previous legislation dealing with discrimination, including:*
  - the Sex Discrimination Act 1975
  - the Race Relations Act 1976
  - the Disability Discrimination Act 1995
  - the Employment Equality (Age) Regulations 2006
- The law is based on EU directives. It covers discrimination in employment, education, transport, and the provision of goods, facilities, and services. It brings together all the anti-discrimination legislation into one comprehensive statute
- The Equality and Human Rights Commission oversees and polices the Act
- The employment provisions are enforced through EmTs
- A claim of unlawful discrimination must be commenced in an EmT within 3 months of the act complained of or, where there are a series of complaints, within 3 months of the last incident. The initial approach must be to Advisory, Conciliation and Arbitration Service which offers to conciliate, though the parties are not obliged to agree to conciliation
- The Equality Act does not apply to Northern Ireland where the old legislation is, for the time being, still in force with some amendments

### Characteristics protected by the act

The following are characteristics protected by the act:

- Age
- Disability
- Gender reassignment
- Marriage and civil partnership
- Pregnancy and maternity
- Race
- Religion or belief
- Sex
- Sexual orientation

# Disability discrimination 1: The definition of disability

A disabled person is one with a physical or mental impairment that has a substantial and long-term adverse effect on his/her ability to carry out normal day-to-day activities. These activities may be carried out in employment or outside employment, but must be activities common to many jobs, such as reading, writing, walking, and climbing stairs, not those special to a particular job, such as assembling a watch or playing a violin in an orchestra.

- Physical impairment includes sensory impairments such as those affecting sight or hearing
- Mental impairment includes learning difficulties and any mental disorder. Since 2005 it is unnecessary to show that a mental illness is clinically well recognized
- A substantial adverse effect is one that is more than minor or trivial
- Long term means having lasted for 12 months or more, likely to last for 12 months or more, or terminal
- The Equality Act removes the need to prove impairment of one of a list of capacities, e.g. mobility, manual dexterity, or memory. It is now ultimately for the EmT to decide what is a normal day-to-day activity
- Pain and fatigue must be taken into account, and the fact that disabled people develop coping mechanisms to avoid tasks they find difficult
- Where a condition would be disabling if not controlled by drugs (e.g. epilepsy, diabetes) or assisted by prosthesis or other aid (e.g. hearing aid, counselling), it counts as a disability under the Act. Only exception to this is defective eyesight assisted by spectacles or contact lenses
- A severe disfigurement is treated as a disability (unless self-inflicted), even though it does not interfere with normal day-to-day activities
- Cancer, human immunodeficiency virus (HIV), and multiple sclerosis are disabilities from diagnosis
- Other progressive conditions, e.g. muscular dystrophy, dementia, are disabilities from when the impairment has some effect on the ability to carry out normal day-to-day activities, even though not yet substantial
- Recurrent disabling conditions, e.g. rheumatoid arthritis, are disabilities despite periods of remission if a substantial adverse effect is likely to recur
- Where a person has suffered from a substantial and long-term disabling condition in the past and has now recovered, he/she will be protected by the Act if discriminated against because of the past disability. This is particularly important to those who have had a mental illness
- The Equality Act 2010 (Disability) Regulations 2011 provide that a person is disabled if certified as blind, severely sight impaired, sight impaired, or partially sighted by a consultant ophthalmologist
- *These regulations also provide that certain conditions are to be treated as not amounting to impairments, i.e.*
    - a tendency to set fires
    - a tendency to steal
    - a tendency to physical or sexual abuse of other persons
    - exhibitionism
    - voyeurism

- Seasonal allergic rhinitis is to be treated as not amounting to an impairment unless it aggravates the effect of another condition
- Addiction to alcohol, nicotine, or any other substance is to be treated as not amounting to an impairment unless originally the result of administration of medically prescribed drugs or other medical treatment
- Where addiction causes a disabling medical condition, e.g. alcoholism and liver cirrhosis, the consequent impairment is a potential disability under the act

## Occupational health reports

- A medical report on a worker should not state definitively that he/she is disabled, since that is a legal question for an EmT. However, it is acceptable for a doctor or HCP to state that in his/her opinion it is likely or unlikely that the worker is likely to be regarded as disabled, without making a definite ruling
- If it is appropriate, a report should set out whether there is an impairment, the effect on normal day-to-day activities, and how long it is likely to last
- It may also recommend adjustments to the working environment, working practices, or the provision of auxiliary aids that could enable worker to do the job, despite the disability. The latter is good employment practice even when there is doubt about whether the worker is disabled, and this is supported by the Equality and Human Rights Commission's Code of Practice on Employment 2011
- In order to be legally defensible, occupational health reports must be written by a suitably qualified expert, based on evidence, and must be logical and reasoned. Suitable expertise would include being an accredited specialist in occupational medicine[1]

## Further information

*Guidance on Matters to be Taken into Account in Determining Questions Relating to the Definition of Disability* (2011). Office for Disability Issues, DWP London.

Kloss D (2020). *Occupational Health Law*, 6th edn, Chapter 8. Wiley-Blackwell, Oxford.

# Disability discrimination 2: Employers' duties

The disability provisions of the Equality Act apply to all employers, except for the armed forces. They apply to job applicants, employees, workers, contract workers, and office-holders, but not to volunteers. A complaint of unlawful disability discrimination must be made to an EmT within 3 months (of the act or the last incident).

## Direct discrimination

- This is treating someone less favourably because of the fact of the disability—a 'blanket ban', e.g. 'job is not open to those with epilepsy'
- Direct discrimination is unlawful and cannot be justified. Each job applicant or employee must be treated as an individual
- Direct discrimination against a non-disabled person because of association with a disabled person is unlawful, e.g. mother of a disabled child rejected because of fear she will take time off to care for her child

## Pre-employment screening

- Employers must not normally ask health questions, including questions about sickness absence, before offering a job applicant work
- However, an offer of work can be made conditional on satisfactory health clearance and health questions can then be asked
- *The employer is allowed to ask an applicant, before offering work*:
  - if he/she needs adjustments to the selection process, e.g. an interview
  - questions about functions intrinsic to the job, e.g. eyesight
- Health questionnaires should be drafted, processed, and interpreted by health professionals and stored as confidential medical records. Nothing in the pre-employment health questionnaire should be disclosed to the manager without the consent of the worker, or a court order. Such information should only be disclosed to managers with consent in so far as this is necessary for them to undertake their management responsibilities

## Disability-related discrimination

- This is treating someone unfavourably because of something that arises in consequence of his/her disability, e.g. rejecting a wheelchair user for a job as a firefighter. This discrimination is justifiable if the employer can prove it is a proportionate means of achieving a legitimate aim. The employer is not liable unless they either knew or ought reasonably to have known that the worker had a disability
- Employers should consider reasonable adjustments before rejecting someone for a disability-related reason, e.g. dismissal for unacceptable sickness absence without considering adjustments to the attendance management procedure may be unlawful discrimination. However, employers are not obliged to continue to employ a disabled worker whose attendance or performance has been seriously unsatisfactory for a long period

- An employer may be able to justify discrimination on health and safety grounds, but only if it is proportionate to the risk. Decisions must be based on a risk assessment and reasonable adjustments must be made
- Employers must not exclude a disabled person if there is no explicit statutory prohibition and no clear evidence that the risk to the disabled person is substantially greater than the risk to the non-disabled worker, or employment would create a significant hazard to others

## The duty to make reasonable adjustments

- There is a duty to consider adjustments to the working environment and practices, and the provision of auxiliary aids (including services)
- There is a duty to consider adjustments in the course of recruitment
- The duty only arises when the employer either knows or ought reasonably to know of the disability
- The employer only has to do what is reasonable. Reasonableness depends on practicability and cost. The extent of an employer's resources, the nature of its activities, and the size of the undertaking are relevant. Financial assistance through the Access to Work scheme, or sponsorship by a charity or local authority, must also be explored
- The employer must not seek payment from a disabled worker for the costs of complying with the duty of reasonable adjustment
- *Examples are given in the Code of Practice on Employment 2011*:
  - making adjustments to premises
  - providing information in accessible formats
  - allocating some of the disabled person's duties to another worker
  - transferring the disabled person to fill an existing vacancy
  - altering hours of work or training
  - assigning to a different place of work or training, or home working
  - allowing the disabled person to be absent during working or training hours for rehabilitation, assessment, or treatment
  - providing training/mentoring for disabled person or other worker
  - acquiring or modifying equipment
  - modifying procedures for testing or assessment
  - providing a reader or interpreter
  - providing supervision or other support
  - allowing a disabled worker to take a period of disability leave
  - participating in supported employment schemes such as Workstep (see ➲p. 446, Rehabilitation and disability services)
  - employing a support worker to assist a disabled worker
  - modifying disciplinary or grievance procedures
  - adjusting redundancy selection criteria
  - modifying performance-related pay arrangements
- Reasonable adjustments include moving a disabled worker to a higher-grade job (if he/she has the necessary qualifications), or to a lower-paid job (if that is all that is available within his/her competence) with the worker's consent
- In general, a disabled employee is not entitled to a longer period of sick pay than the non-disabled. However, the Court of Appeal has held that, where an employer is at fault in not making a reasonable adjustment, they must pay full pay throughout a resulting period of absence

- Disability-related leave, e.g. to attend physiotherapy or counselling, is not sick leave and should be recorded separately
- Failure to make adjustments deemed reasonable by an EmT cannot be justified

## Relevant legislation and further information


- Equality Act 2010 (Disability) Regulations (2010) TSO London
- Equality and Human Rights Commission (2011). CoP on Employment London
- Kloss D (2020). *Occupational Health Law*, 6th edn, Chapter 8. Wiley-Blackwell, Oxford

# Sex discrimination

It is unlawful to treat a person of one sex less favourably than someone of the opposite sex because of their gender. Stereotypical assumptions should not be made about women being weaker and more vulnerable than men. Each person should be treated as an individual.

## Indirect discrimination

- Indirect discrimination is treating a member of one sex unfavourably because of a provision, criterion, or practice which puts members of one sex at a disadvantage, e.g. a requirement to work shifts or to work away from home
- Indirect discrimination can be justified if the employer has used a proportionate means of achieving a legitimate aim, e.g. the needs of his/her business require these methods of working

## Sexual harassment

Sexual harassment is a form of sex discrimination. It is unwanted conduct either of a sexual nature or on the grounds of sex that has the purpose or effect of violating the employee's dignity, or creating an intimidating, hostile, degrading, humiliating, or offensive environment. If not done with that intention it is to be regarded as having such an effect only if it should reasonably be considered as doing so.

## Pregnancy discrimination

- The Equality Act 2010 provides that it is unlawful to treat a woman unfavourably in the protected period because she is pregnant or because of illness suffered by her as a result of it or because she takes statutory maternity leave
- The protected period begins at conception and ends at the end of her statutory maternity leave or, if earlier, when she returns to work after the pregnancy. If she does not have the right to maternity leave it ends 2 weeks after the end of the pregnancy
- After the end of the protected period, the employer is entitled to treat any sickness absence of the woman in the same way as he would treat that of a man, even though it may be pregnancy or maternity related
- Nothing shall render unlawful any act done in relation to a woman if it is necessary to protect women as regards pregnancy or maternity, e.g. work with lead or ionizing radiations or work on a ship or aircraft
- Pregnant employees are entitled to reasonable time off work with pay to attend antenatal care recommended by a doctor, midwife, or health visitor (Employment Rights Act 1996)
- Where a job is hazardous for a pregnant employee or one who has recently given birth, the employer must not dismiss her. Either a suitable alternative must be found, or she must be sent home on full pay
- If a doctor or midwife has certified that night work is hazardous for a pregnant employee, the employer must either offer her suitable day work or suspend her on full pay
- Under the Management Regulations 1999 an employer must carry out a risk assessment of the specific risks posed to the health and safety of pregnant women or new mothers when employing any woman of

childbearing potential. Further risk assessment should be performed when a female employee informs the employer in writing that she is pregnant and be updated as necessary. Failure to do so is unlawful sex discrimination
- *The main hazards are*:
  - physical agents (e.g. shocks, vibrations, handling of loads, noise, non-ionizing radiation, extremes of heat and cold)
  - chemical agents (e.g. mercury, lead, antimitotic drugs, carbon monoxide)
  - biological agents (e.g. listeria, rubella, chickenpox, toxoplasma, cytomegalovirus, hepatitis B, and HIV)
  - working conditions (e.g. mining)
- If the woman informs her employer after her return to work that she is breastfeeding, a risk assessment should be done
- Employers have a duty to provide suitable workplace rest facilities for women at work who are breastfeeding
- There is no statutory right for workers to take time off to breastfeed, but an employer who unreasonably refuses to allow a woman to express milk or to adjust her working conditions to allow her to continue to breastfeed may be liable for unlawful sex discrimination
- *A woman must not be at work within 2 weeks of giving birth*:
  - from 1 April 2007 she has the right to up to 52 weeks maternity leave
  - statutory maternity pay is payable for up to 39 weeks

## Gender reassignment

- Discrimination against a person who is proposing to undergo, is undergoing, or has undergone a process (or part of a process) for the purpose of reassigning sex by changing physiological attributes, or who is living as a member of the opposite sex without undergoing medical treatment, is unlawful under the Equality Act 2010
- Absence from work to undergo gender reassignment must be treated in the same way as absence due to sickness or injury, and the employer must not treat a transsexual's absence less favourably than that of other workers if it is unreasonable to do so, e.g. the transsexual asks to take a day's holiday to attend counselling and the employer refuses without good reason when he would allow another worker to be absent
- Under the Gender Recognition Act 2004 a person who has successfully undergone gender reassignment and has lived in the transgender for at least 2 years can register his/her acquired gender and thereafter is entitled to be regarded for all purposes as possessing that gender, including when undertaking intimate body searches as a police or security officer

## Relevant legislation

- Equality Act 2010
- Workplace (Health, Safety and Welfare) Regulations 1992
- Management of Health and Safety at Work Regulations 1999
- Employment Rights Act 1996
- Gender Recognition Act 2004

# Age discrimination

- Discrimination against employees because of their age is unlawful under the Equality Act 2010 unless the employer can justify it as a proportionate means of achieving a legitimate aim. This applies to both direct and indirect discrimination, and to both young and old
- Employers are permitted to ask for training and experience where it can be shown that this is a genuine requirement for the job, and to refuse to give training where the employer will be unlikely to work for long enough to justify the expenditure on training
- In 2011 the employers' right to force employees to retire at 65 was repealed. Employers now have to justify forcing an employee to retire at any age. However, the Supreme Court decided in 2012 that a policy that specifies a compulsory age of retirement can be defended if it is reasonably necessary to assist workforce planning or to preserve the dignity of older workers
- There is no age limit for the right to claim unfair dismissal and redundancy rights
- Case law from the European Court of Justice has held that assumptions based on statistical averages showing that older workers are likely to be less physically and intellectually competent than younger workers can justify the imposition of age restrictions on recruitment and retirement where public safety is at risk. Compulsory retirement of airline pilots at age 65 has been upheld as lawful
- Employers are justified in imposing fitness testing on older workers, where fitness is a necessary job requirement

## Young workers

- Employers are under a special duty to protect young workers
- No person under 13 may lawfully be employed in any capacity and from 13 to 16 years old only outside school hours and not for more than 2 hours a day, except for approved work experience for children in their last year of school
- The employer must conduct a risk assessment of a young person under 18 years old before he/she starts work and has a duty to take into account inexperience, lack of awareness of risk, and immaturity
- *Young persons must not be employed on work which is:*
  - beyond their physical or psychological capacity
  - involves harmful exposure to agents which are toxic
  - carcinogenic, cause heritable genetic damage or harm to the unborn child, or in any other way chronically affect human health
  - involves harmful exposure to radiation
  - involves a risk of accidents which it may reasonably be assumed cannot be recognized or avoided by young person's owing to their insufficient attention to safety or lack of experience or training
  - or presents a risk from extreme cold or heat, noise, or vibration

## Relevant legislation

- Equality Act 2010
- Management of Health and Safety at Work Regulations 1999

# Working Time Regulations 1998

These provisions are very complex, and only a general account is given, with only a few of the many amendments being considered in this section. Issues around working time inevitably link in with shift working and related health issues.

## Main provisions and definitions

- The regulations impose a limit on working hours, including overtime, of an average of 48 hours for each 7 days, taken over a period of 17 weeks, but there are many exceptions. Doctors in training were included from 1 August 2004. The 48-hour limit applied fully from 2009
- Working hours include hours when the worker is on call on his/her employer's premises, but not when he/she is on call at home. They do not include travel to and from work unless the worker's job involves travel, e.g. a travelling salesman
- Employers are permitted to ask workers to opt out of the 48 hours limit by agreement in writing. Workers must not be penalized for refusing to do so
- Employers must keep records and are subject to inspection by the HSE
- There is a general duty in the Health and Safety at Work Act to prevent risks to health and safety. This applies to overlong working hours
- Young workers (under 18 years old) are prohibited from working more than 8 hours per day or 40 hours per week
- The regulations extend to workers as well as employees

## Night workers

- There are special provisions relating to night workers, defined as working at least 3 hours of daily working time between 23.00 and 06.00 hours
- An employer shall ensure that no night worker, whose work involves special hazards or heavy physical or mental strain, works for more than 8 hours in any 24-hour period during which the night worker performs night work

*Night workers' health assessments*

- Every adult worker assigned to night work must have the opportunity of a free health assessment before he/she takes up the assignment, and at regular intervals as appropriate. This should be done through a screening questionnaire, compiled with guidance from a qualified health professional (see ➲p. 794, Night worker health assessment). Where a potential problem is disclosed, referral to a health professional is advised
- Where a doctor has advised an employer that a worker is suffering from health problems that the practitioner considers to be connected with night work, the employer should, where possible, transfer the worker to suitable day work
- A report by a doctor that a worker is unfit to work nights can only be made with the worker's consent in writing

## Rest periods and holidays

- Adult workers must be given a rest period of at least 24 hours every week and a rest break of at least 20 minutes after 6 hours. They must have a rest period of at least 11 hours in each 24-hour period
- *There are special provisions for workers under 18 years old*:
  - they must have a rest period of at least 48 hours per week and a rest break of at least 30 minutes after 4.5 hours
  - they are entitled to a rest period of at least 12 hours in each 24-hour period
  - young workers should not normally be employed to work at night, but in exceptional cases they may be assigned to night work, e.g. work in hospitals
  - young workers assigned to night work must have the opportunity of a free assessment of their health and capacities before they take up the assignment
- Workers are entitled to a minimum of 28 days a year paid holiday, which includes bank holidays. Part-time workers are also entitled to 28 days paid holidays
- Employees who are absent on sick leave continue to accrue rights to paid holidays which can be taken after they return to work
- The holiday provisions are enforced through the employment tribunals

## Relevant legislation

Working Time Regulations (1998) (as amended)

## Further information

Department of Trade and Industry (2003). *Your Guide to the Working Time Regulations (VRN 00/1068)*. Department of Trade and Industry, London. Available at: http://www.dti.gov.uk/employment/employment-legislation/employment-guidance/page28978.html

HSE (2006). *Managing shift work, HSG 256*. HSE Books, Sudbury.

Chapter 27

# Legislation related to occupational health records

# Legislation related to occupational health records

- Access to Medical Reports Act 1988
- Access to Health Records Act 1990
- General Data Protection Regulation 2016
- Data Protection Act 2018
- Freedom of Information Act 2000

# General Data Protection Regulation 2016 and Data Protection Act 2018

## Purpose

The General Data Protection Regulation (GDPR) was agreed by the EU in Brussels in 2016 and came into force throughout the EU on 25 May 2018. Its intention was to provide common standards of data processing throughout the EU. As an EU Regulation it did not need domestic legislation to bring it into force. It repealed the Data Protection Act 1998. At the same time the UK Data Protection Act 2018 also came into force dealing with matters of detail and ensuring that the new law would survive Brexit. It is important to note that the GDPR is not the only law regulating the processing of personal data and, in particular, that the common law of confidentiality and the ethical rules of the health professions are still in force and run in parallel with the GDPR. Breach of the GDPR may lead to a fine of up to 20 million Euros or 4% of global turnover. In the UK the law is enforced by the Information Commissioner.

## Application

The GDPR applies to the processing of personal data by individuals and organizations based in the UK or processing data in the UK. It applies to data held on computer but to manual records only if in an internally structured filing system, e.g. health records filed according to the name of the patient and internally by date. Data include X-rays, videos, and audiotapes.

## Definitions

*Data controller*: the person who determines the purpose and means of data processing.

*Data processor*: the person who processes data on behalf of the controller.

*Data subject*: the person to whom the data relates.

*Personal data*: information relating to an identified or identifiable natural person. It does not include data which are completely anonymised, data relating to a dead person, or data relating to a company.

*Special category data* (formerly called sensitive data): data revealing an individual's racial or ethnic origin, political opinions, religious or philosophical beliefs, or trade union membership, and genetic data, biometric data for the purpose of uniquely identifying a natural person, data concerning health, or data concerning a natural person's sex life or sexual orientation.

*Caldicott guardian*: a senior health or social services professional responsible for controlling the management, use, and disclosure of health or social services data, mainly in the National Health Service (NHS). A system set up after the report of the Caldicott Committee to the Department of Health in 1997 on the use and transfer of patient identifiable information.

## Main requirements

- Data controllers must pay a fee, depending on their size, to the Information Commissioner's Office (ICO). Failure to pay is a criminal offence
- Where data are being sent abroad to a country which does not have as strict data protection laws as the EU, e.g. the USA, special agreements need to be in force to provide adequate privacy protection. After Brexit the UK will need to put in place similar procedures

- Both controllers and processors must have a lawful basis for processing data under Article 6. In the case of special category (sensitive) data, they must also have a lawful basis under Article 9. Consent as defined by the GDPR is only one of the potential lawful bases and should not be used by occupational health professionals. This does not mean that they do not need consent or a court order to report to managers or other third parties like solicitors or the police (other than in exceptional cases where there is a legal duty or in the public interest), because the common law of confidentiality and the ethics of the regulators continue to apply. The ethical guidance on confidentiality of the Department of Health, the General Medical Council (GMC), and the Faculty of Occupational Medicine remains in force. The definition of consent at common law is less restrictive than the GDPR definition, e.g. the common law recognizes implied consent. If not using consent as a lawful basis there is no need to comply with the GDPR definition: common law consent is sufficient
- Data controllers must comply with the data protection principles

*The six data protection principles*

These are set out in Article 5 GDPR and are as follows:

(a) Data must be processed lawfully, fairly, and in a transparent manner
(b) Data must be collected for specific purposes and not further processed in a manner incompatible with those purposes (other than for statistical or research purposes)
(c) Data must be adequate, relevant, and limited to what is necessary
(d) Data must be accurate and kept up to date
(e) Data must be kept for no longer than is necessary
(f) Data must be processed in a manner that ensures appropriate security

*Subject access requests (SAR)*

- The data subject has a right to access his own data, including health records, and to be provided with a copy of his records free of charge and normally within a calendar month of making a request. The controller should confirm the identity of the subject. Where a request is made by someone acting on the subject's behalf, like a solicitor, they should ask to see a written authorization. All requests should be acknowledged, logged, and tracked to completion
- Data may be withheld if they would cause serious harm to the subject's physical or mental health or that of another person. A health professional should carefully document the reason for denying access. Access may also be denied to data which reveal the identity of a third party who does not wish to be identified (other than another health professional) unless it is reasonable to disclose without their consent. Identifying information of third parties may need to be redacted (blacked out)

## Legislation and guidance


- Confidentiality: NHS Code of Practice, Department of Health (2003) DH Publications London
- Data Protection: Employment Practices Code (2011) Information Commissioner's Office Cheshire.
- General Data Protection Regulation and Data Protection Act 2018 UK Government TSO Norwich.
- Website of the Information Commissioner. ) Information Commissioner's Office Cheshire. Accessed at: http://www.ico.gov.uk/

# Access to Medical Reports Act 1988

## Purpose

The Access to Medical Reports Act 1988 (AMRA) applies to requests by a patient or insurance company for a report (not the full record) from a doctor who is or has been responsible for clinical care. It is not a data protection subject; access is requested and the doctor can charge a reasonable fee for a report.

## Application in occupational health (OH)

In OH practice it applies to a request by an OH professional for a report from a general practitioner (GP) or consultant physician.

- AMRA provides that the employee must give written consent to obtaining a medical report; the employee is given the option of asking to see the doctor's report before it is sent to the employer and at that stage withdrawing consent to its disclosure to management. He is allowed 21 days to access the report. As an alternative to refusing consent, he may ask for a statement of his views to be added. A doctor can withhold information if it would seriously damage the patient's physical or mental health or reveal the identity of a third party (other than another health professional) who does not wish to be identified
- The report must be retained by the doctor for at least 6 months
- A request for a *report* is not a request for subject access to the full medical *record* and a GP or consultant who provides a printout of the entire record when a report has been requested is providing excessive information in breach of the GDPR

*Reports produced by an OH professional*

- AMRA does not in most cases apply to a request for a report *from* an OH professional because most such reports are written by nurses and not doctors and, even if by an occupational physician, not a doctor *responsible for clinical care*

*OH reports to management*

- An OH professional should not report to managers or their lawyers without consent or a court order. Consent does not need to be in writing, but you are strongly advised to obtain written consent, if possible, for reasons of proof. This is a common law rule which has not been overruled by the GDPR. The consent should be informed which means that the worker should know, at least in broad terms, what the report contains. Exceptionally, where the worker reveals information that discloses a risk to others, it can be reported without consent to the proper authorities in the public interest
- The GMC advises that the worker should be asked whether they wish to see a written report before it is sent to management and, if so, the report should be given or sent to the worker, allowing a short period to allow them to consider it and make representations if they wish. It is common to send the report by email and allow the worker 48 hours to comment. They can be told that if they do not reply within that time frame the report will be sent. There is no need to ask at that stage for a positive approval of the written report, though some cautious physicians do so. Any mistake of fact, or opinion based on a mistake of

fact, should be corrected, but the health professional should not change his or her professional opinion at the behest either of the worker or the employer
- The worker should be warned that if they do not consent to a medical report the manager can act without medical evidence
- A report to management that a worker has not attended or has refused consent to a report can be made without consent

## Access to Health Records Act 1990

Where records relating to a deceased person are requested, they should only be disclosed to either the executor or administrator of the deceased's estate or to a person with a claim arising from the death. The GDPR does not apply. If the close relatives do not fall within these categories, they have no right of access to the records despite their relationship with the deceased. Records can be disclosed by order of a coroner.

## Legislation and guidance

Access to Health Records Act 1990 UK Government TSO Norwich
Access to Medical Reports Act 1998 UK Government TSO Norwich
Faculty of Occupational Medicine (2018) *Guidance on Ethics for Occupational Health Practice*. FOM, London
GMC (2017). *GMC Supplementary Guidance. Confidentiality: Disclosing Information for Insurance, Employment and Similar Purposes*. GMC, London
GMC (2019). *Confidentiality, Revised to Include the GDPR*. GMC, London
Kloss D (2020). *Occupational Health Law*, 6th edn, Chapter 3. Wiley-Blackwell, Oxford

# Freedom of Information Act 2000

The Freedom of Information Act 2000 provided for public access to information held by, or on behalf of, publicly funded bodies in England, Wales, and Northern Ireland. Similar legislation applies in Scotland: the Freedom of Information (Scotland) Act 2002. These pieces of legislation were intended to create a culture of openness among public bodies. The Freedom of Information Act 2000 created the ICO whose role is to enforce the act. The Act was subsequently updated by the Environmental Information Regulations 2004. In Scotland the Scottish Information Commissioner fulfils the ICO's role.

## Definitions

- *Public authorities include*:
  - central government
  - local authorities
  - police
  - prison service
  - health authorities
  - NHS GPs, dentists, opticians, and pharmacists
  - educational establishments

## Main requirements

- All public bodies must produce a publication scheme (approved by the Information Commissioner) stating what information they routinely make available (e.g. annual reports, committee minutes) and how to obtain it
- An information request may be made verbally, in writing, or by email
- Public bodies must respond promptly to such information requests and in any event within 20 days
- *There are 23 exemptions from disclosure in the Act. Some are absolute while others are qualified exemptions*:
  - information covered by an absolute exemption includes personal information
  - information covered by a qualified exemption may only be withheld where the public interest is best served by withholding it. The presumption is that disclosure is preferred
- Where a public body refuses to release information application may be made to the Information Commissioner to review the decision. Where the ICO disagrees with the decision not to release information, the public body can be required to release the information
- Where an individual or a public body disputes the ICO's decision, an appeal can be made to the Information Tribunal
- Failure to comply with a decision of the Information Tribunal may be held to be contempt of court

## Legislation and guidance


- HMSO (2000). *Freedom of Information Act 2000*, Chapter 36. Stationery Office, London
- HMSO (2002). *Freedom of Information (Scotland) Act 2002*, asp 13. Stationery Office, London
- HMSO (2004). *The Environmental Information Regulations 2004*. Stationery Office, London
- Information Commissioner's Office. Regularly updated. Information Commissioners Office Cheshire. Available at: http://www.ico.gov.uk/
- Scottish Information Commissioner. Regularly updated Scottish Information Commissioner's Office St Andrews Scotland. Available at: http://www.itspublicknowledge.info/

# Chapter 28

# Environmental legislation

# Environmental Protection Act 1990

The Environmental Protection Act 1990 aimed to improve control of pollution arising from industrial processes by integrating pollution control. It represents the most recent in a series of laws that began with the Alkali Acts in the nineteenth century. This legislation covers air, water, and soil pollution, and also covers the release of genetically modified organisms. The Act gave the Secretary of State power to prescribe substances subject to controls on their release into the environment. The Act was subsequently updated by the Environment Act 1995, which created the Environment Agency (EA) (England and Wales) (see ➔ p. 622, The Environment Agency) and its equivalent Scottish body, the Scottish Environment Protection Agency.

## Definitions

- *Pollution*: of the environment means release into air, water, or land of any substance capable of causing harm to living organisms, e.g. humans
- *Release*: includes emissions into the air, discharge of substances into water, and the disposal, deposit, or keeping of substances in or on land
- *Waste*: includes any scrap material, effluent, or unwanted substance
- *Controlled waste*: means household, industrial, or commercial waste
- *Special waste*: is controlled waste that is so dangerous to keep, treat, or dispose of, that special provision is required for dealing with it

## Main requirements

- No one may carry out a prescribed process unless authorized by the enforcing authority (Regulation 6)
- When carrying out a prescribed process, the operator should employ the best available techniques, not entailing excessive cost ('Batneec') to prevent the release of prescribed substances, to minimize any release, or to render harmless any substance released (Regulation 7)
- If a prescribed process has not been carried out for >12 months, the enforcing authority may revoke the authorization (Regulation 12)
- If a prescribed process is carried out in breach of its authorization, an enforcement notice can be served
- If there is an imminent risk of serious pollution, a prohibition notice may be served
- An appeal against an enforcement or prohibition notice may be made to the Secretary of State
- The enforcing authorities are required to maintain a register of prescribed processes available for inspection by the public (Regulation 20)
- Any organization that carries on a prescribed process without authorization, fails to notify a transfer of undertaking involving a prescribed process, or fails to comply with a prohibition or enforcement notice is liable on conviction to a fine not exceeding £50,000 and/or 6 months' imprisonment, or if convicted on indictment to an unlimited fine and/or imprisonment for up to 2 years
- Directors, senior managers, the company secretary, or similar officers can also be prosecuted if the offence was committed with their consent or connivance or was attributable to their neglect

- Disposal of controlled waste is prohibited (Regulation 33) except in accordance with a Waste Management License. This excludes storage of household waste in domestic premises
- Transport by road of controlled waste, except in accordance with the controls imposed by a Waste Management License, is an offence
- Regulation 34 creates a duty of care for any person or organization producing, carrying, keeping, or disposing of controlled waste, to prevent the escape of waste from his control, and on transfer of the waste to ensure the transfer is only made to an authorized person
- A written description of the waste must be provided to the waste collection authority or a holder of a waste management license
- Where controlled waste is deposited on land in breach of the regulations, the enforcing authority may require the occupier to remove the waste. Where the occupier did not deposit the waste, the authority may remove the waste from the land

## Legislation and guidance

- Environmental Protection Act 1990, Chapter 43. Stationery Office, London
- Environment Act 1995, Chapter 25. Stationery Office, London

# The Environment Agency

## Background

- The (EA and the Scottish Environmental Protection Agency (SEPA) were created by the Environment Act 1995 and came into being in 1996
- The EA is a non-departmental public body of the Department of Environment, Food and Rural Affairs and an Assembly Sponsored Public Body of the National Assembly for Wales
- The Agency exists to protect the environment of England and Wales. It covers all of England and Wales including the land, rivers, and coastal waters
- SEPA has a similar role in Scotland to the EA south of the border

Both agencies work with the HSE in the licensing of major industrial sites under the Control of Major Accident Hazards Regulations 1999 (COMAH) (see ➲ p. 621).

## Structure of the EA

- *Supervised by a board of 12 members*:
  - eleven members are appointed by the Secretary for Environment, Food and Rural Affairs
  - one member is appointed by the National Assembly for Wales
- Managed by a Chief Executive and six directors
- Employs ~12,000 staff
- Operates through six regional offices in England and one in Wales (Environment Agency Wales) and 21 area offices

## Role of the EA

The EA is a regulatory body which has a wide remit covering issues such as the following:

- Water resources and water quality
- Flood prevention and management
- Leisure and recreation
- Navigation
- Fisheries
- Soil quality and land contamination
- Air quality and air pollution
- Waste transport and disposal
- Radioactive substances
- *Pollution prevention and control, which involves the enforcement of environmental regulations in a range of industries*:
  - agriculture
  - chemical
  - food and drink
  - power stations, fuel stores, etc.
  - metals
  - minerals, e.g. cement works
  - nuclear waste
  - radioactive substance users
  - pulp and paper
  - wood
  - waste management
  - textiles and tanneries

## Relevant legislation

Environment Act 1995, Chapter 25. Stationery Office, London. Available at: http://www.opsi.gov.uk/acts/acts1995/Ukpga_19950025_En_1.htm

# Control of Major Accident Hazards Regulations 2015

## Purpose

COMAH implements the European Commission's Seveso III directive on the control of installations that may pose a major accident hazard. The aims of the regulations are:

- To identify sites where a major accident may occur
- To put in place control measures to prevent such an accident
- To mitigate the impact of an accident should it occur
- COMAH 2015 repealed and replaced COMAH 1999

## Application

The COMAH regulations apply to any lower tier or top tier site as defined in the regulations.

## Definitions

- *Competent authority*: because of the overlap between workplace health and safety and environmental protection, the competent authority for the COMAH regulations comprises:
    - HSE and the Environmental Protection Agency in England and Wales
    - HSE and SEPA in Scotland
- *Major accident*: means an uncontrolled event at a site covered by the COMAH regulations that lead to serious danger to people or the environment, and involves an agent defined in the regulations

## Main requirements

- Operators shall take all measures needed to prevent accidents (Regulation 4), and to limit the harm caused by any accident that may occur, by reducing risk to a level as low as is reasonably practicable
- All operators must produce a major accident prevention policy and keep it up to date (Regulation 5)
- Operators of new or planned installations must notify the competent authority as soon as possible, to allow planning of assessments
- Operators of existing installations must notify the competent authority if a significant change is anticipated, such as an increase in dangerous substances on site, a change to processes, or closure of the site
- Where an installation is a top-tier site, its operator must prepare a safety report (Regulation 7) demonstrating that all necessary measures to prevent an accident have been taken
- *The safety report must be revised*:
    - every 5 years (Regulation 8)
    - when there is a change in the safety management system
    - when new knowledge dictates that a review is needed
    - COMAH 2015 increased requirements for public information including a duty for lower tier establishments to provide public information

## Legislation and guidance

- HSE (2015). *A Guide to the Control of Major Accident Hazards Regulations 2015*. HSE Books, Sudbury

# Environmental impact assessment

European Council Directive 97/11/EC on the assessment of the effects of certain public and private projects on the environment came into force in 1999. It extended the range of development projects for which Environmental Impact Assessment (EIA) was required under Council Directive No. 85/337/EEC. A range of planning regulations has since implemented the amended directive in the UK, and The Town and Country Planning (EIA) Regulations 2010 and its Scottish equivalent are expected to come in to force in 2011.

## Purpose

- To ensure that the planning authority, when giving consent for a project, is aware of any likely environmental impacts of the development
- EIA is a procedure for systematically assessing the environmental impacts of land use change (development), including ↑ noise, ↑ pollution, ↑ traffic, etc. It is a multidisciplinary activity that requires a range of expertise, as each project raises different issues
- EIA may indicate the ways in which a project can be modified to ↓ or eliminate adverse impacts, ideally by designing out the nuisance at source

## Application

- Planners may require developers to prepare an EIA prior to giving *development consent*. It is the developer who then commissions and pays for the EIA
- All Schedule 1 projects must have an EIA carried out. Schedule 1 includes major hazards such as oil refineries and nuclear power stations, as well as motorways, waste incineration plants, and large quarries
- Schedule 2 projects are only required to have an EIA if the project is likely to cause significant environmental impact[1]

## Definitions

- EIA, when applied to the environmental impact of government or other public policy, is termed *Strategic Environmental Assessment*
- *Development consent*: the decision of the competent planning authority to allow the development to proceed
- The *competent authority* is the public body giving the primary consent for a particular project
- *Economic impact assessment* (cost-benefit analysis) forms part of an EIA in some circumstances
- *Health Impact Assessment*: the requirements for this component of an EIA in the UK vary depending on the specific development, but broadly cover two areas:
  - social effects of a development (e.g. access to amenities from a new bridge). These can be beneficial or deleterious, and will embrace quality of life as well as more direct outcomes
  - adverse effects of the development (e.g. hospital admissions due to factory emissions)

1 See Town and Country Planning (Environmental Impact Assessment) (England and Wales) Regulations 1999 for a full list of Schedule 1 and 2 projects.

## Main requirements

- *EIA can be*:
  - prospective for a new development
  - retrospective for an existing situation
- In some cases, prospective assessments should include a monitoring component to quantify the *actual impact* and compare that with the *estimate of impact* made in the EIA

*Quantification of impacts*

Should be attempted wherever possible. Use established effects size coefficients, as has been done for air pollution, applying these to the specific population at risk.

Bear in mind the dangers of applying health data gathered from one population to a different population.

## Relevant guidance and legislation

This is not an exhaustive list of the regulations relating to EIA.

- Town and Country Planning (EIA) (England and Wales) Regulations 1999
- The EIA (Scotland) Regulations 1999
- Planning (Environmental Impact Assessment) Regulations (Northern Ireland) 1999

# Section 6

# Occupational hygiene

# Chapter 29

# Occupational hygiene overview

# Role and function of occupational hygienists

## Introduction

Occupational hygienists have a role in identification, evaluation, and management of work-related hazards. Occupational hygiene is one of the core disciplines within the occupational health team.

## Definition of occupational hygiene

The British Occupational Hygiene Society (BOHS) defines occupational hygiene as the discipline of protecting worker health by controlling workplace hazards that can cause harm. It also helps in maintaining worker well-being and safeguarding the community at large.

Through science and engineering, occupational hygienists identify, evaluate and control exposure to workplace hazards that may include chemicals, dust, fumes, noise, radiation, vibration and extreme temperatures, to name a few. The Faculty of Occupational Hygiene within BOHS develops and maintains the professional standards of occupational hygienists.

## Scope and functions

- *Hazard identification*:
  - anticipate and recognize health hazards that may result from operational processes, work tasks/method, equipment, tools, and the work environment
  - identify the location and nature of hazards and number exposed
  - understand the possible routes of entry of hazardous agents into the human body, and the potential health effects of such agents
- *Exposure evaluation*:
  - evaluate work processes and methods of work so as to understand exposure pathways and factors affecting the level of exposure
  - design suitable sampling strategies
  - assess workers' exposure to hazards including exposure measurement (personal or static) and interpretation of data
- *Management/control of hazards*:
  - evaluate effectiveness of administrative, organizational, and engineering controls used to minimize exposure to hazards
  - advise on risk control strategies including prioritization and ranking of risks
  - advise on the selection of risk management measures
  - understand the legal framework for occupational hygiene practice
  - educate, train, inform, and advise persons at all levels in all aspects of hazard and risk communication
  - record findings and review
- *Environmental risk management*: recognize agents and factors that may have environmental impact; understand the need to integrate occupational hygiene practice with environmental protection

## Code of ethics and qualifications

BOHS code of ethics are available at: https://www.bohs.org/app/uploads/2020/11/BOHS-Code-of-Ethics.pdf. 2020

# Classification of occupational hazards

Hazards in the working environment can be divided into five main categories (Table 29.1). These may produce an immediate or delayed response dictated largely by their inherent characteristics and the intensity and frequency of exposure.

**Table 29.1** Types of occupational hazard

| Hazard category | Examples |
|---|---|
| Chemical | Solids (dusts), liquids, fibres, gases, vapours, fumes, mists, and smoke |
| Physical | Noise, vibration, ionizing and non-ionizing radiation, extremes of temperature, humidity, pressure, electricity, illumination, and visibility |
| Biological | Viruses, bacteria, fungi, protozoa, nematodes |
| Ergonomics and mechanical | Frequent loading/lifting, repetitive action, poor / awkward posture, excessive force<br>Strains/sprains, cuts, shearing injuries, crushing injuries, puncturing (object penetrates body), entanglement (loose clothes caught in machinery) |
| Psychosocial and organizational | Excessive workloads, conflicting demands, poor environmental conditions (excessive noise, poor lighting), poorly managed organizational change, psychological harassment, job insecurity, lack of involvement in decision making, and poor communication |

# Use of occupational hygiene exposure data

Exposure monitoring may be conducted for the following reasons:

- To identify hazards
- To demonstrate compliance with occupational exposure limits (OEL)
- As part of health risk assessments/investigations
- When conducting epidemiological studies
- When designing and selecting appropriate control measures
- When assessing the effectiveness of control measures
- To identify individuals for inclusion in health surveillance programmes
- Litigation and insurance purposes

## Hazard identification

- Information sources/techniques include inventories of materials and material safety data sheets, understanding processes and work environments, and observing actual work practices
- This may not enable the identification of all hazards, particularly those generated from non-routine activities or as a result of chemical processing, e.g. thermal degradation
- Exposure monitoring can provide useful information on the location and spread of contaminants in the workplace

## Monitoring compliance

- The most common reason for sampling is to determine whether the exposure of an individual or group of individuals exceeds an OEL
- In the case of hazardous substances, monitoring is necessary in the following circumstances as defined in the Control of Substances Hazardous to Health (COSHH) Regulations 2002 (amended):
  - when an initial monitoring exercise is necessary to reach an informed decision/judgement about the risks
  - when failure or deterioration of the control measures could result in a serious health effect because of the toxicity of the contaminant, or the extent of potential exposure, or both
  - when measurements are necessary to ensure that workplace exposure limits are not exceeded, and always in the case of the substance or process specified in schedule 5 of COSHH (exposure to vinyl chloride monomer and chromium acid mist from electroplating tanks)
  - as an additional check on the effectiveness of the control measures provided
  - when any changes occur in the conditions affecting employees' exposure, which could mean that adequate control is no longer being maintained, e.g. changes in work methods or systems of work, increase in quantity of substances used

## Standard setting

Occupational exposure data are used to draw and understand dose–response relationships when deriving OELs for different hazards. Dose–response data are used to determine the no observed adverse effect level (NOAEL). The measured exposure level for the hazard is compared with its derived NOAEL to determine whether it presents a risk to health for defined workplace scenarios (see ➲ Chapter 33).

## Epidemiological study

Ideally, occupational epidemiological studies should include exposure estimates of all employees to essentially all contaminants over all of the time period of the study. Data on the degree of exposure will help the epidemiologist to identify a dose–response relationship, which can aid the confirmation of a causal relationship between an agent and a disease. Various surrogates for exposure have also been used, such as job title, which is crude and can lead to misclassification of employees and exposure categories. Retrospective exposure assessment can be impaired by recall bias, and by poor quality or missing data. Prospective exposure assessments may be hindered by data which is not representative of the whole study population.

## Monitoring the effectiveness of controls

Control measures such as engineering need to be assessed for their continued effectiveness. This can be achieved by comparing the performance of the control measure against its design specification, e.g. for ventilation systems (velocities, pressure, and flow rates) or by monitoring changes in exposure level for the pollutant that the system is designed to control/minimize (see ➲ Chapter 32, Prevention and control of exposure).

## Informing the process of litigation

Exposure data may be used in medico-legal cases. The relevance and reliability of the measured data may have an impact for both the plaintiff and the defendant.

## Further reading

American Industrial Hygiene Society (AIHA). Available at: https://www.aiha.org/
Australian Institute of Occupational Hygienists (AIOH). Available at: https://www.aioh.org.au/
British Occupational Hygiene Society (BOHS). Available at: http://www.bohs.org/

# Chapter 30

# Monitoring exposure

# Sample types for workplace pollutants

Measurement of exposure in occupational hygiene normally involves collecting a sample from the breathing zone using personal sampling equipment. However, in some cases air-sampling techniques alone may not provide a reliable indicator of exposure, e.g. where there is potential for skin absorption or ingestion, or where respiratory protective equipment is used to control exposure (see ➲ p. 686, Selecting respiratory equipment and see ➲ p. 657, Biological monitoring). Examples of sampling instrumentation for airborne pollutant are shown in Chapter 2, Chemical hazards (see ➲ p. 45).

## Monitor

Monitoring techniques for airborne pollutants can be divided into several categories.

- *Instantaneous monitoring (direct reading)*: provide read time data, may be used to detect explosive concentrations of solvents, oxygen deficiency, or physical hazards such as noise and light levels. The instrument may be linked to an alarm device or data downloaded to a computer to examine the exposure profile with time (see Fig. 30.1)
- *Integrated monitoring*: provides a single time-weighted average (TWA) concentration over a defined sampling period, i.e. averaging peaks and troughs, e.g. when sampling personal exposure for compliance purposes.
- *Personal sampling*: involves the placement of a monitoring device within the individual's 'breathing zone' (approximately 20–30 cm from the nose/mouth) to sample the microenvironment from which the person breathes
- *Static (area or fixed) samples*: can be taken to check the effectiveness of process controls, to identify emission sources, to determine background concentrations in the work environment (mapping), and in some cases as a surrogate for personal sampling
- *Active and passive monitoring*: active monitoring techniques involve use of a sampling pump to pull airborne pollutant through a sampling device, while the passive technique relies on molecular diffusion, e.g. diffusion badges for sampling airborne pollutants
- *Bulk samples*: large volume of air, liquids, or settled particulates collected, e.g. for qualitative analysis to determine the nature/composition of pollutant

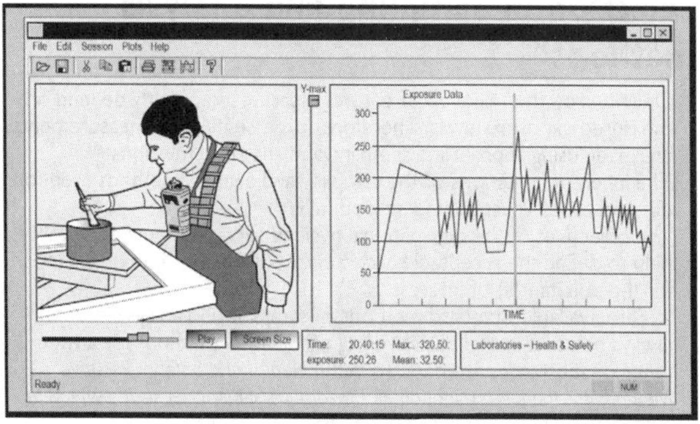


**Fig. 30.1** Video exposure monitoring. Combining a direct reading monitor with a video to examine the relationship between work practices and exposure.

# Selection of sampling and analysis methods

- Decisions on the selection of control measures frequently depend on measured exposure levels. Therefore, it is essential that measurements are made using appropriate sampling and analytical methods
- The inherent limitations of the sampling and analysis methods used for data collection must be understood fully
- The objectives of the occupational hygiene survey and its design will help to define the acceptable accuracy, precision, and limit of detection for the pollutant(s) of interest
- Where available, standard methods of sampling and analysis should always be used. In the UK, sampling and analysis methods for a wide range of substances are detailed in the *Health and Safety Executive Methods for the Determination of Hazardous Substances* series which are available on line at: http://www.hse.gov.uk/pubns/mdhs
- The International Standard Organization, the European Committee for Standardization, and various national bodies, e.g. the US National Institute for Occupational Safety and Health, also publish methods for the measurement of workplace contaminants
- *In the absence of a recommended reference sampling method, the following factors should be considered when selecting an appropriate method*:
  - nature of the pollutants (gases, vapours, mists, fibres, particles, etc.) to be collected and the stability of the sampling medium
  - compatibility of the sampling medium with the subsequent analytical technique, e.g. gas chromatography, atomic absorption spectrometry, X-ray diffraction
  - capacity and collection efficiency of the sampling medium
  - intrinsic safety of the sampling equipment, its ease of use, and portability for personal sampling

## Analytical definition of terms

- *Specificity*:[1] the ability of the assay to measure one particular substance in the presence of another substance in the sample
- *Sensitivity*:[3] smallest amount of substance in a sample that can be accurately measured by an assay
- *Accuracy*: difference between the measurements and the true or correct value for the quantity measured
- *Precision*: closeness of agreement between the results obtained by applying the method several times under prescribed conditions. Precision can be expressed by the standard deviation
- *Limit of detection*: the smallest amount of a substance that can be reliably measured by the instrument which is distinguishable from the background

1, 3 The definitions of sensitivity and specificity are those used in occupational hygiene practice and differ from those used in epidemiological surveys.

## Minimum sampling volume

When sampling it is important to ensure that a sufficient quantity of sample is collected to enable the analyst (laboratory) to determine the amount of contaminant accurately. The minimum sampling volume (time) can be calculated from the following equation:

$$\text{Min. sampling vol. } (m^3) = (10 \times \text{LOD (mg)}/\text{OEL } (mg/m^3)).$$

LOD is for analytical technique.

## Sampling and analysis errors and corrections

When comparing measured exposure data with relevant occupational exposure limits (OELs) it is important to consider the following:

- Instrumental and analytical errors
- Potential for contamination of sampling device
- Sampling efficiency of collecting devices and desorption efficiency of solid adsorbents
- Ensure that the measurements and OELs are expressed at standard temperature and pressure. For example, as the exposure limits are based on a temperature of 20°C and a pressure of 760 mmHg, the concentrations of any measured pollutant not measured at these values should be corrected as follows:

$$C_{corr} = C(760/P)(T/293),$$

where $C_{corr}$ is the corrected concentration, $P$ (mmHg) is the actual pressure of air samples, and $T$ (K) is the absolute temperature of air sampled

## Quality assurance (laboratory analysis)

When sending samples to analytical laboratories for analysis (after an exposure monitoring survey), e.g. analysis of sorbent tubes for solvents include:

- 'Field blanks' for analysis. 'Field blanks' are samples taken to the worksite and treated and handled in the same way as other samples with the exception that no air is drawn through the sampling media
- Samples that are 'spiked' with a known amount of the substance(s) sampled in the workplace

For information on practical methods for sampling hazards (chemical, physical, and biological agents) in the workplace, see further reading.

## Further reading

Cherrie J, Coggins MA, Semple S. (2021). *Monitoring for Health Hazards at Work*, 5th edn. Wiley-Blackwell, Oxford.

# Workplace exposure survey types

## Three stages

The design of the exposure monitoring programme will be strongly influenced by the aim of the survey. The HSE has produced an outline for monitoring exposure, which includes three stages (initial appraisal, basic survey, and detailed survey). These are summarized here. The structured approach is summarized in Fig. 30.2.

*Initial appraisal*

This step helps to establish the need for, and the extent of, monitoring. Information is required on the following factors:

- The substance to which individuals are exposed
- The hazardous and physical properties of the substance
- The airborne form of the substance
- The process or operations where exposure is likely to occur
- The number, type, and position of sources from which the substance is released
- The groups of employees who are most likely to be exposed
- The pattern and duration of exposure, including exposure routes (inhalation, dermal, ingestion)
- Actual work practices
- The means by which the release of the substance is controlled
- Whether personal protective equipment is used and its effectiveness
- The OELs for the substances involved

*Basic survey*

This step involves identifying and monitoring exposure of employees who are likely to be at significant risk. The exposure is estimated using either semiquantitative or validated laboratory-based sampling and analysis methods. The survey also includes an indication of the efficiency of process and engineering controls.

*Detailed survey*

This is conducted when:

- The extent and pattern of exposure cannot be confidently assessed by a basic survey
- Exposure is highly variable between employees doing similar tasks
- Carcinogenic substances or respiratory sensitizers are involved
- *The initial appraisal and basic survey suggest that*:
    - TWA personal exposure may be very close to the OEL
    - costs of additional control measures cannot be justified without the evidence of the extent of exposure variability
    - specific non-routine tasks are undertaken which require further investigation

## Prioritization of sampling needs

Having determined the need and reasons for sampling, it may be necessary to make an a priori prioritization of contaminants and/or processes to be assessed. The following factors should be considered when prioritizing sampling:

- Number of individuals potentially exposed to the substance
- *Toxicity of the substance(s)*: acute and chronic effects

- Quantities (substance) used over some arbitrary reference period
- Pattern and estimate of exposure levels
- Existence and effectiveness of control measures used to minimize exposure
- Reported symptoms (health surveillance programmes)
- Findings from previous risk assessments

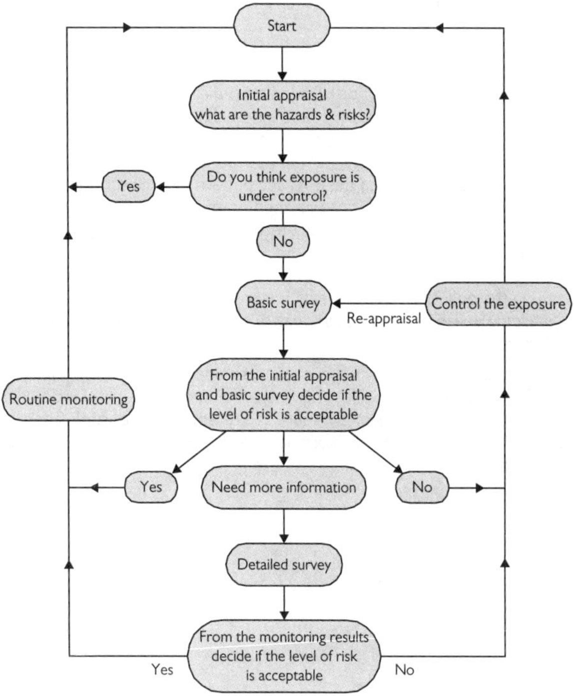


**Fig. 30.2** Structured approach for assessing exposure to substances hazardous to health

Reproduced from HSG173. HSE Books under Open Government Licence 3.0

## Exposure variability

Exposure to hazards (e.g. chemicals, noise, vibration.) in the workplace can vary both within and between individuals, days, shifts, etc. In order to obtain representative exposure data for risk assessment these variables need to be understood and considered carefully in the design of occupational hygiene sampling surveys.

- *Factors which influence the release and airborne concentrations of substances include*:
    - physical and chemical properties of the substance
    - number of sources
    - rate, speed, and duration of release from each source
    - variation in the process, job, and tasks carried out
    - dispersion and mixing of agent in the workplace
    - ambient work conditions (air movement, temperature, humidity)
- Employees may influence the level and pattern of exposure by their individual work practice (posture, method of work) and attitudes towards risks (use of personal protective equipment) and systems of work
- Identification of variations of exposure within days is of importance when the pollutant has potential to cause acute health effects
- Seasonal variations in exposure may occur due to differing production demands

It is important to document circumstances under which the exposure occurs. This information enables the interpretation of the data and understanding the determinants of exposure and reasons for exposure variability. Table 30.1 lists the types of information to be collected during exposure measurement.

**Table 30.1** Information to be collected during exposure measurement

| Category | Information |
|---|---|
| Strategy | Reason for collecting measurements<br>Worst case or randomly chosen worker<br>Task-specific or full-shift based<br>Duration of sample<br>Sampling and analytical method |
| Location | Type of industry<br>Department<br>Number of employees in the department |
| Worker | Personal identification code<br>Gender, age<br>Worker behaviour (e.g. tasks performed)<br>Personal protective equipment used<br>Machines and tools used<br>Pace of work<br>Degree of training<br>Mobile or stationary work |
| Process | Level of automation<br>Continuous or intermittent<br>Control or exposure-reducing measures |
| Environment | Indoors or outdoors<br>Temperature, atmospheric pressure, relative humidity<br>Weather conditions (for outdoor work)<br>Local and/or general ventilation<br>Room volume (e.g. confined space < 50 m3)<br>Day or night shift |
| Agents | Likely source (e.g. composition of raw materials)<br>Physical characteristics (e.g. particles, vapours, mists, fibres, etc.) |

Source: Based on Kromhout H (2002). Design of measurement strategies for workplace exposures. *Occup Environ Med*, 59, 286, 349–54.

# Designing exposure monitoring programmes

Occupational exposure monitoring programmes should address the following questions:

- Whose exposure should be measured?
- Where to collect the sample?
- When to measure?
- How long to sample?
- Number of samples?
- How often?
- How to interpret the data?

When evaluating these questions, consider the following points:

- For compliance purposes, sampling can be carried out on a group basis where groups of employees are performing identical or similar tasks and are exposed to similar risks to health, i.e. homogenous groups
- For the assessment of human health risks personal sampling is preferred, as this is most likely to reflect the individual's exposure. In fact, assigned OELs are specific to personal exposure only
- When locating personal samplers consideration must be given to source(s) of exposure, work tasks, and individual work practices. Studies have shown up to twofold differences in dust level for samples placed equidistant from the nose/mouth on each lapel
- Start-up procedures at the beginning of the shift and end-of-shift such as clean-down as well as unplanned events (chemical spillage) can make an important contribution to daily exposures
- When sampling exposure to demonstrate compliance with OELs, the duration over which the sample should be taken is dictated by the reference period of the OEL. In the UK, OELs are expressed over two reference periods, i.e. 15 minutes and 8 hours. Given the variability of occupational exposure data, one or two samples taken on one day may be insufficient to reach reliable exposure estimates. The sample size requirements can be related to closeness of measured mean personal exposure levels to OEL for the contaminant of interest (Table 30.2)
- The decision on the frequency of monitoring should be based on factors such as reliability of controls, closeness of exposure levels with limits (Table 30.3), changes in work practices, work equipment, work environment, and reported symptoms
- Exposure data are usually log normally distributed and can be expressed as a range, arithmetic mean, geometric mean and geometric standard deviation, or as a log probability plot to estimate percentiles points

**Table 30.2** Sample size requirements for testing mean exposure from log normal distribution of 8-hour TWAs (95% significance and 90% power)

| | Sample size, n | | | | |
|---|---|---|---|---|---|
| Mean/OEL | SD = 1.5 | SD = 2.0 | SD = 2.5 | SD = 3.0 | SD = 3.5 |
| 0.1 | 2 | 6 | 13 | 21 | 30 |
| 0.25 | 3 | 10 | 19 | 30 | 43 |
| 05 | 7 | 21 | 41 | 67 | 96 |
| 0.75 | 2 | 82 | 164 | 266 | 384 |
| 1.25 | 25 | 82 | 164 | 266 | 384 |
| 1.50 | 7 | 21 | 41 | 67 | 96 |
| 2.00 | 2 | 6 | 11 | 17 | 24 |
| 3.00 | 1 | 2 | 3 | 5 | 6 |

SD, geometric standard deviation.

**Table 30.3** Minimum frequency of regular monitoring

| Shifts to be sampled (per 10 employees) | Exposure/occupational exposure |
|---|---|
| 1/month | 1–2 |
| 1/quarter | 0.5–1 or 2–4 |
| 1/annum | 0.1–0.5 or 4–20 |
| None | <0.1 or >20 |

# Data interpretation 1: Calculating time-weighted average concentrations

Airborne concentrations of substances are calculated using the following equation:

$$C = M / V,$$

where $C$ is the concentration (mg/m$^3$), $M$ is the mass of substance (mg), and $V$ the volume of air sampled (m$^3$).

## Calculating 8-hour TWA

If exposure is measured by collecting a number of samples over an 8-hour period, then the 8-hour TWA is calculated by multiplying each exposure concentration by the corresponding exposure duration,

$$8\text{h TWA} = \left(C_1 \times T_1 + C_2 \times T_2 .|.|.|.CnTn\right) / 8$$

where $C$ (mg/m$^3$) is the concentration and $T$ the time (h).

*Example*

A machinist in a wood workshop works an 8-hour shift. A personal sample was taken using an IOM sampling head connected to a sampling pump for 2 hours. The sampling pump was calibrated at a flow rate of 2.0 l/min. The difference (gain) in the weight of the sampling filter before and after sampling was 5 mg.

Personal sampling was conducted for two further periods on the same day, i.e. 2 hours and 4 hours which produced TWA concentrations of 6.0 and 2.0 mg/m$^3$, respectively.

*Question*

- What is the 2-hour TWA personal dust concentration for the first sampling period?
- What is the 8-hour TWA?

*Calculation*

- 2-hour TWA =
  - mass (mg)/volume (m$^3$)
  - 5.0 mg/0.24 m$^3$
  - 21.0 mg/m$^3$
- 8-hour TWA = (21.0 × 2.0) + (6 × 2) + (2.0 × 4.0) = 8.0 mg/m$^3$

## Period of work >8 hours: Adjustment of OEL

- The use of unusual work schedules is now fairly common. Consequently, workers will not experience occupational exposure over the traditional 8 hours per shift, 5 days a week, which is that used in setting OELs
- A work-shift longer than 8 hours will result in additional exposure and also a shorter period of recovery before the next insult. This may not be a problem with substances with very short half-lives. However, the body burden for substances with half-lives approaching or exceeding 16 hours (the period of recovery for an 8-hour working day) may rise over the week/shift period

- A number of sophisticated models utilizing pharmacokinetics have been put forward to adjust for exposures greater than the reference period of 8 hours. Unfortunately, they require a great deal of substance-specific information, which is very rarely available. A more simplistic equation is given here which can be used to adjust the 8-hour OEL:

$$\text{OEL multiplication factor} = 8/H\,[(24-H)/16],$$

where $H$ is the number of hours worked.

▶▶ Note that the formula does not apply to continuous 24-hour exposure, work periods of <7–8 hours/days or 35 hours/weeks, or concentration-dependent acute toxicants.

# Data interpretation 2: Exposure to chemical mixtures

Occupational exposure seldom involves exposure to a single substance. Exposure to mixtures is of concern in both measuring exposure and estimating their biological significance. Potential adverse effects may be greater than, less than, or equal to the sum of the effects of the individual components of the mixture.

## Evaluating exposure to mixtures

- The majority of the substances encountered in occupational settings are assigned an individual workplace exposure limit (WEL). Some WELs relate to substances commonly encountered as complex mixtures, e.g. welding, rubber, and solder fumes
- When individuals are exposed to mixtures, the first step is to ensure adequate control of each individual substance. It may then be necessary to assess whether further control is needed so as to counteract any increased risk due to presence of other substances in the mixture. Interaction should be considered in the following order:
  - synergistic effect: occurs when the combined effect of the two agents is greater than the effect of each agent given alone. Antagonistic effects occur when the combined effect of two agents is less than the sum of the effects of each agent given separately
  - additive effect: is an example of a non-interaction, i.e. the combined effect of two agents is equal to the sum of the two effects of each agent given alone
  - independent effects: i.e. the other components do not add, enhance, or diminish the effect of the most active component, e.g. where each component acts on a different organ in the body and the magnitude of each effect is not influenced by the other effects
- When there is reason to believe that the effects of constituents are additive, and where the WELs are based on the same health effects, the mixed exposure should be assessed using the formula:

$$C_1/L_1 + C_2/L_2 + C_3/L_3 + \ldots < 1.0,$$

where $C_1$, $C_2$, etc. are the airborne TWA concentrations and $L_1$, $L_2$, etc., are the corresponding WELs

# Dermal exposure

Workers may be exposed to hazardous substances by inhalation, ingestion, and contact with the skin or eyes. Exposure by the dermal route may result in local (skin irritation, non-melanoma skin cancer) as well as systemic effects (neurotoxicity, hepatotoxicity).

- *Dermal exposure to chemicals occurs in a number of jobs, examples include*:
  - agricultural workers (pesticide sprayers)
  - painters (solvents)
  - hairdressers (dyes)
  - engineers (metalworking fluids)
  - construction workers (cements, solvents, resins)
  - cleaners (solvents, skin irritants)
- Wet-work is an important cause of irritant contact dermatitis
- Chemicals diffuse through the stratum corneum because of the concentration gradient between the skin contamination layer (SCL) (mixture of sweat, sebum, and other material on the skin) and the tissue around the peripheral blood supply
- Most gases/vapours are not taken up by the skin in significant quantities as the concentration gradient is too low
- Volatile substances partly evaporate from the skin before being absorbed
- Most solids must dissolve in the SCL before they can be taken up via the skin
- *The mass (surrogate for concentration) of a substance absorbed through the skin depends on the following properties of the substances, which are used to predict the permeability coefficient of the substance (Kp)*:
  - solubility in oils and water
  - chemical structure
  - and molecular weight
- Disruption of the skin barrier, e.g. caused by dermatitis, increases absorption of chemicals or particles
- High molecular weight liquids (>500 Dal) with an octanol–water partition coefficient <–1 or >4 are unlikely to permeate skin
- *Dermal exposure assessment should include information on the following*:
  - substance type
  - intensity (concentration or mass of substance on skin) of exposure
  - duration and frequency of exposure
- Occlusion of the exposure site by clothing or personal protective equipment may ↑ absorption through the skin.

### Skin notation 'Sk'

Many national authorities publish occupational exposure limits and assign a 'skin notation' to substances when they judge that dermal exposure may make a significant contribution to total exposure. List of chemicals (more than 100) assigned 'skin notation' can be found in the HSE guide note EH40.

Examples of Hazard Statements relevant to dermal exposure include H312 (harmful in contact with skin), H314 (causes severe skin burns), H315 (cause skin irritation), and H317 (may cause an allergic skin reaction). See ➲ Appendix 1 for health hazard statements.

# Conceptual model of dermal exposure

- Dermal exposure can be conceptualized according to a number of compartments and transfer routes (Fig. 30.3)
- Key transfer routes depend on the particular work situation, e.g. someone handling pesticide in a container may have direct splashes onto the SCL and the outer clothing contaminant layer from the source, together with direct contact of these layers with surfaces contaminated by pesticides
- Use of this conceptual model can help in the analysis of the main routes and compartments for different workplace exposure scenarios

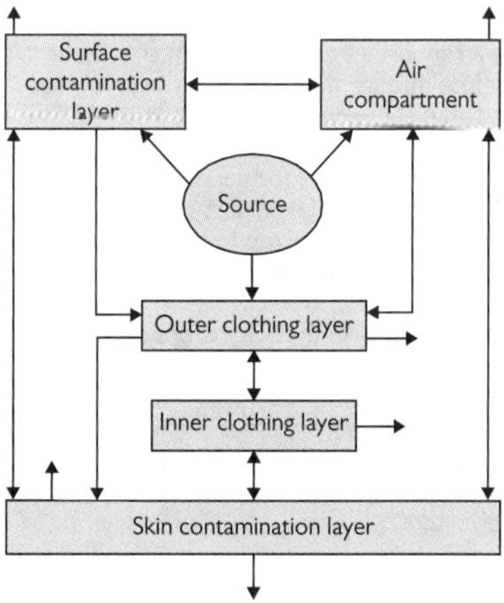


**Fig. 30.3** Conceptual model of dermal exposure

# Dermal: Exposure measurement and estimating uptake

## Assessing the contribution of skin exposure to systemic uptake

Several methods are used to measure dermal exposure, although the results from these techniques are not directly comparable:

- Intercepting contaminants before they land on the SCL or clothing
- Removal of contaminants from the SCL after exposure
- *In situ* methods, e.g. use of fluorescent tracer compounds
- *Biological monitoring*, see ➲ p. 657

## Qualitative assessment of dermal exposure

To investigate skin exposure, collect good descriptive information:

- Record contact with contaminated surfaces (number of contacts, area of SCL in contact, duration of each contact)
- Evidence of splash (liquids) or powder (solids) on surfaces
- Large particles/droplets that may impact on worker or work surfaces
- Type of clothing worn (note visible contamination), glove type, whether gloves are worn continuously, reuse of gloves

► Videos are useful in analysing worker behaviour and dermal exposure

## Interception methods

*Patch sampling*

- Widely used to sample low-volatility liquids, e.g. pesticides
- Specially constructed gauze patches are attached to workers' clothing or the skin
- Patches attached outside clothing are said to assess potential exposure
- Samples inside clothing are said to assess actual dermal exposure
- Patches are analysed to assess contaminant mass (and total body contaminant mass by multiplying the area of the body part by contaminant mass on the patch and summing overall)

*Suit sampling*

- An alternative interception sampler is the cotton 'suit sampler'
- Suit analysis gives a direct estimate of whole-body contaminant mass landing on the SCL and/or clothing

## Skin stripping

- Skin stripping is a removal technique which can assess contaminant, e.g. acrylate, jet fuel, metal, that has started to permeate skin
- Adhesive tapes are used to remove ('strip') sequential layers of stratum corneum and any contaminant residues present in the skin

## Removal techniques

- Hand washing
- Rinsing with distilled water or other liquid
- Skin wiping with moist hand wipes, dry cotton fabric, etc.

### *In situ* methods

- Fluorescent tracer methods are highly specialized research tools
- Small amounts of a fluorescent agent are added to the contaminant source
- After work the skin is imaged with ultra violet (UV) light using a video camera linked to a computer system to estimate tracer mass and hence contaminant mass

### Biological monitoring and dermal exposure

- Biological monitoring provides indirect assessment of dermal exposure, but without contextual exposure information it is of limited value
- Biological monitoring is often limited by availability of suitable method to measure the substance (parent compound or its metabolite) in the body
- Biological monitoring provides an assessment of personal protective equipment efficacy where data are available for workers with and without protective clothing

### Surface monitoring

- Surface contamination and transfer to skin play an important part in many dermal exposure situations (see Fig. 30.3)
- Surface contamination monitoring provides a measure of workplace contamination and its probable contribution to dermal exposure
- Surface wipe sampling is extensively used, but has high variability
- Techniques are similar to those described for skin removal sampling
- Estimating dermal uptake

The dermal uptake (mass) of a chemical can be estimated from the following equation:

$$U_{sk} = K_p \times C_{sk} \times A \times t$$

where $K_p$ is the permeability coefficient (cm/h), $C_{sk}$ is the concentration of the substance on the skin (mg/cm$^3$), $A$ is the area of skin exposed, and $t$ is the duration of exposure (hours).

For a defined exposure scenario the relative uptake of a substance by both the dermal and inhalation route can be compared, i.e. contributions to total boy burden. The inhalation uptake ($U_{inh}$) can be estimated from the following equation:

$$U_{inh} = C_{air} \times B \times t$$

where $C_{air}$ is the air concentration (mg/m$^3$), $B$ is the breathing rate (m$^3$/h), $t$ is the exposure time (h).

Mathematical models can be used to assess dermal exposure uptake (Cherrie 2018).

### Further information

Cherrie J, Semple S and Coggins and Coggins (2021). Dermal and inadvertent ingestion exposure. In: *Monitoring for Health Hazards at Work*, 5th edn. Wiley-Blackwell, Oxford.

Cherrie JW (2018). How to quantitatively assess dermal exposure to volatile organic compounds. *Ann Work Expos Health* 62:253–254.

# Chapter 31

# Biological monitoring

# Biological monitoring and biological effect monitoring

## Definitions

*Biological monitoring (BM)*

The measurement and assessment of hazardous substances or their metabolites in tissue, secretions, excreta, expired air, or any combination of these in exposed workers. Examples of blood and urine BM are shown in Table 31.1.

*Biological effect monitoring (BEM)*

The measurement and assessment of a biological effect (early consequences of exposure) in exposed workers, caused by absorption of chemicals. Unlike BM, BEM is not a surrogate of absorbed dose but provides evidence of exposure. Examples of BEM include measuring the following biochemical responses:

- Cholinesterase activity following an acute exposure to organophosphorus pesticides
- Urinary $\beta_2$-microglobulin proteins following exposure to cadmium
- Free erythrocyte protoporphyrin in blood or $\delta$-aminolaevulinic acid in urine for workers exposed to inorganic lead

## Benefits of BM

- Unlike air monitoring (external inhalation exposure) BM integrates exposure received from all routes
- Provides estimate of total body burden
- Evaluates the effectiveness of control measure including personal protective equipment
- May provide a biomarker for potential health effects
- Provides additional information for individual or group risk assessment
- Can provide an estimate of accumulate exposure for some substances, e.g. mercury
- BM can be a useful complementary technique to air monitoring, particularly when exposure via the dermal route is significant. Examples of chemicals which have the potential to penetrate skin include those assigned the 'Sk' notation
- Provide value information when communicating risks

## Limitations of BM

- Some sampling techniques are invasive, e.g. blood samples
- Few validated sampling and analysis methods
- Difficult to differentiate between occupational and non-occupational exposure to the same substance
- Exposure limits may not be health based, e.g. biological monitoring guidance values (BMGVs)
- Need to consider practical and ethical issues (see the following)
- Interpretation requires knowledge of confounders, e.g. smoking, drinking alcohol (see Table 31.1)

**Table 31.1** Biological (blood and urine) samples and analyses

| Biological sample | Example of parent compound | Examples of metabolite |
|---|---|---|
| Urine | *Metals*: mercury, lead (organic), cadmium, chromium, cobalt, vanadium<br>*Organic solvents*: methyl ethyl ketone, acetone, phenol, pentachlorophenol, 4,4′-methylene bis-2-chloroaniline | *Aromatic compounds:* phenylmercapturic acid (for benzene), hippuric acid (for toluene), methyl hippuric acids (for xylene), mandelic acid (for styrene and ethyl benzene), 1-hydroxypyrene (for polyaromatic hydrocarbons), di-amines (for Isocyanates) |
| | | *Chlorinated solvents*: trichloroacetic acid (for trichloroethylene, perchloroethylene, 1,1,1, trichloroethane) |
| | | *Other organic compounds*: e.g. dialkylphosphates (for organophosphorous pesticides), 2,5-hexanedione (for *n*-hexane) |
| Blood | *Metals*: inorganic lead, mercury, cadmium, cobalt<br>*Organic solvents*: aromatic compounds, e.g. toluene, styrene<br>*Chlorinated solvents*: trichloroethylene, tetrachloroethylene, 1,1,1 trichloroethylene | *Inorganic gases and chlorinated solvents*: carboxyhaemoglobin (for methylene chloride and carbon monoxide), trichloroethanol (for trichloroethylene) |

# Interpretation of data

## Units and creatinine correction

- *Blood samples*: in micrograms (µg) or milligrams per litre (mg/l).
- *Urine levels*: in milligrams per gram (mg/g) of creatinine or millimoles per millimole (mmol/mmol) of creatinine. Urine concentration can vary widely because of variation in fluid intake and sweat. Concentration/dilution effects are corrected by adjusting for specific gravity or creatinine correction. Creatinine correction is not advised if the creatinine <3 or >30 mmol/l

## Biological exposure limits

BM data are usually compared with biological exposure standards/guidelines set by national authorities. Examples include the following:

- The Threshold Limit Value (TLV)® list of the American Conference of Governmental Industrial Hygienists (ACGIH)® contains Biological Exposure Indices (BEIs®).[1] The BEI® are advisory reference values and represent the concentration of a substance that is likely to be found in the sample of a worker who was exposed through inhalation to the TLV®
- The Deutsche Forschungsgemeinschaft (DFG, the German Research Foundation) publishes an annual list of biological tolerance values (BAT). A BAT is defined as a maximum permissible quantity of a substance which does not generally impair the health of a worker
- In the UK there is a statutory requirement for monitoring lead under the Control of Lead at Work (CLAW) Regulations. Under CLAW, action and suspension levels are assigned for lead workers. However, for other substances hazardous to health, the Health and Safety Executive (HSE) has adopted non-statutory BMGVs

## Biological monitoring guidance values

- BMGVs are non-statutory. Where the BMGVs are exceeded, this indicates that work practices and controls need to be investigated. It does not imply that health effects will occur or that the WEL is exceeded. Table 31.2 gives a list of chemicals and their assigned BMGVs. For each substance, a free leaflet is available from the HSE describing the analytical method, sampling strategy, quality assurance schemes, and interpretation of results
- BMGVs are used to adequate control of exposure
- BMGVs are based on 90th percentile value of BM data from workplaces employing good occupational hygiene practices
- HSE researchers develop methods for BM and Health and Safety Laboratory (HSL) analyses biological samples. Exposure data from occupational hygiene studies of workplace are stored in HSL's Biological Monitoring Database

1 ACGIH (2021). *Threshold Limit Values for Chemical Substances and Physical Agents & Biological Exposure Indices*. ACGIH, Cincinnati.

**Table 31.2** BMGV values

| Substance | BMGV | Sampling time |
|---|---|---|
| Butan-2-one | 70 µmol butan-2-one/l in urine | Post-shift |
| 2-Butoxyethanol | 240 mmol butoxyacetic acid/ mol creatinine in urine | Post-shift |
| Carbon monoxide | 30 ppm carbon monoxide in end-tidal breath | Post-shift |
| Chromium VI | 10 µmol chromium/mol creatinine in urine | Post-shift |
| Chlorobenzene | 5 mmol 4-chlorocatechol/mol creatinine in urine | Post shift |
| Cyclohexanone | 2 mmol cyclohexanol/mol creatinine in urine | Post-shift |
| Dichloromethane | 30 ppm carbon monoxide in end-tidal breath | Post-shift |
| *N,N*-dimetylacetamide | 100 mmol *N*-methylacetamide/ mol creatinine in urine | Post-shift |
| Glycerol trinitrate | 15 µmol total nitroglycols/mol creatinine in urine | At the end of the period of exposure |
| Isocyanates (applies to hexamethylene diisocyanate, IPDI, toluene-2,4-diisocyanate, and methylene bisphenyl isocyanate) | 1 µmol isocyanate-derived diamine/mol creatinine in urine | At the end of the period of exposure |
| Lindane | 35 nmol/l (10 µg/l) of lindane in whole blood (equivalent to 70 nmol/l of lindane in plasma) | Random |
| 4,4′-Methylene bis-2-chloroaniline | 15 µmol total MbOCA/mol creatinine in urine | Post-shift |
| Mercury | 20 µmol/mol creatinine in urine | Random |
| 4-Methylpentan-2-one | 20 µmol 4-methyl pentan-2-one/L in urine | Post-shift |
| 4,4-Methylene dianiline (MDA) | 50 µmol total MDA/mol creatinine in urine | Post-shift for inhalation and pre-shift next day for dermal exposure |
| Polyaromatic hydrocarbons | 4 µmol 1-hydroxypyrene/mol creatinine in urine | Post-shift |
| Xylene, o-, *m*-, *p*-, or mixed isomers | 650 mmol methyl hippuric acid/ mol creatinine in urine | Post-shift |

## Interfering factors

The following factors can affect BM results:

- Diet (fish increases arsenic/mercury level)
- Sex (females have higher erythrocyte protoporphyrin levels than males)
- Age (cadmium levels increase with age among smokers)
- Alcohol intake affects the metabolism of organic solvents, e.g. styrene
- *Ethnic groups*: evidence for difference in metabolism of solvents
- A metabolite of interest may be produced by more than one substance

## Further information

HSE (2005). *Workplace Exposure Limits*, EH40. HSE Books, Sudbury. Available at: https://www.hse.gov.uk/pubns/priced/eh40.pdf

Threshold Limit Values (TLV) and Biological Exposure Indices (BEI) (2021). *American Conference of Governmental Industrial Hygienists (ACGIH)*, Cincinnati, Ohio, US. Available at: https://www.acgih.org/forms

# Practical and ethical considerations

## Practicalities

Several practical considerations must be taken into account before starting a BM programme:

- *The reason for collecting samples*:
  - compliance
  - risk assessment
  - health surveillance
  - epidemiological studies
- Appointment of a competent person to oversee the development and implementation of the programme
- Criteria for selecting individuals for monitoring
- Provision of information for subjects and obtaining individual consent
- *Development of a suitable BM strategy*:
  - timing of sample collection in relation to the beginning and end of shift or working week (see Table 31.3)
  - number of samples to be taken
  - type of biological sample to be collected
  - substance or metabolite to be measured
  - amount of sample required
- *Selection of suitable laboratory*:
  - experience of specific analysis
  - quality assurance schemes
  - validated analysis method
- Any special precautions for the collection, storage, stability, packaging, and dispatch of samples to a laboratory
- How the data will be interpreted including non-occupational exposure
- Feedback of grouped anonymized results to the workforce
- Storage of data, and who has access to the data
- Use of the data and likely benefits to the employees

## Ethical considerations and access to data

- Since BM involves taking samples from individuals it is essential that the rights of individuals are safeguarded
- The need for the monitoring, collection of samples, associated risks, and the use of data should be discussed and agreed with all concerned, employees, employers, and workers' representatives
- Workers must be made aware of what will be analysed in the sample taken and what action may follow based on the results
- Results must be treated as confidential and disclosed only to those health professionals the worker has agreed should have the results
- The individual tested is entitled to his/her results together with an explanation of them
- Group data can be provided to management and unions ensuring that any specific identifiers are removed
- Under the UK Control of Substances Hazardous to Health Regulations, the results should be kept for at least 40 years from the date of last entry
- When companies cease operation, they are advised to offer the data (both biological and personal inhalation) to the HSE

**Table 31.3** Half-life of chemicals and optimum sampling time: general relationship as a guide for monitoring

| Half-life (h) | Optimum sampling time |
|---|---|
| <2 | End of exposure |
| ~2–10 | End of exposure at the end-of-week shift or beginning of the next shift |
| ~10–100 | End of exposure at the end of the working week |
| >100 | Random (sampling time not critical) |

## Further information

HSE (1997). *Biological Monitoring in the Workplace*, HSG 167. HSE Books, Sudbury. Available at: https://www.hse.gov.uk/pubns/priced/hsg167.pdf

# Chapter 32



# Prevention and control of exposure

# Exposure prevention and control

## Prevention and control

As far as exposure to hazardous agents is concerned, there is a legal duty to prevent or, where this is not reasonably practicable, to control exposure adequately. Adequate control of exposure to contaminants can be achieved by:

- ensuring that exposure is below occupational exposure limits
- reducing the exposure to as low as reasonably practicable for substances carcinogens
- implementing the control measure listed
- adopting principles of good practice for the control of exposure (listed in the following section)

## Control measures

- *Where it is not reasonably practicable to prevent exposure, the employer must apply protection measures appropriate to the activity including, in order of priority*:
  - design and use of appropriate work processes, systems of work, engineering controls, and the provision of suitable work equipment and materials
  - the control of exposure at source including use of ventilation systems and appropriate organizational measures to minimize the risks
  - where adequate control of exposure cannot be achieved then suitable personal protective equipment (PPE) should be used in addition to measures listed here
- *The measures used to control exposure should include*:
  - arrangements for safe handling, storage, transport, and disposal (waste materials) of substances hazardous to health
  - suitable maintenance procedures
  - reducing the number of employees exposed, the level and duration of exposure, and the quantity of material used
  - general ventilation
  - appropriate hygiene measures including adequate washing facilities

When making decision about selection, design, installation of measures to control exposure (engineering, administrative methods, or PPE) it is important to consider the nature of work, requirement of the job, the work environment, and how the employees will use the control measures.

## Controlling exposure to carcinogens

Where exposure to carcinogens cannot be prevented, the following control measures are required in addition to those described here:

- Total enclosure of process and handling systems
- Prohibition of eating, drinking, and smoking
- Cleaning floors, walls, and other surfaces at regular intervals
- Designating those areas and equipment which may be contaminated
- Storing, handling, and disposing of carcinogens safely, including use of closed and clearly labelled containers

## Principles of good practice for controlling exposure

In the UK a set of principles of good control practice are used as a basis for judging whether control is adequate for hazardous substances. These include:

- Design and operate processes and activities to minimize emission and the spread of agents
- Take into account all relevant routes of exposure when developing control measures
- Control exposure by means that are proportional to health risk
- Choose the most effective and reliable control options that minimize the emission and spread of health hazards
- Where adequate control cannot be achieved by other means, provide suitable PPE, in combination with other control measures
- Check and review regularly all aspects of control measures for their continuing effectiveness
- Inform and train employees about the hazards and risks from the agents with which they work, and the use of control measures developed to minimize risks
- Ensure that the introduction of any control measures does not increase the overall risk to health and safety

## Use of controls

- Every employer who provides control measures is required to take reasonable steps to ensure that they are properly used
- Employees must make full and proper use of any control measures provided and report defects to their employer

## Maintenance, examination, and testing of controls

- Employers are required to maintain plant, equipment, engineering controls, and PPE in an efficient state, in efficient working order, and in clean condition
- All control measures including systems of work and supervision should be reviewed
- All local exhaust ventilation (LEV) should be examined and tested every 14 months unless another interval is specified, e.g. in Schedule 4 of the Control of Substances Hazardous to Health (COSHH) Regulations
- Where respiratory protective equipment (RPE) (other than disposable RPE) is used to control exposure, the employer should ensure that it is examined and, where appropriate, tested at suitable intervals

# Control hierarchy: Source, transmission, and the individual

Controlling exposure is a fundamental to protecting workers from risks. The control hierarchy (Fig. 32.1) shows methods for exposure reduction from the most to least effective. Other hierarchies of control include in turn: (1) control at source; (2) prevent or control transmission of the pollutant to the individual; and (3) protect the worker.

## (1) Control at source

- *Eliminate the hazard by*:
  - changing the process or method of work so that the hazard is not created
  - substitute hazardous with non-hazardous substances
- Modify the process to reduce the frequency, intensity, or duration of emission
- Substitute substance with one of lower toxicity or different form of the same substance
- Enclose the process/sources of emission
- Provide extraction ventilation
- Improve process/equipment maintenance
- Limit areas of contamination, e.g. spills, leaks

**Hierarchy of control: Examples for noise and vibration**

- Use alternative tools (altered frequency and amplitude)
- Introduce or increase damping; isolate machine from floor (noise)
- Avoid/cushion impact

## (2) Prevent/control transmission

- Shielding between the worker and source
- Increase distance
- Housekeeping
- Sufficient dilution ventilation

**Hierarchy of control: Examples for noise and vibration**

- Reflective and absorbent barriers
- Active noise control

## (3) Individual

- Automatic or remote control of process
- Enclose the worker
- Safer work practice and systems of work
- Education, training, supervision
- Provide PPE
- Reduce exposure time
- Reduce number of workers exposed
- Health surveillance for exposed individuals

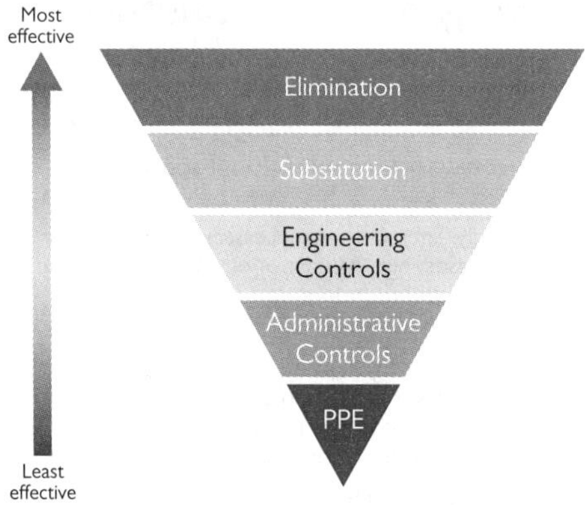


**Fig. 32.1** Hierarchy of control
https://www.cdc.gov/niosh/topics/hierarchy/default.html

# Software/organizational solutions

Options for controlling exposure to hazards in the workplace can be categorized broadly as software (management solutions) and hardware (engineering) methods. Selection and use of PPE is discussed on ➔ pp. 684–700.

## Hierarchy of software/organizational solutions

*Elimination*

Elimination is usually limited to unnecessary operations or poor work practices. In some cases, high-risk activities are subcontracted to another operator.

*Substitution*

- *By a less toxic substance*: e.g. in painting using water-based solvents or organic solvents of lower vapour pressure
- *By the same substance*: but in a form that reduces exposure, e.g. use material in pellet form rather than as a powder

*Designing or redesigning the process*

Reductions in exposure may be achieved by adjustments to the way the job is performed or modifying the layout of the process and the operator's work procedures.

*Suppression of the substance*

Suppression can be achieved in a number of ways. For example, water is used as dust suppressant. Evaporation of vapour from volatile solvents in tanks can be suppressed by using a refrigerated strip just above the surface, creating a cool layer of concentrated vapour, and reducing further evaporation. In electroplating, the surfaces of tanks can be covered by floating plastic spheres, which reduce the surface area available for evaporation, or by adding low-density liquid surfactants.

## Other software methods

- Good work practice and systems (including good housekeeping)
- Appropriate supervision
- Job rotation
- *Information, instruction, and training*: the worker must be made aware of the following:
  - hazards to which they are exposed, and the risks to health
  - factors (process, equipment, method of work, environment) which may affect their exposure
  - any relevant occupational exposure limits
  - significant findings of risk assessments
  - appropriate precautions and actions to be taken in order to safeguard health
  - the correct use of control measures provided and how to recognize and report defects, e.g. PPE, engineering controls
  - the signs and symptoms associated with the hazards and reporting requirements

# Hardware/engineering solutions

The hierarchy of engineering control systems is:
- Total enclosure under negative pressure
- Partial enclosure with extraction
- General dilution ventilation (see ➔ p. 676)

## Classification LEV hoods

LEV are designed and work effectively when the airborne contaminant is contained, received, or captured by the hood. There are three types of hoods (see Fig. 32.2) in order of effectiveness are: enclosing hoods, receiving hoods, and capturing hoods.

## Enclosing hoods

*Full enclosure*

To reduce exposure to very toxic substances the contaminants should be handled in an enclosure under negative pressure, e.g. hot cells for radioactive materials, glove boxes, and abrasive blasting cabinets.

*Partial enclosure extraction booths*

A partial enclosure contains the process with opening for material handling or operator access. Examples include chemical fume cupboards and paint spray booths. Air velocity at the opening (face velocity) should be sufficient to prevent escape of substance into the environment. Typical face velocities for booths are in the range 0.5–2.5 m/s.

## Receiving hoods

Receiving hood receive the contaminant, i.e. the process takes place outside the hood, e.g. a canopy hood over a hot process. A push–pull systems are special types of receiving hood where a jet of air is blown (pushed) from side of a tank add is sucked (or pulled) by a hood on the opposite side.

## Capturing hoods

The process and the source of the contaminant are outside the hood. Capture hoods are placed at the side or behind the source in relation to the worker. Hoods can be fixed or moveable; examples of hood include downdraught tables, lip extraction, low volume high velocity hoods. Typical capture velocities for pollutants range from 0.25 to 10 m/s.
- For hoods, the velocity decays rapidly with distance from the hood, e.g. for a circular hood the velocity is only approximately 10% of the face velocity one diameter away. For this reason, the process should be conducted close to the hood, i.e. the contaminant source should be within the capture distance of the hood
- Hoods with width to length ratios <0.2 are called slots. Slots are commonly used on degreasing tanks, cleaning baths, and electroplating tanks to remove vapours and mists released from the tank surfaces

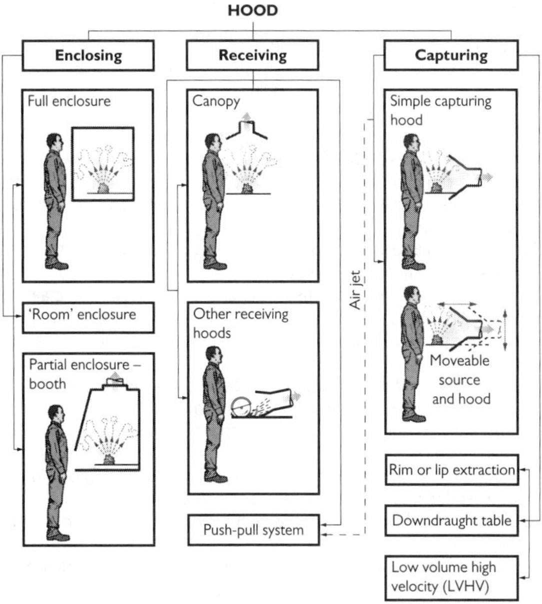


**Fig. 32.2** Classification: Types of LEV hoods

Reproduced from HSG258, Controlling airborne contaminants at work, Fig 10, https://www.hse.gov.uk/pubns/ priced/hsg258.pdf. HSE Books under Open Government Licence 3.0

## General (dilution) ventilation

General (or dilution) ventilation reduces the concentration of the contaminant by mixing the contaminated air with clean, uncontaminated air. Air is supplied to and from an area or building via air exhaust fans placed in the walls or roof of a room or building. The air supply may also be filtered and heated. General ventilation requirements are covered in the Workplace (Health, Safety and Welfare) Regulations 1992:

- Fresh air is required to provide oxygen, remove carbon dioxide, remove excess heat or, if conditioned, provide heat, remove odours, and dilute contaminants arising from workplace activities
- Air introduced into workplaces should be free of contaminants and discharges from nearby extract outlets
- Air may be recirculated to conserve energy costs. Recirculated air, including air conditioning systems, should be filtered to remove impurities and have fresh air added to it before being reintroduced to the workplace
- Mechanical ventilation systems should be regularly cleaned and tested to avoid contaminated air entering the room
- Insufficient air changes may lead to tiredness, lethargy, dry or itchy skin, and eye irritation
- Chartered Institution of Building Service Engineers (CIBSE) produces recommended fresh air supply rates per person (CIBSE Guide A: Environmental Design). The fresh air supply rate should not normally fall below 5–8 L/s/occupant
- Health and Safety Executive (HSE) has published detailed guidance on measures to avoid Legionnaires' disease caused by *Legionella pneumophila* which grows in water-cooling towers[1]

When designing dilution ventilation systems consideration needs to be given to the location of air inlet, position of source of the pollutant, and the position of the worker. Dilution ventilation is more effective if the exhaust fan is located close to exposed worker and the air supply (makeup air) is located behind the worker so that contaminated air is drawn away from the worker's breathing zone (Fig. 32.3).

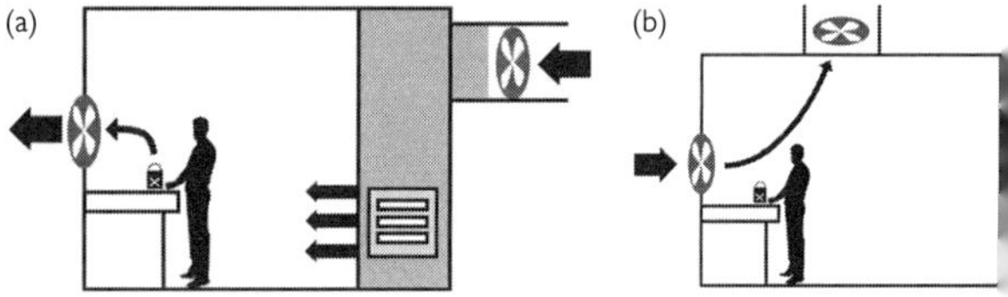


**Fig. 32.3** Example of good (a) and poor dilution (b) ventilation design

Reproduced from HSG258, https://www.hse.gov.uk/pubns/priced/hsg258.pdf, HSE Books under Open Government Licence 3.0

1 HSC (2013). *Legionnaires' Disease. The Control of Legionella Bacteria in Water Systems. Approved Code of Practice and Guidance*. HSE, UK. Available at: https://www.hse.gov.uk/pUbns/priced/l8.pdf

# Factors affecting performance of ventilation systems

LEV systems comprise a hood, enclosure, or slot (negatively pressurized to ensure an inward current of air) connected to a fan via ducting with an air-cleaning device to ensure that the discharged air is fit for recirculation or emission. Fig. 32.4 shows components of an LEV system. Fig. 32.5 shows the effectiveness of various LEV types used to control airborne contaminants.

## Factors leading to poor performance

LEV performance depends on its design, the integrity of its components, and its maintenance and use. Inadequate performance results from:

- Insufficient enclosure
- Low capture velocity
- Extracted air volume is lower than the volume of pollutant released
- Filters and air cleaners blocked
- Restricted, blocked, or damaged ducting
- Ducting too resistant
- Fan of the wrong type or size
- *Fan entry conditions unsatisfactory*: bend or damper close to fan inlet affecting velocity profile
- *Fans badly installed*: the wrong way round or rotating in the wrong direction
- Fan blades dirty or corroded, or motor seized
- *Air discharge to atmosphere affected by wind*: best to discharge vertically. Weather shields must not restrict the airflow from the discharge point
- No provision to allow make-up air to replace that extracted
- Multibranched system not balanced
- Poor maintenance and care
- New workstation added without adjusting fan performance

## LEV system components

- *Inlets*: such as booths, hood, slot, canopy, or enclosure
- *Ducting*: which may contain bends, junctions, dampers; it may be circular or rectangular in cross-section and rigid or flexible
- *Fans*: usually centrifugal type
- *Air cleaners*: such as bag filter, wet scrubber, cyclone, or solvent recovery device
- *Discharge*: to atmosphere via a stack, diffuser, grille, or just open duct

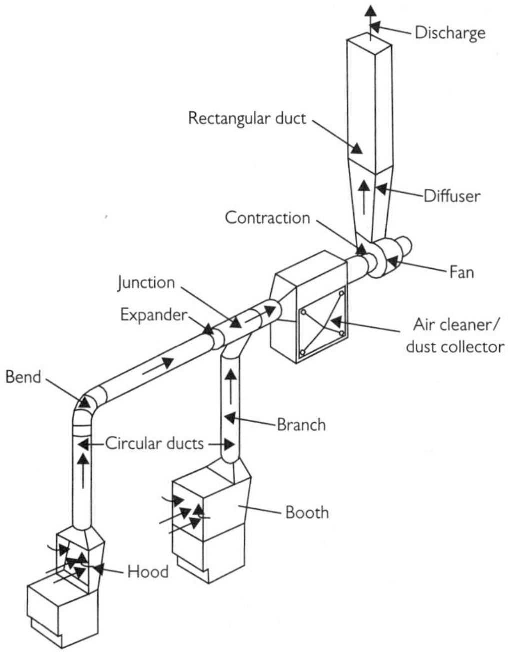


**Fig. 32.4** Components of LEV system. © HSE (1998).

Reproduced from Maintenance, examination and testing of local exhaust ventilation, HSG54 (1998), figure 1, p. 2. HSE Books under Open Government Licence 3.0

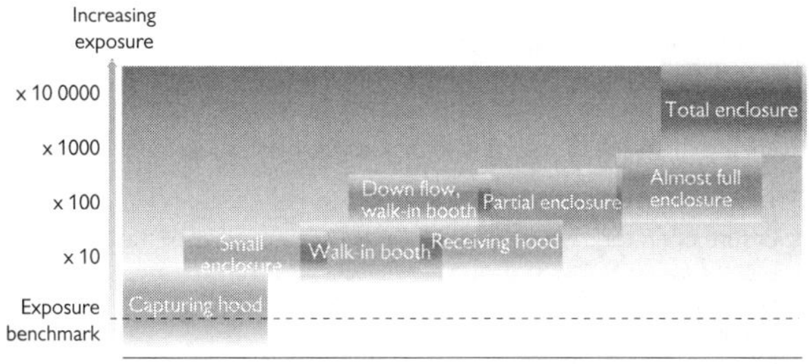


**Fig. 32.5** Effectiveness of various LEV types.

Reproduced from Fig 9, Controlling airborne contaminants at work. HSG258, https://www.hse.gov.uk/pubns/ priced/hsg258.pdf. HSE Books under Open Government Licence 3.0

# Local exhaust ventilation: Assessing performance

## Examination and testing

According to HSG258 (2017) examination and testing of LEV involves three stages:

- A through visual examination to verify the LEV is in efficient working order, in good repair, and in a clean condition
- Measurement and examination of the technical performance of the system against its specification, i.e. comparison with original commissioning report

Assessment to check the control of worker exposure is adequate.

*Visual and structural examination*

- External examination of all parts of the systems for damage, wear, and tear
- Check filter cleaning devices (e.g. mechanical shake down system) are working correctly
- Check pressure (built in) gauges, e.g. located before and after filter
- Check that the monitors and alert/alarms are working correctly
- Check for deposits of settled dust in and around the LEV hood

*Assessment of the technical performance*

- Static pressure measurements taken behind each hood, and across the filter and the fan
- Check velocities (capture, face, and transport) of air at various points in the systems (as specified in the system commissioning manual)
- Calculate the airflow rates ($q$) at the face of the hood or booth and in the duct including at the filter and fan:

$$Q = v \times a,$$

where $v$ is the velocity (m/s), $a$ is the cross-sectional area of hood or the ventilation duct ($m^2$)

- Check speed of fan and motor
- Check the replacement or make-up air supply
- Test the air cleaner performance and any air recirculating systems

Compare the result of testing with the design specification for the system.

## The assessment of control effectiveness

- Ensure operator's working zone is within capture zone of the LEV (Fig. 32.6)
- Dust lamp tests to check escape of fine dust or mists
- Smoke tube or leak tests
- Observe the operator and work practice
- Conduct air sampling to determine whether control is achieved

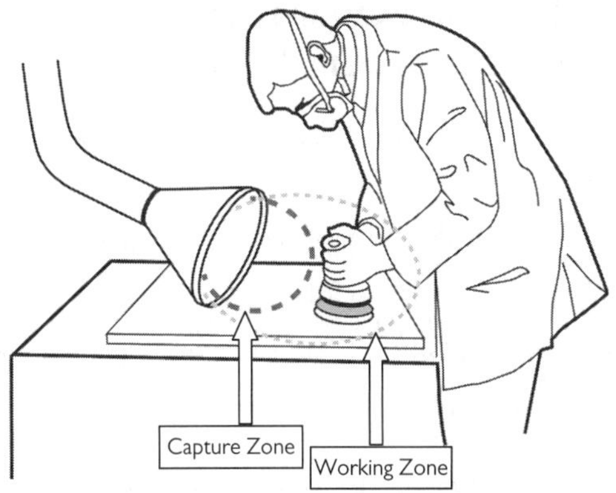


**Fig. 32.6** Capture and working zone. Note: The *capture zone* is the space in front of the hood where the air velocity is sufficient to capture the contaminant. The *working zone* is defined as the space where the activity generates the contaminant. For effective control, the working zone must lie within the capture zone of the hood

Reproduced from HSG258, Controlling airborne contaminants at work, Fig 9, https://www.hse.gov.uk/pubns/priced/hsg258.pdf. HSE Books under Open Government Licence 3.0

## Definitions

- *Capture velocity*: the air velocity required at the source of emission sufficient to cause the pollutant to move towards the mouth of the extractor and thus be successfully captured
- *Face velocity*: the air velocity at the opening of a hood or enclosure
- *Transport velocity*: minimum velocity required in the system, including ductwork and extract devices, to keep collected particles airborne and to prevent them from being deposited in the system
- *Static pressure*: the pressure exerted by a fluid in motion at right angles to the direction of flow
- *Velocity pressure*: the pressure equivalent of the kinetic energy of a fluid in motion. It is calculated from the expression $Pv = 0.5\, pv^2$, where $p$ is the density of air ($kg/m^3$) and $v$ is the velocity of air (m/s)
- *Total pressure*: the sum of the static and velocity pressures at a point in an air stream. It can be +ve or –ve relative to atmospheric pressure

## Further information and guidance

HSE (2017). *Clearing The Air—A Simple Guide to Buying and Using Local Exhaust Ventilation (LEV)*, INDG408. HSE, Sudbury. Available at: http://www.hse.gov.uk/pubns/indg408.pdf

HSE (2017). *Controlling Airborne Contaminants at Work—A Guide to Local Exhaust Ventilation (LEV)*, HSG258. HSE, Sudbury. Available at: http://www.hse.gov.uk/pubns/priced/hsg258.pdf

# Recording the examination and testing of local exhaust ventilation plant

**A suitable record of each thorough examination and test of LEV should contain the following details**

- The name and address of the employer
- The identification (and location) of the LEV, and the process and substances concerned
- The dates of the examination and test
- The process conditions at the time of test, e.g. normal
- Diagram of the LEV system showing position of hood, filter, fan, and test points
- Information about the LEV plant which shows:
  - its intended operation performance for controlling adequately
  - exposure to hazardous substances
  - whether the LEV is still achieving the same performance
  - if not, the adjustment or repairs needed to achieve that performance
- Methods used to make the judgement of performance
- Results of any air sampling relevant to LEV performance
- Name, job title, and employer of the person carrying out the examination and test
- Observation on the way the operator used the LEV
- Signature of person carrying out the test

- The employer should have a LEV 'user manual' and a system 'logbook'
- These documents should be supplied as part of the design, installation, and commissioning process
- The maximum time between tests for most LEV systems is 14 months (see ➔ Schedule 4 of Control of Substances Hazardous to Health Regulations 2002 for frequency of examination and testing of LEV plant used of specific processes)
- The employer should keep the examination and test report for at least 5 years

# Personal protective equipment: Legal requirements and use

## Definition

PPE is defined as all equipment (including clothing) that is intended to be worn or held by a person at work, and which protects him/her against one or more risks to his health or safety.

## Legal requirements

See PPE at Work Regulations 1992 (as amended) *Personal protective equipment: legal requirements and use, PPE at Work Regulations 1992*. The law governing the use of PPE in other specific regulations is contained in:

- PPE at Work Regulations 1992
- COSHH 2002 (as amended)
- Control of Asbestos at Work Regulations 2012
- Control of Lead at Work Regulations 2002
- Ionizing Radiation at Work Regulations 2017
- Confined Spaces Regulations 1997
- Control of Noise at Work Regulations 2005

⚠ PPE is considered as the last resort to protect against risks to health and safety. Thus there is a need to demonstrate first that the risk cannot be controlled adequately by other means, i.e. PPE is provided as additional measures to minimize

## Use of PPE

- *PPE is used widely, but should be considered as the last resort as*:
  - it only reduces exposure for the individual wearer, whereas control at source protects all those in the area
  - the actual level of protection is difficult to assess
  - it may interfere with work tasks/practice
  - it may be uncomfortable and restrict the wearer, limiting movement, and visibility
  - effective protection can only be when the selected is suitable, correctly fitted, properly used, and maintained
- PPE should only be used where it provides additional protection from residual risks as identified by the workplace risk assessment. The use of PPE must not increase the overall level of risk
- The following factors should be considered when selecting PPE: the job type and risk for which protection is required, the physical effort needed to do the job, the work environment (noise, temperature, confined space), and the person wearing the PPE for instance if they know allergies to materials such as latex gloves
- The PPE purchased (by employer) must bear the (CE) mark and comply with PPE Regulations with regard to its design and manufacture
- Employees are required to use any PPE provided by the employer to meet the requirements of PPE at work Regulations.

- *PPE should be selected and used after justification for its use has been made in the risk assessment. For example RPE can be used in the following situations:*
  - where inhalation exposure remains despite use of other controls, i.e. used minimize residual risk
  - where there is short-term or infrequent exposure and use of other controls is not practical
  - as an interim measure, e.g. when putting in place other controls
  - for emergency response, e.g. safe exit or emergency rescue
  - for emergency work/when there is temporary failure of controls

## Setting up an effective PPE programme

Having assessed the risk and implemented all reasonable control measures, the following steps should be considered when setting up a PPE programme:

- Identify individuals/tasks/environment where PPE is needed
- Select appropriate PPE to control residual risks
- Involve worker in the PPE selection process
- Match PPE to each individual wearer
- Carry out fit tests for RPE
- Ensure the use of PPE does not create additional risks
- Ensure that the PPE is compatible with other PPE
- Minimize PPE use time by defining when it should be used, e.g. particular tasks
- Inspect PPE to ensure it is correctly maintained, cleaned, and replaced
- Provide suitable storage facilities to prevent contamination
- *Record*: PPE issue, maintenance, inspection, and RPE fit-testing data
- Inform individuals of the following: the need for PPE, how (and when) to wear and store the PPE, consequences of PPE failure, and the importance of reporting PPE defects

## Further information and guidance

HSE (2013). *Consulting Employees on Health and Safety: A Brief Guide to the Law*, Leaflet INDG232. HSE Books, Sudbury. Available at: www.hse.gov.uk/pubns/indg232.htm

HSE (2015). *Personal Protective Equipment at Work Regulations 1992*, L25, 3rd edn. HSE Books, Sudbury. Available at: https://www.hse.gov.uk/pubns/priced/l25.pdf

# Respiratory protective equipment

RPE is provided to protect individuals against exposure to harmful airborne substances (gases, vapours, dusts, fumes, and fibres) or from oxygen-deficient atmospheres when (a) residual risk to health remains after implementation of other control measures, (b) other controls cannot be used/practical, e.g. when working in a confined space.

## RPE types

- RPE can be divided into two main types:
  - respirator (filtering device): i.e. filter used to remove contaminants; do not use for protection in situations with reduced oxygen levels
  - breathing apparatus (BA): requiring a supply of breathing quality air from an independent source, e.g. air compressor, air cylinder
- Both types are available with different face pieces. Masks (Fig. 32.6) rely on a good seal with the wearer's face. Hoods, helmets, and visors (loose-fitting face pieces) rely on clean air being provided to the wearer to prevent leak-in of contaminants (Fig. 32.7)

## Selecting RPE that is adequate and suitable

The decision to use RPE should be justified in a risk assessment. RPE must be both *adequate* (right for the hazard and reduces exposure to the level required) and *suitable* (right for wearer, the job tasks and work environment, and not create additional risks due to RPE).

HSG33 (HSE, 2013) describes a stepwise process that can be followed to select RPE. In summary this include the following:

- Identify the hazardous substance(s) that individuals are exposed to
- Identify the form of the airborne pollutant, i.e. vapour, gas, dust, fume, fibre, or mist
- Match the nature (form) of the airborne pollutant to the filter type, e.g. particles filter or gas/vapour filters
- Decide on the level of protection factor required (see below RPE required protection factors)
- *Select RPE taking account of following*:
  - the individual wearer: e.g. pre-existing medical conditions, wears glasses/contact lenses
  - the job tasks: e.g. work-rate, wear-time, mobility, vision, and communication requirements
  - the work environment: e.g. temperature, humidity, confined space
  - other head-worn PPE: e.g. eye and ear protection, and safety helmets
  - legal requirements: e.g. CE marking, employer and employee duties
  - costs: e.g. equipment, training, testing, repair/replacing storage

## RPE protection factors

The effectiveness of RPE is indicated by the assigned protection factor (APF). The APF is the level of respiratory protection that the respirator (or class of respirators) is expected to provide to employees when it is used correctly.

> *Example*: A respirator with an APF of 10 should reduce the workers' exposure by a factor of 10, i.e. to one-tenth of exposure level in the breathing zone (outside the mask).

APF values assigned to different types of RPE are given in HSG 53 (HSE, 2005). Examples of RPE are shown on ➲ p. 690, Table 32.1, Protective equipment. RPE devices are rated a APF value of either 4, 10, 20, 40, 200, or 2,000. It is important to choose an APF above the calculated value.

## Required protection factor

*Example*: A worker is exposed to dust assigned a workplace exposure limit (WEL) 8 hours time-weighted average concentration (TWA) = 5 mg/m³. The daily TWA exposure is measured to be 30 mg/m³. In order to reduce the personal exposure to the WEL, the required protection (PF) is: PF = 30/5 = 6.

In this case select RPE device with APF of 10, i.e. above the required protection.

## Filter for respirators

There are three main types of filter: particle filter, gas/vapour filter, and combined filter. Examples of different types of RPE available are shown in Tables 32.1 and 32.2.

- Particle filters are marked with a 'P' sign and filtration efficiency number 1 (low), 2, or 3 (high). If the filter is reusable with fan-assisted respirators they will also have a sign 'TH' or 'TM'
- Gas/vapour filters are categorized by the substance type they can be used against. The filter is marked with a letter indicating type, a number to indicate capacity (1 = low, 2 = medium, 3 = high), and a colour code. See Table 32.2
- Combined filters are marked for both particles and gas/vapour, e.g. A1P3—organic vapour with capacity class 1 and high efficiency particle filter

## RPE fit testing

A major cause of leaks for RPE equipment is poor fit. To ensure adequate protection all tight-fitting RPE must be fit tested as part of the initial selection stage. Since individuals have facial differences (shape, size), fit testing will also identify RPE types which are not suitable for certain individuals. There are two types of RPE fit testing:

- Qualitative fit testing (QLFT) is a pass/fail test based on wearers' subjective assessment of any leakage from the face seal. The test method is based on detecting a bitter or sweet tasting aerosol. The QLFT method is used for disposable and reusable half masks but not suitable for full-face masks
- Quantitative fit testing (QNFT) is an objective test providing a numerical measure of fit (fit factor). The test can be conducted with using two methods: (a) ambient particle counting; (b) controlled negative pressure. The QNFT method is used for full-face masks as well as disposable and reusable half masks
- Fit testing should be conducted by a competent person. Competence can be demonstrated through achieving accreditation under the 'Fit2Fit RPE Fit Test Providers Accreditation Scheme' developed by the British Safety Industry Federation and supported by the HSE. For further details on the scheme, see http://www.fit2fit.org

- For further information on how to conduct fit test for respirators and fit-test report, see https://www.hse.gov.uk/pubns/indg479.pdf
- *The fit-test report should include the following*:
  - name of the person fit tested
  - make, model, type, and size of facepiece tested
  - exercises performed during the test
  - type of filter fitted to the face piece during the test
  - whether the facepiece tested was the subjects or a test facepiece
  - the test method used (qualitative or quantitative)
  - for QNFT the measured fit factor for each individual
  - the pass level used in the test
  - date of test
  - details of person carrying out the test

## Further information

HSE (2013). *Respiratory Protective Equipment at Work: A Practical Guide*, HSG53, 4th edn. HSE, Sudbury. Available at: https://www.hse.gov.uk/pubns/priced/hsg53.pdf

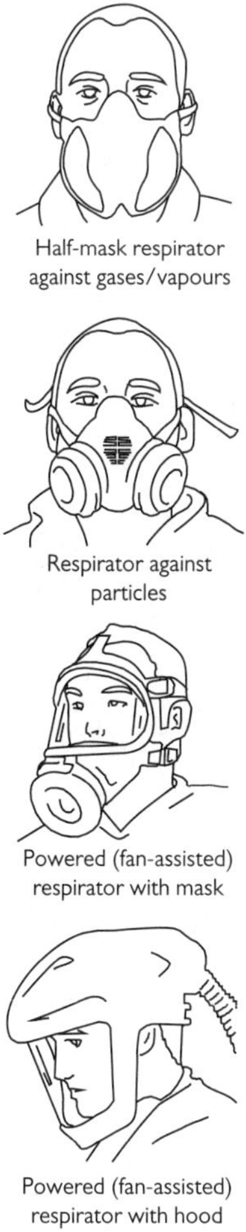

Half-mask respirator against gases/vapours
Respirator against particles
Powered (fan-assisted) respirator with mask
Powered (fan-assisted) respirator with hood


**Fig. 32.7** Types of respirator

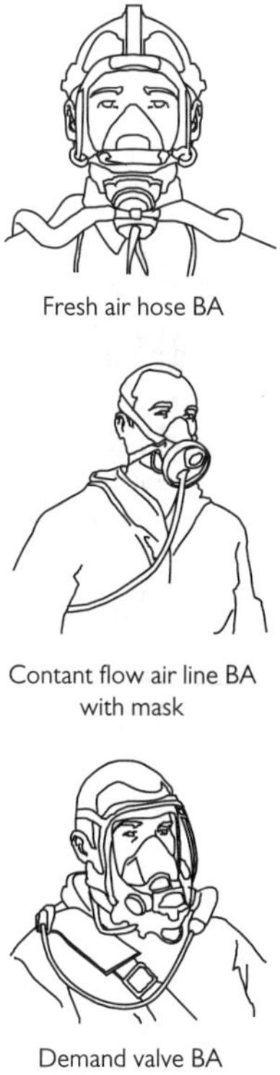


**Fig. 32.8** Types of breathing apparatus

**Table 32.1** Protection values for different types of RPE

| PF required | Respirators | | | | | | Breathing apparatus | | |
|---|---|---|---|---|---|---|---|---|---|
| | Half-mask, particle filters | Half-mask, gas filters | Full face mask, particle filters | Full face mask, gas filters | Powered (fan-assisted) masks | Powered (fan-assisted) hoods | Fresh air hose | Constant flow airline BA | Demand valve BA |
| 4 | FFP1, FMP1, P1 | | P1 | | | | | | |
| 10 | FFP2, FMP2, P2 | FF gas, FM gas, Gas | P2 | | TM1 | TH1 | LDH1 | | |
| 20 | FFP3, FMP3, P3 | | | Gas | TM2 | TH2 | | LDH2, LDM1, LDM2, Half-mask | |
| 40 | | | P3 | | TM3 | TH3 | Full face mask, Hood | LDH3, LDM3, Hood, Full mask | |
| 200 | | | | | | | | Suit | |
| 2000 | | | | | | | | | Airline, self-contained |

Reproduced from Respiratory protective equipment at work, HSG53 (2005). HSE Books under Open Government Licence 3.0

**Table 32.2** Gas/vapours respirator filters

| Filter type | For use against | Colour code |
|---|---|---|
| A | Organic gases and vapours, with a boiling point >65°C, e.g. A1, A2, or A3 | Brown |
| B | Inorganic gases and vapours (excluding carbon monoxide), e.g. B1, B2, or B3 | Grey |
| E | Sulphur dioxide and other acid gases and vapours, e.g. E1, E2, or E3 | Yellow |
| K | Ammonia and its organic derivatives, e.g. K1, K2, or K3 | Green |
| Hg-P3 | Mercury, the filter incorporates a particle filter P3 | Red and white |
| NO-P3 | Oxides of nitrogen the filter incorporates a particle filter P3. Single use only<br>No class number | Blue and white |
| AX | Organic gases and vapours with low boiling point (<65°C), e.g. AXP2, AXP2. Single use only | Brown |
| SX | Substance as specified by the manufacturer | Violet |

Note: The filter must be marked with at least the filter type and with each colour code. For example, AEK2P3 will be marked Brown, Grey, and Green. These figures are based on European standards: EN143 and EN14387

Reproduced from Respiratory protective equipment at work, HSG53 (2005). HSE Books under Open Government Licence 3.0

# Hearing protectors

## Requirements, types, use, and maintenance

- Guidance on hearing protection can be found in the Control of Noise at Work Regulations (CNAWR) 2005 (➲ p. 582, Control of Noise at Work Regulations 2005). More detailed information can be found in BS EN 458:2016, Hearing protectors, recommendations for selection, use, care, and maintenance
- Under CNAWR, if the personal noise exposure is likely to exceed the upper exposure action value, then exposure should be reduced as low as reasonably practicable. If this cannot be achieved using technical and organizational control measures, then the use of personal hearing protectors (HP) is compulsory. Hearing protection is also required for employees working within areas assigned as hearing protection zones and as short-term measure when other control measures are being developed
- HP work most effectively when earmuff seals are not damaged, the tension of the headband is not reduced, compressible earplugs are clean
- HP which reduce the level at the ear to below 70 dB should be avoided; this overprotection may cause difficulties with communication and hearing warning signals
- HPs must be CE marked showing that it meets the European Standard BS EN 352
- HPs include earmuffs and earplugs; the latter can be custom moulded
- Most HPs provide greater protection at higher frequencies than at lower frequencies

## Earmuffs

Easy to fit, reusable, clearly visible, and hence easy to monitor. They may be uncomfortable in warm conditions. Long hair, beards, jewellery, or glasses may reduce protection. More expensive than ear plugs.

- *Seals*: check seals for cleanliness, hardening, and damage
- *Cup*: check for cracks, holes, damage
- *Headbands*: avoid overbending and twisting, check tension
- Store in a clean environment

## Earplugs

Earplugs are more suitable when used with other PPE, e.g. with safety glasses. Workers who suffer from recurrent otitis externa may be unable to tolerate earplugs. Custom-made plugs are more comfortable and are easier to fit for some wearers. However, need to conduct fit tests before putting into use.

- *Reusable plugs*: clean regularly, ensure not damaged or degraded
- *Issue to individual*: not to be shared
- Require careful insertion to ensure effective protection
- Provide greater protection at higher than low frequency
- Risk of infection (dirty hands)
- *Disposable plugs*: use only once

## Special protector types

- *Level-dependent (or amplitude-sensitive) protectors*: designed to protect against noise but allow communication during quieter periods
- *Flat or tailored frequency protectors*: these provide similar protection across all frequencies which can assist communication. Useful where it is important to be able to hear high-frequency sound at the correct level relative to lower-frequency sounds, e.g. musicians
- *Active noise reduction protectors*: incorporate an electronic sound-cancelling system enabling additional noise attenuation. Effective at low frequencies (50–500 Hz)
- *Protectors with communication facilities*: these use a wire or aerial to relay signals, alarms, and messages to the wearer. The signal level should not be too loud, and the microphone should be switched off when not in use

## Selecting hearing protectors

When selecting HPs the following should be considered:

- Personal noise exposure level and exposure variation
- Pattern of exposure
- Noise reduction (attenuation) provided by the protector
- Work environment (temperature, humidity, dust, dirt)
- Compatibility with other PPE worn
- Comfort and wearer preference
- *Hearing needs*: communication, hearing warning sounds, conducting tasks
- *Costs*: equipment, maintenance, training
- *Health problems*: ear infections, discharge, etc.
- Legal requirements

## Further information

BS EN 458 (2017). *Hearing Protectors. Recommendations for Selection, Use, Care and Maintenance.* Guidance Documents. British Standards Institution (BSI), London, UK.

# Predicting noise reduction

The noise level at the ear (L'A) when hearing protection is worn can be estimated using three different methods (octave band method; high, medium, and low frequencies (HML) method; and single rating number (SNR) method). L'A is estimated by subtracting the estimated noise reduction (using manufacturer's performance data) from measured noise data.

## Manufacturers' hearing protection data

The supplier must provide the following information for the HP. An example of supplier data is shown in Table 32.3:

- Mean and standard deviation attenuation values at each octave band centre frequency (63 Hz–8 KHz)
- Assumed protection values at each frequency, i.e. mean protection minus one SD
- H, M, L, and SNR values

## Noise level data required for estimating protection

The following types of noise data should be measured depending on the method chosen (one of three) to calculate the attenuation afforded by the ear protector.

- *Octave band analysis*: requires measurement of noise level at each octave centre frequency for the range 63 Hz–8 kHz
- HML require measurement of the A-weighted (LA) and C-weighted (LC) sound pressure levels
- *SNR*: requires single measurement of LC only

## Predicting attenuation using the HSE electronic spreadsheet

The measured noise levels and manufacturer's data can be entered into an electronic spreadsheet to calculate the attenuation afforded by the chosen ear protector. The spreadsheet is available on the HSE website (http://www.hse.gov.uk/noise). Of the three methods, the octave band analysis method provides the best estimate for L'A.

HP usually give lower protection than predicted by manufactures data due to, e.g. poor fitting. The difference between manufacturers' data and 'real-world data' is accounted for in the HSE calculator by 'derating' the protection by 4 dB.

## Protector use time

If HP is removed in a noisy area, even for short period, amount of protection provided will be significantly reduced. Fig. 32.8 shows that if the HP is worn for 70% of the time the protection afforded is only about 5 dB regardless of the type of HP used (A, B, or C).

## Information for employees

Employees should be provided with information on HPs including:

- Why and where HPs need to be worn?
- How replacements can be obtained?
- How to wear HPs with other personal protection?
- How to check, store, and report damage to HPs?

**Table 32.3** Example of noise attenuation data supplied by manufacturers

| | Octave band centre frequency (Hz) | | | | | | | |
|---|---|---|---|---|---|---|---|---|
| | 63 | 125 | 250 | 500 | 1,000 | 2,000 | 4,000 | 8,000 |
| Mean attenuation | 17.3 | 21 | 24.5 | 27.3 | 27.9 | 33.8 | 36.1 | 40.8 |
| Standard deviation (dB) | 5.4 | 5.3 | 6.7 | 6.6 | 4.8 | 3.7 | 5.2 | 6.5 |
| Assumed Protection Value (APV) | 11.9 | 15.7 | 17.8 | 20.7 | 23.1 | 30.1 | 30.9 | 34.3 |
| Single number values | H | 29 | M | 23 | L | 20 | SNR | 27 |

APV, mean attenuation minus 1 SD.

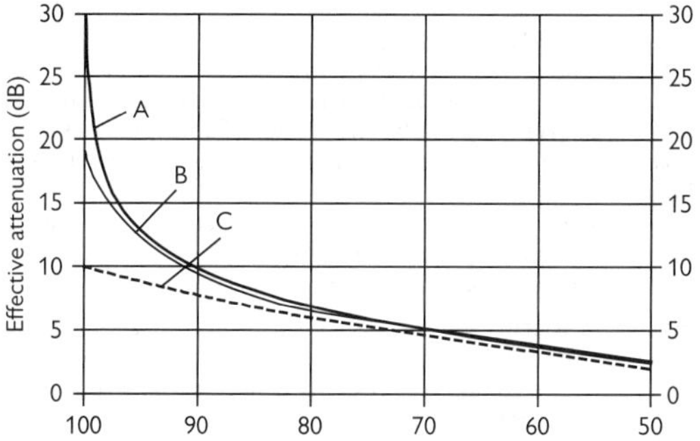


**Fig. 32.9** Effectiveness of hearing protectors in relation to time worn. Protectors providing (A) 30 dB attenuation, (B) 20 dB attenuation, and (C) 10 dB attenuation.

Reproduced from The Control of Noise at Work Regulations 2005. HSE Books, under Open Government Licence 3.0.

# Gloves

## Applications

- Protection from cuts and abrasion, handling sharps
- Keeping hands warm in cold weather when using machines that cause hand–arm vibration syndrome
- Handling chemicals, radioactive materials, hot or cold materials
- Danger of electrical hazards
- Work involving naked flame, welding

## Glove selection and use

Gloves differ in design, material, thickness, and size. The following factors should be considered when selecting gloves to avoid contact with harmful substances:

- *The substance* types handled and their dermal effects (local and systemic)
- *Other hand hazards*: e.g. abrasion, vibration, cuts, or high temperature
- *Type and duration of dermal contact*: e.g. single-use glove may be appropriate for intermittent exposures or thicker reusable glove for longer exposure periods. Wearing gloves for extended periods can lead to excess moisture on the skin which in itself can act as a skin irritant
- *The user*: size (use sizing charts) and comfort. Some chemicals used to manufacture gloves can cause skin allergies, e.g. proteins in natural rubber latex.
- *The tasks*: gloves should not limit the job requirements, e.g. manual dexterity requirements, need for sterile gloves
- Work environment (temperature and humidity)

The HSE glove selection memory aid sheet (from HSG262) can be completed and discussed with the glove supplier and is available on web page http://www.hse.gov.uk/skin/resources/glove-selection.pdf

Gloves used to protect hands against chemical substances should meet the requirements of the European Standard EN374-3. For wet work, gloves marked EN374-2 should be used.

## Glove selection charts

Most glove manufactures produce charts to showing how their gloves perform against a range of single substances. These charts use three key terms: break through time, permeation rate, and degradation.

- *Permeation*: chemical migrates through glove
- *Penetration*: bulk flow of chemical through seams, pinholes, closures, porous materials, or other imperfections
- *Degradation*: change in physical properties of glove material as a result of exposure to a chemical agent

▶ The *breakthrough time* is defined as the time between the initial application of a test chemical to the outside surface of the protective glove and it subsequent presence on the inside of the material.

## Glove performance data

Glove suppliers usually provide chemical resistance charts, with glove performance for different chemicals. Performance is rated using the following data:

- *Breakthrough time*: ranges from 1–10 to >480 minutes
- *Permeation rate*: fast, medium, or slow
- *Degradation*: scale 0–6

## Information and training

Gloves should be checked regularly and replaced if they are worn or have deteriorated. Workers should know: what gloves to wear and when, how to put the gloves on and take them off without contaminating the skin, how to dispose gloves safely, and the limitations of gloves as a measure to minimize dermal exposure.

Need to also ensure that there are adequate facilities for storage, cleaning, replacement, and disposal of gloves. Note: some gloves may need to be disposed of as hazardous waste.

## Further information

HSE (2015). *Managing Skin Exposure Risk at Work*, HSG262. HSE Books, Sudbury. Available at: http://www.hse.gov.uk/pubns/priced/hsg262.pdf

# Protective clothing

Protective clothing includes separates (jacket, trousers), aprons, overalls, coveralls, and body suits.

## Applications

- *Chemical work protecting against accidental spillages*: use aprons
- *Contact with sprays or jets of chemicals*: use coveralls
- *Wet working*: using water sprays for cleaning, use rubbers, plastic, water-repellent coatings, waterproofs, breathable fabrics
- *Radiant heat from welding, foundries*: flame-retardant, insulating, and heat-resistant fabric
- *Electrical and electrostatic hazards*: materials which resist build-up of static electricity

## Precautions

- When selecting protective clothing consider the chemical resistance and protection, protection against mixtures, and breakthrough times recommended by the manufacturer
- Store used/contaminated clothing separate from clean clothing
- Inspect for wear and tear/loose seams and damage
- Do not wear loose protective clothing close to moving machines
- Clean clothing following the manufacturer's instructions

⚠ If protective gloves or clothes are worn incorrectly this may increase the risk to the individual.

- Contaminant may get inside the protective device (glove) and be occluded, resulting in higher exposure
- Prolonged use may cause moisture (sweat) on skin which can act as an irritant
- Reduces heat loss, which may increase likelihood of heat stress
- Latex gloves may cause an allergic reaction in susceptible individuals (➲ p. 228, Latex allergy)
- Gloves worn near moving equipment and machinery parts may be caught in the equipment, drawing the worker's hand into the moving machinery

## Further information

HSE (2000). *Selecting Protective Gloves for Work with Chemicals: Guidance for Employers and Health and Safety Specialists*, Leaflet INDG330. HSE Sudbury. Available at: www.hse.gov.uk/pubns/indg330.htm

HSE (2015). *Managing Skin Exposure Risks at Work*, HSG262, 2nd edn. HSE, Sudbury. Available at: www.hse.gov.uk/pubns/books/hsg262.htm

HSE (2015). *Preventing Contact Dermatitis and Urticaria at Work*, Leaflet INDG233 (rev2). HSE, Sudbury. Available at: www.hse.gov.uk/pubns/indg233.htm

# Eye and face protection

## Types of eye and face protection

Eye protection can be divided into three basic types:

- *Safety spectacles*: separate lenses in metal or plastic frame with side shields
- *Goggles*: flexible plastic frame with one or two lenses and flexible headband. With the rim in contact with the face, goggles provide eye protection from all sides
- *Face shields or visors*: one large lens with a frame and adjustable head harness or mounted on helmet. Can be worn with prescription lenses. Protects the face, but eyes are not fully enclosed

## Applications

Eye protection is required for the following hazards:

- Splashes of chemicals, e.g. acids or body fluids
- Chipping and debris from use of power-driven tools on metals, woods, etc.
- Molten metal, radiant heat sparks, or hot liquid splashes from furnaces
- Intense light (lasers) and other optical radiation likely to cause risks to the eye, e.g. ultraviolet (UV) light from welding

## Selecting eye and face protection

Table 32.4 shows examples of eye protection for different hazard types.

**Table 32.4** Eye protection and hazards

| Hazard | Eye protection equipment | Examples |
|---|---|---|
| Impact | Spectacles with toughened lenses/side screens | Flying swarf<br>Chiselling |
| Dust | Goggles<br>Air-fed positive pressure hood with visor | Grinding<br>Shot-blasting |
| Molten metal | Goggles<br>Face shield or visor | Casting and pouring |
| Radiation (non-ionizing) | Goggles, tinted<br>Face shield or visor with correct protective shade<br>Sunglasses | Welding and lasers (UV radiation)<br>Casting and pouring molten metal/glass (IR radiation)<br>Outdoor work (UV radiation) |
| Chemical or biological | Goggles<br>Face shield or visor | Exposure to gases, vapours, liquids, dusts, biological agents |

## Precautions

- Issue eye protection on a personal basis and ensure that it fits properly
- Stored in a protective case
- When cleaning, follow manufacturer's instructions
- Do not use when the visibility (scratched and worn lenses) is reduced, or the headband is damaged or worn
- *Lens may mist*: use anti-mist sprays or ventilation eye protection

## Standards for selection, use, and maintenance

BS 7028: 1999. *Eye Protection for Industrial and Other Uses. Guidance on Selection, Use and Maintenance.*

## Further information and guidance

*British Standards on Eye Protection.* British Standards Institution (BSI), London. Available at: https://shop.bsigroup.com/products/personal-eye-protection-specifications

# Section 7

# Toxicology

# Chapter 33

# Principles of toxicology

# Toxicology and dose–response

Toxicology is the study of the adverse effects of chemicals in humans and other living organisms. It plays a fundamental role in chemical risk assessment.

## Dose–response relationship

The dose–response relationship refers to the correlative relationship between exposure to a chemical (dose) and the effect that occurs (response).

## Types of dose–response

Two types of dose–response relationship exist.

### *Graded dose–response*

This relates to the occurrence of effects in an *individual*, with the response varying in severity according to dose

### *Quantal dose–response*

This relates to the distribution of a specific response within a *population*.

For many chemicals, the quantal dose–response relationship is characterized by a normal frequency distribution represented in a frequency histogram by a bell-shaped curve. This distribution reflects differences in susceptibility to chemicals within a population (biological variation), indicating the presence of *sensitive* individuals and *resistant* individuals.

## Dose–response parameters

Several parameters can be derived from the dose–response relationship.

- *No observed adverse effect level (NOAEL)*: the dose, determined experimentally, at which there is no statistically significant or biologically significant increase in adverse effects
- *Lowest observed adverse effect level (LOAEL)*: the lowest dose at which there is a significant increase in adverse effects
- *Threshold*: the dose below which the probability of an individual responding is zero
- *LD50*: median lethal dose, a single dose of substance that can be expected to cause death in 50% of experimentally exposed animals. This value is determined in acute systemic toxicity tests and is used to indicate the relative acute toxicity of a substance

## Patterns of dose–response

- With essential elements and vitamins, the shape of the graded dose–response relationship in an individual is U-shaped, representing adverse effects which occur at low doses (deficiency) and at high doses (toxicity) (Fig. 33.1)
- With genotoxic carcinogens, the response (development of cancer) is considered not to have a threshold (i.e. there is no dose that is associated with zero risk) (Fig. 33.2)

Threshold dose and NOAEL will occur in this part of curve; actual values will depend on experimental dose levels used

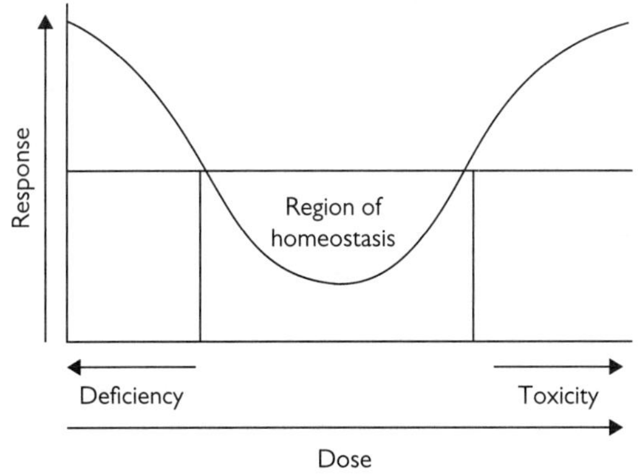


**Fig. 33.1** Dose–response relationship for an essential substance.

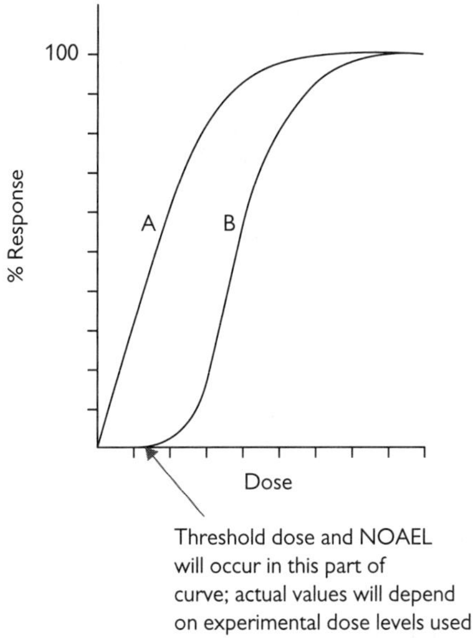


**Fig. 33.2** C omparison of dose–response for two compounds (A) with no threshold and (B) with threshold.

# Toxicokinetics and types of toxic effect

## Toxicokinetics

The toxicokinetics of a substance is the quantitation and time course of four components:

- Absorption
- Distribution
- Metabolism
- Excretion

The toxicokinetics of a substance determines its concentration at the target organ/tissue and consequently determines its toxicity.

### *Absorption*

This is the process by which substances cross membranes in the body and enter the bloodstream. Main routes of absorption are the respiratory tract (inhalation), the skin (dermal), and the GI tract (oral).

### *Distribution*

This is the translocation of substance within the body after it has been absorbed into the blood.

### *Metabolism (or biotransformation)*

This is the process by which a substance, once it is absorbed, is changed into one or more chemically different substances (metabolites).

### *Excretion*

This is the process by which a substance and/or its metabolites are eliminated from the body. Route and rate of excretion vary according to the substance, the most common routes being:

- Urine
- Faeces
- Exhaled breath

Excretion of the substance (or its metabolites) may be used for biological monitoring purposes.

## Types of toxic effect

Several terms are used to describe the toxic effects that are associated with exposure to a substance. Frequently used terms are defined in the following section.

- *Acute effects*: resulting from short periods of exposure to a relatively high concentration/dose of chemical, e.g. irritation of eyes, skin, and respiratory tract (toluene, arsenic), and central nervous system depression (*n*-hexane)
- *Chronic effects*: caused by repeated or prolonged exposure to a relatively low concentration/dose of chemical, e.g. central nervous toxicity (toluene); cancer of respiratory tract, skin, and liver (arsenic); and peripheral neuropathy (*n*-hexane)
- *Local effects*: occur at the site of first contact with a substance, e.g. eye irritation (formaldehyde)
- *Systemic effects*: occur only after the substance has been absorbed into the body

- *Immediate effects*: these develop soon after exposure takes place. In contrast, *delayed effects* only become apparent some time after exposure has taken place; perhaps months or years later
- *Reversible effects*: subside once exposure ceases
- *Irreversible effects*: remain following cessation of exposure; in some cases, irreversible effects may become progressive

## Specific toxic effects

*Carcinogenesis*

Carcinogenesis is a multistage process in which exposure to a substance leads to genetic damage within the cell, resulting in uncontrolled proliferation of cells and ultimately the occurrence of a tumour. Carcinogenic substances are generally divided according to the mechanisms involved:

- *Genotoxic mechanism*: substances which cause cancer by direct damage to the genetic material
- *Non-genotoxic mechanism*: substances which cause cancer by indirect damage to the genetic material

*Mutagenesis*

This is a permanent change in the genetic material of a cell (DNA), involving a single gene, a block of genes, or an entire chromosome, which is passed on to the next generation of cells. A mutation in germ cells (reproductive cells such as sperm and ova and their precursors) can result in genetic damage that is passed on to offspring (heritable genetic defects). A mutation in somatic cells (non-reproductive cells) may lead to the development of cancer.

*Respiratory sensitization*

A state of specific airway hyper-responsiveness that is induced in some individuals by certain substances (respiratory sensitizers or asthmagens). Immunological or irritant mechanisms may be involved.

*Skin sensitization*

An immunologically mediated skin reaction which occurs in some individuals as a result of skin contact with certain substances.

# Assessment of toxicity and evaluation of toxicological data

## Assessment of toxicity

EU legislation requires that chemicals placed on the market must undergo a risk assessment to determine the risks to humans and the environment. An important part of the risk assessment process involves determining the intrinsic harmful properties of the substance (hazard identification) using toxicological data.

## Toxicological testing

Toxicological data may come from animal, human, or *in vitro* studies, or be based on structure–activity relationships. Toxicological data for new substances and, when necessary for existing substances, are obtained using internationally accepted test methods (https://www.oecd-ilibrary.org/environment/oecd-guidelines-for-the-testing-of-chemicals_72d77764-en)

- *Existing substances*: substances which were commercially available in the EU between January 1971 and September 1981. Under previous legislation these were listed in the European Inventory of Existing Commercial Chemical Substances. Under existing legislation these are listed in the European Community (EC) inventory
- *New substances*: any substance that became commercially available in the EU after September 1981. Under previous legislation these substances appeared in the European List of Notified Chemical Substances. Under existing legislation these substances are listed in the EC inventory and assigned an EC number

Toxicological data for the following endpoints are examined:

- Acute systemic toxicity
- Skin irritation
- Eye irritation
- Skin sensitization
- Repeated dose toxicity
- Mutagenicity
- Carcinogenicity
- Reproductive toxicity

## Registration Evaluation and Authorization of Chemicals (REACH) legislation

This legislation (see ➔ p. 588) emphasizes that unnecessary testing on animals should be avoided. To this end, REACH promotes:

- The use of alternative methods for assessing hazards of substances
- The sharing of toxicological data between registrants

## Evaluation of toxicological data

Toxicological data for many substances involve uncertainties that need to be characterized for risk assessment:

- For most substances, toxicological data are based on animal studies, often using levels of exposure that are higher than would be applicable to humans

- The human population is more diverse than would be expected in a group of laboratory animals, and this variability needs to be taken into consideration
- Toxicological data may incorporate several experimental inadequacies (e.g. inappropriate exposure route, short duration of exposure, or deviations from standardized test methods)

*Uncertainty or assessment factors*

When evaluating toxicological data, these uncertainties are addressed by the use of uncertainty or assessment factors. The intention is that incorporating uncertainty factors will provide some reassurance of protection against the harmful effects of chemicals when limited information is available. Uncertainty/assessment factors are used when establishing occupational exposure limits (OELs) and in determining derived no-effect levels under REACH.

## Classification and labelling

Classification and labelling involve:

- Evaluation of the hazards of a substance (or preparation) in accordance with EU legislation
- Communicating information about the hazard via the label

## Legislation

- The European Regulation on classification, labelling and packaging of substances and mixtures (Classification, Labelling and Packaging (CLP) Regulation) came into force in all EU member states on 20 January 2010
- The CLP Regulation replaces the Chemicals (Hazard Information and Packaging for Supply) Regulations 2009 in the UK, commonly known as CHIP, and is overseen by the European Chemicals Agency
- The CLP Regulation adopts the Globally Harmonized System on classification and labelling (see ➲ p. 46, Chemical hazards)
- The aim of this regulation is to ensure that people who are supplied with any chemical receive information on its hazards and advice on how to protect themselves, others, and the environment. Classification entails evaluating toxicological data for a substance and comparing these against specified classification criteria

# Occupational exposure limits

OEL is a generic term for occupational air standards, used for personal monitoring, as a means of assessing whether or not workers are exposed to unacceptable levels of a substance.

## Purpose

The main purposes of OELs are:
- To demonstrate compliance
- To identify individuals at risk
- To select control measures in order to minimize health risks
- To enable enforcement

Factors considered in setting standards include:
- Where the substance is used
- Identification of critical health effects
- Number of people exposed to the substance
- Typical exposure levels
- Control technology available
- Cost of implementing control systems
- Potential health benefits from exposure reduction

## Workplace exposure limits (WELs)

- WELs are OELs set for substances hazardous to health under the Control of Substances Hazardous to Health Regulations. HSE produces an updated list of WELs in the EH40 publication
- A WEL is the maximum concentration of an airborne substance, averaged over a reference period, to which employees may be exposed by inhalation
- Two limit periods, referred to as the time-weighted average concentration, are used to express the WELs, i.e. the long term (8 hours) and the short term (15 minutes)
- Where a substance is not assigned a WEL, this does not indicate that it is safe. Exposure to such substances should be reduced to a level as low as reasonably practicable, taking account of the toxicity of the substance
- *Substances listed in EH40 may be assigned a 'Sk', 'Sen', or 'Carc' notation*:
    - Sen: substance capable of causing occupational asthma
    - Sk: substance that can be absorbed through skin, i.e. those substances for which there are concerns that dermal absorption will lead to systemic toxicity
    - Carc: substance which meets criteria required for classification as a category 1A or 1B carcinogen (known or presumed to have carcinogenic potential for humans) ) or category 1A or 1B germ-cell mutagen (known to induce or regarded as if it induces heritable mutations in the germ cells of humans)

## Deriving the WEL value: information and stages

- Assessment of the toxicology, i.e. potential of the substance to produce adverse health effects
- Identification of NOAEL/LOAEL from the dose–response relationship
- Application of uncertainty factors (safety factors)

- Estimate the highest exposure at which no adverse effects would be expected to occur in workers following exposure over a lifetime
- The Advisory Committee on Toxic Substances determines whether the derived exposure limit is currently practicable; if so, the WEL is proposed at this level

## Criteria for setting WELs

- The WEL is set at a level at which no adverse effects on human health would be expected to occur based on the known or predicted effects of the substance
- However, if such a level cannot be identified with reasonable confidence or if this level is not reasonably achievable, the WEL would be based on a level corresponding to what is considered to be good control, taking into account the severity of likely health hazards and the costs and efficacy of control solutions

## Compliance with WELs

Substances assigned a WEL fall into two groups:

- Substances that are carcinogens or mutagens, or that cause sensitization
- All other hazardous substances assigned a WEL

For carcinogens, mutagens, or respiratory sensitizers, employers should try to prevent exposure or, if this is not feasible, ensure that exposure is reduced as far below the WEL as is reasonably practicable. For other substances, the employer should ensure that the WEL is not exceeded.

## Units

- Concentration of airborne particles (dusts, fumes) is expressed in milligrams per cubic metre ($mg/m^3$)
- In EH40, limits for dusts are usually expressed as the inhalable or respirable fraction
- Limits for fibres are expressed as fibres per millilitre of air (fibres/ml)
- Volatile organic substances are expressed in both parts per million by volume (ppm) and milligrams per cubic metre ($mg/m^3$)

Airborne concentration can be converted from ppm to $mg/m^3$ (or vice versa) using the following equation:

$$\text{WEL } (mg/m^3) = \text{WEL (ppm)} \times \text{MW}/24.05526$$

where MW is the molecular weight of the substance and 24.05526 is the molar volume of an ideal gas at 20°C and 1 atm pressure (101,325 Pa, 760 mmHg).

Section 8

# Epidemiology in occupational health

# Chapter 34

# Epidemiology

# Measures of disease occurrence

Modern epidemiology is an important pillar of public health, drawing on methods from many scientific fields to systematically study the distribution and determinants of health-related states or events (not just illnesses and diseases) in specified populations. Ultimately, the knowledge is applied to the control and prevention of health problems.

Descriptive epidemiology is concerned with the patterns of disease occurrence in the populations, which involves asking questions on 'person, place, and time'. Based on the observed differences in distribution, analytic epidemiology then attempts to identify the determinants for excess of disease through epidemiological studies of various designs.

Three important aspects need to be considered when measuring disease occurrence: (a) what is being measured; (b) what is the population being described; and (c) the time period during which cases of disease are enumerated. Various measures have been used, but incidence and prevalence are most commonly used. These measures may relate to a population in its entirety (e.g. crude rates), or they may be specific to defined subgroups (e.g. sex- and age-specific rates).

## Case definition

Defining a case of disease may be relatively straightforward. For example, it is usually not too difficult to decide whether or not someone has recently incurred a hip fracture. For some disorders, however, the distinction between normality and abnormality may be less clear-cut (e.g. hypertension, depression). In these circumstances, case definitions should be explicit, even if somewhat arbitrary. Otherwise, measured disease occurrence cannot be meaningfully interpreted and compared (across regions and over time).

## Incidence

The incidence of a disease is the measure of most relevance to studies of disease causation and can be expressed as either a risk or a rate. Incidence risk (sometimes known as cumulative incidence or risk) refers to the proportion of *new* cases of disease having onset or first recognized within a population 'at risk' of contracting the disease during some period of time (typically a year). Incidence risk is always between 0 and 1 (or between 0% and 100%).

$$\text{Incidence risk} = \frac{\text{New cases arising in a specified period}}{\text{Total number of people at risk at the start of the period}}.$$

Incidence rate (also called incidence density or rate) is a measure of frequency with which a disease or other incidents occur over a specified time period. The denominator is the sum of the person-time of the at-risk population. Using person-time rather than just time is useful when the amount observation time differs between people or when the population at risk varies with time (Fig 34.1). Incidence rates are numerically similar to risks for rare conditions, but rates can be greater than one for very common condition.

$$\text{Incidence rate} = \frac{\text{New cases arising in a specified period}}{\text{Total person-time at risk of the disease}}.$$

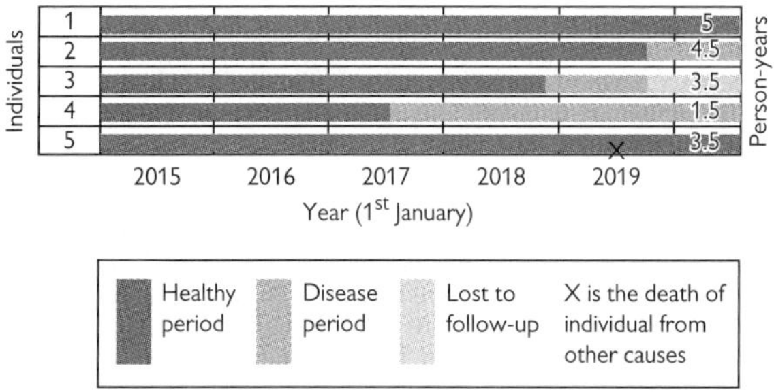


**Fig. 34.1** A hypothetical follow-up study illustrating the 'person-time' concept

$$\text{Incidence rate} = \frac{\text{New cases of disease}}{\text{Total person-time at risk of the disease}}$$
$$= \frac{3}{5+4.5+3.5+1.5+3.5}$$
$$= 0.167 \text{ per person-years}$$
$$(\text{or } 167 \text{ per } 1{,}000 \text{ person-years})$$

It is often not possible to work out individual person-time. Instead, the average number of people in the population during the specified period is used in the denominator. For short period of time, e.g. one year, it is assumed that a population of say, 100,000 people, are all at risk and would contribute 100,000 person-years.

## Mortality

Mortality (death) is mostly measured in counts or rates and is the incidence of death, either from any cause (all-cause mortality) or from a particular disease/disease family (cause-specific). Mortality rates reported from routine data often use a midyear population as the denominator. For diseases in which a large proportion of cases result in fatality (e.g. mesothelioma), mortality serves as a good proxy for incidence.

## Prevalence

The prevalence of a disease is the proportion of a population who are cases at a defined point in time (point prevalence) or during a defined period (period prevalence). For example, the point prevalence of rheumatoid arthritis in a population at the time of a survey might be 1%, and the 1-month prevalence of low back pain 20%. The prevalence of a disease depends upon its incidence and also on the time for which people remain cases before recovery or death.

Prevalence may be relevant to the planning of health services. In addition, they are sometimes used as a proxy for incidence in studies of disease causation. However, findings must be interpreted with caution, since associations with prevalent disease could reflect effects on recovery or fatality as well as on incidence.

Assuming the underlying population is static (i.e. no people moving in or out of the area), prevalence can be approximated by the product of incidence and average duration of the disease (i.e. how long the disease persists before cure or death). This crude relationship holds if incidence and duration are constant over time.

## Proportional rates

Calculation of incidence, mortality, and prevalence requires that the population under study be enumerated. Sometimes this is not possible, but the occurrence of a disease can be related to an indirect index of population size. For example, the proportions of deaths attributed to brain cancer might be compared between two populations. Here the total number of deaths in each population serves as an indirect index of its size. Care is needed, however, in the interpretation of proportional rates. A high proportion of deaths from brain cancer could indicate high mortality from the disease, but it could also reflect an unusually low overall death rate in the population under study.

## Standardized rates

Disease occurrence often varies importantly with sex and age but comparing multiple sex- and age-specific rates between two populations may be unduly cumbersome. Standardization is a method of summarizing disease occurrence in a population that takes account of its sex and age distribution, and thereby allows more meaningful comparison with other populations. It can be applied to incidence, mortality, prevalence, or proportional rates. Two methods of standardization are widely used.

### *Direct standardization*

Directly standardized rates are simply a weighted average of sex- and age-specific rates. The weighting factors being defined by the sex and age distribution of a standard population (often an imaginary population such as the World Health Organization world standard population). The directly standardized rate bears the same unit as the crude rate.

### *Indirect standardization*

Indirect standardization compares the number of cases of disease in a study population with the number that would have been expected had the study population experienced the same sex- and age-specific rates as a specified standard population (e.g. the national population). The comparison is summarized by the ratio of observed to expected cases (and hence bears no unit; sometimes expressed as a percentage). A standardized mortality ratio (SMR) is an example of such a ratio.

## Measures of association

Much of epidemiology is concerned with comparing the occurrence of disease between groups of people according to their exposure to 'risk factors'. A risk factor is a characteristic that is associated with an increase or reduction in the risk (rate) of a disease. The association may be directly causal (e.g. asbestos causes mesothelioma) or indirect because the risk factor is a marker for a cause (e.g. yellow-stained fingers are a risk factor for lung cancer because they are a marker for smoking).

A measure of association quantifies the strength or magnitude as well as indicating the direction of the association between an exposure and disease. Assume there is a population with some of its members exposed to a certain factor. The remaining members of the same population are unexposed. In the same population, not all the people would have the disease of interest. Combining the two together, there will be four mutually exclusive scenarios: (a) exposed and with disease; (b) unexposed and with disease; (c) exposed and no disease; and (d) unexposed and no disease. A contingency (2 × 2) table can be drawn up as follows:

| | | |
|---|---|---|
| Exposure + | *a* | *b* |
| Exposure − | *c* | *D* |

The risk of disease among the *exposed* would be $a/(a + b)$, where $a$ is the number of individuals with disease given exposed and $a + b$ is the total number of exposed individuals. Likewise, the risk of disease among the *unexposed* would be $c/(c + d)$, where $c$ is the number of individuals with disease given unexposed, and $c + d$ is the total number of unexposed individuals. The comparison of risks between exposed and unexposed groups can be made by division, i.e. ratio (relative) measures, or by subtractions, i.e. difference (absolute) measures.

## Ratio (relative) measure

Risk ratio, rate ratio, and odds ratio are often collectively known as 'relative risk' (RR), which is a commonly reported measure of association from epidemiological studies.

*Risk ratio*

A risk ratio is simply the ratio of risks in people exposed and unexposed to a risk factor.

$$\text{Risk ratio} = \frac{\text{Risk in exposed}}{\text{Risk in unexposed}} = \frac{a/(a+b)}{c/(c+d)}.$$

*Rate ratio*

If rates are compared instead, the relative measure is called a 'rate ratio'. Provided risk is small and the time period is short, risk ratio and rate ratio are approximately equal.

$$\text{Risk ratio} = \frac{\text{Risk in exposed}}{\text{Risk in unexposed}}.$$

*Odds ratio*

An odds ratio is defined as the odds of disease in a person exposed to a risk factor divided by the odds in someone who is unexposed.

$$\text{Odds ratio} = \frac{\text{Odds in exposed}}{\text{Odds in unexposed}} = \frac{a/b}{c/d} = \frac{ad}{bc}.$$

## Difference measures

The disease risk in the unexposed group can be seen as the background risk—in other words, the risk in the absence of the exposure of interest. This is because although unexposed to the exposure of interest, the unexposed individuals can possess other risk factors that may confer some risk of disease.

*Attributable (excess) risk*

Attributable risk is the additional risk above and beyond the background risk associated with the exposure and is calculated as the difference in risk between people with and without exposure to a risk factor. It is the measure of association that is most relevant to decisions in risk management for individuals. For example, in deciding whether the risk of cancer from a specified occupational exposure to ionizing radiation is acceptable, we need to know the absolute increase in cancer incidence that is caused by the exposure.

*Population attributable risk*

Population attributable risk is defined as the rate of disease in a population minus the rate that would apply if everyone in that population were unexposed to the risk factor. It depends on the attributable risk in individuals and also the prevalence of exposure in the population. It is relevant to risk management for populations, giving an indication of the burden of disease that might be prevented by eliminating exposure to a causal factor.

*Attributable proportion (aetiological fraction)*

Attributable proportion is the proportion of all cases of disease in a population that would be prevented if the risk of disease in exposed persons were reduced to that of the unexposed. Again, its use is in risk management for populations. The attributable fractions for different causes of a disease may sum to more than 100%. This is because where an individual is exposed to more than one cause, removing any one of the exposures might be sufficient to prevent him getting the disease.

# Statistical inference

## Populations and samples

Most epidemiological studies use observations in a sample of people to draw conclusions in a wider population from which the sample derived. For example, the odds ratio for welders in a case–control study of pneumonia might be taken as an estimate of the association with pneumonia in welders more generally. A sample statistic (the odds ratio in the sample of people who participated in the case–control study) is used to estimate a population parameter (the odds ratio in the population of welders more generally).

One of the limitations on this extrapolation is that sample statistic may be a biased estimate (over- or underestimate) of the true population parameter simply by chance, especially if the sample is small in size. Statistical inference is the process by which uncertainties from chance variation between samples are taken into account when drawing conclusions about populations. Two methods are commonly used—hypothesis testing and estimation with confidence intervals.

## Hypothesis testing

The aim of hypothesis testing is to investigate whether sample data are consistent with an assumption about the population from which the sample was drawn. It starts with a *null hypothesis* that there is no association between exposure and disease and an alternative hypothesis, often the negation of the null hypothesis. A calculation is then made of the probability that the association in a sample of the size studied would be as much as (or more than) the observed findings, if there were really no difference between the groups (as expected under the null hypothesis). If this probability ('*p*-value') is sufficiently low (i.e. the observed findings are sufficiently unlikely under the null hypothesis), the null hypothesis may be rejected and the alternative hypothesis (i.e. there is an association/a difference) be accepted. The findings are therefore deemed to be 'statistically significant'.

When reporting hypothesis tests, it is more informative to report the level of their statistical significance (i.e. the magnitude of the *p*-value) than simply that the *p*-value is below some specified threshold for significance (e.g. $p < 0.05$). It is important to note that the distinction between the *p*-values on either side of the threshold (e.g. 0.05) is purely arbitrary. A *p*-value above the threshold only implies that on the available evidence the null hypothesis cannot be rejected, instead of having enough evidence to support no association/difference. A *p*-value below the threshold also does not indicate invariably the alternative hypothesis is correct.

## Statistical tests

Statistical tests such as the chi squared ($\chi^2$), *t*-tests, and Wald test are a mathematical means of calculating test statistics, from which *p*-values can be obtained. The appropriate test varies according to the study design and the nature of the data collected.

## One- and two-tailed tests of significance

A two-tailed *p*-value is the probability of deviation from the null hypothesis in either direction to the extent that was observed in the study sample. For example, if the null hypothesis were of no association between exposure and disease, a two-tailed *p*-value would be the probability of finding an association, positive or negative, at least as strong as that observed, simply by chance. A one-tailed *p*-value relates to deviations from the null hypothesis in only one direction. Unless otherwise stated, quoted *p*-values are normally two-tailed.

## Confidence intervals

A confidence interval is a range within which a population parameter might normally be expected to lie, assuming that the findings from a study sample are unbiased.

Usually 95% confidence intervals are quoted. The mathematical derivation of a 95% confidence interval is specified in such a way that, on average (and in the absence of bias), 95% of the time the interval so calculated will include the true value for the population parameter. Confidence intervals are more informative than *p*-values and are generally the preferred method of statistical inference in occupational health (OH) studies.

# Interpretation of associations

Epidemiological studies addressing the relationship between an exposure and disease may differ markedly in their findings. There are several possible reasons for this, all of which should be considered when interpreting observed associations. It is important that a valid association be first established before considering whether the association is causal.

## Bias

Bias is a systematic tendency to underestimate or overestimate a parameter of interest because of a deficiency in the design or execution of a study. There are many potential sources of bias, but broadly they arise because the study sample is systematically unrepresentative of the population about which conclusions are to be drawn (e.g. because of inappropriate selection criteria or incomplete participation of selected subjects)—also known as *selection bias*, or from inaccurate information about participants (*information bias*).

Because of the practical and ethical constraints on research in humans, bias is inevitable in epidemiological studies. The aim should be to minimize its occurrence by optimizing the design (e.g. random sampling, prospective data collection using standardized, objective tools) and then allow for its potential impact when interpreting results.

## Chance

Even if there is no systematic bias in the selection of a study sample, it may be unrepresentative simply by chance. Spurious findings may also arise due to the play of chance. Chance findings may be minimized if the sample size is sufficiently large (e.g. 0.5 million in the UK Biobank) and the threshold for significance is set at a lower level (e.g. 0.01 rather than 0.05). However, in occupational epidemiology this is not often feasible.

Gauging the potential impact of chance variation between samples entails techniques of statistical inference (confidence intervals or hypothesis testing). In addition consideration should be given to what is known from other studies (including relevant non-epidemiological research). If an association is biologically implausible or incompatible with a large body of prior research, it may be reasonable to attribute it to chance even if it is highly significant statistically.

## Confounding

Confounding occurs when a risk factor under study is statistically associated with another exposure or characteristic ('confounding factor') that independently determines the risk of disease. It can lead to spurious associations in the absence of direct causation or cause true causal associations to be under- or overestimated. For example, lorry drivers might have an unusually high incidence of lung cancer, not because lorry driving causes the disease, but because they tend to smoke more than the average. Here smoking would be the confounding factor. The impact of confounding can be minimized when the potential confounding factors have been measured and incorporated in the design (restriction, matching) and statistical analysis (stratification, multivariable regression models).

## Causal inference

Cause and effect may be directly observed from randomized-controlled interventions, but in most cases, especially in occupational medicine, experimental data are rare. Decisions about causation have to rely on observational data obtained from cohort, case–control, and cross-sectional studies (described later in the chapter) where only associations between the exposure and the disease of interest may be observed. Such associations could be spurious, under- or overestimated due to bias, chance, or confounding inherent to all observational study designs. Therefore, one should first assess whether the association could have been otherwise explained by the flaws (bias and confounding) and chance, before looking at attributes of the study to decide whether causality may be inferred.

There are some generally accepted aspects that could be considered in the evaluation of causality, although it should be noted that many of these are not absolute requirements.

- *Temporality*: exposure should precede the development of disease. However, the order of exposure and effect cannot always be established with certainty. For example, changes in a certain biomarker may be observed prior to the detection of tumour, leading to suggestions that the biomarker change is a cause of cancer. In fact, it could well be carcinogenesis and/or subsequent malignant progression (*disease*) that really causes the changes in biomarker levels (*exposure*). This *reverse causation* is more likely to be observed in diseases with long latency
- *Strength of association*: strong association (typically RR greater than two is considered moderately strong) is less likely to be 'explained away' by bias and confounding. However, weak association should not be dismissed as non-causal
- *Dose–response relationships*: the absolute risk of disease is likely to be dependent on the dose (intensity, duration) of exposure if the agent or circumstance causes disease. The nature of exposure should also be considered, since there may be a 'threshold' effect, whereby exposure above (below) certain level will (not) lead to disease
- *Consistency*: if the same association can be observed from studies of different designs across different settings, it is less likely to be an artefact. Consistency can be more easily noticed in meta-analyses (statistical pooling of findings). However, it is entirely possible that heterogeneity could arise because an exposure may have specific effect in a particular population (see following effect modification)
- *Biological plausibility*: associations that are be supported by plausible biological mechanisms lend more credibility than those that are not

## Effect modification

Effect modification occurs when the RR associated with a risk factor varies according to the presence or level of another characteristic or exposure (an effect modifier). For example, the RR of skin cancer from occupational exposure to sunlight might vary according to skin colour. Effect modification is a biological phenomenon that needs to be described, by reporting the stratum-specific RRs rather than one single summary estimate.

# Routine health statistics

## Purpose

Routinely collected health statistics are used for several purposes in OH:

- Monitoring the impact of known occupational hazards and the effectiveness of control measures
- As an alert to previously unrecognized hazards
- As a background against which to assess the occurrence of disease in occupational groups (e.g. in cohort studies or in the investigation of occupational clusters of disease)

## Reporting schemes and registers of occupational disease

Reporting schemes are used to collect and register information about cases of definite or probable work-related illness. They are applicable to health outcomes that can be linked to occupation with reasonable confidence in the individual case. Attribution to work may be made in two ways:

- *On the timing and other clinical features of the illness*: e.g. acute injuries and poisoning may be linked to work through their temporal relation to an exposure incident, and occupational asthma may be diagnosed through the demonstration of sensitization to an agent encountered only at work
- From knowledge that the individual has been exposed to an agent or circumstance that carries a high RR of the health outcome

## Sources in the UK

Various sources of routine health statistics may be useful to OH professionals practicing in the UK:

- *Reporting schemes for occupational injuries and diseases*: these include data reported to the Health and Safety Executive under Reporting of Injuries, Diseases and Dangerous Occurrences Regulations 2013; and various voluntary reporting schemes coordinated by the Centre for Occupational and Environmental Health at the University of Manchester, as part of The Health and Occupation Reporting Network (THOR)
- *Periodic surveys* of health and work conducted by the Health and Safety Executive (HSE), including the Labour Force Survey and Workplace Health and Safety Survey (WHASS)
- Statistics of social security compensation for occupational injuries and prescribed industrial diseases
- *Statistics of mortality and cancer incidence by occupation*: these are published periodically by the Office for National Statistics (ONS) and in the past were produced by its predecessor, the Office of Population Censuses and Surveys
- *General statistics of mortality and cancer incidence*: published by ONS, these may provide useful background data against which to evaluate patterns of disease observed in occupational populations
- *Hospital Episode Statistics*: curated by the National Health Service (NHS) Digital, these relate to hospital admissions by cause and procedure. They do not include information on occupation, but include useful data on, for example, admissions for accidental pesticide poisoning

All of the statistical sources listed have their individual strengths and limitations which must be taken into account when they are used.

**Voluntary reporting schemes within The Health and Occupation Reporting Network (THOR)**

- Occupational Physicians Reporting Activity (OPRA)
- Surveillance of Work-Related and Occupational Respiratory Disease (SWORD)
- EPI-DERM Occupational Skin Surveillance
- Musculoskeletal Occupational Surveillance Scheme (MOSS)
- Surveillance of Occupational Stress and Mental Illness (SOSMI)
- Surveillance of Infectious Diseases at Work (SIDAW)
- Occupational Surveillance Scheme for Audiological Physicians (OSSA)
- Occupational Surveillance of Otorhinolaryngological Disease (THOR-ENT)

## Further information

HSE. *Self-reported Work-Related Illness (SWI) and Workplace Injuries (LFS)*. HSE Books, Sudbury. Available at: http://www.hse.gov.uk/statistics/publications/swi.htm

HSE. *Workplace Health and Safety Survey (WHASS) Programme*. HSE Books, Sudbury. Available at: http://www.hse.gov.uk/statistics/publications/whass.htm

ONS Health and Social Care. Available at: https://www.ons.gov.uk/peoplepopulationandcommunity/healthandsocialcare

Statistics at DWP. Available at: https://www.gov.uk/government/organisations/department-for-work-pensions/about/statistics

University of Manchester. Available at: http://research.bmh.manchester.ac.uk/epidemiology/COEH/research/thor/

# Planning epidemiological research

Unlike many other types of OH research, epidemiological investigations often do not require expensive equipment or facilities. However, even the simplest studies must be carefully planned and rigorously conducted.

The starting point for any investigation is one or more study question(s). These should be both worthwhile and answerable. In other words, depending on what is found, the information generated by the study should have the potential to affect how things are done in the future.

## Protocols

A protocol is essential for any epidemiological study. It is used in seeking ethical approval, permissions, and funding; as a guide to data collection and analysis; and as a reference when preparing reports of the study findings. The original study protocol, together with a note of any deviations that occurred as the study progressed, should be retained so that they are available if required for the purposes of audit and governance.

If the investigator is inexperienced in epidemiological research, or lacks relevant expertise (particularly in statistics), help should be sought in preparing protocols. The main elements of a protocol are:

- *Background*: this sets up the study question(s), summarizing relevant information from earlier research, the current gaps in knowledge, and why it is important to address these gaps. It may also describe new technical advances that allow the gaps in knowledge to be addressed in a way that was not previously possible
- *Study question(s)*: these should be explicitly stated
- *Methods*: this section should describe how the study questions will be addressed. It should include details of which subjects will be eligible for study, and how they will be recruited; what data will be collected about participants and how these data will be analysed to answer the study question(s). It may also be relevant to include information about the validity of methods for data collection
- Plans for publication
- *Statistical power*: this gives an indication of confidence that the study sample will not be unrepresentative simply by chance
- *Ethical considerations*: any ethical issues associated with the research, and if so, how they will be addressed
- Permissions and agreements (if relevant)
- Funding (if relevant)

## Ethical and regulatory approvals

Most epidemiological studies (by virtue of their nature involving human participants and personal data) require formal review by a properly constituted research ethics committee (where there is doubt advice can be sought from the chair of the committee to which the study would be referred). The relevant committee will depend on who is conducting the study, from where subjects will be recruited, and the type of data to be collected.

In the UK, any research that involves the NHS premise, patients or staff in England and Wales will require a 'Health Research Authority and Health and Care Research' approval, which brings together the review of ethics and the assessment of governance and legal compliance. This streamlined process is done via the Integrated Research Application System. Separate systems are in place for research based in NHS Scotland and Health and Social Care in Northern Ireland.

For research outside the NHS, researchers should apply to one of the higher education research ethics committees. Ethics committees normally specify the format in which they wish to receive applications.

## Questionnaires

Questionnaires are often used to collect epidemiological data. They may be self-administered or administered at interview. Questions may be open-ended (i.e. with free text answers) or closed-ended (i.e. with a finite set of options from which the answer is chosen). Important considerations in the design of questions are their validity (will they provide accurately the information that is sought?), understandability, and the ease with which the answers can be analysed. Use of previously developed questions (e.g. from widely used questionnaires) is often an advantage. Questionnaires should collect the information that is likely to be needed to address the study question(s), but unnecessary detail should be avoided.

# Investigation of disease clusters

A cluster of disease is an unusually high number of cases in a defined population over a time period during which fewer than one or two cases would be expected.

Disease clusters are not infrequent in occupational populations. Occasionally they result from exposure to a hazardous agent or activity in the workplace, but much more often they simply represent a chance coincidence. Nevertheless, they require proper assessment.

The assessment of occupational clusters entails a staged approach, the extent of investigation depending on the level of scientific suspicion that an occupational exposure is responsible and also the level of concern in the workforce and management.

## Characterization of index cases

A first step is to characterize the index cases that have given rise to concern. The aim should be to establish:

- The precise diagnosis of each case
- The occupational exposures that the cases share in common

If the cases, in fact, suffer from different diseases that are unlikely to have the same causes, or they do not share any potentially hazardous occupational exposures, then the level of scientific suspicion is low, and more detailed investigation may not be necessary.

## Further investigation

If further investigation is required, the next steps are to:

- Search readily accessible sources of information (e.g. company pension files and OH records) for any additional cases with the same diagnosis/diagnoses and exposure(s) as the index cases
- Estimate the expected frequency of the relevant diagnosis/diagnoses in all employees with the same exposure(s) as the index cases. This gives an indication of how unusual the cluster is
- Review published scientific literature regarding known and suspected causes of the disease(s) suffered by the index cases. Look for indications that a shared occupational exposure might have a causal role
- *Establish how frequently the shared exposures of the index cases occur elsewhere, and what is known about their potential adverse effects*:
  - if the same exposures commonly occur in other occupations or circumstances, then any increased risk of disease might be expected to apply also in these other situations
  - if the shared exposures have known toxic effects that are consistent with an increased risk of the disease(s) in the index cases, then the level of scientific suspicion is increased. (For example, a cluster of cancer would be more suspicious if there were shared exposure to a known mutagen.)

## Formal epidemiological studies

If additional investigation is required, then often it will take the form of a formal epidemiological study. Such a study may be conducted in the workforce that experienced the cluster, with the aim of providing more precise estimates of risk in relation to specific exposures. However, it must be remembered that clusters only come to attention because they are unusual, and therefore a study in a workforce with a disease cluster can be expected to show elevated risks for the disease concerned. For this reason, a stronger design is to conduct a study in a separate population with similar exposures to the index cases. If a study of this sort provides independent evidence of excess disease, the case for an underlying occupational hazard becomes more compelling.

## Cross-sectional studies

In a cross-sectional study information is collected at a single point in time (or over a short period) about the prevalence of health outcomes and/or their determinants in a defined population.

In OH, information from cross-sectional studies may be used for several purposes:

- *Planning and prioritizing interventions*: e.g. the prevalence of stress-related illness might be assessed in a workforce to decide whether changes were needed in working methods or styles of management
- *Monitoring the impact of measures to control hazardous exposures*: e.g. the prevalence of sensorineural deafness might be assessed to check the effectiveness of controls on noise exposure, or personal exposures to an airborne pollutant might be measured to check that local exhaust ventilation was working as intended
- *Investigating associations between exposures and disease*: e.g. whether the prevalence of dermatitis is unusually high in workers handling a new material

## Cross-sectional studies of disease causation

As cross-sectional studies typically collect data on various risk factors as well as on health outcomes, it may sometimes be appropriate to look for associations between these variables (odds ratios of prevalence are obtained). Cross-sectional studies as a means of investigating causes of disease are attractive in that they can often be conducted relatively quickly and cheaply.

However, special care is needed in their interpretation, given in cross-sectional studies both risk factor and health outcome are assessed simultaneously.

- Risks may be underestimated because of biases in the selection of subjects for study. This is a particular concern when the disease of interest is sufficiently disabling that it causes people to leave the job in which it arose, or where its symptoms are exacerbated by continuing exposure to the causal agent, again leading people to move from the job that caused it. For example, the risk of asthma from an occupational allergen might be missed if sensitized individuals rapidly moved to other work and therefore were not included in a cross-sectional sample of exposed workers
- The cross-sectional design may make it difficult to distinguish cause from effect. For example, a high prevalence of pathological drinking in publicans might occur because heavy consumers of alcohol preferentially seek employment in bars, or because work as a publican makes people more prone to drink heavily, or both

For these reasons, cross-sectional studies of disease causation work best for less serious diseases that are unlikely to cause a change of job and are unlikely to impact on the exposures under investigation.

# Cohort studies

A cohort is a general term for any group of individuals who share some common characteristic. A cohort study involves the follow-up of two or more cohorts (often one group exposed to a risk factor and the other not exposed or at a lower level), and the subsequent health or mortality is compared between these groups. Ideally the cohorts should be as similar as possible except for the single putative risk factor.

Also known as prospective or longitudinal studies, cohort studies can be used to estimate both relative and attributable risks. This is a powerful design as it allows collection of risk factor information at the start and tracing the natural history of a condition over time. The method has been widely used to investigate known and suspected causes of occupational cancer but can be applied to many other types of health outcome. One major challenge of the design is that large numbers of individuals may need to be followed up over many years, if the disease is uncommon, increasing cost and logistical complexity. Over time, differential attrition of participants may lead to bias undermining the validity of the findings.

## Assessment of exposure

Exposures must be assessed not only to the risk factor(s) of prime interest, but also to potential confounding factors. Depending on the study question and the practicality of data collection, the exposure ascertained may be at a single point in time (most often the time of entry to follow-up), over a period up to a specified point in time, or right through to the time of exit from follow-up (this requires repeated assessment of exposures throughout the follow-up period). Many different methods of exposure assessment may be employed, including the use of questionnaires, employment records, and occupational exposure measurements. Often a job-exposure matrix is applied to translate job titles into agent-specific exposures.

## Assessment of health outcome

The methods by which health outcomes are ascertained will depend on the study question, and on practical and ethical limitations. They may be assessed continuously throughout follow-up or at one or more time points during the follow-up period. Methods include the use of death certificates, cancer registrations, follow-up questionnaires, physical examinations, and clinical investigations. To prevent bias, methods for ascertaining health outcome should not vary in relation to the risk factors under study.

## Retrospective cohort studies

Particularly in the study of occupational carcinogens (where prolonged follow-up is usually required to obtain statistically meaningful results), cohort studies are often conducted retrospectively. This requires that cohort members can be identified retrospectively, and their exposures assessed in a way that it is not biased in relation to subsequent health outcome. It is also necessary that the relevant health outcomes can be reliably assessed in retrospect.

## Comparisons with the general population

Occupational cohort studies of mortality and cancer incidence commonly use disease rates in the general population (national or regional) as a comparison. This has the advantage of giving statistically robust control data at relatively low cost and is valid provided it can reasonably be assumed that the exposures of interest are negligible in the general population when compared with those in the study cohort.

## Healthy worker effect

In cohort studies that compare mortality in an occupational group with that in the general population, bias may arise from a 'healthy worker effect'. This occurs because employed people tend on average to be healthier than the population at large. In particular, people with chronic disabling disease are liable to be selectively excluded from employment. Thus, when followed up over time, employed populations tend to have lower than average death rates from causes, such as chronic respiratory disease, for which death is often preceded by a prolonged period of disability.

## Statistical analysis

Various statistical methods are applied in the analysis of cohort studies, depending in part on the exact study design and the type of health outcome. Generally speaking multivariable Poisson and Cox proportional hazards regression models are used in the analysis of cohort studies, yielding rate ratios and hazard ratios, respectively. One technique that is widely used when comparing mortality or cancer incidence in an occupational cohort with that in the general population is the 'person-years method'. This entails first summing the number of years for which cohort members were under follow-up in different combinations of age and calendar period. The age- and calendar period-specific disease rates in the general population are then applied to these person-years of follow-up to obtain an 'expected number' of cases for each combination of age and calendar period. Next, the expected numbers are summed across all combinations of age and calendar period. Finally, the observed number of cases is divided by the total expected number to give a SMR or standardized incidence ratio.

# Case–control studies

In a case–control (case–referent) study people with a disease of interest (cases) are identified, and their past exposure to known or suspected causes is compared with that of controls (referents) that do not have the disease, associations generally being summarized by odds ratios. Sometimes case–control studies are 'nested' within a larger cohort investigation. Essentially, exposure information is collected about all of the cases of disease in the study population and time period, but about only a representative sample of those who are not cases.

The case–control approach is particularly useful when the disease of interest is rare (one selects the cases directly). However, it does not provide an estimate of incidence in the population and how one selects and studies the cases and controls could greatly influence the validity of the findings.

## Recruitment of cases

The source of cases and method of ascertainment should be explicitly defined. Ideally, cases should have incident (newly presenting or newly diagnosed) disease. Prevalent or fatal cases may be used as an alternative, but associations may then reflect influences on recovery or fatality as well as on incidence. Often an attempt is made to recruit all cases in a defined study population and time period, but this is not essential, and the source population for the case group may only be notional (e.g. the catchment population of a hospital).

## Selection of controls

Controls should be representative (in terms of their exposures to risk factors and potential confounders) of the non-cases in the population (defined or notional) that gave rise to the cases. A second objective is that they should provide information on exposures of similar quality to that for cases (the ideal of perfect accuracy is rarely achievable). Often it is impossible to achieve both of those aims simultaneously, and compromise is necessary. Two sources of controls commonly employed are patients with other diseases and people selected at random (or effectively at random) from the study population.

Controls are sometimes matched to cases (either individually or in groups) according to the presence or levels of potential confounding factors such as sex and age as a means to control for confounding. Where matching is used, the exposures of controls should represent those of all non-cases in the source population with the relevant matching criteria.

## Ratio of controls to cases

Where exposure information can be obtained as easily from cases as controls and there is no practical limit to the available pool of cases, statistical efficiency will be maximized by recruiting equal numbers of cases and controls. Where cases are in limited supply or control data can be ascertained more easily than data from cases, the statistical power of a study may usefully be enhanced by taking a higher ratio of controls to cases. However the return from this diminishes as the ratio increases, and control to case ratios greater than four are rarely worthwhile.

## Exposure ascertainment

Exposures must be assessed both to risk factors of interest and to potential confounding factors. Various sources of information are used including questionnaires, historical records, and biomarkers (provided these reflect exposures before disease onset and are not modified by the occurrence of disease). If exposures are ascertained by questionnaire and the recall of cases is more complete than that of controls, bias may result with spurious inflation of risk estimates.

## Statistical analysis

Case–control studies are typically analysed using logistic regression, which offers the adjustment of multiple confounding factors that is otherwise not possible with the conventional Mantel–Haenszel method. Odds ratios are obtained from the logistic regression analysis and are interpreted the same way as risk or rate ratios from cohort studies.

# Experimental studies

An experimental study assesses the effect of a planned intervention on outcomes of interest. Outcomes that may be relevant in OH research include:

- Disease incidence, prevalence, or mortality
- Incidence of other adverse events (e.g. dangerous occurrences or near-miss accidents)
- Biomarkers of subclinical health effects (e.g. acetyl cholinesterase activity)
- Biomarkers of exposure to hazardous agents
- Measures of attitude or behaviour

Comparisons may be between a new intervention and standard practice or between two or more different interventions.

## Study designs

Various study designs may be employed depending on the nature of the intervention(s) and outcome(s) of interest.

*Simple 'before and after comparisons'*

Outcome measures are assessed in the same subjects or groups before and after an intervention, looking for changes that might be attributable to the intervention. The weakness of this design is that results may be confounded by other determinants of outcome that change over time in parallel with the intervention.

*Non-randomized, controlled comparisons*

Subjects or groups receiving an intervention are compared with controls that receive a different intervention or are managed according to standard practice. At baseline (i.e. prior to the intervention), controls should be as similar as possible to the subjects receiving the intervention in characteristics that are known or likely to predict the outcomes under study. This may be easier to achieve if the outcome is the change in a parameter following the intervention rather than its absolute value.

*Randomized controlled interventions*

People or groups with similar baseline characteristics are randomly assigned to receive the intervention or to serve as controls, and their subsequent outcomes are compared. If there is marked heterogeneity of subjects or groups at baseline, they should be stratified before randomization according to likely predictors of outcome, and then randomized within strata. The advantage of randomized controlled interventions is that when randomization is applied to large numbers of individuals or groups; it tends to eliminate confounding effects even for unrecognized confounders. However, when only a few individuals or groups are available for study, the benefits of randomization are minimal, and it is usually better to use a non-randomized companion.

## Blinding

Sometimes it is possible to 'blind' subjects, those implementing an intervention, and/or those assessing outcome measures as to whether an individual or group received a particular intervention. This can have two advantages:

- Prevention of confounding that might occur if knowledge of the intervention led to other parallel changes (either deliberate or subconscious)
- Reduction of potential bias in the assessment of outcomes (e.g. from placebo effects)
- Blinding is particularly important where the assessment of outcomes depends on subjective judgment by the participant or an investigator

Section 9

# Environmental medicine

# Chapter 35

# Environmental protection

# Environmental medicine

The World Health Organization (WHO) defines environmental health as: those aspects of human health, including quality of life, that are determined by physical, chemical, biological, social, and psychosocial factors in the environment and the theory and practice of assessing, correcting, controlling, and preventing those factors in the environment that can potentially affect adversely the health of present and future generations. There is substantial overlap between environmental and occupational health and, while occupational health professionals are not expected to be specialists in this area, they may be called on to advise on environmental health risks arising from industrial activities and must be able to recognize and manage these issues.

## General principles

- Environmental exposures are often more subtle than workplace exposures, and are generally of much lesser degree (e.g. pesticide exposure in farming communities, outdoor air pollution), and effects are often less easily attributable to the exposure
- Where an environmental exposure is recognized to affect health, the aim is to protect the population by removing or reducing exposure, e.g. reducing ambient air pollution by improvements in engine and fuel technology
- *This exposure, effect, control paradigm* (Fig. 35.1):
  - provides a framework for understanding how a specific exposure might lead to an individual health effect
  - identifies where control measures might be instituted, e.g. by reducing personal exposure or reducing emissions by legislation
- The response is likely to be multidisciplinary and may require involvement from public health, environmental health, and emergency medicine specialists

## Exposures

- Pathway from source to receptor normally via environmental media e.g. air, water (except electromagnetic radiation, which requires no carrier)
- Route of exposure via inhalation, ingestion, or dermal absorption, or other routes (noise, vibration, ultraviolet (UV) light)
- Quantification of exposure/dose related to concentration of hazardous substance, magnitude and duration of exposure, and individual characteristics of receptor (e.g. age, body weight, comorbidities)
- Estimation of exposure may be by questionnaire/structured interview, direct measurement (e.g. personal air sampling), exposure reconstruction with biological monitoring/biological effects monitoring, and indirect assessment using existing information to model exposure scenarios

## Control

- The main principles for control require identification of the critical agents, pathways, and populations at risk
- Route(s) of exposure and may be multiple (e.g. organophosphates may be dermally absorbed, inhaled, or ingested). An understanding of the proportion of the total dose from each route is essential when considering control
- The *precautionary approach* is usually used, where, without waiting for cast-iron proof that exposure A via route B causes disease C, action is taken to reduce overall exposure

## Practicalities of assessing environmental exposures and health impacts

The effect of an environmental exposure may come to notice through the following:

- *Increased exposure*: recognition that a population is exposed to a specific substance or pollutant mix, e.g. particulate air pollution in cities
- *Disease clustering*: recognition of a cluster of a specific disease in time and/or place (e.g. outbreaks of infectious disease)
- *By analogy*: with exposure to other proven exposure/outcome situations elsewhere, e.g. current concerns around exposure to nanomaterials bearing in mind the proven adverse effects of asbestos and the considerable delays in accepting the true health impact of that material

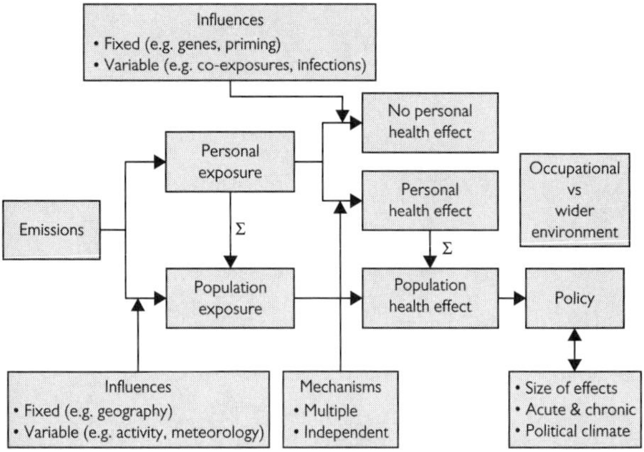


**Fig. 35.1** Health effects of an environmental hazard

## UK Health & Security Agency

As from 1st October 2021 UK Health Security Agency (UKHSA) became responsible for planning, preventing & responding to external health threats as well as operational leadership. It is an executive agency, sponsored by the Department of Health & Social Care. PHE was replaced by UKHSA and the Office of Health Improvement & Disparities.

# Public Health England

## Structure

Public Health England (PHE) was formed in 2013 as an executive agency of the Department of Health and Social Care under statutory changes passed in the Health and Social Care bill. PHE assumed many of the tasks of its predecessor, the Health Protection Agency (HPA), although several key functions have been handed to local authorities to run. PHE was tasked with the investigation and management of outbreaks of infectious diseases and environmental hazards, and ensuring effective emergency preparedness, resilience, and response for health emergencies.

PHE had the following public-facing divisions:

- Health Protection
- Health Improvement
- Knowledge and information
- Operations
- Regional units (South/Midlands/North/London)

## Role of the PHE Health Protection Division

The Health Protection Division's role was to protect the public health. Its remit remains broadly the same as that of the HPA, i.e. radiation protection services, infectious disease surveillance, coordination of investigation of national and uncommon outbreaks, advice to government on risks posed by various infections, and response to major public health incidents and international health alerts.

The Health Protection Division was made up of the following elements:

- Centre for Radiation, Chemical, and Environmental Hazards
- Centre for Infectious Disease Surveillance and Control
- Major Incident Response Unit
- Field Epidemiology Unit

Despite its name, PHE retained some health protection responsibilities for Scotland, Wales, and Northern Ireland, especially on chemicals, poisons, and radiation. The UK Government and the devolved administrations have designated PHE to act as the National Focal Point for all of the UK and only PHE should communicate directly with supranational health bodies such as the European Centre for Disease Control and the WHO. PHE also works closely with other relevant agencies, notably the Office for Environmental Protection, and the Department for Environment, Food and Rural Affairs (DEFRA).

Website for UKHSA www.gov.uk/government/organisations/uk-health-security-agency

Transforming the public health system; Department of Health & Social care March 2021

## Relevant legislation

- UK Statutory Instrument; Open Government Licence. *Health and Social Care Act 2012*. London. Available at: http://www.legislation.gov.uk/ukpga/2012/7/contents

# Outdoor air pollution

- Air pollution arises from a variety of sources, being a mix of different particles, gases, and chemicals, the proportions of which vary by source and by site
- *Air pollutants are emitted from both man-made and natural sources, including*:
  - combustion of fossil fuels
  - industrial processes and solvent use (e.g. chemical and mining industries)
  - agriculture (e.g. ammonia and methane emissions)
  - waste treatment
  - natural sources (volcanic eruptions, sea salt, disturbed dust)
- Continued exposure to polluted air confers a greater risk to health than discrete episodes, although the Great London Smog of December 1952, which killed at least 4,000 individuals, was critical as it led to the introduction of the Clean Air Act 1956

## Content and sources

### *Particulate matter*

*Sources*

- Vehicle emissions
- Industry
- Power generation
- Natural sources

*Measures*

- *Concentration:*
  - gravimetric method: direct measurement of mass (μg/m³ of air); also allows for chemical analysis
  - optical: light scattering, absorption, extinction; allows for real-time measurement of particle concentration
- *Size distribution*:
  - electron microscopy: offers broad range of detail on particulates, but time-consuming
  - impactor: separates particulates based on aerodynamic diameter
- *Particulate size fractions*:
  - inhalable fraction: particulate matter with diameter approximately 30–10 μm that can be inhaled but do not generally penetrate further than the bronchi (e.g. wood dusts)
  - thoracic fraction: particulate matter <10 μm in diameter ($PM_{10}$), can penetrate terminal bronchioles (e.g. cotton dusts)
  - respirable fraction: particulate matter <2.5 μm in diameter ($PM_{2.5}$), can penetrate alveoli (e.g. crystalline silica dusts)
- *Nanoparticles*:
  - ultrafine particles of 1–100 nm diameter
  - inhaled nanoparticles may pass into the systemic circulation and animal studies suggest may result in cardiovascular health effects

*Gases*
- *Sulphur dioxide*: largely from industry or power generation
- *Nitrogen oxides*: 2° pollutant from vehicles
- *Ozone*: 2° pollutant from action of UV light on oxides of nitrogen and hydrocarbons
- *Carbon monoxide*: from vehicles

*Other substances*
- *Carcinogens*:
  - benzene, 1,3-butadiene, polycyclic aromatic hydrocarbons (PAHs)
- Lead

## Health effects

*Diffuse pollution*
- ↑ Particles are associated with ↑ morbidity and mortality from cardiorespiratory disease on a day-to-day basis, particularly affecting those with other risk factors (e.g. old age, pre-existing disease)
- Similar health effects are seen with ozone and sulphur dioxide (particularly asthma and bronchitis)
- Effects of long-term exposure on disease prevalence and severity may be more marked
- Although occupational exposures to diesel engine exhaust emissions and benzene known to increase risk of cancer, there is no direct evidence of an increased risk from lower-level environmental exposures

*Point source pollution*
- Emissions from point sources can cause clusters of disease. The worst recorded peacetime incident occurred in Bhopal, India, in 1984, when an incident at the Union Carbide (India) Ltd plant led to the release of a cloud of methyl isocyanate gas causing over 3,800 deaths
- More usually, concerns arise about the potential for an identified source to be a cause of disease clusters. See ➲ Chapter 34, Epidemiology, in Investigation of disease clusters
- Many disease clusters are chance events unrelated to point sources of pollution, but understandably generate considerable public concern

## Control
- Air quality standards are based on health effects worldwide
- Responsibility for meeting national air quality standards falls to local councils in the UK

## Relevant guidance and legislation
- *Department for Environment Food And Rural Affairs, DEFRA UK Air Information Resource*. Available at: https://uk-air.defra.gov.uk/
- *GOV.UK Clean Air Strategy 2019*. London. Available at: https://www.gov.uk/government/publications/clean-air-strategy-2019

# Indoor air pollution

- In the developed world 90% of time is spent indoors
- In parts of the developing world much greater time is spent outdoors, although morbidity and mortality are greater in low-income countries due to lack of access to clean cooking fuel
- Indoor air quality is not subject to legislation except in the workplace, where occupational exposure standards apply in some settings

## Indoor pollutants

- Environmental tobacco smoke (ETS)
- Allergens, including moulds, pollen, animal dander
- Indoor penetration of pollutants from outside (notably particles)
- Cooking fume
- Microorganisms and endotoxins
- Nitrogen dioxide from gas cookers and fires
- Carbon monoxide faulty gas appliances
- Ozone
- Biomass fuel combustion, e.g. plant material or agricultural waste
- Low volatile organic compounds (VOCs), e.g. acetone and formaldehyde in cleaning products
- Radon

## Health effects

- *ETS exposure*: respiratory symptoms in children, lung cancer
- *Biomass fuel*: lung cancer, chronic obstructive pulmonary disease
- *Cooking fume*: lung cancer, possibly exacerbation of asthma
- *Radon*: lung cancer
- *Sick building syndrome*: the exact cause is unknown, but it appears to relate to air exchange rates and temperature. It presents with an ill-defined collection of symptoms (see ➲ p. 370, Sick building syndrome)

## Control

- There are no indoor air quality standards, although smoking has been banned in all enclosed public spaces since 2007
- Control of outdoor emissions lowers levels of indoor air pollution
- By law anyone installing or servicing gas appliances must be gas safe registered
- Landlords are required to have gas appliances and flues serviced annually, and retain a landlord gas safety record
- Selection of low VOC building products

## Relevant legislation and guidance


- UK Statutory Instrument; Open Government Licence 1998. *Gas Safety (Installation and Use) Regulations 1998*. Available at: http://www.legislation.gov.uk/uksi/1998/2451/contents/made
- National Institute for Clinical Excellence (NICE) (2020). *Indoor Air Quality at Home*, Guidance NG149. NICE, London. Available at: https://www.nice.org.uk/guidance/ng149

# Water pollution

The WHO estimate that 2.2 billion people do not have access to safely managed drinking water. Microbiological contamination is well recognized, but contamination by heavy metals, etc., also occurs. Pollution follows spills, industrial discharges, mining (especially abandoned mines), agricultural run-off, and leachate from landfill. Naturally occurring metals may affect water quality. Pollutants may be point sources such as industrial discharges or diffuse pollutants including agricultural run-off of animal wastes. Contamination of estuarine and inland seas may lead to severe impacts. Water is divided into surface waters (streams, rivers, lakes) and ground water (~98% of available fresh water). These are closely linked and exchange occurs between them.

## Heavy metals

*Arsenic*

Naturally present in high levels in groundwater in some countries (Bangladesh, Chile, India, etc.). Chronic ingestion causes:
- Thickening of the skin (hyperkeratosis) and ↑ pigmentation
- Skin, bladder, and lung cancer
- Peripheral neuropathy
- Diabetes
- Adverse pregnancy outcomes and infant mortality

*Arsenic remediation*
- Test water for arsenic and mark supplies with ↑ arsenic, e.g. by painting handpumps a different colour
- Educate people as to risks of drinking high arsenic water
- *Source low arsenic water*:
  - rainwater harvesting
  - deep boreholes to aquifers with low arsenic
  - sand filtration

*Fluoride*
- Fluoride in water is mostly of geological origin, although can also be caused by discharge of gaseous industrial waste
- Fluoride in drinking water at ~1 ppm prevents dental caries
- Exposure to fluoride >2 ppm as a child <8 years old → dental fluorosis
- Children >8 years cannot develop dental fluorosis
- Mild dental fluorosis → white spots on teeth (hypomineralized enamel); severe dental fluorosis is rare → heavily mottled and stained teeth
- Chronic ingestion of water with >10 ppm fluoride → osteofluorosis—back pain, calcified ligaments, bone thickening

Severe cases of osteofluorosis resemble ankylosing spondylitis

*Fluoride remediation*
- Removal of fluoride from water is difficult and expensive
- Use low fluoride water supplies where possible
- Defluorination may be carried out using contact precipitation

## Lead (Pb)

- Water may be contaminated by inorganic lead in houses with lead pipes (pre-1970s UK housing) or copper pipes joined with lead-solder
- Soft water areas ↑ lead levels as acidic water ↑ plumbo-solvency
- ~25% of UK houses still have lead water pipes

*Lead remediation*

- Water suppliers ↓ plumbo-solvency by adding lime to low-pH supplies (to ↑ pH) and/or orthophosphate (a corrosion inhibitor), if water at the consumer's kitchen tap is likely to have lead >10 μg/l
- Remove all lead pipes and tanks from potable water supplies
- Run kitchen tap for 1 minute if it hasn't been used for >6 hours
- Never use water from hot water taps for drinking or cooking

## Organic chemicals

*Pesticides*

- Spills or run-off from agriculture → ground water contamination
- Main threat is to aquatic life, rather than human health

*Solvents*

Contamination of ground water by organic solvents may occur where chemicals spill or underground fuel storage tanks leak.

*Polychlorinated biphenyls*

Polychlorinated biphenyls (PCBs) are persistent organic pollutants (POPs) that may contaminate water supplies, e.g. PCBs from abandoned electrical equipment.

## Other contaminants

*Nitrates*

- Occur in ground water due to fertilizers and animal wastes
- Nitrates → nitrites → methaemoglobinaemia ('blue baby syndrome') in bottle-fed infants <3 months of age (see ➲ p. 362, Methaemoglobinaemia)
- *Nitrate remediation*: reverse osmosis, distillation, or anion exchange

*By-products of water treatment*

- Water is often treated with chemicals such as chlorine or chloramines
- Trihalomethane is generated by organic material reacting with chlorine. Whether it is a carcinogenic hazard is disputed

*Endocrine disruptors*

- Phthalates, human sex hormones, and pharmaceutical agents in water have been linked with abnormal sexual developmental in some species
- Whether exposure leads to adverse effects in humans is unclear.

## Relevant legislation

WHO Factsheet. *Drinking Water*. WHO, Geneva. Available at: https://www.who.int/news-room/fact-sheets/detail/drinking-water

# Soil pollution

## Introduction

- Soil pollution may occur due to industrial, military, or agricultural releases of pollutants
- Municipal waste disposal is a significant source in many countries
- May be point source or diffuse (e.g. oil run-off from roads)
- Contamination may arise locally, but deposition of pollutants from distant sources may also occur (e.g. acid rain from coal burning power plants, heavy metals, and dioxins from waste incineration)
- *Disposal of sludge and sediments*:
  - sewage sludge containing heavy metals such as lead
  - growth promoters containing copper in pig farming can lead to copper contamination of soils when slurry is applied to land
  - heavy metal contamination from disposal on land of silt and sediment dredged from harbours or river estuaries
- *Industrial activities in an area may leave a legacy of soil pollution for future generations*:
  - mining, e.g. mine tailings
  - metal refining
  - leather tanning (chrome)
  - demolition (asbestos)
  - town gas production
- Poor or non-existent records of waste disposal further complicate remediation in such cases

## Soil contaminants

- *Heavy metals*: arsenic, chromium, cadmium, lead, mercury, nickel
- Cyanide
- *POPs*: pesticides, organic solvents, PCBs, PAHs, dioxins
- Asbestos
- Radioactive substances

## Example of soil pollution

*Love canal*

- One of the best-known examples of soil pollution occurred in Love Canal (now called Black Creek Village) in upstate New York
- Approximately 22,000 tons of industrial chemical waste was buried in a disused canal near a residential area over many years
- Chemicals leached into the basements of some of the homes
- Studies reported ↑ miscarriages and birth defects
- >800 families had to be relocated
- One consequence of Love Canal was the creation of the US 'Superfund' programme in 1980 set up to protect human health and the environment by cleaning up contaminated land sites

# Food contamination

Food may be contaminated at any stage during production, processing, or distribution. The potential for contamination of food by microorganisms or toxins is well recognized and will not be considered further. Less commonly, chemical or metal contaminants lead to food poisoning outbreaks. Thus, food acts as one pathway for pollutants in the environment to act on human health. Animals may be affected by pollutants (e.g. lead-poisoned wildfowl), become ill and so easier to catch, and pose a hazard to human health if eaten.

## Groups at ↑ risk

- Producers and their families who largely consume their own produce
- Children and unborn children are at ↑ risk if exposed to neurodevelopmental toxins, e.g. methyl mercury

## How pollutants enter the food chain

- *Pollutants enter the food chain through contamination of air, soil, or water*:
  - discharges from factories
  - mines (e.g. heavy metals)
  - agriculture (e.g. pesticides)
  - waste dumps
- *Food may be contaminated during*:
  - production
  - processing
  - distribution
  - storage
  - preparation/cooking
- Sale of food not intended for human consumption
- Intentional adulteration of foodstuffs

## Agents implicated

- Cadmium-contaminated mine discharges entered the Jinzu River basin in Japan. Water used for irrigation of rice paddies led to cadmium entering the food chain. Consumption of cadmium-contaminated rice has led to *itai-itai* ('ouch ouch') disease, principally among post-menopausal women. Sufferers developed osteoporosis and proximal renal tubular dysfunction
- *Fish may absorb methyl mercury. Fishermen and their families who consume these catches are at special risk*:
  - in the Great Lakes area of North America mercury contamination has led to health advice being issued on fish consumption
  - in the 1950s, fishermen's families around Minamata Bay, Japan, who ate fish contaminated with methyl mercury experienced ↑ neurological illness. For several years, an electronics factory had discharged mercury in the bay, so contaminating marine life
  - lead: rarely, lead poisoning may arise from food contamination (e.g. spices, flour). Flour can be contaminated when a damaged millstone is repaired with lead. Illegal alcohol (moonshine) may be lead contaminated; life-threatening poisoning can occur in heavy drinkers

- *Consumption of adulterated oil sold as olive oil in 1981 led to Spanish toxic oil syndrome*: severe myalgia, eosinophilia, and pulmonary infiltration. Research points to the toxin being fatty acid esters of 3-(N-phenylamino)-1,2-propanediol. Approximately 20,000 people were affected and 300 died. Others were left with chronic paraesthesia and musculoskeletal and skin complaints
- 'Rice oil disease', termed '*yusho*' in Japan and yucheng in Korea, due to PCBs accidentally contaminating rice oil occurred in Japan in 1968 (1,800 cases) and Korea in 1978 (~2,000 cases). Unborn children exposed to PCBs and their breakdown products, polychlorinated dibenzofurans (PCDFs), showed developmental delay, behavioural problems, and ↓ growth. Chloracne and liver disease occurred

## Pesticides entering the food chain

*Organomercurials*

Following a series of bad harvests in the late 1960s and early 1970s, Iraq imported wheat treated with mercurial fungicides. The wheat arrived too late for planting that year and so the people consumed seed never intended for human consumption. More than 10,000 people died, and ~100,000 people suffered long-term health effects.

## Adulteration of foods

Unscrupulous producers, wholesalers, and shopkeepers may adulterate foodstuffs to maximize profits; this kind of fraud flourishes where food testing and enforcement are weak. Activities such as adding illegal dyestuffs to spices occasionally come to light. Food adulteration is principally an economic issue but depending on the adulterant used such food may affect human or animal health.

# Environmental impact assessment

Environmental impact assessment (EIA) is a tool used to identify the potential environmental, health, and social effects of a proposed project or development before the decision is taken on whether to proceed. The objective is to ensure that the environment is taken into consideration in planning and decision making, and that decision makers are fully informed and accountable. Legislation and practice vary around the world; in the UK it is a legal requirement for certain town and country planning projects, but for business and industry it is a non-mandatory part of corporate social responsibility.

## Components of an EIA

- *Screening*: identification of projects requiring formal EIA
- *Scoping*: identification of which potential impacts must be assessed, consultation with stakeholders, and development of terms of reference for EIA
- *Impact prediction*:
  - hazard identification: project broken down into stages/processes to produce a hazard matrix
  - exposure assessment: to determine which hazard exposures are likely to be minor, and which require formal assessment—consider concentration in air, water, etc., intensity (of noise, radiation, etc.), duration of exposure, exposure–response relationship (e.g. stochastic, deterministic), characteristics of affected population
  - health risks estimate: the nature and severity of the harm, numbers at risk, time scale over which harm will occur, latency of health effect, communication of risks to stakeholders
  - identification of mitigation measures: feasible, cost-effective measures to reduce risk. May be structural (e.g. design or location change, engineering controls) or non-structural (e.g. legal restrictions, economic incentives, provision of community services and training)
- *Determination of cost*: assessment of costs of mitigation vs costs of legal, financial, and reputational damage of not mitigating risk
- *Communication of findings*: communicate significance of findings to range of stakeholders including decision makers, regulatory bodies, and the wider public
- *Decision making*: whether to approve the project or not, and under what conditions
- *Monitoring, compliance, and enforcement*: monitoring whether predicted impacts and proposed mitigations occur as defined in the EIA and ensure unsuccessful mitigations are identified and addressed in a timely manner

## Relevant legislation and guidance

- UK Statutory Instrument; Open Government Licence. *The Town and Country Planning (Environmental Impact Assessment) Regulations 2017*. Available at: www.legislation.gov.uk/uksi/2017/571/introduction/made

Section 10

# Safety science

# Chapter 36

# Safety science

# Health and safety management framework

Employers are required to put in place suitable arrangements to manage for health and safety and to control health and safety risks. As a minimum, processes and procedures should meet legal requirements (see ➔ p. 556, Management of Health and Safety at Work Regulations 1999).

A formal management system or framework can help employers manage health and safety. These are known as occupational health and safety management systems. The Health and Safety Executive (HSE) in their document *Managing for Health and Safety (HSG 65)* provides guidance to leaders, owners, and line managers on a framework that can be adopted for health and safety arrangements. This edition of the HSE's guidance revised a traditional health and safety system known as Policy, Organising, Planning, Implementation, Measuring, Audit, and Review to a 'Plan, Do, Check, and Act' approach. This revised approach can help organizations achieve a balance between the systems and behavioural aspects of management, and it helps health and safety management to be seen and treated as an integral part of business management. The HSE Plan, Do, Check, Act cycle is shown in Fig. 36.1. The Plan, Do, Check, Act approach has also been adopted by, and utilized within, the international standard ISO 45001:2018 *Occupational health and safety management systems—Requirements with guidance for use*. ISO 45001 is not a normative standard. Its structure aids integration with other management systems such as environmental management and quality management. Further details about some of the key steps are covered in Chapter 19, Policies, and on ➔ pp. 388–391, Quality and audit in OH and ➔ p. 774, Measuring performance.

Organizations have a legal duty to put in place suitable arrangements to manage health and safety. HSE's core elements managing health and safety are:

- Leadership and management (including appropriate business processes)
- A trained/skilled workforce operating in an environment where people are trusted and involved

## Further information

HSE (2013). *Managing for Health and Safety*, HSG65, 3rd edn. HSE Books, Sudbury. Available at: http://www.hse.gov.uk/pubns/priced/hsg65.pdf

HSE. *Managing for Health and Safety*. HSE Books, Sudbury. Available at: https://www.hse.gov.uk/managing/index.htm

HSE (2013), Plan, Do, Check, Act An introduction to managing for health and safety. INDG275. HSE, UK. Available at: https://www.hse.gov.uk/pubns/indg275.pdf

HSE(2013). Leading health and safety at work. Actions for directors, board members, businhttps://www.hse.gov.uk/pubns/indg417.pdfess owners and organisations of all sizes. INDG417, HSE, UK. Available at:

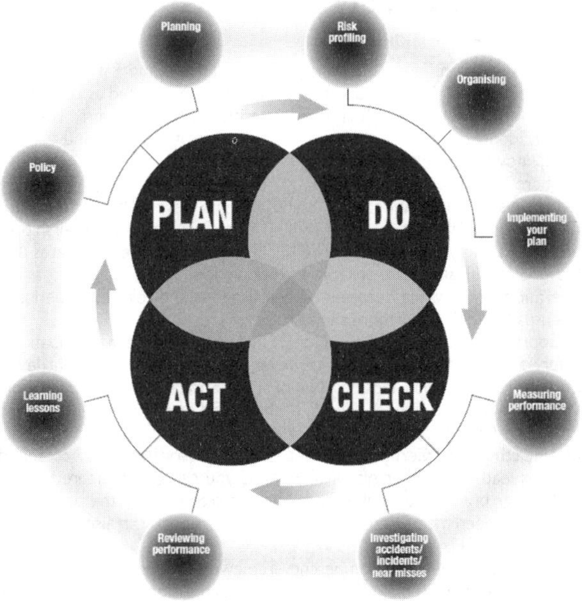


**Fig. 36.1** The Plan, Do, Check, Act cycle

Reproduced from HSG65, Managing for health and safety, p. 9. HSE Books (201. HSE Books under Open Government Licence 3.0

# Health and safety specialists

## Training and qualifications

Under Regulation 7 of The Management of Health and Safety at Work Regulations 1999, health and safety specialists are appointed as competent person(s) to provide health and safety assistance to employers. The HSE (2019) identifies competence as the combination of 'practical and thinking skills, knowledge and experience'.

There are several routes of entry into health and safety. There are two levels of qualification: level 3 and a degree level. The Institution of Occupational Safety and Health (IOSH) offers chartered membership to health and safety professionals. The IOSH membership website states that 'Level 3 qualifications are suitable for people looking to move into a first operational role, while degree level qualifications and relevant experience are usually required for more senior roles'.

Courses accredited by the National Examination Board in Occupational Safety and Health are available; however, there are many different levels of qualification which includes National Vocational Qualifications/Short Vocational Qualifications at Level 5, bachelor and master's degrees, and the Northern Council for Further Education Institute of Occupational Safety and Health Level 3 Certificate in Safety and Health for Business. Accredited courses lead to membership of IOSH, and you can gain chartered health and safety practitioner status once the requirements of the application stage have been met. Occupational health professionals can also gain membership of IOSH.

IOSH has reviewed the competency framework, *Professional standards for safety and health at work*, for health and safety professionals. The framework details a number of competencies relating to technical skills, core skills, and behavioural skills. The competencies include, for example, legislation and standards, policy, risk management, sustainability, human capital, ethical practice, strategy, leadership, etc. These competencies demonstrate the direction of travel for the health and safety specialist role and the business skills also required.

There have been several reviews of health and safety in the last few years, led by Professor Löfstedt. One recommendation, outlined in the *Common Sense, Common Safety Report*, was to professionalize health and safety consultants. An Occupational Safety and Health Consultants Register has been established to list consultants who can offer advice to UK businesses to help them manage health and safety risks.

## Duties of health and safety specialists

### *Advice on health and safety policies*

Health and safety specialists/professionals (e.g. health and safety managers, advisors, and safety officers) help to formulate policies related with:

- Risk profiling, organizational assessment, and the management and control of health and safety risks
- Safe plant and systems of work
- Safe work environment to reduce physical injuries and ill health (which includes physical health and mental health)
- Emergency preparedness and response procedures
- Incident, accident, and near miss investigation and reporting procedures

- Monitoring and reviewing performance
- Health and safety training (i.e. competency requirements)
- Legal requirements and compliance
- Fire safety (see ➔ p. 776, Fire safety)

*Other duties*

- Understand the application of the Health and Safety at Work, etc. Act 1974 and other legislation as relevant to the business
- Advising management on the design and safe use of plant and equipment
- Periodic inspections to identify unsafe plant, unsafe working conditions, and unsafe practices
- Worker consultation and involvement, e.g. communicating with trade union appointed safety reps or representatives of employee safety (➔ p. 552) through the Health and Safety Committee (as part of the worker involvement and consultation process)
- Facilitating or undertaking risk assessments
- Advising on compliance with current and new legislation
- Risk management, with initial focus on prevention
- Communicating finding/solutions at different levels
- Promoting and delivering occupational health and safety awareness, communication, learning/development/education programmes through toolbox talks, formal training sessions, briefings, etc.
- Providing information on incident/accident prevention techniques/ controls
- Recording, monitoring, analysing incident statistics
- Accident, incident, and near miss investigation
- Advising about the need to report incidents to HSE in compliance with Reporting of Injuries, Diseases, and Dangerous Occurrences Regulations (RIDDOR) (see ➔ p. 569, RIDDOR Regulations)
- Advising on work-related ill health instances in conjunction with occupational health and human resources
- Assessment of the work environment and work equipment
- Audit of health and safety systems (either using an inhouse process or a formal process against an international system such as ISO 45001: 2018)
- Measuring performance (including setting performance measures)
- Liaison with occupational health departments, government inspectors, local authorities (including fire services), and environmental protection agencies

## Further information

HSE (2019). *Competence*. HSE Books, Sudbury. Available at: https://www.hse.gov.uk/managing/competence.htm

HSE. *Delivering Health and Safety Reform*. HSE Books, Sudbury. Available at: https://www.hse.gov.uk/aboutus/health-and-safety-reform/index.htm

IOSH. *Competency Framework*. Leicester, UK. Available at: https://www.iosh.com/competencyframework

IOSH. *Membership*. Leicester, UK. Available at: https://www.iosh.com/membership/about-membership/membership-faqs/

Occupational Safety and Health Consultants Register (OSHCR). Available at: http://www.oshcr.org/

# Accident and incident investigation and management

## Definitions

HSE (2014) defines the following.

*Accident*
- An event that results in injury or ill health

*Incident*
- *Near miss*: an event, while not causing harm, has the potential to cause injury or ill health
- *Undesired circumstance*: a set of conditions or circumstances that have the potential to cause injury or ill health

*Dangerous occurrence*
- One of a number of specific, reportable adverse events, as defined in the RIDDOR 2013

## Purpose of investigation

Accidents/incidents need to be investigated for the following reasons:
- Ensuring legal compliance
- To identify and take appropriate actions to prevent reoccurrence
- To collect data required for accident reporting/notification to enforcing authority
- To collate information required to defend an insurance claim
- To identify the cause

Investigating near misses and learning lessons from them can prevent costly accidents. Other benefits of investigation include worker morale and attitude towards health and safety, preventing further business losses.

## Causes of accidents/incidents

Most accidents/incidents involve multiple, interrelated causal factors and occur as a result of deficiencies, errors, omissions, or unexpected changes. The HSE classifies causes as:
- *Immediate causes*: the agent of injury or ill health
- *Underlying causes*: unsafe acts and unsafe conditions
- *Root causes*: an initiating event or failing from which all other causes or failings spring. Root causes are generally management, planning, or organizational failings

## Consequences of accidents/incidents

- Damage only, e.g. to plant and machinery, and products, etc.
- Minor injury
- Serious injury/ill health
- Major injury/ill health
- Fatal
- Loss of production
- Breach of legislation and prosecution, fines, fee for intervention
- Civil claims
- *Environmental impact*: spillages, discharge
- Damaged reputation
- Lowered employee morale

## Outcome of a health and safety investigation

A risk control action plan should be designed. Where possible the risk control measures to recommend and their priority should be chosen in the following order:

- Measures which eliminate the risk
- Measures which combat the risk at source
- Measures which minimize the risk by relying on human behaviour

Management actions as a result of an investigation can include the following examples:

- Identification of specific instruction and training needs
- Need for detailed job safety analysis to identify the hazards and precautions
- Improving systems of work (safe design, safe work procedures, permit to work, safety rules, and review of risk assessments)
- Improve the level of supervision
- Identify areas/tasks where personal protective equipment (PPE) is required and/or the correct type of PPE
- Preparation of safety guidance notes for particular activities
- Setting up committees and feedback to all concerned
- Improvement in the working environment, e.g. lighting levels, ventilation, workplace layout
- Improvement in information and its provision
- Review health and safety responsibilities

## Further information

HSE (2014). *Investigating Accidents and Incidents: A Workbook for Employers, Unions, Safety Representatives and Safety Professionals.* HSE Books, Sudbury. Available at: https://www.hse.gov.uk/pubns/hsg245.pdf

# Cost and reporting of accidents

All organizations should determine the costs of accidents. This process helps to identify causes and consequences as well as providing useful information on strategies and drivers for future accident prevention.

All accidents have both direct and indirect costs and incur insured and uninsured costs.

- *Insured costs include*:
  - claims on employers and public liability insurance
  - damage to building, equipment, or premises
- *Uninsured costs include*:
  - lost time
  - extra wages for overtime working, temporary labour
  - sick pay
  - production delays
  - fines
  - legal costs and excess on any claims
  - investigation time
  - clerical effort
  - reputation and loss of image

The total cost of an accident can be determined by considering both direct and indirect costs.

## Direct costs

- Increase in liability premiums
- Claims for injury, or for defective or unsafe products
- Fines and damages awarded in criminal courts for breaches of law
- Court and legal costs
- Costs of absence (e.g. salary of absent employee, overtime worker, loss of output)

## Indirect costs

- *Treatment*:
  - first aid
  - transport
  - hospital attendance
- *Lost time*:
  - injured person
  - management
- *Production*:
  - loss of production
  - damage to plant
  - training
  - supervision
- *Investigation (time and manpower)*:
  - management
  - safety advisors
  - safety representatives
  - liaison with external agencies
- *Others*:
  - administration
  - costs incurred by witnesses attending court

## Legal requirements to report and keep records

A RIDDOR report is required only when the accident is 'work related'; and it results in an injury of a type which is 'reportable'. Consideration of 'work-related' relates to the way the work was organized, carried out, or supervised; any machinery, plant, substance, or equipment used for work; and the condition of the site or premises where the accident happened. The following must be reported:

- *Work-related accidents which cause death*:
  - to workers and non-workers must be reported.
- *Work-related accidents which cause certain serious injuries*:
  - the list of 'specified injuries' are detailed in Regulation 4 of RIDDOR 2013
- *Diagnosed cases of certain industrial diseases*:
  - diagnoses of certain occupational diseases, where they are likely to have been caused or made worse by their work as detailed in Regulations 8 and 9 of RIDDOR 2013
- *Certain 'dangerous occurrences' (incidents with the potential to cause harm)*
  - there are 27 categories of dangerous occurrences that are relevant to most workplaces
- *Over 7-day injuries to person at work*: a written report must be sent to the enforcing authority within 15 days of the accident
- *Reportable gas incidents*
- *Non-fatal accidents to non-workers*
  - if there is an injury and the person is taken directly from the scene for treatment at hospital for that injury

## Recording

Records of incidents covered by RIDDOR are also important. They ensure you collect sufficient information to allow you to properly manage health and safety risks. You must keep records of:

- Any accident, occupational disease, or dangerous occurrence which requires reporting under RIDDOR
- Any other occupational accident-causing injuries that result in a worker being away from work or incapacitated for more than 3 consecutive days (these only get reported under RIDDOR when incapacitation goes on to exceed 7 days)

## Reporting

- Online at http://www.hse.gov.uk/riddor and complete appropriate online report form
- *Telephone*: remains available for reporting fatal and specified injuries only via the incident contact centre

## Documentation

Copies of all forms sent to the authorities must be kept.

## Further information

HSE (2013). *Reporting Accidents and Incidents at Work, A Brief Guide to the RIDDOR 2013*. HSE Books, Sudbury. Available at: http://www.hse.gov.uk/pubns/indg453

HSE. *Economics of Health and Safety*. HSE Books, Sudbury. Available at: http://www.hse.gov.uk/economics

HSE. *Health and Safety Statistics*. HSE Books, Sudbury. Available at: http://www.hse.gov.uk/statistics/

HSE. *How to Make a RIDDOR Report*. HSE Books, Sudbury. Available at: http://www.hse.gov.uk/riddor/report.htm

HSE. *RIDDOR—Reporting of Injuries, Diseases and Dangerous Occurrences Regulations 2013*. HSE Books, Sudbury. Available at: http://www.hse.gov.uk/riddor

# Injury frequency rates

Injury frequency rates enable analysis of trends, facilitating comparison between one organization and another, or between different parts of the same organization.

## Examples of accident rate measures

- Incidence rate = (total number of injuries per year/number of persons employed) × 100,000
- Frequency rate = (total number of injuries per year/total number of hours worked per year) × 1,000,000
- Incident frequency rate = (total number of injuries per year/average hours per week + weeks per year + employment) × 1,000,000

## Standardization of data

When comparing incident rates it is important to ensure that the following elements are standardized:

- Definitions of what has to be reported
- Reporting procedures
- Methods of calculation

In addition to the industry data, certain industry associations provide their members with accident statistics, which may be used for 'benchmarking', i.e. comparing performance data with competitors.

## National accident statistics

The HSE produces the health and safety statistics and annual *Summary Statistics*. This contains summary data on fatal injuries to workers, subdivided into employees and self-employed, and non-fatal injuries to workers.

## Further information

HSE (2015). *Injury Frequency Rates*. HSE Books, Sudbury. Available at: https://www.hse.gov.uk/statistics/adhoc-analysis/injury-frequency-rates.pdf

HSE (2021). *Health and Safety Statistics*. HSE Books, Sudbury. Available at: https://www.hse.gov.uk/statistics/

# Measuring performance in health and safety management

Performance needs to be measured to provide information on the progress and current status of the strategies, processes, and activities used by an organization to control risks to health and safety. It also identifies whether you are achieving your aims and objectives. Monitoring also reinforces management commitment to health and safety, and it must add value and not just be a tick-box exercise.

Two types of monitoring systems are used, and effective monitoring arrangements will include a balance of both types of measures:

- *Active methods* (*leading indicators*), which monitor the design, development, installation, and operation of management arrangements
- *Reactive methods* (*lagging indicators*), which monitor evidence of poor health and safety practice but can also identify better practices that may be transferred to other parts of a business

## Active (proactive) monitoring data

- Staff perception of management commitment to health and safety
- Routine inspection of premises, plant, equipment
- Periodic review of documents, e.g. risk assessments, maintenance programmes
- Exposure and health surveillance data to assess adequacy of controls
- Extent of compliance with standards
- Observation of work and behaviour
- *Training in health and safety*: the impact/outcome of the training and its effectiveness
- Knowledge among staff of risks and controls
- Time taken to implement actions
- Actual use of personal protective equipment
- Frequency of inspections, safety tours, audits
- Competence of staff with responsibilities for health and safety
- Number of staff suggestions for health and safety improvements
- Staff attitudes to risk and use of controls
- Employee engagement score

## Reactive monitoring data

- Regulatory agency enforcement action
- Ill health and sickness absence data/records
- Reported accidents, incidents, and injuries
- Damage to property

## Outcome of performance assessment

For the risks that are identified during active and reactive monitoring, actions should include the following:

- Identify reasons for under-performance
- Identify underlying failure in health and safety management systems
- Prevent recurrence
- Satisfy legal requirements, e.g. reporting under RIDDOR

## Links to business performance

The health, safety, and well-being of employees is aligned to business performance. IOSH has produced a report, *The Healthy Profit*, which illustrates the financial, ethical, and sustainability benefits of businesses investing in the health and safety of their workforce and encourages transparency in how they report against safety and health performance. These considerations can help identify performance measures.

## Further information

HSE website for information about health and safety management, including leadership actions for directors and boards; safety climate tool; risk assessment tools for slips, trips, and falls; industry-specific advice on machine safety; and other aspects. Available at: https://www.hse.gov.uk/

IOSH. *The Healthy Profit*. Available at: https://www.iosh.com/more/iosh-means-business/healthy-profit/

# Fire safety

Most fires are preventable and can be avoided if those responsible for workplaces and other buildings adopt the right behaviours and procedures. For a fire to start there must be a source of fuel (something that burns), a source of oxygen, and a source of ignition (heat). A fire risk assessment must be carried out and kept up-to-date.

Fires may start accidentally, but the threat of arson should also be considered, and appropriate measures are taken to reduce this risk. Good housekeeping, effective maintenance (especially of electrical equipment), rigorous health and safety procedures, effective fire detection, warning systems, and firefighting equipment all reduce fire risks.

## Fire regulations

- Current regulations governing fire prevention in England and Wales came into force from October 2006—the Regulatory Reform (Fire Safety) Order 2005. Similar legislation applies in Scotland—the Fire (Scotland) Act 2005
- Fire authorities no longer issue fire certificates
- *The regulations cover non-domestic premises*:
  - offices and shops
  - factories and warehouses
  - residential care
  - sleeping accommodation
  - education
  - places of assembly
  - theatres/cinemas
  - outdoor events
  - health care
  - transport facilities
- Enforcement of the Fire Safety Regulations is the responsibility of the local fire and rescue service, except for Crown property where HM Fire Safety inspectors take this role

## Other relevant regulations

Where a workplace contains dangerous substances, which can create an explosive atmosphere, e.g. petrol, gas, solvents, paints, flour, or wood dusts, then Dangerous Substances and Explosive Atmospheres Regulations, 2002, and the Equipment and Protective Systems intended for use in Potentially Explosive Atmospheres Regulations 1996 will likely also apply.

## Main requirements

The main requirement is to carry out a fire risk assessment (this is the responsibility of the 'responsible person'). The Department for Communities and Local Government (DCLG) website has advice on the legislation including guidance on fire safety and fire risk assessments.

*Identify the fire hazards*

- The person in control of premises must undertake a fire risk assessment
- This assessment should identify sources of fuel, ignition, and oxygen

*Identify people at risk*

- Employers need to consider all persons who may be affected in the event of a fire on their premises including staff, visitors, and the public
- Particular consideration needs to be given to making adequate provision for those at greater risk (such as lone workers) and vulnerable people such as disabled people, elderly people, and children or parents with babies

*Evaluate, remove, or reduce the risks*

The employer must provide adequate fire prevention measures and maintain them.

*Record your findings, prepare an emergency plan, and provide training*

- Keep a record of any fire hazards and what you have done to reduce or remove them
- Employers must have a clear plan of how to prevent fire and how people will be kept safe in the event of a fire (evacuation plan)
- Staff must be provided with sufficient information, instruction, and training on fire prevention and the actions necessary in the event of a fire. This may include measures such as training in the use of fire extinguishers, fire safety briefings, and regular fire drills to rehearse fire evacuation procedures

*Review and update the fire risk assessment regularly*

The fire risk assessment must be kept under regular review. Any significant changes, e.g. to premises or work practices, to your plan, or to risks, requires review of the emergency plan and you must inform others of those changes.

## Legislation and guidance

- DCLG. *Fire Safety in the Workplace*. Available at: https://www.gov.uk/workplace-fire-safety-your-responsibilities
- DCLG. *Fire Safety Law and Guidance Documents for Business*. Available at: https://www.gov.uk/government/collections/fire-safety-law-and-guidance-documents-for-business
- DCLG. *Fire Safety Risk Assessment: 5-Step Checklist*. Available at: https://www.gov.uk/government/publications/fire-safety-risk-assessment-5-step-checklist
- HSE. *Fire*. Guidance on fire safety in the construction industry. Available at: www.hse.gov.uk/construction/safetytopics/fire.htm
- Scottish Government. Available at: www.gov.scot/policies/fire-and-rescue/non-domestic-fire-safety/

# Electrical safety

We use electricity in our everyday life; however, electricity can kill or severely injure people and cause damage to property.

## General principles

- Risk assessments should cover electrical hazards
- Electrical equipment should be suitable for the work, the way it is going to be used, and for the environment in which it is used
- Managers should establish a system of rules and procedures wherever electrical work is to be carried out or ensure that contractors brought in to do electrical work have appropriate rules
- Electrical systems and equipment must be maintained, so far as reasonably practicable, to prevent danger. This includes portable equipment as well as fixed equipment
- In environments that are damp or wet, electrical equipment should be suitably insulated to prevent electrocution
- Where electrical equipment is to be used in areas where there is a potential for explosion, risk assessments must be undertaken, and suitable equipment should be employed
- Only competent persons should be allowed to work on electrical equipment, machinery, or installations
- The normal policy should be that work is only undertaken on equipment or installations known to be dead and electrically isolated
- Live system/equipment working should be the exception rather than the rule. It should only be carried out where it is unreasonable for work to be done on dead systems/equipment and where a suitable risk assessment has been carried out by a competent person
- Any equipment provided, e.g. voltage meters, should be suitable for use and adequately maintained
- Before commencing work on electrically isolated equipment it should be confirmed, through the use of a suitable test procedure by a competent person, that the equipment is dead
- Wherever possible, equipment should be disconnected (and protected against accidental reconnection) from electrical power before any work is attempted
- Any equipment to be worked on should be isolated and secured by 'locking out' using an inter-lock. In addition, a notice should be posted at the point of disconnection so that all personnel are aware that electrical work is being undertaken on the dead system
- Any high-voltage equipment should be earthed so that, in the event of equipment failure, the operator will be protected
- Where work has to be carried on any high-voltage electrical equipment/installations a permit to work system will be required

## Legislation and guidance


- HSE (2013). *Electricity at Work: Safe Working Practices*, HSG 85, 3rd edn. HSE Books, Sudbury. Available at: https://www.hse.gov.uk/pubns/priced/hsg85.pdf

## Work-related road safety

Driving at work activities are undertaken by professional/vocational drivers; drivers driving fleet, lease, or hire vehicles; or drivers driving their own privately owned vehicle.

### Epidemiology

The independent Work-Related Road Safety Task Group estimated that:

- One third of all road accidents involve someone at work
- ~1,000 people die in work-related road crashes in the UK each year
- 250 people are seriously injured each week in work-related road crashes

### General principles

- All road users on the public highway must comply with road traffic legislation
- Health and safety law applies to work activities on the road in the same way as it does to all work activities
- The Health and Safety at Work, etc. Act 1974 places duties on employers to manage risks to employees who drive at work (i.e. on-the-road work activities) to prevent harm to workers and the public and this includes road safety. The organization's health and safety policy should address road safety—a specific road safety policy may be required
- Health and safety law does not apply to commuting (i.e. travelling between their home and their usual place of work)
- Employers should undertake a risk assessment of their work-related road safety, consult with employees and their representatives, and act on their findings. Risks must be prioritized and controlled
- The provision of training and instruction where necessary

Following the hierarchy of control, the need for road travel should be considered and either video/teleconferences be used instead to prevent the travel, or a safer transport method such as rail is used to substitute/reduce the risk.

### Safe vehicles

- Vehicles should be fit for purpose
- Well maintained and in road-worthy condition
- Safety and ergonomic features should be considered when purchasing new fleet vehicles
- Tachographs, where fitted, should be regularly inspected to confirm professional drivers are complying with legislation, e.g. speed limits
- Privately owned vehicles must be insured for business use and if over 3 years old, have a valid Ministry of Transport test certificate

### Safe drivers

- Drivers should be competent for the vehicle and any special equipment on the vehicle
- Medically fit to drive that category of vehicle
- Hold a valid license for the country being driven within. Licenses should be inspected upon employment and regularly reviewed thereafter

*Drivers should be*:
- trained in the safe operation of their vehicle, e.g. pre-journey checks of warning lights, tyre pressures
- trained in adjusting seating and head restraints
- trained in securing loads and ensuring their correct distribution in the vehicle
- aware of their vehicle height, width, and weight (laden and unladen)
- trained to respond to a vehicle breakdown safely

## Safe journeys

The journey plan should take an appropriate route (e.g. large vehicles should avoid low bridges and narrow roads)

Where possible avoid rush hours

Should take account of prevailing weather and road conditions

Work patterns and delivery timetables should be realistic to avoid placing inappropriate demands on drivers, which might lead them to speed

Driving rosters should take account of total hours worked and not just hours at the wheel to reduce driver fatigue

Long journeys should be broken by an overnight stop

## Legislation and guidance

HSE (2014). *Driving at Work: Managing Work-Related Road* Safety, HSE INDG 382(rev1). HSE Books, Sudbury. Available at: 🖱 http://www.hse.gov.uk/pubns/indg382.pdf

## Section 11

# Practical procedures

# Chapter 37

# Clinical tasks and procedures

# Recording an occupational health consultation

Every new consultation should start with an explanation to the patient/employee of the role of occupational health and the rules of communication (see ➲ p. 396, Ethical principles in clinical occupational health practice, ➲ p. 398, Confidentiality, consent, and communication, ➲ p. 482, General principles of fitness for work assessments).

## Checklist for clinical consultations

*Handwritten notes*

- Notes should be written clearly (preferably in black ink) or dictated and typed
- Every sheet should be labelled with the patient/client's name, and at least one other identifier (e.g. date of birth (DOB) or address) or preferably a unique serial number
- *Essential details of referral*:
  - by whom? (self, manager, other)
  - reason (short-term absence, long-term absence, performance issues, other)
  - job title, employer, duration of employment
  - membership of pension scheme if applicable
- *Clinical history with a focus on current symptoms and function*: ask about day-to-day activities in enough detail to judge whether the Equality Act applies

⚠ Ask routinely about alcohol and recreational drug intake. Alcohol is often used as a maladaptive coping strategy by those with anxiety or depression.

- Previous medical history and sickness absence history
- *Details of the current job including information about tasks, or preferably a job description*: remember to consider psychosocial (demand, control, support, job satisfaction) as well as physical aspects of the job
- *Occupational history including duration of previous similar jobs or exposures*: episodes of job change or loss because of health problems; any applications for compensation or Industrial Injuries Benefit. Be alert for relevant coexposures
- *Clinical examination*: relevant physical examination, and mental state examination where appropriate
- *Summary and conclusions*: it is useful to include a brief formulation or justification of conclusions, especially where there is likely to be dispute
- *Output*:
  - list in handwritten record all outputs from the consultation including telephone calls, other conversations, written reports, or letters
  - always record a brief summary of the content of verbal outputs
  - see ➲ p. 442, Long-term sickness absence, ➲ p. 482, General principles of fitness for work assessments, for the content of outputs to the referring manager
- Print your name and job title
- Sign and date every record

- Record that the employee has been informed about their rights of access to the report from the consultation, whether they wish to have a copy of the report, and (if so) if they wish to see the report before it is released

*File copies of the following documents*

- *Informed consent for referral*: this is sometimes included on a referral *pro forma*. Where consent has not been gained prior to referral, it is good practice to obtain it at the beginning of the consultation. This is particularly important if the occupational health (OH) physician is concerned that the employee is unhappy or poorly informed about the referral. An example of an information sheet for referred clients is given in ➲ p. 881, Appendix 2: Consent for an occupational health assessment
- Written referral from employer
- *Supporting material where appropriate*: e.g. job description, musculoskeletal or mental health symptoms questionnaires if used in the clinical assessment, relevant test results (e.g. lung function)
- Reply to manager
- Letters to general practitioners (GP) or specialist consultant where applicable
- Written consent for reports (see ➲ p. 616, Access to Medical Reports Act 1988)

*Workplace visits*

- Workplace visits should be carried out, where indicated by the initial clinical assessment. Functional assessment in the workplace can be very useful in offering practical advice about adjustments to work
- File handwritten notes of the visit (including interview with manager or coworkers) and typed report
- File any supporting material, e.g. Control of Substances Hazardous to Health or other risk assessments, occupational hygiene data

# Assessing mental health: Tools

## Things to ask yourself before using assessment tools

- Why am I using a tool?
- Am I clear about the distinction between a screening tool and a diagnostic tool?
- Do I refer a patient just because of their score?
- What will I do if my clinical impression differs from the score on the tool?

## Advantages of using assessment tools

- *As an* aide memoire: ensure all important questions asked
- To provide an 'objective' measure of severity
- To generate a score to assist communication with other health professionals
- To measure response over time, e.g. following treatment
- Can be completed by the patient at home or in waiting room

## Disadvantages of using assessment tools

- *Crude measures*: patients can score highly without being especially 'ill'
- *Falsely reassuring*: distinction between screening and diagnosis
- Don't consider your own clinical impression of the patient
- Have the potential to lead to unnecessary referrals
- Only examine symptoms in one (occasionally two) domains, e.g. most depression tools ignore anxiety and vice versa
- Tools assess symptoms rather than function
- Many tools are under copyright

## Checks and calibration

Depression and anxiety assessment tools have not been validated in the occupational health setting. Ad hoc use is to be discouraged. Many psychiatrists do not use rating scales at all. There is a recognition, e.g. in medico-legal circles, that several factors, including occasionally frank exaggeration, can contribute to the score on a questionnaire.

The choice of rating scale needs consideration; the choice will vary depending on why a scale is thought necessary. The use of assessment tools may be best considered as part of a wider strategy for identifying and managing depression in the workplace. Training might be needed. Policies for how to respond to high scores or unexpected scores should be established before they occur.

## Examples of assessment questionnaires

- *Patient Health Questionnaire*: commonly used in 1° care in the UK so may assist communication with GP. Is free and accessible online. Limited range of questions and possibility of overscoring—false positive. No anxiety questions
- *Beck Depression Inventory*: lengthier more detailed questionnaire but takes longer to complete. Includes questions about somatic symptoms. No anxiety questions. Copyright
- *Hospital Anxiety and Depression Scale*: specifically designed for use in hospital settings where patients have several possible causes for somatic symptoms such as fatigue—*is this your patient population?* Includes anxiety symptoms which can be scored separately. Utility of cut-offs (8 and 10) not clear. Copyright

## Further information

Mitchell AJ, Coyne JC (eds.) (2010). *Screening for Depression in Clinical Practice: An Evidence-Based Guide*. Oxford University Press, New York.

# Psychological therapies

## Overview

Psychological interventions are best viewed in the same way as pharmacological or physical interventions. There are many to choose from:

- An evidence-based approach, where available, is recommended
- Benefits and adverse effects need to be carefully weighed
- Specific interventions are effective for specific disorders
- Cost is likely to be part of any treatment decision

► One difference to consider is that the effectiveness of many psychological therapies depends in part on the relationship between the patient and the therapist

## Counselling

*Pros*

- Readily available
- Can be relatively inexpensive
- High reported levels of patient satisfaction

*Cons*

Little good evidence to suggest effective in treatment of psychiatric disorder (compared to lower levels of distress or upset)

### Further information

BACP. Regularly updated website. Available at: http://www.bacp.co.uk

Henderson M, Hotopf M, Wessely S (2003). Workplace counselling. *Occupational Environmental Medicine* 60:899–890.

McLeod J (2010). The effectiveness of workplace counselling: A systematic review. *Counsel Psychotherapy Resolutions* 10:238–248.

## Cognitive behavioural therapy

*Pros*

- Excellent evidence base
- Effective for a wide range of common mental disorders including depression, phobias, post-traumatic stress disorder
- Also effective for chronic fatigue syndrome and irritable bowel syndrome
- Provides patients with 'tools' they can use should difficulties recur
- Can be delivered effectively online (e.g. beating the blues)

*Cons*

- Is hard work! Patients need to do homework and keep detailed diaries
- Trained therapists in short supply
- Can be expensive
- Patients require a minimum of six to eight sessions; some need many more

### Further information

Beating the Blues (2006–2012). *Beat Depression and Anxiety*. Regularly updated web resource Available at: http://www.beatingtheblues.co.uk

Gilbert P (2009). *Overcoming Depression: A Guide to Recovery with a Complete Self-Help Programme* Constable & Robinson, London.

LTTFF. *Living Life to the Full*. Self-help web resource. Available at: http://www.llttf.com

Royal College of Physicians London (2012). *Cognitive Behavioural Therapy*. Available at: http://www.rcpsych.ac.uk/mentalhealthinfoforall/treatments/cbt.aspx

## Psychodynamic psychotherapy

*Pros*

- Can help with complex and longstanding difficulties
- Allows patients time to think *why* things might have happened as well as how they might make changes

*Cons*

- *Is a major commitment*: sessions are at least weekly and continue for many months or longer?
- Model not necessarily easily understood
- Many different forms (e.g. Freudian, Jungian, Lacanian, etc.) and not always clear which is indicated
- Can be expensive
- Relatively little evidence of benefit for diagnosable psychiatric disorders

## Further information

Royal College of Physicians. London. *Psychotherapies*. Regularly updated web resource. Available at: http://www.rcpsych.ac.uk/mentalhealthinfo/treatments/psychotherapies.aspx

Tavistock and Portman. London. Regularly updated web resources. Available at: http://www.tavistockandportman.nhs.uk

## Improving access to psychological therapies

- National Health Service programme to improve the delivery of treatment for common mental disorders according to National Institute for Clinical Excellence (NICE) guidelines
- Since 2011, its remit has broadened to include support to patients of all ages and patients with long-term physical conditions
- Widely though not yet universally available in England
- Cognitive behavioural therapy (CBT) and other talking therapies available in a range of different intensities
- Keeping patients in or returning patients to work is a priority and trial of employment advisors working alongside improving access to psychological therapies therapists is underway

## Further information

NHS (2018). The Improving Access to Psychological Therapies (IAPT) Pathway for People with Long-term Physical Health Conditions and Medically Unexplained Symptoms. Available at: https://www.england.nhs.uk/wp-content/uploads/2018/03/improving-access-to-psychological-therapies-long-term-conditions-pathway.pdf

# Chronic pain

Persistent pain in the absence of signs of tissue injury is now recognized as reflecting a dysfunctional sensory system. Changes occur at receptor level in both the peripheral and central nervous system. Although there is no specific predisposing personality type, pain is associated with catastrophizing (excess worry about a situation).

## Classification of pain

- Somatic
- Visceral
- Neuropathic (nerve injury)
- Idiopathic

## Epidemiology of chronic pain

- In the UK, 7.8 million people have chronic pain; 50% have depression
- 50% of loss of quality of life is attributable to pain
- Low back pain is the commonest pain-related cause of work loss
- Of the top ten health problems impacting productivity, three specifically relate to pain (back/neck pain, other chronic pain, and arthritic pain)

## Risk factors for disability and sickness absence

- High pain intensity
- High perceived disability
- Beliefs and fears about the harmful effect of work
- High physical job demands
- Inability to modify work
- High job stress
- Poor workplace social support or dysfunction
- Poor job satisfaction

**New Zealand yellow flags system predicts absence risk:**

- Have you had time off work in the past with pain?
- What do you understand is the cause of your pain?
- What are you expecting will help you?
- How is your employer responding to your pain? Your coworkers? Your family?
- What are you doing to cope?
- Do you think that you will return to work? When?

⚠ If the worker expects the pain to be a sign of harm or they are reliant on passive behaviours to manage pain, then they are at risk of long-term absence from work.

The Keele STarT Back Tool identifies those at risk of chronic disability.

## Pain management

Based on three key principles—reassurance if it is safe to move, rehabilitation to support movement, and relief of pain. General approach includes:

- Referral to local exercise initiatives and simple analgesia
- Paracetamol for mild to moderate pain
- Anti-inflammatories for inflammatory pain (⚠ but side effects)
- Amitriptyline, and other tricyclics or anticonvulsants (gabapentin or pregabalin) as first line medication for neuropathic pain
- Referral to specialist pathways and services for those who fail to improve or have complex pain issues
- CBT approach if significant psychosocial factors are present
- Unless specific serious medical pathology is suspected (red flags), diagnostic tests such as X-ray or magnetic resonance imaging scans are not appropriate
- Facilitate modifications to work, including limits to the duration of concentrating on a task or a reduction in physical demands
- The Pain Toolkit describes 12 steps to managing pain

► The prognosis for return to work falls dramatically after 12 weeks, so the focus should be on early, rapidly phased, goal-based, rehabilitation.

### The pain toolkit

- *0–2 weeks*: provide support and reassurance to stay active
- *2–6 weeks*: develop a specific plan which identifies obstacles and provides a structure to return to work, including modifications
- *6–12 weeks shift up a gear*: provide vocational rehabilitation and cease ineffective health care interventions
- *12+ weeks*: establish communication between all players, avoid unnecessary medical interventions, and ensure social solutions in place

## Difficult cases

These should be managed by a multidisciplinary pain service.

- *Pain medications*:
  - opioids

⚠There is little evidence for the efficacy of strong opioids in many pain conditions. Long-acting preparations are recommended and avoidance of variable effect medications such as pethidine

- Radiofrequency denervation can be cost effective in highly selected cases
- Management of depression including CBT and other cognitive approaches including meditation techniques
- If struggling at work, explore reduction in hours, retraining/redeployment, or (as a last resort) ill-health retirement

## Further guidance

Keele University. *Keele STarT Back Tool*. Available at: http://www.keele.ac.uk/sbst/

NICE. *Low Back Pain: Early Management of Persistent Non-specific Low Back Pain*, CG88. NICE, London. Available at: http://publications.nice.org.uk/low-back-pain-cg88

NICE. *Management of Long-Term Sickness and Incapacity for Work*, PH19. NICE, London. Available at: http://www.nice.org.uk/PH19

# Night worker health assessment

Under the European Working Time Directive employers must offer a health assessment to night workers (➔ p. 608, Working Time Regulations 1998).

## Process

A night worker's assessment is a two-stage process consisting of:

- A screening questionnaire
- A medical examination for those in whom the screening questionnaire identifies a medical problem that might be caused or made worse by night work, and which needs further detailed assessment

## Role of occupational health

This will depend upon the arrangements for access to OH services:

- Where there is an in-house OH department, both screening questionnaires and subsequent examinations will usually be carried out by the OH team
- However, in organizations which have contracted or ad hoc access to OH advice, the screening questionnaire is often administered by the HR department or a manager. This is permissible under the Working Time Regulations provided that the advice of an appropriate health professional is sought when designing the questionnaire
- Medical examinations (where appropriate) must be carried out by a suitably medically qualified person
- To review the health effects in shift and night work (see also ➔ Chapter 5, Psychosocial hazards)

## Communication of results

- The rules that apply to all OH reports are relevant for communicating the outcome of night worker health assessments. Medical or confidential information should not normally be disclosed (and if so, only with the individual's consent). Conclusions should be confined to practical advice about fitness for night work and any adjustments required, including transfer to day work
- Where there is no OH department (and the screening questionnaires are handled by HR officers or others), the screening questionnaire should be designed to protect confidentiality. One method is to ask workers to tick a single box (following a checklist of health problems that are relevant for night work) to declare the *existence* of a health problem, but not to disclose its *nature*. This approach is supported by the Department of Trade and Industry

## Health assessment questionnaire for night workers

*Example of night worker health assessment questionnaire*

The purpose of this confidential questionnaire is to enquire if you have any health problem which could be affected by night work, so that where necessary an appropriate medical review can be arranged.

*Personal Details*

- Surname
- Forename/s
- DOB
- Gender
- Job title
- Manager
- Contact address (internal or home address)

*Health declaration*

Please indicate if you have any of the following health disorders:

- Diabetes
- Heart or circulatory disorders
- Depression or anxiety
- Stomach, intestinal, or bowel disorders
- Chronic chest conditions
- Any disability affecting mobility which will cause difficulties in arranging night work
- Any condition that causes recurrent or continuing difficulty with sleeping
- Any medical condition for which you are taking medicines according to a strict timetable
- Any specialist care requiring attendance at hospital clinics for treatment

*Next steps*: if you have declared a health problem, you may be referred to a doctor or nurse for further assessment. This will be done in confidence, and no medical details will be passed to your employer without your consent. The medical adviser will make a simple declaration of your fitness for night work and the need for any adjustment to working hours on health grounds.

# Methods for alcohol and drug screening

Managers are responsible for the health, safety, and welfare of those working under their supervision. This responsibility includes ensuring employee fitness for work. The appropriate legislation for most work situations is covered by one of the following in most cases: Health and Safety at Work etc. Act, the Misuse of Drugs Act 1971, and The Road Traffic Act 1988.

Crucial before testing is the establishment of appropriate policies and procedures. Managers must be alert to intoxication from alcohol or drug misuse. This can be established by simple observations and assessment of cognition, speech, posture, and movements without recourse to screening tests.

## Screening tests

Testing for drugs and alcohol should not be undertaken lightly and must be part of a substance abuse policy (see ➲ p. 416, Substance abuse policies).

- *There are many different forms of screening tests for alcohol and drugs of misuse that may be conducted* (see Table 37.1):
  - directly at the 'point of contact'
  - indirectly using specialist laboratory services
- Alcohol may be measured by breath, saliva, or urine testing
- Drug testing may use blood, saliva, hair, or urine with differing considerations as shown in Table 37.1

⚠ All test subjects must be invited to predeclare any prescribed or over-the-counter medicines and any special foods or supplements that they have taken, to enable accurate test interpretation.

**Table 37.1** Summary of screening methods

| | Breath | Saliva | Urine | Blood | Hair |
|---|---|---|---|---|---|
| Advantages | | | | | |
| Easy to collect | + | + | + | | + |
| Observable test | + | + | | + | + |
| Minimal training | + | + | + | | |
| Equipment readily available | + | + | + | + | + |
| Low cost | + | + | + | | |
| Long-term detection | | | | | + |
| Disadvantages | | | | | |
| Difficult to collect | | | | + | |
| Potential for deliberate interference by subject | | | + | | |
| Limited application (substances that can be tested) | + | + | | | + |

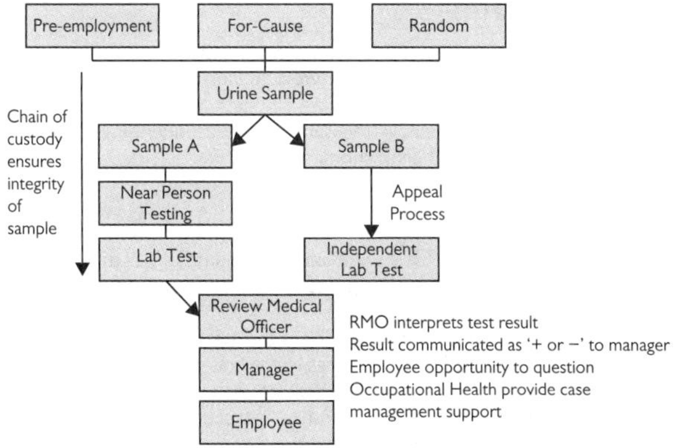


**Fig. 37.1** Alcohol and drug screening process

## Chain of custody

- This is the process for managing the collection, handling, storage, and testing of biological samples to prevent any possible contamination or interference (see Fig. 37.1)
- Normally, the sample is divided at collection into samples A and B and sealed, with a tamper evident seal, in the presence of the test subject

In the event of a positive sample A test result, the test subject can arrange an independent test of sample B.

## Who should be tested?

- The selection of test subjects must be clearly defined in the policy and selection procedures should avoid any possible discrimination
- *Possible options may include*:
  - announced or unannounced testing of all employees
  - only those in defined safety critical roles
  - those involved in accidents ('for cause')

## Positive test results

- Alcohol testing often uses the Road Traffic Act standards to define fitness for work
- Drug testing reports only the presence of an illicit drug as a marker for drug-taking behaviour
- The Review Medical Officer will interpret and report test results, but managers are responsible for deciding possible employment implications

## Further information

BMA (2016). Alcohol, drugs and the workplace—The role of medical professionals. Available at https://www.bAlcohol, drugs and the workplace—The role of medical professionals

# Lung function

In occupational medicine lung function is most measured:

- During the assessment of fitness for work in individuals with respiratory disorders
- As part of respiratory health surveillance and subsequent investigation (➔ p. 464, Respiratory health surveillance)
- Detection of occupational asthma

## Common measurements and definitions

- Forced vital capacity (FVC) is the maximum volume of gas that can be expired from the lungs during a forced expiration from a position of full inspiration
- Forced expiratory volume in 1 s ($FEV_1$) is the maximum volume of gas that can be expired from the lungs in the first second of a forced expiration from a position of full inspiration
- $FEV_1$/FVC gives an indication of airways obstruction. A ratio below 70–75% indicates significant obstruction
- Peak expiratory flow (PEF) is the maximum flow achievable from a forced expiration starting at full inspiration with an open glottis. It occurs early in the expiratory manoeuvre, when the lungs are expanded, and the airway diameter is large
- Simple self-paced tests of walking distance can be used in the objective assessment of functional disability. However, such tests depend on motivation. The gold standard test is to measure $VO_2$ max directly. This requires standardized testing and for routine clinical OH work indirect $VO_2$ max using the Chester Step Test or similar procedures are more commonly used

## Nomograms

$FEV_1$, FVC, and PEF vary with height, age, and sex, and with ambient temperature and pressure. Conversely, $FEV_1$/FVC is useful because it is self-normalizing (unaffected by height, age, and sex). Individual recordings of lung volumes should be compared with nomograms (reference graphs of the normal readings in healthy adults for a given age, height, and sex). This can be done using standard graphs, but most modern automated spirometers provide a printout that includes a comparison with normal 'expected' values. Results printed on thermal paper need to be photocopied or scanned.

## Quality control in lung function testing

It is important that measurements are reproducible. This is particularly important for health surveillance, where serial measurements are used to identify temporal changes in function. Therefore, lung function testing should be governed by a written protocol such as those from the British Thoracic Society recommends the following:

- Spirometers and peak flow meters must be maintained and calibrated according to the manufacturer's instructions
- Quality check on the volume time and flow volume printout
- Record the greatest $FEV_1$, FVC, and PEF from at least three technically acceptable manoeuvres. The variability between readings should not exceed 5%. On some machines this is referred to as A or B levels

**Rejection criteria for lung function measurements**

- Leak at the mouthpiece
- Poorly coordinated start to the manoeuvre
- Cough during the manoeuvre
- Early termination of the expiration including 'glottic closure'
- Submaximal effort

## Interpretation

Having achieved acceptable levels of variation between readings interpretation relies not just on numerical values but on the scrutiny of both volume time (V/T) and flow volume (F/V) graphs to ensure compliance with spirometry procedure and the enhance detection of abnormalities. Z scores which relate to standard deviations are increasingly used to determine if individuals' results are abnormal.

## Further information and guidance

American Thoracic Society (2002). Guidelines for the six-minute walk test. *American Journal of Respiratory Critical Care Medicine* 166:111–117. Available at: http://ajrccm.atsjournals.org/cgi/content/full/166/1/111

British Thoracic Society and the Association of Respiratory Technicians and Physiologists (1994). *Guidelines for the measurement of respiratory function.* Recommendations of the British Thoracic Society and the Association of Respiratory Technicians and Physiologists. *Respiratory Medicine* 38:165–194.

# Serial peak flow testing

Method of choice for suspected cases of occupational asthma.

## Protocol

It is important that readings are as reproducible as possible. The patient should first be instructed in basic PEF technique by a suitably qualified professional. The patient should be observed and corrected on poor technique. Readings taken at the same time should be within 5% before the technique is deemed satisfactory.

*Recording regime*

- The best of three PEF readings should be recorded every 2 hours during waking time. Measurements should be continued at home and at work
- Reading should continue for a period of at least 4 weeks, including at least a 1-week period away from work
- *A standardized sheet should be used by the patient to record the timing of*:
  - symptoms
  - medication, in particular bronchodilators
  - significant exposures, e.g. work activity (noting that coexposure to more than one allergen can occur), leisure time exposure to smoky rooms, cold air, exercise
- Patients should be instructed not to enter missing or very late readings, but to leave blanks if readings are inconvenient or inadvertently forgotten

Tampering and non-compliance are feasible

## Recording and interpreting results

- Serial PEF charts are usually plotted graphically to show the minimum, maximum, and mean peak flow readings each day. Note on the graph treatments and exposures, and presence at work or home
- Various computer programmes are used by specialist centres. Some are freely available for use by OH practitioners, including the Obstacle Avoidance System (OASYS) software. OASYS uses a scoring system to assess serial PEF records, and preset cut-off scores to determine occupational asthma cases (94% specificity and 75% sensitivity)
- *The diagnostic features of occupational asthma on a serial PEF record are*:
  - variable airflow obstruction, with >20% variation in PEF values
  - consistent falls in peak flow on work days compared with non-work days

## Further information and guidance

OASYS. *Oasys and Occupational Asthma*. Software is available at: http://www.occupationalasthma.com/default.aspx Midlands Thoracic Society UK 2021 Birmingham

# Screening audiometry

## Purpose

Hearing conservation programmes employ industrial audiometry to confirm the effectiveness of existing noise control measures. Health surveillance is required for all employees exposed at the upper action value and those workers at ↑ risk between the lower and upper action values (see ➲ p. 582, Control of Noise at Work Regulations 2005). Most OH services offer screening with air conduction (AC) rather than diagnostic audiometry. The latter involves tests of both AC and bone conduction. By measuring hearing thresholds (the faintest sound perceived at that frequency) the aim is to detect deterioration before the individual is aware of any deficit.

► The test–retest reliability of industrial audiometry is limited. There are many causes of hearing loss other than noise-induced hearing loss (NIHL) (see ➲ p. 334, Noise-induced hearing loss). Do not assume that hearing loss in a noise-exposed worker is necessarily NIHL (see ➲ p. 466, Classification of hearing loss, and ➲ p. 476, Patterns of hearing loss).

## How to perform screening audiometry

*Tools required*

- *Pure tone audiometer*: several audiometers are available for industrial audiometry including the Bekesy self-recording audiometer and computer-based automatic systems. Frequencies tested are 500 Hz and 1, 2, 3, 4, 6, and 8 kHz, and intensity of tone ranges from 0 to 120 dB HL
- Matched earphones with insulating ear muffs

► Ideally audiometry tests are carried out in a soundproof booth or room to decrease ambient noise. Background noise should not exceed that stated in EN 26189.

*Screening questionnaire*

- *The employee should complete a short questionnaire to record*:
  - occupational and hobby noise exposure (e.g. music, shooting, motor sport) and use of hearing protection
  - risk factors for hearing loss (use of ototoxic drugs, head injury, meningitis, ear disease, ear surgery, family history of deafness)
  - symptoms such as dizziness, tinnitus, ear discharge, or communication difficulties due to hearing impairment

*Clinical examination*

- Otoscopy
- Record evidence of otitis externa, tympanic perforations, etc.
- Tuning fork testing (Rinne and Weber tests)

*Exposure enquiry*

Employees should not be noise exposed in the 16 hour prior to test to reduce the risk of temporary threshold shift (TTS). Alternatively, wear personal protective equipment if noise exposed prior to testing.

- Record noise exposure in the 16 hours before testing
- Where there is doubt as to the presence of TTS, repeat audiometry later when not noise exposed

*Procedure*

Detailed information on audiometry methods is available in EN 26189.

- Explain the procedure to the employee and give clear instructions
- The tester should check to confirm that the employee has understood
- The employee should don the earphones and the tester should check fitting
- Once test commences, observe the employee's performance to confirm that he/she is correctly responding to the screening audiometry
- Poor attention and lack of understanding make testing impossible
- If audiogram is at odds with speech communication, repeat the test
- Once the test is complete, it should be reviewed with the employee

*Checks and calibrations*

- Test ambient noise level with a noise meter to confirm that background noise is within recommended limits
- *A three-stage approach to calibration is advised*:
    - Stage A: daily inspection (e.g. loose/damaged headphone wires); self-test audiogram identifies gross changes in performance.
    - Stage B: 3-monthly on-site objective test of calibration
    - Stage C: annual workshop calibration check/recalibration if required. If daily/quarterly checks raise doubts, recalibration is indicated

## Retention of audiometry records

Records of health surveillance should be retained for as long as the employee remains in employment. As claims for NIHL may arise many years after employment ends, it is prudent to retain records for longer.

## Relevant standards and guidance


- BS EN 60645–1 (2001). *Audiometers. Pure-Tone Audiometers Published by European Standards*
- EN 26189 (1991). *Specification for Pure Tone Air Conduction Threshold Audiometry for Hearing Conservation Purposes; Published by European Standards*
- HSE (2005). *Controlling Noise at Work. The Control of Noise at Work Regulations 2005*, L108. HSE Books, Sudbury, Sudbury.
- *The British Society of Audiology*. Bathgate Available at: http://www.thebsa.org.uk/

# Colour vision testing

Pre-employment or pre-placement testing for colour vision deficits may be required in safety critical jobs (aviation, firefighting, railways) or in jobs requiring good colour matching (printing, textiles). One example of a safety critical job is seafaring, where deck crew must distinguish other ships' red and green navigation lights at night to avoid collisions.

Congenital red/green colour vision deficits occur in 8% of men and 0.4% of women, reflecting the X-linked inheritance of this condition. Although such people are often termed 'colour blind' this is a misnomer as most show altered colour recognition.

## Procedure

The accuracy of colour vision testing is influenced by the test employed, the individual's visual acuity, and the adequacy of lighting. There are many colour vision tests, but few are widely used in occupational health practice.

What matters is whether an employee's colour perception is adequate, in terms of safety and performance, for the proposed role. In recent years some industry bodies have reviewed colour vision demands in their industry and revised guidance on colour vision standards and testing for specific occupations, notably the UK's Maritime and Coastguard Agency for seafarers, the Civil Aviation Authority for flight crew, and the Fire Services for firefighters. These revised standards should avoid unnecessarily excluding some individuals with colour vision deficits who are, in fact, fit for that work.

### Ishihara test

- Ishihara plates were designed as a screening test for congenital red/green colour vision deficits. This test is the one most employed in the occupational setting
- Several different versions of this test exist, including the full 38 plate, an abbreviated 24 plate, and a concise 14 plate edition
- The 38-plate edition consists of an introductory plate, transformation plates (2–9), vanishing plates (10–17), hidden digit plates (18–21) and classification plates (22–25). The numbers on transformation plates are read as different numbers by those with colour vision deficits when compared with those with normal colour vision. Vanishing plate numbers are invisible to those with red–green deficits. Classification plates are used to classify those screening positive on plates 2–17. Birch recommends that the hidden digit plates are unhelpful and should be omitted
- The 24-plate edition has an introductory plate, transformation plates (2–8), and vanishing plates (9–13)
- The Ishihara test should be viewed at arm's length in daylight or similar artificial setting
- Many with normal colour vision will misinterpret some plates, and these misinterpretations should be distinguished from true errors
- The individual should be asked to read and identify the number on each plate
- Undue delay (>4 s) in identifying a number suggests a mild deficit. Three or more errors on plates 2–17 of the 38-plate edition or two errors on plates 2–13 of the abbreviated 24-plate test indicate red/green colour deficit

## City University test

- The City University test (3rd edn) is a two-part test. Part 1 is a sensitive screening test of four pages, with four lines of coloured dots arranged in columns of three. The individual is asked to identify differences in colour (where they exist) in each column. It may be used to identify tritan deficits based on specific errors made on the lower half of pages 2, 3, and 4
- Part 2 is a series of six plates, each of which has a central, coloured dot and four coloured dots arranged around the central dot. The individual must identify which of the four surrounding dots is the closest colour match to the central dot
- Part 2 will classify subjects as protan, deutan, tritan, or normal colour perception
- Those with mild deficits score normally or make few errors in Part 2

## 15D Farnworth Testing

This is a relatively quick and convenient test to define the nature of the colour deficiency by arranging tablets of different saturated hues in sequence and plotting on a circular diagram. The test discriminates between congenital and acquired retinal defects.

## Lantern tests (Holmes Wright and CAM)

These have been replaced by the computer-based Colour Assessment and Diagnosis Test.

## Relevant standards and guidance

- HSE (1987). *Colour Vision Examination: A Guide for Occupational Health Providers*, MS7. HSE Books, Sudbury. Available at: http://www.hse.gov.uk/pubns/ms7.pdf

## Further information

Birch J (2001). *Diagnosis of Defective Colour Vision*, 2nd edn. Butterworth Heinemann, Oxford.

HSE (2005). *MS7 Colour Vision Examination—A Guide for Occupational Health Providers*, 3rd edn. HSE Books, Sudbury.

# Clinical assessment of hand–arm vibration syndrome clinical grading

The vascular and neurological components of hand–arm vibration syndrome (HAVS) are graded according to scales first developed by a workshop in Stockholm. These scales have been modified by Lawson and McGeogh[1] (see Tables 37.2 and 37.3) and are used internationally and by the HSE and UK Faculty of Occupational Medicine to frame advice on avoidance and career counselling. Stage 2 is divided into early and late. Although stage 2 v refers to the frequency of attacks as well as the extent, it is generally accepted that cold exposure is the major determinant of frequency of attacks rather than severity of the HAVS. The Griffin score (see Table 37.2) is also helpful in applying a Stockholm grade. It is widely agreed that stage 4 v is likely to reflect the effects of underlying disease such as scleroderma rather than HAVS.

For the sensorineural assessment, it is important to note that reduced sensory perception and dexterity refer to examination findings rather than symptoms. For both the vascular and sensorineural scale each hand is assessed and staged separately.

**Table 37.2** Workshop scale for classifying vibration white finger

| Stage | Griffin score | Description |
|---|---|---|
| 0 v | 0 | No attacks |
| 1 v | 1–4 | Attacks affecting only the tips of the distal phalanges of one or more fingers |
| 2. (early) | 5–9 | Occasional attacks affecting distal and middle (rarely also proximal) phalanges of one or more fingers |
| 2. (late) | 10–16 | Frequent attacks of whiteness affecting the distal and middle (rarely also proximal) phalanges of one or more fingers |
| 3 | 18 or more | Frequent attacks affecting all phalanges of most fingers all year |
| 4 | | In stage 3, with trophic skin changes in the As 3 v with trophic changes |

Occasional = 3 or less attacks per week.

Frequent = more than 3 attacks per week.

1. Lawson IJ, McGeoch KL (2003). A medical assessment procedure for a large number of medico-legal compensation claims for hand–arm vibration syndrome. *Occupational Medicine* 53:302–308

**Table 37.3** Stockholm workshop scale for classifying sensorineural HAVS

| Stage | Symptoms |
|---|---|
| 0S sn | Exposed to vibration but no symptoms |
| 1 sn | Intermittent numbness and/or tingling |
| 2 sn (early) | Intermittent numbness and/or tingling reduced sensory perception |
| 2 sn (late) | Persistent numbness and/or tingling, reduced sensory perception |
| 3 sn | Constant numbness and or tingling, reduced sensory perception, and manipulative dexterity in warmth |

Constant = present all the time.

Persistent = lasting more than 2 hours.

Intermittent = not persistent.

Additionally, the vascular effects are sometimes allotted a score, widely known as the Griffin score, based on the phalanges in which blanching symptoms are reported (see Fig. 37.2).

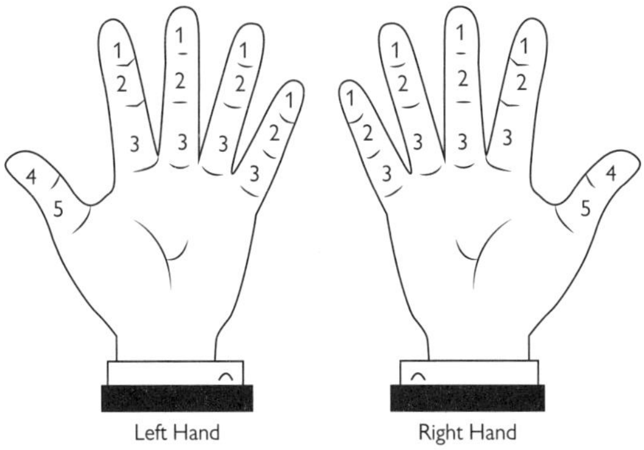


Left hand:

| Score: | Th | 1 | 2 | 3 | 4 |
|---|---|---|---|---|---|
| Total: | | | | | |

Right hand:

| Score: | Th | 1 | 2 | 3 | 4 |
|---|---|---|---|---|---|
| Total: | | | | | |

**Fig. 37.2** Griffin blanching score

# Chapter 38

# Non-clinical tasks and procedures

# Occupational hygiene report

Occupational health (OH) professionals must be able to assess the quality and relevance of occupational hygiene reports, interpret them, and advise the employer on further action. This checklist summarizes the structure and content of an occupational hygiene survey report.

## Title page

- Name and address of client
- *Consultant*: name (printed legibly), qualifications, signature
- Date of issue
- Report reference number

## Executive summary

- One-page summary of purpose, main work activities investigated, findings, and conclusions including response to specific questions raised by client when requesting the work

## Introduction

- Background to the investigation
- Who requested the survey and the purpose of survey
- Information provided by client
- Date on which the work (survey) was conducted
- Description of plant, its layout, workforce, and main processes

## Information on processes assessed

- Types of processes and/or tasks assessed
- Equipment/tools/chemical substances used by workforce
- Patterns of work (shift work)
- Control measure available and whether they are used
- Relevant health and safety legislation
- Occupational exposure limits for hazards identified
- Summary of potential health effects, e.g. acute and chronic

## Assessment methodology

- Techniques used to evaluate exposure; both sampling and analysis methods, e.g. Methods for the Determination of Hazardous Substances published by the Health and Safety Executive (HSE)
- Sampling strategy including selection of individuals for sampling and sampling periods
- Techniques used for evaluating effectiveness of control measures
- Instrument type used and their calibration

## Results and discussion

- Tables of results showing the following: number of employees' monitored, actual exposure monitoring period (time), activity conducted by employees during sampling period, calculated exposure level, and adjusted results (time-weighted average concentrations).
- Data on the effectiveness of control measures used, e.g. engineering controls, personal protective equipment (PPE)
- Interpretation of results with reference to objectives and relevant legislation and exposure standards

- *Explanation for the following*:
  - variations in measured exposure levels
  - exposure patterns/trends
  - outliers
- Sources of error in data collection and uncertainties in estimating exposure levels

## Recommendations

- Key actions based on findings, e.g. improved control measures
- Prioritization of action including resources, expertise, and timescale
- Further exposure monitoring and justification

## Appendices

- Diagrams, drawings, photographs
- Equipment specification
- Certificates of analysis
- Additional detailed information on exposure data

⚠ Remember that if you are not an occupational hygienist, you should only interpret hygiene data to the extent of your competence. Most OH professionals have general training in the principles of occupational hygiene. However, always ask for clarification or explanation of results from the occupational hygienist who produced the report, particularly if the conclusions are not clear and/or well justified.

# Document a workplace inspection

### Part A Background information

- Name of company visited
- Department(s) inspected
- Purpose of inspection
- Name and qualifications of inspector
- Date of inspection

### Part B Inspection checklist

1. *Plant, process, materials*

- Site plan
- Processes and tasks conducted (routine and non-routine)
- Hazard types identified (including methodology). (*Hazard types*: physical, chemical, biological, psychosocial, and ergonomic/mechanical)
- Materials handled (raw materials, products, by-products, and waste products)
- Control measures available and their use, e.g. PPE, engineering controls, and administrative controls

2. *Personnel*

- *Workforce*: number, job titles, and gender
- Working hours and shift patterns
- Sickness absence, risk assessment, Reporting of Injuries, Diseases, and Dangerous Occurrences Regulations reports, and health surveillance data

3. *Services and records*

- Welfare facilities (canteen, changing rooms, showers, etc.)
- OH staff and clinical facilities
- OH services provided
- *Record*: types, format, safe keeping, confidentiality, and access

### Part C Findings

- Summary of processes and activities observed on site hazards types identified including their sources (location)
- Individuals exposed to hazards, when exposed, duration, and pattern of exposure
- Potential health effects associated with hazards identified
- Ranking/prioritization of risks to health
- Agreed list of actions, responsibilities, and timescale

Signature
Review data

# Carry out a noise assessment

The noise assessment can be divided into three stages.

### Background information

- Define purpose of the survey, e.g. collection of noise exposure data for compliance with the Control of Noise at Work Regulations 2005
- *Gather background information*:
  - plan of work/layout to be assessed
  - tasks performed and patterns of work
  - time spent on specific tasks and variability in exposure time
  - previous records of noise surveys/assessments
  - control measures available, e.g. ear muffs, noise refuge and control rooms, acoustic screens
  - any recent relevant health concerns/reported symptoms

### Preliminary site visit and static noise measurements

- Systematically identify all noise sources
- *Collect exposure information*: who is exposed, when, for how long, and how often
- Identify control measures used and their effectiveness
- Take measurements with a handheld sound-level meter at workers' position(s) relative to a noise source
- Plot noise levels on a site map (noise mapping) showing position of machines and workers. This helps to understand the distribution of noise levels for the area being assessed
- Estimate the LAeq for the job/task levels from information on tasks performed by workers and exposure time
- The LAeq for each job/task is then combined with its duration during the working day to determine the $L_{EP,d}$. The calculation can be performed using the electronic spreadsheet available on the HSE website www.hse.gov.uk/noise

### Detailed noise survey: Personal dosimetry

- *In certain situations the $L_{EP,d}$ and peak sound pressure level are best determined by personal dosimetry*:
  - fluctuating noise exposure levels
  - high exposure variability
  - sources of impulse noise
- Where $L_{EP,d}$ is likely to exceed the noise exposure limits, carry out octave band analysis (noise frequency pattern) for tasks performed by the workers. These data will assist with the selection and design of control measures
- Identify steps needed to reduce noise exposure as far as reasonably practicable by examining in turn the noise source, the transmission of noise from the source, and the individual exposed
- Keep records of assessment (see Table 38.1) and review

**Table 38.1** Noise monitoring survey data form

| | | | | | |
|---|---|---|---|---|---|
| a. *Premises*: name, address | | | | | |
| b. *Survey*: conducted by, date of survey | | | | | |
| c. *Survey equipment*: type, model, calibration, sound level meter settings, e.g. weighting, response time | | | | | |
| d. *Workplace*: layout, processes, noise sources | | | | | |
| e. *Individuals exposed*: number, shift pattern, tasks conducted | | | | | |
| f. *Ear defenders*: type available, actual use time, protection afforded by ear defender | | | | | |
| ***Estimate of personal exposure levels*** | | | | | |
| Tasks and location | Individual (name) | Noise level $L_{Aeq}$ | Exposure duration | $L_{EP,d}$ dB(A) | Peak pressure ($L_{Cpeak}$) |
| **Octave band analysis—dB levels at different frequencies** | | | | | |

| | | | | | | | |
|---|---|---|---|---|---|---|---|
| Frequency | 63 Hz | 125 Hz | 500 Hz | 1 KHz | 2 KHz | 4 KHz | 8 KHz |
| dB level | | | | | | | |

dB values, e.g. for a noise source (machine), need to be measured using an octave-band analyser as part of the survey, and record on the form for each frequency.

# Carry out a display screen equipment assessment

All organizations are likely to possess at least some equipment that falls under the terms of the Health and Safety (display screen equipment (DSE)) Regulations 1992, as amended (see ➔ p. 562, Health and Safety (DSE) Regulations 1992). These regulations require that every employer shall perform an assessment of workstations to assess and reduce risk for DSE users.

## Procedure

- The assessor should be trained regarding the requirements of the DSE regulations and how to undertake a DSE assessment
- Use a checklist or online questionnaire to gather operator feedback
- Implement reasonably practicable adjustments to mitigate risks
- Record the key findings and adjustments made for retention until the next DSE assessment

A home worker's workstation should be assessed even if the employer did not provide the workstation

## Elements to be considered in a DSE assessment

*Equipment*

- Workstation should be of sufficient size to permit adjustment of the equipment and should be non-reflective
- Chair should be height adjustable with an adjustable backrest that offers good lumbar support
- A footrest should be provided if the user so desires
- Display screen/monitor should give a clear image with adjustable contrast and brightness
- Keyboard should be adjustable, with sufficient space in front of the keyboard to support wrists/arms
- Keys should be legible, and the keyboard layout should facilitate use
- Document holder should be provided where required
- Non-keyboard input devices (mouse/tracker ball, etc.) should be suitable for the task and the user

*Environment*

- Adequate space
- Keep workstation tidy and free from clutter
- Adequate room/task lighting
- No direct glare or reflections on screen
- Adjustable window blinds
- Comfortable humidity levels
- Low noise levels from equipment
- Avoid trailing cables

*Equipment/user interface*

- Software should be fit for purpose
- 'Help' functions should be provided
- *User must be adequately trained in*:
  - use of equipment/software
  - setting up the workstation correctly

- *Poor user posture is a risk of musculoskeletal disorders (MSDs)* (see ➲ p. 286, Work-related upper limb disorders 1; ➲ p. 288, Work-related upper limb disorders 2):
  - avoid slouching
  - avoid work at an angle
  - avoid very small fonts; use 'zoom' function
  - minimize keystrokes by use of 'macro' functions
  - regular breaks from keyboarding ↓ fatigue
  - keyboarding skills course ↓ risk of MSDs

*Psychosocial hazards*

Identify if psychosocial hazards are present as these may result in stress or MSDs. Consider the elements of the HSE management standards:

- *Demands*: this includes issues such as workload, work patterns, and the work environment
- Control: how much say the person has in the way they do their work
- *Support*: this includes the encouragement, sponsorship, and resources provided by the organization, line management, and colleagues
- *Relationships*: this includes promoting positive working to avoid conflict and dealing with unacceptable behaviour
- *Role*: whether people understand their role within the organization and whether the organization ensures that they do not have conflicting roles
- *Change*: how organizational change (large or small) is managed and communicated in the organization

## Frequency of review

The DSE assessment should be reviewed where:

- The workstation is moved
- The hardware or software is upgraded
- There is a substantial change to task demands
- The environment around the workstation is changed, e.g. new lighting
- There is a change to the user's capacity/abilities due to injury or ill health

## Relevant legislation and guidance

- HSE (2003). *Work with Display Screen Equipment: Health and Safety (Display Screen Equipment) Regulations 1992 as Amended by the Health and Safety (Miscellaneous Amendments) Regulations 2002. Guidance on Regulations.* HSE Books, Sudbury. Available at: ☞ www.hse.gov.uk/pubns/books/l26.htm
- HSE. *Display Screen Equipment (DSE) Workstation Checklist.* HSE Books, Sudbury. Available at: ☞ https://www.hse.gov.uk/pubns/ck1.htm
- HSE. *Management Standards.* HSE Books, Sudbury. Available at: ☞ https://www.hse.gov.uk/stress/standards/

# Carry out an ergonomics assessment

Remember that if you are not an occupational hygienist, you should only interpret hygiene data to the extent of your competence. Most OH professionals have general training in the principles of occupational hygiene. However, always ask for clarification or explanation of results from the occupational hygienist who produced the report if the conclusions are not clear and/or well justified.

A comprehensive ergonomics assessment covers the range of ergonomics hazards including physical (posture, loading, repetition), psychosocial, and organizational factors.

## Monitoring and analysis techniques

There are numerous methods for assessing ergonomics risks (Table 38.2). The simplest combinations for most basic assessments are a self-administered questionnaire to a population of exposed workers (or a sample thereof) plus direct observation of work tasks. Further information about specific aspects of risk assessment is given on ➲ p. 136, Lifting and handling; ➲ p. 134, Posture; ➲ p. 140, Repetitive work; ➲ p. 816, Carry out a display screen equipment assessment; ➲ p. 146, Organizational psychosocial factors; ➲ p. 340, Stress 1: recognition and assessment; ➲ p. 344, Stress 2: interventions/risk controls.

## Ergonomics assessment tools

A number of generic ergonomics assessment tools are available for use in workplace and task assessment (see Table 38.2). As with most practical methods of risk assessment, there is a compromise between scientific validity and usability.

**Table 38.2** HSE tools

| Name of tool | What to assess? |
|---|---|
| MAC Lift | Lifting and handling tasks |
| MAC Carry | Carrying tasks |
| MAC Team Handling | Team handling tasks |
| V-MAC | Repetitive handling or carrying with varying weights |
| RAPP | Pushing and pulling tasks |
| ART | Repetitive upper limb tasks |
| RULA | Postural hazards in repetitive upper limb tasks |
| REBA | Postural hazards in repetitive whole-body handling tasks |
| QEC | Lifting tasks<br>Repetitive tasks |
| Nordic Musculoskeletal Questionnaire | General screen. Can be used to evaluate MSD problems and identify clusters within a workplace |
| Musculoskeletal discomfort assessment tool (body map) | General screen. Used to identify MSD location and intensity. Helpful do identify clusters within a workplace |
| General Wellbeing Questionnaire (GWBQ) | General screen. Used to evaluate sub-optimal health (associated with work related stress) and identify clusters within a workplace |

# Assess and interpret a research paper

In order to make the best use of research evidence and avoid being misled by poor science, it is advisable to appraise published original research papers critically.

The majority of research papers in occupational medicine are observational studies.[1] A checklist for identifying common problems with cohort and case–control studies, divided by each main section of a paper, is given here. The list is intended for readers of single scientific papers following publication, rather than as a guide for peer reviewers at the stage when a manuscript can be revised, or for those who are compiling evidence tables for guideline development.

## Introduction

- Is the existing state of knowledge adequately described?
- Is the study well justified?
- Is it relevant for your own practice?

## Methods

*Study sample*

- Are the target population and the sample well defined?
- *Is the sample sufficiently large?*
  - ideally, a power calculation should be shown
  - wide confidence intervals are an important clue to inadequate sample size
- Are there any obvious sources of bias in the selection of subjects (e.g. volunteers, patients seen for medico-legal purposes)?

*Selection of controls*

Are the comparison groups appropriate?

- Controls in case–control studies should be selected from the same population as the cases (e.g. clinic attenders from the same hospital catchment area)
- Care should be taken that unexposed groups in cohort studies are not inadvertently exposed, e.g. through proximity to exposed workers

*Tools*

Are the methods of case ascertainment standardized?

- Case definitions should be stated clearly. It is useful if definitions are used widely, as the results are more easily compared with previous literature
- Methods should be valid and repeatable. It is not always possible to validate subjective outcomes, e.g. pain or mental ill health, as there is no gold standard. However, questionnaires and other tools should at least have acceptable repeatability
- *Confounding*: have possible confounding factors been considered, and attempts made to measure them for inclusion (adjustment) in later analysis?

1 Randomized controlled trials (RCTs) are rare in occupational medicine research and are not covered here. Methods for assessing RCTs are available. Improving the quality of reporting of RCTs: The CONSORT statement. Available at: https://www.sciencedirect.com/science/article/pii/S0140673600043373

*Exposure assessment*

Consider the quality and accuracy of exposure assessment.

- Using job title as a proxy for exposure is common, but rather inaccurate
- Retrospective exposure assessment from hygiene records varies in quality
- Recalled exposure can be subject to bias if the subject has the disease of interest

*Statistical methods*

Statistical techniques must be stated clearly (but not necessarily described in detail). Check that they are appropriate for the format of data presented.

## Results

*Response rates*

Rates >55% are desirable. Lower response rates are acceptable, but the impact of response bias on the results should be discussed.

*Presentation of results*

- Look for an indication of the magnitude of effect or risk (odds ratio, relative risk, prevalence rate ratio). Consider whether an increased risk is likely to be important clinically
- Look for an estimate of statistical uncertainty (the likelihood that the results could have occurred by chance). Traditionally, *P*-values have been used to express statistical significance, but they do not give a feel for the size of an effect. Confidence intervals around a risk estimate give more information about the scale of a finding

## Discussion and conclusions

- Were limitations acknowledged and discussed? These must be borne in mind when making the link to practice
- Are the conclusions drawn appropriate?
- Are the results related to other evidence from the existing literature?
- If a study has added new knowledge, is this generalizable to your local population?
- Do the results suggest that a change in practice is indicated?

# Conducting a media interview

## Circumstances

The press may question occupational health professionals because they are named as a contact in a press release or are participants at a press conference. In addition, a journalist pursuing a story may approach them without advance warning. Contacts may take various forms:

- Requests for non-attributable background information
- Interviews to be used in the preparation of written articles
- Live or recorded interviews on radio or television
- Social media contacts

## Preparation

As for a professional examination, when dealing with the media, it is important to be adequately prepared. In particular, it is essential to have a good understanding of the relevant facts. If you get things wrong, you lose credibility and may damage the reputation of occupational health. Where media contact is expected (e.g. following a press release or because a newsworthy event has occurred), it is helpful to anticipate the questions that might be asked. And when an approach is received from a journalist, it is useful to establish at the outset the intended readership/audience, and the planned scope and format of the communication. Asking for the likely questions in advance may be helpful.

## Talking to journalists from the written media

- Assume that anything you say is 'on record' and attributable, unless otherwise agreed (most journalists can be trusted to respect such agreements)
- If you do not know the answer to a question, an offer to find out may be appreciated (but be sensitive to the journalist's deadline)
- If you are unable to answer a question (e.g. because of confidentiality), try to explain why rather than simply decline to comment
- Most journalists are happy to let you check quotes that they wish to attribute to you (often they are paraphrases of what was actually said)
- Where deadlines allow, some journalists are happy to receive feedback on the draft text of their article (but remember that final responsibility for the content is theirs)
- Check that your name and affiliation are correctly noted
- Remember that once you are quoted in one article, follow-up enquiries may come from other journalists

## Broadcast interviews

- Pre-recorded interviews have the advantage that if you lose your thread, you can start again. However, be mindful that your contribution may be edited and interspersed with other material. Consider whether you trust the producer to do this sympathetically
- Establish in advance the planned format of the programme including its length, who will be the other participants, and in what capacity you are contributing (representing a group or giving your personal view)
- Think through your main message in advance, and try to ensure that you get it across as early as possible in the interview

- Use language appropriate to the audience and do not talk too fast
- Avoid jargon or technical phrases without explanation
- Practical examples may help to illustrate theoretical points
- Avoid appearing defensive
- Avoid saying things that you might regret, even after completion of the interview (if in doubt, assume that the tape is still running)
- Ensure that your name and affiliation have been correctly noted
- Dress appropriately for television appearances (wear plain, muted, colours)
- Maintain eye contact with the interviewer and avoid fidgeting

## Training

Various courses are available for health professionals on interactions with the media. They provide a good opportunity to develop and practice techniques and are strongly recommended for those who expect frequent or difficult media contacts.

It can be helpful to rehearse or practice likely questions with an informed colleague before the interview.

# Writing a press release

## Purpose

Press releases are issued to draw the attention of journalists to new information which may be of interest to their readership/audience. They may be directed at specialist publications (e.g. trade magazines) as well as the more general media (newspapers, radio, and television). They help to maximize publicity and also give the instigator some control over its timing.

## Sources of assistance

OH professionals normally issue press releases with assistance from experts in media relations, who can advise on their format, and optimize their circulation to journalists. Depending on the circumstances, assistance may come from:

- *The editorial staff of a scientific journal*: many journals these days like to publicize their content beyond specialist readers, and have well developed systems for promoting publicity
- *Academic institutions*: most major academic institutions have a press office
- *Conference organizers*: it is common practice to highlight selected presentations at medical and scientific conferences, which may be of wider interest
- *Media relations departments of employing companies*: many larger companies have such departments
- *Government press offices*: relevant to occupational health professionals working for government departments, agencies, and advisory committees
- *Social Media*: is increasingly used to release information

## Advance preparation

In planning a press release, several questions should be considered.

- What is the main message?
- Who is the message for? This will influence both the content and also the way in which the press release is circulated
- What will be the best timing? There may be little choice about this (e.g. because there is a need to coincide with publication of a paper or a presentation at a meeting). However, where there is flexibility, factors to consider include the timing of other events that are likely to compete for media attention (e.g. a royal wedding) and the availability of an appropriate person to answer any follow-up questions from journalists (which usually come over several days)

## Format

In compiling a press release, it is important to bear in mind the way in which journalists work. Some may wish to interview the originators to get additional information, but others will prepare their piece simply from the content of the press release, perhaps supplemented by readily available information from the internet. Requirements include:

- An attention-grabbing headline
- A clear statement of the main message in understandable language

- A short amplification of the main message. It is often helpful to include attributable quotes that can be incorporated into articles
- Useful background information (e.g. brief details of the committee that has issued a report or the conference where paper will be presented)
- Useful references for further information (particularly to websites)
- Contact details for someone who can give further information
- It is important to ensure accuracy of information provided

## Press conferences

Where it is anticipated that new information will be of special interest to the general media, it may help to accompany a press release with a press conference. Such conferences are best organized by media professionals. The important thing for participating health professionals is to ensure that they are well prepared to answer questions.

Section 12

# Emergencies in occupational health

Chapter 39

# Acute poisoning

# General principles and contact details for specialist advice

*All substances are poisonous; there is none which is not a poison. The right dose differentiates a poison and a remedy.*

Paracelsus (1493–1541)

## Role of occupational health

- Be aware of the general principles of first aid for substances that can cause acute poisoning in the workplace. In many organizations, occupational health (OH) lead on first aid, particularly first aid for acute poisoning at work
- In the workplace, adequate numbers of staff should be trained first aiders. The number of trained first aiders required depend on the hazards identified on site (see ➔ p. 570, First Aid at Work Regulations 1981)
- A suitable and sufficient risk assessment of the work environment may indicate some staff need to be trained in immediate life support (ILS)
- Know your workplace/work area and identify chemical hazards
- Identify possible sources of chemical exposures/poisoning (do a risk assessment)
- Identify remedial actions needed (controls)
- Liaise with the nearest acute admitting hospitals when there are highly toxic chemical hazards in the workplace, e.g. cyanide, hydrofluoric acid
- Formulate and document immediate first aid/treatment protocols, consider aspects such as ambulance call-out times and transfer times to acute hospitals

## Contact details for specialist advice

- Telephone advice from UK National Poisons Information Service (NPIS) or National Poisons Information Centre (NPIC) of Ireland (if needed):
  - *UK NPIS*—0344 892 0111
  - *Ireland NPIC*—(01) 809 2566

Register with TOXBASE® (the primary clinical toxicology database of the NPIS. Available at: https://www.toxbase.org/)

## Immediate management of poisoning in the workplace

- *Assess the situation*: risk assessment
- Is it safe to approach the casualties?
- ⚠ Remove the casualties from further exposure *if it is safe* to do so
- Contact the emergency services
- *Assess the route of exposure*:
  - inhalation
  - skin contamination/burns
  - eye contamination/burns
  - ingestion (unlikely in the occupational setting)
  - injection

- Assess the need for personal protective equipment (PPE)
- Start decontamination if necessary
- Start first aid
- *With known or suspected case of exposure/poisoning instigate airways, breathing, circulation (ABCs):*
  - airway
  - breathing
  - cardiac support

## Management of chemical exposures to the eye

⚠ Chemicals splashed or sprayed into the eyes are an ophthalmological emergency.

*Features*

- Pain, blepharospasm, lacrimation, conjunctivitis, palpebral oedema, blurred vision, and photophobia
- Acidic and alkaline solutions may cause corneal burns
- *Alkaline solutions may penetrate all layers of the eye and cause:*
  - iritis
  - anterior and posterior synechia
  - corneal opacification
  - cataracts
  - glaucoma
  - retinal atrophy
- Eye injury due to alkaline solutions is usually more severe and if untreated continues to cause damage long after the incident

### Management of chemical exposures to the eye

- Remove contact lenses if necessary and immediately irrigate the affected eye thoroughly with lukewarm water or 0.9% saline for at least 15–20 minutes. Continue until the conjunctival sac pH is normal (7.5–8.0). Use pH-sensitive paper (litmus) to check pH, retest after 20 minutes, and reirrigate if necessary
- If exposed to strong acids or alkalis, arrange for urgent referral to nearest acute admitting hospital for ophthalmological assessment
- Any particles lodged in the conjunctival recesses should be removed
- Repeated instillation of local anaesthetics (e.g. amethocaine) drops may reduce discomfort and help more thorough decontamination (apply only if trained to administer)
- Corneal damage may be detected by instillation of fluorescein drops (if trained to examine the eye), ulceration show up green under a bright light with blue filter
- If corneal damage is detected, arrange for urgent referral to nearest acute admitting hospital for ophthalmological assessment
- Mydriatic and cycloplegic agents (e.g. cyclopentolate, tropicamide) may reduce discomfort (apply if trained to administer). Do not use in patients with glaucoma
- If symptoms do not resolve rapidly, arrange for urgent referral to nearest acute admitting hospital for ophthalmological assessment

# Carbon monoxide poisoning

## Properties

- Colourless odourless gas
- Unlikely to be encountered in the occupational setting in isolation
- Product of incomplete combustion including diesel oils, petroleum products, and domestic gas

► Leaks of *domestic gas* do *not* involve carbon monoxide (CO).

## Mechanism of toxicity

- CO combines with haemoglobin to reduce the oxygen-carrying capacity of the red blood cells in blood
- Haemoglobin binds with CO easier than with oxygen (200–300 times greater affinity for CO)—see the oxyhaemoglobin dissociation curve (see Fig. 24.1) to shift to the left, impairing tissue oxygen delivery
- CO may also inhibit cytochrome oxidase in cells
- The short-term exposure limit is 200 ppm (232 mg/m3)
- The long-term exposure limit is 30 ppm (35 mg/m3)

## Poisoning features

*Immediate features*

- Headache
- Nausea/vomiting
- Irritability
- Weakness
- Tachypnoea

*Intermediate features*

- Dizziness
- Ataxia
- Agitation/irritability
- Impairment of consciousness
- Respiratory failure

► Cerebral oedema and metabolic acidosis may develop in serious cases. Less common features include skin blisters, rhabdomyolysis, acute renal failure, pulmonary oedema, myocardial infarction, retinal haemorrhages, cortical blindness, choreoathetosis, and mutism.

*Late features*

- The majority recover uneventfully
- Rarely, neuropsychiatric features after periods of several weeks free of symptoms. More common in those >40 years of age and includes memory impairment, disorientation, apathy, akinetic mutism, irritability, inability to concentrate, personality change, parkinsonism, and parietal lobe lesions. Urinary and/or faecal incontinence and gait disturbance are common. Fortunately, the great majority will recover completely or to a considerable extent within a year

## Indication of severity

- Severity increases with one or more of the following
- Any new objective acute neurological signs, e.g. ↑ tone, upgoing plantar reflexes
- Coma
- Need for ventilation
- Electrocardiogram (ECG) indication of infarction or ischaemia
- Clinically significant acidosis
- Initial carboxyhaemoglobin >30%

▶ The link between carboxyhaemoglobin level and clinical outcome is weak.

## Management of CO poisoning

- Remove from exposure
- Maintain a clear airway and adequate ventilation
- Give oxygen in as high a concentration as possible
- Transfer to hospital if severely compromised
- Correct metabolic acidosis by increasing oxygen delivery to the tissues
- Give mannitol 1 g/kg (as 20%) IV over 20–30 minutes if cerebral oedema suspected
- Monitor the heart rhythm (record ECG)
- Measure the carboxyhaemoglobin concentration as an emergency. A carboxyhaemoglobin percentage of 30% indicates severe exposure. However, concentrations less than this do not exclude significant poisoning, and the relationship between carboxyhaemoglobin and severity of poisoning and/or clinical outcome is poor
- In patients who have been unconscious look for extrapyramidal features and retinal haemorrhages to assess the severity of central nervous system (CNS) toxicity
- The role of hyperbaric oxygen therapy (HBOT) is controversial. Consider and discuss with a Poisons Information Centre (p. 830) if carboxyhaemoglobin percentage >20% and any of the following:
  - loss of consciousness at any stage
  - neurological symptoms (other than headache)
  - myocardial arrhythmia/ischaemia diagnosed by ECG
  - pregnancy

## Further information

*Carbon Monoxide Poisoning: Needless Deaths, Unnecessary Injury*. Letter from the Chief Medical Officer/Chief Nursing Officer. Available at: https://assets.publishing.service.gov.uk/government/uploads/system/uploads/attachment_data/file/485581/CO_diagnosis_algorithm_2015.pdf

Department of Health Heath Protection Agency (2013). *Carbon Diagnosing Poisoning: Carbon Monoxide Poisoning: Recognise the Symptoms and Tackle the Cause (CO)* (amended October/November 2013). Letter from the Chief Medical Officer/Chief Nursing Officer. Available at: https://assets.publishing.service.gov.uk/government/uploads/system/uploads/attachment_data/file/260211/Carbon_Monoxide_Letter_2013_FinalforPub.pdf; http://www.hpa.org.uk/webc/HPAwebFile/HPAweb_C/1236845874045

Public Health England, Department of Health (2013). *Diagnosing Poisoning: Carbon Monoxide (CO)*. Updated 2015. DH, London.

# Cyanide 1: Poisoning

## Properties

- Naturally occurring toxin in a variety of compounds
- Important examples are hydrogen cyanide (HCN) gas, salts, e.g. potassium and sodium cyanide (KCN, NaCN), and nitriles (R–CN), which are used widely as solvents and in the manufacture of plastics (e.g. acrylonitrile)
- Cyanogenic glycosides are produced by many plants and when digested produce HCN

## Sources of exposure

- *Industrial*: metal treatment and ore processing, printing, electroplating, photoengraving, electronics, production of acrylics, plastics, and nylon, petrochemical industry
- Fumigants and rodenticides
- Acrylic nail remover and metal polishes
- *Fires*: combustion of polyurethane, rubber, nylon, etc.
- Tobacco smoke
- Drugs, e.g. sodium nitroprusside
- *Natural sources*: cassava, some grasses, flax, lima beans, linseed

## Toxicity

- Highly toxic by inhalation, ingestion, or dermal or eye exposure
- Soluble cyanide salts (e.g. Na, K, Ca, NH3) are more toxic than lower solubility salts (mercury, gold, copper, and silver cyanide)

*Onset of toxicity*

- Toxicity can occur within a few seconds of HCN gas inhalation, with death occurring within minutes
- Ingestion of soluble cyanide salts can cause toxicity within minutes, but continued absorption can cause toxicity for several hours
- Toxicity from skin exposure requires a large surface area to be affected. Onset of toxicity may be delayed for several hours

## Estimated lethal doses

- *Hydrocyanic acid*: 50 mg (single dose)
- *NaCN/KCN ingestion*: 150–300 mg (~3 mg/kg)
- *Median lethal dose for skin contamination with HCN*: 100 mg/kg

*UK short-term occupational exposure limits (15 minutes)*

- *HCN*: 4.5 ppm (5 mg/m3)
- *Cyanogen chloride*: 0.3 ppm (0.77 mg/m3)

*UK long-term occupational exposure limits (8 hours time-weighted average concentration)*

- *HCN*: 0.9 ppm (1 mg/m3)
- *Other (except HCN, cyanogen, and cyanogen chloride)*: 5 mg/m3

## Clinical findings

- Dyspnoea
- Dizziness
- Headache

- Hypotension
- Convulsions
- Coma
- Death

⚠ It can be difficult to diagnose cyanide poisoning.

## Acute poisoning

Cyanide, cyanogen chloride, acetonitrile, and other cyanide releasing substances.

*Ingestion or inhalation of large amounts*

Cyanide concentration >3 mg/l (>114 μmol/l)

- Immediate unconsciousness
- Convulsions
- Death within 1–15 minutes

*Ingestion, inhalation, or skin absorption of moderate amounts*

*Cyanide concentration 1–3 mg/l (38–114 μmol/l)*

- Dizziness
- Rapid respiration
- Vomiting
- Flushing
- Headache
- Drowsiness
- Hypotension
- Rapid pulse
- Unconsciousness
- Death in convulsions within 4 hours except sodium nitroprusside where death may be delayed for 12 hours

*Ingestion, inhalation, or skin absorption of small amounts*

*Cyanide concentration <1 mg/l (<38 μmol/l)*

- Nausea
- Dizziness
- Drowsiness
- Hyperventilation
- Anxiety

## Acute poisoning: Acrylonitrile

*Inhalation*

- Nausea and vomiting
- Diarrhoea
- Weakness
- Headache
- Jaundice

Note that skin contact can cause epidermal necrosis.

# Cyanide 2: Treatment

⚠ Rescuers should not put themselves at risk and avoid self-contamination. Moisture on some cyanide salts can liberate HCN.

**Immediate first aid**

- Maintain clear airway and adequate ventilation
- Give 100% oxygen to all patients
- Monitor pulse, blood pressure, respiratory rate, oxygen saturation, and cardiac rhythm (ECG if available)
- Transfer all definite cases to hospital as rapidly as possible
- Consider starting treatment on site if transfer to hospital is likely to be prolonged, depending on severity of exposure

## Diagnosis

In the absence of a blood cyanide concentration the following features suggest cyanide poisoning:

- Lactate >7 mmol/l
- Elevated anion gap acidosis
- Reduced arteriovenous oxygen gradient

## Mild poisoning

- Observe asymptomatic and mildly symptomatic patients for at least 6 hours after ingestion of cyanide salt and at least 12 hours after ingestion of acetonitrile
- Give 50 ml of 25% sodium thiosulphate (12.5 g) IV over 10 minutes if patient's condition worsens and is deemed to be life-threatening and if transfer to hospital likely to be prolonged

## Moderate and severe poisoning

- Patients with moderate or severe poisoning (e.g. coma) should be managed in a critical care environment
- Treatment with antidote therapy is necessary in all cases of moderate or severe poisoning
- It is important that the admitting hospital is informed if any antidote therapy has been given in the pre-hospital setting since repeat doses of some antidotes can cause unwanted side effects
- ⚠ If treatment is started on site the doctor should accompany the casualties to the admitting hospital
- Give 20 ml of 1.5% dicobalt edetate solution (300 mg) IV over 1 minute followed immediately by 50 ml of 50% dextrose. If there is only a partial response to dicobalt edetate 300 mg or the patient relapses after recovery, a further dose of dicobalt edetate 300 mg should be given. If a second dose of dicobalt edetate is administered, there is a danger of inducing cobalt toxicity, if the diagnosis is *not* cyanide poisoning
- In addition, the administration of 50 ml of 25% sodium thiosulphate (12.5 g) IV over 10 minutes may be beneficial
- *Or*, if dicobalt edetate is not available, give 10 ml of 3% sodium nitrite solution (300 mg) IV over 5–20 minutes *and* 50 ml of 25% sodium thiosulphate (12.5 g) IV over 10 minutes

- A further dose of sodium thiosulphate 12.5 g IV over 10 minutes may be needed. A second dose of sodium nitrite should *not* be given because of the risk of excessive methaemoglobinaemia
- Response to treatment in the pre-hospital setting can be assessed by improved haemodynamic status
- Single brief convulsions do not require treatment. If frequent or prolonged, control with IV diazepam (10–20 mg) or lorazepam (4 mg)
- Correct hypotension by raising the legs of the patient and/or expanding the intravascular volume

# Hydrogen sulphide poisoning

## Properties

- Colourless, flammable, and explosive gas with characteristic 'rotten egg' smell
- CAS No. 7783–06–4
- UN 1053

*Synonyms*

- Sulphuretted hydrogen
- Sulphur hydride
- Hydrosulphuric acid

## Toxicity

- Irritant gas with systemic asphyxiant effects
- Reversibly inhibits cytochrome oxidase, which impairs cell respiration
- Rapidly absorbed by inhalation
- Little absorption occurs through the skin
- Irritating to the eyes
- Occupational short-term exposure limit is 10 ppm (14 mg/m$^3$)
- Long-term exposure limit is 5 ppm (7 mg/m$^3$)

| | |
|---|---|
| 0.02–0.025 ppm | Odour threshold |
| 10 ppm | Unpleasant smell, sore eyes |
| 100 ppm | Loss of smell after 3–15 minutes, eyes and throat sting |
| 250 ppm | Prolonged exposure—pulmonary oedema |
| 1,000 ppm | Rapid collapse, respiratory paralysis, coma, and death within minutes |

## Features

Prolonged exposure causes:

| | |
|---|---|
| • Respiratory tract irritation | • Bronchitis |
| • Rhinitis | • Dyspnoea |
| • Pharyngitis | • Pulmonary oedema |

## Systemic effects

| | |
|---|---|
| • Vomiting | • Drowsiness |
| • Diarrhoea | • Tremor |
| • Headache | • Muscular weakness |
| • Nystagmus | • Seizures |
| • Dizziness | • Tachycardia |
| • Agitation | • Hypotension |

### Inhalation of high concentrations

Leads rapidly to:

| | |
|---|---|
| • Olfactory fatigue<br>• Collapse | • Seizures |
| • Respiratory paralysis | • Coma |
| • Cyanosis | • Cardiac arrhythmias |
| • Convulsions | • Death within minutes |

### Eye effects

May be delayed and include:

| | |
|---|---|
| • Irritation | • Photophobia |
| • Inflammation | • Conjunctivitis |
| • Lacrimation | • Keratitis |
| • Conjunctival hyperaemia | • Blepharospasm |

Recovery is usually complete, but there may be permanent damage.

### Skin effects

- Skin discoloration
- Pain, itching, erythema
- Local frostbite (exposure to liquified gas)

### Management of $H_2S$ poisoning

- Remove from exposure (rescuers must wear PPE)
- Oxygen in as high a concentration as possible, if necessary, via an endotracheal tube (if trained to intubate)
- Skin decontamination is usually not necessary because it is a gas. Removing patient's clothing and washing the skin with water and a mild detergent may reduce the risk of odour-related complaints in rescuers, but this is *not* a priority if dealing with a critically ill patient
- Maintain a clear airway and adequate ventilation
- Monitor pulse, blood pressure, and oxygen saturation
- If the patient has clinical features of bronchospasm treat conventionally with nebulized bronchodilators and steroids (if trained to administer)
- Transfer to hospital
- Correct hypotension with IV fluids
- Convulsions are unlikely to require treatment by the time the patient reaches medical care but IV diazepam 10–20 mg could be given if necessary

# Organophosphate poisoning

See also ➲ p. 328.

### Immediate management and decontamination

- ⚠ *Avoid contaminating yourself*: organophosphates are rapidly absorbed through skin
- Wear appropriate protective clothing
- Supportive measures are vitally important

► Most products are dissolved in hydrocarbon solvents. Aspiration of these products will cause severe aspiration pneumonia with high mortality, and for this reason gastric aspiration should be avoided.

### Management of organophosphate poisoning

- Prevent further absorption according to route of exposure
- Remove to fresh air
- Remove soiled clothing and wash contaminated skin with washing-up liquid in water (see ➲ p. 830)
- Consider hospital transfer early
- Protect the airway
- Monitor BP and pulse
- In symptomatic patients establish intravenous access
- Collect blood samples in an ethylenediamine tetra-acetic acid tube for measurement of erythrocyte and plasma cholinesterase activities to confirm the diagnosis
- If bronchorrhoea develops, administer atropine 0.6–2 mg IV every 10–30 minutes until secretions are minimal and the patient is atropinized (dry skin, sinus tachycardia, and dilated pupils). In severe cases very large doses of atropine may be required if hospital admission is likely to be delayed
- Moderately or severely poisoned patients should be given pralidoxime mesilate 1–2 g IV over 5 to 10 minutes to reactivate phosphorylated enzyme (repeat every 4 to 6 hours if necessary)
- Diazepam 5–10 mg IV is useful in controlling apprehension, agitation, fasciculation, and convulsions. The dose may be repeated as required

### Skin decontamination: Pesticides

- ⚠ Safety first
- Avoid contaminating yourself
- Wear protective clothing
- Do *NOT* allow smoking nearby. There may be a risk of fire if a solvent is involved
- Carry out decontamination in a well-ventilated area, preferably with its own ventilation system
- The patient should remove soiled clothing and wash him/herself if possible
- Put soiled clothing in a sealed container to prevent escape of volatile substances

- Wash hair and all contaminated skin with liberal amounts of water (preferably warm) and soap
- Pay special attention to skin folds, fingernails, and ears

Note: The intensity of the odour is not necessarily an indication of the toxicity of the pesticide. It may be due to the solvent or have been added as a deterrent against ingestion.

# Mercury poisoning

## Properties

Mercury occurs in three forms:
- *Elemental mercury*: highly mobile silvery liquid, volatile even at room temperatures. Rapidly absorbed by lungs. Usually only toxic by inhalation
- *Inorganic mercurial salts or minerals*: white crystals or powders, e.g. mercuric chloride, mercuric iodide, mercuric oxide, mercuric sulphide, mercurous chloride
- *Organic mercury*: combines with carbon, e.g. ethylmercury, methylmercury, merthiolate

## Toxicity

Can occur from ingestion, injection, inhalation, or dermal absorption.

## Acute inhalation of mercury vapour

- Cough
- Breathlessness
- Chest tightness
- Pulmonary irritation
- Pneumonitis, pulmonary oedema, necrotizing bronchiolitis, and acute respiratory distress syndrome
- 'Influenza-like' symptoms with muscle pains, fever, and tachycardia
- Gastrointestinal (GI) upset may occur within a few h

## Elemental mercury

- *Inhalation of elemental mercury globules may cause*:
  - pneumonitis
  - haemoptysis
  - respiratory distress
  - oliguric renal failure
- Systemic mercury toxicity is unlikely to occur following a single ingested dose

### Management of elemental mercury poisoning

- Remove from source of exposure
- Give supplemental oxygen
- Transfer to hospital if appropriate

## Inorganic mercurial salts or minerals

*Toxicity*
- Inorganic salts are highly *corrosive*
- Fatalities have occurred after ingestion of 0.5 g of mercuric chloride

*Features*

- GI mucosa and kidney are the main target sites
- Burning of the mouth and throat
- Abdominal pain
- Nausea
- Vomiting followed by haematemesis
- Bloody diarrhoea
- Colitis
- Intestinal mucosal necrosis

**Management of inorganic mercury poisoning**

- Remove from source of exposure
- Give supplemental oxygen
- Give pain relief if necessary
- Transfer to hospital as soon as possible

## Organomercury compounds

*Toxicity*

Systemic mercury poisoning results typically from acute inhalational exposure or chronic/repeated ingestion of contaminated foods.

*Features*

- *Ingestion causes*:
  - retching, coughing, and choking
  - ingestion of aryl mercury salts causes nausea, vomiting, and abdominal pain
  - systemic mercury poisoning may ensue
- *Inhalation may cause*:
  - mucous membrane irritation
  - repeated or substantial exposures can result in systemic toxicity

*Skin exposure*

Mucous membrane irritant at high concentrations.

**Management of organomercury poisoning**

*Ingestion*

- Supportive measures provide the mainstay of therapy
- Save blood and urine for mercury concentration determination in symptomatic patients
- Specialist referral is indicated in patients with systemic features of mercury poisoning. Chelation therapy with dimercaprol propane sulfonic acid may be required in these cases

*Inhalation*

- Remove from exposure
- Oxygen/bronchodilators may be required
- Symptomatic and supportive measures dictated by patient's condition

*Skin exposure*

*Decontamination priority*: use standard decontamination procedures

# Phenol poisoning

## Properties

Phenols (CAS No. 108–95–2) are chemicals with a colourless to light pink appearance and with an acrid, sweet odour. Phenols are used in various industries such as for production of disinfectants, antiseptics, biocides, and adhesives. Phenols are used in various forms:

- UN 2821 phenol (solution)
- UN 2312 phenol (molten)
- UN 1671 phenol (solid)

## Synonyms

| | |
|---|---|
| • Carbolic acid | • Phenolum |
| • Hydroxybenzene | • Phenyl hydrate |
| • Phenyl hydroxide | • Phenic acid |
| • Phenyl alcohol<br>• Monohydroxybenzene | • Tar acid<br>Tar oils |

## Toxicity

- Corrosive to body tissues
- Rapidly absorbed following skin contact, leading to systemic toxicity
- Inhalation is not the normal route of exposure
- Ingestion is *very toxic*

*Occupational exposure limits*

- *Long-term exposure limit*: 2 ppm
- *Short-term exposure limit*: 4 ppm

## Phenols and cresols: Features and management

- Exposure by any route can cause irritation, burns, and systemic effects
- *Ingestion*:
  - causes irritation of mucous membranes and the GI tract
  - significant ingestion causes white/brown skin and mucosal burns which may be painless
  - laryngeal oedema can occur, and oesophageal stricture may be a late complication
- *Skin contact*: even dilute solutions (1%) can cause irritation, dermatitis, burns, and necrosis of the skin following prolonged contact. Often presents as relatively painless white or brown necrotic lesions. The brown discoloration may remain after healing. Exposure to even a small surface of the skin can rapidly cause systemic effects (see ➔p. 104)
- *Eye contact*: causes irritation, conjunctival and corneal oedema, and blindness

## Systemic features

- Nausea
- Vomiting
- Diarrhoea
- Abdominal pain

- Hypotension
- Tachycardia
- Cardiac arrhythmias (such as atrial fibrillation)
- Metabolic acidosis
- Shock
- Bronchospasm
- Pulmonary oedema
- Late CNS features include excessive sweating, drowsiness, respiratory depression, convulsions, coma, and death

**Management of acute poisoning with phenols**

- Remove patient from exposure
- Ensure a clear airway and adequate ventilation
- Give oxygen if clinically indicated
- Monitor pulse, blood pressure (BP), and cardiac rhythm
- Transfer to hospital
- Single brief convulsions do not require treatment. If frequent or prolonged control with IV diazepam 10–20 mg or lorazepam 4 mg

### Phenol: Skin contamination

Wash all contaminated areas of the skin with copious quantities of water.

### Phenol splashed or sprayed into the eyes

See ➔ p. 830, General principles of acute poisoning and contact details for specialist advice for eye decontamination procedures.

# Methaemoglobinaemia (acute treatment)

Characterized by increased quantities of haemoglobin in which the iron of haem is oxidized to the ferric ($Fe^{3+}$) form, i.e. leads to oxidation of haemoglobin (and a decreased oxygen carrying capacity of the haemoglobin). Methaemoglobin causes a variable degree of cyanosis. See ➲ p. 362, Methaemoglobinaemia for clinical features and causal exposures.

Exposure to a large amount of these agents can lead to the development of 50–60% methaemoglobin. The symptoms of acute anaemia develop because methaemoglobin lacks the capacity to transport oxygen

### Treatment of acute methaemoglobinaemia

Acute toxic methaemoglobinaemia presents a serious medical emergency:

- Remove from the toxic agent
- Arrange for immediate admission to hospital
- Assessment with ABCs
- Methylene blue (methylthioninium chloride) should be administered in a dose of 1–2 mg/kg intravenous (IV) as 1% solution over 3–5 minutes. Repeated doses may be needed
- Methylene blue (methylthioninium chloride) should not be used if the methaemoglobinaemia is due to chlorate poisoning as it may convert the chlorate to hypochlorite which is an even more toxic compound
- In cases of acute methaemoglobinaemia with intravascular haemolysis, haemodialysis with exchange transfusion is the treatment of choice

# Hydrofluoric acid exposure

## Properties

A colourless fuming liquid used in metal extracting, refining, polishing, and glass etching. An industrial chemical but also present in some household rust removers. A solution of hydrogen fluoride in water.

## Synonyms

- Hydrogen fluoride
- Fluoric acid

## Toxicity

See Table 39.1:

- *Corrosive (acid)*: readily penetrates intact skin, nails, and deep tissue layers
- Skin exposure or ingestion of any quantity can be dangerous and can result in severe hypocalcaemia, hypomagnesaemia, and hyperkalaemia
- Ingestion or skin contact alone or with inhalation can be fatal
- There may be sudden deterioration and fatal arrhythmias can occur within 90 minutes
- Hydrofluoric acid solutions with concentrations as low as 2% may cause burns if they remain in contact with the skin for long enough because of ability to penetrate lipid layers and release toxic fluoride ions (Table 39.2)

## Further information

True B-L, Dreisbach RH (eds.) (2002). *Dreisbach's Handbook of Poisoning Prevention, Diagnosis and Treatment*, 13th edn. Parthenon Publishing, Lancaster.Warrell DA, Cox TM, Firth JD, Benz EJ, Conlan C, Cox T (2020). *Oxford Textbook of Medicine*, 64th edn. Oxford University Press, Oxford.

**Table 39.1** Toxicity of hydrofluoric acid

| Mode of entry | Signs/symptoms | Management (all transfer to hospital) | Possible systemic effects to be aware of |
|---|---|---|---|
| Ingestion | Burning of mouth, throat<br>Retrosternal/abdominal pain<br>Laryngeal burns<br>Hypersalivation<br>Vomiting<br>Haematemesis<br>Hypotension<br>Oesophageal/gastric perforation | Urgent assessment of airway, intubation/tracheostomy may be needed<br>Do *not* induce vomiting<br>Transfer to hospital<br>Treat hypocalcaemia (calcium gluconate 10–30 ml of 10% sol IV)<br>Treat hypovolaemia<br>Opiates may be needed | Hypocalcaemia<br>Hypomagnesaemia<br>Hyperkalaemia<br>Metabolic acidosis<br>Pulmonary aspiration<br>Myoclonus<br>Tetany<br>Convulsions<br>CNS depression |
| Inhalation | Irritation upper airway<br>Cough<br>Chest tightness<br>Headache<br>Ataxia<br>Confusion<br>Dyspnoea/stridor<br>Haemorrhagic pulmonary oedema (late sign) | As above | Cardiac arrythmias<br>Prolonged QT interval/Ventricular Tachycardia/Ventricular Fibrillation |

| Mode of entry | Signs/symptoms | Management (all transfer to hospital) | Possible systemic effects to be aware of |
|---|---|---|---|
| Skin contact | Severe and deep burns<br>Pain disproportionate<br>Blue-grey discoloration in severe cases<br>Time for burn to develop (Table 39.2) | Remove clothing<br>Irrigate with water for 15–30 minutes<br>Opiates may be needed<br>Apply calcium gluconate gel (in surgical glove for hand burns) | See ingestion |
| Eye contact | Conjunctivitis<br>Chemosis<br>Corneal epithelium coagulation ± necrosis | Remove contact lenses<br>Irrigate with water or 0.9% saline for at least 20 minutes<br>Calcium gluconate solution should not be used in eyes<br>Local anaesthetics (e.g. amethocaine) may help decontamination<br>Mydriatic and cycloplegic agents (e.g. tropicamide), may help (avoid in glaucoma) | See ingestion |

**Table 39.2** Concentration and onset of skin symptoms (hydrofluoric acid)

| Concentration | Time to symptom onset |
|---|---|
| Anhydrous or >50% | Immediate |
| 20–50% | Up to 8 hours |
| <20% | 12 to 24 hours |

Chapter 40

# Non-chemical emergencies

# Management of anaphylaxis

## General considerations

In occupational health (OH) practice, anaphylaxis can occur in association with the administration of immunizations. All OH departments that administer vaccines must have adequate facilities for resuscitation. Resuscitation equipment should be latex free, particularly in the health care industry where the incidence of type 1 hypersensitivity to latex among employees is significant. OH staffs who administer vaccines should be retrained in resuscitation protocols annually.

## Prevention of anaphylaxis

- Seek history of known allergy to vaccine components prior to immunization
- Vigilance in individuals who have a strong history of atopy, although immunization is not contraindicated

## Diagnosis of anaphylaxis

Anaphylaxis is likely when all of the following three criteria are met:

- Sudden onset and rapid progression of symptoms
- Life-threatening airway and/or breathing and/or circulation problems (wheezing and dyspnoea, collapse with hypotension, tachycardia)
- Skin and/or mucosal changes (flushing, urticaria, angioedema)

The following supports the diagnosis:

- Exposure to a known allergen for the patient

## Treatment of anaphylaxis

The specific treatment of an anaphylactic reaction depends on:

- Location
- Training and skills of rescuers
- Number of responders
- Equipment and drugs available

## Treatment

- Mild (itching, but no features of angio-oedema or shock). Oral anti-histamines
- *Moderate to severe*:
  - position and maintain airway and circulation if cardiovascular collapse (30 chest compressions to two ventilations if cardiorespiratory arrest)
  - 100% oxygen, via mask, insert airway if unconscious
  - adrenaline 0.5 ml of 1:1,000 (0.5 mg) intramuscular (IM); can be repeated at 5 minutes intervals according to pulse and blood pressure
  - establish venous access and start intravenous (IV) colloids
  - give hydrocortisone 200 mg by IM or slow IV injection (can be repeated) and chlorpheniramine 10 mg IM or slow IV injection
- Hydrocortisone and antihistamine in anaphylaxis are not life-saving but may help prevent or shorten protracted reactions
- Moderate to severe cases will require admission because of risk of prolonged reactions and recurrence. Individuals who experience mild reactions can be discharged with oral antihistamines

## Reporting adverse reactions

- Report to Committee on Safety of Medicines (CSM) using yellow card scheme. http://medicines.mhra.gov.uk/ 2015
- Record in OH notes and counsel individual about avoidance
- Report to general practitioner (GP) with the individual's consent

## Further information

Department of Health (2020). *Immunization Against Infectious Disease* (The Green Book). DH, London. Available at: http://www.dh.gov.uk/prod_consum_dh/groups/dh_digitalassets/@dh/@en/documents/digitalasset/dh_128623.pdf

Resuscitation Council (UK). *Anaphylaxis Algorithm for HCW*. London May 2021 Available at: https://www.resus.org.uk/anaphylaxis/emergency-treatment-of-anaphylactic-reactions/

# Management of needlestick and contamination incidents 1

## Hazards associated with needlestick injury

- *Main hazards*: hepatitis B virus (HBV), hepatitis C virus (HCV), human immunodeficiency virus (HIV) (➲ p. 170, Hepatitis B; ➲ p. 174, Hepatitis C; ➲ p. 176, Human immunodeficiency virus)
- Any blood-borne infection (e.g. malaria) can be transmitted by needlestick injury (NSI)
- For prevention of NSIs, see ➲ p. 118, Human tissue and body fluids

## Classification of contamination incidents

- *Percutaneous*: when a contaminated sharp breaches intact skin
- *Mucocutaneous*: when blood or body fluids splash onto mucous membranes or non-intact skin
- ▶ Intact normal skin is an effective barrier against blood-borne virus (BBV)

## Immediate first aid

- Wash wound with soap and water; encourage bleeding gently
- Irrigate exposed mucous membranes copiously with water

## Risk assessment (see Tables 40.1–40.3)

**Table 40.1** Risk estimates derived from historical data on occupational transmissions

| Specific BBV | Risk of transmission after percutaneous exposure to infected source material |
|---|---|
| HBV | Up to 30% for HBeAg positive source<br>1–6% for HBeAg negative source |
| HCV | 1.9% (range 1–7%) |
| HIV | 0.3% (0.2–0.5%) |

## Source testing

Source patients should generally be tested for HBV, HCV, and HIV:

- *Pre-test discussion and informed consent* are essential, and may be carried out by any appropriately trained and competent health care worker
- *The unconscious source patient* should not normally be tested until consent has been obtained. If necessary, post-exposure prophylaxis (PEP) should be commenced until the patient awakes. If a source patient has died, consent should normally be obtained from a relative

**Table 40.2** Risk estimates can be refined according to two aspects of the NSI

| | Higher risk | Lower risk |
|---|---|---|
| Injury details | Hollow needle<br>Exposure to blood<br>Puncture to ungloved hands<br>Deep wound<br>Sharp visibly blood-stained<br>Needle had been directly in the source's blood vessel | Solid needle<br>Exposure to other fluids*<br>Puncture through gloves<br>Superficial wound<br>Sharp not visibly blood-stained<br>Mucocutaneous exposure |
| Source infectivity | HBeAg positive<br>High HIV viral load/low CD4 count (terminal AIDS) | HBeAg negative, anti-HBe positive<br>Low/undetectable HIV viral load/high CD4 count |

*There is no evidence of transmission from non-blood-stained urine, saliva, faeces, or tears.

**Table 40.3** Follow-up of NSI recipients

| NSI (high risk or known +ve source) | Baseline | 6 weeks | 12 weeks | 24 weeks |
|---|---|---|---|---|
| HbsAg | | HbsAg | HBsAg | HBsAg |
| HCV | | HCV RNA<br>LFTs | HCV RNA<br>Anti-HCV | Anti-HCV |
| HIV | | | Anti-HIV | * |
| All | Store serum (for 2 years) | | | |

Follow-up highlighted in bold is quoted in published guidance from the Health Protection Agency or Expert Advisory Group on Acquired Immune Deficiency Syndrome (AIDS).

*Coinfection (HIV + HCV) in the source patient has been associated with late seroconversions in the recipient HCW, so 24-week follow-up should be considered in these cases.

## Post-exposure prophylaxis

- *HBV*, *HIV*: see ➲ p. 860, Management of needlestick injury 2: hepatitis B virus post-exposure prophylaxis, ➲ p. 862, Management of needlestick injury 3: human immunodeficiency virus post-exposure prophylaxis
- *HCV*: at present there is no effective PEP against HCV, but follow-up aims to identify seroconversion early so that intervention with interferon can be offered

## Counselling and psychological support

Despite the generally low risk of infection, NSIs are extremely anxiety-inducing. Careful risk communication, counselling, and support are vital.

## Restrictions from work

Recipients of high-risk NSIs should not be restricted from work (or exposure-prone procedures (EPPs)) during follow-up but advised to practice safe sex and avoid blood donation. Fitness for EPPs (if seroconversion occurs) is covered in ➲ Chapter 24.

## Reporting procedures

Exposure incidents from sources that are positive for BBV are reportable:

- To Health and Safety Executive under Reporting of Injuries, Diseases, and Dangerous Occurrences Regulations 1995
- Eye of the needle report London 2020 https://www.gov.uk/government/publications/bloodborne-viruses-eye-of-the-needle
- In England, as a serious untoward incident to the Strategic Health Authority

## Further information and guidance

*Communicable Disease Report: Exposure to Hepatitis B Virus: Guidance on Post-exposure Prophylaxis.* Available at: https://www.hse.gov.uk/biosafety/bloodborne-viruses/risk-healthcare-workers.htm London 2021

GMC (2012). *Guidance on Issues Regarding Consent.* General Medical Council, London. 2020 Available at: http://www.gmc-uk.org/guidance/ethical_guidance.asp

Green Link to Guidance: Chapter 18. Available at: https://www.gov.uk/government/publications/hepatitis-c-guidance-on-the-investigation-and-management-of-occupational-exposure London 1999

*National Institute for Occupational Safety and Health Bloodborne Pathogens Website.* London 2016. Available at: http://www.cdc.gov/niosh/bbppg.htm; https://www.gov.uk/government/publications/occupational-exposure-to-bloodborne-viruses-initial-report-form

# Management of needlestick and contamination incidents 2: Hepatitis B virus post-exposure prophylaxis

## Indications

Significant occupational exposure to HBV positive source material.

## Regime

- Treatment depends on whether the recipient has been immunized against HBV and (if so) whether they have achieved adequate immunity. See Table 40.4
- Hepatitis B specific immunoglobulin (HBIG) is usually provided by Bio Products Laboratory. If you provide cover for managing NSIs, ensure that clear arrangements are in place to access HBIG promptly if indicated

## Further information and guidance

Guidance on management of potential exposure to blood-borne viruses in emergency workers For occupational health service providers and frontline staff 2019 Public Health England, London ➚ https://assets.publishing.service.gov.uk/government/uploads/system/uploads/attachment_data/file/815106/Human_hepatitis_B_immunoglobulin_specific-post_exposure.pdf

Chapter 18, Department of Health (2020). *Immunization Against Infectious Disease* (The Green Book). DH, London ➚ https://assets.publishing.service.gov.uk/government/uploads/system/uploads/attachment_data/file/628602/Greenbook_chapter__18.pdf

**Table 40.4** Summary of post-exposure treatment for hepatitis B

| HBV status of person exposed | Significant exposure | | | Non-significant exposure | |
|---|---|---|---|---|---|
| | HBsAg positive source | Unknown source | HBsAg negative source | Continued risk | No further risk |
| ≤1 dose HB vaccine pre-exposure | Accelerated course of HB vaccine* HBIG × 1 | Accelerated course of HB vaccine* | Initiate course of HB vaccine | Initiate course of HB vaccine | No HBV prophylaxis Reassure |
| ≥2 doses HB vaccine pre-exposure (anti-HBs not known) | One dose of HB vaccine followed by second dose 1 month later | One dose of HB vaccine | Finish course of HB vaccine | Finish course of HB vaccine | No HBV prophylaxis Reassure |
| Known responder to HBV vaccine (anti-HBs > 10 mIU/ml) | Consider booster dose of HB vaccine | Consider booster dose of HB vaccine | Consider booster dose of HB vaccine | Consider booster of HB vaccine | No HBV prophylaxis Reassure |
| Known non-responder to HB vaccine (anti-HBs < 10 mIU/ml 2–4 months post-vaccination) | HBIG × 1 Consider booster dose of HB vaccine. A second dose of HBIG should be given at 1 month | HBIG × 1 Consider booster dose of HB vaccine. A second dose of HBIG should be given at 1 month | No HBIG Consider booster dose of HB vaccine | No HBIG Consider booster dose of HB vaccine | No prophylaxis Reassure |

* An accelerated course of vaccine consists of doses spaced at 0, 1, and 2 months. A booster dose may be given at 12 months to those at continuing risk of exposure to HBV. Reproduced from Public Health Lab Service, Hepatitis Subcommittee, Communicable Disease Report. 1992: 2, R97–R101. Permission granted. (Further details and explanation of terms used are contained in this article.)

# Management of needlestick and contamination incidents 3: Human immunodeficiency virus post-exposure prophylaxis

## Indications

Significant occupational exposure to source material that is known to be infected with HIV, or high risk of infection and HIV test is not obtainable.

## Drug regime

A combination of at least three oral anti-retroviral agents for 4 weeks, including both nucleoside analogue reverse transcriptase inhibitors and protease inhibitors.

### The Expert Advisory Group on AIDS (EAGA) recommends the following standard regime

The preferred first-line regimen for PEP (for occupational and non-occupational use) is Raltegravir/Truvada for 28 days.

- One Truvada tablet (245 mg tenofovir disoproxil (as fumarate) and 200 mg emtricitabine (FTC)) once a day plus
- One Raltegravir tablet (400 mg) twice a day

If the source patient has been treated with anti-retrovirals, OH professionals are strongly recommended to seek advice from an expert genitourinary physician with experience in treating HIV disease.

## Timing of PEP

The EAGA recommends that PEP is given as soon as possible after exposure and certainly within 48–72 hours of exposure and continued for at least 28 days. It is not generally recommended to commence PEP beyond 72 hours post-exposure, but this is a matter for the judgement of local experienced clinicians.

## Side effects of PEP

- Serious side effects are rare, but one death has been reported with a previous PEP regime for an occupational exposure
- Unpleasant minor side effects (gastrointestinal (GI) upset, headache) common; treatment with adjuvant anti-emetics and anti-diarrhoeals often required
- The newer PEP regime generally better tolerated than previous combination therapy, but there is still a high incidence of failure to adhere

## Efficacy of PEP

- Advice on HIV PEP is based on indirect evidence of efficacy in the prevention of vertical transmission of HIV, and on surveillance data following occupational exposures
- PEP with Zidovudine has been shown (in a case control study) to reduce the risk of occupational transmission by 80%
- There have been documented cases of occupational transmission of HIV despite appropriate PEP

## Further information and guidance

Public Health England (2019). Guidance on management of potential exposure to blood-borne viruses in emergency workers. For occupational health service providers and frontline staff. Available at: https://assets.publishing.service.gov.uk/government/uploads/system/uploads/attachment_data/file/835888/Guidance_on_management_of_potential_exposure_to_blood__2_.pdf

# Psychiatric emergencies

## General points

- Psychiatric emergencies are relatively common among people who have an established diagnosis of serious mental disorder, but unusual in the general working population
- *A situation can be considered as an emergency when there is a serious and current risk to the safety of the person and/or others. This danger may be*:
  - a consequence of deliberate planning
  - or the risk can be unintentional

## Immediate assessment of emergencies

- Ensure the safety of the person
- Try to speak with the person, recognizing that it is usually impractical to carry out a detailed psychiatric assessment in these circumstances
- Ensure the safety of others (including yourself) while doing so

⚠ When there is an immediate and serious risk of harm, there should be no delay in calling the police

- If possible, try to establish some dialogue with the person. However, avoid confrontation and disagreement. This may calm the situation, enable further evaluation of the problem, and perhaps give an initial indication whether there is an underlying psychiatric disorder
- A more detailed assessment of the person's mental state can be arranged thereafter in a more secure and specialist setting
- *When talking with the person, it may be useful to ask about*:
  - what they are planning to do?
  - why they wish to harm themselves or others?
  - what, if anything, has happened very recently to them to prompt the crisis?
  - whether they have had previous mental health problems?
- *Take any account of suicidal thoughts seriously. Particular concern is raised when a person makes clear statements of intent to kill themselves, particularly*:
  - if they have made firm plans of how to kill themselves
  - if they have current significant symptoms of depression
  - and/or if they have experienced recent serious loss
- *Colleagues and management may have some knowledge, ask about*:
  - recent stress (whether or not work-related)
  - and any history of previous mental disorder

► A person whose behaviour is considered dangerous as a result of a current mental disorder does not need to be detained using the Mental Health Act in order for them to be restrained in an emergency. This can be carried out under common law. Subsequent specialist assessment and treatment may require the person to be legally detained in hospital.

## Lower risk situations

Some situations that cause alarm may not be regarded as medical emergencies that require immediate and assertive intervention. However, they may make it impossible for the person to continue working, and they would benefit from early medical assessment. Such situations may include:

- Acts of self-harm without suicidal intent
- Symptoms of mild or moderate mood disorder
- Overwhelming symptoms of anxiety

It will be useful to ensure the person agrees to be seen urgently by their GP, out-of-hours medical services, or at the Accident and Emergency department, and if necessary to make arrangements for them to be transported there

## Particular psychiatric disorders

- Behaviour that is dangerous to self or others does not in itself indicate that a person is mentally ill. In many situations, such behaviour arises at times of crisis, and the person may well have behaved similarly in the past when faced with overwhelming difficulties
- Current intoxication with alcohol and/or drugs may increase impulsivity and disinhibition
- *In a minority of situations, current symptoms of an untreated serious mental disorder present a serious risk*:
    - people who have delirium may be disorientated, aroused, hallucinated, and irrational
    - those who have acute schizophrenia may be violent as a result of command hallucinations, or because of their persecutory beliefs
    - symptoms of acute mania may include irrational thinking and extreme excitement and irritability
    - symptoms of severe depression may result in acts of serious self-harm

It is very unlikely that a confident diagnosis can be made in the setting of an acute emergency. This will usually be possible only after further assessment and observation, physical examination and appropriate investigations, interviews with others who know the person, and knowledge of any previous psychiatric and medical history.

https://cdn.mentalhealthatwork.org.uk/wp-content/uploads/2018/07/05111111/line_managers_resource.pdf

Chapter 41

# Terrorism and crime

# Terrorism (deliberate use of chemical, biological, radiation, or nuclear weapons)

Terrorism, while difficult to precisely define, has as its core the intent to generate a psychological impact beyond the immediate victims. The likelihood of a successful chemical, biological, radiological, or nuclear (CBRN) terrorist attack remains remote although could cause massive damage and extensive human suffering with little or no warning. The response to such an event must be multiagency and multidisciplinary, and address the following considerations:

- Rescue and treatment of victims, and control and containment of fire or other hazards are complicated. Sites may be contaminated with CBRN substances
- The impact of CBRN weapons may stretch much further than the scene of disaster. Exposed personnel can spread contamination into other areas as they depart from the scene
- As well as the physical injuries, there is major public fear over any use of such weapons, with the risk of significant psychological casualties. Public reassurance and health risk communication forms an essential part of the management of any incident
- Thorough contingency planning is necessary by all organizations likely to be involved

## Immediate incident management

- *CBRN incidents may present covertly. When the cause of an incident is unknown, first responders should adopt the 'Step 1, 2, 3+' approach*:
  - Step 1: one casualty. Approach using NORMAL procedures. CBRN contamination unlikely
  - Step 2: two casualties. Approach with CAUTION, CBRN contamination possible. Report on arrival, update control. If possible or suspected, follow advice for Step 3
  - Step 3+: three casualties or more. DO NOT APPROACH, CBRN INCIDENT CONTAMINATION LIKELY. Identify hazard, control scene, report to control. Perform risk assessment and give assistance to non-ambulant casualties if safe to do so
- *First responders must not compromise their own safety or that of the public when attending a potential CBRN incident*:
  - consider the possibility of a secondary device or exposure designed specifically to affect or injure emergency responders
  - be aware of local policies and relevant major incident practices including use of personal protective equipment (PPE)

# Other factors

- In the event of a mass casualty scenario, first responders will need to dynamically prioritize treatment according to triage category
- Decontamination of casualties may be necessary before treatment can be administered
- PPE must be appropriate to the hazard. Clinicians likely to be involved in CBRN incidents must be trained in correct use of PPE and be aware that protective equipment limits movement and carries risks of hyperthermia

## Specific terrorist weapons

Each main class of weapon is covered as a separate topic (see ➔ p. 870, Chemical weapons; ➔ p. 872, Biological weapons; ➔ p. 874, Radiation and nuclear weapons).

## Further information and guidance

Guidance is available from Public Health England.

CRBN incidents: clinical management & health protection. Gent N, & Milton R, editors. 2nd ed. London: Public Health England; 2018. PHE Publications gateway number 2018080 Available at: https://assets.publishing.service.gov.uk/government/uploads/system/uploads/attachment_data/file/712888/Chemical_biological_radiological_and_nuclear_incidents_clinical_management_and_health_protection.pdf/

# Chemical weapons

Terrorist attacks using chemical weapons have the potential to cause large numbers of casualties. The 1995 sarin attack in a Tokyo subway, e.g. killed 12 people and caused over 1,000 casualties. Chemical weapons can be dispersed in a gas, liquid, and solid forms, and numerous agents exist, each with different symptoms and effects. Although some may require extensive laboratory facilities to manufacture, others can be fabricated relatively simply. Much of the efficacy of such a weapon depends on its ability to disperse the material.

## Types of chemical weapons

- *Nerve agents*: affect the individual's nervous system. Most belong to the family of organophosphates, and act by blocking acetylcholinesterase. Highly toxic, a small drop on skin can be fatal. Examples include organic pesticides, sarin, tabun
- *Blister agents/vesicants*: attack exposed skin, resulting in blisters and skin burns, as well as respiratory distress if inhaled, e.g. mustard gas and lewisite
- *Blood agent/cyanides*: rapidly absorbed into the bloodstream, attack the capacity of the blood to hold and deliver oxygen, causing the victim to suffocate. Cyanide gases and compounds are most common
- *Choking agents*: attack lungs, primarily causing pulmonary oedema, e.g. chlorine, phosgene, nitrogen oxides
- *Incapacitating agents*: usually irritate skin, mucous membranes, eyes, nose, lips, and mouth; causing vomiting or intolerable pain. While this may lead to serious medical situations, it is not designed to kill or cause permanent harm. Used alone, the intention is to temporarily incapacitate and force people to leave an area. However, these agents can be used in combination with other chemical weapons to force removal of protective equipment. Examples include pepper spray, tear/CS gas, and other riot control agents

## Risks to emergency personnel

Chemical contamination can offer a major and immediate hazard to responders who must be correctly trained and equipped. All agents have the potential for 2° contamination of ambulances, fire, and medical equipment, thereby affecting anyone in contact with them. Therefore, proper decontamination is necessary before casualties leave the area.

### Management of casualties with chemical exposure

- Provide respiratory protection
- Remove from hazard area
- Decontaminate externally by showering
- Control movement to avoid spread of contamination
- Administer specific antidote if available

# Biological weapons

Bioterrorism presents serious challenges. Biological weapons can be easy to develop and have utility across the spectrum of conflicts and targets.

- Their release may be:
  - *Overt*: announced openly by the perpetrators
  - *Covert*: i.e. unannounced without a warning or indication of the organism
- Many organisms could be used deliberately and distributed through food, water, or air
- Depending on the organism, intentional release may be indistinguishable from natural outbreaks, either using naturally occurring pathogens or because symptoms are identical. Therefore, early recognition of outbreaks can only be achieved if clinicians are aware of the possibility and take appropriate measures before a definite diagnosis is reached
- *The US Center for Disease Control has identified 30 agents that may be weaponized, and has categorized them as follows:*
  - A: highest priority. Easily transmitted, high morbidity and mortality, e.g. anthrax, smallpox
  - B: moderate priority. Lower morbidity and mortality, more difficult to disseminate, e.g. salmonella, brucellosis
  - C: high priority. Potential to cause significant morbidity and mortality; emerging pathogens that could be engineered for mass dispersion, e.g. severe acute respiratory syndrome, human immunodeficiency virus
- Agent used and mechanism of delivery will depend on whether terrorists are state sponsored. A group with access to biotechnology and laboratory infrastructure more likely to cause mass casualties. However, a lone operative involved in deliberate contamination of food may still have devastating impact, albeit on a smaller scale
- These weapons may be much more effective when used against civilian populations than when deployed against agile and relatively healthy military organizations. There is a real risk that public panic will lead to swamping of medical care

## Types of biological weapons

*Pathogens*

- Disease-causing organisms that can reproduce and keep spreading long after the attack
- Potential for many thousands of casualties, but likely to be much less because of difficulty in efficiently spreading material to reach large populations

*Toxins*

- Poisonous substances produced by living things, e.g. botulinum toxin and aflatoxin
- Many are lethal in small quantities and can kill very large numbers of people
- Presents more like a chemical attack than a biological one

## Recognition of a bioterrorism incident

Any confirmed case of smallpox, plague, pulmonary anthrax, glanders, tularemia, Venezuelan equine encephalitis, or viral haemorrhagic fever in the UK without history of travel to an endemic area should be assumed to be the result of a deliberate release until proven otherwise.

### Bioterrorist attack

The following findings indicate the possibility of a bioterrorist attack:
- Unusual illness
- Unusual numbers of patients with same symptoms
- Illness unusual for time of year
- Illness unusual for patient age group
- Illness in an unusual patient
- Illness acquired in an unusual place
- Unusual clinical signs or disease progression

## Prophylaxis and treatment

- Prophylactic vaccination is possible for certain agents. Once the threat is known, vaccination may be used to contain spread of a weapon used strategically. However, it will always involve risk–benefit assessments, and post-exposure measurements may be more relevant
- The delay in detection means those handling initial casualties will be unaware of hazard and may be unprotected

### Management of biological exposures

- *Dependent on the pathogen*: identification of the agent is critical, and will facilitate measures to protect responders (such as vaccination)
- A suspected casualty should be isolated, and medical staff should wear full protective clothing
- Treatment should include general supportive measures as well as agent-specific treatment
- Medical personnel should be familiar with the local response plan for handling biological emergencies
- Specialist help should be sought; in the UK this is available from Public Health England or the public health agency for the relevant devolved administration
- Monitoring of others exposed and if appropriate post exposure prophylaxis/will be necessary

# Nuclear and radiological weapons

Although terrorist use of an improvised nuclear device cannot be ruled out, it is thought to be very unlikely. More probable scenarios include the use of conventional explosives to attack nuclear facilities, or to spread radioactive materials directly over a large area ('dirty' bomb), and the targeted use of small quantities of radioactive material (e.g. Litvinenko polonium poisoning 2006). In most such cases, it is the fear of the unknown effects of these weapons (rather than any short-term health risks) that is likely to be the major problem.

## Radiation sources

- Radiation can present an external or internal hazard
- The terrorist scenario can involve alpha, beta, or a gamma radiation (but not neutrons which would only be released from operating nuclear reactors or nuclear weapon yields)
- External hazards, which are predominantly gamma and penetrating, are removed when the source is taken away
- However, contamination by radioactive dust will persist and can damage the skin (beta and gamma only) and internal 'target' organs from inhalation, ingestion, or skin penetration. In these circumstances (unless internal contamination is very major), the main effects are likely to be long term, predominantly involving excess risk of malignancy

## Type of incident

- Exposure to penetrating radiation, e.g. from a gamma emitting source. These patients are not radioactive and pose no threat to the rescuer
- External contamination following release of radioactive material. The patient and their clothes may be contaminated and may present a risk to the rescuer
- Internal contamination due to ingestion, inhalation, or absorption of radioactive substances. Body fluids may present a risk to the rescuer

## Risk controls

- *The principles of time, distance, and shielding are essential in minimizing exposure to rescue staff*:
  - reduce time spent in radiation area
  - increase distance from radiation source
  - use effective shielding (concrete or metal if possible)
- It is important that first responders use full PPE to avoid breathing in radioactive dust and prevent contamination of skin

## Further information and guidance

*Public Health England Radiation Protection Services*. Available at: https://www.phe-protectionservices.org.uk/services

*Resources from US Radiation Emergency Assistance Centre/Training Site (REAC/TS)*. Listed on https://orise.orau.gov/reacts/index.html

# Crime

In an increasingly globalized world, sending employees abroad is often an essential part of business. For workers, this can mean exposure to significant personal security risks, including that of kidnap, ransom, and extortion (KRE). While previously mostly confined to terrorist groups in defined high-risk lawless states, KRE is increasingly being adopted by criminal gangs in more stable locations as a funding and intimidation tactic. The methods employed are as varied as the motives although three broad types predominate.

## Types of kidnap

*Virtual*

- An extortion scheme in which the victim is tricked into paying a ransom to free a loved one they believe has been kidnapped. No one has actually been taken and instead, through deceptions and threats, the victim is pressured into paying a quick ransom before the scheme falls apart

*Express*

- A high-volume, low-value process in which the victim is forcibly taken to an ATM and made to withdraw cash. Normally the criminal will free the victim immediately after receiving the cash

*Traditional*

- A person is taken, and a message sent to their loved ones and/or employer demanding a large sum of money for their safe release from hostage situation. Almost 80% of reported traditional kidnappings last for <7 days

## Health effects

- The physical and psychological impact of a kidnapping can be severe for the victims and their families, friends, and coworkers
- The development of Stockholm and London syndromes in captivity
- *Shorter-term*: anxiety and post-traumatic symptoms such as insomnia, hyper-arousal, and hypervigilance
- *Longer-term*: post-traumatic stress disorder is the most prevalent issue, and may be exacerbated by torture, starvation, or other violence, while captive

## Treatment of kidnap victims

- Cognitive behavioural therapy and exposure therapy shown to be beneficial
- Positive social support aids recovery

## Further information and guidance

Foreign and Commonwealth Office. (Now Foreign, Commonwealth & Development Office (FCDO) *Operating in High-Risk Environments: Advice for Business*. 2014 London Available at: https://www.gov.uk/guidance/operating-in-high-risk-environments-advice-for-business

Kidnaping The Basics; Overseas Security Advisory Council, US Dept of State. Washington 2019 Available at: https://www.osac.gov/Content/Report/ec9e4092-cbf6-4fb7-b301-15f4ae161d01

# Appendix 1

# The Global Harmonization Systems (GHS), Safety Data Sheets (SDS), and Health Statements

- The globally harmonized system (GHS) for the classification and labelling of chemicals is used internationally to standardize and harmonize the classification and labelling of chemicals
- Hazard statements are a key element for labelling under GHS. Each hazard statement (for physical, health, and environmental hazards) is designated a code, starting with the letter H and followed by three digits. Statements for health hazards are shown in this appendix
- The Safety Data Sheet (SDS) is an essential component of the GHS providing information about a substance or mixture for use in the workplace. Information is presented under 16 standard heading shown in this appendix

## Hazard statements for health effects

*H300*: Fatal if swallowed
*H301*: Toxic if swallowed
*H302*: Harmful if swallowed
*H303*: May be harmful if swallowed
*H304*: May be fatal if swallowed and enters airways
*H305*: May be harmful if swallowed and enters airways
*H310*: Fatal in contact with skin
*H311*: Toxic in contact with skin
*H312*: Harmful in contact with skin
*H313*: May be harmful in contact with skin
*H314*: Causes severe skin burns and eye damage
*H315*: Causes skin irritation
*H316*: Causes mild skin irritation
*H317*: May cause an allergic skin reaction
*H318*: Causes serious eye damage
*H319*: Causes serious eye irritation
*H320*: Causes eye irritation
*H330*: Fatal if inhaled
*H331*: Toxic if inhaled
*H332*: Harmful if inhaled
*H333*: May be harmful if inhaled
*H334*: May cause allergy or asthma symptoms or breathing difficulties if inhaled
*H335*: May cause respiratory irritation
*H336*: May cause drowsiness or dizziness
*H340*: May cause genetic defects
*H341*: Suspected of causing genetic defects
*H350*: May cause cancer
*H351*: Suspected of causing cancer
*H360*: May damage fertility or the unborn child
*H361*: Suspected of damaging fertility or the unborn child
*H362*: May cause harm to breast-fed children
*H370*: Causes damage to organs
*H371*: May cause damage to organs
*H372*: Causes damage to organs through prolonged or repeated exposure
*H373*: May cause damage to organs through prolonged or repeated exposure

# SDS—16 standard sections

For an SDS to be valid it must have 16 sections. SDS are required by the UK REACH Regulations.

1. Identification (chemical name, recommended uses, and supplier contact information)
2. Hazards identification (classification of substance/mixture, label elements, other hazards)
3. Composition/information on ingredients (substances/mixtures)
4. First-aid measures
5. Firefighting measures
6. Accidental release measure (personal protective equipment, emergency procedures, environmental precautions, methods, and materials for containment and clean up)
7. Handling and storage (precautions for safe handling, condition of storage)
8. Exposure controls/personal protection
9. Physical and chemical properties
10. Stability and reactivity (chemical stability possibility of hazardous reactions)
11. Toxicological information (potential health effects)
12. Ecological information (persistence and degradation, bio-accumulative potential)
13. Disposal considerations (water treatment method)
14. Transport information (transport hazard class, environmental hazards)
15. Regulatory information (safety, health, and environmental regulations/legislation specific for the substance/mixture)
16. Other information

# Appendix 2

# Consent for occupational health assessment

## Essential information about your assessment

*What is the purpose of an occupational health (OH) assessment?*

The purpose is to assess health problems that may be caused (or made worse) by work or are having an effect on your ability to work. We aim to give fair and impartial advice to *both you and your manager* about:

- Your fitness for your job
- Any risks to your health that arise from your duties or your workplace

The main aim of the OH assessment is not to diagnose or treat disease, however, in some circumstances we may just help to ensure that you are receiving the right medical tests or treatment

*When is an OH assessment needed?*

Depending on your circumstances, it might be needed:

- When starting a new job
- When returning to work after a period of time off work due to illness
- If you have problems carrying out your job or are not performing as well as would be expected
- If you have a high level of absence from work due to sickness
- If there is a concern that you might have a health problem that is caused or made worse by work

*Who will carry out the assessment?*

Your appointment will be with an OH doctor or nurse. The OH doctors and nurses who carry out assessments have skills in assessing the relationship between health and work.

*What will happen at my appointment?*

The doctor or nurse will ask you questions about your health and your job and may carry out a medical examination.

- They will sometimes arrange to visit your workplace and see your activities for themselves
- They may ask for your written permission to obtain further medical information from a general practitioner or other doctor who has been treating you. If they ask to do this, the doctor or nurse will explain the reason for requesting a report, and what will happen to the information that your doctor provides

*What will happen after my assessment?*

At the end of the consultation we will usually send a report to the person who referred you (usually your manager or a personnel officer).

If you referred yourself, we may or may not want to send a report to your manager, but this would depend on your own situation and wises.

*What information will be sent to my manager?*

The sort of information that will be included in the manager's report depends on the reason for your referral, but would usually include practical advice about fitness for work, e.g.

- Whether you are fit for work
- If not fit now, an estimate of how long it might be before you are fit
- Whether adjustments or changes need to be made to your job in order to help you to return to work, or to protect your health. These changes may be short term (for rehabilitation) or longer term

- The likelihood of further health problems leading to absence from work in the future
- The report does not usually contain confidential personal or medical information. Rarely, it might be useful to include some medical details, but this is exceptional and is only done with your consent

*Will I know what is being said about me in a report?*

Yes, you have open access to all information that will pass from OH as a result of your assessment. At the end of your appointment, the doctor or nurse will tell you what they are going to say in the report and to whom it will be sent. You will have an opportunity to discuss the report with the doctor or nurse. You can also have a copy of the report if you wish. You can choose to have a copy either before it is released or at the same time.

*Can I refuse to see the doctor or nurse, or refuse to have a report released to my manager?*

Yes, you are quite free to decline the assessment. You can also refuse to have a report released at the end of the consultation. However, it is often not in your best interest to do so, as your employer will not be able to take your health problem into account properly. If you are worried about the OH consultation or report, please discuss with someone in the OH team. They will help you to understand the likely consequences of consenting or refusing in your own particular case.

*Finally*

It is important to remember that the OH professionals do not take sides with either an employee or their manager—but aim to give careful advice to both.

Please do not hesitate to ask for more information or explanation if you need it.

Please sign below to indicate that you have read this information sheet and consent to your occupational health assessment.

Name (in capitals):

Signature

Date:

# Appendix 3

# Informatics in occupational health

The use of information technology in occupational medicine is continually increasing. A great deal of practical information is available on the world-wide web. Wherever possible, useful websites and web references for guidance documents have been quoted within specific topics throughout this handbook. Listed here are websites that are useful for occupational health (OH) practice.

## UK professional bodies in OH

- Faculty of Occupational Medicine (FOM). Available at: www.fom.ac.uk
- Society of Occupational Medicine (SOM). Available at: http://www.som.org.uk/
- British Occupational Hygiene Society (BOHS). Available at: http://www.bohs.org
- Institution of Occupational Safety and Health (IOSH). Available at: http://www.iosh.co.uk

## Specialist/industry-specific practitioner groups

Some require a membership subscription, but selected material is free.

- Association of NHS Occupational Physicians (ANHOPS). Available at: http://www.anhops.com/
- Association of Local Authority Medical Advisers (ALAMA). Available at: http://www.alama.org.uk/
- Commercial Occupational Health Providers Association (COHPA). Available at: http://www.cohpa.co.uk/

## Discussion forum

Occenvmed. Available at: http://www.occmed.free-online.co.uk/page5.html

## Academic departments of occupational medicine

- The Institute of Occupational and Environmental Medicine, University of Birmingham. Available at: http://www.birmingham.ac.uk/schools/haps/departments/ioem/index.aspx
- Centre for Occupational and Environmental Health, University of Manchester. Available at: http://www.medicine.manchester.ac.uk/oeh/
- Medical Research Council Epidemiology Resource Centre, University of Southampton. Available at: http://www.mrc.soton.ac.uk/index.asp?page=33

- Department of Occupational and Environmental Medicine, National Heart and Lung Institute. Available at: http://www.lungsatwork.org.uk/clinical.php
- Other university departments of occupational and environmental medicine can be located through the respective university websites

## Occupational and environmental medicine journals

- *Occupational and Environmental Medicine*. Available at: http://oem.bmjjournals.com/
- *Occupational Medicine*. Available at: http://occmed.oxfordjournals.org/
- *Scandinavian Journal of Work, Environment and Health*. Available at: http://www.sjweh.fi/
- *Journal of Occupational and Environmental Medicine*. Available at: http://www.joem.org/pt/re/joem/home
- *Annals of Work Exposures and Health*. Available at: http://academic.oup.com/annweh/

## Links to other occupational health disciplines

- British Thoracic Society. Available at: http://www.brit-thoracic.org.uk/
- Ergonomics Society. Available at: http://www.ergonomics.org.uk/
- Division of Occupational Psychology - The British Psychology Society. Available at: http://www.bps.org.uk/divsion-occupational -psychology

## Other useful UK websites

- Health, Environment and Work (HEW). Available at: http://www.agius.com/hew/index.htm
- UK Health and Safety Executive (HSE). Available at: http://www.hse.gov.uk
- HSE statistics. Available at: http://www.hse.gov.uk/statistics/
- UK Health Protection Agency. Available at: http://www.hpa.org.uk
- Clinical evidence. Available at: http://www.clinicalevidence.com/ceweb/conditions/index.jsp
- National Institute for Health and Clinical Excellence (NICE). Available at: http://www.nice.org.uk/
- NHS Plus. Available at: http://www.nhsplus.nhs.uk/
- UK Department for Work and Pensions. Available at: http://www.dwp.gov.uk/
- Council for Work and Health. Available at: http://www.councilforworkandhealth.org.uk
- Advisory, Conciliation and Arbitration Service (ACAS). Available at: http://www.acas.org.uk
- Public Health England. Available at: http://www.gov.uk/government/organisations/public-health-england

## International websites

- European Agency for Safety and Health at Work. Available at: http://europe.osha.eu.int/OSHA
- National Institute for Occupational Health and Safety (USA). Available at: http://www.cdc.gov/niosh/homepage.html

- World Health Organization (WHO). Available at: http://www.who.int/en/
- International Research on Cancer (IARC). Available at: http://www.iarc.fr/
- European Chemical Agency (ECHA). Available at: http://www.echa.euopa.eu
- The National Institute for Occupational Safety and Health (NIOSH). Available at: http://www.cdc.gov/niosh/index.htm
- The Canadian Centre for Occupational Health and Safety (CCOHS). Available at: http://www.ccohs.ca

# Index

Notes
Tables, figures, and boxes are indicated by *t*, *f*, and *b* following the page number
Abbreviations used in the index.
COSHH - Control of Substances Hazardous to Health Regulations 2002
LEV - local exhaust ventilation
PTSD - post-traumatic stress disorder
RIDDOR - Reporting of Injuries, Diseases, and Dangerous Occurences Regulations 2013

## A

## D

## F

## G

## H

## M

## N

## U